CRUISING GUIDE TO THE
NORTHERN GULF COAST

Other Cruising Guides from Pelican:

CRUISING GUIDE TO THE NORTHERN GULF COAST:
Florida, Alabama, Mississippi, Louisiana

FOURTH EDITION

By Claiborne S. Young

PELICAN PUBLISHING COMPANY
GRETNA 2003

First edition, 1991
Second edition, 1995
Third edition, 1998
Fourth edition, 2003

*The word "Pelican" and the depiction of a pelican are trademarks
of Pelican Publishing Company, Inc., and are registered
in the U.S. Patent and Trademark Office.*

Maps typeset by Heathyr Davis
Cover photo by Claiborne Young
All text photographs by Karen and Claiborne Young

Library of Congress Cataloging-in-Publication Data

Young, Claiborne S. (Claiborne Sellars), 1951-
    Cruising guide to the northern Gulf Coast : Florida, Alabama,
Mississippi, Louisiana / by Claiborne S. Young.— 4th ed.
        p. cm.
    Includes index.
    ISBN 1-58980-093-1 (pbk. : alk. paper)
    1. Boats and boating—Gulf States—Guidebooks. 2. Inland navi-
gation—Gulf States—Guidebooks. 3. Intracoastal waterways—Gulf
States—Guidebooks. 4. Gulf States—Guidebooks. I. Title.
    GV776.G85 Y68 2003
    797.1'0976—dc21
                                                    2003002368

Information in this guidebook is based on authoritative data available at the time of printing. Prices and hours of operation of businesses listed are subject to change without notice. Readers are asked to take this into account when consulting this guide.

Please note that channel conditions, depths, aids to navigation, and almost all on-the-water navigational data is subject to change at any time. While author has been careful to verify firsthand all navigational information, on-the-water conditions may be quite different by the time of your cruise. Failure to follow current on-the-water reality, even when it differs from the instructions contained in this guide, can result in expensive and dangerous accidents. The author has worked hard to help minimize your risk, but there are potential hazards in any cruising situation, for which captains, navigators, and crew are solely responsible.

Pelican Publishing Company and the author make no guarantee as to the accuracy or reliability of the information contained within this guidebook and will not accept any liability for injuries or damages caused to the reader by following this data.

Printed in the United States of America

Published by Pelican Publishing Company, Inc.
1000 Burmaster Street, Gretna, Louisiana 70053

This book is dedicated to

my frequent companion and research

assistant,

ANDY LIGHTBOURNE—

a friend and sailor for ALL seasons

Contents

Acknowledgments

First and foremost I want to thank my first-rate first mate, Karen Ann, without whose help as an experienced navigator, photographer, research assistant, and partner this book would not have been possible. I would also like to extend a warm thanks to my mother for all the help with the stories of Florida in the good old days.

A very special thanks is extended to my dear friend and research assistant, Andy Lightbourne, to whom this book is dedicated. Without his many selfless hours spent in research and tracking down the endless bits of information needed by this writer, *Cruising Guide to the Northern Gulf Coast* would not have been possible. I would also like to thank Andy's first mate, Wendy (a true "river rat"), for all her warm and much-appreciated hospitality. Truer friends no one has ever had!

Thanks also to my ace research assistant, Bob Horne. No one could ask for a better companion or friend during all the many on-the-water hours of research necessary to put together a new and comprehensive edition such as this.

A very special acknowledgment is also paid to Ms. Mary Boshart of Bay Sails in Mandeville, Louisiana, for all her tireless help in getting the story right about the northern shores of Lake Pontchartrain, as well as her enthusiasm for all my guidebooks. Stop by Bay Sails and tell Mary I sent you!

Chris Moser, dockmaster for Panama City Marina, and Susan Payne, dockmaster for the all-new St. Andrews Bay Marina, were extremely helpful in helping me to acquire the latest data for Panama City waters. I gratefully acknowledge their assistance.

I also gratefully acknowledge the assistance of the many other dockmasters and marina managers throughout the Northern Gulf Coast who gave so much of their time and wisdom to me while I was researching the region.

Finally, I would like to thank Dr. Milburn Calhoun, Nancy Calhoun, Kathleen Calhoun Nettleton, Nina Kooij, and the rest of the staff of Pelican Publishing Company. It has been a genuine pleasure to again work with the "Pelican Bunch," and I hope our relationship will continue for many years to come.

Introduction

It is still a landscape of incredible and heart-stopping beauty, with its dark pines, its flashing water, its vivid yellow sun and the iridescent feathers of its birds. History still waits at the end of every road, whether a paved super-highway . . . or a narrow sand track like those near the little towns. . . . Before twilight the dark clouds have disappeared, and the world is a sparkling mass of raindrops on green leaves as the long rays of the sun play over them. Choruses of frogs and crickets are singing as the evening comes, and in the magenta crepe myrtles brown thrashers buzz. The smell of the grass is damply sweet and the smell of the night cestrums hangs thick and pungent in the blackness that finally descends.

Thus does Gloria Jahoda describe Panhandle Florida in her now classic book *The Other Florida.* While, to be sure, Ms. Jahoda's description is meant to apply to the little-populated areas of northwestern Florida, she herself notes that the Florida Panhandle is far more akin to the other Northern Gulf states of Alabama, Mississippi, and Louisiana than the boisterous eastern coast of the Sunshine State.

Cruising captains have long ignored this stretch of green shores and backwater anchorages. Only within the last decade have mariners begun to appreciate its pristine beauty, within easy range of a bevy of marina facilities and uncounted anchorages. The relative isolation of the region has not been all bad news. Cruisers have been able to (and still can) chart their way to many a pleasant overnight stop between Carrabelle and New Orleans and drop their hook where few have been before them. This can be a very, very special experience in our modern, well-planned world, and I am proud to do my small part to make these waters more accessible to my fellow cruisers.

It must be noted, however, that the last five years have seen a marked increase in development along the Northern Gulf coastline. This writer was shocked to see two low-rise condo complexes on the shores of once-sleepy Carrabelle as we began research for this new edition. While, to be sure, there are still, thankfully, many stretches of the Northern Gulf ICW that remain in their natural state, cruisers who have not plied these waters for several years will be more than slightly surprised to see all the new construction and far more crowded shoreside highways.

The cruising grounds of the Northern Gulf Coast between Carrabelle and New Orleans are truly waters of great contrast. Where else can captain and crew cruise for a single day and pass from the gin-clear, emerald green waters of the Florida Panhandle to the mud-rich brine of Mobile Bay? Another few miles lands you in the wide-open reaches of Mississippi Sound, while another day's cruise will introduce mariners to the almost secret backwater recesses of the wilderness rivers separating Mississippi and Louisiana.

There is something for every cruiser on the varied waters of the Northern Gulf. Those who enjoy anchoring off for the evening will discover a mind-boggling array of overnight havens, particularly on the Florida Panhandle. Many of these anchorages are well off the beaten path and provide a tangible feeling of isolation. Occasionally it is a long run between stops, but marina facilities are excellent, and cruisers can always be assured that a good marina and/or boatyard is within a few hours' run at most.

In the past, this writer has always shied away from any listing of overnight transient- dockage rates for marinas. These sorts of charges change at such a dizzying speed that any such tabulation would be long out of date by the time the ink in this book was dry. However, for the first time, in this new edition, we are going to institute a very simple transient-dockage fee-rating system. All marinas that provide overnight transient berths will be rated "Above-Average," "Average," or "Below-Average." Hopefully, this simple system will give you at least some idea of what to expect when it comes time to pony up your overnight-dockage bill.

The waters of the Northern Gulf from Carrabelle to New Orleans have many wonderful attributes to recommend them to cruisers. The Florida Panhandle is surrounded by some of the clearest water that this writer has ever witnessed, which, together with the beautiful white-sand beaches of the region, make it all too easy to understand why some skippers simply forget to ever come home. Additionally, Panhandle waters are pocked with more gunk holes, side waters, and overnight anchorages than you could shake a gaff at. Seldom before have I seen such a collection of potential havens. Some are located miles from the most remote vestiges of civilization.

Mobile Bay is famous for its rich history and heavy commercial traffic. With appropriate caution, it can be an impressive sight to watch the BIG boys passing carefully up and down the bay.

Mississippi Sound is blessed with some of the most historic cities in the nation. The roads lining the sound's northern shore harbor one of the largest collections of antebellum mansions in the South. Biloxi (say, "bill-LUCK-see") is the second-oldest settlement in the continental United States. Its past is prominently on display for visitors to enjoy. Pascagoula, Gulfport, and Bay St. Louis all have their own fascinating heritage, which the historically minded among us can savor with the greatest relish. During times of fair weather, several anchorages bordering the Mississippi Sound barrier islands to the south can also make for a memorable overnight stay.

A decade ago, the state of Mississippi legalized gambling. This has resulted in the construction of more and more mammoth casino complexes along the sound's shoreline, where once there were only charming shrimp trawlers, pleasure-craft facilities, and more than a fair share of historic buildings. If you are one of those cruisers who enjoys gambling and glitzy night life, then this change will be welcome. Everyone else will be far less than happy.

Louisiana offers another round of backwater cruising on the streams around Pearl River and along the northern shores of Lake Pontchartrain. When discussing the attractions of Louisianian waters, however, the lion's share of the attention must fall on New Orleans. We shall explore this fascinating city in the last chapter of this guide. For now we need only note that it is one of the most colorful, historic, changeable, confusing, and fun-loving cities that America has ever known.

In closing this brief review of the Northern Gulf's attractions, we would be remiss without a word about the succulent food available all up and down the coast. If there is another region of our nation that produces such a consistent supply of gastronomical delights, this writer does not know of it. Whether your pleasure is simple, but ultra-fresh, fried seafood or Creole gumbo or Cajun rice, few palates will come away from the Northern Gulf with anything less than complete satisfaction.

The history of the Northern Gulf Coast is as fascinating as it is complex. The Florida Panhandle was settled by the Spanish and remained, except for a brief (but important) period of British rule, under their control until 1821, when the region finally came under American ownership. What we know today as the states of Alabama, Mississippi, and Louisiana were settled by an unforgettable collection of Frenchmen. Though the region was to know Spanish rule for many years before coming into the American fold by way of Thomas Jefferson's Louisiana Purchase, the French left their indelible stamp, which can still be heard and seen today in some of the native accents and customs.

Within the body of this guide, I have endeavored to present a cross-section of this rich heritage. Wherever possible, readers are referred to various historical accounts for additional information.

Weather along the Northern Gulf Coast is very different from what might be expected by mariners from more northerly climes. Springs are warm and often humid, with relatively frequent thunderstorms. Nevertheless, this season is considered one of the best cruising times in the region. In the absence of any major storms, there is usually just enough wind for a good sail, and many days are clear and sparkling. Of course, cold fronts and other weather systems can mar this pattern of good weather, but most skippers will find spring cruising along the Northern Gulf to be a genuine delight.

The long, hot, humid summers can leave cruisers used to cooler climates breathless from the heat. From June through August and well into September, there are many days of calm air, which leave sweltering sailcraft plodding along under auxiliary power. As if that weren't problem enough, frequent afternoon thunderstorms can, and often do, reach violent proportions. They can seemingly come out of nowhere. This writer has huddled miserably in his boat, anchored in the middle of a marsh, while fearfully watching lightning strikes all around his craft. Yet, as little as fifteen minutes before the storm struck, the sun had been shining and the breezes rather light. In another thirty minutes, the maelstrom had departed as if it had never been. Truly, summer cruising along the Northern Gulf should be planned with a ready ear to the latest weather forecast. No matter what the weather folks say though, if a dark cloud comes over the horizon, abandon everything and head for the nearest shelter.

If it were not for one very serious flaw, the weather from October through the first part of December would be a serious contender with the spring months as the best cruising season on the Northern Gulf. The great big exception to this is, of course, the furious tropical giants which we call hurricanes. The season for these great storms stretches from July through November. Any student of the region's history can readily tell you of the many, many hurricanes that have battered the Northern Gulf in years past. In 1995 Hurricanes Erin and Opal dealt a serious blow to the Florida Panhandle, while in 1976 Hurricane Camille laid waste to a goodly portion of the Mississippi coastline. If the weather service detects one of these giants heading your way, don't muck about. Head for the deepest shelter you can find and don't stick your nose out before the all-clear is sounded.

Winters along the Northern Gulf are short and sweet. While freezes occasionally descend on the coastline, this is a rare happening. Nevertheless, cold weather can sometimes appear, as demonstrated by the ice on Mobile Bay's Dog River in December 1989. Most of the time, captains and crews with time on their hands can pick and choose their days and continue sailing and cruising right on through the winter months. Of course, if you have a schedule to keep and the weather turns nasty, it could make for a very different story.

Before leaving our consideration of the Northern Gulf weather behind, this writer must mention one additional meteorological phenomenon. Time and time and time again, while performing research for this guide and its subsequent editions, it was brought forcibly to our attention that weather forecasting in this region is anything but accurate. During one two-week period, it finally reached the point where we planned on just the opposite conditions of those predicted by the NOAA broadcasts. I don't know what the problem is, but captains should know that they must take weather forecasts in this region with more than a few grains of salt.

In this guide I have endeavored to include all the information skippers may need to take full advantage of the Northern Gulf's tremendous cruising potential. I have paid particular attention to anchorages, marina facilities, and danger areas. All navigational information necessary for a successful cruise has been included, and these data have been set apart in their own subsections and screened in gray for ready identification.

Each body of water has been personally visited for the very latest depth information. However, remember that bottom configurations do change. Dockside depths at marinas seem to be particularly subject to rapid variation. Cruisers should *always* be equipped with the latest charts and "Notice to Mariners" before leaving the dock. The gray-scale maps presented in the body of this text are designed to locate anchorages and facilities and give the reader a general knowledge of the coastline. They are not intended for and should not, under any circumstances, be used for navigation.

This guide is not a navigational primer and it assumes that you have a working knowledge of piloting and coastal navigation. If you don't, you should acquire these skills before tackling the coastal waters.

Successful navigation of the Northern Gulf's waters is yet another study in contrasts. To the east, the waters spread about the Florida Panhandle are mostly deep and forgiving. Often, on bright, sunny days, the clear waters allow you to see just where the good depths drop off and shoaling begins. While this "eyeball navigation" cannot always be relied upon to keep you out of trouble, it is an invaluable tool in many instances.

While some bodies of water in the Florida Panhandle can produce a healthy chop when winds exceed fifteen knots (St. George Sound, Apalachicola Bay, and Pensacola Bay spring immediately to mind), much of the route is well sheltered from inclement weather.

Mobile Bay introduces cruising captains and their crew to muddy and mostly shallow waters that call for more than their share of navigational caution. Navigators should plan their cruises carefully and plot any necessary compass courses well ahead of time before venturing out on the bay's open waters.

Mississippi Sound sometimes has the "worst" of both worlds. Not only is the water wide open to the effects of wind and wave, it is also peppered with shoals and underwater obstructions. The ICW runs through the middle of the broad sound. A lengthy run to the north is necessary in order to reach the various sheltered ports of call along the northerly shoreline. Cruising the Mississippi Sound portion of the ICW calls for an attentive ear to the latest forecast and careful advance planning. Check your sounder often and keep a sharp lookout for lateral leeway.

Louisiana again introduces visiting cruisers to mostly deep waters, with the exception of Lake Pontchartrain. This unusually large lake has depths that seldom exceed 15 feet. Couple this relatively thin water with strong afternoon thundershowers and you can readily understand why captain and crew must approach Pontchartrain with the greatest respect.

With some isolated exceptions, currents flow swiftly along the inland waters of the Northern Gulf. All mariners should be alert for the side-setting effects of wind and current. Sailcraft, particularly when cruising under auxiliary power, and single-engine trawlers should be especially mindful of the quickly moving waters.

Cruisers familiar with Florida's eastern coastline will be deliriously happy to learn that there are far fewer no-wake zones and bridges with restricted opening schedules than on their home waters. *Sailcraft should be warned, however, that there are still some **fixed** bridges on the Gulf Coast ICW that have only 50 feet of vertical clearance.* Fortunately,

several of these spans are now being replaced by 65-foot structures, but for the moment at least, sailors who need more than 50 feet of clearance are doomed to frequent offshore jaunts to reach the various ports of call along portions of this coastline.

All navigators should have a well-functioning depth sounder on board before leaving the dock. This is one of the most basic safety instruments in any navigator's arsenal of aids. The cruiser who does not take this elementary precaution is asking for trouble. An accurate knotmeter/log is another instrument that will prove quite useful. It is often just as important to know how far you have gone as to know what course you are following.

The modern miracle of satellite-controlled GPS (Global Positioning System), particularly when interfaced with a laptop computer loaded with the latest digitized nautical charts, is yet another powerful navigational aid. Many captains have already discovered that these electronic marvels can be of immense value when cruising the Northern Gulf coastline, particularly on the wide waters of Mobile Bay, Mississippi Sound, and Lake Pontchartrain.

Since we have been talking about electronic navigation, this would be a good time to announce a new feature in this guide. For only the third time in our series of guidebooks, approximate latitude and longitude positions of marinas and many anchorages have been included. All of these lat/lon positions are included strictly for informational purposes; they must NOT be used as GPS or Loran C way points!

With the phenomenal increase in popularity of computerized navigational software, we thought it important to provide lat/lon information. For instance, this data can be plugged into Nobeltec's "Navigational Suite" or the "Cap'n" software, and the program will immediately place an icon on the digitized image of the appropriate nautical chart, almost exactly where the marina or anchorage you are making for is located. That's a real, on-the-water advantage, but to be repetitive, *please* don't use this data as simple way points.

There are several reasons why. Loran C and GPS readings give mariners a straight-line distance or bearing to the intended way-point destination. Straight-line tracks do NOT take into account such vagaries as shoals you will need to avoid, peninsulas you will be unable to cross, or islands that just seem to get in the way.

In this guide, lighted daybeacons are always called "flashing daybeacons." I believe this is a more descriptive term than the officially correct designation, "light," or the more colloquial expression, "flasher." Also, to avoid confusion, daybeacons without lights are always referred to as "unlighted daybeacons." Similarly, lighted buoys are called "flashing buoys."

Cruisers who are (or become) regular visitors to the wide and varied waters of the Northern Gulf Coast might want to seriously consider another publication complementary to this guide. *Southwinds* magazine, published out of St. Petersburg, Florida, is a great source for cruising and racing (under sail) news along this coastline. This publication does a most commendable job of keeping its readers informed about the latest happenings in the boating world from Florida to New Orleans. If all this sounds interesting, subscriptions can be ordered by writing to *Southwinds,* P.O. Box 1190, St. Petersburg, FL 33705 or calling (813) 825-0433.

I can only hope that you, my fellow cruisers, will have as much fun exploring the waters between Carrabelle and New Orleans as I have had in researching them for you. It is my sincere belief that you will never find so many contrasting waters in so short a space of coastline anywhere else in the world. And, just in case your appetite is not yet sufficiently whetted, consider Gloria Jahoda's immortal description of her first autumn along the Northern Gulf Coast:

> The pines were shining and soughing in the hottest of early autumn winds, fat mullets were jumping in the slow brown river, and the unknown people had begun to smile back at me when I unwrapped the line from my bamboo fishing pole and smiled at them. Wild buckwheat blossoms were starting to go to seed in empty meadows, and down in the roadside ditches near the Gulf red Catesby lilies were flamboyant in a sun I was sure would blaze relentlessly forever.

Good luck and good cruising!

CRUISING GUIDE TO THE
NORTHERN
GULF COAST

CHAPTER 1

From Carrabelle to Panama City

Remember that cold night last winter when the wind was flinging the sleet against your window and you were perched in your easy chair, eyes closed, dreaming of cruising somewhere, anywhere? Chances are that in your mind's eye you pictured wide, sparkling waters, so clear that you could see the bottom in 6- to 8-foot depths. Then, if your imagination was really up to snuff, you might have dreamed of these waters being surrounded by wonderfully undeveloped shores buffered with snow white sands, and overlooked by abundant pines and hardwoods. Of course, a sheltered branch of the Intracoastal Waterway would be close by for quick access to and from this imaginary cruising paradise. You might perhaps wish to include two historic communities nearby, with just enough marina facilities to cover all a cruiser's needs but without being so numerous as to intrude on your idyllic scene. Finally, you might liberally sprinkle the waters with isolated anchorages far from civilization.

Ah, if it could only be. Well, open your eyes, my friend. We have just managed to conjure up a mental picture of the Northern Gulf Coast ICW's easterly genesis. Indeed, the waters about the charming villages of Carrabelle and Apalachicola contain all these many wonderful qualities and much more. Cruisers should make every effort to include plenty of time in their plans to fully enjoy this sunny stretch's tremendous cruising potential.

Of course, it is only fair to note that "progress" is making its presence known more and more in both Carrabelle and Apalachicola, though not to an extent that detracts from the town's backwater character (at least not yet). Cruising visitors to Carrabelle's shoreline will now note two low-rise condo complexes, and Apalachicola's population of gift and antique shops seems to be ever growing.

The easternmost waters of the Gulf Coast ICW consist of an improved, well-marked channel leading through broad St. George Sound and Apalachicola Bay. The charming village of Carrabelle, boasting first-rate, recently expanded marina facilities, sits just north of the Waterway's eastern tip.

After traversing the sometimes choppy waters of the sound and bay, the ICW turns sharply north into the sheltered reaches of the Apalachicola River. The town of Apalachicola beckons cruisers from the river's banks to stop awhile at its growing selection of marinas and explore the community's many beautiful homes. There are perhaps no better examples of early Floridian (Victorian and antebellum) architecture anywhere in the Sunshine State.

Eventually the Waterway winds its way past several smaller streams offering additional anchorage opportunities, and enters the Jackson River, which in turn leads to Lake Wimico. This is an extraordinarily beautiful section of the Gulf Coast ICW. The completely undeveloped, deep green, cypress-laden shores seem to exude an atmosphere of mystery and secrecy which is all too rare in our modern, fast-paced world.

Northwest of Lake Wimico, the Waterway enters a mostly man-made canal. Parts of this passage are certainly not as pleasing to the eye as the waters to the south and east. However, another canal does provide reliable access to St. Joseph Bay and peninsula. Adventurous captains can follow this passage to a new, topnotch marina and a remote harbor where it is possible to dinghy ashore to enjoy some of the most magnificent beaches in the Florida Panhandle.

Finally, the ICW continues to snake its way west to East Bay. Abundant anchorages are found along the westerly portion of this passage. East Bay leads, in turn, to Panama City and its astonishing array of marina facilities, which will be covered in the next chapter.

Cruisers making the offshore jump from Dog Island or Government Cut Inlet to Panama City should be advised that the restricted military areas shown on the NOAA charts are for real. Frequent excercises are conducted on these waters, often with live weapons. Several years ago at the Sail St. Petersburg boat show, this writer spoke to a cruising couple who graphically described just such an incident that took place far too close to their sailcraft for comfort. Please be sure to stay clear!

Many Panhandle skippers cruise the waters between Panama City and Pensacola for years and never even see the easternmost portion of the Gulf Coast ICW. Little do they realize that their cruising plans are omitting what just may be the state's most magnificent waters. If you are one of those cruisers who relishes the feeling that every turn of the screw or puff of wind carries you a bit further from civilization and the madding crowd, run, don't walk to the marina and gear up for a cruise on the waters between Carrabelle and East Bay!

Charts Mariners traveling the easterly section of the Gulf Coast ICW will only need the first four charts listed below. Captains running the various inlets or those approaching from the open sea may require one or both of the larger coverage charts.

11404—small craft, ICW type chart which gives good details of Dog Island, the Carrabelle entrance channel, East Pass Inlet, Government Cut Inlet, and the ICW into Apalachicola Bay

11402—ICW chart that outlines the southern reaches of Apalachicola Bay, the town of Apalachicola's waterfront, and follows the Waterway west to Lake Wimico

11393—details the ICW from Lake Wimico to the easterly reaches of East Bay, near Panama City. Also gives excellent details on St. Joseph Bay and the anchorages off St. Joseph Peninsula

11390—follows the Waterway through East Bay to Panama City

11405—small-scale, large coverage chart that details the entrances into St. George Sound through the passage east of Dog Island and East Pass Inlet

11401—another broad-scale chart that covers the western reaches of St. George Sound and all of Apalachicola Bay. This chart is useful for navigators entering Government Cut Inlet from the open waters of the Gulf.

Bridges
Carrabelle River Bridge—crosses Carrabelle River at the village of Carrabelle—Fixed—40 feet
St. George Island Bridge—crosses ICW at standard mile 361—Fixed—50 feet—new bridge under construction at this location to replace existing bridge—when complete, new

span will have 65 feet of vertical clearance and older bridge will be removed
John Gorrie Memorial Bridge—crosses ICW at standard mile 351—Fixed—65 feet
Apalachicola Northern Railroad Bridge— crosses ICW at standard mile 347—Swing bridge—11 feet (closed)—usually open unless a train is due
White City Bridge—crosses ICW at standard

mile 329—Fixed—65 feet
Gulf County Canal/Port St. Joe Bridge— crosses Gulf County Canal at its intersection with St. Joseph Bay—Fixed—75 feet
Overstreet Bridge—crosses ICW at standard mile 315—Fixed—65 feet
Dupont Bridge—crosses ICW at standard mile 295—Fixed—50 feet

Entering or Leaving St. George Sound and Apalachicola Bay

Mariners cruising to Apalachicola Bay from points west will, of course, enter the region by way of the well-marked ICW passage. However, for those arriving from the open waters of the "Big Bend" and the Gulf of Mexico, or planning a departure to Anclote Key and other ports of call to the south, the situation is very, very different. As mentioned above, the Northern Gulf ICW begins its passage to the west in St. George Sound (soon leading west to Apalachicola Bay). *To the east and south, there is no protected waterway.* Skippers cruising north from Florida's West Coast or departing Carrabelle to cruise south must contend with an open-water passage of better than 130 nautical miles. Whether you choose to hug the coastline or cut the corner and swing far out into the Gulf's waters, this memorable voyage calls for caution and careful planning.

Captains contemplating a cruise of Florida's Big Bend region might want to consult this writer's *Cruising Guide to Western Florida* (or check out *Cruising Guide to Florida's Big Bend,* the newest cruising guide from Rick Rhodes). The entire passage as well as in-depth accounts of all the Big Bend rivers are covered in this volume.

This guide's coverage of the Panhandle waters begins at St. George Sound and Dog Island. Cruisers entering or leaving the sound have three fairly reliable means of putting out into (or coming in from) the Gulf waters. Both East Pass Inlet, to the west of Dog Island, and the wide swath of deep water east of the land mass are convenient for cruising craft whose captains wish to enter the easterly reaches of St. George Sound. The shoal waters of Dog Island Reef, to the east of Dog Island, and the shallows associated with South Shoal off Alligator Harbor make the latter route a bit more complicated. The wonderfully isolated anchorages along Dog Island and the excellent marina facilities at Carrabelle are convenient to both of these passages. Either channel calls for navigational caution and close attention to business.

Tall sailcraft that cannot clear the 50-foot St. George Island fixed bridge separating St. George Sound and Apalachicola Bay must either forego cruising the sound's waters or leave St. George by way of East Pass and enter Apalachicola Bay via Government Cut Inlet. Eventually, a 65-foot fixed span will replace the current 50-foot bridge, but construction is just getting underway as this account is being tapped out on the keyboard.

Cruisers wishing to berth at Apalachicola or sailcraft wanting to avoid the round-about trip described above would do better to enter the bay by way of Apalachicola/Government Cut Inlet, almost due south of the town. This passage is subject to shoaling, but on-site research in 2002 revealed minimum depths of 8 feet.

If you are planning to cruise south and east from Apalachicola Bay or St. George Sound, these three inlets will serve as your departure points as well. Be sure to take a long and careful listen to the NOAA weather forecasts before venturing out onto the open waters of the Gulf.

St. George Sound and Apalachicola Bay

It's hard for this writer to be objective about the waters of St. George Sound and Apalachicola Bay. To be succinct, I consider them some of the most beautiful on which it has been my privilege to cruise. Whether you seek good marina facilities in small, quaint (not to mention historic) villages, or isolated anchorages within a stone's throw of deserted, white sand beaches, these twin bodies of water on the eastern end of Florida's Panhandle never fail in their abilities to reward.

St. George Sound and Apalachicola Bay flow directly into each other and are separated only by the long bridge and causeway between Cat Point and St. George Island. While there is certainly more shallow water to be found in Apalachicola Bay than in the sound, most cruisers can think of the twin bodies of water as being essentially similar in character.

The Northern Gulf Coast ICW officially begins at flashing daybeacon #2, just west of Dog Island (though the latest edition of chart 11404 shows the magenta line leading all the way to the Carrabelle approach channel). Cruis-ers entering St. George Sound via East Pass Inlet will find themselves in close proximity to this initial aid marking the southwestward-flowing Waterway channel. If it's late in the day, or if you have had a long passage across the Big Bend, you might consider turning north to the facilities at Carrabelle or east toward the anchorages along Dog Island's northerly shoreline.

Cruisers entering St. George Sound via the broad channel northeast of Dog Island will face a cruise of some 6 nautical miles from the island's eastern tip to the beginning of the ICW's track and the channel to Carrabelle. The previously mentioned overnight havens along Dog Island are within an easy jog of this entrance into the sound.

Apalachicola Bay eventually flows north into a broad body of shallow water spanned by the 3.4-nautical mile John Gorrie Memorial Bridge. All but small craft should avoid this portion of the bay. Shallow St. Vincent Sound leads west from Apalachicola Bay to shoal-filled and treacherous Indian Pass Inlet. Again, the vast majority of cruising craft will want to stick to the bay's deeper waters and the ICW channel.

Two inlets serve Apalachicola Bay. West Pass is practically impassable but Government Cut, mentioned earlier, can be used by cautious cruising craft.

After mentioning all the fortunate qualities of St. George Sound and Apalachicola Bay, it must be said that both can foster a healthy chop when winds exceed 15 knots. However, on fair-weather days, a voyage down this stretch of the ICW can make for one of the most pleasurable cruising experiences between the Panhandle and New Orleans!

Dog Island (Standard Mile 376.5)

Dog Island is an oblong body of land and

marsh located due southeast of Carrabelle on the far side of St. George Sound. The island remains one of the most beautiful and least developed of the privately owned Gulf Coast isles, thanks to a determined effort by the four-teen full-time residents. In the early 1970s, it appeared that developers were poised to snatch up this gem of sand and grass much as had been done all up and down the Northern Gulf Coast. Thankfully, the island's con-stituents united to resist these efforts and per-suaded the Nature Conservancy to purchase a large majority of the available land. Today, with the exception of the Pelican Inn, there are only a limited number of houses along the beaches and inland areas. Visitors are mostly free to wander the magnificent sand dunes topped by pines, hardwoods and scrub growth without constraint or the visual encroachment of modern, unsightly development. Those with an eye for nature's beauty will surely agree that this is a preciously rare experience.

Cruisers are some of the prime beneficia-ries of this natural bonanza. The only access to the island is by water taxi and private boat. With three excellent anchorages (see informa-tion below), most any mariner who is of a mind to do so can throw out the hook, blow up the dinghy, and journey ashore to this sub-tropical paradise.

Those cruisers who desire an even more inti-mate view of this unusual island can arrange for overnight (or longer) stays at the Pelican Inn (800-451-5294, http://www.thepelicaninn.com). This rustic hostelry features eight apartment-like accommodations and is located near the southeastern shores of Tysons Harbor (near the island's northeasterly tip). There are no restau-rants or stores on Dog Island, so bring all your food and necessities. Believe me, the magnifi-cent sunsets, surffishing, great shell hunting, and superb isolation more than compensate for any lack of amenities.

After coming ashore, cruisers will find a wide variety of landside conditions. Part of the shoreline northeast of Tysons Harbor and the beach south and west of Ballast Cove exhibit notable sand dunes. Some have been swept bare by the Gulf winds while others are sur-prisingly topped with substantial pine and oak trees. Perched between the dunes are lower, sandy stretches leading into grassy marshes. The astonishing variety of birds and small mammals is enough to set any nature lover to dreaming. If you are numbered amid the happy ranks of this naturalistic fraternity, make every effort to give Dog Island your full attention.

Before leaving Dog Island, let us review one word of warning. Many cruisers have discov-ered that it's almost impossible not to tarry on the shores of this remarkable isle. Good weather and breathtaking sunsets seem to invite more and more exploration. If all you have to do is jump aboard and take a quick cruise back to Carrabelle, Apalachicola, or even Panama City, so much the better. How-ever, if you must cross the Gulf for points east and south, don't let all the good weather pass you by before making the jump. As beautiful as these tranquil shores are, they may seem less appealing while running before a 40-knot gale headed for Anclote Key or Clearwater.

Dog Island Anchorages (Standard Mile 376.5) (Various Lats/Lons—see below)

Three first-rate anchorages are available to cruisers along the northerly banks of Dog Island when the fickle winds choose to blow from the south or east. Only one of these havens is safe from fresh northerly breezes or heavy westerly blows.

Moving east to west, the first anchorage is discovered on the correctly charted patch of 8- and 9-foot water partially enclosed by the hook on the island's northeastern tip (near 29 49.478 North/084 34.997 West). While care must be exercised to avoid encroaching on the shoal water to the southwest, most boats up to 48 feet will find plenty of swinging room— amidst minimum 8-foot depths and good shelter if the winds are blowing from the east, northeast, southeast, or south. The shoreline consists of small, well-vegetated sand dunes and white-sand beaches. There is no development within sight. Many cruisers will want to get the anchor down as fast as possible and break out the dinghy to head ashore. During the summer months, make sure to take along the insect repellent.

Dog Island's most sheltered set of anchorages is found on the eastern shore of Tysons Harbor, just west of the haven discussed above. This deep cove boasts a privately marked channel that is used by the local ferry. The cut maintains minimum 5½-foot depths (with soundings of 7 to 8 feet being more the norm) from its northerly mouth to the docks that line the cove's southerly tip (see below). Because of the channel's narrow width at certain points along its track, this passage is not recommended for boats over 38 feet in length or those drawing more than 5 feet.

The charted bubble of 8- and 9-foot water flanking the easterly side of the Tysons Harbor channel can make for a very snug overnight anchorage in most winds. Try dropping the hook near 29 49.049 North/084 35.184 West. Care must be taken to leave the

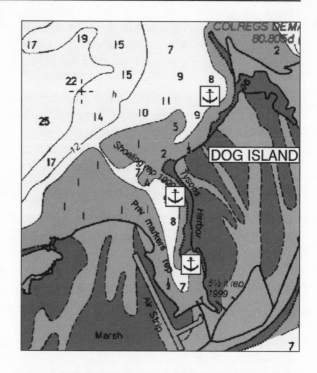

channel directly abeam of this position. Check out our navigational account of Tysons Harbor in the next section of this chapter for more helpful hints. Minimum depths of 6 feet run to within 50 yards of shore. Typical soundings are in the 7- to 9-foot range. Swinging room should be sufficient for vessels up to 40 feet. Shelter from foul weather is excellent except during times of strong northwesterly breezes. The banks are lined by the usual white sand beaches watched over by tall, stately pines. Seldom has this writer found a more lovely or secure overnight stop. It is heartily recommended.

South and southeast of the just-described anchorage, the privately marked cut continues on to a set of docks lining the cove's southernmost shores. Depths remain good, typically 5½ feet or better, if and only if you remain in the

channel. Depths to either side of the cut deteriorate rapidly.

Cruisers approaching the southerly docks
may see some local sailcraft swinging on
mooring buoys east of the approach channel.
Depths run to 5 feet or even slighly less on
these waters, but if these soundings are not a
problem for your vessel, it is quite possible to
anchor near 29 48.720 North/084 35.103
West. Be sure to leave plenty of swinging room
between your vessel and the resident craft on
the mooring buoys. The space is a bit cramped,
so this inner anchorage is not suggested for
vessels larger than 35 feet. In any case, this
writer much prefers the outer anchorage
reviewed above. Unless there is some com-
pelling reason to drop the hook at the inner

haven, we suggest you opt out of this anchorage in favor of the outer (northerly) haven.

Intrepid explorers who push on to the
southern docks will probably see two signs on
the outer face of these piers. One states in
unequivocal language, "No Trespassing"—
translation: "Don't even think about tying up
here." The second sign denotes these piers as
property of the Dog Island Yacht Club. We
have learned through our knowledgeable con-
tacts in Carrabelle that this is not a yacht club
in the traditional sense but rather an association
of Dog Island property owners. Obviously, visitors are not welcome at these piers.

On the other hand, there is a public ramp
and finger pier immediately to the west of the
"yacht club" piers. Here, you can tie up a

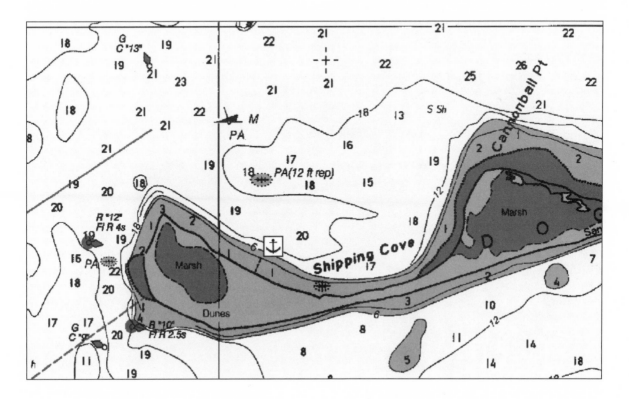

dinghy or smaller power craft, which greatly facilitates a trip ashore. Just be sure you are mooring your dinghy to the public pier and not the private docks.

With winds from the south or east, pleasure craft of almost any size can anchor in the 10-plus feet of water on broad Shipping Cove, found near Dog Island's westerly terminus. A single house with a long, dilapidated pier that fronts the cove's shore makes a good navigational reference point. Good depths of 6 to 10 feet run to within 100 yards of the old dock. Try anchoring near 29 47.075 North/084 39.722 West. The shoreline here is noticeably more barren than that found on the havens to the east. Nevertheless, a dinghy trip ashore puts the visitor within easy walking distance of several large sand dunes on the Gulf-side beaches to the east and west. This is a very popular weekend stopover during the spring, fall, and summer months. Mariners who happen to drop anchor during these times of the year will most likely be joined by a host of their fellow cruisers.

Carrabelle and the Carrabelle River (Standard Mile 380.5) (Various Lats/Lons—see below)

The small town of Carrabelle sits perched on the eastern and northern banks of a river known by the same name. A deep, well-marked channel leads from St. George Sound past several large spoil shoals off the river's southerly entrance. A quick cruise upriver reveals the town's delightful marinas and village waterfront.

Until just a few, short years ago, commercial fishing was clearly king in Carrabelle. While cruising visitors will still discover quite a collection of picturesque shrimp trawlers lining the still-

Carrabelle waterfront

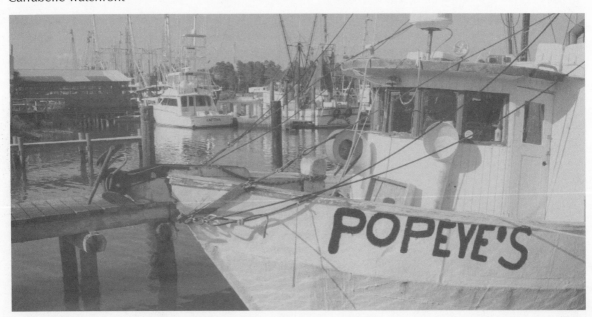

quaint village waterfront, the winds of change are beginning to blow through once-sleepy Carrabelle. Within the last three years, two low-rise condo complexes and a new marina have sprung up. There is also more automobile traffic, and generally, things seem to be moving at a bit of a faster pace than in years past.

All this is not to say that Carrabelle has lost its charm. To the contrary, this village still retains its backwater character, but unless the local authorities carefully manage new development, things could change within the next five years. Let's hope that this never comes to pass and that Carrabelle's local leaders will follow the example of other successful seaside communities such as Beaufort, North Carolina, which has accommodated development but still retains the air of an earlier, far more gracious era.

Here are some phone numbers and Web sites to know in Carrabelle:

> Carrabelle-area Chamber of Commerce—
>   850-697-2585, http://www.Carrabelle.org
> Tow Boat/U.S. Carrabelle—
>   850-697-8909 , 850-508-5268 (cell)
> Florida Marine Patrol—850-697-3741

Carrabelle Facilities

Until 1989, transient berths were at a premium in Carrabelle. Only one marina provided any significant transient dockage, and that was often strained to the limit, particularly in foul weather. Have things ever changed for the better. First, the Moorings at Carrabelle opened, followed just this past year by C-Quarters Marina. Now, transient slips are far easier to come by in Carrabelle, though the wise mariner will still call ahead for advance dockage reservations.

Carrabelle entrance channel

Let's now take a detailed look at Carrabelle's marinas. We will not proceed geographically but rather in the various facilities' order of importance to visiting cruisers.

First among any discussion of local pleasure-craft meccas must be the Moorings at Carrabelle (29 51.110 North/084 40.370 West). This large, obviously well-managed marina, located west of unlighted daybeacon #17, features modern wooden, fixed piers with a substantial number of transient slips. Berths on the inner portion of the harbor are particularly well sheltered. Depths alongside have an impressive range of 6 to as much as 10 feet. Gasoline, diesel fuel, plus 30-50-amp dockside power and fresh water connections are readily available. Mechanical repairs can be arranged for both gasoline and diesel power plants. For those with prop or shaft problems, the marina dockmasters can make arrangements for repairs with a local, independent dive service (but no haul-outs are available at the Moorings). There is a small ship's and variety store (plus dive shop) on the premises. Just to show how serious the Moorings is about great service, cruisers will find a phone set aside for their use in the ship's store.

The local IGA supermarket, two convenience stores, and several other helpful shoreside businesses (see later in section) are found within easy walking distance of the piers.

Newly remodeled, climate-controlled showers are located in a free-standing building on the western side of the complex. Reaching them can be a bit of a trek for captain and crew berthed on the eastern end of the complex, but the walk is more than worth the effort. This same building houses a brand-new cruiser's lounge on its upper floor, com-

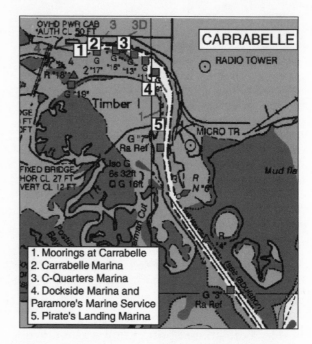

1. Moorings at Carrabelle
2. Carrabelle Marina
3. C-Quarters Marina
4. Dockside Marina and Paramore's Marine Service
5. Pirate's Landing Marina

plete with pool table, color television, and high-speed Internet access. How's that for a fine addition to an already first-rate facility?

The Moorings also offers waste pump-out services, a Laundromat, and an adjacent motel. The motel is extra-nice with large rooms and efficiencies that overlook the harbor. This would be a great spot to take a break from the live-aboard routine, particularly after a rough Big Bend crossing. There is even an on-site swimming pool at which to while away a few hours during a hot summer afternoon.

The marina staff will be glad to help with transportation to local restaurants, though the dining spots described later are within walking distance.

With all these amenities and services, it's not difficult to imagine why the Moorings at Carrabelle has become the most popular marina in this region. Advance dockage reservations would be a very wise precaution.

The Moorings at Carrabelle (850) 697-2800
http://www.mooringscarrabelle.com

Approach depth—10-17 feet
Dockside depth—6-10 feet
Accepts transients—yes
Transient-dockage rate—average
Fixed wooden piers—yes
Dockside power connections—30 and 50 amp
Dockside water connections—yes
Showers—yes
Laundromat—yes
Waste pump-out—yes
Gasoline—yes
Diesel fuel—yes
Mechanical repairs—yes
Ship's store—yes
Restaurant—several nearby

The new kid on the block in Carrabelle is C-Quarters Marina (29 51.140 North/084 40.150 West). This marina's 67 slips are spread out single file along the Carrabelle waterfront, east and west of the combination dockmaster's building, ship's store, and restaurant. C-Quarters guards the northerly banks between unlighted daybeacons #13 and #15. There was originally a fresh seafood market in this complex as well, but that part of the operation is now closed.

C-Quarters is primarily in the business of supplying dockage to resident craft, but there are usually two to three slips set aside for transients. Berths are composed of new, fixed wooden piers complete with fresh-water and

The Moorings at Carrabelle

30- to 50-amp power hookups. Good dockside depths of 7 to as much as 16 feet should be enough for even long-legged vessels. Gasoline, diesel fuel, and waste pump-out service are also readily available. Good, nonclimate-controlled showers and an adequate Laundromat are located on the premises, as is a large and well-stocked ship's store. Some mechanical repairs can usually be arranged through local, independent technicians. The on-site Crabby Nick's Seafood House (850-697-5300), which is also reviewed in this chapter, has good food and is obviously quite convenient for crews staying at C-Quarters.

There are also four shoreside rooms and one apartment for rent within this complex. We have not yet had a chance to evaluate these landlubber lodging services.

All in all, C-Quarters struck us as a good facility that cruisers can consider as a more-than-adequate alternative in Carrabelle. However, with only two to three transient slips in the offing, wise captains will check on availability prior to arrival.

> **C-Quarters Marina (850-697-8400)**
>   http://www.cquarters.com
> Approach depth—10-12 feet
> Dockside depth—7-16 feet
> Accepts transients—2-3 slips usually available
> Transient-dockage rate—average
> Fixed wooden piers—yes
> Dockside power connections—30-50 amp
> Dockside fresh-water connections—yes
> Waste pump-out—yes
> Showers—yes
> Laundromat—yes
> Gasoline—yes
> Diesel fuel—yes
> Mechanical repairs—local, independent technicians
> Ship's store—yes
> Restaurant—on site and others nearby

Several other pleasure-craft facilities are to be found in Carrabelle, though none of these offers anything in the way of transient dockage. A short hop upstream of unlighted daybeacon #7, Pirate's Landing Marina (850-697-2778) overlooks the westerly banks near 29 50.773 North/084 39.959 West. This facility is now dominated by the local commercial-fishing crowd. While gasoline and diesel fuel can be purchased here by cruising craft (dockside depths run 10+ feet), we strongly suggest the above reviewed marinas farther upstream for an overnight stay.

Dockside Marina and Boatworks (850-697-3337) is prominent on Carrabelle River's southern flank opposite unlighted daybeacon #9, near 29 50.956 North/084 40.001 West. While this facility sports a few wet slips fronting onto the channel, its primary focus is on the manufacture of small johnboats. No services are available to cruising craft.

Paramore's Marine Service (850-697-3666) makes its home on the same site as Dockside Marina. This firm offers haul-outs by way of both a 30-ton travelift and a 50-ton marine railway. Do-it-yourselfers are welcome. The staff can also arrange for mechanical repairs through local, independent contractors. Painting, fiberglass work, and bottom jobs are also very much available at Paramore's.

Incidentally, all three of the above reviewed facilities—Pirate's Landing Marina, Dockside Marina, and Paramore's Marine Service—are located on Timber Island. This body of land borders the western and southern flank of the Carrabelle River as it makes its way past the village waterfront. Strong local rumor has it that Timber Island will soon be the site of a large condo complex. If this turns out to be

C-Quarters Marina, Carrabelle

true, all this new development could potentially have a negative impact on these three
pleasure-craft oriented firms.

Carrabelle Marina (850-697-3351) guards
the Carrabelle River's northern banks abeam of
unlighted daybeacon #17, at 29 51.137
North/084 40.308 West. Its position lies
between C-Quarters Marina and the Moorings
at Carrabelle. This small but friendly facility has
now completely abandoned the transient-dockage business. As the owner put it to this writer,
"Our wet slips are really designed for boats 30
feet and smaller." Dry-stack storage, gasoline,
a small ship's store, and some outboard repairs
are available, however. Resident craft at the
marina's wet slips will discover fresh-water

and 30- to 50-amp power hookups.

Captains whose craft are in need of mechanical repairs will be interested to learn of a relatively new firm on the Carrabelle waterfront.
While Marine Systems (850-697-2660) lacks
any wet-slip space of its own, it does have an
arrangement with nearby C-Quarters Marina to
make use of two berths for its service customers.

Marine Systems' motto is "You break it,
we fix it." Judging by our observations, this is
not just a brag. It appears these people are in
the serious mechanical-repair business. We
saw mammoth diesel-power plants being
serviced as well as transmission and marine
generators. In our collective opinion, if you
are in need of mechanical servicing, your

search in Carrabelle is ended. Give Marine Systems a call!

Carrabelle River Anchorages
(29 51.823 North/084 41.008 West)

Navigators studying the Carrabelle River Extension insert on chart 11404 might conclude that good anchorage can be found on the upper reaches of the stream, north and west of the town waterfront. However, the marked channel between unlighted daybeacons #22 and #25 has shoaled to 4-foot depths just where you would least expect to find shallow water.

Adventurous captains whose craft can stand this relatively thin water may choose to continue upstream to the end of the charted track at unlighted daybeacon #68. Be warned, however, that care must be exercised to stay in the improved cut, or even shallow-draft vessels may find the bottom.

Carrabelle Marina

Marine Systems, Carrabelle

West-southwest of #68, you can follow the southerly fork of the river for a short distance and drop the hook in 6 to 7 feet of water near 29 51.823 North/084 41.008 West. There should be enough swinging room for boats as large as 36 feet. The shores are lightly developed and provide good protection from all winds. In fact, this would make a good foul-weather hidey hole, always supposing you can reach the anchorage without finding the bottom.

Frankly, considering the good marina facilities at the village of Carrabelle and the long cruise necessary to reach the anchorage discussed above, most captains will wisely choose to ignore this potential overnight spot. However, for those of our cruising brethren who insist on dropping the hook for the evening, the upstream portion of the Carrabelle River is the only game in town.

Carrabelle Ashore

Carrabelle exhibits a surprisingly complete collection of supermarkets, convenience stores, and drug stores, as well as several excellent restaurants. This is a good port in which to restock after crossing the Gulf or to take on stores in anticipation of the passage south.

While you are shopping, ask one of the locals to point out "the world's smallest police station." It consists of a phone booth! Actually, there is now a larger police station, but the old phone booth is still there to remind visitors of when it was used in an earlier day.

Two convenience stores and the local IGA Supermarket (812 NW Avenue A, 850-697-2710) are found directly across the street from the Moorings at Carrabelle and C-Quarters Marina.

Ace Hardware (712 North Avenue, 850-697-3332) is just next door to the IGA (as is the one-and-only local bank), or you could hike several additional blocks into the downtown business district and visit with the good folks at Ganders Hardware (90 Tallahassee Street, 850-697-3688). The local post office and Burda Rexall Drugstore (108 SE Avenue A, 850-697-3630) are located within a half-block of Ganders as well.

For one of the best seafood meals you will ever enjoy, take a stroll across the Carrabelle River Bridge, just west of the town waterfront. Soon after crossing the span, Julia Maes Restaurant (1558 Highway 98, 850-697-3791) will be spotted on the eastern side of the road. The mixed-seafood platters are absolutely spectacular, and everything else is just as good, and we mean GOOD. Don't miss this one folks, unless you happen to dislike all forms of ultrafresh seafood.

Another, far newer dining choice on the Carrabelle waterfront is Crabby Nick's Seafood House (501 NW Avenue A, 850-697-5300). This eatery is located on the front side of the same building that houses the dockmaster and ship's store of C-Quarters Marina (see above), and fronts onto the path of Highway 98, the principal artery of automobile traffic through Carrabelle. We found the food good and the service exemplary at Crabby Nick's, but to be honest, the fare is not as spectacular as the offerings at Julia Maes. However, if

you're in town for more than one night, this would be an excellent second choice.

When it comes time for breakfast or the midday meal, consider giving the nod to Harry's Restaurant (113 St. James Avenue, 850-697-3400). Believe you me, all the locals do (particularly for breakfast) and there is no better recommendation for any dining spot. Harry's is located in the heart of the downtown district, a pleasant walk of six to eight blocks from the principal village marinas.

If life afloat has begun to wear a bit thin, and it's time to spend a night or two with solid ground under your feet, there are several good choices in Carrabelle. The Moorings marina (see above) is fortunate enough to boast its own shoreside motel. Our stays at this facility have always been enjoyable, and we can recommend it without reservation.

Another good choice is the Georgian Motel (850-697-3410). Located in the downtown Carrabelle business district, hard by Harry's Restaurant, the Georgian is a small but utterly charming little hostelry. The owners, Ray Finn and his first-rate first mate , simply can't seem to do enough for their guests. To be succinct, the hospitality here is absolutely outstanding!

Carrabelle Events

The village of Carrabelle features several special events throughout the course of the year that warrant visiting cruisers' attention:

Riverfront Festival—an exhibition of local arts and crafts plus plenty of food. Usually held the fourth Saturday in April

Tallahassee Builders Fishing Tournament—first of June

Grady White Fishing Tournament—late September

Carrabelle sunset

Boat Parade of Lights—second Saturday in December

Carrabelle History

Shortly after the Civil War, an industrious pioneer by the name of Oliver Kelley came to live near the banks of what was then known as the Crooked River. Though stories vary, it seems that Kelley must have lost his wife or sweetheart in the war. Her name was Carrie. He named the settlement after his lost love and added the word "belle" to recall her beauty. Thus the unusual moniker of Carrabelle was born.

Carrabelle's first post office was founded in 1878. This new federal facility served the fifty families living around the mouth of the Crooked River.

Lumbering and the timber harvesting industry soon came to be the mainstay of this struggling but optimistic settlement. Vast quantities of logs and loads of turpentine were floated down the river and dispatched aboard ocean-going sailing vessels, which anchored in the secure coves of nearby Dog Island.

A severe hurricane in 1898 destroyed much of the town. The lumbering business fell off and the local economy was depressed for a time as the residents strove to rebuild their community a bit farther upstream. The new version of Carrabelle rose on the shores of St. James Island, sandwiched between the Crooked and New rivers. The town continues to occupy this site today.

During World War II, Carrabelle experienced a short-lived boom. Camp Gordon Johnston was established five miles out of town, and new recruits trained for amphibious landings on the shores of Dog Island. In these later days, some of those who trained at Camp Johnston have returned to visit their onetime home. Some have been so impressed with the region's natural beauty that they have chosen to retire in Carrabelle.

Following the war, Carrabelle lapsed more and more into the role of an isolated but charming fishing village. Shrimp, crab, and freshwater fish are harvested for sale locally, as are grouper and red snapper in the offshore waters. This commercial fishing tradition continues into modern times. Several sport fishing boats now operate from Carrabelle, lending a new flair to the area angling.

Within the last two decades, Carrabelle has also become something of an artist's colony. Several lucky individuals with a flair for the brush and an appreciation of nature's beauty have settled in the town. Carrabelle now boasts three galleries.

Today, Carrabelle sits quietly on the shores of the river renamed in its honor, much as it has been for the past hundred years. To this writer, the town is reminiscent of Oriental in North Carolina or the charming tree-lined lanes of McClellanville in the South Carolina Low Country. Steeped in its own simple but honorable history and bathed in abundant sunshine, Carrabelle stands ready to greet cruising visitors with its excellent marina facilities. I suggest that you heed the call!

East Pass Inlet (Standard Mile 376.5)

Most local captains consider East Pass Inlet a reliable passage to and from the open sea. This cut currently boasts 8-foot minimum depths (with most soundings being considerably deeper) and five charted navigational aids, a sure sign that the inlet is at least relatively stable.

As you would expect, when wind and tides oppose one another, East Pass is nothing if not rough. Strong storms in the Gulf can also send a considerable swell rolling through the inlet. However, these problems are certainly not unique to this seaward cut. The same could be said for almost any other inlet on the Northern Gulf. So, if you are of a mind, pick a day of fair weather and make use of East Pass Inlet with as much confidence as any mariner can ever place in those often fickle barriers between inland waters and the Gulf of Mexico.

St. George and Little St. George Islands

Modern-day St. George Island is now separated into two distinct land masses by artificial Government Cut Inlet (also known as Bob Sike's Cut). The westerly portion is known alternately as Little St. George Island or Cape St. George Island State Preserve, while to the east is larger St. George Island. St. George can be reached by landlubbers traveling over the long Cat Point Bridge, west of flashing daybeacon #40. Little St. George Island is accessible only by boat.

Much like its northeasterly sister, Dog Island, St. George has mostly escaped the ravages of modern development. In earlier times, the numerous island pines were slashed for turpentine. If you search diligently, you may still be able to find evidence of this previously flourishing enterprise. During World War II, the island was the staging ground for extensive army training and maneuvers. With the dawn of the latter half of the twentieth century, St. George has come under the watchful care of its four hundred year-round residents. These devoted admirers of the island's great natural beauty have fought long and hard to resist multi-unit condominiums and other unsightly and environmentally unwise construction. So far, they have succeeded admirably in their self-appointed task, with the result that St. George Island is now the largest essentially undeveloped barrier island in all of Florida.

With this natural character in mind, it's easy to understand why visitors can still wander the beaches and find a pirate's ransom in beautiful shells.

This writer has had the opportunity to take an early morning stroll on the beaches of St. George. As the sun rose, I stopped for a few moments and looked about. As far as the eye could see and the ear could hear, there was no evidence whatsoever of man's existence.

St. George Island features the magnificent white-sand beaches of the Florida Panhandle, so commonplace to the natives and so awe-inspiring to visitors. A goodly portion of the beach is bounded to the northwest by tall sand dunes backed by pines and hardwoods. Hiking among this magnificent natural setting is highly recommended for those who have seen one too many waves.

The most easily accessible, yet totally natural, beaches on St. George Island are the strands of the Dr. Julian G. Bruce/St. George Island State Park. The park encompasses over 1880 acres on the island's northeastern tip. Hiking trails, an observation deck, and a small boat launch are also available within the park's boundaries. Perhaps the greatest attraction for nature lovers are the huge flights of migrating birds often observed during the spring and fall. To quote the park brochure, "On such days, the oak hammocks may be alive with small birds while the hawks and falcons patrol above."

Little St. George Island is very similar in character to its bigger brother, save that it remains completely undeveloped and lacks any residents whatsoever. Fortunately, this island is now owned by the state of Florida and its future as an unspoiled barrier island is assured.

The Cape St. George Lighthouse is perched atop the southerly sand dunes on Little St. George's southernmost reaches. The tower seen today is actually the second lighthouse to be erected in the area. The first was constructed in 1833 but was destroyed by the great hurricane of 1850. By 1852 the present-day light was erected and outfitted with a "third-order" lens. Standing 72 feet tall, the light is visible for nine miles under ideal conditions.

During the Civil War, cannon fire from Confederate forces temporarily disabled the light. However, it was soon repaired and again gazing benignly over the nearby waters.

Today the light is totally automated and the ancient keeper's quarters are in ruins. A very long hike is required to reach the lighthouse from the nearest anchorage. However, on days of fair weather when the torrid sun is not too hot, this is a trip many cruisers will certainly want to consider. The first sight of the old, snow white sentinel set amidst the tall dunes, with no other man-made structure in sight, is a moment which has to be experienced to be understood.

St. George and Little St. George Island Anchorages (Various Lats/Lons—see below)

Sadly, there are only a limited number of places for mariners to drop the hook while visiting St. George and Little St. George Island. All of these temporary havens have minimal shelter from winds blowing across St. George Sound (from the north). In fact, winds from any quarter exceeding 15 or 20 knots call for a delay in visiting the islands.

None of the spots described below are suggested for an overnight stay with foul weather in the forecast. Pick a day of fair breezes and sunshine for your visit, drink in the island's beauty to your heart's content, but be ready to retreat to the docks of Carrabelle or Apalachicola if a black cloud appears over the horizon.

Moving east to west, the first potential St. George Island refuge is found on the waters of the second cove indenting the island's northwesterly shore, northeast of charted Pilot Harbor (standard mile 373). Minimum 6-foot depths can be found on the waters near 29 44.971 North/084 42.935 West. There is plenty of swing room, and some shelter from eastern and southeasterly breezes. Don't approach to within less than 400 yards of the adjoining shoreline. A broad band of shallows shelves out from these banks.

Once the hook is down, you can carefully dinghy ashore and walk across to the beaches of St. George Island State Park. The sand dunes and trees described earlier will be very much in evidence.

Some might consider dropping anchor in the charted bubble of deep water well west of (charted) Sugar Hill, near 29 43.514 North/084

45.114 West (standard mile 369). Drop the hook before coming within 200 yards of the shoreline. Again, swinging room is almost unlimited, but shelter from foul weather is minimal. The sand dunes guarding the beach on this portion of the island are particularly tall and absolutely magnificent. Break out the dinghy and get ready for an unforgettable day.

Cruisers piloting pleasure craft 45 feet and smaller, and who are intent on visiting Little

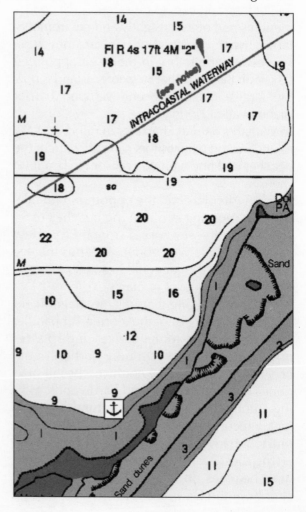

St. George Island and the St. George Lighthouse, can drop the hook just south of flashing daybeacon #12. These waters lie north of charted Cape St. George (near 29 36.161 North/085 02.062 West). Minimum 7-foot depths are held only to within 400 yards of the southern banks. Do not attempt a closer approach on any vessel larger than a dinghy! A long dinghy trip through 2-foot water is necessary to reach the attractive, well-wooded shoreline, followed by an even longer walk to the lighthouse. You just may find the extra effort more than justified. Be warned that this anchorage is particularly subject to rough water when winds are blowing from the north.

While any navigator studying charts 11404 and 11402 can pick out a host of other spots to drop the hook along St. George and Little St. George islands, the three anchorages described above take maximum advantage of the scant natural shelter. All have been selected to allow the closest possible approach to the shoreline.

Eastpoint

The small channel serving the village of Eastpoint is found on the northern shores of St. George Sound, east of Magnolia Bluffs and well north of flashing daybeacon #40 (on the ICW). This tiny village is renowned for its active fishing and oystering fleet. Locals will tell you that the sweetest oysters in the world come from Apalachicola Bay and Eastpoint. Unfortunately for us cruisers, the entrance channel only carries low-tide depths of 3 to 5 feet, and you must follow an exacting route through unmarked shoals to reach the cut. Also, there are no services catering specifically to pleasure craft in Eastpoint. Dockage is practically nil for visiting craft. Consequently, most

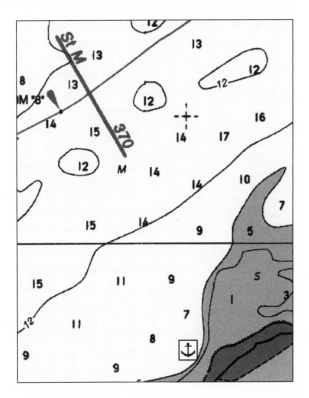

mariners would do far better to enjoy the seafood brought into this quaint port at one of the several fine restaurants in Carrabelle or Apalachicola.

Government Cut Inlet (Standard Mile 355)

Artificial Government Cut Inlet (known locally in Apalachicola as Bob Sike's Cut) is found almost due south of flashing daybeacon #76 on the Waterway. The interior of the inlet is bounded on both shores by broken stone, obviously placed there by the Army Corps of Engineers to retard bank erosion. This well-marked, artificial channel is subject to periodic shoaling, and a check in the spring of 2003 revealed some shallow spots along the northeastern side of the channel. With luck,

5- to 6-foot depths can be held if you avoid these shoals. It's still a good idea to play it safe and check at one of the local marinas in Apalachicola. As always, try to time your passage for fair weather and light breezes. The fillings in your teeth will be ever so thankful.

St. Vincent Island and Anchorage (29 38.295 North/085 05.590 West)

St. Vincent Island, lying west of the ICW's 90 degree turn to the north on its way to Apalachicola, is a sprawling land mass covering more than 12,000 acres. While most of the island is composed of sandy, higher ground, several large marshes are also found on the interior and northeastern banks. St. Vincent is bounded to the southeast by shallow West Pass Inlet, and to the west by treacherous Indian Pass. Both of these inlets are shoal and should not be attempted by either visiting or local cruisers.

St. Vincent Island is a national wildlife refuge and is therefore protected from development. It is almost completely uninhabited at the present time. As on Dog and St. George islands, sand dunes front much of the oceanside beach. Most of this land mass is surrounded by the shoal waters of St. Vincent Sound, but fortunately, there are exceptions.

Don't be shocked if, while anchored on the haven described below, you happen to spot what appear to be unusually large deer patrolling the St. Vincent shoreline. These are actually "Sambar Deer," an unusually mammoth version of this gentle species that was imported from Southeast Asia between 1900 and 1910. The U.S. Fish and Wildlife Service is currently using St. Vincent Island as a protected breeding ground for bald eagles and red wolves. We wish them well in their efforts.

In fair weather and light winds (only), adventurous cruisers might consider anchoring vessels up to 45 feet in the charted patch of 5- to 7-foot water southeast of Back Slough, near 29 38.295 North/085 05.590 West. These waters are subject to rough conditions when fresh winds are blowing from the east, northeast, and north, but in light airs this spot should do for a few hours to allow exploration ashore. The adjacent shoreline is absolutely magnificent, fringed with a thin ribbon of white sand beach and backed by a deep pine woods. The whole area begs to be explored by foot, but take along a liberal supply of insect repellent if you heed this siren call.

West Pass Inlet

West Pass Inlet is a broad but shoal-prone passage that separates Little St. George and St. Vincent islands. Do not attempt this seaward cut! During his original on-site research some eleven years ago, this writer observed a local fisherman in an intense struggle to move his grounded vessel to deeper water. Unless you cherish the thought of running aground, you'll leave this wayward channel strictly to the locals.

St. Vincent Sound and Indian Pass Inlet

Shallow St. Vincent Sound borders the westerly reaches of Apalachicola Bay. While much of the sound carries 4 to 6 feet of water, there are numerous unmarked shoals with less than 3 feet of depth waiting to trap the unwary cruiser. While the local fishermen out of Apalachicola make regular use of the rich fish and shellfish populations of St. Vincent Sound, visiting cruisers are advised to make discretion the better part of valor and avoid its waters.

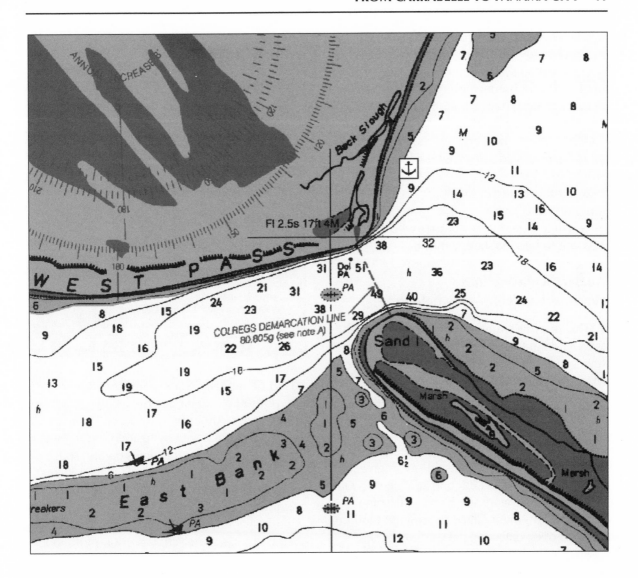

The westerly reaches of St. Vincent Sound eventually lead to ultrashallow Indian Pass Inlet. No pleasure craft, even in an emergency, should attempt to use this impassable cut. Depths run to 2 feet or less. The strong tidal currents and resulting breakers would quickly swamp and capsize any boat foolish enough to attempt the cut.

Apalachicola (Standard Mile 351.5)

I always think of a visit to the village of Apalachicola as a time warp to Florida's Victorian and antebellum past. Strolling down the village's incredibly tranquil lanes while watching the lazy sunlight play about the beautifully restored mansions and homes, it requires little effort to believe that you have somehow slipped back to a simpler, more gracious era. Apalachicola may well be Florida's best and last reminder of those now far-removed times when life was a bit slower and concerns seemed less pressing. Many cruisers make annual treks to the docks of this timeless village to sample these rarefied airs. This writer urges every mariner who reads this account to join that happy throng.

Apalachicola Marinas
(Various Lats/Lons—see below)

The marina situation in Apalachicola has taken a definite turn for the better over the past few years with the opening of Scipio Creek Marina. Now, between this facility and Deep Water Marina (see below), visiting cruisers can be pretty well assured of finding quality overnight dockage in this charming community.

The ICW runs north via a dredged, well-marked channel from the shallow intersection between Apalachicola Bay and St. Vincent Sound to the village's waterfront. North of flashing daybeacon #TM, the local pleasure-craft facilities begin to open out along the westerly banks.

First up are the docks of the Apalachicola Municipal Marina, located in the charted, L-shaped offshoot northwest of #TM (29 43.385 North/084 58.923 West). This public facility has three big disadvantages for visiting cruisers. First, there is no regular dockmaster on duty at the harbor. (Though the city of Apalachicola does employ an official dockmaster, he does not have an office or headquarters at the city dockage

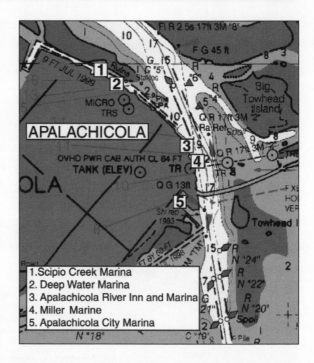

1. Scipio Creek Marina
2. Deep Water Marina
3. Apalachicola River Inn and Marina
4. Miller Marine
5. Apalachicola City Marina

basin). Secondly, depths on the inner, northeasterly portion of the harbor run as thin as 3½ feet at low water. And, finally, most of the available slip space is taken up by resident craft. Nevertheless, occasionally, transients do find space for overnight or temporary dockage at the city marina's fixed, wooden piers. As alluded to above, soundings alongside in the innermost portion of the L-shaped harbor run to 3½ feet, but berths on the outer, southeasterly portion of the dockage basin have better depths of 5 to 6 feet. Power connections of the 15- to 20-amp variety, fresh-water hookups, and a public waste pump-out service are available if you should happen to find an available slip. No fuel, repairs, or other shoreside marine services are to be had.

Apalachicola Municipal Marina
(850) 653-9319 (City)

653-7274 (Dockmaster)

Approach depth—6-13 feet
Dockside depth— 3½-6 feet
Accepts transients—limited
Transient-dockage rate—average
Fixed wooden slips—yes
Dockside power connections—15 and 20 amp
Dockside water connections—yes
Waste pump-out service—yes

Battery Park, a small, low-key, city recre- ation facility with a few public rest rooms, is found just across the street from the dockage basin. This park plays host to a community building that serves as the center for the Florida Seafood Festival (see below). The local restaurants reviewed below are within easy walking distance of the city docks.

Two other Apalachicola marina facilities are located along the Waterway's western shores just north of the John Gorrie Memorial Bridge's

Apalachicola City Marina

fixed, high-rise span. Moving south to north, you will first encounter Miller Marine Service (29 43.595 North/084 58.863 West). This small facility features one long, wooden-face dock that also doubles as a fuel pier. One or two transient craft (overnight only) can sometimes be accommodated here, but Miller Marine works closely with its next-door neighbor, Apalachicola River Inn and Marina, and often sends visiting overnighters its way. Low-tide dockside depths at Miller Marine are an impressive 10 feet. Fresh-water and 30- to 50-amp hookups are found dockside, and full fueling services are readily available. A well-stocked ship's store is maintained on the premises. The restaurants at Apalachicola River Inn are just next door, and a slightly longer hike will lead you to the central downtown district with its wealth of restaurants and other retail businesses.

Miller Marine Service (850) 653-9521
www.hometown.com/millermarine/index.htm

Approach depth—12 feet
Dockside depth—10 feet
Accepts transients—very limited
Transient-dockage rate—average
Fixed wooden-face dock—yes
Dockside power connections—30 and 50 amp
Dockside water connections—yes
Gasoline—yes
Diesel fuel—yes
Ship's store—yes
Restaurant—several nearby

The docks of Apalachicola River Inn and Marina (formerly Rainbow Inn) are found immediately adjacent to Miller Marine, near 29 43.615 North/084 58.882 West. Though the name of this combination motel, marina, and restaurant has recently changed, the ownership remains the same. Apalachicola River Inn has gotten a bit of an unhappy reputation among the cruising community of late because of its failure to answer VHF calls under its former moniker. Also, it must be noted that the marina's fixed wooden piers are not in the best of condition, though they are certainly serviceable. These docks have never been an ideal arrangement for larger cruising craft anyway, and their shelter from really foul weather is also suspect.

Transients are accepted for overnight accommodations. As already noted above, the width of these berths may not be appropriate for vessels larger than 45 feet. All slips feature fresh-water and 30- to 50-amp power connections. Boat clubs should note that Apalachicola River Inn and Marina no longer accepts large groups for weekend dockage. There has apparently been a bit of a problem with too much dockside partying in the past.

A single shoreside (heated and air-conditioned) shower is available, and mechanical repairs can often be arranged through independent, local contractors.

The "inn" part of the complex consists of a large two-story motel with many rooms overlooking the Waterway. Obviously, these lodging accommodations are extremely convenient for anyone wanting to spend a few days ashore off their trusty craft. Apalachicola River Inn features three on-site dining choices. Caroline's Fine Dining overlooks the water just behind the docks. This restaurant is open for all three meals of the day and boasts full menus including some fine seafood for the evening repast. The breakfasts are absolutely

Miller Marine, Apalachicola

first rate, as evidenced by this writer's satisfied palate. Upstairs, the Roseate Spoonbill
Lounge is a great place to unwind after a long day
on the water. The lounge is open seven nights a
week and sometimes features live entertainment.
A package liquor store is also located on site.

Just next door, and under the same ownership, is Boss Oysters (850-653-9364). Besides
the succulent oysters, visitors can choose from
fine steaks, smoked seafood, and barbecue.
This establishment also has some very attractive
outside dining, with a host of tables overlook-

ing the Waterway.

Cruisers with a need for restocking their
larders will probably have to take a taxi. The
closest Piggly Wiggly Supermarket is some twelve
blocks away, with an IGA Supermarket a bit farther out. Try calling Crooms Taxi (850-653-8132).

Apalachicola River Inn and Marina (850) 653-8139
    http://www.apalachicolariverinn.com

Approach depth—12 feet
Dockside depth—9-12 feet
Accepts transients—yes
Transient-dockage rate—average

Fixed wooden slips—yes
Dockside power connections—30 and 50 amp
Dockside water connections—yes
Showers—yes
Mechanical repairs—yes (independent contractors)
Restaurant—three on site and others nearby

The charted Scipio Creek offshoot, which runs northwest from the town waterfront (northwest of flashing daybeacon #2), leads to what this writer considers to be the finest marina facilities in Apalachicola. Whether you find a berth at petite Deep Water Marina or

Apalachicola River Inn and Marina

ultrasheltered Scipio Creek Marina, your stay is almost sure to be a real pleasure.

One word of warning, though: the long, correctly charted shoal separating the ICW-Apalachicola waterfront channel and the southeasterly entrance to Scipio Creek is very real. First-timers should be *sure* to read the navigational account of these waters, presented in the next section of this chapter, before attempting entry.

Moving southeast to northwest, cruisers will first come upon Deep Water Marina (29 43.915 North/084 59.279 West). Out of all the hundreds and hundreds of marine facilities that this writer has reviewed, I can truthfully say that I have never found anything quite like

Deep Water Marina. Visiting cruisers can be assured of a warm and knowledgeable welcome at this facility guarding the creek's southwesterly shoreline. It was founded by two long-time cruisers, Harold and Dee Rudd, and the present owners, Richard and Nancy Clifton, have continued the tradition of service above and beyond the call.

The entrance channel holds minimum 8-foot depths, and at least 6 to 7 feet of water can be expected dockside. Transients are welcomed at modern, floating, wooden-decked piers featuring fresh-water connections and 30- and 50-amp power hookups. Some 4 to 5 slips are usually set aside for the use of visitors. Call ahead of time to avoid disappointment.

Apalachicola waterfront

Cruisers in search of personal cleanliness will find what they seek in the form of a unique *A*-shaped building just behind the docks, which houses some fine (non-air-conditioned) showers. A Laundromat is located on the marina grounds as well.

Full-service mechanical repairs for both gasoline and diesel-power plants are available on site, as are haul-outs via a 25-ton travelift. Deep Water also features mast installation for sailcraft via a sturdy crane. The marina maintains a good parts store and all the Apalachicola restaurants are accessible via a walk of several blocks. Again, those needing groceries will probably want to take a cab (Crooms Taxi—850-653-8132), or you might make use of several bikes thoughtfully provided by the marina management for the use of visitors.

After your lines are coiled, take a moment to check out the marina's main building. This old edifice was saved by the original owners. They jacked it up off its pilings, straightened the frame, and then sat it back on a secure footing. The tin roof and exterior walls were repaired and the entire interior received a thorough cleaning. Now visitors can stroll about this venerable building with the friendly smell of the old timbers in their nostrils and admire some of the huge cypress planks that were cut from several sunken cypress logs discovered while dredging the dockage basin. Cruisers can also make use of this building as a safe and dry spot to perform some of their own work that is best accomplished out of the weather.

This writer heartily urges his fellow cruisers to give Deep Water Marina their most serious consideration. Your cruise will be ever so much richer for a day or two spent at this wonderful stopover. Oh yes, if you do lack for anything during your stay, just tell Duke, the marina's black labrador. He's the one really in charge!

Deep Water Marina (850) 653-8801
http://www.deepwatermarina.com

Approach depth—8 feet
Dockside depth—6-7 feet
Accepts transients—yes
Transient-dockage rate—average
Floating wooden docks—yes
Dockside power connections—30 and 50 amp
Dockside water connections—yes
Showers—yes
Laundromat—yes
Mechanical repairs—yes
Below-waterline repairs—yes
Parts store—yes
Restaurant—several nearby

Scipio Creek Marina is the newest pleasure-craft facility in Apalachicola and arguably one of the very best firms of its type in the Florida Panhandle. It was a fortunate day for the cruising community when Scipio Creek opened its doors (or slips, as it were) for business.

The marina's dockage basin cuts into the southerly shores of Scipio Creek, a short hop upstream (northwest) of Deep Water Marina, near 29 43.964 North/084 59.382 West. Additionally, a long face dock fronts directly onto the creek. The marina's wonderful restaurant (see below) sits just behind this pier.

Scipio Creek's inner basin was originally a commercial-fishing-craft hub, but it has been newly dredged and converted to the almost exclusive use of pleasure craft. This upstream portion of the creek is actually quite sheltered, and it would take some really nasty weather to disturb even those boats moored to the outer, face pier. The inner berths boast enough shelter for anything short of a hurricane.

Scipio Creek Marina is glad to accept transients. Minimum, low-water depths at the outer pier run around 8 feet, with at least 4½ to 6 feet of water on the inner slips (with typical soundings of 6 to as much as 10 feet). Dockage is provided at excellent, fixed wooden piers, featuring ultramodern 30- and 50-amp power and freshwater hookups. Waste pump-out service is available, as is gasoline and diesel fuel.

Shoreside, cruisers will discover one fair, nonclimate-controlled shower, a small Laundromat, and a nice ship's/variety store. The marina's mammoth, dry-stack storage building will also be quite obvious, just behind the dockage basin.

Some outboard and I/O repairs are available from the marina staff, while heavier repair work can be readily referred to local, independent mechanics. Scipio Creek is not in the haul-out business, except as it applies to the dry-stack storage portion of the operation.

One of the real delights at Scipio Creek is its on-site (but under separate ownership) restaurant, Pappa Joe's Oyster Bar and Grill (850-653-1189). Believe you me the oysters are spectacular, and the seafood platters are also more than memorable. It's a bit ironic that what is now one of Apalachicola's best dining spots is located in this somewhat (at least by land) out-of-the-way location. Trust us, though, you won't find better seafood anywhere in Apalachicola.

Galley slaves in need of stock will probably want to take a taxi to the either the local Piggly Wiggly or IGA supermarket. This is a lengthy trek by foot (as with all the other Apalachicola marinas) but a very quick taxi ride.

Over and above all these impressive statistics, we were struck time and again by the Scipio Creek Marina staff's "can-do" attitude. We think you will be similarly pleased. Tell Shane we sent you!

Scipio Creek Marina (850-653-8030
   http://www.scipiocreekmarina.com

Approach depth—8-12 feet
Dockside depth—8 feet outer pier (MLW)
   4½-10 feet inner basin (MLW)
Accepts transients—yes
Transient-dockage rate—average
Fixed wooden piers—yes
Dockside power connections—30 and 50 amp
Dockside water connections—yes
Waste pump-out—yes
Showers—yes
Laundromat—yes
Gasoline—yes
Diesel fuel—yes
Mechanical repairs—mostly independent contractors
Ship's/variety store—yes
Restaurant—on-site

Apalachicola Ashore

The beautiful Victorian homes that grace Apalachicola's quiet lanes are clearly this community's star attraction. There is perhaps no better example of these bygone structures than the magnificently restored Gibson Inn (850-653-2191 http://www.gibsoninn.com). Located at the corner of Highway 98 (Market Street) and Avenue C, the inn is only a short step from all the waterfront marinas.

Built by James Fulton Buck in 1907 from the finest heart pine and black cypress, this grand dame of Apalachicola was originally opened as the Franklin Inn. Incidentally, any of you who are familiar with the history of the South Carolina Low Country will recognize the name of Buck as being associated with a great

Scipio Creek Marina, Apalachicola

lumbering dynasty founded near Georgetown before the Civil War.

The original structure was heated by steam and featured thirty-three rooms. Twin porches wrapped the first and second floors. A widow's walk and cupola on the roof completed the classic Victorian look.

After passing through the hands of a succession of owners, the inn was acquired by two sisters, Annie and Mary Ella ("Sunshine") Gibson, in 1923. All the local stories indicate that these two were real characters, and they soon renamed the inn for themselves, a designation that survives to this day.

The Gibsons ran the inn until 1942, at which time the army acquired it for an officers' club. Following the war, the building col-

lapsed into a sad state of disrepair until the present owners discovered it in 1983. One year of renovation and a cool million dollars later, the Gibson Inn was restored to its original glory, and glorious it is! Each room has its own special decor appropriate to the time of the inn's construction. Downstairs, the large, airy lobby with its heart pine floors is flanked by the reconstructed bar. Just behind is the restaurant, which serves all three meals.

To say that a visit to the Gibson Inn is memorable is to understate the obvious. This writer urges all his fellow cruisers to take advantage of this unique hostelry. I promise that it will be a stay you will never forget. Even if you should choose to remain aboard, consider dining at the restaurant. The more sophisticated dishes are the star gastronomical attraction during the evening meal. The breakfast is first-rate, with the hot cakes earning a particular note of praise. It's not going too far to say that those who have not visited the Gibson Inn have not really seen Apalachicola. To be succinct, don't miss it!

In addition to the Gibson Inn and the restaurants reviewed as part of our marina coverage above, there are several other dining spots that should attract your notice. Delores Sweet Shop (29 Avenue E, 850-653-9081) serves a wonderful breakfast and lunch. Then again, you might want to try the Apalachicola Seafood Grill (100 Market Street, 850-653-9510). As its name implies, the seafood is first rate.

New restaurants seem to be springing up almost on a daily basis in the revitalized

Gibson Inn, Apalachicola

downtown Apalachicola business district. Don't be surprised to find even more choices than the long list presented in this account.

After you have finished slaking your appetite, stroll west on Avenue C for a view of the town's many restored Victorian and antebellum homes. Sixth and Seventh streets, running off Avenue C to the north and south, display many other restored abodes that are well worth a look. On a warm, sun-splashed day, the light filtering through the tall trees and playing about the roofs, walls, and lawns of these venerable old homes makes for a sight that is almost dreamlike in its serenity.

Eventually, you may want to make your way to the John Gorrie Museum on 6th Street. Dr. Gorrie practiced medicine in Apalachicola dur-ing the mid-1800s. While trying to find some way to cool the rooms of victims of yellow fever, he invented the modern-day ice machine. In addition to his medical and inventive pursuits, this famous citizen of Apalachicola also served as mayor, postmaster, city treasurer, council member, band director, and founder of Trinity Church. Strangely enough, he died without ever finding a commercial market for his invention.

After visiting the museum, take a few moments to stroll across the street to Trinity Episcopal Church. Shipped section by section to Apalachicola from New York in 1837, this old house of worship reminded this writer of Prince George Church in Georgetown, South Carolina. The church still retains the original hand-stenciled ceiling and pipe organ.

John Gorrie Museum, Apalachicola

Respectful visitors are welcome to view the interior unless a service is in progress.

Now walk back to Market Street (Highway 98), the main thoroughfare running through the downtown business district. There is so much to see and experience along this street and its tributaries.

Be sure to drop by the Apalachicola Chamber of Commerce at 99 Market Street (850-653-9419, www.baynavigator.com). Here you will find all sorts of brochures and a friendly staff ready to help with any needed information.

Visitors up for the best reading material in town will want to check out Hooked on Books (54 Market Street, 850-653-2420) and Betsy's Downtown (67 Commerce Street, 850-653-1290). Both of these small, but well-supplied bookshops have all the latest bestsellers as well as many titles of regional interest.

Another shop we found to be of particular interest is the Apalachicola Bay Trading Company (52 Avenue D, 850-653-4889). Here, visitors can ooh and ahhh at some exquisite examples of handcrafted furniture. Of course, they'll be glad to sell you a few pieces to cart back home.

Forgotten Coast Outfitters (94 Market Street, 850-653-9669) features an excellent selection of outdoor-oriented clothes plus fly-fishing equipment, gifts, and books of local interest.

There are many other shops, particularly of the antique persuasion, and restaurants along Market Street and its adjoining lanes. Visiting these tiny establishments is almost like taking a step back to the turn of the century.

All mariners will want to pay a call to Wefing's Marine (850-653-9218) at 252 Water Street (www.wefings.com). Water Street parallels the path of the Apalachicola River and the ICW. Wefing's position along this track puts it within easy walking distance of all the Apalachicola marina facilities.

Wefing's is the largest, independent marine store in this region. Chances are, if you need anything nautical, the good people here will have what you seek or, at worst, be able to acquire it shortly.

Wefing's also has a second bait-and-tackle location at 58 Market Street (Highway 98), in the heart of downtown Apalachicola. The original Water Street store will be of more interest to cruising yachtsmen.

Another Water Street business of interest is the Seafood-2-Go Retail Market (123A Water Street, 850-653-8044). Here, just a quick step north of the Apalachicola River Inn, visitors can purchase the freshest catch of the day. Soon your galley will be filled with the wonderful smell of frying fish!

And if that's not enough for you, don't miss the Grady Market (850-653-4099) at 76 Water Street. This complex boasts a varied assortment of gift, gourmet food, antique, art, and garden shops. They are all more than fascinating!

Finally, consider making your way back to the waterfront on Bay Avenue, which borders the shores of Apalachicola Bay. Often you can catch a cooling breeze from the nearby waters. The view of the bay to the right, with more of the village's magnificent houses to the left, is not to be missed.

Cruising visitors may well want to time their visit to Apalachicola for the first weekend in November. During this happy time the community hosts the Florida Seafood Festival. This event is an entertaining extravaganza of arts and crafts, recreational activities, and, of course, mouth-watering seafood. There is

Wefing's Marine Supply, Apalachicola

also an annual "Spring Tour of Homes" held during the first weekend in May.

Numbers to know in Apalachicola include

Crooms Taxi—850-653-8132
Apalachicola Car Rental—850-653-2211
Apalachicola Chamber of Commerce— 850-653-9419
Wefing's Marine Supply—850-653-9218

Apalachicola History

The charming village of Apalachicola has a rich past full of color and dashing figures. The name is Native American and is translated by most authorities as "the land beyond." If the local native Americans meant "beyond the ordinary," they could not have been more truthful.

The first Europeans to establish themselves

Apalachicola homeplace

in the Apalachicola region were Franciscan friars from Spain. Moving east from Pensacola, this order established ten missions in the region during those early Colonial days.

Following the English victory in the Seven Years' War (1763), known as the French and Indian War in this country, Spain ceded Florida to Great Britain. The English lacked the manpower to exploit all their new territory. Private trading companies took over much of the lucrative Indian trade that was the mainstay of the region's economy. This arrangement continued even after the American Revolution, when Florida was returned to the Spanish.

By 1835 the Panton & Leslie Company, originally based in Saint Augustine and having been granted most of northwestern Florida by the Spanish, had evolved into the Apalachicola Land Company. Some years earlier the Indian troubles had at last been brought to an end by Andrew Jackson during his campaigns of the War of 1812. This process had set in motion a chain of events which would eventually bring all of Florida into the American fold.

By the mid-1830s Apalachicola had become established as a major cotton-shipping center. The young town grew into the third largest port on the Gulf Coast. Vast sums of wealth were accumulated and many beautiful homes were built to house the wealthy residents. In 1836, 51,673 bales left the docks of Apalachicola. This colorful era is recalled by a historical marker along the village waterfront that carries the caption "When Cotton Was King."

The heyday of the cotton merchant and planter lasted, as elsewhere, until the Civil War. Early in that tragic struggle, the town was blockaded by Union forces. The Confederates retreated up the Apalachicola River, outmatched by the numerically superior Northern forces. A traditional legend of Apalachicola claims that local residents would signal the home troops with a lamp in one of the town's tallest houses whenever the Yankees left on an expedition. The Southerners could then steal quickly back into town for supplies and a home-cooked meal.

After the war the cotton industry was laid waste. Many of the beautiful old homes sat empty and silent. The village's residents took more and more to fishing and oystering for their livelihood. This proved to be a lucrative industry. During the late 1800s oysters from Apalachicola Bay gained the reputation as the finest in the nation. Locals will argue that fame is still deserved to this very day.

During the last decade, farsighted individuals have been discovering Apalachicola and its old homeplaces in ever-increasing numbers. Many a fine Victorian and antebellum home which once rang with the joyous shouts of a cotton shipper's children has now been restored to its former glory. The old river village of Apalachicola is unquestionably undergoing a latter-day renaissance. How fortunate for us all that it is a new beginning without the need for modern, unsightly construction.

ST. GEORGE SOUND AND APALACHICOLA BAY NAVIGATION

The easternmost reaches of the ICW running through St. George Sound and Apalachicola Bay traverse some of the most open inland waters between Carrabelle and New Orleans. While fair-weather passage of the sound and bay is a true cruising delight, winds over 15 knots can raise a most unwelcome chop. Blows over 25 knots can be downright dangerous. Prudent skippers will plan their cruise from Carrabelle to Apalachicola with careful attention to the latest weather forecast.

The easterly portion of this run does not stray near too many shoals and is relatively easy to navigate. The situation is quite different as you approach the long East Pelican Reef and Rattlesnake Cove adjacent to St. George Island. Visiting cruisers must now pay close attention to the Waterway's ample markers or risk a most unpleasant grounding.

Nevertheless, this is not a navigationally difficult portion of the Gulf Coast ICW. Cautious skippers armed with the appropriate charts and the latest *Notice to Mariners* should be able to come through with nothing worse than a bit of eye strain from staring intently at their charts.

Entering St. George Sound   There are two possible entrances from the deep water of the Gulf of Mexico into St. George Sound. The more easterly route is particularly convenient to the anchorages on the northern shores of Dog Island, though it is more complicated than East Pass Inlet, which is just west of the island. Both entrances require careful navigation and constant attention to the sounder.

If you choose to enter St. George Sound to the east of Dog Island, you will need chart 11405 for navigation. First, you must clear the shallows of South Shoal, which lies to the south of Alligator Harbor and Lighthouse Point, by passing well to the south of flashing buoy #26. A long, slow turn to the north is then necessary to skirt the shoal known as Dog Island Reef. To avoid the reef, set your course to eventually come abeam of and pass flashing daybeacon #1 by several hundred yards to its easterly quarter. A sharp turn to the west will then carry you into the deeper waters leading to St. George Sound. Flashing daybeacon #3 helps you along the way. Set a course to come abeam and pass #3 by some 50 yards to its northerly side.

While making the trek between #1 and #3, a marked channel will be passed north of your course line. This cut serves some local, private piers and is of no interest to visiting cruisers.

Once abeam of #3, the sound's deeper waters are within sight to the west and the anchorages associated with Dog Island are only a short cruise away.

To continue on your way, point to eventually pass to the north of flashing daybeacon #5 and come abeam of flashing daybeacon #7 by some 100 yards to its northwesterly quarter. Once abeam of #7, the first of Dog Island's superb anchorages will come abeam to the south.

Visiting cruisers are advised against using the shortcut that runs between Dog Island Reef and the shallows abutting the easterly tip of Dog Island, marked by unlighted nun buoy #2. Leave this cut to the local fishermen who know where the shoals are. The longer passage around Dog Island Reef's easterly quarter is much safer.

Dog Island Anchorages   To enter the easternmost anchorage on Dog Island, set a careful compass course for the deep waters just inside the hook on the island's northnortheasterly tip. For best depths, favor the easterly banks slightly. This maneuver will help to avoid the charted patch of 5-foot water to the southwest. Watch your sounder. If depths fall below 7 feet, slow down, assess the situation, and make appropriate corrections before grounding depths are reached.

Be sure to drop the hook before moving to within 100 yards of shore. Closer in, depths deteriorate to 3 feet or less. As usual with Panhandle waters, bright, sunny days allow for easy visual identification of the shallows. Even so, be sure to leave enough swinging room between the shoals and your anchordown spot to avoid swaying into the shallows.

Remember that neither this anchorage nor the haven in Shipping Cove features adequate shelter when winds are blowing from the north, or in foul weather. On the plus side though, the strong currents so prevalent north of Apalachicola seem to be mostly absent in this region.

Skippers who choose to make use of the excellent Tysons Harbor anchorage should continue cruising on the sound's deeper waters until the cove's entrance is directly abeam to the southeast. Then, turn into the mid-width of the cove and proceed at idle speed until you see the first of the private markers denoting the channel leading inward. If for some reason you don't spot these privately maintained aids, don't attempt to enter the cove on your own. The channel (without the markers) is much too tricky for strangers. Nighttime entry, for the same reason, is not recommended for visiting cruisers.

Cruise into Tysons Harbor by passing to the appropriate side of the various aids to navigation. Some are unadorned pilings, but the others are daymarkers, with far more red aids to navigation in evidence than green marks. As you would expect, pass all red markers to your starboard side and take their green counterparts to port.

To reach the superb anchorage along the harbor's easterly banks, depart the marked cut between the third and fourth set of markers, and set course for the correctly charted bubble of 8- to 9-foot waters to the east. Feel your way carefully with the sounder to within 75 yards of the eastern banks. Drop the hook, leaving a good buffer against the shallows around the shoreline.

South and southeast of the above-described anchorage, the marked Tysons Harbor channel continues upstream to the private docks of the Dog Island Yacht Club and the public pier near the launching ramp. Continue to follow the various markers to these piers.

The inner anchorage will come up to the east after coming abeam and passing the last marshy point to the east. If you do choose to make use of this questionable haven, cruise carefully in between the resident craft you will spy moored here, and drop the hook before making a close approach to the shoreline. Be sure to leave adequate swinging room between your vessel and its neighbors. This can be a real challenge in these close quarters.

The westernmost Dog Island anchorage in Shipping Cove is the easiest to enter. Look for a single house on shore in the very back of the cove and use this structure as a navigational reference. Head directly toward the house and pier, dropping the hook at least 75 yards short of the banks.

On St. George Sound West of #3, off Dog Island's northeasterly tip, begin using chart 11404. This map's larger scale gives far better resolution.

Once abeam of flashing daybeacon #3, you have a cruise of 5.8 nautical miles in front of you before intersecting the Carrabelle River-ICW channel. Fortunately, this is a mostly open run with few shallows to worry with. Be sure to avoid the charted 2-, 3-, and 4-foot patches north of the "Dol rep" designation on chart 11404 by cruising well to the south of these hazards. Also, be on guard against the charted sunken wreck. Note the "Masts" designation, denoting that the derelict's masts are above the waterline.

Don't attempt to take the shortcut that runs north of the just-discussed shoals and intersects the Carrabelle Channel near unlighted daybeacon #1. On-the-water research revealed this route to be confusing. The various aids on the channel are very hard to spot when approaching Carrabelle from this angle. Cruising craft larger than 26 feet are specifically warned against making use of this passage.

Instead, follow a course that will eventually bring you abeam of unlighted can buoy #13 well to its southerly side. At this point you must decide whether to continue on to the west to the beginnings of the Gulf Coast ICW, eventually leading to Apalachicola, or turn northeast into the Carrabelle channel. This account will first review Carrabelle and its river, followed by a discussion of the Waterway channel leading to the sheltered waters of the Apalachicola River.

Carrabelle and Carrabelle River   The channel to Carrabelle is flanked by large spoil islands to the east. During high water, a goodly portion of these hazards are underwater and, on choppy days, are not readily visible. Fortunately, the Carrabelle Channel markers allow most navi-

gators to avoid these hazards easily. There is also a wide buffer of deep water between the channel and the spoil islands. Minimum depths in the marked cut are a very respectable 12 to 20 feet.

To enter Carrabelle, continue on the deep waters of St. George Sound until you are some .2 nautical miles southwest of unlighted can buoy #13. Then, turn sharply back to the northeast and set course to come abeam of flashing daybeacon #15 to its fairly immediate easterly side. From this point, navigation of the channel is straightforward until coming between unlighted can buoy #1 and the unnumbered 20-foot flashing forward range marker. The range denoted by this aid to navigation can be very useful in keeping to the outer portion of the approach cut.

From #1, the channel swings sharply to the northwest. Make the turn when you are between #1 and the unnumbered range marker, and point to come abeam of unlighted daybeacon #3 to its northeasterly quarter. Another range, northwest of unlighted daybeacon #4, is useful when running this portion of the channel.

At unlighted nun buoy #6, the channel swings to the north. Now, it becomes a fairly simple matter to follow the deep, well-marked channel as far as the Moorings at Carrabelle Marina.

At unlighted daybeacon #6, visiting cruisers should take note of the "Idle Speed, No Wake" sign. This restriction is in force throughout the entire Carrabelle waterfront.

You will spy Paramore's Marine Service and Pirate's Landing Marina guarding the southwestern banks, south of unlighted daybeacon

#9. The headquarters of C-Quarters Marina will come abeam along the northerly shoreline, between unlighted daybeacons #13 and #15. Carrabelle Marina will be spied to the north abeam of unlighted daybeacon #17, followed closely by the extensive piers of the Moorings.

Upstream on the Carrabelle River   Many cruisers will choose to discontinue their explorations of the Carrabelle River at the Moorings. However, a few captains may decide to continue upstream to the anchorage described earlier, southwest of unlighted daybeacon #68. Remember, though, the channel only carries 4 feet of depth between unlighted daybeacons #21 and #25. Unless future dredging removes this trouble spot, you must be sure your vessel can handle this thin water before making the upstream trek. Note also that the Carrabelle River fixed bridge has a vertical clearance of only 40 feet, preceded by a power line with 50 feet of height. This restriction, along with the shallow depth, will serve to bar most larger and medium-sized sailcraft from the river's upper reaches.

Even captains who can stand the 4-foot stretch must take great care to stay in the channel. A goodly current flows through the Carrabelle River, and it's not too hard for leeway to ease you out of the deeper water, even when it seems as if you are heading directly for the next marker. Be sure to watch your stern as well as the track ahead to avoid this problem.

To proceed upstream, continue on your former course after passing unlighted daybea-con #17 for some 25 to 30 yards. Then, cut sharply to the southwest and point to pass unlighted daybeacon #18 to its immediate southeasterly side. Once pass #18, begin slowly curling your course around to pass through the mid-width of the Carrabelle River fixed bridge. Along the way you will pass to the north of unlighted daybeacon #19.

Between #19 and the Carrabelle fixed bridge, passing cruisers will spy a canal cutting into the southerly banks. This stream sports quite a collection of pleasure craft and private docks. These local captains must know some trick. We tried to enter this body of water twice, only to be turned back by extremely shallow depths on each occasion. Based on this experience, it would seem a far better plan to leave this errant creek to those with definite local knowledge.

Once through the fixed span, carefully set course to come abeam of unlighted daybea-con #21 to its immediate northerly side. There seems to be a tendency to drift into the shallow waters to the north between the bridge and #21. Such a mistake can land the hapless mariner in 3 to 4 feet of water.

Between #21 and unlighted daybeacon #25, cruisers will discover the shallowest portion of the Carrabelle River channel. Even when staying directly in the channel, you can expect consistent 4-foot depths. Once abeam of unlighted daybeacon #26, soundings again deepen to 6 feet or more.

A no-wake zone is in force between unlighted daybeacons #25 and #40. This prohibition protects the extensive waterfront development lining the western banks along this stretch of the river.

The marked channel continues on to unlighted daybeacon #68. Farther upstream, there are no other aids to navigation. To enter the anchorage, carefully set course from #68 for the southerly branch of the river. Favor the easterly shore slightly.

Consider dropping anchor in the stream's mid-width shortly after coming abeam of the point, lying northwest of your position, separating the river's two branches. Depths should be in the 7- to 10-foot range. Swinging room can be a bit tight, so use only enough anchor rode for a 6-to-1 scope.

Uncharted shoals are *soon* encountered west of the above described anchorage. In spite of soundings shown on chart 11404, cruisers are specifically warned against proceeding any farther up either branch of the river.

East Pass Inlet   Many cruisers entering St. George Sound make use of East Pass Inlet. This relatively deep seaward cut boasts five charted markers, a sure sign of a pretty stable channel. At this printing, navigators can count on minimum 8-foot depths, with most soundings showing considerably more. However, remember that inlets are notorious for quick depth changes. It might be wise to call one of the Carrabelle marinas on the VHF and check on conditions before entering the channel.

Also note that the charted wreck, southeast of flashing buoy #12 is for real. During our last sojourn of this channel in the fall of 2002, a portion of this derelict was visible above the water line. We were able to identify it as a sunken fishing trawler. This wreck is a real hazard at night or in low-light conditions.

On the ICW   Flashing daybeacon #2 marks the official beginning of the northern branch of the Gulf Coast ICW. Come abeam of this aid to its southerly side and set course to come abeam of flashing daybeacon #6 by about the same distance to its southerly quarter. A run of 2.8 nautical miles separates #2 and #6. Fortunately, the run does not stray near any shallow water. Nevertheless, it would be a good idea to follow a careful compass course between the two aids.

The ICW continues on its southwesterly trek by passing to the south of flashing daybeacon #8 and then entering a long, improved channel denoted by numerous aids to navigation. Unlike in past years, many of these markers are now unlighted daybeacons, supplemented by a few floating aids to navigation. This cut leads past several shoals to the central pass-through of the fixed Cat Point-St. George Island Bridge.

As chart 11404 clearly shows, there are numerous unmarked shallows outside of the Waterway channel east of the fixed span. Prudent navigators will only leave the ICW along this stretch after careful planning and chart work. Between flashing daybeacons #2 and #14, two anchorages can be found on the northwesterly shores of St. George Island, southeast of your course line.

St. George Island Anchorages   To make good your entry into the cove anchorage northeast of charted Pilot Harbor, abandon the ICW channel some .7 nautical miles southwest of flashing daybeacon #2. Turn to the south and cruise carefully along for about 1 nautical mile. You should then begin feeling your way carefully toward the shoreline. Be *sure* to drop the hook before approaching to within less than 200 yards of the southern and southeasterly St. George Island shoreline.

Cruisers making for the anchorage south-southeast of flashing daybeacon #8 should set a careful course from #8 for the deeper waters well west of charted Sugar Hill. Drop the hook at least 400 yards short of the shoreline. Farther in, depths become too shallow. Take care to stay well west of the large bubble of shoal that ranges north and northwest of Sugar Hill.

On the ICW   Don't attempt to enter Rattlesnake Cove southeast of unlighted daybeacon #26. While these waters look good on chart 11404, the bay's entrance is surrounded by numerous unmarked shallows, including a large oyster bank, and is much too troublesome for strangers.

West of flashing daybeacon #40, the ICW hurries through a dredged cut in Bulkhead Shoal and soon passes under the fixed Cat Point-St. George Island Bridge. Vertical clearance is set at 50 feet. Sailcraft that cannot clear this height must reenter the Gulf through East Pass Inlet and then cruise back into Apalachicola Bay through Government Cut.

As this account is being tapped out on the keyboard, construction has just gotten well underway on a new, higher version of this span. For the next several years, passing cruisers will undoubtedly have to dodge a whole series of work barges, cranes, and other construction equipment. Take extra care when approaching the Cat Point-St. George Island Bridge, and expect the unexpected until this lengthy construction project reaches fruition.

Don't be tempted to try the entrance to the charted "Yacht Basin" south-southeast of unlighted can buoy #49, just west of the St. George Island Bridge. While 11404 would lead you to expect a broad and deep cut, this channel has narrowed and shoaled extensively. It is only appropriate for very small craft.

The ICW continues west down a well-defined channel. There are now far more daybeacons and less floating aids to navigation along this stretch than was true just a few short years ago.

The Waterway follows a near 90 degree turn to the north just west of flashing daybeacon #76. South of #76, skippers have access to Government Cut Inlet and, to the southwest, the anchorages associated with Little St. George and St. Vincent islands.

Government Cut Inlet   Be warned that Government Cut Inlet is subject to shoaling and periodic dredging, but this channel is normally passable for pleasure craft. Cautious navigators will check at one of the Apalachicola marinas about present conditions before attempting this seaward cut. Also, try to pick a day of fair weather and light to moderate winds. Strong southerly blows can raise a particularly threatening chop.

As mentioned earlier, there is some recent

shoaling on Government Cut Inlet along its northeastern flank. We suggest that you deviate from the charted range marker and slightly favor the inlet's southwestern sign between unlighted daybeacon #1A and the gap between unlighted daybeacons #3 and #4.

Little St. George and St. Vincent Anchorages To reach the anchorage to the north of Cape St. George, set course from either flashing daybeacon #76 or unlighted can buoy #77 to come abeam of the charted Higgins Shoal shallows by some .4 nautical miles to their northerly side. You can then set a direct course for flashing daybeacon #12. This bisected course will allow you to avoid the extensive shallows jutting northwest from Pilot Cove.

Once abeam of #12, you can work your way carefully towards the southerly shoreline, keeping an eagle eye on the sounder. If depths drop below 7 feet you are encroaching on the shallows buffering the banks. Retreat to deeper water and, as always, leave plenty of swinging room between your craft and the shoal water.

Remember, shallow water extends out for a good 400 yards from the banks of Little St. George Island into the bay. Take great care to avoid this extensive hazard.

If you should choose to continue west to the anchorage abeam of St. Vincent Island, track your way to the western tip of Little St. George, known incongruously enough as Sand Island. Along the way, stay well to the north and northeast of flashing daybeacon #10 and unlighted daybeacon #8 to avoid the shallow water abutting the shoreline.

Once abeam of #8, set a careful compass course for a position just south-southeast of the charted location of Back Slough. This run will lead you across the northeasterly reaches of West Pass Inlet. As you might expect, the waters can be more than slightly choppy in this area.

Watch your depth sounder carefully. When depths reach the 7-foot level, drop the hook.

To return to the ICW channel, retrace your steps to the east. The seemingly more direct course to the northeast will lead even small craft to grief on the 2- and 3-foot waters of St. Vincent Bar.

On the ICW North of unlighted nun buoy #6, the ICW begins to run through an improved channel, cut amidst the shallower waters of northern Apalachicola Bay. Spoil shoals line a goodly portion of this run, particularly to the west.

Stick to the marked cut. This is not the place to go exploring outside of the Waterway. Fortunately, the numerous floating buoys make it a relatively simple matter to stay in the channel.

At flashing daybeacon #TM the ICW intersects a local channel running first west and then south into the northwesterly reaches of Apalachicola Bay and the eastern genesis of St. Vincent Sound. Local fishing craft use this cut extensively. However, there are no facilities for pleasure craft anywhere along the passage. Depths vary widely, ranging to as little as 4 feet or less at lower tide. Visiting cruisers are advised to bypass this wayward cut and leave it to the knowledgeable locals.

North of #TM the docks of Apalachicola Municipal Marina will be found on the charted *L*-shaped harbor cutting into the northwestern banks. After leaving this harbor behind, the channel quickly passes under the fixed high-rise section of the John Gorrie Memorial Bridge (also known as the Highway 98 Bridge). Fortunately, vertical clearance for this span is set at 65 feet. Soon after passing under the bridge, Miller Marine and Apalachicola River Inn and Marina will be spotted along the westerly shoreline.

A charted channel strikes northwest into Scipio Creek from the Waterway along the Apalachicola waterfront, northwest of flashing daybeacon #2. This cut leads to Deep Water Marina and Scipio Creek Marina, both of whose docks guard the creek's southwestern banks.

When entering this stream, be very sure to avoid the long, long correctly charted tongue of shoal water striking southeast from the creek's northeasterly entrance point. For best depths, depart the Waterway abeam of flashing daybeacon #2, and favor the western and southwestern banks as you enter Scipio Creek. You can cruise back to the mid-width after working your way upstream some 50 yards pass the northeasterly entrance point.

Apalachicola River to Gulf County Canal

The Gulf Coast ICW between Apalachicola and the Port St. Joe/Gulf County canal is one of the wildest and most scenic stretches of the Waterway from Carrabelle to New Orleans. Deep stands of age-old cypress trees surrounded by marsh and other hardwoods brood over the dark-colored waters. Birds by the hundreds are often observed along the banks. There are overnight anchorages readily available to most cruising craft which seem about as far removed from civilization as one is likely to get in our modern, well-planned world. A night spent on one of these lonely creeks, washed in the glow of countless stars unhindered by the clear coastal air, may lead one to conclude that this is what cruising is all about.

Several years ago this writer was privileged to pass the night in one of these memorable sanctuaries. I stood in the cockpit long after dark staring with amazement at the vast heavens above. The only sound that came to my ears save the crickets was the light sighing of the wind. I hope you too will have the opportunity to experience a night spent along this unforgettable portion of the Gulf Coast ICW.

The Waterway follows the delightful waters of the Apalachicola River northwest for some 5 nautical miles from the village sharing its name and then enters the almost equally charming Jackson River. Several side waters are available for anchorage along this stretch, but currents do run swiftly.

The Jackson River leads, in turn, to gorgeous Lake Wimico. While lacking any gunk holes, the run through this lake may just be the most beautiful of the entire trek. Northwest of Lake Wimico, the Waterway follows portions of Searcy Creek to the White City Bridge. When the

Waterway was developed, several branches of this creek were joined by man-made canals. Some of the stream's abandoned loops provide first-rate overnight havens.

West of White City the ICW follows a mostly dredged land cut with decidedly less beauty than the waters to the east. Some 1.4 nautical miles past the bridge, the ICW intersects the Port St. Joe/Gulf County Canal. Captains can follow this stream to the community of Port St. Joe and beyond to the wide waters of St. Joseph Bay. Here mariners will discover a shiny new first-rate marina, while the bay's waters to the west offer one of the most dramatic fair-weather anchorages in the Florida Panhandle.

While anchorages along this section of the ICW are fairly numerous, there are no readily available facilities catering to pleasure craft directly on the Waterway short of Panama City, some 38 nautical miles west of Apalachicola. Of course, you can always spend the night or top off your tanks at Port St. Joe (see below), but otherwise, you're on your own over the course of this entire run.

Four Tree Cutoff (Standard Mile 348.5)

The charted entrance to the Little St. Marks River southeast of unlighted can buoy #13, known as "Four Tree Cutoff," has shoaled far more than indicated on the edition of chart 11402 available at the time of this writing. Entrance depths are now less than 4 feet. All craft, even of the outboard variety, are advised to bypass this errant offshoot.

Upper Apalachicola River and St. Marks River Anchorage (Standard Mile 345.5) (29 49.522North/085 00.900 West)

The ICW abandons the Apalachicola River between unlighted daybeacon #30 and flashing daybeacon #2. While the Waterway begins its trek up the Jackson River, the upper reaches of the Apalachicola strike northeast toward an eventual intersection with the St. Marks River. The mid-width of the Apalachicola carries minimum 8-foot depths to its charted limits (at least). In fact, we discovered some depth soundings that exceeded 20 feet in places.

The upstream portion of the Apalachicola River is reasonably well-marked with uncharted aids to navigation that greatly facilitate avoiding the few shoals flanking the shoreline. The presence of these marks is not really surprising, as this stream supports a good amount of barge traffic. In fact, while it falls far beyond the scope of this guide, we are told that this river is navigable far inland to Columbus, Georgia. Fellow cruising guide author Capt. Rick Rhodes is currently working on an in-depth guide for the upstream reaches of all the Florida Big Bend and Panhandle rivers. The upper section of the Apalachicola River will be covered in this work, to be released in 2003.

The lower section of the Apalachicola River, within several miles of its intersection with the ICW, has an unfortunate (and prodigious) 2-knot-plus current. The water movement is so strong that yachts passing the river's entrance on the Waterway have been shoved to the south and southwest. Sailcraft and single-screw trawlers who choose to make the passage upriver, described below, must take this current into account and watch for leeway like the proverbial hawk.

In light of the frequent commercial-barge traffic, and the strong currents reviewed above, it is a decidedly *bad* idea to attempt anchoring along the course of the Apalachicola River. Nightmares of dragging anchors are bound to fill the dreams of any cruiser dropping the hook on these waters.

Fortunately, for those willing to take a 3-nautical-mile jaunt upriver, there is a ready solution to this problem. The river current lessens noticeably (but does not disappear entirely) on the extreme upstream reaches of the St. Marks River, which intersects the Apalachicola River north of St. Marks Island. If you can avoid one shoal at the St. Marks' westerly mouth, this stream carries 8 to 16 feet of water and features enough swinging room for vessels up to 38 feet. Try dropping the hook on the St. Marks, some .3 nautical miles east of the intersection between the two rivers, near 29 49.522 North/085 00.900 West (where chart 11402 indicates a 14-foot sounding). This anchorage has excellent shelter and is appropriate for the heaviest weather.

The banks of the St. Marks rivers are almost totally devoid of development, and the swampy, well-wooded shores so typical of this area very much in evidence. In short, the natural scenery is magnificent. Few mariners who enjoy getting off the beaten path will begrudge a trip up this fascinating stream.

There is one lone house perched on the point separating the two rivers, but this solitary structure tends to add to the ambiance rather than detract from it. We did note several houseboats secured semi-permanently on the upper reaches of the St. Marks River. This novel alternative to weekend fishing camps is quite prevalent all along the Northern Gulf.

Adventurous cruisers can follow the St. Marks River east and then south from the Apalachicola to a point just short of the river's intersection with East River Cutoff. Past this point, the twin streams become too small for cruising-size craft.

Saul Creek (Standard Mile 345) (29 47.539 North/085 03.118 West— lower anchorage) (29 48.340 North/085 03.127 West—upper anchorage)

Saul Creek boasts what just may be the best overnight anchorage between the village of Apalachicola and Lake Wimico. This stream makes into the ICW's northeasterly banks just northwest of unlighted daybeacon #6. Entrance depths from the ICW are an impressive 10 feet plus, soon deepening to soundings of 19 to 30 feet on the interior.

The stream's lower reaches immediately adjacent to the Waterway are large enough to allow the passage of pleasure craft up to 48 feet, but are a bit skimpy on elbow room while swinging on the hook.

Have faith. Some .4 nautical miles northwest of its intersection with the ICW, Saul Creek splits. The easterly branch, known as Saul Creek Cutoff, is too narrow for most cruising craft, but the principal western fork is another story. After passing through a brief, uncharted hole with depths of 20 to 30 feet, the stream temporarily widens out into a broad pool with depths of 8 to 9 feet on the centerline. Boats up to 36 feet will find plenty of swinging room to let down the hook near 29 47.539 North/085 03.118 West, in about as sheltered a spot as you are ever likely to find. Depths on this portion of the creek seem to run around 12 to 14 feet. Indeed, if I had a boat in Apalachicola and heard that a powerful storm was headed our way, my choice for shelter would most likely be this very spot.

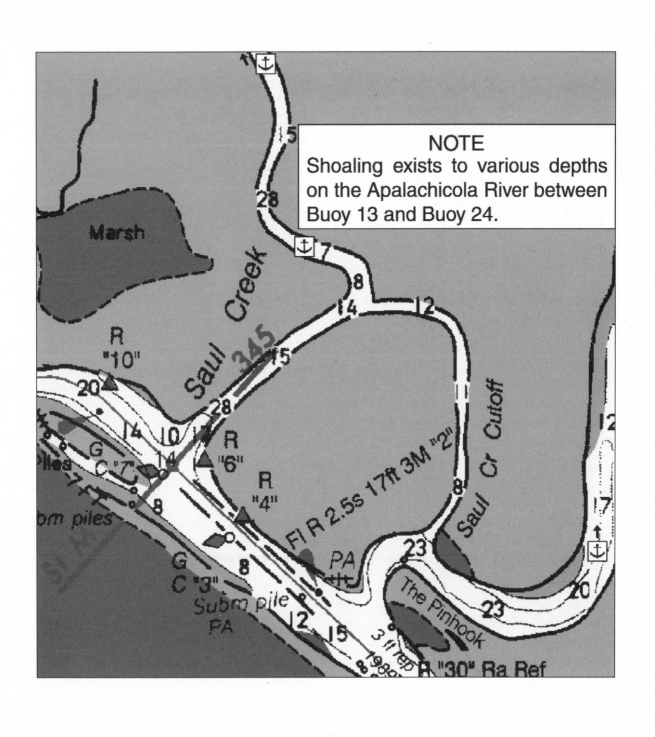

NOTE
Shoaling exists to various depths on the Apalachicola River between Buoy 13 and Buoy 24.

The wanderers among us might also consider dropping the hook even farther upstream, just short of Saul Creek's second split, near the position of charted (but tiny) Cedar Creek. Depths on this portion of Saul Creek run 15+ feet, but swinging room is only sufficient for boats as large as 34 feet. Try dropping the hook near 29 48.340 North/085 03.127 West, in some 13 to 17 feet of water.

While water movement on Saul Creek is certainly not as swift as that on the upper Apalachicola River, there is still some current. Be sure your anchor is well set before heading below for a well-earned toddy.

To say that the shores of Saul Creek are attractive is to do the stream an injustice. Of all the side waters east of the Bay County Canal, the deep, swampy cypress shores of this creek are without peer. Tall cypress trees, trailing their long beards of gray moss, look benignly over the river as they have for time uncounted. Even cruisers who normally spend their evenings afloat at marinas ought to consider this unusually beautiful and well-sheltered haven.

Several of the floating, fishing-camp-type weekend retreats, so typical of these waters, will be spied along the shores of Saul Creek. The presence of these structures certainly does not impede anchorage on Saul Creek in any way, shape, or fashion, but in former times, there was no development along the stream's shores whatsoever.

Lake Wimico (Eastern Entrance–Standard Mile 340.5) (Western Entrance—Standard Mile 335.5)

Northwest of flashing daybeacon #1, the combined path of the ICW and Jackson River flow out into the wider waters of Lake Wimico. This fortunate body of water has long had

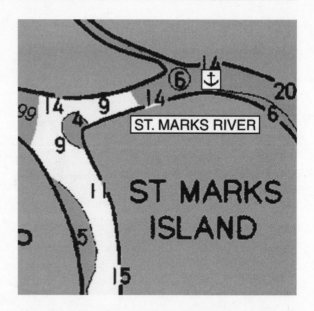

the reputation of being one of the most visually appealing settings along the Gulf Coast ICW. Indeed, if you are lucky enough to visit during a day of little wind (as was this writer) and see the shoreline unbroken by any human hand, mirrored in the dark but shining waters, you will most certainly be a believer as well.

For all its natural beauty, Lake Wimico lacks any accessible side waters for cruising-size craft. While a portion of the lake carries respectable depths of 5 to 6 feet, shallow water abuts the edges of the Waterway channel. Captains of larger vessels should follow the marked cut.

There seems to be a long-standing tendency toward lateral leeway on the ICW channel traversing Lake Wimico. Please review the navigational account of the lake later in this chapter for more information.

Eventually the ICW channel leads across Lake Wimico and then passes into the Searcy Creek section of the Waterway. This body of water reintroduces superb shelter. It would take some truly nasty weather to raise any sort of chop on Searcy Creek.

Long Loop Anchorage (Standard Mile 334.5) (29 49.688 North/085 11.370 West)

Northwest of standard mile 335, the first large loop cutting into the Searcy Creek-ICW's northeastern banks can make for an excellent anchorage if your craft can fit the size requirements. While the southeastern entrance shoals to 4 feet or less, the northwesterly entrance

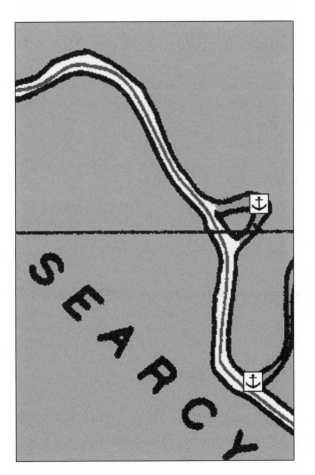

from the ICW carries 7 to 8 feet of water. Soundings temporarily improve to 9 and 10 feet at the rear of the loop.

Maximum swinging room is found near the northwesterly intersection with the ICW and the rearward section of the stream, just before it loops back to the east and south. There should be enough room for vessel as large as 34 to 36 feet in these two areas. Craft up to 38 feet might be able to make use of this anchorage by employing a Bahamian-type mooring. In heavy weather, this would also be a wise practice for smaller vessels.

Protection is quite good from all winds, and the shoreline is the usual undeveloped cypress swamp. One feature of this creek is the many fishing-camp-type houseboats permanently moored on the rear portion of the loop. There is certainly not enough swinging room for cruising craft to anchor near the houseboats, and depths soon deteriorate to 4-foot levels, moving back south and southwest toward the Waterway. Most mariners will want to anchor well before reaching the houseboats, in one of the two havens described above. Then, if you so desire, you can break out the dinghy and explore the rest of the loop.

Island Anchorage (Standard Mile 334) (29 50.051 North/085 11.380 West)

Perhaps the best anchorage between Lake Wimico and White City is also found on the ICW's northeastern shore, just north of the anchorage described above. While much shorter than its southerly sister, this stream has minimum 6-foot depths at both entrances, with 8 to 12 feet of water on the back portion of the loop. Swinging room, particularly on the northerly section of the loop, is sufficient for vessels up to 40 feet. However, boats in the upper end of this size range might want to put down a Bahamian moor for maximum protection.

Shelter is near perfect from all winds and the attractive shoreline is completely undeveloped. It was on this loop that my mate and I passed the memorable evening described at the beginning of this section. To say the least, we recommend it heartily to our fellow mariners.

Another Loop Anchorage (Standard Mile 332.5) (29 50.651 North/085 12.466 West)

The loop creek that cuts into the Waterway's northeastern shore, and is charted just below the designation "Impenetrable swamp" on 11393, carries 6 to 7 feet of water on the initial portion of its northwesterly leg *only*. However, depths drop off to 3 feet or less at the rear of the loop and on the southeasterly leg leading back to the ICW. In mid-1997 we stirred considerable mud

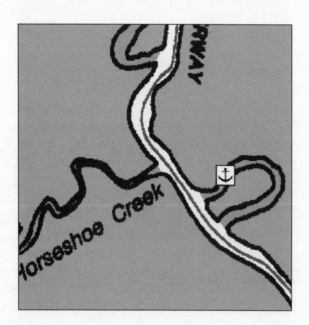

on the southeasterly portion of this creek in a small, shallow-draft power craft.

Unfortunately, the deeper northwesterly portion of the loop also has the least swinging room. There is probably only enough space for a 32-footer to fit in comfortably. With two other superior anchorages so close by, most navigators will choose to bypass this questionable loop.

White City (Standard Mile 329.5)

The fixed, high-rise (65 feet of vertical clearance) White City Bridge crosses the ICW just northeast of standard mile 330. Passing cruisers will note a public launching ramp and an adjacent fixed, wooden pier flanking the Waterway's northeasterly banks, immediately southeast of this span. Depths on the outer part of this dock run 6 to 7 feet, with about 4 to 4½ feet of water lying alongside the interior section. While we did not see any signs prohibiting overnight dockage, this pier appears to have been primarily constructed with small power craft in mind, and cruising-sized vessels will now find little to recommend a stopover at White City.

Just northwest of the White City span a small, charted stream cuts back to the northeast. There is an older, now-disused launch ramp and some private docks guarding this tiny creek's shores. Even so, we sounded less than 4 feet of depth at its entrance. All but shallow-draft vessels are strictly advised to keep on trucking down (or up) the Waterway.

Time Change

At White City, cruisers do a bit of time travel—from Eastern into Central time. Be sure to set your watches back an hour, or you could be a bit early for that special dinner in Panama City.

APALACHICOLA RIVER TO GULF COUNTY CANAL NAVIGATION

The run along the ICW from Apalachicola to the Gulf County Canal is comprised of the familiar, well-marked Gulf Coast Waterway channel. A new factor is inserted, however, east of Lake Wimico via the strong currents flowing from several small rivers. Sailcraft proceeding under auxiliary power and single-screw trawlers must be particularly alert for the effect of side-setting current. Check your course over the stern regularly to quickly note any lateral slippage.

Entrance into the various side waters along the way presents no unusual difficulties except for the strong water flows just discussed. Captains entering the upper reaches of the Apalachicola River must be especially ready for this problem.

For most cruisers, power and sail alike, this is a portion of the ICW that will not present enough navigational problems to detract from the region's great natural beauty. Nevertheless, don't become so entranced with the scenery that you fail to watch your stern. Such a mistake could result in a most unpleasant grounding far from any helpful facilities.

On the ICW   The ICW channel remains well marked north of the 65-foot, fixed John Gorrie Memorial Bridge. Observe all beacons and floating aids to navigation carefully as there is shoal water lying to the east between the bridge and the ICW's turn to the northwest at flashing daybeacon #8.

Pay particular attention to the long, charted spit of shoal water cutting southeast from the northeasterly entrance point of Scipio Creek (west of unlighted can buoy #5). These shallows seem to be building outward and are littered with semisubmerged debris. Be *sure* to pass east of #5.

Northwest of flashing daybeacon #10, there are no further markers for some 2.4 nautical miles. Simply stick to the mid-width and you will not encounter any problems.

Finally, unlighted can buoy #13 breaks the monotony at the charted location of Bay City. A series of floating markers directs navigators northwest toward the Apalachicola Northern Railroad Bridge. This span has a closed vertical clearance of 11 feet but is usually open unless a train is due.

West of the railroad bridge, the Waterway cuts a bit to the northwest and continues following a few aids to navigation to the Jackson River. Unlighted daybeacon #26 will be spotted surprisingly close to the easterly banks. Pass #26 by a good 25 yards to its westerly side.

ICW—Upper Apalachicola River Intersection   Northwest of unlighted daybeacon #30, the Waterway leaves the confines of the Apalachicola River. The upper section of this river, abandoned by the ICW, splits off to the north. As mentioned earlier, the current leaving the Apalachicola is so strong that it has been known to shove ICW boats onto the southern side of the channel. Be ready for this current by favoring the north-northeastern side of the Waterway somewhat when passing.

Another navigational problem with the intersection of the Waterway and the upper portion of the Apalachicola comes up by way of the southernmost, uncharted aids to navigation defining the latter stream's upstream channel. It's all to easy to mistake the southernmost, unlighted nun buoy on the upper Apalachicola as an ICW aid to navigation. Skippers following the Waterway's track, who are not interested in exploration of the Apalachicola River's upper reaches, should ignore the nun buoy and set course to come abeam of the ICW's flashing daybeacon #2 to its southwesterly side.

Upper Apalachicola River Remember that current flow often exceeds 2 knots between the Apalachicola River's intersection with the ICW and the forks at the St. Marks River. Boats with limited maneuverability, such as sailcraft with low-powered auxiliaries or single-screw trawlers with small diesels, should think long and hard before committing to an upriver voyage. If you do make the attempt, keep an eagle eye out for leeway and be on maximum alert for other problems caused by the swift waters.

Be on guard against barge traffic while cruising on Apalachicola. During our last visit in late summer 2002, we spotted two barges and tugboats within a single hour.

A few of the upper Apalachicola River's daymarks are actually nailed to trees along the shoreline. Needless to say (but let's say it

anyway), these errant aids to navigation need to be given a wide berth.

To enter the mouth of the upper Apalachicola, depart the Waterway by favoring the eastern side of the entrance slightly. Soon you should spy one red, unnumbered, and unlighted nun buoy. For best depths, pass this aid to navigation fairly close to your starboard side.

As you begin cruising through the first sharp turn, known as "the Pinhook," the narrow waters of Saul Creek Cutoff will come abeam to the north. This stream (at least this part of it) is too narrow for all but skiffs and outboard-powered craft.

After passing through the Pinhook, you will begin to pick up the uncharted markers denoting the river channel. Most of these aids consist of floating buoys, while a few are daybeacon (signs) affixed to trees along the shoreline.

Follow the buoyage system carefully! As suggested on chart 11402, there are more than a few shoals abutting the river's banks. Fortunately, the various aids to navigation vastly simplify the task of circumventing the shallow water. None of the aids on the upper Apalachicola River is lighted. Consequently, it is decidedly unwise for strangers to attempt entry after dark or even in conditions of low visibility.

The numerous buoys and daybeacons finally lead upstream to the intersection with the St. Marks River. If you choose to enter (or anchor on) the St. Marks, be sure to avoid the large bubble of 4-foot water correctly charted on the southern point of this stream's western mouth. Once past this problem area, select any likely spot on the mid-width to drop anchor. Boats drawing less than 6 feet can continue exploring the St. Marks as it winds its way to the southeast. Hold to the mid-width for best depths. Eventually the stream splits at the fork with East River Cutoff. Cruising-size craft should halt their gunk-holing at least 100 yards short of this split. Both streams narrow and depths become too unreliable for larger vessels.

Continuing upstream, the Apalachicola soon leaves the confines of chart 11402. Further upstream passage is probably best left to the professional towboat captains, at least until Capt. Rick Rhodes' detailed guidebook of these waters is available to the cruising community.

Saul Creek   The delightful waters of Saul Creek strike northeast between unlighted daybeacons #6 and #10. For best depths, enter the stream on its mid-width and continue to follow the centerline as you work your way upstream.

Eventually Saul Creek splits. The easterly branch, known as Saul Creek Cutoff, is too narrow for cruising-size vessels. However, the main branch of the creek, just north of the split, leads to the best anchorage on the stream. While cruising through the northerly fork, you will first sound your way through a small patch of 20 to 30 feet of water. These rather astounding depths soon give way to more conventional 8- and 9-foot readings. Drop the hook before passing through the stream's next turn to the northwest, and settle in for a night of peace and security.

It is possible for boats as large as 36 feet to continue exploring upstream on Saul Creek until the waters again split at the intersection with Johnson Creek. A good spot to anchor is found just short of this intersection where chart 11402 notes a sounding of 17 feet.

Further passage north on either branch of Saul Creek is not recommended due to the relatively narrow character of the streams. As fascinating as they undoubtedly are, these waters are best left to the locals.

On to Lake Wimico   The Gulf Coast ICW follows the wide, deep, but mostly unmarked track of the Jackson River as it works its way west to Lake Wimico. No unusual navigational concerns are to be found between Saul Creek and the lake.

The Waterway channel across Lake Wimico, however, calls for greater caution. A good portion of the cut is lined by spoil shoals. In spite of soundings of 4 to 6 feet shown on chart 11402 in the lake's interior reaches, captains should make every effort to stay well within the ICW channel.

On-site research and talks with fellow cruisers has revealed a tendency to wander off the marked track between the various aids to navigation. This problem is probably due to two factors. First, the daybeacons marking the channel through the lake are located a bit too far apart. Some pairs are separated by almost a full nautical mile. Also, there seems to be some low-profile current in the lake, even though it is not readily apparent from looking at the water. These two factors make it imperative for all navigators to watch the markers they have just left behind as well as their course ahead to quickly note any lateral slippage.

While the channel through most of the lake is straight as an arrow, prudent mariners will pre-plot a compass/GPS course between the markers. This precaution will help you keep to the marked cut.

To enter the lake from the east, come abeam of flashing daybeacon #1 to its northeasterly side. Be particularly mindful of the charted shoal flanking the ICW's northeasterly side at flashing daybeacon #1. On-the-water observations have led us to believe that this shoal is growing larger.

The run across Lake Wimico then lies straight before you through the various pairs of aids until reaching a point between flashing daybeacon #13 and unlighted daybeacon #14. Westbound craft might have some difficulty in sighting #13 and #14. These aids to navigation seem to blend with the shoreline. Use your binoculars to help locate the markers.

Farther to the northwest, the channel cuts a little to the south. Point to come abeam of flashing daybeacon #15 to its fairly immediate northeasterly side. The entrance into Searcy Creek to the northwest will then be quite obvious.

Once the lake is behind you, switch to chart 11393 for continued navigation of the ICW track.

On the ICW—Searcy Creek   The Searcy Creek section of the ICW running west to the White City Bridge is narrow, well sheltered, and unmarked. Successful navigation of the cut is the usual elementary matter of holding to the middle.

The charted loop creek that makes into the Waterway's northeasterly banks, a short hop northwest of flashing daybeacon #15, is certainly deep enough, with typical soundings of 8+ feet, but it is too narrow for anchorage by any vessel larger than 24 feet. Additionally, this small stream plays host to quite a collection of floating, fishing-camp-type houseboats. Cruising-size craft would do well to bypass this body of water entirely.

Large Loop Anchorage   The first large loop *northwest of standard mile 335* should be entered only by way of its northwesterly branch. Depths of 4 feet or less are quickly encountered on the southeasterly entrance.

Enter the creek on its mid-width. The waters featuring maximum swinging room are found just past the creek's mouth. Good depths continue as the stream follows a slow bend to the north. Another wide section of the creek will be encountered just before it swings back to the southeast.

Do not attempt to follow the rear portion of the loop east to the houseboat moorings described earlier. As the southeasterly branch of the creek is approached, depths drop off to 4-foot levels.

Island Loop Anchorage   The excellent anchorage on the smaller loop circling the island found a short distance north (and west) of the anchorage reviewed above can be entered by either of its mouths. As you might expect, hold to the centerline throughout the entire stream for best depths. Maximum swinging room is available on the northerly branch, but small craft can select any likely spot to drop the hook and settle in for the evening.

Another Loop Anchorage   The loop cutting into the Waterway's northeastern banks almost opposite charted Horseshoe Creek can only be accessed via its northwesterly mouth. Enter on the mid-width. Depths of 6 to 7 feet continue for only about half the passage toward the rear of the loop. Past this point, 2- to 3-foot soundings are the norm all the way through the stream's southeasterly entrance.

On the ICW   Do not attempt to enter any of the other loops off the Waterway between Horseshoe Creek and the White City Bridge. Without exception they are quite shoal, as this writer's bent prop can well attest.

The charted pontoon bridge east of the White City span was removed long ago. Maybe NOAA will one day gets its act together and remove this designation from future editions of chart 11393. Just before reaching the White City Bridge, a public launching ramp and an adjoining single, fixed-pier will come abeam on the northeastern banks.

The White City fixed bridge has an impressive vertical clearance of 65 feet. Once through the bridge, it's a quick trek of some 1.4 nautical miles on the Waterway to the intersection with the Gulf County/Port St. Joe Canal.

Gulf County Canal, St. Joseph Bay, and St. Joseph Peninsula

Whoever decided to dredge the canal between the ICW and St. Joseph Bay certainly did a good turn for all of us pleasure cruisers. While this stream was most certainly constructed to allow barge traffic ready passage from the now-defunct pulp mill at Port St. Joe to the ICW, the canal provides three very important benefits for cruisers. First, it allows for ready access to a brand-new, absolutely first-class marina on the Port St. Joe waterfront. Secondly, this stream also allows for easy passage from the Waterway to the very navigable St. Joseph Bay Inlet channel. Finally, careful captains can drop the hook in Eagle Harbor and dinghy ashore to some of the most magnificent beaches anywhere on the Florida Panhandle. How's that for some fortunate qualities?

Gulf County/Port St. Joe Canal (Standard Mile 328.5)

The arrow-straight canal provides 10-foot minimum depths from the ICW to the open waters of St. Joseph Bay. Depths range as high as 40 feet, with typical soundings around 10 to 12 feet.

The northeasterly portion of the canal cuts through the usual swampy ground. Southwest of the charted power cables, commercial development begins to become evident on both shores.

The southwestern foot of Gulf County Canal is spanned by a fixed bridge with 75 feet of vertical clearance, preceded by a power line with 85 feet of clearance. Cruisers approaching this high-rise span will sight a few docks abutting the northwesterly banks, where local fishing craft are regularly moored. Unfortunately, there are no facilities for pleasure craft.

There are no anchorages, docks, or shelters of any kind on the canal. Once committed to this passage, you are obligated to traverse its full length before you can hope to find any shelter at Port St. Joe and on St. Joseph Bay.

Port St. Joe and Port St. Joe Marina (29 48.881 North/085 18.557 West)

After many years without pleasure-craft facilities of its own, St. Joseph Bay, and the community of Port St. Joe in particular, can now boast truly world-class services. Port St. Joe Marina sits on a man-made, currently uncharted, but well-sheltered harbor east-southeast of flashing daybeacon #30.

Perhaps the only down side to this marina (and its a rather minor quibble) is that the entrance can be a bit difficult for first-timers to identify. You will find the outer mouth of the approach cut near 29 48.817 North/085 18.630 West. Captains lacking the miracle of GPS should simply keep a close watch on the easterly banks as they cruise south on the broad, correctly charted "Harbor Channel," east of flashing daybeacon #30. Eventually, you will spy the harbor's entrance, flanked by twin stone jetties.

Once you have spotted the entrance to Port St. Joe Marina, the rest is sure to be a real on-the-water pleasure. We simply can't say too many good things about this facility. It is, quite simply, one of the best marinas in all of the Florida Panhandle.

The Port St. Joe Marina dockage basin consists of an artificial harbor surrounded on three and one half sides by a substantial land berm. A large combination ship's store, restaurant, and dockmaster's building overlooks the easterly banks.

Transients are gladly accommodated at Port St. Joe Marina. Dockage consists of sturdy, fixed-wooden piers featuring the latest freshwater and 30- to 50-amp power hookups. Some slips feature canvas coverings to protect vessels from inclement weather.

Entrance depths run to 8 feet or better, with minimum 6½-foot soundings dockside. Typical depths in the dockage basin run around 8 feet. Waste pump-out service, gasoline, diesel fuel, and extensive dry-stack storage are also available. Some mechanical repairs can be accommodated through local, independent technicians.

Shoreside, visiting cruisers will discover superclean, air-conditioned showers and a small but adequate Laundromat. These facilities are located in the same building as the marina's extensive ship's and variety store.

Here you will also find the Dockside Cafe and Raw Bar (850-229-5200). This on-site dining attraction is open for lunch and the evening meal seven days a week. Breakfast is served on weekends. There's lots of open-air dining available. It's ever so nice to sip on a cool drink under one of the tiki-type roofs while watching the harbor traffic after a long day on the water.

Several other restaurants are to be found within walking distance in downtown Port St. Joe. Check out our review of this community's central business district below.

Cruisers in need of galley supplies are not forgotten. A new Piggly Wiggly supermarket is located a mere two blocks from the marina. Another block or two will lead visitors to a drugstore set along the side of Highway 98 and the downtown shopping district along Reid Avenue (see below).

To paraphrase an old television commercial, "If you can find a better marina, stay

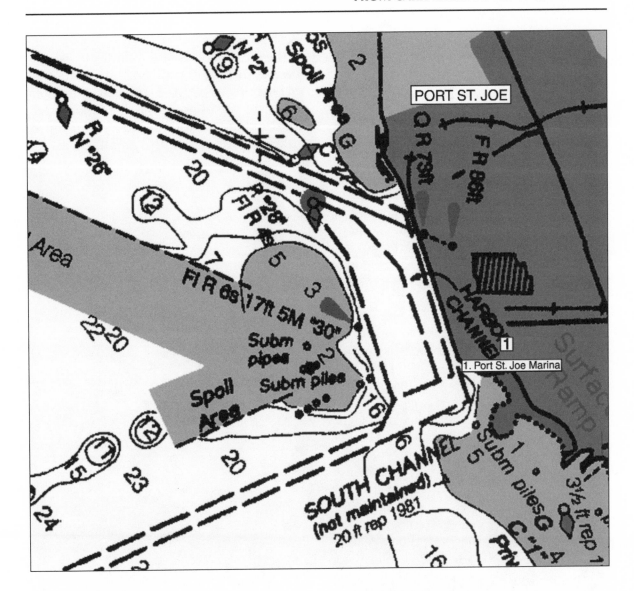

there." We don't think you will, and to be at least a little bit succinct, Port St. Joe Marina receives this writer's highest recommendation.

Port St. Joe Marina (850) 227-9393
www.brandymarine.com/psjmarina.index.htm

Approach depth—8-24 feet (MLW)

Dockside depth—6½-8 feet (MLW)
Accepts transients—yes
Transient-dockage rate—average
Fixed wooden piers—yes
Dockside power connections—30 to 50 amp
Dockside fresh-water connections—yes
Waste pump-out—yes

Gasoline—yes
Diesel fuel—yes
Showers—yes
Laundromat—yes
Mechanical repairs—some can be arranged
through local, independent technicians
Ship's/variety store—yes
Restaurant—on-site and others nearby

Port St. Joe

The city of Port St. Joe guards the easterly reaches of St. Joseph Bay. This town offers excellent motels, restaurants, and at least one historical site of note. The first Florida state constitution was formulated by a group of political pioneers in this small, backwater

Port St. Joe Marina

town. This historic achievement is now aptly remembered by a museum.

For years, the big knock against Port St. Joe was its huge pulp and paper mill, so prominently visible from the waters of St. Joseph Bay. When this plant was in operation, the smell of progress was not so sweet.

The pulp mill has been closed for some years now, and while its demise was most certainly a blow to the local economy, the air has been ever-so-much purer since.

Rumors continue to abound as to this property's future. One line of thought has the Walt Disney company developing the land as a major recreation complex. Only time will tell if any of these grandiose plans come to fruition.

In the meantime, the downtown Port St. Joe business district has gone through a tasteful redevelopment, centering along Reid Avenue. This area is easily accessible by way of a four- to five-block walk from Port. St. Joe Marina.

Visitors strolling along Reid Avenue will find, among others, an antique mall, the Port Side Trading Company (an interesting-looking gift shop), a package store, and the Sugar Shack (an ice-cream parlor and restaurant).

Perhaps Reid Avenue's greatest attraction, however, is the Flower Mill Bakery Cafe (226 Reid Avenue, 850-229-6050). These good people serve a wonderful breakfast and the baked goods—well, words just fail me. Trust me, they are scrumptious.

There are also several motels spread up and down the track of Highway 98 as it passes through Port St. Joe. At least one is within walking distance of the marina.

Port St. Joe struck this writer as a community in transition from the old paper-mill economy to something very different in the future.

Just what that future may turn out to be should be answered over the next several years.

St. Joseph Bay

The large body of water known as St. Joseph Bay spans an impressive length of some 11.5 nautical miles and is as much as 5.5 nautical miles in width at its widest point. As you might expect, winds over 10 knots from any quarter can foster a very healthy chop. Keep an eye on the weather as you plan your voyage on the bay.

While the southerly portion of St. Joseph Bay is quite shoal, the northern two-thirds are mostly deep. There is a large shelf of shallow water extending east from St. Joseph Peninsula, but fortunately Eagle Harbor penetrates this barrier.

The southern ⅓ of St. Joseph Bay is an official aquatic preserve. Sensitive sea-grass beds are marked by orange and white buoys. Be *sure* to stay well away from the shallows defined by these low-key aids to navigation.

Except for the anchorage described below, the bay lacks any sheltered havens. Despite its scant supply of sheltered, overnight havens, a cruise on St. Joseph Bay is certainly not to be discounted out of hand. With the exception of Port St. Joe, the shoreline is practically undeveloped. If you cruise the bay during the fall, spring, or winter months, you will most likely be the only pleasure craft in sight on the wide waters. This potential for privacy, coupled with the considerable charms of Eagle Harbor and St. Joseph Peninsula State Park, discussed below, may just make this noteable body of water the best-kept secret on the Florida Panhandle.

St. Joseph Bay Inlet

The northern section of St. Joseph Bay presents

a wide-open face to the Gulf of Mexico. The waters are crossed by a well-maintained and marked channel, originally designed to serve the commercial needs of the Port St. Joe pulp mill. Fortunately, pleasure cruisers piloting even the largest craft can also make use of this well-situated cut to leave the Gulf and gain ready access to the ICW or depart the Panhandle's inland waters and strike out for the open sea. Sailors should find this channel particularly helpful, as it provides a well-spaced alternative for those needing seaward access between Apalachicola Bay and Panama City.

Eagle Harbor Anchorage
(29 45.975 North/085 24.126 West)

A wide tongue of deep water cuts through the shoal waters buffering the eastern shores of St. Joseph Peninsula and leads fortunate mariners to a cove known (and charted) as Eagle Harbor. Care is needed to avoid the shallows to the north and south, but careful navigation should see you safely inside.

Try anchoring within some 100 yards of the deeper water's southwesterly tip, near 29 45.975 North/085 24.126 West. Shelter is excellent for westerly winds, while light to moderate breezes from the north and south are also acceptable. There is no protection from easterly blows, however. Strong winds from this quarter would make for a most uncomfortable, possibly dangerous, stay.

Captains and crews dropping anchor in this haven may well spot what seems to be a small marina and partially enclosed harbor lying just to the south, near 29 45.855 North/085 24.147 West. On-site research revealed this to be a pontoon-boat rental facility associated with the adjacent state park (see below).

While there are 5-foot depths in the harbor, approach soundings of only 3 feet, or even slighly less at low water, relegate this tiny facility to small, very shallow-draft craft. About the only interest it might hold for visiting cruisers is the possibility of temporary dinghy dockage, but even this service is not assured.

Once the hook is down, take a moment to admire the undeveloped shoreline. As you survey the white-sand dunes of St. Joseph Peninsula State Park, it won't be long before the inspiration hits to break out the dinghy and journey ashore for some of the best beach-combing to be found anywhere.

Sadly, because of the unmarked surrounding shoals, this writer must discourage captains and their mates who pilot craft drawing more than 5½ feet, or which are more than 45 feet in length, from entering Eagle Harbor. In very light airs, you could possibly anchor in the deeper waters to the east, but a very long dinghy ride would then be required to reach the shoreline.

Of course, this navigational channel would be so much simpler if you are lucky enough to have a GPS aboard, interfaced with a laptop computer, running appropriate navigational software. All of us are not so lucky; however. So lacking these electronic marvels, be ready to practice your best DR navigation.

St. Joseph Peninsula State Park

"Miles of white sand beaches, striking dune formations, a heavily forested interior, and a favorable climate for year-round outdoor recreation characterize this pristine state park.

"The 2,516-acre park is almost entirely surrounded by water. . . . The park is best known for its beaches and huge barrier dunes. The shallow waters of St. Joseph Bay teem with a

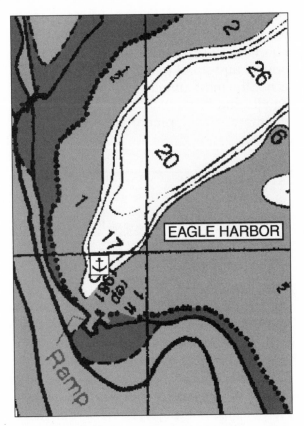

EAGLE HARBOR

variety of marine life. Bay scallops, hermit crabs, fiddler crabs, horseshoe crabs, and octopi are frequently encountered in the bay."

The description presented above is taken directly from the official St. Joseph Peninsula State Park brochure as produced by the Florida Department of Natural Resources. It is entirely accurate. Indeed, one cannot wander these unspoiled beaches without remembering that all of Florida was once like this. With the rampant commercial development since World War II, sanctuaries such as this state park are now all too rare. How fortunate that cruisers have such ready access to this memorable park. This writer urges all his fel-

low mariners to allow sufficient time in their plans to fully enjoy this special treat!

Mexico Beach

The resort community of Mexico Beach actually looks out over the open Gulf waters northwest of St. Joseph Bay, but as it does not connect with any inland waters, the small canal known as Salt Creek, which serves the town, can only be reached from the bay or Gulf. While some small facilities are available to pleasure craft, entrance depths are a meager 3 feet and sometimes less.

Those few cruisers who successfully negotiate the relatively shallow entrance will quickly spot the city docks just to port. These fixed wooden piers are free for all to use. Unfortunately, dockside depths are only 2½ to 4 feet and there are no power or water connections.

Farther upstream, Marquardt Marina offers better services, including three transient slips. However, you must be able to clear a fixed, culvert-type bridge with only about 12 feet of vertical clearance before reaching this facility. This restriction confines Marquardt's patrons to smaller power craft.

If you can clear the bridge, visiting cruisers will find respectable dockside depths of 5 to 6 feet next to the fixed wooden piers with power and water connections. Gasoline and diesel fuel are available, as is a large ship's and tackle store. Mechanical repairs are in the offing for outboards and I/O-powered craft. Boats up to 30 feet can be hauled out, though this service is provided mainly to serve the dry-docked power craft stored at the marina.

Marquardt Marina (850) 648-8900

Approach depth—4 feet (or less)

Dockside depth—5-6 feet
Accepts transients—3 slips usually open
Fixed wooden piers—yes
Dockside power and water connections—20 amp
Gasoline—yes
Diesel fuel—yes
Mechanical repairs—limited
Below-waterline repairs—limited
Ship's store—yes
Restaurant—several nearby

The town of Mexico Beach itself, along with its side-by-side sister community Beacon Hill, consists of a long row of beach houses and small retail stores. Frankly, this is not the most attractive section of the Panhandle and this writer was rudely reminded of mass development in southeastern Florida.

GULF COUNTY CANAL AND ST. JOSEPH BAY NAVIGATION

Successful navigation of the Gulf County Canal and St. Joseph Bay is an elementary study in coastal piloting. Passage of the canal is about as simple as it gets. St. Joseph Bay calls for more caution.

As is true with any water body of its size, St. Joseph Bay can carry a very respectable chop when winds exceed 10 knots. Entrance into the Eagle Harbor anchorage adjacent to the St. Joseph Peninsula is complicated by the absence of any aids to navigation. On the other hand, the marked channel leading from St. Joseph Bay into the Gulf is exceedingly well marked with floating buoys, most of which are lighted.

Captains and crews visiting St. Joseph Bay for the beautiful beaches of the St. Joseph Peninsula should make every effort to pick a day of fair weather with light breezes. If you are leaving for the open waters of the Gulf or arriving from those same reaches, the bay's entrance channel should serve you well.

Gulf County/Port St. Joe Canal   Enter the Gulf County Canal from the ICW on its mid-width. Don't cut either corner. Some shoaling seems to be occurring on both the northwestern and southeastern points. Once inside the canal, cruisers will be surprised to see their sounders showing 40-foot depths. These readings soon rise to 10- and 12-foot levels. Simply hold to the centerline for best depths all the way to the Highway 98/Port St. Joe Bridge.

Some .9 nautical miles north of this span, you will begin to encounter industrial development along the canal's shoreline. While the large barges often moored along the canal are not subject to injury from the wake of passing pleasure craft, the same may not be true of the commercial fishing vessels sometimes docked along the canal's northwestern banks just short of the bridge. Slow down if there is any question. Remember, you are legally responsible for any damage caused by your wake.

The intersection between the southwestern tip of the Gulf County Canal and St. Joseph Bay is crossed by a 75-foot fixed bridge. Fortunately, the well-marked passage from the canal out into the deeper waters of St. Joseph Bay is now a wide, easily followed passage. This was not always true in times past. Nevertheless, leeway is still possible, courtesy of the strong tidal currents that regularly dog these waters, so watch your track over your stern as well as the path ahead to detect any lateral slippage on your vessel's part.

As you pass out of the Gulf County Canal, point to pass between unlighted daybeacons #5 and #6. Continue on course, pointing for the gap between flashing buoy #4 and unlighted can buoy #3. Shoal water with depths of less than 3 feet guards both sides of the dredged channel between the canal's southwesterly mouth and #4. Take great care to stay in the marked cut. Once abeam of flashing buoy #4, you can relax. The deep waters of St. Joseph Bay stretch out in front of you for miles in most directions. Now you must decide whether to turn south to Port St. Joe Marina, set off across St. Joseph Bay to Eagle Harbor, or run the bay's well-marked inlet channel.

Route to Port St. Joe Marina Continue cruising to the west for some 100 yards past the gap between flashing buoy #4 and unlighted can buoy #3. Then, turn 90 degrees to the south, and point to pass unlighted nun buoy #2 fairly close to its westerly quarter. Be advised that #2 is a very low-lying aid to navigation, and it can be difficult to spot.

Continue on the same course for .18 nautical miles past #2, then swing to the southeast. Use your binoculars to help pick out flashing buoy #28 and unlighted can buoy #27. Cruise between these two aids to navigation, and remain on this track for another 100 yards or so. Now turn south on the charted Harbor Channel, paralleling the old industrial waterfront. The former pulp and paper mill will be more than obvious to the east during this run.

Be sure to stay well east of flashing daybeacon #30. Very shallow 2- and 3-foot waters lie west, northwest, and southwest of #30.

Eventually, you will pass #30 well west of your course line. Begin watching the easterly banks for the somewhat hard-to-find entrance to Port St. Joe Marina. Use your binoculars to help pick out the approach cut, which is defined by twin stone jetties. You will find this channel's westerly mouth near 29 48.817 North/085 18.630 West. Once you have the entrance in your sights, cut into the channel's centerline, and cruise into the mostly enclosed marina dockage basin.

Out into St. Joseph Bay Cruisers bypassing Port St. Joe Marina should consider setting a course from a position between flashing buoy #4 and unlighted can buoy #3, to come abeam of flashing buoy #24 on the main bay channel to its northerly quarter. You can then either follow the marked cut out to sea or begin your trek toward the anchorage along the St. Joseph Peninsula.

Cruisers are warned against entering the bay's southerly reaches. The recorded soundings of ½ to 3 feet on chart 11393 are for real. Even small outboard fishing craft regularly find the bottom in this treacherous area.

Eagle Harbor To visit the enchanting anchorage on the St. Joseph Peninsula at Eagle Harbor, depart from the main bay channel at flashing buoy #24. Set your course directly across the charted spoil bank for the cove's entrance. On-site research revealed that minimum 8- to 9-foot depths can be held over this spoil, with soundings of 10 to 11 feet being more the norm. It is a run of just slightly less than 5 nautical miles from #24 to the Eagle Harbor anchorage.

As you approach the entrance between the shallows to the north and south, slow to idle speed. Keep up just enough speed for ready maneuverability. Using your compass, chart 11393, and hopefully a GPS-plus laptop computer, carefully cruise into the deep tongue of 20-foot-plus water leading into the interior of Eagle Harbor. Watch your sounder. If readings get above 15 feet, you are encroaching on the shallows to either the north or south. Stop and make corrections before grounding depths are reached.

Eventually you will spot a launching ramp and the tiny boat-rental concession described earlier on the cove's southwestern corner. Carefully bend your track a bit to the southwest and drop anchor near 29 45.975 North/085 24.126 West. Don't even think about making a closer approach to the boat-rental harbor. Depths soon rise to 3 feet or less at MLW. Also be sure to stay at least 250 yards off the adjoining banks.

As can be readily appreciated by any competent navigator, the above-described procedure is delicate and not to be undertaken lightly. The absence of any markers renders the task far more complicated than need be. Only two or three buoys placed at strategic points would vastly simplify the navigation of Eagle Harbor. It is hoped that in the future the Coast Guard will take note of this deficiency.

Cruisers visiting Eagle Harbor during the spring and winter months should note that the late-afternoon sun will be shining directly into their eyes. This makes it almost impossible to visually identify surrounding shoals.

St. Joseph Bay Inlet Channel   The St. Joseph Bay channel to and from the Gulf of Mexico is exceedingly well marked and easy to follow, night or day. The only unusual portion of the passage is found abeam of flashing buoy #16. Here the channel runs hard by St. Joseph Point to the west. Be sure to pass to the east of #16 to avoid the shoal waters surrounding the point.

Once past flashing buoy #14, the marked passage begins a long, slow turn to the southwest. After leaving flashing buoy #12 behind, deep, open water spreads out in every direction. Pleasure craft need not follow the marked channel any longer, but its westerly tip at flashing buoy #2 does make a good navigational reference point for those putting out on the Gulf.

Mexico Beach   Those few boats whose shallow draft allows them to visit Mexico Beach should consider setting a course from flashing buoy #8 (on the main St. Joseph Bay Inlet channel) to the southern mouth of Salt Creek. Leaving the channel from this aid rather than a buoy farther to the west results in a shorter run across unmarked water. Your course will be almost due north from #8 and the run covers some 3.2 nautical miles. There are no shallows along the way to be concerned with until you are within 150 yards of the Salt Creek entrance.

At the current time, two flashing buoys (#1 and #4), and a flashing daybeacon (#1) mark this very uncertain channel. The markers at the entrance to Salt Creek have been changed repeatedly during the last several years, and there's no guarantee that the scheme of aids to navigation will be the same when you arrive. This channel is NOT recommended without very specific local knowledge, and even then, its thin water is only appropriate for very shallow-draft vessels.

Once past the concrete-enclosed entrance, depths remain pretty much the same until you pass under the culvert bridge. Farther upstream, cruisers will find 5 to 6 feet of water leading to Marquardt Marina.

ICW TO East Bay

The run from White City to the easterly reaches of East Bay and the approach to Panama City is one of contrast. From the White City Bridge, cruisers follow a mostly man-made canal for some 12.5 nautical miles to the narrow confines of Wetappo Creek's South Prong. The Waterway then flows through Wetappo Creek for some 4.5 nautical miles before it empties into the wide waters of upper East Bay. This portion of the ICW is well sheltered and rough water will not be a problem. There is but one side-water capable of providing minimal overnight anchorage on this entire run.

Conversely, East Bay is a large body of water that can get quite choppy if winds exceed 15 knots. However, there are several first-rate anchorages to be found on the creeks and bayous flowing into the bay. Several of these feature excellent shelter and magnificent, undeveloped shores.

Finally, the Waterway passes under the Dupont fixed bridge (vertical clearance 50 feet) near standard mile 295. West of this span the sprawling community of Panama City spreads out before you. The many facilities and anchorages associated with this active city will be reviewed in the next chapter.

There are no pleasure-craft marinas or facilities of any kind between White City and the Dupont Bridge. Fortunately, the extensive marinas of Panama City are just a short cruise west of this fixed span. Be sure your tanks are topped off before leaving Apalachicola behind.

Wetappo Creek—North Prong (Standard Mile 314.5) (30 00.642 North/085 22.431 West)

The North Prong of Wetappo Creek cuts into the Waterway's eastern shore just north of standard mile 315. This wilderness stream boasts natural shorelines with enough depth and swinging room to accommodate smaller cruising craft overnight. Even if you aren't ready to stop for the evening, Wetappo Creek makes a wonderful gunk hole. The marshy shores, backed by pines and hardwoods, are a sight that few cruisers will soon forget.

The westernmost reaches of North Prong maintain 6 to 7 feet of water and there should be enough swinging room for vessels as large as 34 feet. As the stream follows its first sharp turn to the south, soundings increase to the 10-foot level. Soon the creek takes another sharp turn, this time to the east. After passing through this curve, skippers will find a good stretch to drop the hook. There should be enough elbow room here for vessels up to 34 feet in length.

Both anchorages provide excellent shelter from even the heaviest weather. In really strong blows (over 25 knots), you might want to consider a Bahamian moor, or even stringing a line to a shoreside tree to avoid swaying into the banks. Otherwise, you could look long and hard without finding an anchorage as protected as this one.

California Bayou (Standard Mile 302) (30 05.294 North/085 29.637 West)

California Bayou is the first in a series of three good anchorages on East Bay's northern shores. The bayou's mouth cuts the northeastern banks opposite the gap between the ICW's flashing daybeacons #35 and #37. The entrance channel is unmarked and calls for caution, but careful navigators should be able to arrive safely during periods of fair weather. While not quite as sheltered as the others, California Bayou can make a good overnight haven, except when winds are blowing from the southwest. The shoreline is comprised of the high, little-developed, well-wooded banks so typical of this entire region. The stream has a rich feeling of isolation to it. Cruisers who, like this writer, enjoy getting off the beaten path will want to give California Bayou their most serious consideration.

Minimum entrance depths are around 6 feet with soundings of 7 feet being more the norm. Depths outside of the channel rise markedly.

Boats up to 38 feet long can drop the hook in 7 feet of water about 100 yards upstream from a point abeam of the northwesterly

entrance point. Moving even farther to the northeast, 30- to 32-foot vessels can follow 5- to 6-foot soundings for a short distance and find even better shelter. Be warned that the upstream limits of the bayou carry only 2 to 4 feet of water, as correctly forecast on chart 11390.

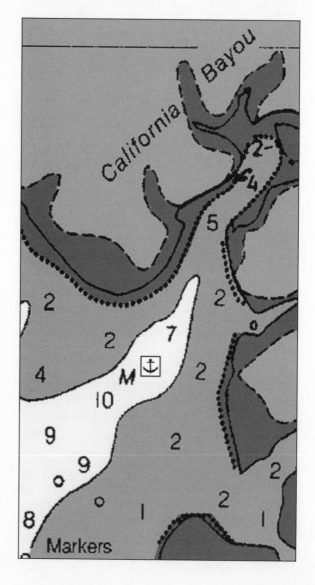

Laird Bayou (Standard Mile 300) (Various Lats/Lons—see below)

The unmarked entrance to Laird Bayou is found well northeast of flashing daybeacon #43.

This may just be the best anchorage on all of East Bay. While there are a few shoals flanking the bayou's entrance to avoid, careful cruisers should be able to enter without undue difficulty.

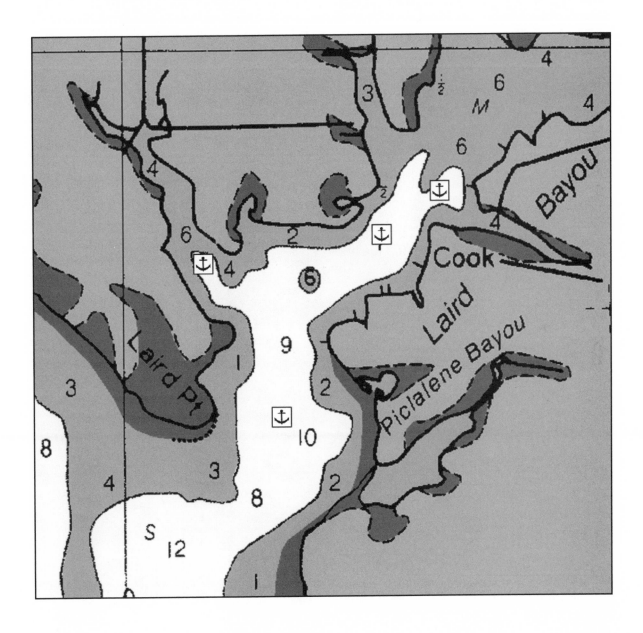

Once inside, there are at least three good places to set the hook. Protection is excellent from all winds and should be sufficient for any blows short of hurricane force. There is a single house perched on the eastern shores of the stream. Otherwise the shoreline is lined by tall pines and hardwoods. On still days, the trees reflect beautifully on the water.

Vessels over 45 feet can drop the hook in the broad tongue of 10-foot water east of Laird Point, near 30 07.190 North/085 31.592 West. However, there are better sheltered spots farther upstream which are appropriate for many cruising craft.

About .3 nautical miles upstream, an unnamed branch of Laird Bayou breaks off to the northwest. Minimum 6-foot depths are held on the mid-width of this stream, and there is enough space for a 36-footer to drop the hook near 30 07.535 North/085 31.788 West. This spot boasts maximum shelter.

Larger boats can anchor on the main body of the bayou abeam of the charted location of Cook, near 30 07.593 North/085 31.324 West. Depths run from 6 to 9 feet and vessels as large as 45 feet should have enough room to swing to and fro on the hook.

Of all the potential anchor-down spots on the bayou, however, the best seems to be found abeam of the unnamed creek that cuts the eastern shores of its larger sister, just north of the designation "Cook" on chart 11390 (near 30 07.701 North/085 31.175 West). Waters with 5½ to 8 feet of depth spread almost from shore to shore. Swinging room should be more than adequate for a 48-footer.

Except for its shallower upper reaches, Laird Bayou is one of those places where mariners can suit their fancy when selecting a spot to

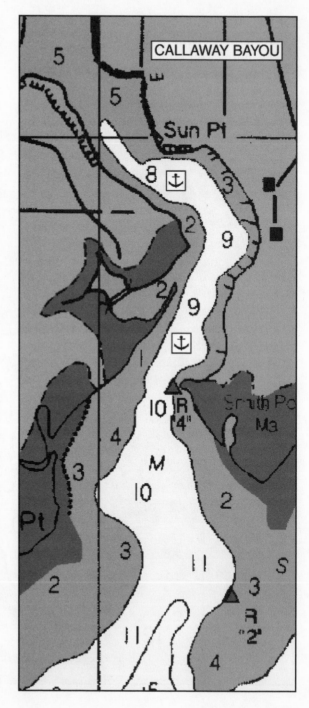

anchor. While the list of specifically recommended anchorages above is extensive, this writer has no doubt that enterprising cruisers will find even more spots to spend the night on this enchanting side-water.

Callaway Bayou (Standard Mile 298) (Various Lats/Lons—see below)

Callaway Bayou lies along East Bay's northern shore between the ICW's flashing daybeacons #43 and #45. This stream offers excellent protection and good overnight anchorage, but as seems to be the case with most side waters adjoining East Bay, there are some flanking shoals at the bayou's entrance to worry with.

Careful skippers can enter Callaway Bayou with minimum 6-foot depths, but *be sure* to read the navigational account of this stream presented in the next section of this chapter before attempting it.

Once past the troublesome entrance, visiting cruisers will be greeted by shores with moderate but not unattractive residential development. Skippers piloting pleasure boats of most any size can anchor in the patch of deep water north of unlighted daybeacon #4, near 30 07.554 North/085 33.789 West. You can expect 8- to 9-foot depths in this area.

Better sheltered is the broad bubble of deep water south of Sun Point (30 07.912 North/085 33.802 West). Here, cruising craft can anchor amidst depths of 7 to 8 feet, abeam of a housing development on the eastern banks. There should be enough swinging room for most pleasure boats.

Fred Bayou (Standard Mile 297)

Fred Bayou makes into the southerly banks of the ICW just west of flashing daybeacon #45. The well-marked channel maintains minimum 12- to 13-foot depths and eventually leads upstream to an Air Force barge loading facility. There is not enough room to anchor off the channel. Most pleasure craft will probably choose to bypass Fred Bayou. However, if you are one of those captains who just has to see it all, feel free to explore the creek. Just be sure to stay well out of the path of any commercial traffic you might encounter.

ICW TO EAST BAY NAVIGATION

This little stretch of the Gulf Coast ICW is generally a pleasure to navigate. However, there are a few small but thorny problems that do require your attention. Care must be taken to follow the Waterway's true track in Wetappo Creek. The shallow, false mouths of the intersecting streams and loops can be confusing. On East Bay there is some shallow water, and on the easterly portion of the run, one must be careful to stay in the marked passage. The bay's width exceeds 2 nautical miles near the Dupont Bridge; it does not require too much imagination to see that things can get a trifle ugly when winds are over 15 knots. So, as always, keep charts 11393 and 11390 close at hand to quickly resolve any questions, maintain a steady watch on the sounder, and you should enjoy your cruise to Panama City.

On the ICW It's a straight run down the unmarked but well-sheltered canal comprising the ICW between the entrance to the Gulf County Canal and the Overstreet fixed bridge, just short of standard mile 315. This span has a vertical clearance of 65 feet.

Somewhere during this run, the man-made canal flows unnoticed into the southeasterly reaches of Wetappo Creek's South Prong. A few more turns appear and there are some small loops abutting the waterway's shores. Do not attempt to enter any of these wayward offshoots. They are quite shoal.

North of standard mile 315 passing cruisers will come upon the entrance to North Prong, Wetappo Creek on the eastern shore and the southeasterly entrance to a large loop creek on the western banks. *Do not* attempt to enter the loop creek even though you may see several old boats docked at the rear of the stream. The southeasterly entrance has practically no water at all and even the northwestern mouth has very questionable depths.

You can, however, choose to enter the North Prong of Wetappo Creek to the northeast.

Wetappo Creek—North Prong Enter the North Prong on its mid-width. For best depths, you need only hold to the centerline for the entire passage upstream to the charted 12-foot power lines. Obviously, most any cruising craft will want to avoid these shocking obstructions like the black plague.

While this is a fascinating gunk hole, only boats 34 feet and (preferably) smaller should attempt to cruise this far. Pleasure craft up to 34 feet can drop anchor in the wider section between the ICW and the stream's first sharp turn to the southeast, but farther upstream the turns become a bit sharp for larger craft.

On the ICW Study the Waterway northwest of Wetappo Creek's North Prong on chart 11393 for a moment. You will quickly note that the various side waters entering this unmarked portion of the ICW could cause confusion, particularly for *eastbound* navigators.

The small, shallow bay abutting the Waterway's southwestern shore, a short distance southeast of unlighted can buoy #1A, seems to be especially troublesome for cruisers headed east. Slow down between #1A and the entrance to Wetappo Creek, and be sure to pick out the actual path of the ICW before proceeding ahead. This passage would be acutely difficult after dark. Nighttime passage is strictly not recommended for visitors.

On East Bay Unlighted can buoy #1A ushers westbound cruisers into the upper reaches of East Bay. This easternmost portion of the bay exhibits very shallow depths. Often soundings rise to as little as 1 foot. Be sure to stick strictly to the marked ICW channel, at least until you reach flashing daybeacon #14, east of Strange Bayou. Fortunately, the numerous floating markers, supplemented by an ample supply of daybeacons, vastly simplify this process. Be sure to pay close attention to all the various aids to navigation, and keep charts 11393 and 11390 within reach.

Both Horseshoe Bayou, northeast of flashing daybeacon #19, and Sandy Creek, north of flashing daybeacon #28, are much too shallow for cruising craft. Don't attempt to enter either stream unless you want to have a clear and unforgettable memory of what the local bottom sounds like.

It is possible for cruising craft to get off the ICW channel on the outer reaches of Walker Bayou, southwest of flashing daybeacon #42. However, you will hit 4-foot waters before reaching the sheltered interior portion of the creek. Considering the fine anchorages only a short cruise to the west, this bayou can only be considered an emergency haven.

Note that west of unlighted daybeacon #46, the numbering sequence of the Waterway's aids to navigation begins anew. Flashing daybeacon #1 lies almost opposite #46, followed by a pair of markers, flashing daybeacon #2, and unlighted daybeacon #3.

After easing past flashing daybeacon #2, look towards the northern shoreline. You will sight a few buildings associated with the charted community of Allanton. North of unlighted daybeacon #10 a marked channel leads into a commercial boatyard. While there are no facilities for pleasure craft at this yard, passing cruisers can often view one or more huge fishing trawlers being built on the ways.

Northwest of flashing daybeacon #14, deeper waters abut a goodly portion of the Waterway channel. These improved depths spread out in an even broader path north and west of flashing daybeacon #25. This condition holds throughout the remainder of East Bay into Panama City. While there are still some shallow patches to be avoided, sailcraft skippers making careful use of charts 11393 and 11390 can tack off the ICW channel in many places.

Between flashing daybeacon #15, east of Blind Alligator Bayou, and unlighted daybeacon #17, watch for leeway to the west. An errant current could ease unsuspecting skippers onto the 1-foot waters to the west.

During a sojourn of these waters several years ago, this writer found himself eastbound on this portion of the Waterway. It was quite a shock to pass flashing daybeacon #15 during the early morning hours and realize how difficult it was to make out the next set of markers to the southeast. Captains cruising east along this stretch when the sun is in their eyes should take extra caution and have the binoculars ready to help with aids to navigation identification.

Visiting cruisers can continue on the Waterway's easily followed path as it moves to the northwest until coming abeam of flashing daybeacon #35 to its northeasterly side. From #35, mariners have access to the area's first good anchorage, California Bayou.

California Bayou   Use chart 11390 for navigation in California Bayou. For some reason, this version is clearer than the corresponding sketch on chart 11393.

Set a careful compass (or GPS) course from flashing daybeacon #35 for the midwidth of the deeper water leading into the creek's interior reaches. Be on guard against the large 4-foot patch of water abutting the northwesterly side of the entrance. You must also take care to avoid the charted 2-foot shoals to the southeast. Proceed at a slow speed and keep a steady watch on the sounder. If depths rise above 6 feet, you are approaching the surrounding shallows. Halt your forward progress and make the appropriate corrections.

As you enter California Bayou, look toward the southeasterly banks and you should see a series of private markers of the piling and stake variety denoting several commercial oyster beds. Be sure to stay well to the west and northwest of these informal aids to navigation. As can be readily appreciated, oyster beds are founded in shallow water, and are known to be tough on gelcoats.

Once pass the entrance point, begin favoring the northwesterly banks slightly. As can be seen from a study of chart 11390, this maneuver will help to avoid the ribbon of 2-foot water flanking the eastern and southeasterly banks.

Discontinue your upstream explorations as the first blunt point of land comes abeam on the southeastern shore. Past these waters depths become much too unreliable for cruising craft.

On the ICW   After passing flashing daybeacon #35, switch to chart 11390 for continued navigation west on East Bay to Panama City.

Be sure to pass well to the southwest of unlighted daybeacon #38 off Piney Point. This point seems to be building outward.

Similarly, come abeam of and pass flashing daybeacon #40 by at least 25 yards to its southwesterly quarter. Chart 11390 correctly forecasts a small shoal surrounding #40. For best depths, you should also pass well to the northeast of unlighted daybeacon #41. This aid marks a 6-foot oyster bank. From #41, mariners have access to the best anchorage between White City and the Dupont Bridge.

Laird Bayou   The only real problem encountered in navigating Laird Bayou is caused by the two shoals flanking the bayou's mouth. As can be seen from a quick study of 11390, there is a large shoal abutting Laird Point which guards the bayou's western entrance, and a smaller belt of 1- to 2-foot shallows along the eastern banks. To avoid these hazards, set course from unlighted daybeacon #41 to come abeam of the Laird Point shoal by some 50 yards to its southeasterly side. As you make your approach to the creek, be on guard against the 1- and 2-foot waters to the east. As the unnamed entrance point comes abeam east and southeast of your course line, cut a bit farther to the east to avoid the Laird Point Shoal. Once this maneuver is completed, you can follow the wide swath of deep waters almost due north into the creek's inner section.

You need only continue holding to the centerline on the main body of Laird Bayou for good depths as far as the large patch of charted 7-foot water north and west of the "Cook" designation on chart 11390. Do not attempt to cruise farther upstream. Depths begin to rise and the presence of unmarked shoals renders these waters much too unreliable for larger boats.

If you choose to enter the unnamed offshoot that cuts into the western bank north of Laird Point, continue up the middle of Laird Bayou until the stream's entrance is directly abeam to port, then cut into the entrance, favoring the southwestern shore slightly. Don't cut either corner. Following this procedure will help to avoid the charted shoals flanking the entrance to the north and south. Consider dropping the hook between the northeasterly entrance point and the next point on the starboard shore. Farther upstream water levels rise to 4 feet or less.

On the ICW   It's only a short hop west to flashing daybeacon #43. Between #43 and the next western aid, flashing daybeacon #45, navigators may choose to enter Callaway Bayou on the northern shore.

Callaway Bayou   Entrance into Callaway Bayou is complicated by the large tongue of (at long last) correctly charted shallows striking south and southwest from unlighted daybeacon #2. Earlier editions (before the September 28, 1996 edition) of chart 11390 did not correctly portray this potentially troubling shoal.

For best depths, set your course to come abeam of unlighted daybeacon #2 by some 30 to 40 yards (no closer) to its westerly side. Be on guard against the tongue of 4-foot water south and southwest of #2. Once abeam of #2, point to come abeam of un-lighted daybeacon #4 fairly close to its westerly side. Between #2 and #4, be mindful of the correctly charted 2-foot shoal waters to the east. Also, be on guard against the equally threatening 3-foot shoals to the west. Once pass Smith point, good depths are easily held on the stream's centerline to Sun Point. Exploration pass here is not recommended for cruising-size craft.

On the ICW   As you approach the Dupont fixed bridge, watch for flashing daybeacon #2 off Long Point. During our on-site research, this aid seemed much farther out from land than one would expect from studying chart 11390. Be sure to pass #2 to its southerly side.

Southeast of the Dupont span, visiting cruisers will note that the two flanking sections of the old, low-level bridge have been left in place for fishing purposes. Of course, the center span has been removed to allow for easy passage of all waterborne vessels. You will encounter the old span immediately after passing between unlighted can buoy #3 and unlighted nun buoy #4. Continue on almost dead ahead to the Dupont span's central pass-through.

The fixed Dupont Bridge itself has a vertical clearance of 50 feet. While other 50-foot fixed bridges along the Northern Gulf Coast are in the process of being replaced by 65-foot high-risers, there is no sign of new construction here. Sailors will have to contend with this troublesome span's 50-foot clearance for many years to come(at least).

CHAPTER 2

Panama City to Choctawhatchee Bay

Captains and crew visiting Florida's Panhandle for the first time will be surprised by Panama City and its pleasure-craft facilities. If you expected to find a somewhat larger version of other sleepy Panhandle communities, think again. Quite simply, Panama City is the yachting capital of northwestern Florida.

The reliable Panama City/St. Andrew Bay Inlet leads to the Gulf of Mexico just southwest of the town. Mariners bent on putting out into the open Gulf waters between Apalachicola and Pensacola Bay should plan on making use of this advantageous cut.

North of Panama City, the Waterway flows first north and then west into the split between North and West bays. Both these large water bodies have surprisingly few anchorages or opportunities for side-water exploration and gunk-holing.

The ICW meanders its way through the heart of West Bay and enters a long canal for some 17 nautical miles on the way to Choctawhatchee Bay. This track is protected from even the most inclement weather.

Soon the Waterway flows west into gorgeous Choctawhatchee Bay. Of the many beautiful, gloriously undeveloped waters in the Florida Panhandle, the Choctawhatchee is clearly one of the best. Shores crowded with hardwoods and pines overlook quite a collection of protected anchorages. Cruisers who cannot find an overnight haven suited to their tastes on the Choctawhatchee might as well give up anchoring off forever.

East of Fort Walton Beach, there is just enough development on Choctawhatchee Bay to provide good services for cruising craft. Excellent marina facilities are found on Rocky and Boggy bayous. Some cruising services are also available along the Destin City waterfront and at Sandestin, flanking the Choctawhatchee's southerly shoreline.

Destin, the only community of any size between Panama City and Fort Walton Beach, sits astride artificial East Pass Inlet on the southwestern corner of Choctawhatchee Bay. An active charter fishing fleet and the beautiful white-sand beaches (not to mention the gin-clear water) draw ever-increasing hordes of tourists year after year. While the channel leading from the bay to Destin is anything but reliable, careful captains can follow the marked track to several marinas in Destin Harbor, only one of which accepts transients.

West of Destin the ICW traverses the westerly reaches of Choctawhatchee Bay. Here captains will find the ample facilities and the inviting waters of Fort Walton Beach. This region will be covered in the next chapter.

Quite honestly, there are few other stretches of the Gulf Coast ICW between Carrabelle and New Orleans that can lay claim to as many delightful attributes as can the run between the Dupont Bridge and Fort Walton Beach. Whether you enjoy anchoring out, berthing overnight at well-appointed marinas, or simply cruising between attractive, undeveloped shorelines, you will surely delight in this portion of the ICW!

Charts   Most navigators should purchase the first three charts outlined below. The fourth chart will only be needed for those making offshore passages.

11390—ICW chart that details the waters from East Bay through Panama City and into West Bay. St. Andrew Bay, Grand Lagoon, and the Panama City (St. Andrew) Inlet also receive detailed coverage

11385—follows the Waterway from West Bay to the westerly limits of this chapter's coverage in western Choctawhatchee Bay. This chart gives the best details for side waters off the Choctawhatchee.

11391—intermediate coverage chart that gives good, detailed coverage of St. Andrew Bay and inlet, as well as the Panama City waterfront

11389—small-scale, offshore chart useful for approaching St. Andrew (Panama City) Inlet from the Gulf

Bridges

Dupont Bridge—crosses ICW at standard mile 295—Fixed—50 feet

Massalina Bayou Bridge—crosses entrance to Massalina Bayou hard by the Panama City Marina—Bascule—7 feet (closed)—opens on demand

Hathaway Bridge—crosses ICW at standard mile 285—Fixed—50 feet—new bridge currently under construction to replace this span

West Bay Creek Bridge—crosses ICW at standard mile 272—Fixed—65 feet

Choctawhatchee Bay/Highway 83 Bridge—crosses ICW at standard mile 250—Fixed—65 feet

Mid-Bay Bridge—crosses ICW and Choctawhatchee Bay at standard mile 235—Fixed—64 feet

Rocky Bayou Bridge—crosses upstream reaches of Boggy Bayou east of Nelson Point—Fixed—20 feet

East Pass Inlet Bridge—crosses East Pass Inlet west of Destin—Fixed—48 feet (officially listed as 49 feet)

Panama City

Any landside or waterborne visitor to Panama City will gain the swift and sure impression that this is a community on the move. The U.S. military installations in the immediate area certainly provide an impetus for progress, but this ready source of federal money is amply supplemented by a strong private economy. Visiting cruisers are some of the chief beneficiaries of this vigorous economic climate.

Boasting more than a dozen marina facilities, many of which are large, first-class operations, Panama City has more boating services than any other community between Carrabelle and New Orleans. Whether seeking overnight (or seasonal) dockage or extensive repairs, pleasure-craft mariners in Panama City can be assured of finding whatever is needed.

There are also numerous opportunities for sheltered anchorage on the waters surrounding Panama City. The many bayous indenting the ICW at regular intervals afford excellent overnight havens. Some are sheltered enough for the heaviest weather.

Ashore, Panama City offers a huge selection of businesses of all descriptions, including marine parts suppliers. There is an excellent array of fine restaurants, ranging from those that serve traditional seafood fare to one of the funkiest (and best) on-the-water dining attractions we have ever reviewed. Dining should never become monotonous in this exciting community.

To be succinct, Panama City should rate a red circle on every Gulf Coast ICW cruiser's charts. Skippers who bypass this delightful community will, quite simply, miss one of the real delights afforded on the entire run from Carrabelle to New Orleans.

Panama City Waters and Facilities

As alluded to above, the waters surrounding Panama City are chock-full of good overnight anchorages and first-rate marinas.

Basically, the local facilities and overnight havens can be divided into two groups. One set of marinas and yards is located along the principal city waterfront stretching from a position north and west of the Dupont/Long Point fixed bridge to the Hathaway fixed span. There are now two topnotch Panama City municipal marinas included in this collection of facilities. Between these two bridges, cruisers will also discover a delightful collection of bayous affording protected anchorage lining the northern and northeastern shoreline.

Alternately, a large group of marinas and yards pepper the shores of Grand Lagoon, just northwest of the St. Andrew/Panama City Inlet. Several of these facilities can meet any of the cruising craft's normal needs.

Dupont Bridge to St. Andrew Bay

Between Dupont Bridge and the ICW's intersection with St. Andrew Bay, the first of Panama City's facilities and anchorages are readily available to passing cruisers. Visitors will find quite a collection of sheltered overnight havens and full-service marinas on this relatively small stretch. Whether you want to anchor off in a secluded cove or coil your lines at a large, full-service marina, you need look no further than the Waterway east of St. Andrew Bay.

Numbers to know in Panama City include

Yellow Cab—850-763-4691
Executive Taxi—850-784-6611
Your Taxi—850-784-6611
Enterprise Car Rentals—850-747-1110
Budget Car Rental—800-527-7000
West Marine (1388 W 15th Street)—
    850-763-1844
Chamber of Commerce—850-785-5206

Pearl Bayou (Standard Mile 295)
(30 06.102 North/085 37.277 West)

The main body of Pearl Bayou intersects the ICW to the southwest, immediately after passing through the Dupont Bridge. The entrance is found just southwest of flashing daybeacon #2. Good anchorage for boats up to 38 feet is found on the creek's western arm. While there are a few shoals to avoid along the way, careful captains should be able to maintain minimum 7-foot depths, with most soundings in the 10- to 13-foot region. Be sure to read the navigational information presented later in this chapter before attempting to enter the bayou or set the hook.

The bayou's entrance borders a military recreation park, associated with nearby Tyndall Air Force Base, on its eastern banks. Conversely, the shoreline of the westerly arm is delightfully undeveloped. The well-forested banks give good protection in all winds, though the stream is less sheltered from strong easterly blows.

While not as long on swinging room as some other creeks in the Panama City region, Pearl Bayou is nevertheless a good anchorage that may fit very well into the visiting cruiser's itinerary.

Pitts Bayou and Pier 98 Marina (Standard Mile 295) (30 07.110 North/085 35.808 West—Marina) (30 07.166 North/085 35.873 West—Anchorage)

Pitts Bayou indents the ICW's northeastern banks between the ICW's unlighted nun buoy #8 and flashing daybeacon#29. This navigationally simple creek offers the twin rewards of a marina facility offering fuel and an exceptionally well-sheltered overnight anchorage. Minimum 7-foot depths are carried well upstream past Pier 98 Marina. The shoreline exhibits moderate to heavy residential development. Protection is good from all winds, particularly on the bayou's upstream limits. If the wind should be blowing directly from the pulp mill on Watson Bayou, there could be an odor problem on the stream. However, this situation has not developed during our several visits to this bayou.

Pier 98 Marina is found on the creek's eastern banks in the body of the first sharp bend to the north. This facility now has new owners. We were amazed to discover a large, new shoreside gasoline station plus convenience store and deli just behind the dockage basin. The marina is now managed through this facility, but this firm does not employ a dockmaster.

Transients are occasionally accepted for overnight dockage at the marina's fixed wooden piers. Cautious skippers will give the marina a call ahead of time to make sure space is available. These docks have undergone some repairs under the new owners and have been considerably improved. This same bunch has also added a modern fuel dock offering both diesel fuel and gasoline.

Depths alongside run about 7 feet at mean low water. Many of the available slips are of the covered variety (not appropriate for sailcraft), and most are occupied by long-term dockers. Those who do find a berth will be able to hook up to 30-amp power and fresh-water connections.

The old dockmaster's office just behind the piers is now an interesting custom fishing-rod and reel shop. We were fascinated to inspect some of the *very* expensive hardware being turned out of this operation.

Come dinnertime, the adjacent Rodeo's Steak Pit restaurant (850-872-0034) specializes (surprise, surprise) in beef dishes. The deli portion of the convenience store also offers breakfast.

Our take on this new creation of Pier 98 Marina is that the physical plant has been upgraded, but the docks are at least somewhat of an afterthought to the filling station/convenience store portion of this enterprise. Without a full- or even a part-time dockmaster, cruisers may expect to have some difficulty in securing a temporary slip, and they should be ready to undertake all tasks, including docking, on their own.

Pier 98 Marina (850) 874-8723

Approach depth—14-15 feet
Dockside depth—7 feet
Accepts transients—limited

Transient-dockage rate—average
Fixed wooden piers—yes
Dockside power connections—30 amp
Dockside water connections—yes

Laundromat—nearby
Gasoline-yes
Diesel fuel-yes
Restaurant—on site

Pier 98 Marina, Pitts Bayou

Captains preferring to anchor off for the evening can make use of Pitts Bayou with every confidence. One of the best spots to set the hook is found on the large bubble of deep water abeam of Pier 98 Marina (near 30 07.166 North/085 35.873 West). Swinging room should be sufficient for craft as large as 45 feet. Protection is good from all winds, though a particularly strong southwesterly breeze could blow straight up the bayou, giving rise to an uncomfortable chop.

In really nasty weather boats up to 35 feet can cruise upstream to the charted patch of 10-foot water. Cruisers who set the hook on this stretch of the creek should be adequately sheltered from any weather short of a full gale.

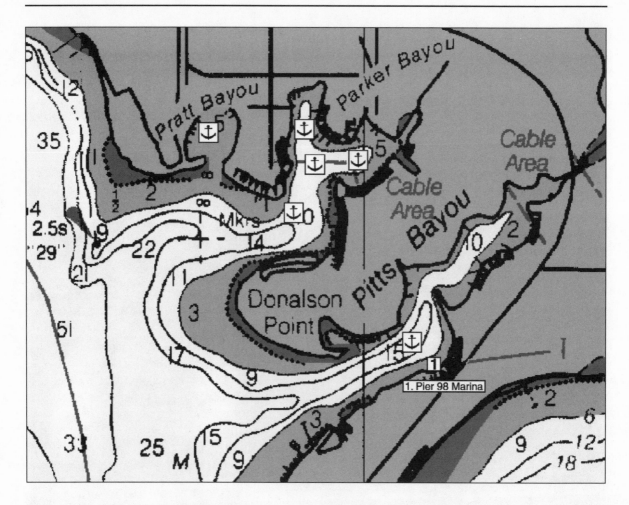

Parker Bayou (Standard Mile 294.5) (Various Lats/Lons—see below)

The entrance to Parker Bayou indents the Waterway's northeastern banks east of flashing daybeacon #29. This is yet another of the many superior anchorages found along the ICW as it approaches the principal Panama City waterfront. Minimum depths of 6 feet, with 8 to 11 feet of water being more the norm, are held into the upstream branches of the creek. Four (at least) possible havens are overlooked by moderate residential development. One is sufficient for heavy weather.

Large boats can anchor in the charted patch of 10-foot water in the mid-width of the bayou's sharp swing to the north, near 30 07.451 North/085 36.160 West. Our on-site research revealed some 9-foot depths on this portion of the creek. While there is sufficient shelter from most winds, westerly breezes over 10 knots could result in a very uncomfortable night.

Farther upstream, Parker Bayou splits into

two arms. Boats as large as 45 feet will find plenty of elbowroom amid the 8- to 11-foot waters immediately southwest of the split, near 30 07.563 North/085 36.128 West. This spot is better sheltered than the waters downstream, but for maximum protection from foul weather, consider setting the hook a bit farther upstream on one of the two upper arms of Parker Bayou.

The easterly branch is the better of the two for overnight anchorages, and the shoreline gives excellent protection from all winds. Care must be taken to avoid the charted shallows to the northeast. This would be a great spot for craft as large as 38 feet to ride out heavy weather. Try anchoring near 30 07.574 North/085 35.997 West.

The northwesterly arm of Parker Bayou is a bit more open than its eastern sister, but it would still afford good protection in most winds. Numerous private docks spring out from the shoreline at regular intervals. There is some shallower water on the eastern banks, but elementary precautions should be more than sufficient to avoid this hazard. We found good anchorage near 30 07.658 North/085 36.151 West.

Pratt Bayou (Standard Mile 294.5) (30 07.617 North/085 36.386 West)

Pratt Bayou is a small, lakelike body of protected water that opens into the northern banks of the entrance to Parker Bayou. The entrance is quite narrow, but it is reasonably well marked by privately maintained, obscurely charted piles and carries 5-foot minimum depths.

Once past the narrow entrance, the waters spread out into a broad pool with depths of 5 to 7 feet on the mid-width. There should be

sufficient elbowroom for boats up to 36 feet to anchor comfortably. The banks are overlooked by fairly heavy, but not unattractive, residential development.

While it is well sheltered and fairly attractive, Pratt Bayou is not particularly recommended for craft over 36 feet or those drawing more than 4½ feet by virtue of its narrow entrance. If your boat meets these requirements, you need not hesitate to make use of the creek as an anchorage or gunk hole.

Watson Bayou and Associated Facilities (Standard Mile 292.5) (Various Lats/Lons—see below)

Watson Bayou cuts the north banks of East Bay, just north-northwest of flashing buoy #25. This body of water is clearly a case of good news and bad news for visiting cruisers. On the plus side, there are three marinas (plus a repair yard) on the creek, one of which offers transient dockage. There are also at least two good anchorages. The upstream haven is well protected and offers enough swinging room for practically any sized craft. Minimum depths of 7 feet run from the creek's mouth to the low-level fixed bridge well upstream. Most of the bayou's shores have moderate residential development, but as noted below, there is an industrial complex on the bayou's southernmost, eastward-flowing offshoot.

On the other hand, the charted "stacks" east of Millville herald the presence of a huge wood-pulp processing mill near the bayou's shores. The two easterly offshoots of Watson Bayou near its southerly entrance are best avoided due to the offensive stench belching from the mill.

The western branch of Watson Bayou, just

north of the creek's entrance, is known as Lake Van Vac. While there are several unmarked shoals to be avoided along the way, careful captains piloting craft less than 38 feet in length can cruise cautiously into the charted patch of 9-foot water flanking the lake's southern

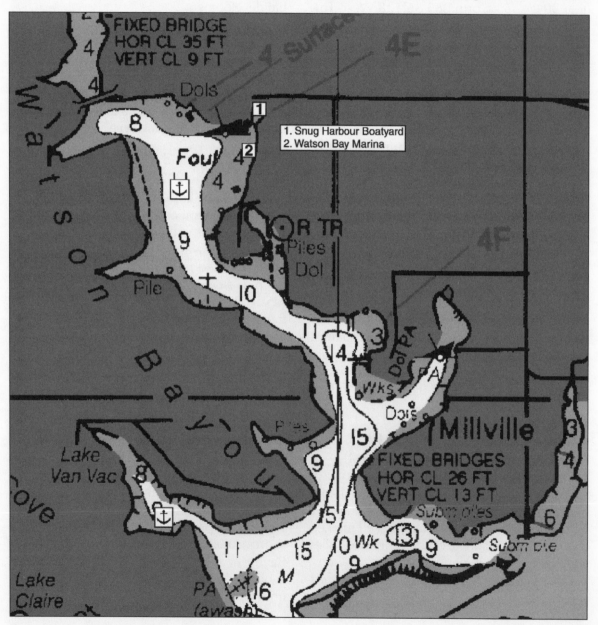

shore and drop anchor near 30 08.509 North/085 38.467 West. Minimum entrance depths are in the 7-foot range if you keep to the unmarked cut. Protection is good enough for even gale-force winds from any quarter. The shoreline supports moderate, but not unattractive, residential development.

The southernmost eastern branch of Watson Bayou holds minimum depths of 7 feet well upstream, but as mentioned earlier, the stream leads directly to the pulp mill. Mariners who possess any crumb of their olfactory senses will avoid this creek like the plague.

Moving upstream, the next eastward-flowing creek is also best avoided. It, too, is uncomfortably near the pulp plant. The shores are lined with commercial fishing vessels. Any pleasure craft anchored on the stream might be obliged to move aside quite early in the morning to allow for the passage of these fishing boats.

Still farther to the north, cruisers will discover two marine facilities on the large cove that indents the bayou's easterly banks, well northwest of the charted "R TR." First up is Watson Bayou Marina (850-872-8617, 30 09.299 North/085 38.234 West), flanking the cove's entrance along the easterly shores. This facility's entrance channel carries at least 5½ to 6 feet of water and sports a good set of markers that greatly facilitate successful entry by deeper-draft vessels.

New owners have taken over Watson Bayou Marina since the last edition of this guidebook. The entire facility, including the docks and showers, have been considerably upgraded, but unfortunately, overnight transients are no longer accepted. Long-term residents will find depths alongside in the 6½- to 7-foot MLW range. Fresh-water and 30-amp power hookups are on hand, as are newly revamped, air-conditioned showers and a Laundromat. There is even a nice captain's clubhouse with a color television. Alas, if only we nonresident cruisers could take advantage of all these nice services. Maybe there'll be room for cruising visitors again some time in the future, but for now, we can only wave as we slip past the piers.

Snug Harbour Boatyard (30 09.382 North/085 38.191 West) occupies the most upstream section of the cove well northwest of the charted "R TR." This facility is accessed by continuing to track your way along the channel that initially leads to Watson Bayou Marina. Cruisers entering Snug Harbour will find an extremely well-sheltered harbor with fixed wooden piers and 6-foot depths. Transients are accepted on a space-available basis. There is usually at least one spot open for visitors, but again, the wise mariner will call ahead for advance reservations. Full-service mechanical (gas and diesel engines) and below-waterline repair services are featured. You will spot the yard's large 35-ton travelift just to the rear of the marina's fixed wooden piers. An on-site marine carpentry-repair firm and a steel-cable supplier add to the yard's offerings. Good showers are found on site, and the Laundromat at Watson Bayou Marina is within walking distance. There are no restaurants worth talking about withing walking distance, nor are there any supermarkets. You'll need to take a taxi for dining or any any serious foodstuff shopping, though there is a convenience store that may be accessed by foot.

Snug Harbour Boatyard (850) 769-8884

Approach depth—5½-6 feet (minimum)
Dockside depth—6-8 feet
Accepts transients—yes (advance reservations recommended)
Transient-dockage rate—average
Fixed wooden piers—yes
Dockside power connections—15-30 amp
Dockside water connections—yes
Showers—yes
Mechanical repairs—yes
Below-waterline repairs—yes
Restaurant—nearby

Abeam of the entrance to Snug Harbour and Watson Bayou marinas, Watson Bayou opens out into a broad pool of deep water. Even the largest pleasure craft will find plenty of swinging room near 30 09.237 North/085 38.413 West. The surrounding shoreline gives excellent protection. Anchored craft should be secure in any winds short of hurricane force.

The few docks of the Gulf Marina of Panama City (850-763-1844) overlook the northeastern shores of Watson Bayou at facility designation #4 on chart 11390. This

Snug Harbour Marina, Watson Bayou

small-scale facility offers dry storage for small craft and some outboard and I/O mechanical repairs. No transient dockage for cruising craft is available.

St. Andrew Bay Yacht Club
(Standard Mile 290.5)
(30 08.543 North/085 38.977 West)

The docks of active St. Andrew Bay Yacht Club overlook the ICW's northeastern banks, well northeast of flashing buoy #20. This facility is glad to accept members of other yacht clubs, with appropriate reciprocal agreements, at their fixed concrete piers. Depths alongside

run some 5½ to 6 feet at the outer berths with 4- to 4½-foot soundings at the innermost slips. The dockage basin is partially protected by wooden slats set vertically across the outermost pier, but strong winds from the south or southwest could still make for bump-and-grind action at the docks. Fresh-water and 30-amp power connections (two 50-amp hookups are available) are on hand. Shoreside, visitors will discover a large clubhouse with showers and a fine dining room (lunch Tuesday through Sunday, 11:30 to 2:00; dinner Tuesday through Saturday, 5:30 to 9:00). Otherwise, you will need to take a taxi (or a fairly long walk) into

St. Andrew Bay Yacht Club, Panama City

Panama City to find a nearby Laundromat, provisions, or other restaurants. It would be a wise practice to call ahead of time for dockage arrangements.

St. Andrew Bay Yacht Club (850) 769-2453

Approach depth—7-15 feet
Dockside depth—4-6 feet (MLW)
Accepts transients—members of other yacht
    clubs with reciprocal privileges
Fixed concrete piers—yes
Dockside power connections—15-30 amp
Dockside water connections—yes
Restaurant—on site

Smack Bayou (Standard Mile 290.5) (30 07.830 North/085 39.987 West)

One of the finest anchorages found on Panama City waters, or anywhere else for that matter, lies southwest of flashing buoy #20. Smack Bayou is an almost-hidden body of water that boasts minimum 6-foot depths, almost perfect shelter, and untouched shores overlooked by dense collections of pines and hardwoods. It's really hard to believe that there can be such an isolated, all-natural anchorage literally within sight of the Panama City waterfront, but this is indeed the happy state of affairs.

The unmarked entrance to Smack Bayou is flanked by large patches of shallow water, but the channel is broad enough that careful navigators should be able to enter without too much difficulty.

With fair weather in the offing, larger cruising craft (45 feet and up) can anchor amidst the large, correctly charted ribbon of deep water just west of Smack Bayou's east-side entrance point. Depths of 12 to 18 feet will be discov-

ered near 30 08.046 North/085 39.829 West. This is clearly not a foul weather hidey-hole, and cruisers should pick another haven if there is a hint of foul weather in the forecast.

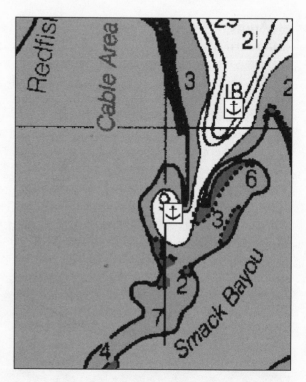

After cruising south of the twin entrance points, captains can take a lazy 180 degree turn to the north and drop the hook amidst 8-foot depths in the correctly charted bubble of deep water enclosed by the long, west-side entrance point. Shelter from all winds is super in this haven, and the scenery will keep you coming back time and time again. There should be plenty of swing room for a 38-footer.

Captains and crew jockeying for an anchor-down spot in Smack Bayou will most likely spy a concrete-hulled sailcraft swinging tranquilly on its hook behind the shelter of the east-side entrance point. This vessel has been swinging on the hook here for many years. In times past, its crew were infamous. By the time you got the anchor down, they were alongside trying to sell all sorts of "crafts." Happily, we can report that this less-than-happy crew has now long departed the scene. The Smack Bayou "craft show" is now only a bad, distant memory.

Wherever you choose to anchor, Smack Bayou is an overnight stop that true dyed-in-the-wool cruisers will not want to miss. Even if you usually frequent marinas during your evening stays on the water, give this anchorage a try. It may just change your mind!

Redfish Point Anchorage
(Standard Mile 290)
(30 08.362 North/085 40.086 West)

Sometimes we discover new anchorages by simply copying our fellow cruisers. That's exactly what happened during our on-the-water research for this new edition. While cruising through East Bay, we noticed two sailcraft anchored in the charted deep water east of Redfish Point and south-southeast of flashing daybeacon #18. Upon investigation, we determined that 8-foot minimum depths could be maintained within 100 yards or so of the southwestern and western shoreline. We dropped our anchor near 30 08.362 North/085 40.086 West, amidst 11- to 12-foot soundings and almost unlimited swinging room. The adjoining shoreline appears untouched and makes for a great backdrop while swinging tranquilly on the hook.

Shelter is very good from western, southwestern, and, to a lesser extent, northern winds. However, this is not the spot to be

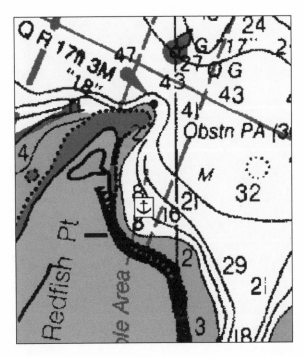

caught with fresh breezes wafting from the northeast, east, or southeast.

If the fickle winds choose to cooperate, this is a superior anchorage and far easier to navigate, particularly if you pilot a cruising craft 45 feet and larger, than nearby Smack Bayou.

Massalina Bayou and Facilities
(Standard Mile 290)
(Various Lats/Lons—see below)

Access to well-protected Massalina Bayou is gained by a marked channel found northeast of flashing buoy #17. A bascule bridge with only seven feet of closed vertical clearance spans the entrance and opens on demand. This small body of water is home to three boating facilities and numerous anchorage possibilities. Good depths of 8 to 12 feet are maintained in the entrance cut, but soundings quickly rise

Massalina Bayou, Panama City

outside of the scantily marked channel. Minimum depths on the interior reaches of Massalina Bayou run 5½ to 8 feet short of the T-shaped split in the creek. Upstream of the split, soundings rise to 4-foot levels.

First up are the piers of the Sailor's Supply Company Marina (30 09.107 North/085 39.566 West) on the southern shores of the large westward-flowing cove near the stream's entrance. The marina also owns a second tier of docks that bisect the cove's centerline.

There has been a de-emphasis on transient dockage at this facility over the past two years. Overnight or temporary visitors are now only accepted on a space-available basis. Call in advance to check on slip availability.

Sailor's Supply Company is still managed by friendly and knowledgeable personnel. The company's office and marine store are found a quick step to the northwest on East Beach Drive, which crosses the bayou bridge.

Dockage is provided at fixed, wooden piers and slips with fresh water hookups. Some slips have 20-amp power connections while others offer 30-amp service. Depths alongside run about 6 feet. Fair, nonclimate-controlled showers and a small Laundromat are found in a shoreside supply building just behind the piers, adjacent to the Massalina Bayou Bridge.

Mechanical repairs are offered through Sailor's Supply Company for Yanmar sailcraft diesel engines and Honda outboards, while independent technicians can be called for other sorts of power-plant servicing. Sail repair is in the offing as well. This firm is also one of the very few on the entire Northern Gulf Coast that services inflatable dinghies.

Sailor's Supply Company is now the only NOAA chart dealer in Panama City offering a full line of these official cartographical aids. The on-site ship's store is unusually well stocked, including an extensive selection of spare parts, plus a CNG refill station. Cruisers should be able to quickly fill almost any conceivable marine-supply need. The managers, Paul and Emily Pritchard, are exceptionally helpful and friendly.

The downtown business district is close at hand, but the nearest grocery store (The Grocery Outlet, 300 E 6th Street, 850-784-1326) is some three-fourths of a mile away. Those not up for this rather long walk can always take a taxi.

A host of fine restaurants are within an easy step of the slips at Sailor's Supply Company. Check the text below for your choices.

Sailor's Supply Company (Tarpon Dock) Marina
   (850) 769-5007

Approach depth—8-12 feet
Dockside depth—6 feet
Accepts transients—limited
Transient-dockage rate—economy
Fixed wooden piers—yes
Dockside power connections—20 and 30 amp
Dockside water connections—yes
Showers—planned
Laundromat—yes
Mechanical repairs—yes
Ship's store—yes (extensive)
Restaurant—several nearby

Sailor's Supply Company Marina, Massalina Bayou

The docks and work yard of Tibbett's Boat Works (850-785-9262, 850-769-0035, 30 09.041 North/085 39.541 West) lie opposite Sailor's Supply Company Marina. Full mechanical repairs for both gasoline and diesel motors, as well as haul-outs via a 70-ton travelift or a 100-ton marine railway, are all readily available. Hull repairs, welding, machine ship service, and painting (Awlgrip and Imron) are also an integral part of the yard's offerings. To be succinct, if you can't get it fixed here, better see how the new-boat market has been doing lately.

The totally charming and utterly unique facility known as Bayou Joe's (850-763-6442, 30 09.172 North/085 39.541 West) overlooks the northern shores of the same westward-flowing cove shared by Sailor's Supply Company Marina. Veteran Northern Gulf cruisers will remember this establishment as bearing the unusual moniker of "Dock at J.R.'s and Eat at Joe's."

Since Rema and Tom Herndon took over, and changed the name to Bayou Joe's, the food has gotten ever better. The utterly funky atmosphere remains unchanged. If you only have

Tibbett's Boat Works, Panama City

the opportunity to eat at one place in Panama City, let this be the one!

Bayou Joe's is open for all three meals of the day, seven days a week. For breakfast, don't dare miss the "garbage potatoes." This utterly delectable blend of cheese, veggies, sausage, eggs, and potatoes is a real belt-buster. There are often some very taste-pleasing specials for the evening meal, and the luncheon "trash-burgers" are sure to be a wonderfully choles-terol-enriching experience.

In fair weather, the open-air, dockside din-ing overlooking the bayou's placid waters is absolutely delightful. Inside seats are also offered for dining during more inclement weather.

The wet-slip dockage at Bayou Joe's (6½-foot depths) is now pretty much taken up by month-to-month patrons, but there is almost always room to tie up temporarily while you dine. As a general rule, overnighters are no longer accepted, though the ultrafriendly own-ers may be able to accommodate a vessel or two if no other dockage is available in the area.

Massalina Bayou also features yet another on-the-water restaurant convenient for dockside

Bayou Joe's Restaurant, Panama City

dining. The Hawk's Nest (850-872-1333, closed Mondays) overlooks the extreme southwesterly corner of Massalina Bayou's westerly arm, just southwest of Bayou Joe's. Currently, most of the slips adjacent to this dining spot are occupied by resident sailcraft. However, there might be room for one or two vessels under 36 feet in length to tie up while dining at the fixed, wooden piers. Depths alongside run about 6 to 7 feet.

Dining at the the Hawks Nest is a bit more formal than at Bayou Joe's, but we did find the seafood to be quite good. This dining spot is also very convenient (as is Bayou Joe's) to those berthing at the Panama City Marina (see below).

Visiting cruisers sometimes anchor on Massalina Bayou amidst its excellent shelter and minimum 5½- to 6-foot depths. There are at least two spots to consider. First up is the wide, correctly charted bubble of deep water just southeast of Bayou Joe's (near 30 09.112 North/085 39.516 West). Here you can anchor in 6 to 8 feet of water with excellent protection. As the bayou supports a moderate amount of pleasure-craft traffic, particularly on the weekends, be sure to show a bright anchor light at night.

Cruisers wanting to get a bit more off the beaten path can track their way upstream on Massalina Bayou past the stream's hooklike turn to the northeast. Depths of 5½ to 6 feet run to within 75 yards of the *T* split in the creek, and there is room enough for a 45-foot vessel to swing comfortably near 30 09.207 North/085 39.375 West. Protection is even better here, but the shores continue to be flanked by heavy, but not unseemly, residential development.

Panama City Marina (Standard Mile 290) (30 09.000 North/085 39.884 West)

Panama City Marina is easily identified by the twin-charted, breakwater-enclosed harbors north of flashing buoy #17. This is one of the largest and best-managed city marinas ever visited by this writer. Captain Chris and her staff simply can't do enough for you. Visiting cruisers can be assured of a warm and knowledgeable welcome at this topnotch municipal marina.

Of course, now mariners have *two* choices in regards to Panama City-owned pleasure-craft marinas. As we will see later in this chapter, the old St. Andrew Bay Marina has been renovated, expanded, and reoriented toward pleasure craft. However, you still can't do better than the Panama City Marina, and this basin has the added advantage of being located in the heart of the downtown Panama City business district.

Transients are eagerly accepted at Panama City Marina's extensive, fixed wooden (concrete pilings) docks, which feature 30- and 50-amp power hookups and fresh-water connections. Cable television and telephone outlets are also available. Depths alongside run an impressive 10+ feet. Mechanical repairs can be arranged through local, independent technicians.

The city marina dockage basin is divided into northwestern and southeastern harbors by a central street. Some larger transient boats are rarely moored along a face dock fronting the Waterway between the two dockage basins. Obviously, berths along this outer pier do not provide the shelter enjoyed by boats in the inner dockage basins.

The marina's combination ship's store, dockmaster's office, Laundromat, and one set of showers overlook the southwesterly shores of

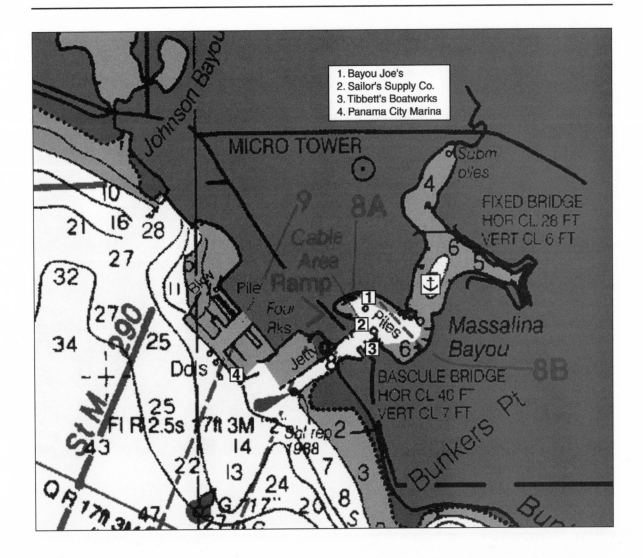

the southeasterly dockage basin. Here, you will also find the floating fuel dock, dispensing both gasoline and diesel fuel. Waste pump-out service is also available.

The marina's ship's/variety store is extensive and offers a nice selection of nautical gifts and basic foodstuffs. Here, you will also discover a small paperback exchange library.

Panama City Marina features two banks of showers, one located in the ship's store (reviewed above), while a second is to be found in a free-standing building on the shore of the northwesterly dockage basin. Both sets are air conditioned, in first-class condition, and feature 24-hour access for registered cruisers only.

The downtown Panama City business district

Panama City Marina

is readily accessible by foot from the city marina. You can easily track your way to several restaurants and other shoreside businesses (see below), as well as the previously reviewed dining choices on nearby Massalina Bayou (see above).

Cruising chefs in search of groceries will be glad to learn that the friendly staff of Panama City Marina can usually provide transportation to a nearby supermarket. There is also an inexpensive (50 cents) city trolley system that boasts service straight to the local shopping mall. Captain Chris informs us that many visiting mariners take the trolley to the mall and return in a taxi. Free bicycles with attached grocery baskets are kept on site for the use of visiting cruisers as well. The local library is located within a block of the dockage basin. Ask for directions at the marina office and ship's store.

Phew! Are your eyes tired from reading about all that is available in and around Panama City Marina? Trust me, you can't do much better than coil your lines here for a few days!

Panama City Marina (850) 872-7272

Approach depth—12-20 feet
Dockside depth—10 feet plus
Accepts transients—yes
Transient-dockage rate—above average
Fixed wooden piers (concrete pilings)—yes
Dockside power connections—30 and 50
   (and some 100) amp
Dockside water connections—yes
Showers—yes
Laundromat—yes
Waste pump-out—yes
Gasoline—yes
Diesel fuel—yes
Mechanical repairs—yes (independent contractors)
Ship's and variety store—yes
Restaurant—several nearby

Downtown Panama City Restaurants and Other Attractions

Cruisers who find berths on either Massalina Bayou or at the Panama City Marina are in for a real treat. The downtown central business district is only a quick step away. Featuring a potpourri of fine restaurants, gift shops, art galleries, and three antique malls, visitors will find much to see, do, and eat along the highways and byways of downtown Panama City.

When it comes time to slake a healthy appetite, garnered from a looong day on the water, downtown Panama City is ready for you! A host of some-new and some-old favorite restaurants graces Panama City's downtown business district. All are within walking distance or, at worst, a very quick taxi ride of your overnight berth. Of course, you could (and probably should) choose to partake of the fare at one of the two previously mentioned dining spots overlooking Massalina Bayou (the Hawk's Nest or Bayou Joe's), but let's pause for a moment to consider two other possibilities.

Ferrucci Ristorante (231 Harrison Avenue, 850-913-9131) serves up some simply wonderful Italian-style cuisine. We found the pasta dishes memorable.

Chef Imondis Bakery and Cafe (4438 Harrison Avenue, 850-913-1933) boasts some yummy bread and sandwiches, as well as a mean cup of she-crab soup. It is open for breakfast and lunch, Monday through Saturday.

The good people at Panama City Marina swear by the food at the Warehouse Cafe and Market (540 Harrison Avenue, 850-913-9266), though we have not yet had a chance to dine here. This gastronomical attraction is apparently located in an antique mall.

How about a good cup of coffee, a cappuccino, or even an espresso? Then check out Panama Java at 233 Harrison Avenue (850-763-8220). We found the atmosphere associated with this coffeehouse to be absolutely delightful.

Cruisers who grow bored of the various dining experiences in Panama City are in real trouble. If you can't find what you're looking for between Bayou Joe's, the Hawk's Nest, Ferrucci Ristorante, or Panama Java, then perhaps it's time to get your palate inspected.

Once your hunger pangs are satisfied, it's time to stroll about and see what else downtown Panama City has to offer. We particularly recommend the Antique Mall (437 Harrison Avenue, 850-763-9993) and Second Edition Antiques and Uniques (445 Harrison Avenue, 850-215-1420). You could spend hours here browsing through all the many historic artifacts. Up for a little new reading material? Don't miss Books by the Sea (571 Harrison Avenue, 850-769-2317). This is a great new-and-used bookstore with a broad selection. Art lovers will want to check out the Gallery of Art (36 West Beach Drive, 850-785-7110) and the Visual Arts Center (19 East Fourth Street, 850-769-4451).

Downtown Panama City is the site for a crowded schedule of special events through-out the year. In the spring of 2002, for instance, April 13 saw a "Marine Flea Market and Marina Clean-up" at St. Andrews Marina, while the Cobia Classic Fishing Tournament took place in April as well. Later that same month, a "Downtown Arts and Antiques Fair" came to call, while May saw a Spring Art Festival.

DUPONT BRIDGE TO ST. ANDREW BAY NAVIGATION

Successful navigation of the ICW between the Dupont span and the Waterway's intersection with St. Andrew Bay is a relatively simple matter of holding to the mid-width on East Bay's westerly reaches. Markers and daybeacons are fairly few and far between, but there are enough to keep the visiting navigator clearly on his path. While it is unlikely that stiff winds will produce dangerous waves in this section, fresh breezes can set up a chop that can be decidedly uncomfortable for small craft. Otherwise, simply study chart 11390 ahead of time, plan a few compass/GPS courses for the longer runs between aids to navigation, and you should find the waters approaching Panama City to be a genuine cruising delight.

The various side waters, creeks, and bayous lying between the Dupont Bridge and St. Andrew Bay call for more navigational caution than the Waterway itself. While most of the various creeks have deep entrances, there are usually just enough unmarked surrounding shoals to make matters interesting. Be sure to study chart 11390 and the information presented below before attempting to enter any of these auxiliary bodies of water.

On the Waterway Immediately after passing under the Dupont fixed bridge, the ICW channel is currently outlined by a pair of floating markers, unlighted can buoy #5 and nun buoy #6. While there is a broad channel of deep water on either side of the marked cut, prudent captains will pass between the two buoys. Set course to pass between #5 and #6. As you pass between this pair of markers, look east and you may catch sight of some uncharted wreckage abutting the shoreline. After leaving #5 and #6 behind, the waterway angles to the north and northwest and passes between unlighted can buoy #7 and unlighted nun buoy #8. Westbound craft will sight no further markers for quite some distance after leaving #7 and #8 in their wake.

Before leaving the Dupont span too far behind; however, two excellent anchorage opportunities present themselves. Cruisers may choose to enter Pearl Bayou to the southwest or Pitt Bayou to the northeast.

Pearl Bayou   Study chart 11390 and you will quickly spy the large shoal abutting the northwestern flank of Pearl Bayou's entrance. Fortunately, flashing daybeacon #2 marks the shallows. Shoaling has encroached on #2 and extends farther to the south and southeast than is shown on the edition of chart 11390 available at the time of this writing. Be sure to come abeam of and pass #2 by at least 30 yards to its southeasterly side.

Shoaling has also encroached on the next upstream aid, flashing daybeacon #3. Stay at least 25 yards to the west of #3.

South of #3, Pearl Bayou splits into two branches. As mentioned earlier, the southerly arm seems to be used as a recreation area and crash boat dock by military personnel from nearby Tyndall Air Force Base. You will spy the recreation park and some large wharves on the banks of the eastward-running cove, south of #3. Pleasure craft should probably avoid this section of the stream.

Passage into the delightfully undeveloped westerly arm of Pearl Bayou is gained by turning into this stream's mid-width soon after passing #3. Be on guard against the sharp point bordering the entrance's northerly shore. This promontory has built much farther out into the stream than is shown on the current edition of chart 11390. Favor the southerly banks a bit when passing the sharp point, but don't approach the charted shallows abutting the southerly shoreline either. Once pass the entrance, stick to the stream's centerline. Shoal water flanks both banks. Drop the hook at any likely spot on the mid-width and settle down for an evening of peace and security. Be sure to discontinue your upstream explorations of the creek before reaching the split in the stream to the west. Past this point shoaling is very much in evidence.

Pitts Bayou   Pitts Bayou is easily entered by avoiding the considerable charted shoal flanking the southern quadrant of the stream's mouth. To bypass this hazard, favor the northern banks when passing through the creek's entrance.

Continue favoring the port-side banks until reaching the bayou's first sharp turn to the north. Here you will see the docks of Pier 98 Marina on the eastern banks. There is plenty of room to drop the hook on the charted pool of 15-foot water abeam of this facility.

To continue cruising upstream, hold to the mid-width as the stream takes a jog to the east and then turns back to the northeast. Be sure to discontinue your explorations at least .1 of a nautical mile southwest of the charted 2-foot patch of water on the creek's extreme upper reaches. As correctly forecast on chart 11390, the channel narrows considerably well short of the 2-foot waters.

Parker Bayou   Parker Bayou has a broad entrance that is mostly free of shoals. Be sure to stay well away from flashing daybeacon #29, which marks the westerly reaches of the creek's mouth. Shoal water has encroached on this aid from the adjacent northerly point.

Cruise into the bayou on its mid-width. Soon the creek will take a sharp turn to the north. Favor the southern shore slightly as you cruise into the loop to avoid the charted shoal water abutting the northern banks. As you pass through the turn, begin favoring the western banks slightly. This maneuver will avoid a small patch of shallows flanking the easterly shoreline.

About .1 nautical miles upstream from the sharp northerly turn, Parker Bayou splits into two baylike arms. To enter the northeastern branch, the better of the two for overnight anchorage, favor the northwestern side of the creek slightly. This maneuver will help you to avoid the first sharp point of land guarding the southerly shoreline which seems to be building outward.

Feel your way to the northeast, watching the sounder carefully. When depths rise to the 7- to 9-foot level, drop the hook. Cruising farther upstream will lead careless navigators into shoal water of 4 feet or less.

Favor the western shore heavily when entering the northwestern arm of the creek. Avoid the point of land separating the two branches of the creek. As correctly forecast on chart 11390, a large buffer of shoal water abuts the eastern banks and the separating point of land. For best depths, drop the hook and discontinue your upstream cruising well short of the stream's northern tip.

Pratt Bayou   Pratt Bayou empties into the northern shores of the entrance to Parker Bayou. A narrow, piling-marked channel holding 5-foot minimum depths leads to the bayou's deeper interior waters. The pilings marking the Pratt Bayou entrance channel are a bit worse for wear. Currently, the outermost marker is a single piling that you pass to your starboard side. From this point into Pratt Bayou, the cut is outlined by pairs of pilings. Proceed at idle speed between the remaining piles. Because of its narrow width, this cut is not recommended for sail- or power craft over 36 feet or those drawing more than 4½ feet.

Once through the entrance, cruisers will find a broad pool of 5- to 7-foot water. Select any likely spot to drop the hook, but don't approach any of the shorelines too closely.

On the ICW   North of unlighted nun buoy #8, the ICW follows the westerly reaches of East Bay, first to the north, and then sharply west at the twin promontories of Ferry and Military points. Before reaching this turn, the Waterway skirts to the west and southwest of flashing daybeacon #29. As mentioned in the discussion of Parker Bayou, the shoal marked by #29 is building outward. Be sure to pass #29 by at least 150 yards to its westerly side.

Navigators should take note that at flashing daybeacon #29, off the mouth of Parker Bayou, the ICW color scheme reverses in response to the nearby Panama City Inlet. Westbound craft should now begin to take green, odd-numbered aids to navigation to their (the cruisers') starboard side and pass red, even-numbered markers to port. This new scheme holds until the ICW passes the inner reaches of St. Andrew Bay Inlet. The usual color configuration begins anew for westbound craft at flashing buoy #5 off Courtney Point.

Flashing daybeacon #28 marks a building shoal at Military Point on the Waterway's southerly flank. Stay well away from #28 by passing it to its northern and northeasterly sides.

North-northwest of flashing daybeacon #28, chart 11390 correctly forecasts deep water running almost to the banks along the northerly shoreline, just west of the closed entrance to Lake Martin. While it would be a simple matter to drop the hook within 100 yards or less of this shore, protection from all but northerly breezes would be minimal. With so many protected anchorages nearby, it probably makes sense to bypass this open cove.

The ICW continues west by passing well to the south of flashing buoy #25. As you approach #25, look north and you will see a large barge-loading facility associated with the pulp mill on Watson Bayou. To the northeast, you should also catch sight of the twin smokestacks of the mill spewing pollution into the air. Hold your nose if the wind happens to be blowing from the north.

North-northwest of flashing buoy #25, visiting mariners have access to Watson Bayou, home of three marine facilities and an excellent anchorage (in spite of the pulp mill).

Watson Bayou   The entrance into broad and mostly deep Watson Bayou is pinched between two sharp points of land. To enter the mouth of the creek, set a course to pass between the two sharp points, favoring the westerly point ever so slightly. As the westerly promontory comes abeam, bend your course a bit to the northwest to avoid the small, charted shoal abutting the eastern point. Once pass this obstruction, deep water opens out before you. Large, deep-draft boats requiring maximum swinging room can anchor here, but be on guard against easterly breezes blowing from the mill.

To the west, the bayou's first offshoot is known as Lake Van Vac. Be warned that the entrance channel is not as it appears on the current edition of chart 11390. The chart would lead you to believe that good water runs hard by the first point on the southern banks. On-site research revealed that this point is building outward. So, while you should favor the southerly banks for best depths, care must also be exercised to avoid this south-side point. On a clear, sunny day, it's easy to spot the shallows by the change in water color.

West of the sharp point, skippers will discover a large pool of mostly deep water, though a few shallows continue to plague the northerly shoreline. This is a great spot to anchor.

Do not attempt to explore upstream from the deep-water bubble. Farther to the northwest, the channel narrows and shoal water is eventually encountered.

Back on the main body of Watson Bayou, skippers can follow a broad, deep track to the north, bypassing the first two eastward-striking arms of the creek. As discussed earlier, these two small creeks are best avoided due to the paper mill and considerable commercial waterborne traffic.

As you cruise through the charted patch of 15-foot water west of the second eastern offshoot, you may catch sight of a commercial boatyard on the eastern banks. No services seem to be available for pleasure craft at this facility.

Soon the bayou takes a sharp turn to the northwest. For best depths, favor the southwestern banks slightly until the stream turns to the north again.

After cruising through the stream's northerly turn, described above, the marked but uncharted channel running east to Snug Harbour and Watson Bayou marinas will be spotted off the main track.

As you would expect, simply pass all red, even-numbered aids to navigation to your starboard side and take green markers to port. You may be surprised, when rounding unlighted daybeacon #3, to discover that this course runs you almost dead ahead into the first rank of piers at Watson Bayou Marina. Keep the faith. On-site soundings showed that best depths are maintained by rounding #3 to your port side. The channel then takes a hard swing to port and parallels the westerly face of the marina dockage basin. To continue upstream, point to pass unlighted daybeacon #4 to your starboard side. At low water, expect some 5½- to 6-foot soundings between #3 and #4.

Cruisers bound for Snug Harbour Marina should come abeam of #4 and then swing to starboard, pointing for this facility's entrance. One last decrepit marker, unlighted daybeacon #6, should be passed to your starboard side just before entering Snug Harbour's ultraprotected dockage basin.

Cruisers continuing north on the main Watson Bayou channel will eventually follow the stream's track through a sharp turn to the north. Past this point the bayou opens out into a wide body of deep water. The piers of Gulf Marina of Panama City will be found on the northeastern banks in this area. Drop the hook anywhere you fancy in the middle, but don't approach either shoreline too closely. As clearly shown on chart 11390, shoal water abuts both banks, particularly to the east. Farther upstream, passage is barred by a low-level, fixed bridge with only 9 feet of vertical clearance.

Smack Bayou   To make good your entry into the superb anchorage on Smack Bayou, depart the ICW some 300 yards northwest of flashing buoy #20. Use your binoculars to pick out the creek's entrance to the south-southwest. Cruise directly for the mid-width of the entrance. Be mindful of the correctly charted shallows to the east and west.

Continue holding to the centerline until coming abeam of the southerly extreme of the twin entrance points (lying to the east and west respectively). Cruisers making for the sheltered haven in the cove to the west can take a lazy turn around the starboard-side (western) entrance point and turn north into the charted deep water. Don't get near the western point itself, as a shoal seems to be building south from this promontory. Do not attempt to approach to within less than 75 yards of the cove's northerly tip. Shoals shelve out from this shoreline. Similarly, don't get too close to the western banks.

Cruisers entering Smack Bayou in the late evening or nighttime should keep a sharp watch with a searchlight for crab pots. We spotted several of these potential prop-tying pests during our on-site research.

Redfish Point Anchorage   To access the anchorage east and south of Redfish Point, depart the Waterway some .13 nautical miles southeast of flashing daybeacon #18. Cruise to the southwest, feeling your way along with the sounder. When depths rise to 8- and 9-foot levels, drop anchor. Don't approach to within less than 100 yards of the adjoining shoreline. A small ribbon of shoals makes out from these banks.

On the Waterway   The ICW continues to be wide and easily followed to flashing buoy #17, which marks the Waterway's intersection with the northeasterly reaches of St. Andrew Bay. While pleasure craft will find plenty of water to either side of #17, depths of 20 feet or better are held by passing between #17 and flashing daybeacon #18 (southwest of #17). Before entering the headwaters of St. Andrew Bay, cruisers may choose to visit Massalina Bayou or the Panama City Marina, north of #17.

Massalina Bayou   For best depths, set a course from flashing buoy #17 to come abeam of flashing daybeacon #2 by some 15 yards to its northwesterly side. Once abeam of #2, adjust course to head directly for the mid-width of the creek's entrance. Watch your stern as well as your progress ahead to make note of any lateral leeway. Don't allow an errant current to sweep you out of the dredged cut.

Take particular care to avoid the channel's northwesterly edge. An underwater, stone jetty lies waiting to trap navigators who make this error. Take our bent prop's word for it, this can be a rocky (and I don't mean of the Balboa variety) encounter.

Immediately after passing into the bayou's mouth, your progress will be barred by a bascule bridge with only 7 feet of closed vertical clearance. Fortunately, this span opens on demand, and the bridge tender monitors VHF Channel 9. Once through the bridge, good water opens out almost from shore to shore, and the creek's marina and yard facilities are easily entered.

Captains choosing to anchor on the upper reaches of Massalina Bayou should hold to the centerline as the stream turns first to the southeast, and then sharply northeast. As you round the northeasterly turn, stay away from the port-side point. A single, unmarked piling warns of an oyster bank building out into the creek from this point of land.

Cease your explorations before approaching to within less than 100 yards of the stream's *T*-like split. Depths fall off to the 4-foot range upstream of this point, and the channel, such as it is, becomes too unreliable for visitors without specific local knowledge.

Panama City Marina   Access to Panama City Marina can be quickly gained by following a course directly from flashing buoy #17 to the southeastern dockage basin. The dockmaster's office, ship's store, and fuel dock will be spotted along the southwesterly wall of the southeast basin.

St. Andrew Bay, Grand Lagoon, and St. Andrew Inlet

St. Andrew Bay, its associated inlet, and northwestward-slashing Grand Lagoon together offer something of all the good cruising qualities that captains might ever expect to find. Whether you seek overnight berths, a ready outlet to the sea, or even a pristine anchorage overlooked by beautifully natural shores, few mariners will leave the waters of St. Andrew without a backward glance.

St. Andrew Bay Inlet is deep, well marked, and used regularly by oceangoing ships. Keeping in mind that while the easily run inlet has yet to be invented, cruising captains can put to sea on this cut with as much confidence as is ever possible on those often uncertain strands where inland waters meet the Gulf.

Grand Lagoon offers some of the finest marina and yard facilities on the entire run between Carrabelle and New Orleans. Whether you seek only dockage at a large, full-service marina with every amenity, or complete repair services, you may be sure of finding what is needed on Grand Lagoon.

Finally, the main body of St. Andrew Bay, sweeping southeast from the inlet, allows access to several protected anchorages along Shell Island. Over a thousand acres of pristine beaches have been set aside along St. Andrew Inlet as St. Andrew State Park. Portions of these barrier islands were swept clean by Hurricane Opal, leaving behind only flat beaches where there were once sprawling sand dunes, pine woods, and marshes. Fortunately some of the wooded areas have survived, but visitors who have not laid eyes on this portion of the Panhandle coastline since Opal are in for quite a surprise.

Although the developed section of the park is found northwest of the inlet, the westerly section of Shell Island (southeast of the inlet) is protected. This lovely barrier island has wonderful beaches and only minimal development. The white sands and clear waters beg you to break out the dinghy and go exploring ashore. This writer suggests that you heed the call. Your voyage will be far richer for the time spent among these timeless sands and waters.

St. Andrew Bay Inlet (Standard Mile 289)

St. Andrew Bay Inlet (also known as Panama City Inlet) is wide, deep, well marked, and carefully charted. This is by far the most reliable seaward passage between Port St. Joe and Pensacola. If you are planning to put to sea or return from the Gulf between St. Joe and Pensacola, this cut should be your primary choice. By all accounts, it is far more reliable than East Pass Inlet at Destin.

The inlet's aids to navigation are clearly charted, usually evidence of a stable cut. Of course, when winds and tide oppose each other, it can still be a bumpy ride, but in fair weather you should come through with nothing worse than a little salt spray.

Visiting cruisers and resident skippers alike should not attempt the shallow seaward cut on the southeasterly reaches of St. Andrew Bay. The channel (what there is of it) is shifting, unmarked, and surrounded by breakers. Don't even think about it.

Grand Lagoon Facilities and Anchorages (Various Lats/Lons—see below)

The southeasterly reaches of Grand Lagoon

flow into the St. Andrew Bay Inlet channel near flashing buoy #9. While the lagoon's entrance has become somewhat prone to shoaling over the last several years, most skippers should be able to pilot their craft safely through the narrow entrance channel with minimum 6½-foot depths into the deeper water to the northwest.

While most mariners entering Grand Lagoon will continue northwest to the lagoon's many facilities, cruisers should be aware that this notable body of water can boast of having a popular anchorage as well. Boats of most sizes and drafts can safely drop the hook in the charted bubble of deep water just inside (northwest of) the lagoon's southwesterly entrance point. We found minimum MLW soundings of 12+ feet near 30 07.809 North/085 43.465 West. This good water runs to within 75 to 100 yards of the cove's shoreline. There is good shelter from southwestern and southeastern breezes and some protection to the east and west as well. Fresh winds from any other direction call for a different choice of stops.

Once the anchor is down, you can then break out the dinghy and row ashore to the St. Andrew State Park recreation area. Camping grounds, nature trails, and a snack bar vie with the magnificent white sand beaches as top attractions at the park. During the warm weather months, this is a very popular weekend stop for Panama City cruisers. If you visit during these times, you will almost certainly be joined by a host of local pleasure cruisers.

A marked channel leads upstream on Grand Lagoon to a host of facilities. The first is Bay Point Marina (30 08.614 North/085 43.691 West), located at the terminus of the charted, extremely well-marked channel leading north-east from flashing daybeacon #5. In spite of the "2 ft. rep" symbol on chart 11390, entrance depths at Bay Point are a very respectable 6 feet, with dockside depths about the same or slightly deeper. Most power and sail craft will find plenty of water under their keels.

Bay Point is one of the largest marinas in the Panama City area. As impressive as this facility is on its own merits, the marina is only a part of a huge Marriott resort complex. Within the development are eight restaurants, all types of shopping, first-rate lodgings, a golf course, swimming pool, and numerous tennis courts. Transient cruisers are welcome to make use of this wide array of amenities. How's that for perks!

Mariners who have not visited Bay Point for the last two years are in for a few surprises. The former ship's store and dockmaster's building now houses the Bay Point Yacht Club. The new dockmaster's headquarters—plus good, climate-controlled showers and a small but adequate Laundromat—are now located in a smaller building just to the south of the older structure. There is no more ship's store at Bay Point. Dockside cable-television connections are now open to transient use, and there is also a new, on-site swimming pool that welcomes visiting cruisers.

The Bay Point Marina harbor is surrounded by the Bay Town shopping complex containing a bank, post office, laundry, clothing store, gift shop, and an unusually well-stocked deli, known as the Butler's Pantry (850-236-2055). This dining attraction serves up some yummy-looking sandwiches.

Besides the deli, one of the complex's other dining spots is to be found within walking distance of the dockage complex. The 30 Degree

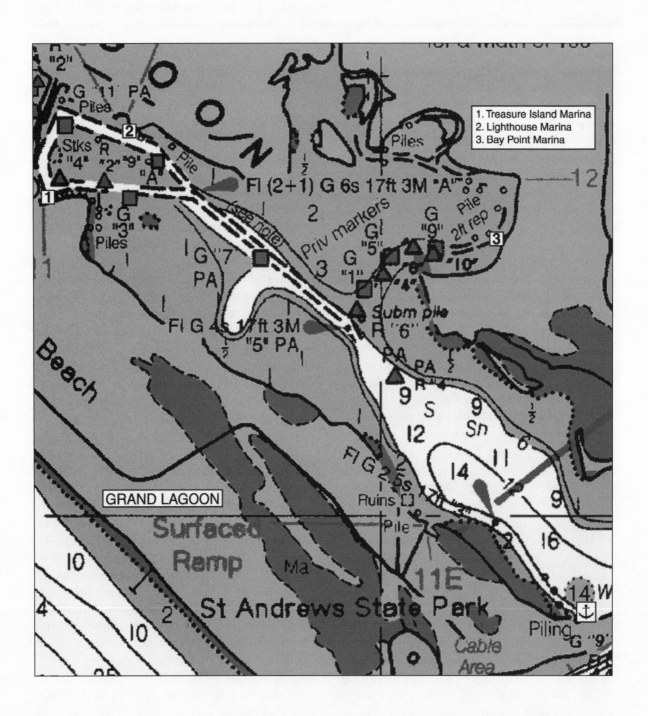

Blue restaurant (850-235-6903) has been described to this writer as a "fine dining establishment." We have not yet had a chance to sample its offerings. (Darn!) Complimentary transportation is cheerfully provided to the complex's other restaurants, as well as to the golf and tennis facilities. To say the least, you would have to look far and wide to find a marina that can offer such a variety of shoreside attractions and activities.

Bay Point Marina itself features plentiful transient dockage at fixed wooden piers. Depths alongside run at least 6 to 7 feet. Every slip boasts 30- and 50-amp power and freshwater hookups. The harbor is well sheltered from northern, northeastern, and eastern blows, but strong winds from the west or southwest could make for a bumpy night. Gasoline, diesel fuel (via high-speed pumps), and a waste pump-out service are readily available. Mechanical repairs can be arranged through independent local contractors. During the spring, summer, and early autumn, advance reservations at this popular facility would be a wise precaution.

Over and above all these impressive statistics and attributes, this writer found the staff and management of Bay Point to be friendly and very much in tune with the needs of visiting cruisers. If you enjoy well-appointed marinas (and who doesn't?), then Bay Point Marina deserves a red circle on your chart.

By the way, if you have any problems at Bay Point, just ask for Harris, the dockmaster's yellow Labrador retriever. He's the one who really knows how to get things done!

Bay Point Marina (850) 235-6911
   http://www.baypointmarina.com

Approach depth—6-12 feet
Dockside depth—6-7 feet
Accepts transients—yes
Transient-dockage rate—above average
Fixed wooden piers—yes
Dockside power connections—30- and 50-amp
Dockside water connections—yes
Showers—yes
Laundromat—yes
Waste pump-out—yes
Gasoline—yes
Diesel fuel—yes
Mechanical repairs—independent technicians
Restaurant—several on site

Moving farther upstream on the main body of Grand Lagoon, the marked channel circles a shoal on the mid-width of the lagoon's northwesterly cruising limits. Continued passage to the west on the lagoon is blocked by a fixed bridge with only 8 feet of vertical clearance. Marina facilities are found on both the northeastern and southwestern shores in this area.

Beginning on the northern channel, visiting cruisers will first encounter Lighthouse Marina and Boatyard (30 08.852 North/085 44.687 West) between unlighted daybeacons #9 and #11. This facility's location is easily identifiable, courtesy of the tall, faux red-and-white, candy-striped lighthouse that overlooks the on-site restaurant and dockage basin.

Lighthouse Marina has undergone a significant expansion during the last several years. Visitors will now discover a full-service marina, fuel dock (gasoline and diesel fuel), complete repair yard, and an extensive dry-stack storage building on this site.

Bay Point Marina, Grand Lagoon

Transients are now accepted at the marina's fixed wooden piers. Good depths alongside of 7 to 8 feet can be expected. Fresh-water and 30- and 50-amp power connections are available at every slip. Some berths also feature cable-television hookups.

Smaller vessels are usually placed at the slips near the restaurant (and "lighthouse"), while larger craft generally find dockage at larger slips a short hop farther to the southeast.

Shoreside, cruisers will find new, air-conditioned showers housed with a small variety and ship's store. The on-site restaurant was closed for renovation during our last visit in the summer of 2002, but it may well be reopened by the time this account finds its way into your hands. There are also at least two other restaurants within walking distance.

Lighthouse also features full mechanical and haul-out repair services. One 30-ton travelift should be able to handle haul-outs for most pleasure craft. Gasoline-power plants are serviced by the Lighthouse yard personnel, but diesel repairs are usually farmed out to local independent technicians.

The hikers among us can undertake a half-mile (or so) trek to a nearby Winn-Dixie supermarket. Ask any of the marina staff for walking directions.

Lighthouse Marina and Boatyard (850) 234-5609

Approach depth—10-12 feet
Dockside depth—7-8 feet
Accepts transients—yes

Transient-dockage rate—above average
Fixed wooden piers—yes
Dockside power connections—30- and 50-amp
Dockside water connections—yes
Showers—yes
Gasoline—yes
Diesel fuel—yes
Mechanical repairs—yes
Below-waterline repairs—yes
Ship's and variety store—yes
Restaurant—2 nearby

Lighthouse Marina and Boatyard, Grand Lagoon

Farther upstream on the northern portion of the circular channel, visiting cruisers will find a host of charter craft docks fronting two popular seafood restaurants. The easternmost dining spot is known as Mako's Restaurant, while Captain Anderson Restaurant and Marina occupies the large building just to the west. While tourists can most certainly book offshore fishing charters here and even take passage on a harbor tour boat, no dockage seems to be available for transients. Even those wishing to tie up for dinner might find a slip hard to come by. Your best bet is to dock at nearby Lighthouse Marina and take the short walk to reach the two eateries. Both serve the freshest of fried and broiled seafood, and they enjoy excellent reputations with the local crowd.

Turning our attention to the two marinas on the southwestern side of the lagoon, Pirate Cove Marina (850-234-3939) resides at the end of a pile-marked channel that strikes south from unlighted daybeacon #2. This facility had just come under new ownership at the time of this writing. Big changes are in the forecast, and we will forego any more mentioning of this marina until the next edition of this guide, at which time we can check out all the new services and structures by eye.

Finally, let us take a look at what is one of this writer's favorite marinas in Panama City. The fixed, wooden piers of Treasure Island Marina guard the cove southwest of unlighted daybeacon #4 (30 08.704 North/085 44.870 West). To paraphrase an old television commercial, if you can find a friendlier marina, then stay there. Resident and visiting cruisers alike can be assured of a warm welcome at this medium-sized facility.

Transients are accepted for overnight dockage, but resident craft have priority over visitors. Advance reservations are strongly advised. Dockage is at fixed piers, with excellent depths of 7 to 10 feet. Fresh-water and 30-amp power connections are available, as are fair, nonclimate-controlled showers, a Laundromat, waste pump-out service, gasoline, and diesel fuel. The fuel dock is open 24 hours a day year round! How's that for service over and above the usual?

Treasure Island maintains a very well-stocked ship's, tackle, and variety store. Full mechanical repairs are available and boats up to 37 feet or 16,000 pounds can be hauled with a forklift. The adjacent Treasure Ship Restaurant is housed in a huge re-creation of an old, bare-pole sailing ship.

Cruisers up for a mile-long hike can find their way to the Winn-Dixie supermarket mentioned above. Otherwise, you can take a quick taxi ride or visit the convenience store that is just across the street from the marina grounds.

Treasure Island Marina (850) 234-6813
Approach depth—7-11 feet
Dockside depth—7-10 feet
Accepts transients—yes
Transient-dockage rate—above average
Fixed wooden piers—yes
Dockside power connections—30 amp
Dockside water connections—yes
Showers—yes
Laundromat—yes
Waste pump-out—yes
Gasoline—yes
Diesel fuel—yes
Mechanical repairs—yes
Below-waterline repairs—limited
Ship's and variety store—yes
Restaurant—next door

Treasure Island Marina, Grand Lagoon

St. Andrew Bay and Shell Island
(30 05.677 North/085 41.052 West)

The main body of St. Andrew Bay sweeps southeast from the head of the inlet channel. There is a wild host of unmarked shoals to avoid, but with care (or, better yet, the use of a GPS interfaced with a laptop computer), you can safely guide your craft to any number of wonderful anchorages bordering Shell Island.

Fortunately, the western portion of Shell Island is part of St. Andrew State Park and is protected from development. The island exhibits some wooded sections contrasting with flat, sandy beaches. Most of the former sand dunes were utterly erased by a hurricane in 1998.

The Gulf-side beaches of Shell Island are absolutely magnificent, and since the park can only be reached by water, they are usually uncrowded. Anchoring on the bay side of the island and then dinghying ashore is a truly wonderful experience. A walk across the island to the beautiful beaches is a slice of paradise.

East of Spanish Shanty Point, deep water runs quite close to Shell Island's northeasterly shoreline. On a clear, sunny day, it's a simple matter to identify where the deep water ends and the shoaling leading into the beach begins. Be sure to set the hook well short of the shallows so as not to swing onto the shoal if the wind or tide change directions.

One of the best spots to anchor is found on the waters of the second cove southeast of Spanish Shanty Point, near 30 05.677 North/085 41.052 West. Mariners can safely cruise to within 200 yards or so of the shoreline with 10-foot minimum depths. An old dock sometimes used by tour boats abuts the shoreline in the mid-width of this anchorage. This structure makes a good navigational reference point.

While the anchorages adjacent to Shell Island are well sheltered from southern winds, strong blows from the north or particularly the east or west could make this a downright uncomfortable spot to be swinging on the Danforth. Pick a fair day of light to moderate winds for your visit to St. Andrew Park and Shell Island. Cruisers should not even consider anchoring on the water of St. Andrew Bay if bad weather is forecasted. Instead, retreat to one of the many facilities or sheltered anchorages discussed earlier in this chapter.

ST. ANDREW BAY, GRAND LAGOON, AND ST. ANDREW INLET NAVIGATION

St. Andrew Bay is certainly broad enough for winds over 15 knots to create a sizeable chop. On fair days a cruise on the bay is a real pleasure, although visiting and resident cruisers alike must take special care to avoid the two charted but unmarked shoals bisecting the water body's mid-width. Be sure to read the navigational information presented below and study chart 11390 carefully *before* attempting to cruise into the southeastern portion of the bay.

As for the inlet, while it is generally quite passable, the ride can be bumpy when the tide or wind acts up. The numerous flashing buoys make for simple navigation of the cut itself.

Grand Lagoon has suffered some on-and-off shoaling at its southeastern mouth over the last decade. While this condition certainly calls for caution, dozens upon dozens of local pleasure craft enter and exit Grand Lagoon day after day without any difficulty. Just be sure to read the navigational information presented below before making a first-time attempt.

Entrance from the ICW From a position between the ICW's flashing buoy #17 and flashing daybeacon #18, set a bisected course to eventually come abeam of flashing buoy #15 at the northeastern entrance into the main body of St. Andrew Bay. A straight course from #17 to #15 will encroach on the shoal waters west of Redfish Point. Instead, cruise west along the ICW channel for several hundred yards before making your cut to the southwest.

Pleasure craft can pass #15 to either side, but the deepest depths are found southeast of the buoy. Once abeam of #15, you must make a choice. You can continue cruising southwest on the inlet channel toward the seaward cut and Grand Lagoon or cut southeast into the delightful eastern arm of St. Andrew Bay.

St. Andrew Bay—Southeastern Arm Those who choose to visit the southeastern arm of St. Andrew Bay and explore its anchorages along Shell Island must turn southeast and set a careful compass course to carry you between Davis Point and the charted but unmarked shoal north of Spanish Shanty Point. Once abeam of Davis Point, bend your course farther to the south in order to bypass the long shoal bisecting the bay

north and northeast of Spanish Shanty Point. Aim for the mid-width of the broad swath of deep water between the long shoal and the northeastern banks of Shell Island. Once having passed well beyond the western tip of this shoal, you can bend your course to the south and begin a careful approach to the Shell Island banks.

As mentioned earlier, one of the best anchorages will be discovered on the waters of the second cove southeast of Spanish Shanty Point. Identification of these waters is helped by the presence of an old dock, which will be spotted by overlooking the southerly banks.

For maximum safety and best depths, continue cruising southeast on the bay until the cove is directly abeam to the south. You can then cut to the south and feel your way carefully with the sounder to within 200 yards of the shoreline with minimum 10-foot depths. Be sure to drop the hook well short of the shoal leading up to the beach. Then break out the dinghy and go ashore for some great exploring, shell hunting, and beachcombing.

On to Grand Lagoon Access to Grand Lagoon is gained by following the first half of the St. Andrew Inlet channel. From a position abeam of flashing buoy #15, set course to come between flashing buoys #13 and #14 at the northeastern limits of the improved inlet cut. Follow this well-marked track until you are some 200 yards northeast of flashing buoy #9. The entrance to Grand Lagoon will then be abeam to the west.

As mentioned earlier, shoaling can be a periodic problem on the southeasterly mouth of Grand Lagoon. As usual for Panhandle waters, it's easy to identify the shallows on sunny days, but this eyeball navigation can not be relied upon on cloudy, stormy days or in low-light conditions.

Be prepared to find some temporary and/or uncharted markers at the lagoon's entrance, which have been placed to warn of the shoals. Currently, there is only a single aid to navigation marking the Grand Lagoon entrance channel, flashing daybeacon #2. The entrance cut is comprised of a narrow passage passing between #2 and the southwestern-side entrance point. At the time of this writing, cruisers sticking strictly to the mid-width of this passage can expect MLW soundings of some 6½ feet. Things could be different by the time of your arrival, so proceed with caution.

Point to pass unlighted daybeacon #2 by some 25 to 30 yards to its southwesterly side. Watch your sounder and proceed at a slow speed unless you already know where the channel is located. By following this procedure, you should come through without any major problems.

Once pass the southwesterly point opposite #2, a wide bubble of deep water spreads out over the mid-width of the bay. Continue cruising upstream, pointing to eventually come abeam of unlighted daybeacon #3 by some 30 yards to its northeasterly side. Be on guard against the charted patch of 1-foot water that encroaches on the northeastern flank of the channel between #2 and #3.

To access the anchorage southeast of #3, depart your upstream cruise on the Grand Lagoon channel after cruising some 200 yards northwest of the lagoon's narrow entrance. Cut in toward the southwesterly shoreline and feel your way into the cove behind the hook of land that comprises the entrance's southwesterly point of land. Drop the hook before approaching to within less than 100 yards of the surrounding backs. Closer to shore, depths rise sharply.

To continue cruising northwest on Grand Lagoon from a position abeam of #3 to the plentiful marina facilities, set course to bring unlighted daybeacon #4 abeam fairly close to its southwesterly side. Then point to pass between flashing daybeacon #5 and unlighted daybeacon #6. Shallow water abuts both sides of the channel on this run. Watch your stern as well as your course ahead to quickly note any lateral slippage.

Once between #5 and #6, the marked and charted channel to Bay Point Marina breaks off to the northeast. Those continuing northwest on Grand Lagoon should next point to come abeam of unlighted daybeacon #7 by some 20 yards to its northeasterly side. Once abeam of #7, continue on course directly toward flashing junction daybeacon #A. Some 20 yards before reaching #A, cut either northwest or west-southwest into the appropriate arm of the marked channel. Shoal water occupies the mid-width of the lagoon in this area, and you must take care to stay in the marked cuts. It is possible to completely loop the centerline shoal by following the circular channel, but most captains will want to cruise to the marina of their choice and then reverse their course and leave the way they came.

Cruisers traversing the northerly fork of the channel to visit Lighthouse Marina (or just to explore) should be sure to stay north of unlighted daybeacons #9 and #11, and all should be well.

St. Andrew Inlet To continue seaward on St. Andrew Inlet, simply follow the well-marked channel past flashing buoy #9, where our discussion of Grand Lagoon began. Flashing buoys #5 and #6 mark twin stone jetties. There is a broad channel between the two aids and you would almost have to be asleep at the helm for the jetties to be a problem.

Southwest of #5 and #6, swells and chop usually begin to pick up. From here to the seaward terminus of the channel at flashing buoys #1 and #2, you can expect the roughest water.

Cruisers approaching St. Andrew Inlet from the sea will be hampered by the relative brevity of the marked channel. Unlike many seaward cuts, the buoys outlining the channel do not push very far out into the Gulf's deeper waters. This writer once missed the channel due to a cantankerous Loran C even though two crew members were assigned the task of watching for the markers through binoculars. Approach with caution and be sure to identify the entrance buoys before proceeding inland.

St. Andrew Bay to Choctawhatchee Bay

From its intersection with the main body of St. Andrew Bay near standard mile 290, the ICW skips lightly down a broad passage bordering the suburbs of Panama City. Soon the Waterway passes under the Hathaway fixed bridge and then strikes north to a great parting of the ways.

South of West Bay Point the broad waters divide into North Bay and West Bay. North Bay, abandoned by the ICW, offers a few anchorages and gunk holes, but not nearly as many as you would expect from a water body of this size. In fact, only those intrepid cruisers who must "see it all" will choose to visit North Bay.

The ICW follows the wide waters of West Bay for some 7 nautical miles to a partially man-made canal, which leads, in turn, to Choctawhatchee Bay. On days of fair weather and light breezes, passage across West Bay is a visual delight. Unfortunately, like its sister to the east (North Bay), West Bay boasts a very limited number of overnight anchorages. The few available havens have questionable shelter from inclement weather.

Facilities on this section of the Waterway are grouped around the Panama City suburbs along the southerly section of the run. Once past the Hathaway fixed bridge, North and West bays are completely without marinas. It's a long run indeed to the next facilities on Choctawhatchee Bay. Be sure your tanks are topped off before leaving the Panama City marinas behind.

To be honest, this is a section of the Gulf Coast ICW that many cruisers are glad to get behind them. However, the natural beauty of North and West bays is nothing to disregard too lightly. So, if it's time for the midday meal, ease into one of the protected waters described below, throw out the lunch hook, and admire nature's handiwork.

ICW Marina Facilities
(Various Lats/Lons—see below)

Two marinas and one boatyard are located along the Waterway south of the Hathaway fixed bridge.

First up is the new incarnation of St. Andrews Marina (standard mile 287.5, 30 10.096 North/085 42.235 West). This Panama City-owned facility is found in the charted, breakwater-enclosed harbor north-northeast of flashing buoy #6, in the shelter of Buena Vista Point. Until very recently, this was primarily a commercial-fishing-craft harbor, but *all* that has now changed in a *big* way.

The Panama City local government has expended a whole passel of capital to upgrade all aspects of this marina. While there are still some commercial-fishing vessels in attendance at St. Andrews, clearly the focus is now on pleasure craft.

It's really quite exciting that a community that already possessed a topnotch municipal marina—in the form of Panama City Marina (see above)—would choose to initiate a second city marina that can lay claim to an equally fine reputation. The cruising community should be so lucky at all ports of call!

The first question that probably occurs to you at this point, dear reader, is whether you should choose Panama City Marina or St. Andrews Marina. Well, the answer is clearly, "It depends." As we have already seen earlier in this chapter, the former facility has the considerable advantage of being located within walking distance of the downtown business district. By contrast, St. Andrews Marina is found in the heart of (guess what), the St. Andrews community. You can think of this section as a sub-set of Panama City. St. Andrews offers some excellent restaurants and a few other shoreside businesses, but it is also only fair to say that there are sections of this community that appear to be a bit down on their luck. On the other hand, there is a more free-wheeling attitude to be found here, as opposed to the downtown district. We suggest that you try both marinas during your various sojourns through Panama City and then make future choices based upon your particular sensibilities.

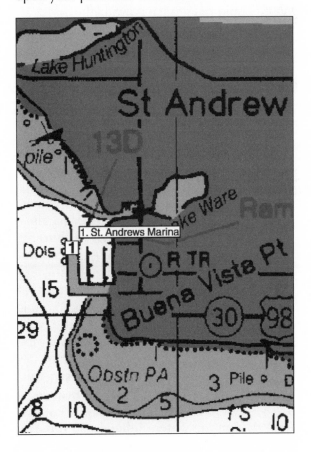

Well, after taking in that overview, let's take a look at St. Andrews Marina itself. The dockage harbor is well sheltered by a concrete breakwater. It would take some really heavy weather to create a problem here. Dockage is comprised of very modern, floating, concrete-decked piers. Depths alongside run a hefty 7 to 12 feet.

Transients are now eagerly accepted at St. Andrews Marina. In fact, some 400 feet of dockage space has been set aside for overnight (or a few-days'-stay) visitors. How's that for a real commitment to transient service?

Each slip is equipped with up-to-date 30- and 50-amp power and fresh-water hookups. Waste pump-out service is available, and both gasoline and diesel fuel can be purchased at the marina fuel dock. A nice ship's/variety store and dockmaster's office building overlooks the northwesterly tip of the dockage basin. At this same location, cruisers will find good, air-conditioned showers and a semi-open-air Laundromat.

A walk of six to seven blocks (or a quick cab ride) will allow access to a "grocery outlet" at the intersection of Highway 98 Bypass and Highway 98 Business. A full-fledged supermarket will require a somewhat lengthier taxi trip.

There are several St. Andrews restaurants within easy walking distance of the marina dockage basin that demand the attention of every cruiser's palette. First and foremost, at least in this writer's gastronomical opinion, is Uncle Ernie's Bayfront Bar and Grill (1151 Bayview Avenue, 850-763-8427). This dining attraction actually overlooks the marina's northeasterly shores and offers extensive outside dining. The restaurant's exterior deck is a great spot to relax with a "cold one" after a long day on the water. Believe you me, the food is nothing to sneeze at either. During our last visit, my almond-encrusted grouper was to die for, and my research assistant's blackened grouper was also done to perfection. Uncle Ernie's is open for lunch and dinner, Monday through Saturday.

The Captain's Table Restaurant and Oyster Bar (1110 Beck Avenue—also known as Highway 98 Business—850-767-9933) serves up some equally good seafood. While we have not sampled the fare here yet, this restaurant comes highly recommended by the staff at St. Andrews Marina. It is open every day, except Sunday, for lunch and dinner.

Beck Avenue Cafe (1316 Beck Avenue—850-914-2777) serves a good breakfast, and the St. Andrews Coffeehouse (1006 Beck Avenue, 850-769-3767) offers some scrumptious pastries. There is also a fresh-bagel shop next door.

Are you beginning to get the idea that St. Andrews Bay Marina and its adjoining, like-named community offer a good alternative in the way of municipal dockage in Panama City? Well, then, you are on the right track! Tell Captain Susan we sent you!

St. Andrews Marina (850) 872-7240

Approach depth—12 feet plus
Dockside depth—7-12 feet
Accepts transients—yes
Transient-dockage rate—average
Floating concrete piers—yes
Dockside power connections—30- and 50-amp
Dockside fresh-water connections—yes
Waste pump-out—yes
Showers—yes
Laundromat—yes
Gasoline—yes
Diesel fuel—yes
Ship's/variety store—yes
Restaurant—many nearby

St. Andrews Bay Marina, Panama City

Sun Harbor Marina (standard mile 285, 30 11.017 North/085 44.002 West) lines the eastern banks of the Waterway, just short of the Hathaway Bridge, southeast of the charted position of Sulphur Point. Transients are accepted at the wide-open dockage basin's fixed wooden piers. There is little in the way of shelter here when fresh winds are blowing from the west, southwest, and south. Depths in the marina's outer slips run an impressive 10+ feet, with some 6 to 6½ feet of water under the innermost portion of the dockage basin. All berths feature 30- and 50-amp power hookups and fresh-water connections. Some slips are covered and thereby only appropriate for power craft, but there are enough open spots to accommodate several sailcraft.

Gasoline and diesel fuel can be purchased dockside. An on-site waste pump-out facility is also available. First-class, climate-controlled showers and a very nice Laundromat are located in a breezeway at the eastern end of the docks. Here, visitors will also spy the ship's and variety store. This small operation can handle basic supply needs, but for more extensive galley resupply, you will probably want to take a taxi ride to one of the local supermarkets.

The newest addition to Sun Harbor Marina is Angler's Bar and Grill (850-763-2021). These people are the latest occupants of the marina's restaurant building, which is actually built out over a portion of the docks. There has been such a turnover in this part of the operation over the past several years that one marina employee referred to their restaurant as the "four month bar."

Sun Harbor Marina (850) 785-0551

Approach depth—12 to 20 feet
Dockside depth—6 feet plus
Accepts transients—yes
Transient-dockage rate—average
Fixed wooden piers—yes (some covered)
Dockside power connections—30- and 50-amp
Dockside water connections—yes
Showers—yes
Laundromat—yes
Waste pump-out—yes
Gasoline—yes
Diesel fuel—yes
Ship's and variety store—yes
Restaurant—on site

Sun Harbor Marina, Panama City

Just next door to (south of) Sun Harbor Marina, Aqua Bay, Inc., boatyard (standard mile 285, 850-785-2567) is ready to handle most any pleasure-craft repairs or maintenance. This full-service repair facility features a 60-ton travelift and full mechanical servicing for both gasoline and diesel power plants.

During times past, there used to be a third marina and restaurant facility on these waters, overlooking the westerly banks just north of the Hathaway fixed bridge. This operation is now pretty much shut down—at least partially due to the new-bridge construction (see below). Just what future, if any, this one-time marina may have could not be determined at the time of this writing.

Bridge Construction

At the very moment that this account is

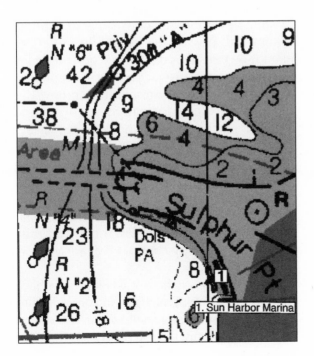

1. Sun Harbor Marina

being pounded out on the keyboard, pilings are being pounded into the bottom strata north of the existing Hathaway bridge. This rather mammoth construction project aims to eventually replace the 50-foot bridge at this location with a new, 65-foot high-rise span. This project will be ongoing through 2002-3. As you might imagine, the Waterway will be festooned with construction barges and equipment during this period. Take extra care when cruising pass.

North Bay (Standard Mile 282.5)

At flashing daybeacon #5 (on the ICW), the Waterway begins a long, slow turn to the west and enters West Bay. Adventurous gunk-holers can cut to the northeast and enter North Bay. This broad body of water boasts a wide, easily followed channel with 6-foot minimum depths. Typical soundings are in the 9- to 15-foot range. North Bay is indented at regular intervals by creeks and bayous, but unfortunately almost all these streams are too shallow for cruising-sized craft to use either as anchorages or gunk holes. Marina facilities are nonexistent.

North Bay's shores are quite pleasing to the eye. With the exception of a commercial plant at the charted position of Lynn Haven, development is more sparse here than along the principal Panama City shoreline. Set as it is amidst the sparkling waters, few true cruising captains would count a fair-weather cruise on North Bay as a visual waste of time. However, those seeking shelter will most likely be frustrated.

Near flashing daybeacon #6, the bay strikes out to the east and eventually leads to a fixed bridge with only 18 feet of vertical clearance. East of this span, good depths continue for some distance, but the bay is eventually blocked by a dam. There are no sheltered side waters with sufficient depth for cruising craft on the easterly side of the bridge. Most visiting cruisers will probably want to confine their explorations to waters west of the fixed span.

All in all, North Bay is rather a disappointment from the cruising point of view. It is unusual in the Florida Panhandle to find a body of water this size without a plenitude of sheltered overnight havens and gunk holes. Consequently, many skippers will wisely choose to bypass this body of water, but for those who must see everything, the two side waters that might invite exploration are detailed below, and navigational information is presented later in this chapter.

Upper Goose Bayou

The creek known as Upper Goose Bayou splits off from North Bay southeast of flashing daybeacon #5. While there is a broad channel with minimum 6- to 7-foot depths along the centerline, this cut is surrounded by unmarked shallows. It is quite easy to stray into 4-foot (or less) waters, even when you are trying to follow the mid-width. Thus, this locale is not recommended for craft that draw more than 4 feet or those more than 36 feet in length. Even then, only adventurous captains should attempt entry.

Those who do manage to negotiate the tricky channel will find a fairly well protected anchorage on the creek's mid-width, abeam of the small, charted offshoot striking northeast. Shelter from western or northwestern breezes is minimal. The shoreline displays moderate but attractive residential development.

Frankly, there are so many other superior anchorages on Panama City waters that Upper Goose Bayou cannot really be recommended as an overnight haven. However, if you are the daring type and want to throw out the lunch hook, you might consider trying, but do so with extreme caution and be sure to read the navigational information presented later in this chapter before making the attempt.

Fanning Bayou

Fanning Bayou cuts into the northern shores of North Bay due north of Haven Point, some .7 nautical miles west of the Mill Point fixed bridge. This creek has a marked entrance channel which maintains minimum 6-foot depths for much of its length. Depths outside of the marked cut quickly rise to grounding levels. The creek supports a fair amount of commercial fishing traffic. Anchoring in the marked channel is not a practical possibility. The shoreline shows light to moderate residential development consisting of modest homes and private docks. While the creek cannot be considered a terrible gunk hole for those intrepid cruisers who insist on poking their bow into every nook and cranny, the channel does call for caution and there is really no place to drop the hook for even a few minutes. Only captains piloting craft less than 36 feet in length should consider entry into Fanning Bayou.

Farther upstream, Fanning Bayou splits into three branches. The westernmost arm is shoal and carries only 4 feet (or less) of water. Cruising craft are strictly cautioned against entering this side-water.

The east-side offshoot has a marked channel, but painstaking navigation is required to avoid the surrounding shallows.

The center branch is the best of the three for

gunk-holing, but, again, you must stick to the marked channel or a quick grounding will be the unfortunate result. Depths drop off to 5 feet or less upstream of unlighted daybeacon #3. Only craft drawing less than 3½ feet should proceed pass #3.

West Bay and the ICW to Choctawhatchee Bay

From the Hathaway fixed bridge, the ICW follows the broad reaches of West Bay through a long, slow turn to the west. Eventually the well-marked channel flows into West Bay Creek, which in turn leads to a long canal connecting the Waterway to the easterly reaches of Choctawhatchee Bay.

West Bay averages over 2 nautical miles in width. This size allows winds over 15 knots more than enough fetch to create a most impressive chop. Strong blows of 20 knots or better can bring on a teeth-jarring passage that, for smaller vessels, can be downright dangerous. If possible, pick a day of fair breezes for your passage through West Bay.

As mentioned earlier, West Bay, like its sister, North Bay, lacks any well-protected anchorages. There are two spots where passing cruisers can at least get off the main portion of the bay, but neither of these (detailed in the next section) is sufficient for heavy weather and both are very much open to southerly blows.

There are no marina facilities of even the most primitive nature on West Bay. It's a long run of almost 40 nautical miles to reach the next available marina on Choctawhatchee Bay. Be sure your tanks are topped off and your craft is in good working order before leaving the many Panama City facilities behind.

West Bay's shoreline is heavily wooded and

quite attractive. Development is light, except for some sort of pulp wood mill northeast of Johnson Bayou. A fair-weather passage of West Bay should be a cruising delight.

The improved ICW channel heads northwest from the westerly reaches of West Bay into West Bay creek at standard mile 273. Some 2.2 miles upstream the Waterway begins following a well-protected, man-made canal which eventually flows into Choctawhatchee Bay. The combined length of West Bay Creek and the canal is better than 17 nautical miles. Strangely enough there is not a single anchorage or marina facility on this entire stretch. While the canal is easy to follow, the stream is mostly unmarked. All one need do to keep to the good water, however, is hold to the centerline.

No one will ever present an eye-appeal or excitement award to the man-made portion of the ICW-West Creek passage. It is clear that this Waterway was artificially cut from the adjoining sandy shores. Portions of the banks rise to clifflike heights. Perhaps the best that can be said for the canal is that it is truly well sheltered from inclement weather.

Johnson Bayou (Standard Mile 280) (30 15.331 North/085 43.626 West)

Johnson Bayou is a very shallow stream found southeast of charted Cedar Hammock. In northerly and easterly breezes, visiting cruisers can depart from the Waterway abeam of flashing daybeacon #9 and cruise towards Johnson Bayou's southerly entrance. Minimum depths of 5 to 6 feet can be maintained to within .2 nautical miles of the stream's mouth. Under no circumstances should you attempt a closer approach.

The well-wooded, high ground to the north

and east give enough protection for northern and eastern winds that do not exceed 15 knots. However, the anchorage is wide open to blows from the south and west.

Burnt Mill Creek (Standard Mile 278) (30 17.956 North/085 45.600 West)

The broad mouth of Burnt Mill Creek lies well north of the ICW's passage through West Bay at flashing daybeacon #1. While this stream certainly affords the most protected anchorage on West Bay, the entrance is surrounded by unmarked shoals that call for very careful navigation. If you can avoid these hazards, boats up to 40 feet can anchor in the broad band of deeper water between Cedar and Graze points, near 30 17.956 North/085 45.600 West. Minimum depths (in the channel) are about 6 feet.

Protection is quite good with winds blowing from the east and west and fair when breezes are from the north. However, southerly winds over 8 knots will begin to cause problems.

The surrounding shoreline is well wooded and delightfully undeveloped. Always supposing that winds are blowing from the proper direction and you can negotiate the tricky entrance channel, this would be a pleasing spot to spend an evening while watching the stars wheel overhead.

ST. ANDREW BAY TO CHOCTAWHATCHEE BAY NAVIGATION

The ICW route follows a wide, deep channel between St. Andrew Bay and West Bay Creek. While running aground along this stretch would result only from the most ham-fisted navigation, shoal water does abut most of the shorelines, so stay alert. The aids to navigation on West and North bays are widely spaced and it is advisable to follow compass/GPS courses between the various markers. As mentioned earlier, winds over 15 to 20 knots can raise a very healthy chop east of West Bay Creek. Your cruise should be planned with the latest NOAA weather forecast in mind.

North Bay, abandoned by the ICW, also boasts a wide channel. However, there are a few shallow spots on this body of water to worry with. Elementary navigation should see you through without mishap. North Bay's side waters are almost universally shallow. The two creeks that might invite exploration are surrounded by shoals.

In fair weather, your West Bay passage along the Waterway should be navigationally simple. Plot compass courses ahead of time, keep chart 11390 ready to resolve any questions, and you need only sit back and enjoy the scenery.

ICW to the Split   From a position between flashing buoy #17 and flashing daybeacon #18, set your course across the northeasterly mouth of St. Andrew Bay, pointing to eventually come abeam of flashing buoy #6 to its southerly side. Along the way, be sure to pass well northeast of flashing buoy #5 and flashing daybeacon #3. You will also pass just south of an unnumbered flashing junction buoy, near standard mile 289.5 Once abeam of #6, you should be able to follow the charted markers to Dyers Point without difficulty.

As noted earlier in this chapter, the usual east to west color configuration of ICW aids to navigation begins anew for west-bound craft at #6. Cruisers heading for points west will now once again begin to pass red, even-numbered markers to their (the cruisers') starboard side and take green aids to navigation to port.

As you approach Dyers Point, watch to the west for Alligator Bayou. This stream and the adjacent shoreline are home to a U.S. Naval testing facility. On several occasions, while performing on-site research, this writer and his assistant have been amazed observing Hovercraft being tested by Navy personnel.

A shoal is building to the west from Dyers Point and is growing towards the easterly flank of the ICW. Give the point a wide berth by passing well south and west of flashing daybeacon #14. Once past the point, alter course to the north and point to pass between unlighted can buoy #1 and nun buoy #2, and then between unlighted can buoy #3 and unlighted nun buoy #4. From these aids, it's a straight shot to the central pass-through of the Hathaway fixed bridge.

The current version of this span has a vertical clearance of 50 feet. Tall sailcraft that cannot clear the bridge must leave by way of St. Andrew Inlet and make their way to Pensacola offshore.

As mentioned earlier in this chapter, construction is well underway at the time of this writing on a new, 65-foot fixed bridge that will eventually replace the present Hathaway span. The new bridge will be located just north of the existing structure. Construction is slated to be complete in very late 2003, but that timetable does not take into account the inevitable delays and the removal of the existing bridge. In the meantime, this section of the Waterway will play host to an impressive collection of work barges, cranes, and other construction equipment. Proceed at idle speed and use maximum caution as you slowly leave all this bridge paraphernalia in your wake.

Once through the span(s), two more sets of unlighted aids help you to avoid the charted shoals to the east. Point to pass between can #5 and nun #6, then between can #7 and nun #8. Just short of #5 and #6, you will pass under an overhead power cable. Vertical clearance in the channel is set at 85 feet, but note that nearer the shorelines, this clearance drops to 45 feet!

Remember that the old Hathaway Landing Marina, which used to guard the westerly banks just north of the Hathaway Bridge, is closed at the time of this writing. Barring some future rejuvenation, cruisers should ignore the old marina channel markers west of unlighted can buoy #5 and #7.

North of #7 and #8, the numerous markers cease for the rest of the passage across West Bay. It's a good idea to already have the various compass/GPS courses on the bay plotted before entering these waters.

From a position between #7 and #8, set a careful compass course to come abeam of flashing daybeacon #5 (east of Shell Point) well to its easterly side. As chart 11390 clearly indicates, there is very shoal water west of #5. Once abeam of #5, cruisers may choose to enter North Bay.

North Bay   Navigational cruising conditions on North Bay are very similar to West Bay. Markers are widely spaced along the broad channel. The few trouble spots plaguing the mid-width of the bay west of the Mill Point Bridge are easily avoided by paying attention to the various beacons.

To enter North Bay, set course to come abeam of flashing daybeacon #3, which marks the bay's southerly reaches, to its easterly quarter. From #3, point to intersect the mid-width of the wide belt of deep water between unlighted daybeacon #4 and flashing daybeacon #5. Stay away from both these aids, as they mark shallow water.

Between #3 and #4, visiting cruisers will note the charted channel running southeast to the Panama City Airport. In a word or two, forget it. Extensive shoaling has taken place and depths of as little as 4 feet can now be expected on this errant cut.

After passing #4, you will soon come abeam of Upper Goose Bayou to the southeast.

Upper Goose Bayou   Remember that entry into Upper Goose Bayou is complicated by numerous unmarked shallows flanking the channel. This creek should only be entered by bold captains in craft 36 feet or smaller and drawing no more than 4 feet.

If you do choose to enter, use flashing daybeacon #5 as a navigational reference point to set a careful compass course for the mid-width of the bayou. Proceed at idle speed and keep an eagle eye on the sounder. If depths start to rise, assess the situation at once and make immediate corrections.

As you enter the bayou, be on guard against the charted 4-foot water to the north and a similar 4-foot patch to the south. Farther upstream, you must be particularly careful to avoid the charted tongue of 1-foot water jutting into the channel from the southwest.

If you can make it past these problem waters, consider dropping anchor where the charted offshoot to the northeast comes abeam. Continued exploration of the upstream reaches to the southeast is strictly not recommended.

On North Bay   North of flashing daybeacon #5, North Bay curves sharply to the east. The bay is traversed by an overhead power cable with *45 feet of vertical clearance. Sailcraft should make careful note of this height restriction.*

Captains approaching the power line will discover that flashing daybeacon #6 appears to be much farther from shore than it would appear from a cursory study of chart 11390. Pass under the power lines by staying well to the north and northwest of #6.

Soon after leaving #6 behind, you will spot the industrial complex at Lynn Haven to the south. Do not attempt to enter Lynn Haven Bayou. This small stream is heavily used by industrial traffic.

Continue following the mid-width of the bay as it curves farther to the east past Lynn

Haven Bayou. Soon the entrance to Fanning Bayou will come abeam to the north.

Fanning Bayou   To enter the main body of Fanning Bayou, point to come between unlighted daybeacons #1 and #2. Keep all red aids to your starboard side and take green markers to port as you cruise upstream to unlighted junction daybeacon #A.

At #A, the bayou splits. Captains in search of danger and excitement might follow the easterly arm, but this channel winds quite a bit and it's all too easy to stray into shoal water even when you think you are following the markers correctly. One of the toughest stretches is between unlighted daybeacons #6 and #7. If you should make it this far, be sure to favor the southeasterly shoreline heavily between #6 and #7.

From #A you can follow the main body of the creek by sticking to the mid-width as far as unlighted junction daybeacon #B. At this point a third arm of the creek comes abeam to the west. Do not attempt to enter this offshoot. Depths immediately drop off to 4 feet or less.

The central section of Fanning Bayou remains marked to the small village of Southport. However, depths begin to rise past unlighted daybeacon #3. Smart captains will discontinue their explorations at #B.

On North Bay   East of Fanning Bayou, the main body of North Bay is spanned by a fixed bridge with 18 feet of vertical clearance. Good depths of 6 feet or more continue to the east for better than 1 nautical mile past the bridge. There are no protected side waters in this region with sufficient depths for cruising craft. The main body of the bay is much too open for overnight anchorage. Most cruisers should terminate their gunk-holing on North Bay west of the fixed bridge.

ICW to West Bay Creek   From flashing daybeacon #5 the ICW follows a lazy turn to the west into the main body of West Bay. Flashing daybeacons #7 and #9 help navigators avoid the charted shallows to the west. Both these aids should be passed well to their easterly sides.

The channel leading west to the twin branches of Harrison Bayou between #7 and #9 may look good on the chart, but it is too open for effective shelter and the passage is surrounded by unmarked shoals. Skippers would do well to avoid this side-water entirely.

Once abeam of flashing daybeacon #9, cruisers in need of immediate shelter from northerly or easterly winds might consider the approach channel to Johnson Bayou.

Johnson Bayou Anchorage   If you do choose to make use of the rather open anchorage on the channel leading to Johnson Bayou, remember above all else to set the hook well short of the charted shallows at the creek's mouth.

Set course from #9 for the centerline of the channel, making northeast towards the bayou's entrance. Watch for leeway and keep a weather eye on the sounder. If depths climb above 7 feet you have either come too close to the creek's mouth or your craft is entering the charted shallows to the north and south. In either case, retreat to deep water and throw out the anchor in depths of at least 7 to 8 feet.

On the ICW   Northwest of flashing daybeacon #9, the Waterway continues its turn to the west. Eventually you should come abeam of flashing daybeacon #1 by some 100 yards (or more) to its northerly side. At #1, adventurous types may choose to visit Burnt Mill Creek to the north.

Burnt Mill Creek   Remember that the entrance to Burnt Mill Creek is flanked by large, unmarked shoals. Proceed at a slow speed and watch the sounder steadily as you make your approach.

Set a careful compass/GPS course from flashing daybeacon #1 for the centerline of the channel leading between Graze and Cedar points. As Cedar Point comes into view to the northeast, be particularly cautious about the charted 3- and 4-foot shallows to the east. If depths start to rise, chances are your course is encroaching on this shoal. Try giving way to the west and see if depths improve.

Stay away from Cedar Point. Chart 11390 correctly identifies a patch of very shallow water building southwest into the main body of the creek.

Consider setting the hook in 6-foot depths as Graze point comes abeam to the west. Farther upstream, depths deteriorate

much more quickly than chart 11390 would lead you to believe.

On the ICW   Some 1.3 nautical miles west of flashing daybeacon #1, the Waterway passes between a large collection of mostly unlighted floating markers. These numerous aids outline the improved channel leading into sheltered West Bay Creek. Westbound cruisers should simply continue to keep all red markers to their (the cruisers') starboard side and take green beacons to port.

There are only three lighted daybeacons in this entire group of markers leading to West Bay Creek and its connecting canal. It does not require too much imagination to conjecture on how difficult nighttime passage would be on this section of the ICW.

Connecting Canal   At unlighted daybeacon #39, the Waterway leaves its prolific markers behind and soon passes into the protecting arms of the canal connecting West and Choctawhatchee bays. It's now time to put our old friend chart 11390 away and break out 11385. The cut flows on for some 20 nautical miles to the easterly reaches of the Choctawhatchee.

The charted bridge northwest of unlighted can buoy #37 and unlighted nun buoy #38 is a fixed structure with 65 feet of vertical clearance. Those of us who remember the old, antiquated 10-foot lift bridge that once crossed the ICW at this location will look thankfully at this newer structure.

Follow the usual Waterway canal running rules. Don't cut any corners and avoid all sharp points of land. By observing these elementary precautions, visiting cruisers can enjoy the passing scenery without undue worry. Continued passage west on the ICW is presented in the next section of this chapter.

Don't even think about anchoring in the charted offshoot that cuts the Waterway's southerly banks, a short hop east of flashing daybeacon #1 and the ICW's intersection with the easternmost reaches of Choctawhatchee Bay. In spite of the 5-foot sounding shown on chart 11385, and in spite of the fact that you may see some local boats moored on the interior section of this stream, we found less than 3 feet of water depth at this entrance from several different angles.

Soon after leaving this errant body of water behind, flashing daybeacon #1 will be sighted ahead. Pass this aid to navigation to its northerly side, and cruise out into the wide, wide waters of Choctawhatchee Bay!

Choctawhatchee Bay

In the interests of peace of mind, cruisers visiting Choctawhatchee Bay for the first time should keep the following thought in their heads: you really have not died and gone to cruising heaven; it just feels that way.

Choctawhatchee is an Indian word meaning "river of the Choctaws." Fortunate indeed were these ancient Native Americans to call this magnificent bay home. Those cruisers lucky enough to visit the Choctawhatchee will find a body of water which combines practically all of the qualities which make the Florida panhandle such a cruiser's mecca. Lovely, heavily wooded, and lightly developed, the bay's shorelines are crisply reflected by the crystal-clear waters. Anchorages are fairly numerous and consistently memorable for their beautiful settings. Most havens are well protected. Marina facilities are more than adequate, though not so numerous as to intrude on the natural scenery. Mariners who don't enjoy a leisurely, fair-weather cruise through Choctawhatchee Bay might as well give up cruising entirely.

And, there is another very significant advantage of cruising this section of the Florida Panhandle as opposed to a land-side visit. Namely, you will be avoiding the section of Highway 98 that runs between Sandestin and Destin. Just a few short years ago, this was a lightly developed section. Now, a mind-bending collection of one tacky strip mall after another rubs shoulders with low- and high-rise condos of all descriptions. There are myriads of people, honking horns, and exasperated tourists everywhere in evidence. To be blunt, this is Florida at its worst, and cruisers can rejoice that their nerves need not be jangled by a drive through this nightmarish portion of Highway 98.

Good depths of 8 feet or better extend to within several hundred yards of both Choctawhatchee Bay shorelines. Although there are a few shallows that must be avoided on the bay's side waters, skippers can, for the most part, take a welcome break from their constant vigil of the depth sounder while traversing the Choctawhatchee's main channel.

Sailors in particular will delight in a cruise of this marvelous bay. The good depths, coupled with a width of 3 nautical miles or more, make for long runs without the need for frequent course changes. With winds from the north or south, you can run up the bay's entire length on a beam reach. How's that for good sailing?

Artificial East Pass Inlet allows uncertain access from the Choctawhatchee's southwesterly reaches to the open sea. While the channel is anything but dependable, many local craft make use of the cut on a daily basis without mishap.

The resort city of Destin guards the easterly shores of East Pass Inlet. Unfortunately, more than a little of the rampant development (referred to above) along Highway 98 has come calling in Destin as well. The waterfront is not exactly cruiser friendly either. One marina, occupying much of Destin Harbor's westerly reaches, does offer some transient dockage. However, the emphasis here is on the community's charter-fishing fleet, so don't look for anything approaching numerous cruising-oriented services. Both East Pass and Destin will be considered in a separate section at the end of this chapter.

Finally, the ICW flows into the westernmost section of the Choctawhatchee and leaves the bay behind near the thriving city of Fort Walton Beach. Details of the Fort Walton region and the Waterway's westerly passage into The Narrows will be covered in the next chapter.

Bridge Anchorage
(30 25.758 North/086 09.100 West)

After leaving the sheltered confines of the West Bay Creek Canal, the Waterway passes out into the easternmost lobe of Choctawhatchee Bay. The profusely marked channel soon approaches the 65-foot Choctawhatchee Bay/Highway 331 Bridge. Just before reaching this span, captains might choose to leave the ICW at unlighted can buoy #25 and track

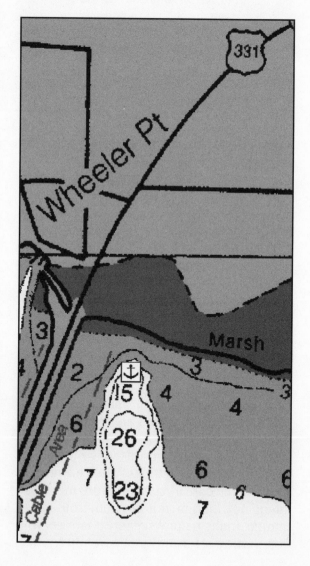

their way north-northeast for some 1.95 nautical miles to a deep anchorage. Study chart 11385 for a moment and notice the correctly charted bubble of 15- to 26-foot waters just east of the bridge/causeway's northerly tip. These deep soundings were probably brought about by dredging up mud and sand to build the adjacent causeway.

However it got there, some 17 to 20 feet of water is found at the northern edge of these deep waters, near 30 25.758 North/086 09.100 West, where cruising craft can anchor. Be *sure* to stay at least 200 yards off the northerly shores and 300 to 400 yards away from the causeway to the west. As correctly indicated on chart 11385, a broad band of shallows buffers these banks, particularly to the west.

This anchorage is well sheltered from all but southern, southeastern, and eastern breezes. The surrounding shores are mostly undeveloped, but there is one building that will be spied just north of the bridge. During the evening hours, we found the automobile traffic on the bridge to be only a minor annoyance, but then again, after a very long day of on-the-water research, it would probably have required a small nuclear device to really disturb our slumber.

Wilderness Rivers

Take another look at chart 11385 and notice the host of streams that make into the northeastern shores of eastern Choctawhatchee Bay, north of the Waterway's unlighted nun buoy #12. We have always avoided these waters due to their questionable depths, but several local cruisers in Destin told us we were missing the boat. So, for this new edition, we checked out these waters on a case-by-case basis. We have one word to describe this entire region: *shal-*

low. Make that *very shallow!* Even Cypress River, which sports one aid to navigation, had only 3 to 4 feet of depth at its entrance. Just to make matters a bit more interesting, the charted "foul" area fronting the various streams is for real. We observed hundreds and hundreds of old pilings along this stretch.

So, while these streams are undoubtedly a gunk-holers paradise for canoes and kayakers, cruising-sized craft should not even consider an exploration of these waters. That is, of course, unless you are intent on giving the good folks at Sea Tow some more business.

La Grange Bayou (Standard Mile 247)

A long, sometimes narrow, but well-marked cut leads northeast from the ICW channel (between the Waterway's flashing daybeacons #46 and #47) to the interior reaches of attractive La Grange Bayou. While minimum depths of 7 feet are maintained over the marked channel's entire length, soundings quickly reach 4 feet or less outside of the marked cut. Consequently, anchoring is not a practical possibility south of unlighted daybeacon #27. Upstream of this aid, good depths open out from shore to shore. However, this stream supports some commercial-barge traffic, so anchoring on these waters is probably a bad idea. In any case, swinging room is not sufficient for vessels over 32 feet.

La Grange's shoreline has very light residential development near its southerly mouth, alternating with mostly undeveloped, well-wooded banks farther upstream. The bayou is typical of the Choctawhatchee's side waters, and most cruisers will find a cruise through here to be a visually appealing trip.

Strangely enough, the upstream, Fourmile

Paddle Wheel Riverboat Repair Yard, La Grange Bayou

Creek section of La Grange Bayou, southeast of the charted fixed bridge, is home to a large boatyard specializing in the construction and repair of paddle wheel riverboats. Even if you can't find a place to set the hook, consider gunk-holing up to the boatyard docks. By proceeding at idle speed, captain and crew may be lucky enough to cruise close by any number of large riverboats moored at the yard's piers. This makes for a very special experience which will not soon be forgotten or repeated.

North of the paddle-wheel boatyard, Fourmile Creek opens out into a pool-like body of water with good depths of 13 to 16 feet. There's enough room for a 38-footer to swing comfortably on the hook near 30 29.435 North/086 08.352 West. Further upstream access is barred by a 5-foot fixed bridge.

However, this same pool of deep water is home to two industrial plants with barge loading and unloading docks. Wouldn't it be awful if you were anchored here, snoozing happily away, only to have a barge come along at 3:00 A.M. and blast you out of slumber with his horn? Worse yet, supposed the tow captain didn't see you in time and barreled right into your anchored craft? With these potential problems in mind, this writer will always find another place to spend the evening on the waters of Choctawhatchee Bay.

Hogtown Bayou (Standard Mile 242.5) (30 23.577 North/086 14.750 West)

Hogtown Bayou winds into the southerly shores of Choctawhatchee Bay between flashing daybeacons #47 and #49. In this particular instance, the so-called bayou resembles a broad bay rather than a narrow creek. There is a wide channel leading first south and then east to the creek's interior reaches, but there are numerous unmarked shoals to avoid. Only bold skippers piloting craft under 36 feet and drawing no more than 4½ feet should attempt entry.

Skippers who successfully navigate the challenging channel can anchor in the bayou's easternmost section, north of shallow Churchill Bayou. Protection from easterly blows is fair, while the northern and southern banks give some shelter when the winds are blowing from either of these directions. Westerly breezes over 10 knots can stir up a wicked chop on the bay.

The northern banks bordering the bayou's interior reaches are mostly comprised of marsh grass backed by some trees, while the southern shores are higher and fairly well wooded. There is some light residential development to the south and east.

While this is certainly not the most sheltered or easily entered of the Choctawhatchee's bayous, it can make for a fine overnight haven in fair weather if you can successfully navigate the unmarked channel. Many mariners may want to consider the deeper, better-sheltered streams to the west as an overnight refuge.

The Tragedy of Santa Rosa

At the turn of the century the so-called Choctawhatchee Peninsula (sandwiched between the bay's waters to the north, the Gulf to the south, and East Pass Inlet to the west) received one of the most iron-willed men that the land would ever know. Charles E. Cessna came to northwestern Florida from Chicago with a dream, and it was not long before he set his plans into motion.

After surveying the land, Cessna laid out the plat for a combination residential community and orange grove just north of Hogtown Bayou. His town was to be known as Santa Rosa Plantation, often shortened in later years to just Santa Rosa. The individual lots sold like proverbial hotcakes to locals and northeastern families hungering for a milder winter.

In the fascinating book . . . And the Roots Run Deep—A Short Story History of Destin, Vivian Foster Mettee presents a fascinating account of those early days in Santa Rosa as seen through the eyes of James Garfield Taylor and his wife, Willie Mae. In describing the village during its formative days, Mr. Taylor states:

> The town of Santa Rosa grew. Homes were built, businesses were constructed, and the farms were cultivated. Crops were produced almost as if by magic in the fertile unused land. Mr. Cessna built a large dry goods and grocery store and also a cold storage plant. A creamery furnished fresh butter, and it was delivered to your home. There was a saw mill, and Mackenzie's logging railroad ran from the mill to the town and down to the landing on the bayou where lumber was shipped out. . . .

The village was also popular with early tourists. By 1910 a sternwheeler riverboat was calling on Santa Rosa twice a week. Guests would lodge at the Santa Rosa Hotel, which was built close to the waters of the Choctawhatchee.

In the early 1920s the dream of Santa Rosa Plantation came to an end. It wasn't a violent hurricane or even a great fire that brought the village to its knees. No, it was a mysterious botanical disease known to the locals simply as "canker." This scourge swept through groves, weakening and sickening the orange trees. Alarmed that the blight would spread to the rest of Florida's lucrative citrus industry, the U.S. Department of Agriculture quarantined the Santa Rosa groves and eventually uprooted and burned the trees.

Many of the residents, who loved their quiet and serene village, tried to stay on. There were attempts at other enterprises but none proved successful. By 1925 most of the valiant citizens of Santa Rosa had either moved to Destin or picked up stakes for parts unknown.

Sometimes when cruising the waters of Florida, it seems easy to think of this state as a modern phenomenon without history. The old, vine-covered homes and cemeteries of Santa Rosa tell a very different story indeed.

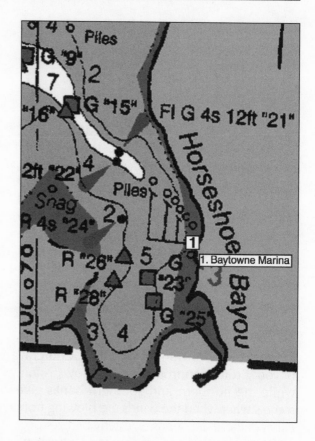

Baytowne Marina at Sandestin (Standard Mile 239) (30 23.267 North/086 19.635 West)

Moving east to west, the first of the Choctawhatchee's marina facilities will be encountered on the easterly shores of charted Horseshoe Bayou, southeast of flashing buoy #SB (southwest of Fourmile Point and the ICW's flashing daybeacon #49). A marked channel leads from the bay's deeper waters to the marina.

Baytowne Marina at Sandestin is part of a huge resort complex that sits astride both sides

of Highway 98. During the last two years, there has been extensive, new development of high-rise condos just behind and within a quick step of the dockage basin. By the time the ink is dry in this book, a new dining/retail center will also have opened in the complex. Complimentary transportation for visiting cruisers will be provided. We understand that there will be *many* dining choices available in this center.

Depths in the Baytowne Marina entrance channel run to 6-foot minimum levels at low tide, with most slips featuring soundings of 5 to 6½ feet. While the Baytowne dockage basin is well sheltered from southerly winds, strong blows from the north or northwest can bring on more than a little dockside chop. This situation is somewhat mitigated by wooden slatting installed on the outer docks, which acts as a partial breakwater. Nevertheless, this is not the place to be caught in really nasty weather blowing out of the north.

Transients are eagerly accepted at Baytowne's fixed wooden piers. Full power (30- and 50- and some 100-amp), water, cable-television, and telephone connections are found at all slips. Gasoline and diesel fuel are available at a new fuel dock on the outer pier. This is a great improvement over the former fueling pier, which required a complicated cruise to the innermost reaches of the dockage basin. The marina also maintains a first-class waste pump-out station. Mechanical repairs can often be arranged through nearby independent technicians.

Shoreside, visitors will find good, air-conditioned showers. There is also an on-site, climate-controlled Laundromat. Hard by these facilities, cruisers will discover an on-site gift and variety store. Ship's store items are noticeably absent.

If you came to Baytowne to have some fun, you're in luck. Visiting cruisers are afforded guest privileges at the complex's two golf courses; numerous, multisurfaced tennis courts; and two swimming pools.

So, all in all, Baytowne Marina at Sandestin is a good bet, unless really foul weather is in the offing. Tell them we sent you!

Baytowne Marina at Sandestin (850) 267-7777
Approach depth—6 feet (low water)

Baytowne Marina at Sandestin, Choctawhatchee Bay

Dockside depth—5-6½ feet (outer two
    piers—low water)
Accepts transients—yes
Transient-dockage rage— above average
Fixed wooden piers—yes
Dockside power connections—30- and 50- and
    some 100-amp
Dockside water connections—yes
Showers—yes
Laundromat—yes
Waste pump-out—yes
Gasoline—yes
Diesel fuel—yes
Mechanical repairs—yes (independent techni-
    cians)
Variety store—yes
Restaurant—transportation provided

Mid-Bay Marina (Standard Mile 235) (30 24.189 North/086 25.388 West)

While performing research on the waters of Choctawhatchee Bay for this new edition, this writer and his ace research assistant thought that someone must have slipped a hallucinogenic into our luncheon tea. Just east of the towering Mid-Bay Bridge (south of flashing buoy #51), we spotted what appeared to be several unbelievably huge metal buildings. Not only that, but the walls of these behemoth structures were festooned with beautiful seascapes, replete with whales and fish of all descriptions. Upon further investigation, we discovered a marked L-shaped channel that ran first west and then cut sharply south, paralleling the easterly face of the bridge. After landing, we found out that this entire complex goes under the moniker of Mid-Bay Marina. The discovery of this complex was truly one of the great surprises that came our way in preparing this edition of CGNG.

It turns out that Mid-Bay Marina's primary business, as you might have guessed from our description of the buildings described above, is dry-stack storage of power craft. And by storage, we mean STORAGE (in big, capital letters). Not only is there room for hundreds and hundreds of boats in the storage building, but the marina also owns the two largest forklifts that this writer has ever seen. We are told that the larger of the two has the highest capacity of any forklift currently in use at dry-stack storage operations across the USA. Boats as large as 43 feet LOA, weighing up to 52,000 pounds, can be picked up by these massive machines.

Mid-Bay also has a few wet slips, though the friendly manager, Scott Roberts, has told me that most of these berths are used mainly to facilitate the comings and goings of their dry-stack customers. Transients are occasionally accepted at these floating concrete piers. You can translate occasionally here to "very seldom." Minimum depths both in the entrance channel and dockside run 8 to 10 feet. There is little in the way of shelter from fresh northern or northeasterly winds.

The marina's wet slips feature 30- and 50-amp power and fresh-water hookups. Waste pump-out service is also available. Full mechanical repairs for both gasoline and diesel power plants are offered, as well as gasoline and diesel fuel.

Mid-Bay boasts a nice ship's/variety store. Within this same building, cruisers will discover first-class, climate-controlled showers. There are no restaurants anywhere within walking distance, and no land-side transportation is readily available. Those few cruisers who do find an overnight slip here will want to come with a fully stocked galley.

Mid-Bay Marine, Choctawhatchee Bay

If you are in the market for dry-stack storage on Choctawhatchee Bay, your search is ended. On the other hand, if you simply seek an overnight berth, be *sure* to call ahead and see if any space is available. Either way, don't miss the chance to oogle the storage building's fascinating murals.

Mid-Bay Marina (850) 337-8200
   http://www.mid-baymarina.com

Approach depth—8-10 feet
Dockside depth—8-10 feet
Accepts transients—limited
Transient-dockage rate—above average

Floating concrete docks—yes
Dockside power connections—30- and 50 amp
Dockside fresh-water connections—yes
Waste pump-out—yes
Showers—yes
Gasoline—yes
Diesel fuel—yes
Mechanical repairs—yes
Ship's/variety store—yes

Rocky Bayou and the Marina at Bluewater Bay (Standard Mile 232.5) (Various Lats/Lons—see below)

Rocky Bayou is the easternmost of the two

major streams which strike northward from the large bay which indents the Choctawhatchee's northern banks west of red nun buoy #56 and flashing buoy #58. This bayou has about everything you could ask for, including first-rate marina facilities, sheltered anchorage, and beautiful shores. It deserves to be included in every cruiser's traveling itinerary.

An exceptionally broad channel boasting 10-foot minimum depths ushers visiting cruisers from the bay into Rocky Bayou. There is very little shallow water on this creek to worry with, and most cruisers will be able to visit every part of the bayou without any difficulty whatsoever. The shoreline exhibits light development set amidst the Choctawhatchee's usual high, well-wooded shores. To be concise, this is about as good as it gets.

Study chart 11385 for a moment and you will quickly note Ward Cove cutting into the eastern shores of Rocky Bayou. This deep off-shoot is home for the fabulous Marina at Bluewater Bay (30 29.735 North/086 26.780 West). It is always a real pleasure to report on first-rate facilities that are getting even better. Happily, that is just the case with the Marina at Bluewater Bay. Since the last edition of this guide went to print, the Hinely family (owners and operators of this fine facility) have purchased the building just behind the dockage basin. It now houses a really nice ship's store (plus paperback-exchange library), new (heated but not air-conditioned) showers, a Laundromat, and L. J. Schooners Dockside Grill and Bar (closed Mondays and Tuesdays). This small eatery is open for lunch from 11:00 A.M. to 2:00 P.M. and from 5:00 P.M. to 9:00 P.M. for the evening meal. For now, the menu is rather basic, but the Hinelys plan to expand the offer-

ing a bit later. If past experience is any guide, L. J. Schooners will also eventually reach topnotch status. There is also a dockside tiki-type bar that is open from 3:00 P.M. until midnight.

Bluewater Bay Marina has almost every service that you might ever require, save haul-out repairs. The marina's entrance channel running the length of Ward Cove is exceedingly well marked. Minimum entrance depths run around 6 feet, though you must make sure not to wander outside of the track defined by the aids to navigation. Depths alongside are an ample 7 to 9½ feet.

Transients are enthusiastically accepted at Bluewater's fixed wooden piers featuring full power and water connections. Some slips also boast cable television and telephone hookups. Gasoline and diesel fuel can be purchased dockside, and free waste pump-out service is available. Mechanical repairs can be arranged through independent contractors. Dry-stack storage for smaller power craft is now in the offing as well. Courtesy transportation is readily available to a nearby supermarket, video store, and several other shops.

Fine recreation facilities are also available at Bluewater Bay. A golf course is complemented by tennis courts and a large swimming pool. Again, the marina staff will be glad to ferry you from the docks to the site of these attractions.

Adding to these impressive statistics, this writer has been repeatedly struck by Bluewater management's exceptionally friendly attitude. If there ever was a marina where the phrase "service with a smile" applies, this is certainly it! If you are anywhere near Rocky Bayou and night is fast approaching, take my word for it; you simply could not do better than to coil your lines for a night, a few days, or even a week at this wonderful facility.

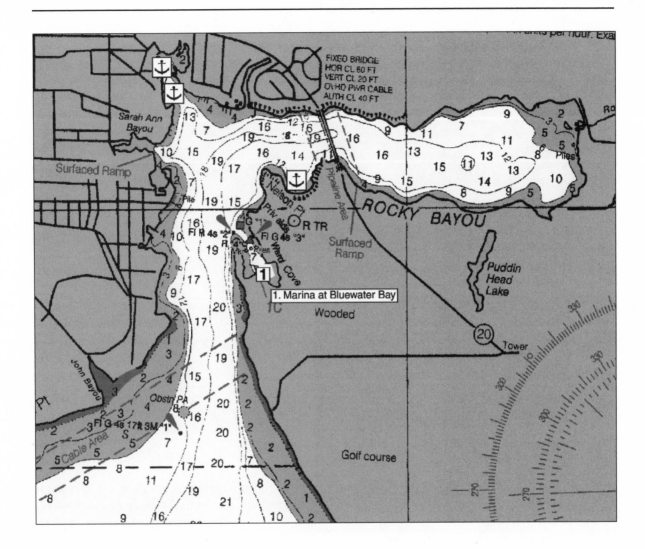

1. Marina at Bluewater Bay

The Marina at Bluewater Bay (850) 897-2821
http://www.bluewaterbaymarina.com

Approach depth—6-8 feet
Dockside depth—7-9½ feet
Accepts transients—yes
Transient-dockage rate—above average
Fixed wooden piers—yes
Dockside power connections—30- and 50-amp

Dockside water connections—yes
Showers—yes
Laundromat—yes
Waste pump-out—yes
Gasoline—yes
Diesel fuel—yes
Mechanical repairs—yes (independent contractors)
Ship's store—yes
Restaurant—on site

Marina at Bluewater Bay, Rocky Bayou

Moving upstream from Ward Cove, the main body of the bayou cuts sharply east at Nelson Point. However, a deep, sheltered stream strikes to the northwest, north of charted Sarah Ann Bayou. While there are two unmarked shoals to avoid, boats up to 45 feet will find plenty of swinging room on the well-protected creek. This is clearly the most sheltered anchorage on Rocky Bayou and, with the appropriate navigational caution, it is highly recommended. Larger, deep-draft boats will probably want to set the hook in the charted bubble of 10-foot water (near 30 30.512 North/086 27.201 West) just

upstream from the creek's entrance. Better sheltered are the waters in the body of the stream's sharp turn to the northeast, near 30 30.618 North/086 27.267 West. Depths of 8 feet or more are found here, and there is ample elbowroom for a 42-footer.

Captains piloting craft up to 36 feet and drawing less than 4½ feet might want to consider anchoring in the ultraprotected patch of charted 6½-foot water near the stream's upper (northeasterly) reaches. Here you can survive any weather short of a hurricane quite nicely.

Hold on, there is yet another anchor-down

spot on Rocky Bayou to consider. With southerly winds in the offing, cruising craft might choose to drop the hook in the charted cove just east of Nelson Point off the main path of Rocky Bayou (near 30 30.115 North/086 26.580 West). The lightly developed shoreline rolls down to the cove's shores in a series of high hills. These banks make a pleasant backdrop and provide wonderful shelter from southern, southeasterly, and (to a lesser extent) southwesterly breezes. Strong northerly blows could make for a bumpy evening, but otherwise you simply can't go wrong by setting the hook in this pristine setting.

The main body of Rocky Bayou leads east to a fixed bridge with 20 feet of vertical clearance. While depths remain good almost to the bayou's upstream limits, these waters are rather broad and would not provide sufficient shelter for anything but light-air anchorage. The stream does remain quite attractive, so if you are interested, feel encouraged to explore the remainder of Rocky Bayou. In all but heavy weather, you can certainly throw out the lunch hook at most any likely looking place and watch the world flow tranquilly by.

Boggy Bayou
(Various Lats/Lons—see below)

Like its sister to the east, Boggy Bayou offers mariners more wonderful cruising. This stream features some marina facilities plus two major side waters that provide snug overnight anchorages. Both Weekley and Tom's bayous will be detailed in separate sections below.

The southerly reaches of Boggy Bayou feature relatively undeveloped shores to the east, while the western banks exhibit fairly heavy development associated with Eglin Air Force Base. Farther upstream, heavy residential development flanks both shores of the bayou at the charted locations of Valparaiso and Niceville. At one point along the Niceville waterfront, a high-rise condo development overlooks the creek. Boggy Bayou is generally attractive, however, and most cruisers will enjoy an exploration of its sparkling waters.

The entrance to Boggy Bayou is relatively narrow, but the cut is well marked and reasonably easy to traverse with good visibility. It's an iffy proposition for strangers to enter the bayou at night or in a driving rainstorm.

North of flashing daybeacon #9, the docks of Giuseppi's Wharf Restaurant will be spotted on the eastern shore (30 30.748 North/086 28.979 West). Giuseppi's is well known for serving the freshest catch of the day, and it is very, very popular with the local crowd. There are few better recommendations.

Cruising patrons at Giuseppi's are welcome to tie to the piers while dining. Overnighters are accepted as well at the fixed, wooden piers, featuring fresh-water and 30-amp power hookups. Several slips are usually available for visitors amidst the crowded docks.

However, Giuseppi's does not employ a dockmaster. Whenever we have stayed here, it has always taken a dedicated search to find someone to ask about where we should dock and to whom the fee should be paid. By the way, this marina, at least at the time of this writing, has the unusual policy of charging an overnight-dockage fee of $20, no matter what sized boat you are piloting.

Depths along the outermost portion of the dockage run around 10 feet, with 7 to 8 feet of water at the middle slips, and around 5 to 6

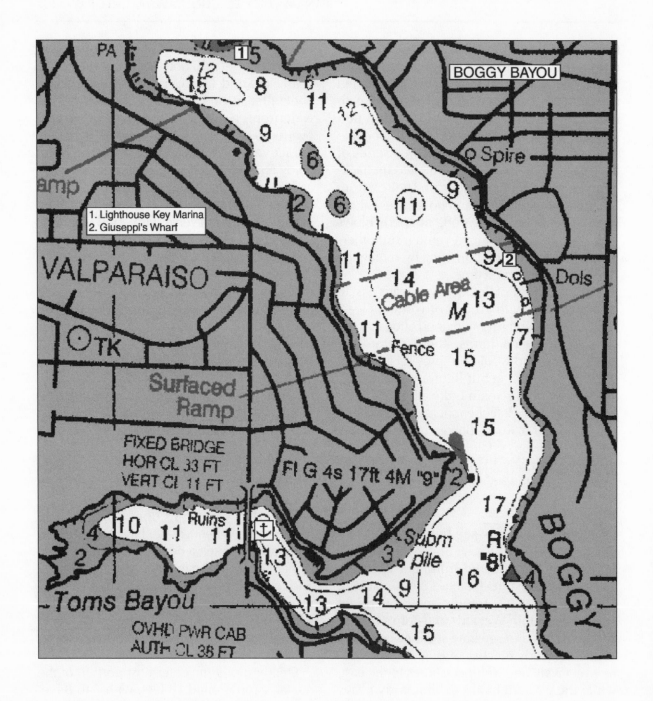

feet of water under the innermost berths. The dockage basin is wide open to wind and wave if foul weather comes calling. This is clearly not the spot to ride out a heavy blow, particularly if winds are wafting from the south. No shoreside facilities such as showers are available and it would be a long walk indeed to reach any grocery or convenience stores.

Giuseppi's Wharf Restaurant and Marina
http://www.giuseppiswharf.com
(850) 678-4229

Approach depth—8+ feet
Dockside depth—10 feet (outermost slips)
7-8 feet (middle slips)
5-6 feet (innermost slips)
Accepts transients—yes
Transient-dockage rate—below average
Fixed wooden piers—yes
Dockside power connections—30-amp
Dockside water connections—yes

Good depths continue on Boggy Bayou into the stream's upper reaches. Eventually, passing cruisers will sight the docks of the Boathouse

Giuseppi's Wharf

restaurant flanking the southwesterly shore-line. This writer can attest to the wonderful cuisine served at this noteworthy dining spot.

While the inner slips at the Boathouse restaurant are occupied by long-time resident craft, the outermost dock is sometimes open to patrons. You can expect 4½- to 5½-foot depths at this pier. There should be enough room for one 40-footer.

Opposite the Boathouse, Lighthouse Key Marina guards the bayou's northeastern shores at Niceville, near 30 31.206 North/086 29.663 West. This facility features fixed wooden slip dockage with 20- and 30-amp power and fresh -water connections. Mechanical repairs are available for gasoline-powered craft, and boats up to 26 feet can be hauled out for below-waterline servicing. Gasoline can be purchased dockside. The marina also features extensive dry-dock storage.

Lighthouse Key Marina (850) 729-2000

Approach depth—11-13 feet
Dockside depth—6-9 feet
Accepts transients—yes
Transient-dockage rate—average
Fixed wooden slips—yes
Dockside power connections—20- and 30-amp
Dockside water connections—yes
Gasoline—yes
Mechanical repairs—yes (gasoline power craft
   only)
Restaurant—several nearby

Weekley Bayou

Weekley Bayou flows from the western shores of Boggy Bayou north of unlighted day-beacon #5. Unfortunately, following the 9/11 terrorist atrocities, this entire stream is now off-limits to pleasure craft. So, don't even

think about entering this bayou, much less anchoring here. These guys can back up their threats.

Tom's Bayou
(30 30.173 North/086 29.618 West)

Tom's Bayou may just provide the single most sheltered and easily accessible anchorage in all of Choctawhatchee Bay. The stream cuts a broad path into the western shores of Boggy Bayou west of unlighted daybeacon #8. Both shorelines present light to moderate residential development alternating with undeveloped areas. Most cruisers will find the stream quite appealing. Minimum entrance depths are 10 feet in the broad channel, with soundings of 13 to 14 feet being more the norm.

While it is quite possible to drop the hook almost anywhere that strikes your fancy within shouting distance of Tom's Bayou's centerline, our favorite spot is the correctly charted pool of 13-foot waters east of the 11-foot fixed bridge barring further upstream passage on the bayou. Swinging room is sufficient for craft up to 48 feet. Vessels and their crews can ride out really nasty weather in this beautiful spot. The high shores give excellent protection from all winds. Good depths run to within 75 yards of the northern banks. In a particularly hard blow you can squeeze a bit to the north for maximum protection.

Joe's Bayou (Standard Mile 230)
(30 24.639 North/086 29.363 West)

The ample mouth of Joe's Bayou flanks the southern shores of Choctawhatchee Bay west of Cobbs Point (south-southwest of flashing daybeacon #59). This stream has a narrow but

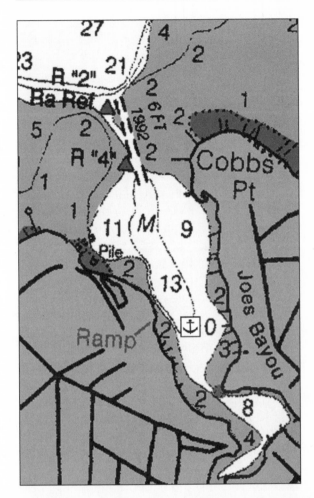

fairly well-marked entrance channel with 10-foot minimum depths. The northerly portion of the stream is comprised of a large pool with 10-foot-plus water stretching to within 100 yards of both shorelines. This portion of the bayou comprises an excellent overnight anchorage. For maximum shelter, cruise upstream until you are some 100 yards south of the public launching ramp that will be spied along the westerly banks. Drop anchor on the mid-width amidst depths of 10 to 13 feet, and settle down for a night of peace and security.

Unfortunately, Joe's Bayou is no longer the backwater stream that it was when the first edition of this guide appeared in 1991. In those days, there was only a house here and there, plus one industrial site, to be seen. No more! Now the shores play host to a dense but not unattractive array of residential development.

We no longer recommend the always hard-to-reach anchorage on the upper reaches of Joe's Bayou, where chart 11385 notes soundings of 8 feet. There are now sooo many private docks along this stretch that swinging room is almost nil.

CHOCTAWHATCHEE BAY NAVIGATION

Fair-weather passage of the Gulf Coast ICW on Choctawhatchee Bay is an elementary matter of following pre-plotted compass/GPS courses between widely spaced aids to navigation. There are very few shoals on the bay to worry with. Most of the few shallow spots flank the bay's shoreline, and almost all are appropriately marked by either unlighted or flashing daybeacons.

With winds of 15 knots or better, the Choctawhatchee's breadth provides plenty of room for waves to get up a head of steam. Blows of 25 knots or better can be dangerous. Considering Choctawhatchee Bay's great natural beauty, it makes sense to plan your passage to correspond with a good forecast. Unless your schedule absolutely demands a run in rain and wind, this writer strongly suggests that you wait out bad weather at one of the fine Panama City or Fort Walton Beach marinas or anchorages, and then begin your memorable passage on this unforgettable body of water.

Entrance into Choctawhatchee Bay   The ICW makes its entrance into Choctawhatchee Bay just west of flashing daybeacon #1 near Point Washington and Tucker Bayou. The improved channel is outlined for the next 5.3 nautical miles by a myriad of markers. With a few exceptions, most of these aids consist of unlighted nun and can buoys. While deep water opens out in an exceptionally broad path west of flashing daybeacon #17, the waters between #1 and #17 border on shoal ground to the south and (to a lesser extent) the north. Nighttime passage of this run by strangers is strictly not recommended.

Old semi-sunken trees, stumps, and other wooden debris line both sides of the Waterway channel between flashing daybeacons #1 and #17. Let this ample evidence be a warning to the wise captain—stick strictly to the marked passage until reaching the deeper waters west of #17.

North of flashing daybeacon #9, a series of small rivers and lesser streams enter the easterly shores of Choctawhatchee Bay. While these various bodies of water usually have good interior depths, depths at their respective entrances run 3 feet or less. Also, note the long, charted "foul" area just southwest of these streams' entrances. On-the-water research revealed hundreds and

hundreds of old pilings along this problem stretch. By all accounts, stay away from these multiple hazards.

For all these unhappy reasons, no other navigational data for these wilderness rivers and creeks will be provided in this guide-book. Anyone piloting a vessel larger than a canoe will enter these waters at their considerable peril.

West of flashing daybeacon #23, the Waterway soon passes under the high-rise Highway 331/Wheeler Point Bridge. Overhead clearance is set at 65 feet. Just before reaching this span, captains might choose to break off to the north-northeast for an overnight anchorage possibility.

Bridge Anchorage   To access the anchorage on the bubble of deep water just east of the Highway 331 Bridge's northerly tip, depart the Waterway abeam of unlighted can buoy #25. Set a careful compass/GPS course for the center section of the charted bubble of 15- to 26-foot water lying to the north-northeast. Be sure to stay a good 200 yards east of the bridge's causeway, and be on guard against the many, many pilings in the long, charted foul area, east of your course line. Split the difference between these two hazards and continue north-northeast into the deep waters.

To avoid the necessity of using a really long anchor rode, we suggest dropping the hook on the northerly end of these artificially deep waters. Depths here run around 17 feet or so. Be *sure* to stay at least 200 yards off the northerly shores, and 300 to 400 yards away from the causeway to the west. As correctly indicated on chart 11385, a broad band of shallows buffers these banks, particularly to the west.

On the ICW   West and northwest of the Highway 331 span, the numerous markers continue for another 1.4 nautical miles. Finally, at flashing daybeacon #46, the abundant aids to navigation cease and it now becomes wise to follow compass/GPS courses between the various beacons as you work your way west on the bay.

Consider setting course from #46 to bring flashing daybeacon #47, north of Live Oak Point, abeam by several hundred yards to its northerly side. Between #46 and #47, the Choctawhatchee's second opportunity for side-water exploration will come abeam to the northeast.

La Grange Bayou   The marked channel running northeast to La Grange Bayou will come abeam some .5 nautical miles northwest of flashing daybeacon #46. While a portion of this cut requires exact navigational caution, most power craft drawing 4½ feet or less and piloted in a cautious manner should be able to traverse the creek with only minimal difficulty. Sailcraft, on the other hand, particularly those with fixed keels and a draft exceeding 5 feet, may want to give long and careful thought before gunk-holing on this particular creek.

To enter the channel, continue on the Waterway until the first aid on the La Grange Bayou channel, flashing daybeacon #1, is almost abeam to the northeast. Then, turn sharply and set course to come abeam of #1 by some 10 to 15 yards to its southeasterly side. From #1 to flashing daybeacon #11, the channel is straightforward and does not border on any shoals.

As you approach #11, the situation changes dramatically. From #11 to unlighted daybeacon #27, over 2 nautical miles upstream, the marked cut borders on very shallow water. Care must be exercised to keep to the channel or a grounding will be the immediate result. Keep all green markers to port and take all red beacons to starboard. Don't cut any corners and keep a constant watch for leeway. Detail a member of the crew to watch the sounder. If depths start to rise, discontinue your forward progress and make corrections.

North of unlighted daybeacon #27, the channel passes into a fairly narrow, but deep, creek. Good depths stretch almost from shore to shore. However, minimal swinging room and the possibility of barge traffic argue against overnight anchorage on these waters.

Continuing upstream another .9 nautical miles will bring the riverboat yard, described earlier, abeam on the eastern banks. Be sure to proceed at idle speed on these waters. Further passage to the northwest is blocked by a low-level fixed bridge with only 5 feet of vertical clearance.

On the ICW   Once abeam of flashing daybeacon #47 by several hundred yards (at least) to its northerly side, set course to come abeam of flashing daybeacon #49, north of Fourmile Point, by some .5 of a nautical mile to its northerly side. This aid marks a broad patch of shoal water surrounding Fourmile Point. Do not approach #49 closely. The shallows seem to be building to the north and have already encroached on the beacon.

Flashing daybeacon #49 can be hard to spot. On-site research revealed several uncharted pilings surrounding this aid. Use your binoculars to pick out #49 from these hazards.

Between #47 and #49 a questionable side-water will come abeam to the south.

Hogtown Bayou   Remember that entrance into Hogtown Bayou is complicated by the presence of many unmarked shoals. Only those piloting boats with a 4½-foot draft, or preferably less, should attempt to make use of this side-water.

If you choose to make the attempt, continue on the ICW until the deepest portion of the bay leading to Hogtown Bayou is directly abeam to the south. Don't try to enter the 7- to 9-foot waters on the easterly portion of the bay's mid-width. These waters abound in pipes and stakes of all descriptions, not all of which are visible above the surface.

Set a careful compass course to follow the charted 13- and 14-foot depths south until the main body of the bayou comes abeam to the east. Then turn sharply to the east, being careful to avoid the charted fingers of 2- and 3-foot waters northeast and east of Hewett Bayou.

Continue on the mid-width into the heart of the large creek's interior reaches. Cruisers seeking to drop the hook would do well to continue upstream to a position between Mussett and Churchill bayous (well to the south of your track). Don't attempt to enter any of these small creeks. They are shoal and treacherous.

On the ICW   From a position abeam of flashing daybeacon #49, it is a long run of 6.5 nautical miles to the next ICW aid to navigation, flashing buoy #51. Set a careful compass/GPS course from #49 to pass between #51 and unlighted nun buoy #52.

Shortly thereafter, cruise between another pair of unlighted aids to navigation, can buoy #53 and nun buoy #54. Immediately west of this pair, the ICW exchanges greetings with the fixed, high-rise Mid-Bay Bridge. This span has a vertical clearance of 64 feet at its central pass-through.

Immediately after passing under the high-rise span, set course to pass between unlighted nun buoy #56 and unlighted can buoy #55, then between flashing buoy #58 and unlighted can buoy #57. There are no nearby shallows to worry with, so, for once, you can be a bit cavalier about identifying these markers.

From #58, it is a lengthy run of some 3.4 nautical miles to a position north of the Waterway's next marker, flashing daybeacon #59. Be sure to come abeam of #59 by at least 400 yards to its northerly side. Shoal water making out from Cobbs Point has encroached on this aid to navigation. By staying well north of its position, passing cruisers can thumb their noses at these shallows!

North of the ICW's track, between #58 and #59, cruisers have access to two of the most exciting side-water gunk-holing opportunities on Choctawhatchee Bay.

Rocky Bayou   Successful navigation of Rocky Bayou is about as simple as it gets. There are very few shoals to contend with, and deep water extends to within 100 yards of most shorelines and sometimes even closer.

The only real shallow patch to worry with is the extensive shoal flanking the westerly reaches of the stream's entrance. Flashing daybeacon #1 warns navigators away from these problem shallows.

To enter the bayou, set course to come abeam of and pass #1 by some 200 yards to its easterly quarter. Stick to the mid-width as you cruise into the creek's interior section and no difficulty should be encountered.

The entrance channel into the Marina at Bluewater Bay is outlined by privately maintained markers on Ward Cove. Two of these aids to navigation (#2 and #3) are lighted. Shoal water does seem to be building out from the south-side point at the cove's entrance. Avoid this hazard, and your visit to this excellent marina will be a snap.

As you cruise upstream on Ward Cove toward Bluewater Bay's dockage basin, be sure to pass between the pairs of various daybeacons. Some of these are uncharted, but they are quite obvious on the water. The innermost markers are unlighted daybeacons #3 and #4. Be *sure* to pass between these aids to navigation *before* making your turn into the dockage basin.

Shoal water flanks the northeasterly section of the entrance into the excellent anchorage north of Sarah Ann Bayou. To avoid this hazard, favor the western and southwestern banks *slightly* when entering this small bay. However, note the charted shoal building out from the west-side point at the entrance. Don't cut too far to the west and get into these shallows. Depths drop off to 8 or 9 feet as the stream takes a jog to the northeast. Be sure to drop the hook well short of the charted shallow water farther to the east.

Rocky Bayou takes a 90-degree cut to the east at Nelson Point. As discussed earlier, the cove on the southerly banks east of Nelson Point is a popular anchorage with local captains. Deep water extends to within 50 yards of the high shoreline. Simply drop the hook at any acceptable spot short of these shallows and settle back for an evening to be remembered.

Farther to the east, Rocky Bayou is traversed by a fixed bridge, with 20 feet of vertical clearance, and a 40-foot power line. While deep water extends for better than 1 nautical mile past the span, this upstream section of the bayou is quite broad and does not afford particularly sheltered anchorage. Most cruisers will wisely choose to confine their explorations to the waters west of the fixed bridge.

Boggy Bayou   While the channel running the length of Boggy Bayou is, in most places, quite wide and well marked, this creek does require a bit more navigational care than its sister to the east. The bayou's entrance, in particular, is bounded by two patches of shoal water. While both are well marked, this is not the place to take a snooze at the wheel. Strangers are also advised against entering the creek at night or in low-light conditions. For the reasons outlined above, it is necessary to pick out the various markers and aids to navigation in order to avoid shallow water. So, while local skippers can probably enter Boggy Bayou blindfolded, visiting cruisers should plan their approach for the daylight hours.

To enter Boggy Bayou from the Waterway, depart from the ICW channel about midway between flashing buoy #58 and flashing daybeacon #59. Set course to come abeam of flashing daybeacon #1, east of Buccaroo Point, by some 100 yards to its easterly quarter.

Note that flashing daybeacon #1 can be hard to spot. Use your binoculars to help pick this marker out of the shimmering haze.

Once abeam of #1, set a new course to pass between flashing daybeacon #3 and unlighted daybeacon #4 at the mouth of Boggy Bayou. Daybeacon #4 can also be hard to spot, as it tends to blend in with a string of trees on Shirk Point. Shoal water is found east and west of #4 and #3 respectively. Be sure to pass directly between the two beacons.

Continue on course and pass to the east of unlighted daybeacon #5. Continued upstream navigation now becomes a fairly simple matter. Observe the various markers and keep chart 11385 nearby to quickly resolve any questions.

Weekley Bayou   Since Weekley Bayou is now off-limits to pleasure craft, we will no longer provide navigational detail on this stream.

On Boggy Bayou   After passing unlighted daybeacon #5, a wide swath of deep water opens out on Boggy Bayou. Eventually you should point to pass unlighted daybeacon #6 to its westerly side, followed quickly by unlighted daybeacon #7, which should be passed to its easterly quarter.

The next upstream aid to navigation, unlighted daybeacon #8, sits fairly close to the easterly shoreline. Come abeam of #8 well to its westerly side for best depths. At #8, Tom's Bayou comes abeam to the west.

Tom's Bayou   Enter Tom's Bayou on its mid-width. Stay away from both shorelines. As chart 11385 correctly indicates, shoal water extends out into the stream from both banks at the entrance. On a clear, sunny day, as usual, it's a simple matter to spot the shallows. In bad weather or low light, be sure to stay on the centerline and keep a steady watch on the sounder.

Once past the entrance, the creek takes a jog to the northwest and flows towards a low-level fixed bridge (11 feet of vertical clearance), which bars further exploration for all but small craft. The stretch between the bayou's mouth and the fixed span makes an excellent overnight haven. Good depths are consistently held to within 50 yards or less of the shoreline.

North on Boggy Bayou   North of Tom's Bayou, cruising captains will encounter flashing daybeacon #9, the northernmost aid to navigation on Boggy Bayou. As you would expect, pass this aid to its easterly side.

North of #9, the waters of Boggy Bayou spread out into an even wider pool of deep water. Soon the bayou begins to bend a bit to the northwest.

Development increases significantly on these waters. Watch to the east for Giuseppi's Wharf Restaurant and Marina, followed farther upstream by the Boathouse restaurant to the southwest and Lighthouse Key Marina to the northeast.

Joe's Bayou   The mouth of Joe's Bayou, lying south-southwest of the Waterway's flashing daybeacon #59, is surrounded by shoal water with depths of 3 feet or less. Fortunately, there is a marked, improved entry channel which carries 10 feet of water or better. To enter, continue on the Waterway channel until unlighted daybeacon #2 comes abeam directly to the south. Set a

new course to come abeam of #2 by some 10 yards to its easterly quarter. Adjust your track to pass the next aid, unlighted daybeacon #4, by about the same distance to its easterly side.

South of #4, deep water spreads out almost from shore to shore on Joe's Bayou for a goodly distance upstream. This is where cruising-sized craft should anchor.

Still farther to the south, chart 11385 indicates soundings of 2 feet just northwest of a pool of 8-foot water. In earlier editions of this guide, we recommended this upstream section as an anchorage for bold skippers who were willing to brave this very narrow, unmarked portion of the bayou channel. However, as discussed earlier, the private docks associated with the recent development on Joe's Bayou now lead us to discourage anchorage here by even those who would hazard the constricted passage.

Destin

The thriving resort community of Destin has become a place where cruising craft are very much an afterthought. On the plus side, Destin Harbor (also known as Old Pass Lagoon) is home to a very large fleet of charter fishing craft. It's not putting too fine a point on it to say that Destin is clearly *the* charter fishing capital of the Florida Panhandle. The waterfront is very crowded with charter-fishing-fleet docks, motels, and seafood restaurants. There is one full-service boatyard catering to pleasure craft. The nearby white sand beaches are legendary and arguably the most beautiful of all the Panhandle's many wonderful seaward strands. More and more tourists are drawn every year to the shimmering waters.

These days there are hordes of people everywhere, honking horns, long long lines of hungry people waiting to be seated at the local restaurants, and a general hurried rush that is, quite frankly, not this writer's idea of a good time.

On the other hand, a wonder of wonders, both the channel leading to Destin from

Choctawhatchee Bay (near standard mile 228) and the channel running from East Pass Inlet into Destin Harbor were fully dredged in the spring of 2002. If past experience is any guide, shoaling began anew as soon as the dredge disappeared over the horizon. Please take the depths quoted below and the scheme of aids to navigation discussed in these pages with a whole box of Morton salt.

Transient dockage has always been a bit hard to come by in Destin Harbor. Currently, only Harborwalk Marina (see below) offers anything in the way of overnight accommodations for visiting cruisers. Even here the local sport-fishing charter vessels are clearly where the action is.

So, Destin is clearly a mixed bag for cruisers. With its many and varied attractions set against the potential navigational difficulty of the various channels and the relative scarcity of transient dockage, every skipper must decide for himself or herself whether this popular port of call will fit into his or her plans.

Destin Geography

Artificial East Pass Inlet (also shown on chart 11385 as "Choctawhatchee Bay Entrance") is the Choctawhatchee's only outlet to the sparkling Gulf waters. This channel cuts the bay's southern shoreline some 3.6 miles east of the ICW's intersection with the Narrows. Perhaps this inlet's greatest claim to fame is the bridge crossing the cut. For many years it was charted as having 50 feet of vertical clearance. Now chart 11385 notes an overhead height of 49 feet, but sailboaters should be forewarned that high-water clearances can be 48 feet *or less*.

Destin Harbor (or Old Pass Lagoon) consists of an elongated lagoon that is protected on all sides by the mainland and wide sand peninsulas. Access to the harbor is gained by a single narrow mouth fronting onto East Pass Inlet. Shoaling is a constant problem at this important intersection.

Depths of 6 to 15 feet are typical in Destin Harbor. However, there is one lump near the Lucky Snapper restaurant that carries only some 3½ feet of water at low tide.

The marked channel that escorts cruisers safely into Destin Harbor is now accurately charted on 11385. Of course, things could be very different by the time you arrive.

The town of Destin is mostly gathered about Highway 98, which skirts just north of the harbor. It is an easy step from any of the area marinas to the many shoreside businesses, including convenience and ship's stores, along this heavily traveled track. If you should happen to become bored with the restaurants on the waterfront, there are many additional dining spots on the highway from which to choose. Just watch out for the incredibly heavy automobile traffic.

The nearest supermarket is located about 1½ miles from Harborwalk Marina, the principal dockage facility for cruising visitors. If this hike is a bit much for your tired feet, call Destin Taxi at 850-654-5700.

Destin History   Looking at the modern city of Destin, one could be forgiven for concluding that this community simply sprang into being during the tourist boom following World War II. However, such a conclusion would overlook this community's interesting past.

Modern-day Destin began in the mid-1830s when Captain Leonard A. Destin, a seafaring New Englander who apparently felt a bit crowded in his native Atlantic waters, moved his family and ship to the eastern shores of East Pass Inlet. From their earliest days in Florida, the captain and his offspring down through the generations pursued the art and science of commercial fishing. As his enterprise grew, men came to work with him during the season. Some were so taken with the charms of nearby Choctawhatchee Bay and the Gulf's clear waters that they chose to stay permanently. Thus the town of Destin was born.

In 1935 Coleman Kelly and his wife, Mattie, emigrated to Destin. This family was to have a profound impact on the town's future. Their first enterprise was a turpentine industry. The strong solvent was still much in demand by the shipwright trade and could be readily gathered from the many pines on the Choctawhatchee peninsula.

The arrival of the Kelly family coincided with the completion of the first Destin high-way bridge. In 1937 Coleman bought the plot of land just east of the bridge on the highway's southern shoulder. Here he built what his wife described in later years as a "many-faceted operation," which they dubbed "The Little Store." There were gas pumps, groceries, and a restaurant in the back from which platters piled high with the most succulent seafood were served daily. The townspeople often gathered here during the evening hours and Mattie relates that the "local fishermen drank enough beer so that the pile of cans stacked on the table in front of them almost hid them from sight."

In August 1939 the Kellys launched the *Martha-Gene* as a deep-sea pleasure fishing craft. One can only wonder if they ever realized where their efforts were to lead. Again Mattie comments:

> Although Coleman Kelly never owned a fishing captain's license, and never sought one,

Approaching Destin from East Pass Inlet

he was fascinated with the idea that sports fishing might be the one activity that would bring people to Destin to enjoy themselves and that they would ultimately stay.

Well, as they say, the rest is history.

The enterprise begun by Coleman Kelly grew and grew until today Destin is the center of charter sportfishing on the Florida Panhandle. Tourists and vacationers arrive by the hundreds during the summer season. High-rise

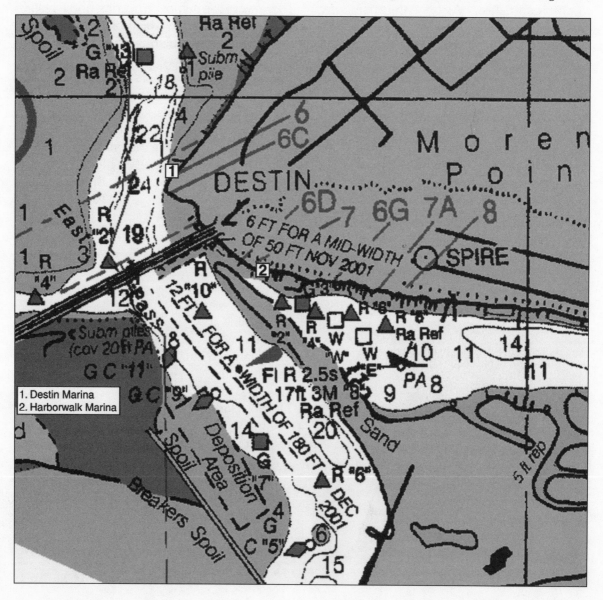

1. Destin Marina
2. Harborwalk Marina

condos overlook the beaches and the hubbub of traffic is heard well into the night. Few of those visitors know that without Coleman Kelly, Destin would have most likely remained a rather obscure Panhandle fishing village.

Destin Facilities and Waterfront Restaurants (Various Lats/Lons—see below)

As noted above, the Destin waterfront does not offer much in the way of transient dockage, though some repairs are available. There is also a dry-stack storage operation fronting Destin Harbor, and sometimes temporary dockage can be found for those interested in satisfying a hearty appetite.

Shortly before reaching the bridge that crosses East Pass Inlet, cruisers entering Destin Harbor from Choctawhatchee Bay will spy a marina facility on the eastern shores of the approach channel. This marina is found near facility designation #6 on chart 11385 (30 23.819 North/086 30.939 West).

Destin Marina (850-837-2470) is a mostly small-craft facility that accepts boats only up to 18 feet for dockage. While the inner slips have 5 feet or less of dockside depth, the outer pier and fuel dock boast 12-foot soundings. Gasoline and diesel fuel are available. Be careful tying up to the docks at Destin Marina, even if it's just for fuel. When the wind has its dander up, we have seen some prodigious waves rolling into these docks.s

Until recently, Sides Marine was found just next door to Destin Marina. During our last visit, this facility was being destructed in preparation for yet another high-rise condo. Just what Florida needs!

The remaining Destin marinas and waterfront restaurants overlook the *north* shore of Destin Harbor. First up is the headquarters of Harborwalk Marina (30 23.614 North/086 30.702 West). As alluded to above, this facility, like everything else in Destin Harbor, has a strong flavor of sportfishing. In fact, several of the local charter craft make their home at Harborwalk.

However, Harborwalk Marina usually has some 6 slips set aside for transient visitors. These are the only berths readily available to cruising craft in all of Destin Harbor, so call ahead to see if any spaces are available.

Visitors and resident craft alike will discover fixed, wooden slips at Harborwalk Marina with fresh-water and 50-amp (only) power connections. Depths at most slips run 6 to 8 feet, but there is one lump in front of the marina's second rank of piers (moving northwest to southeast), near the Lucky Snapper restaurant, that carries only 3½-foot depths at low water. Check the navigational account of Destin Harbor below for hints as to how to avoid this hazard.

Gasoline and diesel fuel are readily available at Harborwalk, but there are no shoreside showers. A large combination ship's, tackle, bait, and variety store overlooks the fuel dock. Both the store and fuel pier are located a short hop from Destin Harbor's westerly entrance, almost abeam of unlighted daybeacon #2. Check here for your slip assignment after making good your entrance from East Pass Inlet.

The popular Lucky Snapper restaurant (850-654-0900) sits in the heart of the Harborwalk dockage complex. A. J.'s Oyster House (see below) is just a few steps farther to the east, or you can take a short walk to one of the many restaurants lining Highway 98.

Cruisers in need of a galley resupply effort

will find plenty of convenience stores within walking distance along Highway 98. The nearest supermarket is a good 1½ miles to the east on Highway 98. You might want to call Destin Taxi at (850) 654-5700.

Harborwalk Marina (850) 337-8250
http://www.harborwalkdestin.com

Approach depth—6-14 feet (except for one 3½-foot spot)
Dockside depth—6-8 feet

Harborwalk Marina, Destin

Accepts transients—6 slips available
Transient-dockage rate—well above average
Fixed wooden slips—yes
Dockside power connections—50-amp
Dockside water connections—yes
Gasoline—yes
Diesel fuel—yes
Ship's and variety store—yes
Restaurant—several nearby

After passing the Harborwalk's ample piers and coming abeam of unlighted daybeacon #4, cruisers will sight another fine dining choice: A. J.'s Oyster House and Restaurant (850-837-1913). This eatery is housed in a multistory building with a grass-roofed Tiki bar perched atop the main restaurant. In good weather, lucky patrons can partake of their seafood outside on this overlook while watching the harbor traffic drift by.

Just behind A. J.'s restaurant is A. J's High and Dry (850-837-3431). This firm specializes in dry-stack storage of small power craft and no services seem to be available for transients.

Immediately east of A. J.'s, passing cruisers will note the Destin branch of the ubiquitous Galati Marine (850-837-0385). This fine firm operates repair yards all over Florida, and their work always seems to be of the first-class variety. No dockage is offered at the Destin location, but complete mechanical and below-waterline, haul-out repairs are readily available. The yard's lift is rated at 50 tons.

A bit farther to the east, East Pass Marina (850-837-2622) overlooks Destin Harbor abeam of unlighted daybeacon #8. Gasoline and diesel fuel can be purchased, but no transient dockage has been available at this facility for several years.

The adjacent Boathouse Oyster Bar (850-837-3645) is a real local hangout with excellent seafood (particularly the grouper sandwiches), plenty of "liquid sunshine" on tap, nighttime entertainment, and genuine dollar-bill wallpaper. The Boathouse is, without a doubt, Destin's most funky dining experience. Don't look for any white tablecloths here. Nevertheless, it is highly suggested by this writer.

Farther to the east in Destin Harbor, there is currently very little in the way of pleasure-craft facilities available for visitors. There used to be some small motels and restaurants offering uncertain dockage, but most of these seem to have fallen to the "condo craze."

There is one fortunate exception. Soon after leaving East Pass Marina in your wake, the headquarters and a few piers associated with Harbor Docks Restaurant (850-837-7559) will come up along the northerly banks. Let's not quibble about this one—the food is simply superb, whether you choose one of the fresh, local seafood dishes, or more landlubber-oriented fare. While some of the available piers are occupied by resident craft, patrons of the restaurant might be able to squeeze in one or two available spots. Dockside depths are an impressive 8 to 13 feet of water.

The southern banks of Destin Harbor are lined by private docks and condominiums. There is a good channel flanking the shoreline that leads back to the harbor entrance. Careful gunk-holers should feel free to explore the harbor's southerly reaches, always keeping in mind the absence of any facilities on this portion of Destin Harbor.

DESTIN NAVIGATION

The channels traversing East Pass Inlet and the entrance from Choctawhatchee Bay into Destin Harbor are not stable and are subject to rapid shoaling. Markers are frequently shifted to follow the ever-changing bottom strata. Habitual dredging usually serves to keep both of these cuts open, but running the channels does call for extra caution and a weather eye on the sounder. Many, many local craft use both the inlet and bay channel on a daily basis without accidents. However, as a stranger to these waters, you must take the extra care that might not be necessary for a local who knows which shoals are building in which direction. Take your time, and if possible, make your approach on a clear, sunny day (so as to better spot shoals). Observe all markers carefully.

As mentioned several times previously, the East Pass Inlet approach from Choctawhatchee Bay and the Destin Harbor channels were dredged in the spring of 2002. For the moment, the correct scheme of aids to navigation is pictured on chart 11385. However, things could be very different by the time you arrive. Be ready for shallower depths and different markers. The rule when running the various Destin channels is to expect the unexpected!

The bridge traversing East Pass Inlet is infamous for having less than its charted vertical 49-foot clearance at or near high water. If you need as much as 48 feet of clearance, be sure to time your passage of the inlet for low tide.

Currently, cruisers approaching either Destin Harbor or East Pass Inlet from Choctawhatchee Bay should set their course to pass between flashing daybeacon #16 and unlighted daybeacon #17. As you are now headed *toward* the open sea, pass all subsequent red, even-numbered aids to navigation to your port side and take all green markers to starboard.

After passing between unlighted daybeacons #13 and #14, the channel angles a bit to the south-southwest and hurries on toward the infamous Destin-East Pass Inlet bridge. Remember that this span usually has only 48 feet or so of vertical clearance at high water in spite of its charted 49-foot height.

From a position between #13 and #14, head for the central pass-through of the East Pass Bridge. Be on guard against the huge, correctly charted shoal of 1- and 2-foot waters lying to the west. This shoal is very much for real! Also, note the correctly charted, far smaller bubble of shallows abutting the northeastern corner of the high-rise span.

Don't be confused by the scantily marked but charted channel that cuts west-southwest immediately north of the Destin-East Pass fixed bridge. This passage serves the Destin U.S. Coast Guard headquarters and is pretty much off-limits to cruising craft.

Once through the bridge, cruising captains bound for Destin Harbor should turn sharply to port and point for the mid-width of the lagoon's entrance, which will be spied to the east-northeast.

The entrance into Destin Harbor was

dredged in the spring of 2002, but make no mistake about it, this portion of the channel *is* subject to shoaling. Proceed with caution. My best advice at this point is to hold scrupulously to the centerline, but pay quick heed to any new aids to navigation that might come your way as you cruise through this cut.

First up you will pass a jet-ski rental dock flanking the northeasterly banks, followed closely by the fuel pier and the first rank of piers associated with Harborwalk Marina (also guarding the northerly shoreline). You should come abeam of unlighted daybeacon #2 to your starboard side just about as you pull even to the Harborwalk fuel dock.

Craft continuing farther into Destin Harbor should point to pass all subsequent red, even-numbered aids to navigation to their (the cruisers') starboard side and take green markers to port (as if you expected something else).

The easterly set of Harborwalk Marina's docks, abeam of the gap between unlighted daybeacons #3 and #4, has a lump in front of the piers that carries only 3½ feet at low tide. To avoid this hazard, stick to the marked channel.

A large shoal occupies the mid-width of Destin Harbor east and southeast of unlighted daybeacon #6. Passing cruisers will spy several "Shoal" signs near #6, warning of this potential hazard. Stay well away from this shallow patch and continue to follow the markers, unless the idae of giving Sea Tow some extra business appeals to you.

CHAPTER 3

Fort Walton Beach to Pensacola Bay

It is understandable that cruisers leaving the wonderful waters of Choctawhatchee Bay might think that the best is behind them. However, mariners will be surprised to learn that many gunk-holing and overnight anchorage opportunities await them between Fort Walton Beach and Pensacola Bay. In fact, for those lucky few who can clear one 19-foot fixed bridge, some of the prettiest anchorages you will ever be lucky enough to find are within easy reach of Fort Walton.

Marina facilities are found here and there between the westerly reaches of Choctawhatchee Bay and the ICW's entrance into Pensacola Bay. The two largest concentrations of marinas are found near Fort Walton Beach and on Little Sabine Bay, hard by Pensacola Beach.

This stretch of the Gulf Coast ICW continues the Florida Panhandle's unvarying tradition of prolific overnight anchorages. In addition to the many havens surrounding Fort Walton, there are also numerous opportunities for passing cruisers to drop the hook in a secure setting throughout Santa Rosa Sound.

The scenery along this portion of the Northern Gulf passage is absolutely magnificent. The northerly shores of Fort Walton Beach seem to have been planned with cruisers in mind. Gorgeous homes with immaculate lawns overlook the surrounding waters and provide a wonderful backdrop for overnight anchorage. Farther to the west, the clear waters of Santa Rosa Sound are set against lightly developed, well-wooded shores to the north and the low sand dunes of Eglin Air Force Base and the Gulf Coast National Seashore to the south. Few cruisers with any eye for natural beauty will be disappointed by this portion of their passage to the west.

By now it's almost becoming a cliché to say that a stretch of water in the Florida Panhandle is "prime cruising ground," but that description remains the most apt of the lot. Whether you enjoy anchoring off or simply admiring clear waters set against beautiful shorelines, you can count on the ICW from Fort Walton to Pensacola Bay to fulfill its smiling promise.

Charts You will only need two charts for successful navigation of this stretch along the Northern Gulf:
11385—covers all waters in the Fort Walton region and details the ICW to Pensacola Beach
11378—follows the Waterway through Santa Rosa Sound to a point just south of Pensacola Bay

Bridges
Shalimar-Garnier Bayou Bridge—crosses Garnier Bayou at the charted location of Shalimar—Fixed—19 feet
Brooks-Fort Walton Beach Bridge—crosses the ICW at standard mile 223—Fixed—48 feet
Navarre Causeway Bridge—crosses the ICW at standard mile 207—Fixed—50 feet
Pensacola Beach Bridge—crosses the ICW at standard mile 189—Fixed—65 feet

Fort Walton Beach Waters

As noted repeatedly throughout the first two chapters of this guide, there are many wonderful cruising grounds to be found in Panhandle Florida and all along the Northern Gulf Coast. However, it's very nice to be surprised by discovering a great cruising region just where you least expected to find it. Fort Walton Beach and its surrounding waters are just such a pleasant surprise.

Take a moment to glance at the northerly waters abutting Fort Walton on chart 11385. The dark orange color signaling urban development covers almost the entire western bank of Garnier Bayou and all of Cinco Bayou. Many years ago, when this writer first entered these waters he expected heavy development. To my astonishment, what I found instead were gracious homes overlooking the shores with impeccably landscaped lawns. Opportunities for sheltered overnight anchorages with lovely backdrops were everywhere in evidence. It was even possible to drop the hook in the lee of very lightly developed or totally natural shores. Quite frankly, it was a bit hard to call it a day and head back to the more developed waters to the west.

Unfortunately, a fixed bridge on the lower reaches of Garnier Bayou with *19 feet of vertical clearance* will restrict a large portion of these lovely waters to power craft.

To the south and west of Fort Walton Beach, the ICW hurries through a dredged channel on the westerly reaches of Choctawhatchee Bay and enters a small body of water known appropriately enough as the Narrows. Here mariners will find the "other" Fort Walton waterfront, crowded with condos, marinas, and boat dealers. Another marina and boatyard guards the southern banks just east of the Narrows' mouth. Additionally, one newly reborn pleasure-craft facility and a large yacht club are located on Fort Walton's attractive northerly waters. One has some transient dockage and offers full repair services. Taken as a group, these Fort Walton Beach marinas offer adequate dockage and some other services for cruising craft.

If by now you have detected a bit of enthusiasm for Fort Walton cruising on this writer's part, then you are indeed on the right track. Captains who race by on the ICW with nary a sideways glance will miss some of the best anchorages in the Florida Panhandle.

Fort Walton History   Modern Fort Walton Beach is built upon grounds that were once sacred to Native Americans. As white settlers slowly filtered into these lands during the early 1800s, they discovered a massive Indian mound and temple. This historic attraction has been preserved and is today open for all to see. Even though it's a healthy walk from any of the town's marinas, this writer urges visiting cruisers to make every effort to view this ancient Native American worshiping place.

By 1821 the future state of Florida had been brought into the American fold largely through the efforts of General Andrew Jackson, who would later become president. It was only natural for this intrepid soldier to be offered the territorial governorship of this latest U.S. acquisition.

One of Jackson's aides was George Walton, son of one of the signers of the Declaration of Independence. In 1842 the Florida legislature created a new county in the northwestern portion of the state and named it "Walton," in George's honor.

As the Civil War drew its dark wings about the Florida Panhandle, the few local citizens occupying the banks north and west of Choctawhatchee formed a military unit to guard Santa Rosa Sound. It was thought that Union forces might use this body of water as a back door to attack nearby Pensacola. The company was stationed at the old Indian temple mound, north of the Narrows. This spot became known as Camp Walton, and the soldiers took on the name of the "Walton Guards."

At the end of The War Between the States, some of the former Confederates came back to the land where they were stationed during the conflict and settled down to a peaceable life. John Thomas Brooks was one of these intrepid pioneers. Almost singlehandedly he formed a town which became known as Brooks Landing. Brooks founded a sawmill and gave the struggling settlement its first commercial enterprise.

In 1915 Walton county was split with Okaloosa County. By some happenstance, the community of Brooks Landing ended up in this latter unit. The town's name was changed to Fort Walton in remembrance of the men who served in the Walton Guards. In 1932 the word "Beach" was added to increase the community's appeal to water-hungry tourists.

In 1937 an event took place which was to have the most profound effect on the future of Fort Walton Beach. The U.S. Air Force acquired a vast tract of land north of the town and much of the barrier island across the Narrows to the south. This military camp was eventually developed into Eglin Air Force Base. Named for Lt. Col. Frederick Eglin, who died in a plane crash shortly after the base was founded, Eglin has been a boon and a source of employment ever since its inception. Soon after its founding, the base was designated as the principal Air Force proving ground. The nation's newest and most modern aircraft are still tested here.

Fort Walton's Northerly Waters (Standard Mile 225) (Various Lats/Lons—see below)

Look at chart 11385 and you will quickly notice an irregular, hand-shaped body of water extending north from the westerly reaches of Choctawhatchee Bay. These waters are comprised of Garnier and Cinco bayous, along with a host of their smaller cousins. The shoreline conditions are nearly ideal. Eye-pleasing residential development alternates with barely populated patches.

For those power captains whose craft can clear the charted, 19-foot fixed bridge, sheltered overnight anchorages are found everywhere you look. Soundings are uniformly deep on all the waters, with only a few small shoals near the entrances of the smaller bayous with which to worry.

One revitalized marina facility is found along the way. Shalimar Yacht Basin (30 26.183 North/086 35.090 West) guards the cove indenting the eastern shore south of the Garnier Bayou Bridge. Due to this facility's advantageous position south of the 19-foot fixed bridge, captains entering this marina need not worry with any height restrictions. This is a distinct advantage for sail- or larger power craft.

As little as two years ago, this writer would have been hesitant to recommend a stay at Shalimar Yacht Basin. However, new owners have taken over and this facility now resembles a phoenix that has arisen from the ashes. Everything has been cleaned up, fixed up,

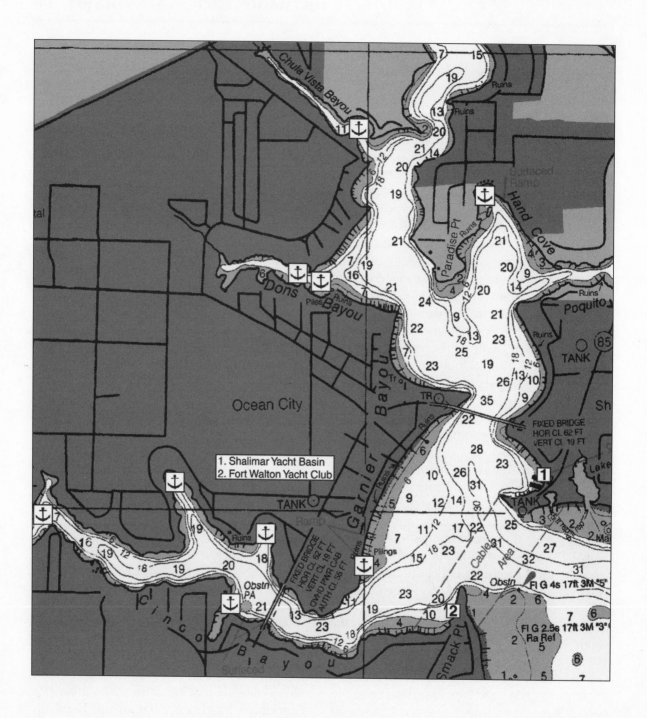

and, generally, put in first-class condition. Once again, we think Shalimar Yacht Basin deserves serious consideration by all our fellow cruisers, whether you are just looking for an overnight berth, or full-service repairs.

Shalimar features twin dockage harbors, each with its own entrance, protected by a wooden breakwater. The marina has both open and covered slips with good, fixed wooden piers. Each berth boasts 20- and 30-amp power and fresh-water hookups. Depths alongside run 6½ feet or better. Waste pump-out service, as well as gasoline and diesel fuel, dispensed by new pumps, are readily available.

Shoreside, captains and crews will discover a single, nonclimate-controlled shower build-ing. This structure had just been repainted with eye-popping reds, yellows, and blues during our last visit, but it was clean as could be. Its position adjoining the southern dockage basin will necessitate a long walk for those cruisers making their temporary home in the north-side harbor. There is no on-site Laundromat presently available, but this service is planned for the future. Shalimar Yacht Basin includes a boat-sales building, which has a very few ship's store and fishing, tackle-type items.

The closest nonfast-food dining spot is yet another branch of the wonderful Giuseppi's Wharf Restaurant, met in the last chapter. It's still a healthy five-block walk to Giuseppi's, and there isn't a supermarket within easy

Shalimar Yacht Basin, Garnier Bayou

walking distance either. That is *not* a problem, however, as Shalimar remains one of the very few marinas that still offers the use of a free courtesy car. We commend the management for this most worthwhile service.

Shalimar Yacht Basin maintains a full-service repair yard. Full mechanical repairs for both gasoline- and diesel-powered plants are in the offing. The yard's travelift is rated at 30 tons.

I'm sure it's quite obvious by now that this writer is most impressed with this new incarnation of Shalimar Yacht Basin. We suggest that every cruiser plying the waters of western Choctawhatchee Bay give this newly minted facility their most serious attention.

Shalimar Yacht Basin (850) 651-0510
   http://www.shalimaryachtbasin.com

Approach depth—10 feet plus
Dockside depth—6½- to 7-foot minimum
Accepts transients—yes
Transient-dockage rate—above average
Fixed wooden piers—yes (some covered)
Dockside power connections—20- and 30-amp
Dockside water connections—yes
Showers—yes
Waste pump-out—yes
Gasoline—yes
Diesel fuel—yes
Mechanical repairs—yes
Below-waterline repairs—yes
Ship's and tackle store—small
Restaurant—long walk (Use the marina courtescar.)

Cinco Bayou and Fort Walton Yacht Club (Various Lats/Lons—see below)

Cinco Bayou enters the western shores of Garnier Bayou well *south* of the charted fixed bridge. Consequently, sailcraft of most sizes can enter the creek without height restrictions. The fixed bridge with a vertical clearance of 19 feet spans the bayou some .9 of a nautical mile farther upstream. It bars most wind-powered boats from the creek's upper limits.

The shoreline of Cinco features heavier residential development than that found on some of the other nearby waters, but the creek is still attractive. Cruisers can throw out the hook for an evening of peace and solitude.

The modern, extensive, fixed piers of Fort Walton Yacht Club (30 25.582 North/086 35.538 West) are found on the eastern banks of the bayou, just south of Smack Point (near the entrance). This most impressive club features expansive shoreside buildings and facilities, including a large clubhouse and restaurant. Members of accredited yacht clubs with reciprocal agreements are readily accepted for overnight dockage. Impressive dockside depths of 6 to (more typically) 8 feet are good news for long-legged sailcraft. During our several visits, we have always observed far more sail- than powerboats. Due to the popularity of this club, it would be a good idea to make your dockage arrangements well ahead of time.

Fort Walton Yacht Club (850) 243-7102
   http://www.fwyc.org

Approach depth—12 feet plus
Dockside depth—6 to 8 feet
Accepts transients—yes (members of accredited
   yacht clubs)
Dockside power and water connections—yes
Fixed piers—yes
Showers—yes
Restaurant—on site

Anchorages abound on the upper reaches of Cinco Bayou. Be aware, however, that you must be able to clear yet another 19-foot fixed span crossing the bayou upstream from Fort Walton Yacht Club to take advantage of the havens discussed below.

Immediately after passing through the Cinco Bayou Bridge, skippers may choose to anchor in the charted cove abutting the northern banks, near 30 25.893 North/086 36.512 West. Minimum 10-foot depths are complemented by excellent protection and enough swinging room for boats up to 36 feet. Shelter is more than adequate for all winds except strong southerly blows. Cruisers will observe a condo development on the starboard shore, with heavy residential development on the opposite banks. A motel guards the rear portion of the cove. Mariners making use of this anchorage must be careful about the charted shoal abutting the eastern banks. Be sure to read the navigational information presented later in this chapter before attempting entry.

Another good anchorage for smaller craft is found opposite the just-discussed haven (30 25.579 North/086 36.697 West). The compact offshoot on the southern banks, just west of the bridge, has 10- to 11-foot minimum depths, but only enough swinging room for boats up to 30 feet. There is another condo project overlooking the eastern banks, and in contrast, a gorgeous southern-style home guards the westerly shoreline. Even if you can't fit in the anchorage, gunk-holers might want to schedule a quick visit to admire this handsome edifice.

One of the best havens on Cinco Bayou is found in the large northerly fork of the stream, charted southwest of the "Ocean City" designation on 11385 (30 26.111 North/086 36.993 West). This sheltered body of water is surrounded by fairly heavy, but nevertheless eye-pleasing, residential development. Minimum

10- to 12-foot depths are held just short of the cove's northwesterly tip. Swinging room is more than sufficient for a 50-footer. Strong southeasterly breezes could raise an unwelcome chop, but cruisers should be safe from all other winds.

West of this anchorage, the main body of Cinco Bayou begins to narrow enough for effective protection. Visitors can drop the hook anywhere that strikes their fancy. One of the best spots is found where the stream takes a sharp turn to the southwest, near 30 25.966 North/086 37.687 West. Here boats up to 40 feet can anchor in about as protected an area as you are likely to find.

Don's Bayou
(Various Lats/Lons—see below)

The creek known as Don's Bayou breaks off from the westerly shores of Garnier Bayou west of Paradise Point. This body of water can be rated as another excellent overnight anchorage opportunity. Minimum depths are 7 feet, with soundings of 9 to 13 feet being more the norm. There are two unmarked shoals at the entrance which must be negotiated. The shoreline holds moderate residential development, interspaced by well-wooded patches along high banks. While not as undeveloped as some of the havens farther upstream, few will find Don's Bayou unattractive. Protection from all winds but particularly strong easterly blows is excellent.

The waters boasting maximum swinging room are found in the charted 12-foot pool just past the entrance, near 30 27.006 North/086 36.234 West. Craft up to 48 feet can drop the hook here with plenty of elbow room. Better protected is the narrower stretch west of the pool (near 30 27.032 North/086 36.362 West). However, there is only enough room for craft up to 38 feet to pitch out the anchor without having to mess with a Bahamian moor.

The creek eventually dead ends into a *T* split. Captains piloting craft up to 32 feet can anchor in the deep water just short of the *T*. Please read the navigational information on Don's Bayou presented later in this chapter before cruising this far upstream.

Poquito Bayou
(Various Lats/Lons—see below)

Poquito Bayou cuts off in an easterly direction well east of Paradise Point. Cruisers entering this creek for the first time from Hand Cove will probably think that it is a bit narrow for comfortable anchorage. Keep the faith! There are some great havens ahead.

Poquito has some stretches of shore with light residential development, while other sections are completely in their natural state. Even in this region of attractive shorelines, this is a particularly appealing body of water. Dropping the hook here for an evening or two should make any skipper breathe a sigh of contentment.

Minimum depths are 7 feet, though again, there are several shoals at the entrance that must be avoided. Elementary navigation should see you safely through.

Protection from all winds, particularly on the northerly, upstream stretches of the creek, is superb. Poquito can be considered a true hurricane hole.

The first spot worthy of consideration as an overnight refuge is found on the charted patch of deep water that opens out to the east just after the creek passes between two sharp points (near 30 27.067 North/086 34.723 West). There should be enough swinging room here for a 45-footer. A few pleasant-looking houses flank the starboard shore, but the port banks are high, well wooded, and completely undeveloped.

Poquito Bayou soon passes through a 90-degree turn to the north. After passing the charted sharp point of land on the eastern shore, the creek opens out into a broad stretch where 45-foot boats will find plenty of room to swing at anchor, near 30 27.318 North/086 34.622 West. Not only is this spot particularly attractive, it's quite well sheltered.

Hand Cove
(30 27.372 North/086 35.384 West)

Perhaps the finest anchorage on all of the various waters lying about Fort Walton is found on the charted deep-water cove behind the small island on the northerly reaches of Hand Cove. Minimum depths are 10 feet, though care must be taken to avoid the shoal water around the island. The banks are overlooked by several gorgeous homes with beautiful lawns. Protection is excellent from all winds and swinging room is acceptable for most pleasure craft. Unless you prefer one of the completely undeveloped anchorages farther upstream, you simply could not do better than Hand Cove.

Chula Vista Bayou
(30 27.660 North/086 36.050 West)

Chula Vista Bayou has more shoaling around its entrance than any of the other creeks leading off Garnier Bayou. There is still a broad, if unmarked, channel that most craft under 40 feet in length should be able to navigate successfully.

Once past the tricky entrance, boats up to 40 feet can drop the anchor in a fairly broad stretch of the creek with good protection from all but strong southeasterly blows. The high, wooded banks are overlooked by the usual attractive, light, residential development.

Farther to the northwest, Chula Vista narrows. There is not enough swinging room for vessels over 28 feet to sway easily at anchor along this stretch.

Upper Garnier Bayou
(Various Lats/Lons—see below)

The northern headwaters of Garnier Bayou fork into two deep-water, bay-like coves separated by a broad patch of shoal water. Both coves make excellent overnight anchorages, but the northeasterly arm is a particularly good haven.

The charted deep-water patch at the upstream end of the northeastern fork (near 30 28.504 North/086 35.315 West) is surrounded by completely undeveloped, heavily wooded shores.

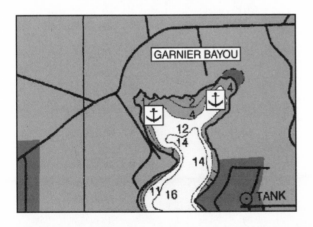

Cypress and other hardwoods overlook the water and provide super protection from all winds. Minimum depths are about 7 feet, with most soundings being considerably deeper. Swinging room is sufficient for most pleasure vessels. Although perhaps not quite as sheltered as the hurricane hole on Poquito Bayou, this spot is one of the finest and most tempting anchorages on Fort Walton's northern waters. If you are one of those cruisers who enjoys anchoring in a beautiful setting, with good marina facilities only a short boat ride away (and what serious cruiser doesn't?), then this just might be the haven you have been searching for.

The northwesterly arm of upper Garnier Bayou is also attractive, though a few homes overlook the banks along this stretch. Minimum depths are 8 feet near our favorite spot at 30 28.442 North/086 35.638 West, and there is enough swinging room for boats up to 45 feet. Protection is also good, though not quite on par with the anchorage that was just discussed. There are a few more unmarked shoals to be avoided at the entrance than are found on the easterly arm, but most navigators will be able to make good their entrance without mishap. For my money, I would choose the northeastern fork every time, but if you don't mind the addition of a few attractive homes in your landscape, the northwesterly haven can also be used with confidence.

NORTHERLY FORT WALTON WATERS NAVIGATION

Navigation of the aforementioned waters is, by and large, a veritable delight. There are a few unmarked shoals to bypass, but on a sunny day it's easy to spot the shallows. The clear water allows you to quickly pick out the sandy color of most shallow patches. On cloudy days or in low-light conditions, you must depend on your chart, compass, GPS, and the information contained in this account. Take your time (as always), keep a sharp watch on the sounder, and keep chart 11385 near the helm.

To enter the mouth of Garnier Bayou, and thereby gain access to all the northerly Fort Walton waters, set a course from the deeper waters of Choctawhatchee Bay to pass between unlighted daybeacon #4 (south of Lake Vivian) and flashing daybeacon #3. As you are cruising towards #3 and #4, be on guard against the shallows abutting Black Point, marked by flashing daybeacon #2, north and northeast of your course line. Obviously you should stay well south of #2 and not approach Black Point.

Be sure to pass well south of unlighted daybeacon #4. Chart 11385 correctly predicts shoal water north of this aid to navigation. Once between #4 to the north of your course line and #3 to the south, begin bending your course to the northwest and point to pass flashing daybeacon #5 by at least 100 yards to its northerly side. Shallows of a mere 2 to 4 feet lie south of #5.

Once abeam of #5, follow the deep water as Garnier Bayou takes a slow turn to the north. Soon you will see a sharp point to the east (marked by the designation "TANK" on chart 11385). A large condo project makes its home on this promontory. You can now turn southwest into Cinco Bayou or continue just a bit to the north and cut east into Shalimar Yacht Basin.

Cinco Bayou   The creek known as Cinco Bayou is easily cruised. Just remember that a fixed bridge with only 19 feet of vertical clearance crosses the stream some .9 nautical miles upstream.

Enter the bayou by cruising into its mid-width. Immediately after coming abeam of Smack Point to the southeast, you will spot the extensive docks and piers of the Fort Walton Yacht Club to port. You can cruise straight into the harbor with good depths. West of the docks there is some shallow water abutting the shoreline. Avoid this area by moving back out into the stream's center from the yacht club docks before continuing upstream.

Excellent depths continue on a broad channel through the fixed bridge. Once past the span, you can enter the small stream to the south on its mid-width, or you might choose the previously discussed anchorage to the north. When entering the northerly offshoot, be on guard against the charted shoal jutting out from the eastern banks. Favor the western shore when entering and picking a spot to drop anchor.

The southerly fork of Cinco Bayou also maintains a broad, deep channel until just shortly before it ends. Skippers cruising anywhere near the centerline should not have any difficulty.

It is an elementary study in navigation to continue upstream on the main southerly branch of Cinco Bayou, at least as far as the charted sharp turn to the southwest. If you choose to anchor in the turn, do not attempt to enter the charted offshoot to the north. It has shoal depths of 4 feet or less. Be sure to set your anchor and adjust your rode so that your vessel will not swing into these waters with a change in wind or tide.

Finally, the bottom begins to climb several hundred yards after the sharp turn to the southwest. Pilots of larger craft should discontinue their upstream cruising before reaching the charted shallows.

Shalimar Yacht Basin   Continue north past the sharp unnamed point west of the charted position of Lake Clyde for some 100 yards or so. You can then swing 90 degrees to the east and enter the yacht basin. There are two separate breakwater-enclosed harbors, each with its own entrance.

On Garnier Bayou   North of Shalimar Yacht Basin, the broad channel of Garnier Bayou sweeps under the previously described fixed bridge. Mariners needing more than 19 feet of vertical clearance must either unstep their mast or forgo cruising farther upstream.

After leaving the fixed span behind, the bayou opens out into a broad body of water. Depths are quite good except around the various points of land jutting out into the stream. Avoid these trouble spots and you should not have to worry about finding the bottom.

Eventually the stream breaks into three major forks. The waters to the east will first be reviewed, followed by Don's Bayou to the west, and finally Chula Vista Bayou and the upper reaches of Garnier Bayou to the north.

Hand Cove   Entry into the wide lower reaches of Hand Cove is facilitated by a spacious channel. As the northerly portion of the cove is approached, you will catch sight of a small island bisecting the waters. Pass this island on the mid-width of the channel to its *easterly* side. Do not attempt the western passage. It is quite shallow.

Once past the island, a broad pool of deep water will be sighted dead ahead. Avoid the extreme northerly end of the cove and you can drop the hook just about anywhere for a secure evening.

Poquito Bayou   Successful navigation of Poquito Bayou is an elementary matter of holding to the mid-width and scrupulously avoiding all points of land. Navigators wise in the ways of cruising off the beaten path will favor the opposite shoreline slightly whenever passing a sharp point.

Eventually, Poquito takes a sharp turn to the north. Minimum 7-foot water continues for quite some distance upstream until finally dropping a bit farther along.

Don's Bayou   When entering Don's Bayou, favor the northerly shore somewhat to avoid the shoal surrounding the charted point of land to the south. Soon you will pass into a large, pool-like area. If you continue upstream from this point, hold strictly to the mid-width between the two charted points constricting the channel to the north and south. There is shallow water surrounding both.

By holding to the centerline, you can continue upstream with good depths to the point where the stream splits into a *T*. Don't attempt to enter either arm of the *T*. While local small craft use this portion of the creek regularly, depths are much too uncertain for larger cruising craft.

Chula Vista Bayou   The entrance into Chula Vista Bayou calls for more caution than most of the other side-waters running off Garnier Bayou. Chula Vista's mouth is squeezed between a large shoal to the northeast and a smaller shallow patch to the southwest.

Cruise slowly into Chula Vista, favoring the southwestern shore, but don't approach these banks too closely. Keep an eagle eye on the sounder. If depths rise to less than 8 feet, you are encroaching upon the surrounding shoals.

On sunny days, it's easy to identify the shallow patches by their lighter color. As usual, the clear Florida Panhandle waters make this sort of "eyeball navigation" a breeze. On cloudy days or during low-light conditions, you must depend on your chart and sounder to stay off the bottom.

Once past the charted sharp point on the northeasterly banks, quickly cruise back towards the mid-width. As correctly noted on chart 11385, a small shoal borders the southwestern banks along this stretch. There is also a larger patch of charted shoals to the northeast.

Once past the shallows at the stream's entrance, you can cruise some .1 nautical miles upstream on Chula Vista and hold minimum 6-foot depths. Farther upstream, soundings drop off to 4- and 5-foot levels.

Most captains will want to anchor in the wide portion of the creek, just northwest of the sharp point on the entrance's northeastern banks. Be sure to favor the southwesterly side of the channel *slightly* when setting the hook in order to avoid the correctly charted shoal abutting the northeastern shoreline.

On Garnier Bayou   Cruising north on Garnier Bayou after leaving the entrance to Chula Vista Bayou behind, you will soon approach a charted point striking out from the western banks. Shoal water has built out much farther into the channel from this point than is shown on the edition of chart 11385 available at the time of this writing. Favor the easterly portion of the channel when passing through.

Upper Garnier Bayou Anchorages   The channel on the northerly extreme of Garnier Bayou resembles a "Y." Two deep arms of the creek extend to the northeast and northwest respectively, separated by a broad patch of shoal water.

As described earlier, the northeasterly fork is the best anchorage. To enter, simply favor the southeasterly banks in order to avoid the shallows to the northwest. Minimum 9-foot depths are carried to within 100 yards of the shoreline at the upstream (northeastern) end of the cove. Consider dropping the hook in the charted patch of 10-foot water.

Navigating the northwesterly arm calls for a bit more caution. The sharp point bordering the southern side of this entrance has built out farther than is shown on the current edition of chart 11385. When entering this portion of the creek, you must give the point a wide berth, yet still guard against slipping into the broad patch of shoal water to the north. On sunny days, "eyeball navigation" greatly simplifies this process.

After cruising for some 100 yards past the southern point, begin favoring the western banks slightly. You can drop the hook anywhere you choose short of the small patch of charted shallows on the arm's northwesterly corner.

ICW from Fort Walton to Pensacola Bay

From the southwestern terminus of Choctawhatchee Bay, the Gulf Coast ICW follows the broadening waters of Santa Rosa Sound to the easterly reaches of lower Pensacola Bay. This is an enchanting passage with beautiful shorelines. The mainland banks exhibit light but sumptuous residential development set amidst beautiful pine and hardwood forests. The barrier islands to the south present a striking contrast. This stretch of shoreline is mostly protected from development by the twin agencies of the U.S. Air Force and the National Park Service. To the east, the banks are part of Eglin Air Force Base, while the westerly section belongs to the Gulf Coast National Seashore. The barrier islands are composed mostly of low-lying sand dunes covered by scrub growth, though some wooded sites occupy the northerly portion of the banks. It is wonderful to discover this natural land just where you would expect heavy development.

Facilities are adequate, though closely grouped. Several marinas and a repair yard serve cruising craft on the easterly portion of Santa Rosa Sound, known as the Narrows. As the Waterway approaches the entrance to Pensacola Bay, two additional facilities are again found on Little Sabine Bay and Pensacola Beach. In between however, cruisers are mostly on their own. Make sure your tanks are topped off before leaving the Fort Walton facilities (in the Narrows) behind.

Sheltered overnight havens dot this portion of the ICW like grains of sand. Everywhere you look there are wonderful places to spend the night tranquilly swinging on the hook. Most of these anchorages are not sheltered from all quarters. Skippers must pick their overnight stops with a ready ear for the forecasted wind direction and speed.

To be sure, the Waterway's run through Santa Rosa Sound continues the Florida Panhandle's tradition of wonderful cruising grounds. Mariners will find more than enough reasons to linger for a while and enjoy the various sights.

Facilities on the Narrows
(Various Lats/Lons—see below)

Actually, the first two facilities cruisers will encounter when leaving the Choctawhatchee behind are located on the bay's southerly banks, east of the entrance to the Narrows.

Deckhands Marina and Marina Motel (also known as Leeside Inn and Marina), south of

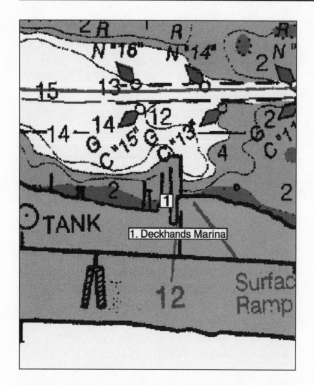

1. Deckhands Marina

Waste pump-out service is on hand, as well as showers and a Laundromat. A restaurant, tiki-bar lounge, and the on-site motel (known as the Leeside Inn) are located just behind the harbor. An adjacent, heated swimming pool is open to the use of transients.

Deckhands Marina (850) 243-1598
http://www.leesideinn.com

Approach depth—7 to 9 feet
Dockside depth—7 to 9 feet
Accepts transients—yes
Transient dockage rate -well above average
Fixed wooden piers—yes
Dockside power connections—30- and 50-amp
Dockside water connections—yes
Laundromat—yes
Showers—yes
Waste pump-out—yes
Mechanical repairs—yes
Below-waterline repairs—yes
Restaurant—on-site

unlighted can buoy #15 (standard mile 225, 30 23.883 North/086 35.005 West), welcomes visitors and offers overnight transient dockage but no fuel. Deckhands boasts full repair services and reasonably good dockage in a slat wooden-plank breakwater-enclosed harbor. Repairs for both gasoline- and diesel-powered plants are offered, and the yard maintains a 35-ton travelift for haul-outs. Depths on Deckhands' entrance channel run between 7 and 9 feet with similar soundings found dockside. Protection should be adequate in all but very strong northerly blows.

Transient berths are provided at fixed wooden slips and piers with 30- and 50-amp power and fresh-water connections. Overnight-dockage rates double (and are well above average) if you do not also rent a room in the adjacent motel.

Just next door, Marina Motel offers overnight transient berths at fixed wooden piers with power and water connections. Protection is not quite as good here as at Deckhands, but it should be adequate in anything except strong northerly winds. The adjacent motel is particularly convenient for water-weary cruisers. Like its neighbor, Deckhands Marina, overnight berth rates double here if you are not also staying at the motel.

Marina Motel (850) 244-1129

Approach depth—6 to 17 feet
Dockside depth—7 to 12 feet
Accepts transients—yes
Transient dockage rates—above average
Fixed wooden piers—yes
Dockside power connections—15- and 20-amp

Deckhands Marina, Fort Walton Beach

Dockside water connections—yes
Laundromat—yes
Showers—yes
Waste pump-out—yes
Restaurant—nearby

Several marinas and one boatyard are grouped along the northerly banks of the Narrows between the Brooks-Fort Walton Beach fixed bridge (this span crosses the Waterway west of unlighted daybeacon #4 near standard mile 223) and flashing daybeacon #21. An alternate channel carrying at least 7 feet of water serves these facilities. Its easterly entrance (standard mile 222.5) is discovered cutting north from the ICW between unlighted daybeacons #6 and #8, while the alternate channel's westerly entrance (standard mile 222) makes off from

the Waterway between unlighted daybeacons #16 and #20.

While some care must be exercised in leaving and entering the Waterway from this cut, the channel carries minimum 7-foot depths, with typical readings of 8 to 14 feet. The passage borders extensive development and numerous docks on the northern shore.

Moving east to west, cruisers will first encounter the fixed piers of Marina Bay Resort (850-244-5132, 30 24.140 North/086 36.637 West). This marina is associated with a large, time-share condo complex. Marina Bay no longer maintains any transient slip space. So, unless you are a condo owner or a guest of an owner, the only option is to keep on trucking.

Passing captains and crew will note the

fixed wooden pier and piling-lined slips of Santa Rosa Sound Brewery and Cafe (850-664-2739) to the west of Marina Bay. This popular restaurant (see below) is happy to allow its waterborne patrons to moor here while dining. No overnight stays are in the offing. Dockside soundings seem to run in the 6½- to 8-foot region.

Next up is the fixed wooden pier of the Summerhouse Restaurant (850-244-1553, see below). In a similar vein to the Santa Rosa Brewery pier, customers are welcome to dock here while partaking of lunch or dinner, but when the meal is over, it's time to move on. Soundings at the Summerhouse pier run 7 feet or better.

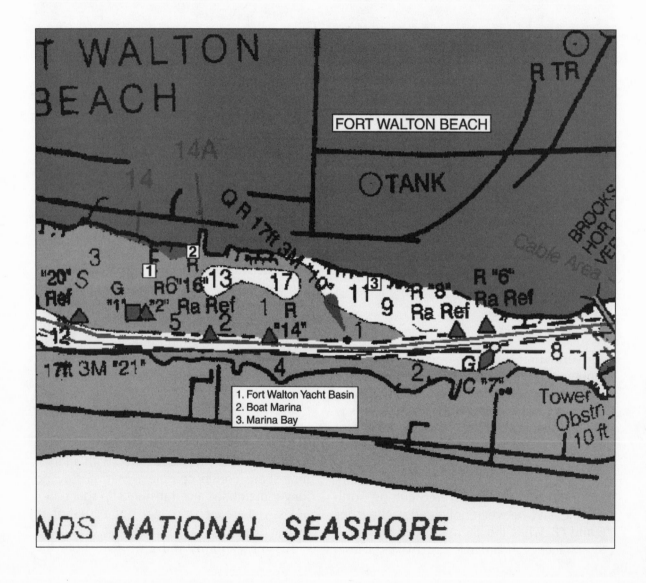

1. Fort Walton Yacht Basin
2. Boat Marina
3. Marina Bay

The Boat Boatyard & Marina is found farther to the west, near 30 24.203 North/086 37.106 West. During out last visit to this facility in the fall of 2002, it was apparent that things had changed at this once-happy marina. In fact, the entire complex had a "down on its luck" feeling. The once-popular ship's store that used to be located in "the Boat" (see below) has long been closed. The on-site (nonair-conditioned) showers were in unacceptably poor condition, and the adjacent repair yard did not seem to be terribly active. While we were unable to talk with the owner, rumor has it that a death in the family has changed the outlook of this marina's management.

On the other hand, the dockage basin still appears to be in good shape. Transient and resident berths are very reasonably priced and composed of fixed wooden piers. Depths alongside run some 6 to 7 feet at low tide. All slips offer 30- and 50-amp power and fresh-water connections. Gasoline and diesel fuel can be purchased dockside. There is also a small-but-adequate Laundromat on the premises.

The Boat's adjacent repair yard features two travelifts rated at 30 and 50 tons respectively. Full mechanical repairs for both gasoline- and diesel-powered plants are available through the on-site firm of Hays Marine (850-243-7873).

The Santa Rosa Brewery and Cafe, reviewed below, is within an easy step of The Boat's docks. There are also several other excellent dining choices which are reviewed in the next section of this chapter.

A convenience store lies just across Highway 98 from the marina grounds. The nearest supermarket is some 1½ miles away. You may want to consider a taxi ride if your galley needs call for a trip to this facility. Check out the "Numbers to Know" section below.

Anyone wanting to spend a night or two with dry ground under their feet will find the Best Inn (100 SW Miracle Strip Parkway, 850-244-0121) very convenient. It is found immediately adjacent to The Boat.

The Boat Marina is named for the huge 150-foot, 600-ton, vintage-1920s, concrete-hulled troop transport that makes its permanent home on the easterly margins of the dockage basin. It is by far the marina's most prominent feature. As you look at the Boat, you may wonder just what it might take to move this mammoth vessel out of its seemingly secure berth. The answer is Hurricane Opal. That great storm picked up this concrete-hulled behemoth and set it back down canted at a crazy angle. Righting the vessel required an intricate and demanding process involving two tugboats and a huge crane. This effort made quite a story in the local press.

The Boat Boatyard & Marina (850) 244-2722

Approach depth—7-14 feet
Dockside depth—6-7 feet
Accepts transients—yes
Transient-dockage rate—below average
Fixed wooden piers—yes
Dockside power connections—30, & 50 amp
Dockside water connection—yes
Showers-yes
Laundromat—yes
Gasoline—yes
Diesel fuel—yes
Mechanical repairs—yes
Below-waterline repairs—yes
Restaurant—several nearby

Westernmost of the alternate channel facilities is Fort Walton Yacht Basin (30 24.178 North/086 37.218 West). This marina offers

The "Boat" at the Boat Boatyard and Marina, Fort Walton Beach

transient dockage at fixed wooden piers with 30- and 50-amp power and fresh-water connections. Many (though not all) of this firm's slips are covered, relegating them to the use of smaller powercraft. However, there are enough open berths lining the outside portion of the dockage basin to accommodate several visitors. These outside docks are not terribly well sheltered, but this would only be a problem in heavy weather. Depths alongside run from 7 to 8 feet. A single shower is located on site, but there is no complimentary laundromat. Full fueling services are readily available as is waste pump-out. Mechanical repairs can sometimes be arranged through independent, local contractors.

The adjacent Original Waterfront Crab Shack restaurant (850-664-0345) is a real favorite with the local crowd. The cuisine here is simply superb! This writer's crab-cake sandwich was absolutely first class, and my first-rate, first mate was equally taken with her grouper sandwich. We plan to return here time and time again! The Crab Shack features both outside and inside dining.

Original Waterfront Crab Shack restaurant, Fort Walton Beach

Fort Walton Yacht Basin (850) 244-5725

Approach depth—7-14 feet
Dockside depth—7-8 feet
Accepts transients—limited number of slips
  available
Transient-dockage rate—below average
Fixed wooden piers—yes
Dockside power connections—30 & 50 amp
Dockside water connections—yes
Waste pump-out—yes
Gasoline—yes
Diesel fuel—yes
Mechanical repairs—independent contractors
Restaurant—on site

Fort Walton Restaurants and Telephone Numbers

Fort Walton Beach can lay claim to many fine dining spots, several of which are convenient to cruising visitors. Several are reviewed below, but this list is by no means exhaustive. Don't be shy about striking out on your own and experimenting. Chances are that your culinary adventures will be rewarded.

Located just west of Marina Bay and featuring its own dockage (see above), Santa Rosa Brewery and Cafe (54 SE Miracle Strip

Parkway, 850-664-2739) has the reputation of being one of the best places to satisfy your appetite in Fort Walton Beach. Succulent seafood as well as sandwiches and delectable beef-chicken dishes are complemented most ably by the restaurant's many varieties of on-site brewed beer. There is a fine view of the Waterway from the rear windows.

If your taste buds call for some of the best catch of the day you will ever enjoy, spare no effort to find your way to the Staff Restaurant (24 SE Miracle Strip Parkway, 850-243-3482, open evenings only). Located a scant two blocks from the Boat Boatyard & Marina, this is the oldest seafood restaurant still in operation on the Florida Panhandle. Trust me on this one, dear reader; the food at the Staff is nothing short of spectacular.

Another good choice is the Summerhouse Restaurant (2 SW Miracle Strip Parkway, 850-244-1553). Featuring its own dockage for customers arriving by water (see above), this dining spot is a striking sight from the water. We have not yet had a chance to sample Summerhouse's bill of fare, but the restaurant has been recommended to this writer by several local marina personnel.

Numbers to know in Fort Walton Beach:

Black and Gold Taxi—850-244-7303
Fort Walton Beach Taxi—850-654-0005
Enterprise Rent-A-Car—850-243-4446
Hertz—850-651-0612
Guardian Car Rentals—850-863-2992
West Marine (248A Eglin Parkway)—
   850-863-8700
West Marine (218 Eglin Parkway)—
   850-664-2254

Santa Rosa Sound Anchorages (Various Lats/Lons—see below)

There are any number of excellent overnight anchoring spots available to cruisers between the alternate Fort Walton channel, discussed above, and Pensacola Beach. As long as they keep in mind the forecast wind direction and speed, visiting captains can be assured of finding many pleasant overnight stops. The best of these anchorages are reviewed below.

The charted patch of deep water east of flashing daybeacon #37 (standard mile 219.5, 30 24.375 North/086 39.381 West) makes a good overnight stop in northerly or light to moderate southerly winds. This would not be an appropriate anchorage in strong easterly or westerly blows. There should be enough swinging room for most sizes of pleasure craft. Skippers anchoring here will be open to the wake of all passing vessels. Minimum 10-foot depths are held to within 50 yards of the northern shores, though care must be exercised to avoid the charted

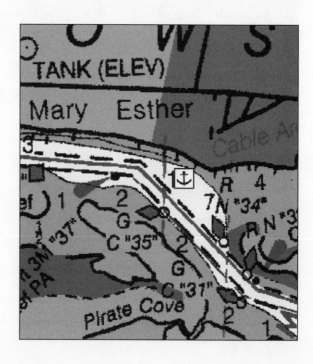

shallows to the east. The anchorage is over-looked by moderate residential development.

Southeast of unlighted can buoy #69 (standard mile 215, 30 24.167 North/086 43.730 West), deep water runs well toward the southerly banks. Minimum depths are 7 feet, but navigators must be careful to avoid the charted finger of shoal water to the southwest. The shoreline exhibits well-wooded banks which give excellent protection in southerly winds. There is even some protection from eastern and western breezes, but not enough for strong blows. Northerly winds above 15 knots would make things a little hairy.

A better choice is found south of flashing daybeacon #71 (standard mile 214.5, 30 24.118 North/086 44.095 West). Minimum depths of 10 to 15 feet run almost to the southerly banks. There is plenty of swinging room for boats as large as 50 feet. The charted point and shoal to the west give good protection from westerly winds, while the heavily timbered banks are a sufficient buffer from even strong southerly blows. Fresh breezes from the northerly or easterly quarter would, however, produce a very different and undoubtedly uncomfortable situation. When the capricious wind is blowing from the appropriate direction, this is a great spot to drop the hook in a beautiful setting. Remember, though, it is open to the wake of vessels passing on the ICW.

The charted cove southwest of unlighted daybeacon #73 (standard mile 214.5, 30 23.994 North/086 44.333 West) makes an excellent haven when winds are not blowing from the north or west. The easterly portion of the cove's shoreline has wooded shores, and some sort of Air Force installation looks out from the charted point to the east. While not quite as protected as

the anchorage discussed below, this is yet another good spot on Santa Rosa Sound to drop the hook when the wind chooses to cooperate.

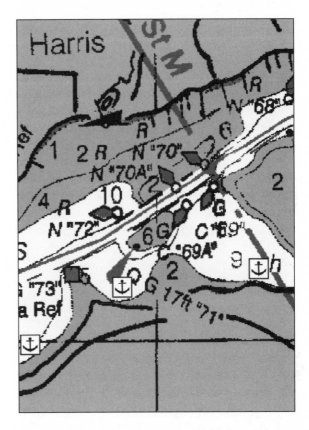

Probably the best overnight anchorage between Fort Walton and Pensacola Beach, in all but particularly strong northerly blows, is found on the charted cove just east of Manatee Point (standard mile 213.5, 30 23.976 North/086 45.267 West), itself immediately east of flashing daybeacon #75. On several occasions we have observed large commercial barges anchored in this haven, waiting for strong winds to subside. There is no better recommendation for any anchorage. You can be assured that such commercial professionals make a point of scouting out the best havens on their selected routes.

Minimum depths of 7 to 10+ feet are held well into the rear of the cove, but skippers must be careful to avoid the charted shoals to the east. On a sunny day, one can spot the shallow water abutting the shoreline by eye. Under these conditions you can cruise quite close to the sheltered banks, remembering always to leave your craft enough swinging room to avoid the shallows should the wind change direction. Pleasure craft as large as 45 feet should find plenty of room. To repeat myself, in all but strong northerly blows above 20 knots, this is without much doubt the best anchorage on this portion of the Gulf Coast ICW. Visiting cruisers should think long and hard before passing it by.

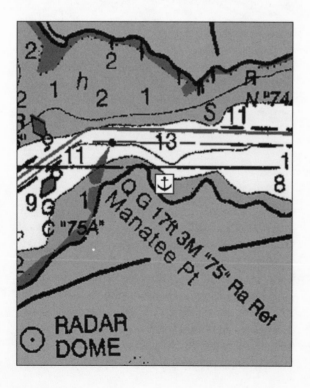

The large bay abutting the northerly banks between flashing daybeacons #78 and #80 may look good on chart 11385, but it is really quite open to all but northerly breezes. Shoal water extends for some distance out from the shoreline, and caution must be exercised to drop the hook well away from the charted 1- and 2-foot shallows. In light airs, captains could cruise far enough from the ICW for a comfortable overnight stay here, but if the winds should freshen during the night, the morning could bring a very different story.

Another good anchorage when southerly winds are blowing is encountered south-southeast of flashing daybeacon #81(standard mile 210, 30 23.599 North/086 48.500 West). The charted point to the west would also give some protection from breezes wafting from this quarter. By cruising southeast from #81, cruisers can take advantage of 7-foot minimum depths to within 150 yards of the southerly banks. The banks are studded with scrub-topped sand dunes and overlooked by some sort of Air Force installation.

Wild-eyed captains piloting craft under 38 feet might consider skirting the unmarked shoals south of unlighted can buoy #83 (standard mile 209, 30 23.455 North/086 49.707 West) and tracking a course to the deep water abutting the southerly banks. Successful navigation of this passage is a tricky process indeed.

If you do successfully bypass the shoal water, minimum 6½-foot depths are held to within 100 yards of shore. The undeveloped banks are composed of the usual sand dunes and grassy growth. The charted radar dome is readily visible to the southwest. All in all, considering the other superior anchorages within a mile or so both east and west on the Waterway, this spot

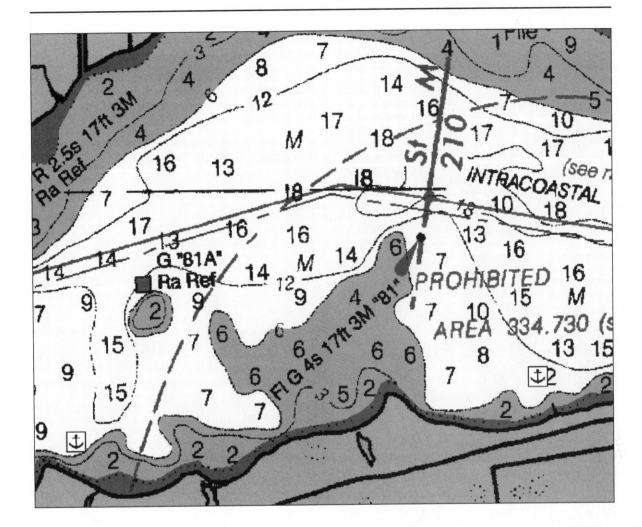

can only be considered as an emergency anchorage or a haven for those skippers who just have to boldly anchor where no man has anchored before.

The best anchorage on Santa Rosa Sound in a northerly blow is found on the charted deep-water cove west of Lower Pritchard Long Point (northwest of flashing daybeacon #82, standard mile 209, 30 24.121 North/086 50.188 West). The enchanting shoreline is ringed by a pretty beach of white sand set amidst a backdrop of tall pines and a few private homes. The waters are so clear that they seem to scream for exploration by mask and snorkel. Even if you don't plan to stop for the whole evening, this would be a great place to set the lunch hook and take a swimming break during warm summer afternoons.

Minimum depths of 6 feet are held to within 100 yards of the banks, while deeper soundings

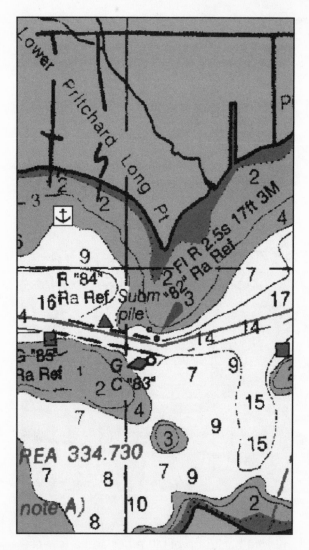

the very best spots on Santa Rosa Sound to spend a night.

Some local boats occasionally anchor on both the eastern and western sides of the Navarre Bridge (standard mile 207) in the charted deeper water to the north. While this area is certainly okay for a lunch stop, the just-discussed overnight havens to the east are much to be preferred.

West of the Navarre Bridge, there are no more anchorage possibilities for some 8.5 nautical miles. West of flashing daybeacon #129 (standard mile 197, 30 21.530 North/087 01.212 West), cautious navigators piloting craft under 40 feet in length can follow the tongue of deep water flowing south toward Santa Rosa Island. With very careful navigation, you can hold minimum depths of 8 feet (with soundings of 10 to 14 feet being the norm) all the way to within 50 yards of shore, west of the charted point of land on the southerly banks. Be sure to read the navigational information concerning this anchorage presented later in this chapter before attempting entry. In calm weather or with winds blowing from the south, this would be a good spot to while away the evening hours. You might even consider breaking out the dinghy and going ashore. The banks here are part of the Gulf Coast National Seashore and are composed primarily of undeveloped sand dunes. They seem to beg for exploration. The point to the east gives some protection in easterly breezes but protection is scant from westerly winds and totally nonexistent in northerly blows. Be sure to consult the latest forecast before choosing this anchorage.

The last two overnight stops worth considering east of Pensacola Beach are found east

of 7 to 9 feet can be expected a bit farther out from shore. There is probably enough swinging room for most vessels. The point to the east gives good protection when winds are blowing from this quarter, and the well-wooded shores provide sufficient lee for any northerly winds short of a full gale. Along with the anchorage east of Manatee Point, this is one of

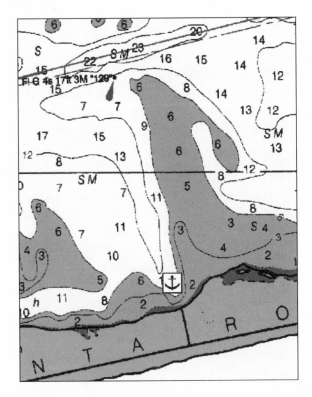

and west of the sharp point protruding out into the sound south of flashing daybeacon #131 (standard mile 193.5). While navigators must be cautious to stay well away from the charted shoal building out from Range Point, minimum 8- to 10-foot depths can be held well in toward shore to the east and west of the shallows. Again, on sunny days, the clear water allows you to see exactly where the depths take a turn for the worse. Obviously, the western cove (near 30 20.832 North/087 04.878 West) would be best with winds blowing from the easterly quarter, and the east-side haven (near 30 21.097 North/087 04.411 West) would be better if breezes are out of the west. Both are very well sheltered from southerly winds, while neither affords any protection

whatsoever from northerly blows. Most boats can make use of these anchorages, as long as the extensive shallows surrounding the point are carefully avoided. The shoreline consists of the usual scrub-covered sand dunes so typical of this area.

Pensacola Beach Facilities (Standard Mile 189)

West of flashing daybeacon #133, the ICW hurries toward the high-rise Pensacola Beach Bridge. Some low-key facilities are still found on the southern banks east of the fixed, high-rise span. Captains piloting craft that draw *less than* 3 feet can follow the deep water south of flashing daybeacon #133 to the southerly shore of charted Fishing Bend cove. Here you

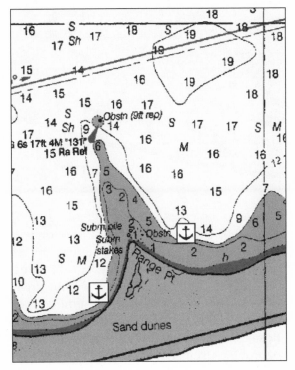

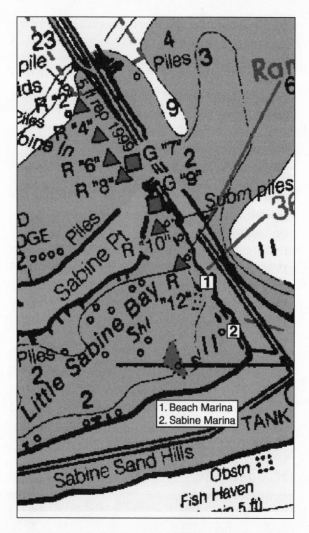

1. Beach Marina
2. Sabine Marina

can tie to a pier associated with a large shopping mall. This is a very popular spot on summer weekends, and waterborne visitors will undoubtedly observe numerous "hobies," water-skiers, and sun worshipers in the area.

The Santa Rosa Yacht Club, formerly Mel's Marina (850-934-1005), fronts onto Santa Rosa Sound's northerly shoreline immediately east of the fixed Pensacola Beach Bridge. This facility is now completely private, and its wet slips are strictly reserved for members.

Little Sabine Bay Facilities

Immediately west of Pensacola Beach Bridge, a well-marked channel skirts south between extensive shoals to Little Sabine Bay. Two marinas are located on the eastern banks near the bay's entrance. One offers services for visitors, while the other is reserved for resident craft.

The Little Sabine Bay entrance channel is subject to periodic shoaling, but it currently carries minimum soundings of 5½ to 6 feet of water, with 6- to 7-foot soundings being the norm. One misstep, however, and you will find waters sporting depths of 4 feet or less outside of the marked cut.

You will first encounter the impressive concrete-breakwater-enclosed harbor of the Beach Marina, south-southeast of unlighted daybeacon #12, near 30 20.189 North/087 08.707 West. This facility used to be known as the Moorings of Pensacola Beach, but the ownership has changed since those days, and the new incarnation has much to offer visiting cruisers.

One look will tell you that Beach Marina is an obviously well-managed facility catering primarily to larger powercraft. Transients are gladly accepted for overnight dockage at fixed concrete piers with full power and water connections. Low-water depths in the basin run around 6 to 7 feet. Advance reservations are recommended. Gasoline and diesel fuel are available, as is a waste pump-out service.

Beach Marina boasts a fleet of rental bicycles. These basic units greatly facilitate a visit to the nearby beach.

The second story of the impressive three-story building just behind the harbor now houses the Market on the Island Deli (850-916-7192). This is actually a surprisingly complete grocery store with fresh meats, some fresh produce, and, of course, a large deli. The market receives our vote as the best on-site food store anywhere along the entire Northern Gulf Coast. Cruising chefs should make every effort to make the acquaintance of this unusually well-supplied and well-sited market and deli!

The top floor is occupied by Bobaloo's on the Beach Restaurant. This location has been the site of an almost dizzying array of restaurants over the last ten years. They seem to come and go almost overnight. We hope that Bobaloo's lasts longer, but to be on the safe side, you'd better call ahead before pinning your exclusive hopes on dining ashore here. By the way, we have not yet had a chance to sample the fare at Bobaloo's.

Beach Marina (850) 932-8466
   http://www.fishpensacola.com

Approach depth—5-8 feet
Dockside depth—6 feet
Accepts transients—yes
Transient-dockage rate—above average
Fixed concrete piers—yes
Dockside power connections—30-, 50-, and a
   few 100-amp
Dockside water connections—yes
Waste pump-out—yes
Gasoline—yes
Diesel fuel—yes
Grocery store and deli—on site
Restaurant—on site

Just south of Beach Marina, you will pass a series of semiprivate piers, followed closely by the fixed, wooden docks of Sabine Marina (850-932-1904, 30 20.083 North/087 08.649 West) overlooking the westerly banks. Even though landside visitors may spot a sign in the adjacent parking lot that advertises transient slips, we have yet to see anything like a dockmaster or any other marina personnel at this facility, even after repeated visits. Based upon this less-than-sterling experience, we encourage our fellow cruisers to look elsewhere for an overnight stop.

Should you ignore this advice and be lucky enough to secure a berth, expect fixed wooden piers, plus fresh-water and 30-amp power hookups. Depths alongside seem to run 5 to 6 feet at low tide. No other services are available on-site.

Little Sabine Bay

The remainder of Little Sabine Bay is not as hospitable as it would appear at first glance. The shoreline is lined by heavy, but not unattractive, residential development. Many houses have their own private piers and both powerboats and sailcraft can be seen docked all around the bay. Be warned that these locals know something that is just hinted at on chart 11378. A huge shoal occupies almost the entire center section of this body of water. While it is possible for local mariners to follow an unmarked channel skirting the entire circumference of the bay, most visiting cruisers will want to confine their travels to the channel leading from Santa Rosa Sound to Little Sabine Bay.

Some boats occasionally anchor in the deep water just south of Sabine Marina. Protection is quite good and depths run from 6 to 10 feet. However, this is far from an isolated haven. Those who prefer swinging on the hook rather than making use of the bay's excellent facilities should probably consider one of the many anchorages to the east on Santa Rosa Sound.

FORT WALTON TO PENSACOLA BAY NAVIGATION

The Gulf Coast ICW in this region calls for more than its share of navigational caution. The channel cuts first one way and then another to bypass the many surrounding shoals. On the easterly portion of the passage, shallow water is quite prevalent and even a small deviation from the Waterway can result in an impromptu dry-docking.

This section of the ICW is quite well marked, but surprisingly, most (though by no means all) of the aids are unlighted. Even some of the critical twists and turns are marked only by lightless buoys and daybeacons. Consequently, nighttime passage is not recommended. Even small, outboard craft would do well to refrain from cruising this portion of the ICW after dark.

A fixed bridge with 50 feet of vertical clearance crosses the ICW just west of the intersection of the Narrows and Choctawhatchee Bay. Tall sailcraft that cannot clear this height must put to sea at Destin or Panama City and make the run to Pensacola Inlet across the Gulf. This is one of the Northern Gulf ICW fixed bridges with a height of less than 65 feet that is *not* currently being replaced.

The easterly portion of Santa Rosa Sound and the Narrows is mostly protected and your passage should not be marred by an unwelcome chop. Farther to the west Santa Rosa Sound opens out into a good-sized body of water. If winds exceed 15, or particularly 20 knots, it can make for a very dusty crossing. If possible, plan your passage to coincide with fair weather.

Leaving Choctawhatchee Bay   From a position abeam of flashing daybeacon #59 on Choctawhatchee Bay (lying off Cobbs Point), cruisers bound westward on the Northern Gulf ICW should set course to eventually come abeam of flashing daybeacon #61, well northwest of the East Pass entrance channel.

Between #59 (north of Cobbs Point) and #61, your course will run within sight of the East Pass Inlet channel to the south. Don't mistake any of the markers on this passage for flashing daybeacon #61.

Be sure to come abeam of flashing daybeacon #61 by at least 200 yards to its northerly side. Shoal waters are building from the south towards this marker. The best plan is to give it a wide berth.

Once abeam of #61, set course for the gap between flashing daybeacon #1 and unlighted nun buoy #2. West of #1 and #2 the Waterway begins its passage through an improved channel leading to the easterly headwaters of the Narrows. While the ICW is well marked with numerous unlighted nun and can buoys (plus a few daybeacons), the surrounding waters are quite shoal. Care must be taken to stay strictly in the marked cut. West of unlighted nun buoy #14 and can #13, depths open out a bit on either side of the ICW channel. However, soundings outside of the Waterway are still suspect and captains would do well to stay in the buoyed route.

On the ICW   A patch of very shallow water encroaches on the northern flank of the ICW as it begins its approach to the eastern face of the Brooks-Fort Walton Beach fixed bridge. Two aids to navigation, unlighted daybeacons #4 and #4A, mark this hazard. Be sure to pass both #4 and #4A to their southerly sides. While cruising along this approach to the Brooks Bridge, watch your stern to make sure leeway is not easing you to the north onto the flanking shallows.

The Brooks fixed bridge crosses the ICW some .3 nautical miles west of unlighted daybeacon #4. Chart 11385 lists the vertical clearance of this span as 50 feet, but conversations with several of the marina operators in Fort Walton Beach lead this writer to conclude that during high water, you can only count on a clearance of 48 feet. Even at 50 feet, this span's clearance is a stumbling block for many sailcraft.

The Narrows Facility Channel   The alternate channel leading to the collection of Fort Walton marinas and boatyards flanking the Waterway's northerly banks cuts to the northwest between unlighted daybeacons #6 and #8. To enter the alternate passage, leave the Waterway soon after passing #6.

Once past #6, simply follow the shoreline on around to the west. Stay no more than 25 yards from the banks, and you will not encroach upon the charted shallows to the south.

To reenter the Waterway on the western end of the alternate channel, pass between unlighted daybeacons #1 and #2 and then head due south out into the mid-width of the ICW passage. You will meet up with the Waterway channel shortly after unlighted

daybeacon #16 comes abeam, well east of your course. Do not attempt to cruise directly from a position between #1 and #2 to either unlighted daybeacons #16 or #20. These maneuvers will land you in 4 feet of water or less.

Cruisers eastbound on the ICW making for the alternate channel should continue cruising east on the Waterway until the mid-width of the alternate passage's westerly entrance, between #1 and #2, is directly abeam to the north. Only then should you cut north and point to pass between #1 and #2.

On the ICW   From unlighted daybeacon #20 to flashing daybeacon #30, the channel is fairly straightforward and reasonably easy to follow.

At flashing daybeacon #30, the ICW takes a sharp jog to the northwest and passes between flashing daybeacon #32 and unlighted can buoy #31. Favor #31 slightly as you pass. Shoaling from the north and northeast seems to creep closer and closer to #32 and the Waterway's next aid to navigation, unlighted nun buoy #32A, between dredging cycles.

Northwest of unlighted nun buoy #34 the Waterway runs quickly towards the charted patch of deep water near "Mary Esther."

Mary Esther Anchorage   This anchorage is easily entered by continuing on the Waterway until you are just short of unlighted can buoy #35. You can then cruise toward the northeasterly shore. Be sure to set the hook before encountering the narrow patch of shoal water abutting the shoreline.

On the ICW   The Waterway passage continues to be well marked and easy to follow for some distance west of flashing daybeacon #37. After passing #42, the residential development associated with Fort Walton begins to fall away and houses break the beautiful landscape less often.

Between unlighted nun buoy #58 and flashing daybeacon #60, a short, charted channel cutting into the northern shore leads to a small marina for the use of military and service personnel associated with Eglin Air Force Base. Gasoline can be purchased by anyone, however. Approach and dockside depths are a minimum of 6 feet.

West of flashing daybeacon #60, a series of nun and can buoys outline a narrow section of the ICW channel. Continue to pass to the south of all red, even-numbered aids to navigation, and north of all green, odd-numbered markers.

South and southwest of unlighted can buoy #61, an alternate channel cuts south and then west, rejoining the ICW near unlighted nun buoy #68. While local captains sometimes use this cut, it is unmarked and borders on very shallow water. Visiting cruisers are strictly advised to stay in the marked Waterway channel.

Triple Anchorages   Three anchorages are available on the southern shores of the Waterway between flashing daybeacons #67 and #74. The first is found on the charted bubble of deep water southeast of unlighted can buoy #69. To enter, cruise south-southeast from #69, being careful to avoid the charted tongue of shoal water to the east. Deep water runs up quite close to shore in this haven. On a clear, sunny day, you can easily see where depths finally begin to rise. Remember to leave plenty of swinging room to avoid the shallows should the wind change directions.

The middle of the three havens comes up southwest of flashing daybeacon #71. Come abeam of #71 to its immediate westerly side, and then set a course to the south. Stay away from the charted point to the west. The shoal water around here seems to be building outward. Navigators must also be on guard against the charted finger of shoal water extending north from the shoreline, just south of unlighted can buoy #69A. Good depths do not run as close to shore here as in the just-discussed anchorage. Be sure to set the hook well north of the banks.

To the west, captains may also choose to enter the deep-water cove southwest of unlighted daybeacon #73. To enter, leave the ICW about midway between #73 and flashing daybeacon #74. Sound your way carefully in toward the southern shoreline. Again, there is a fairly wide band of shallows abutting the shoreline. Drop anchor well short of this problem area.

On the Waterway   The charted shoal southeast of unlighted daybeacon #73 is building outward. Favor the northerly and northwesterly side of the channel when passing and don't approach #73 too closely.

Manatee Point Anchorage   To enter the excellent anchorage east of Manatee Point, continue cruising on the Waterway channel until the mid-width of the cove lying just east of Manatee Point is directly abeam to the south. Then, cut in toward the middle. Consider dropping the hook before approaching to within less than 100 yards of the southerly banks. As correctly forecast on chart 11385, a large shelf of shallow water flanks the shoreline. Good water runs quite close to the westerly banks between the bay's entrance and a midpoint on its north-to-south axis, but you must take care to avoid the charted shoal surrounding the cove's easterly point.

On the ICW   West of flashing daybeacon #78, the ICW passes out into the wider stretches of Santa Rosa Sound. With winds over 15 knots, chop can become quite an annoyance. As you move farther to the west, the sound becomes ever wider and, with strong breezes, ever rougher. While wave conditions are probably not dangerous unless winds exceed 25 knots, the sound's chop can certainly shake the plates around in the galley.

Visiting cruisers studying chart 11385 might look upon the large cove northwest of #78 as an anchorage possibility. However, this body of water is open to all winds save northerly breezes. With so many well-protected havens nearby, it makes sense to choose another spot for an overnight stay.

Study chart 11385 for a moment and you will quickly note the large shoal jutting out from Upper Pritchard Long Point, north of flashing daybeacon #80. This shoal seems to be building outward. Give #80 a wide berth.

Open Anchorages   To enter the somewhat open anchorage south and southeast of flashing daybeacon #81, cut in towards the southern banks some 250 yards east of flashing daybeacon #81. Point towards the charted tower, which you will quickly spy to the south. This course should help you avoid the charted shallows to the west. Be aware of the large shelf of 2-foot water jutting out from the shoreline. Drop the hook well short of this hazard.

The anchorage south of flashing daybeacon #82 is one of the trickiest on Santa Rosa Sound. Only wild-eyed captains piloting boats less than 38 feet in length should attempt entry. If you should decide to brave the entrance, depart from the waterway east of unlighted can buoy #83. Carefully set a compass course to pass between the charted shallows to the southeast and the shoal to the west.

Once past the west-side shallows, you can cruise to within 175 yards of the southerly shoreline with good depths. Be sure to set the hook well north of the shallows adjoining the shoreline.

On the ICW   Study chart 11385 for a moment and notice the patch of 2-foot shallows south of unlighted daybeacon #81A. Be sure to pass north of #81A unless you like the sound of your keel meeting up with the sandy bottom.

Lower Pritchard Long Point Anchorage   Navigation of the excellent anchorage west of Lower Pritchard Long Point is a simple example of coastal navigation. Set a course from either unlighted daybeacon #85 or flashing daybeacon #87 for the mid-width of the wide patch of deep water to the north. As usual, a broad band of shallows flanks the northerly banks.

On the Waterway West of flashing daybeacon #90, the ICW soon passes under the fixed Navarre Bridge. This is another one of those spans with only 50 feet of vertical clearance. Sailcraft skippers take note.

After leaving the Navarre Bridge behind, the Waterway flows through a dredged channel outlined by numerous unlighted nun and can buoys, with a few flashing daybeacons thrown in for good measure. Between the bridge and flashing daybeacon #108, cruisers should stick strictly to the marked cut. Guard against lateral leeway easing you out of the channel into the surrounding shallows.

South and west of unlighted daybeacon #110, a large patch of deep water flows along much of the southern shoreline. This stretch borders numerous unmarked shoals and is better left to those with specific local knowledge.

West of flashing daybeacon #121, the runs between the various daybeacons and other aids to navigation marking the Waterway lengthen considerably. Intelligent navigators will follow pre-plotted compass/GPS courses between the markers all the way to the Pensacola Beach Bridge.

Santa Rosa Anchorage Entry into the overnight haven west of the charted shoal, south of flashing daybeacon #129, calls for navigational caution. As chart 11385 clearly indicates, there is a considerable body of shallower water to the east.

To enter, depart from the ICW at least 150 yards west of #129. Cruise carefully to the south, keeping a constant watch on the sounder. If depths start to rise, you are probably encroaching on the shoal to the east. Give way to the west for better depths. For best protection, follow the deeper water until coming under the lee of the point to the east. Be on guard against the very shoal water stretching north from this point.

Twin Anchorages The two anchorages east and west of Range Point, south of flashing daybeacon #131, are easy to enter if you avoid the considerable shoal stretching north from the point. Leave the Waterway far enough either east or west of #131 to avoid the shallows and cruise carefully toward the southern shoreline. Shoal water extends a bit more out from the point on its easterly quarter. Cruisers entering the east-side anchorage should stay even farther away from the point. As seems to be the case throughout Santa Rosa Sound, be sure to anchor well away from the shoal band along the banks.

On the Waterway Be sure to come abeam of flashing daybeacon #131 by at least 100 yards to its northerly side. Shallow water lies south of this marker.

It is a long run of almost 3.2 nautical miles from #131 to a position north of flashing daybeacon #133. As anyone who bothers to take a perfunctory glance at chart 11378 will readily observe, there is a considerable patch of shoal water south of #133. Be sure to run a careful compass/GPS course between these two aids, pointing to come abeam of #133 well to its northerly side.

As you approach #133, the development surrounding Pensacola Beach will become readily apparent to the southwest. Skippers choosing to make use of the very casual facilities on the southern shores of charted Fishing Bend should carefully skirt their way around the eastern side of the large patch of shallows south of #133. After leaving this currently unmarked barrier behind, you can turn in towards the southwestern shore and carefully follow the deep water flowing to the west. Remember that depths around the various piers in Fishing Bend are only some 3 to 4 feet *or less.*

West of flashing daybeacon #133, the ICW heads toward the fixed Pensacola Beach Bridge. Private Santa Rosa Yacht Club will come abeam along the northerly banks, just before reaching the high-rise span.

A portion of the old, low-level Pensacola Beach Bridge, with its central swinging section removed, has been left in place for local fishermen east of the newer, high-rise bridge. The present-day span has ample vertical clearance of 65 feet.

Once through the fixed bridge, set course to eventually come abeam of flashing daybeacon #142 to its southerly side. Between the high-rise span and #142, you will pass south of flashing daybeacon #140 and north of flashing daybeacon #141.

If you choose instead to make use of the marina facilities on Little Sabine Bay, cut sharply to the south immediately after passing through the bridge.

Little Sabine Bay Entrance and Marinas

The well-marked entrance channel into Little Sabine Bay leads visitors through a dredged cut flanked by very shallow water. Stick strictly to the mid-width and keep an eagle eye on the sounder. As all the channel markers are unlighted, entry after dark could be a real bear.

To enter the bay and thereby gain access to its marinas, come abeam of and pass unlighted daybeacon #2 by some 10 yards to its easterly (your starboard) side. From this point on, keep all red, even-numbered markers to your starboard side and take all green beacons to port.

Next up are unlighted daybeacons #3 and #4. For best depths, favor #4 slightly. This pair of markers is followed by another, unlighted daybeacons #5 and #6. Favor #6 as #5 is actually founded in shoal water.

Unlighted daybeacons #7 and #8 mark the northerly genesis of a narrow stretch in the Little Sabine Bay entrance channel. Stay away from #7. If you were to pass #7 closely, this route would run your vessel headlong into the shoreline.

While cruising through the narrower part of the entrance channel, favor the westerly side of the channel slightly. Soon the broad waters of Little Sabine Bay will open out before you. Point to pass unlighted daybeacon #9 to your port side, followed by unlighted daybeacon #10, which you should bring abeam to your starboard quarter. Finally, unlighted daybeacon #12 marks the southernmost portion of the marked channel. As you would expect, pass #12 to your starboard side.

South of #12, continue heavily favoring

the easterly shores. A very large shoal occupies almost the entire middle of Little Sabine Bay. Cruisers who stray too far to the west are in for a grounding. Soon the docks of Beach Marina will come abeam to the east, followed closely by the docks of Sabine Marina. Both facilities are founded in deep water and can be entered easily.

The rest of Little Sabine Bay is probably best left to the locals. The entire center section of this body of water is quite shallow. While a channel holding 6 feet or more circles the outer edge of the bay, this cut is unmarked and it is all too easy to stray into thin water. On a sunny day, it is sometimes possible to spot the shallows by eye in the clear water, but during cloudy weather or in low-light conditions, well, you've heard the story before. There are no facilities available to visiting cruisers on the remainder of the bay, so unless you just can't stand it, stick to the marina channel on Little Sabine. If you should choose to disregard this advice, please check the present bay channel conditions at one of the marinas before making the attempt. And it might be smart to have a shovel on board.

On the ICW From a position abeam of flashing daybeacon #142 to its southerly side, set a new course to come abeam of flashing daybeacon #144 well to its southern quarter. Be sure to stay to the south of #144. A shoal is building south from Deer Point towards #144.

West of #144 the Waterway darts out into the open reaches of lower Pensacola Bay, which teems with cruising possibilities of its own. Wind and wave can pick up markedly in this open water, so be ready for rougher conditions. Continued coverage of the Gulf ICW is presented in the next chapter.

CHAPTER 4

The Pensacola Area

The thriving city of Pensacola and its surrounding waters comprise one of the Florida Panhandle's true cruising gems. Boasting recently expanded marina facilities and many historical shoreside attractions, the community itself is well worth any cruiser's time. Pensacola Bay, along with its two auxiliary bodies of water, Escambia and East bays, offers open cruising for both sail and powercraft. The lightly developed, heavily wooded shores reflected against the smooth waters on a calm day can quickly lead one to understand why Pensacola has always been a nautically oriented town. As if all that were not enough, the Escambia and Blackwater rivers, major tributaries to East and Escambia bays, offer anchorages and miles of cruising well off the beaten track. Whether you seek full-service marinas, fine shoreside dining and shopping, or just a quiet, isolated pocket in which to drop the hook, chances are that Pensacola and its waters can fill the bill.

Charts Several NOAA charts are needed for complete coverage of the waters lying about Pensacola. Cruisers traveling strictly on the Gulf Coast ICW will only need to purchase the first two charts below, though 11383 would be a wise addition for any navigator.
11378—outlines the ICW through the Pensacola region—also gives excellent detail of the inner harbor channels, Bayou Grande, Bayou Chico, the lower reaches of Pensacola Bay, and Escambia Bay and river
11385—covers upper East Bay and the Blackwater River
11383—good intermediate-scale chart outlining Pensacola Bay Inlet, most of Pensacola Bay, and the city waterfront
11384—highly detailed chart of Pensacola Inlet
11382—offshore sailing chart which may be needed by those putting into Pensacola from the Gulf of Mexico

Bridges
Bayou Chico Bridge—crosses Bayou Chico west of flashing daybeacon #10—fixed—65 feet of vertical clearance
Bayou Grande Bridge—crosses Bayou Grande near its entrance, upstream of unlighted daybeacon #10—Fixed—14 feet
Pensacola Bay Bridge—crosses Pensacola Bay from downtown Pensacola to Gulf Breeze, east of flashing buoy #29 and the large ship's "East Channel"—Fixed—50 feet
Escambia Bay-I-10 Highway Bridge—crosses Escambia Bay north-northwest of Gull Point and unlighted nun buoy #12—Fixed—50 feet
Escambia Bay Railway Bridge—crosses Escambia Bay north-northwest of Gull Point and unlighted nun buoy #12—Fixed—50 feet
Escambia River-Highway 90 Bridge—crosses Escambia River west of East River—Fixed—43 feet
Shields Point-I-10 Bridge—crosses the Blackwater River north of unlighted daybeacon #34—Fixed—45 feet

Pensacola and Pensacola Bay

The city of Pensacola and the waters of Pensacola Bay surrounding the city offer varied opportunities for visiting cruisers. Marina facilities seem to be expanding constantly and are more than adequate. The largest concentrations of pleasure-craft centers are found on Bayou Chico and the downtown Pensacola waterfront. There are even well-protected, secluded anchorages, but few if any of these are located within walking distance of the historic district or principal waterfront.

Numbers to know in Pensacola:

Yellow Cab—850-433-3333
ABC Taxi—850-456-8294
Tucker Black and White Taxi—
    850-432-4151
Budget Car Rental—800-527-7000
Avis Rent A Car—850-433-0011
Enterprise Rent-A-Car—850-456-3070
West Marine (3500 Barrancas Avenue)—
    850-453-0010
Boat/US (3810 Barrancas Avenue)—
    850-456-9955
West Marine (7116 N Davis Highway)—
    850-476-2720

Pensacola Marinas
(Various Lats/Lons—see below)

One group of Pensacola facilities flanks the shores of Bayou Chico. The entrance to the bayou lies northwest of flashing daybeacon #2, itself almost due west of the charted "Inner Harbor Channel." A well-marked, dredged channel with minimum 9-foot depths leads from the deeper waters of Pensacola Bay to the creek's entrance. Any craft with a draft less than 7 feet should be able to enter this cut without difficulty.

The first of the bayou's facilities, the Pensacola Yacht Club (30 23.971 North/087 14.404 West), will come abeam on the northern shore immediately after passing flashing daybeacon #8. This large, long-established club has a partially breakwater-enclosed harbor with 7-foot minimum depths. Another set of slips fronts directly onto the northern shores of Bayou Chico. Maneuvering room at the older, breakwater-enclosed slips is at a minimum, and we have observed some tidal current during our several visits here. Captains should take extra precautions when entering one of the inner slips. A large, white clubhouse with a dining room and bar overlooks the piers and makes for a very impressive sight from the water. Cruisers who are members of accredited yacht clubs, with appropriate reciprocal agreements, are accepted for overnight dockage when space allows. Be sure to make advance reservations by phone. Visitors are allowed use of the dining room, bar, swimming pool, and tennis courts. A fuel dock provides both gasoline and diesel for members and club guests only.

Pensacola Yacht Club (850) 433-8804
   http://www.pensacolayachtclub.com

Approach depth—9 to 12 feet
Dockside depth—7-foot minimum
Accepts transients—members of accredited
   yacht clubs
Fixed wooden slips—yes
Dockside power connections—30-amp
Dockside water connections—yes
Gasoline—yes (members and guests only)
Diesel fuel—yes (members and guests only)
Restaurant—on site

Just upstream from the Pensacola Yacht Club, visiting cruisers will encounter Bahia Mar Marina (30 24.025 North/087 14.493 West) overlooking the bayou's northerly shoreline, east of the new fixed, high-rise bridge.

Pensacola Yacht Club, Bayou Chico

This marina has been under the same owner-ship (Marina Management, Inc.) as the two large, downtown Pensacola marinas (see below) for several years now. This group's highly competent management has continued to improve and expand Bahia Mar.

Bahia Mar does offer transient dockage, but during our last visit in the late summer of 2002, we were told that the marina was "pretty full," and visitors could not always be accommo-dated. Call ahead of time and check on slip availability, rather than risk disappointment.

Berths are provided at both well-founded, fixed, wooden piers and ultramodern, con-crete floating docks. Fresh-water and 30-amp power connections are found at all slips. A few berths also sport 50-amp service. Depths alongside run 6 to 7 feet at low water. About half the available slips are covered, with the other half open and well suited for sailing craft. Shoreside dry storage for smaller vessels is offered. Gasoline and diesel fuel are now available in Bahia Mar's harbor, and there is a small ship's/variety store on the grounds. Cruisers will also discover two small (one per sex), air-conditioned showers and a good, cli-mate-controlled Laundromat.

If you are in the market for a shoreside meal, it could be a bit of a hike. Sam's Seafood (420 S A Street, 850-432-6626) is about a mile away, while Joe Patti's Seafood Deli (foot of A Street, 850-432-3315) is about the same distance. There is a grocery store within a half-mile. Many cruisers will wisely elect to take a taxi to and from these dining and provisioning sources.

Bahia Mar features a full-service repair yard offering mechanical repairs for both gasoline- and diesel-powered plants. Haul-outs are accomplished by a 60-ton travelift.

It almost goes without saying (but let's say it anyway) that the continuous upgrading and expansion of Bahia Mar Marina adds greatly to the marina offerings of Bayou Chico in particular and Pensacola in general.

Bahia Mar Marina (850) 432-9620
http://www.marinamgmt.com/bahia_mar.htm

Approach depth—8 to 12 feet
Dockside depth—6 to 7 feet
Accepts transients—yes
Transient-dockage rate—above average
Fixed wooden piers—yes
Dockside power connections—30- and some 50-amp
Dockside water connections—yes
Showers—yes
Laundromat—yes
Gasoline-yes
Diesel fuel-yes
Mechanical repairs—yes
Below-waterline repairs—yes
Ship's/variety store—yes
Restaurant—taxi ride necessary

Bahia Mar Marina

Mahogany Landing Marina (850-456-9221) guards Bayou Chico's southern shore a bit farther along. In all our visits to this tiny facility over the years, we have yet to actually find anyone on the docks to speak with. It is our strong impression that Mahogany Landing is pleasant setting for a group of local liveaboards, and there is very little here in the way of services for visiting cruisers.

The management of Mahogany Landing has informed this writer by telephone that transients are occasionally accepted for overnight dockage at their fixed wooden piers with fresh-water and 30-amp power connections. Entrance depths are a minimal 4½ feet and dockside soundings are also in the 4½- to 5-foot range. A single, nonclimate-controlled shower and a small on-site Laundromat add to this marina's offerings. My advice is to make definite advance dockage arrangements by telephone before planning on an overnight stop at this facility.

Mahogany Landing Marina (850) 456-9221

Approach depth—4½ feet
Dockside depth—4½ to 5 feet
Accepts transients—limited

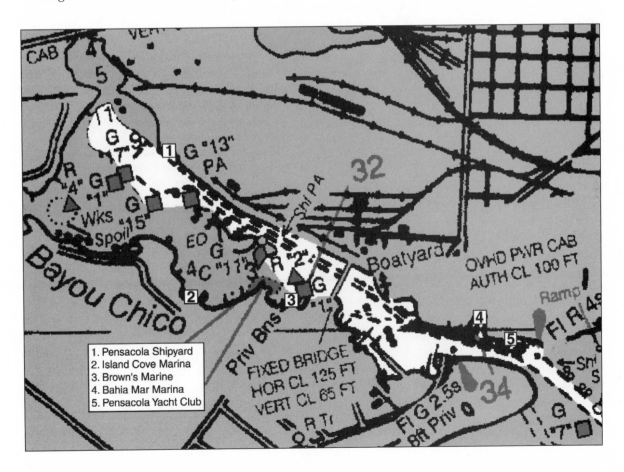

1. Pensacola Shipyard
2. Island Cove Marina
3. Brown's Marine
4. Bahia Mar Marina
5. Pensacola Yacht Club

Transient-dockage rate—below average
Fixed wooden piers—yes
Dockside power connections—30-amp
Dockside water connections—yes
Showers—yes
Laundromat—yes
Restaurant—taxi ride necessary

Harbor View Marine (850-453-3435) guards Bayou Chico's southerly banks just upstream from Mahogany Landing. This firm is in the dry-stack storage business for small craft. The large metal storage building associated with this service will be readily spotted from the water. While there are no dockage facilities for transients, gasoline can be purchased and Harbor View does offer a large ship's store.

Moving a bit farther to the northwest, Bayou Chico is now spanned by a fixed, high-rise bridge will a full 65 feet of vertical clearance. This new structure is a decided improvement over the old, low-level bascule bridge that used to cross the bayou downstream of the new bridge's position. The bascule has now been removed entirely.

The docks, harbor, warehouses, and repair yards of Brown's Marine Service (30 24.076 North/087 14.973 West) are encountered on the southern banks, between the high-rise bridge and unlighted can buoy #11. Brown's maintains a large repair yard and some wet slips.

Transients are accepted for overnight dockage at floating, low-level wooden piers featuring fresh-water and 30-amp power connections. There are also some covered, fixed slips, but these are usually reserved for resident craft. Interestingly, Brown's charges a flat $20 per-night transient-dockage fee no matter what your vessel's size might be.

The marina has good approach and dockside

depths of 6 to 6½ feet. Some of the outermost slips feature 8+-foot soundings. One adequate, nonair-conditioned shower is available shoreside. Cruisers will need a quick taxi ride to reach a restaurant, grocery store, or Laundromat.

Brown's Marine Service features extensive mechanical and haul-out repair services. The list of diesel, gasoline, and hull repair specialists on staff is very impressive indeed. The yard boasts a 60-ton travelift and a marine railway. There is a tiny on-site ship's store to supplement Brown's extensive parts department. Gasoline and diesel fuel can also be purchased dockside.

Brown's Marine Service (850) 453-3471
(800) 234-3471
http://www.brownmarine.com

Approach depth—9 to 10 feet
Dockside depth—6 to 6½ feet minimum
Accepts transients—yes
Transient-dockage fee—below average
Floating wooden docks—yes
Fixed wooden piers—yes
Dockside power connections—30-amp
Dockside water connections—yes
Showers—yes
Gasoline—yes
Diesel fuel—yes
Mechanical repairs—yes (extensive)
Haul-out repairs—yes (extensive)
Ship's store—yes
Restaurant—taxi ride necessary

Lying almost opposite Brown's Marine Service, Day Break Marina (850-434-9022) overlooks Bayou Chico's northerly banks. This facility is very serious about the small-craft, dry-stack storage business. One look from the water at their huge metal storage building will convince you. Gasoline and mechanical repairs are available as is an on-site ship's and tackle shop. Otherwise, no services applicable to visiting cruisers are to be found.

Bell's Marine Service (850-455-7639) is an older repair yard-type facility found on the bayou's southern shores south of the small, charted island which bisects the creek. While visiting many years ago, I was amused to observe huge stacks of seemingly random parts and other nautical junk occupying almost every available square inch of floor space. Yet, when a patron happened in and asked for a particular part, a quick search revealed the requested item. Boat yards seem to have their own peculiar filing systems.

No transient dockage is available at Bell's, but, as you might guess, the marina does offer extensive mechanical repairs. Boats that require long-term servicing are usually docked at Bell's piers without additional charge. Entrance and dockside depths of 4½ to 5 feet may limit the facility's accessibility for deep-draft vessels.

Island Cove Marina (formerly Bayou Chico Marina, 30 24.082 North/087 15.236 West) is the westernmost facility located on Bayou Chico's southerly shores. Its entrance channel cuts back to the south, just upstream of unlighted daybeacon #13.

It is always a happy experience for this writer to update his readers concerning a marina that has undergone a real improvement. That is the happy case with Island Cove. Since new owners took over, things have really looked up. The docks have been rebuilt, the new showers are air-conditioned and really first class, and everything has been repainted and generally spruced up. In particular, the once-difficult entrance channel is now outlined by easy-to-identify floating markers. In the past, we always knew there was a channel out there some place, but it was ever so hard to come by. The old (and we are being charitable to call them that) channel markers consisted of hard-to-see, white, PVC pipes, often lying at drunken angles to the water. If cruisers missed one of these pipes, and believe me that was very easy to do, they could find themselves quite suddenly in 3 feet of water. Now, with the new aids to navigation in place, skippers can confidently expect low-water soundings of 7 to 9 feet in the entrance cut, with 6 to 7 feet dockside.

Island Cove is glad to accept transients for overnight or temporary dockage. Berths will be discovered at newly upgraded, fixed wooden piers with fresh-water and (mostly) 30-amp power connections. A few 50-amp hookups are available in some slips. Shoreside, you will find new, air-conditioned showers and a Laundromat with new machines. Gasoline and diesel fuel are ready for pumping, and waste pump-out service is planned for the future. There is also a very small ship's and variety store in the dockmaster's office.

In its new and happy state, we can now recommend Island Cove Marina to our fellow cruisers without reservation. Just be sure to pick up all the new channel markers as you make good your entry from the main bayou channel to the dockage basin.

Island Cove Marina (850) 455-4552

Approach depth—7-9 feet
Dockside depth—6 to 7 feet
Accepts transients—yes
Transient-dockage rate—above average

Fixed wooden piers—yes
Dockside power connections—30-amp (some 50-amp)
Dockside water connections—yes
Showers—yes

Laundromat—yes
Gasoline—yes
Diesel fuel—yes
Ship's and variety store—very small
Restaurant—taxi ride necessary

Island Cove Marina, Bayou Chico

Finally, for those mariners who persevere and continue upstream, the numerous slips and multifaceted repair facility known as Pensacola Shipyard Marine Complex (or PSMC) will be spotted along the northeasterly shore, northeast of unlighted daybeacon #17 (near 30 24.397 North/087 15.295 West). Pensacola Shipyard is a fascinating place that seems be in a constant state of expansion. Every time we visit, there is more to see and more services for the asking. Whether you seek sheltered dockage (of both the transient and resident variety) or full-service repairs, you might find that this just may be the spot in Pensacola to fill the bill.

The marina portion of Pensacola Shipyard boasts two distinct groups of wet slips. The lower (southeasterly) set has good dockside depths of 6 to 8 feet, while the upper piers maintain only 4½ to 5 feet of water.

Berths are composed of both fixed, wooden piers and new, ultramodern concrete-decked floating docks. Transients are readily accepted, and visiting cruisers can be assured of a warm and knowledgeable welcome. Fresh-water and 30- and 50-amp power connections are at hand, as is a waste pump-out service. Air-conditioned showers and a small Laundromat are located in a separate building behind the dockmaster's office/ship's store. And speaking of ship's store, PSMC now boats a nice ship's/variety store that doubles as the dockmaster's office. This facility is located just behind the southeasterly docks. The ship's store and dockmasters office are currently open from 6:30 A.M. to 3:30 P.M. weekdays and from 6:30 A.M. to 6:30 P.M. weekends.

As good as the marina portion of PSMC is (and we rate it as very good), the repair yard portion of this operation is just about as impres-sive as it gets. Vessels in need of landside service are now hauled out either by way of a new 100-ton travelift or the very impressive 150-ton crane, which is so very, very prominent from the water. This mammoth mechanism was actually purchased years ago as government salvage from Cape Canaveral. One look at the crane and travelift will convince even the most doubting cruiser that Pensacola Shipyard can safely haul just about any-sized ship, be it of the oceangoing or spacegoing variety.

But haul-outs are only a portion of the marine-service story at PSMC. There are also no less than eight on-site contractors that can handle just about any marine repair need.

Ashby Yacht Repair (850-438-1994)—specializing in mast repair and wooden-boat refinishing

Beavercreek Marine (850-887-0496)—general boat contractors specializing in polyester-resin repair, topside and bottom painting

Don Prendergast Enterprises (850-934-1355)—general boat contractors specializing in refinishing, racing finishes, and rigging

Eric Linquist (850-433-1615)—general boat contractor

Stanos Yacht Repair (850-429-8325)—specializing in painting and fiberglass fabrications

Troendle Marine (850-433-1477)—general boat contractors

Watson Ship Repair (850-934-7199)—general boat contractor

Don's Marine Service (850-454-6054)—specializing in marine air-conditioning, refrigeration, electrical, and watermarker repairs

Perhaps now you will believe, along with us, that if you can't get it fixed here, better find out how the new boating market has been doing lately!

Once again, there are no restaurants or grocery supplies within easy walking distance. A quick taxi ride should solve this difficulty.

Pensacola Shipyard
    (850) 202-0170 (dockmaster)
    (850) 434-3548 (main office)
    http://www.psmc.net

Approach depth—9 to 12 feet
Dockside depth—6 to 8 feet (lower slips)
                4½ to 5 feet (upper piers)

Accepts transients—yes
Transient-dockage rate—average
Fixed wooden piers—yes
Concrete floating piers-yes
Dockside power connections—30- and 50-amp
Dockside water connections—yes
Showers—yes
Laundromat—yes
Waste pump-out—yes
Mechanical repairs—yes (extensive)
Haul-out repairs—yes (extensive)
Ship's/variety store-yes
Restaurant—taxi ride necessary

We now move to the facilities along the

Pensacola Shipyard, Bayou Chico

downtown Pensacola waterfront. The owners of the Pensacola-based firm known as Marina Management, Inc., have been busy boys and girls. As if Bahia Mar Marina (see above) and Seville Harbour (see below) were not enough to keep up with, this firm has now constructed an entirely new facility in the downtown Pensacola Palafox Historical District. It goes by the moniker of Palafox Pier Yacht Harbor (30 24.151 North/087 12.819). This marina's dockage basin is located in the middle of the three charted coves north of flashing buoy #PMT2 (which is itself located on the charted "Inner Harbor Channel"). A stone and concrete breakwater has been built surrounding the southerly tip of the dockage cove. This structure combines with a second breakwater to the west and the surrounding shorelines to give superb shelter from foul weather. The entrance into the harbor will be spotted abutting its southwesterly corner.

Palafox Pier incorporates the old "Baylen Slips," which used to overlook the cove's western banks. An entirely new array of 99 ultra-modern slips, composed of concrete-decked floating piers, has now been constructed along the eastern shoreline.

Palafox Pier Yacht Harbor offers transient dockage, featuring full power (30-, 50-, and 100-amp), water, telephone, and cable-television connections at every slip. Waste pump-out service, gasoline, and diesel fuel are all available in the harbor. There are also shoreside showers, but while they are air-conditioned and adequate, we were surprised they weren't a bit larger, considering the first-class nature of everything else at Palafox Pier Yacht Harbor. Cruisers will also find a climate-controlled Laundromat adjacent to the showers.

Lillo's Trattoria Restaurant (850-470-0773) overlooks Palafox Harbor's easterly flank and shares the same building as the shower and Laundromat facilities. We have not been lucky enough to dine here as of yet, but a perusal of the menu and a quick peek inside confirm this dining spot's leaning toward higher-end Italian fare.

Palafox Pier Yacht Harbor has the distinct advantage of being located in the heart of the downtown Pensacola shopping district. There are quite a number of restaurants and retail businesses within easy walking distance of your overnight slip. Among the many choices you might consider are the New World Restaurant (600 South Palafox Street, 850-434-7736) and Mr. Manatees—A Casual Grille (619 South Palafox Street, 850-432-3707). Or, how about Trader Jon's restaurant (511 South Palafox Street, 850-429-1000), complete with its own historical marker.

The shoppers among us will want to check out the Quayside Market (712 South Palafox Street, 850-438-5399). This is an elegant gift shop where one might spend quite some time browsing the many fascinating items.

So, considering its good shelter, ample services, and fortunate location, we think every cruiser plying the waters of Pensacola Bay should draw a big red circle around the position of Palafox Pier Yacht Harbor. It seems destined to become one of the most popular stopovers in this region of interesting stops.

Palafox Pier Yacht Harbor (850-432-9620)
   http://www.marinamgmt.com/Marinas/
   palafox.htm

Approach depth—10+ feet
Dockside depth—8+ feet
Accepts transients—yes

Transient-dockage rate—above average
Floating concrete piers—yes
Dockside power connections—30-, 50-, and
     100-amp
Dockside fresh-water connections—yes
Waste pump-out—yes
Showers—yes
Laundromat—yes

Gasoline—yes
Diesel fuel—yes
Restaurant—on-site and many others within
     walking distance

Pensacola's other major downtown marina facility is known as Seville Harbour (formerly Harbour Village at Pitt Slip marina, 30 24.423

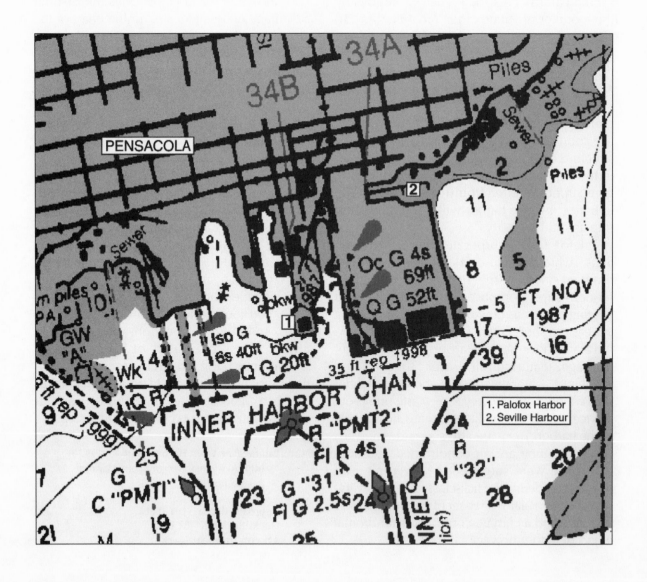

North/087 12.546 West). Like Palafox Pier Yacht Harbor, Seville Harbour (under the same ownership) guards the city's principal waterfront, within a short walk away of the district's many restaurants, shops, and historic homes and buildings. An uncharted, but well-marked, deep channel leads from the bay's deeper waters to the marina docks. This cut is found just north and east of the charted East Channel, east of flashing buoy #PMT2.

Seville Harbour gladly accepts transients at its extensive wooden-decked, floating docks. The most modern power and water connections are very much in evidence, and gasoline and diesel fuel are readily available from a fuel dock that guards the dockage basin's southerly banks. Waste pump-out service is also provided. Mechanical repairs can often be arranged through local, independent technicians.

A large office/retail complex overlooks the harbor and houses the facility's spotless, air-conditioned bathrooms, showers, and laundry. This same structure plays host to a new dining attraction known as the Fish House Dockside Bar and Grill (850-470-0003, http://www.pensacolafishhouse.com). We can attest to the fact that the po'-boy luncheon sandwiches are outstanding. Come time for the evening meal, give every consideration to the Cashew Crusted Softshell Crab. The Fish House features extensive outdoor dining overlooking the dockage basin. There are few better places to spend a beautiful evening after a long day on the water, while watching the light slowly fade from the harbor.

Still not enough to satisfy a famished cruiser's hunger? Well, consider Jamie's Restaurant (850-434-2911). Consistently rated as one of the top dining attractions in all of Florida, it's only a two-block walk away from the dockage basin.

This writer found the Seville Harbour management and dockside personnel prompt and friendly. Visiting and local mariners alike can plan a stay at this facility with complete confidence. Advance dockage reservations are recommended.

About the only negative aspect of the marina is its openness to strong easterly blows. During such times, the "dock rock" can be considerable.

Seville Harbour (850) 432-9620
  http://www.marinamgmt.com

Approach depth—9 feet minimum
Dockside depth—7 to 9 feet
Accepts transients—yes
Transient-dockage rate—above average
Floating wooden docks—yes
Dockside power connections—30- and 50-amp
Dockside water connections—yes
Showers—yes
Laundromat—yes
Waste pump-out—yes
Gasoline—yes
Diesel fuel—yes
Mechanical repairs—yes (independent technicians)
Restaurant—on site and others nearby

Bayou Grande and Mac's Marina (Various Lats/Lons—see below)

Bayou Grande is a large, mostly deep body of water that opens into the westernmost shores of Pensacola Bay, well west of flashing buoy #27. The entrance can be a bit tricky, but captains piloting boats under 45 feet and drawing less than 4 feet (that can clear the 14-foot fixed bridge at the bayou's entrance) should be able to enter safely. Anchorage opportunities abound on the bayou, and one small marina can be found on the creek's northern shores. The wooded, lightly developed

Seville Harbour, Pensacola

banks make for a very pleasant view, whether you are just gunk-holing or dropping the hook for the night.

If it were not for the fixed bridge with only 14 feet of vertical clearance spanning the eastern end of the creek, Bayou Grande would undoubtedly be one of the most popular "hurricane holes" on the Florida Panhandle. Obviously, this span restricts access to smaller powercraft.

Mac's Marina (850-453-3775, 30 22.454 North/087 18.867 West) occupies the charted cove on the creek's northern shore, found near the *u* in *Bayou* on chart 11378. This small facility is primarily a dry-storage marina and does not normally accept transients for overnight dockage. Gasoline and some mechanical repairs are available. In an emergency, you might be able to negotiate an overnight slip if some of the resident craft happen to be away from port, but don't count on it. Mac's does feature a fairly well appointed ship's store, and I found the personnel to be quite helpful.

For those who can clear the bridge, the opportunities to drop the hook amidst the lightly developed shores abound. One anchorage of particular note is Redoubt Bayou, found

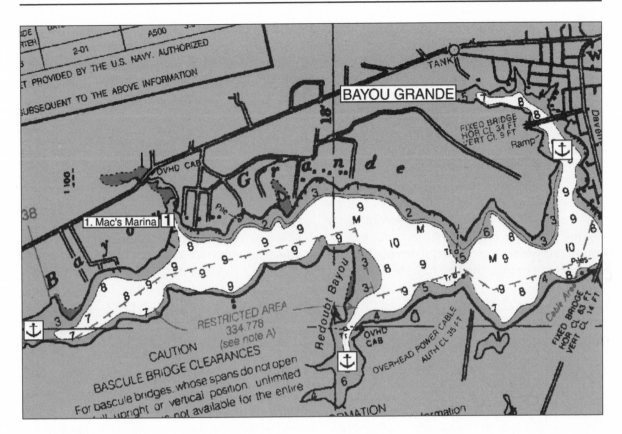

on Grande's southern shore. This creek was named for a redoubt which was supposed to be built as an outwork for Fort Barrancas, overlooking Pensacola Inlet to the south. The work was never finished on this structure and today the bayou's name is the only evidence of this bold plan.

Entering Redoubt Bayou can be a little tough, but there is plenty of swinging room for boats up to 40 feet, with 6-foot minimum depths. (Be sure to read the "Redoubt Bayou" navigation section presented later in this chapter before attempting entry.) The creek provides enough protection for anything short of hurricane-force winds. The shoreline is

beautifully undeveloped and well wooded, with the not disagreeable exception that you can catch a glimpse of the Pensacola Naval Air Station to the south, overlooked by the benevolent eye of the Pensacola Lighthouse. Numerous signs warn that the shore is government property and landing is not allowed. For maximum protection, consider dropping the hook in the pool-like area south of the charted (35-foot) power lines, near 30 21.850 North/087 17.930 West.

Another anchorage of note is found on the large, unnamed creek cutting the bayou's northern shore just west of the fixed bridge. Minimum depths of nine feet are easily maintained until further upstream passage is cut off by a low-level fixed bridge with only 9 feet of vertical clearance. There is enough swinging room for craft of most sizes, and protection is good for all but strong southerly blows. Try dropping the hook near 30 22.779 North/087 16.786 West. The eastern shore exhibits heavy residential development, while the port banks are more pleasingly wooded amidst lighter construction.

Bayou Grande itself, west of Mac's Marina, is sheltered enough for anchorage in all but the heaviest weather. If your craft can stand some 5-foot depths, a really sheltered spot can be found just west of the charted sharp point on the northern shore (past the marina). Here, in a bay-like area (near 30 21.998 North/087 19.583 West), you can cast out the anchor in a beautiful setting with excellent protection from all winds. Just be sure to anchor as close to the center as possible, as the shoreline is somewhat shoal.

Old Navy Cove

In the days of oceangoing schooners, the vessels of the U.S. Navy stationed at Pensacola used to take shelter in the large cove on the bay's southern shore which today comprises the western tip of the town of Gulf Breeze. Old Navy Cove is found east of Fair Point, itself east of unlighted nun buoy #26 on the Pensacola Bay (Main Harbor) channel. While the shoreline now exhibits a rather pleasing blend of wooded areas and residential development, protection is only sufficient when the wind is blowing from the south. Despite all its tradition, most modern cruisers would do well to look elsewhere for a secure haven.

Pensacola Ashore

The thriving city of Pensacola and its adjoining U.S. Naval Air Station present a potpourri of attractions for visiting cruisers. Your main problem may be in picking and choosing which sights to see in the time that is available. It would literally take weeks to sample all the city's offerings, but fortunately many can be visited in a much shorter period of time.

Part of Pensacola's allure for visitors rests in its three historic districts. Located in several portions of the city that were a bit run down and bedraggled until a few decades ago, the renovated historic buildings and homes alongside tasteful new construction are now everywhere in evidence.

The booklet *A Historical Guide to Pensacola,* available from the local Convention & Visitors' Center (850-434-1234), gives a surprisingly penetrating and complete insight into the many attractions available to visitors in all three of Pensacola's historical districts.

The star of this history parade may be the Seville District. During the 1700s and early 1800s the Seville District was the heart of the city's economic life. Lumber mills, brickyards, railway stations, and most of the town's retail businesses were to be found along its narrow cobblestone streets. It is listed on the National Register and contains a "rare concentration of Frame Vernacular, Folk Victorian, and Creole homes. . . . " Located on the eastern side of downtown Pensacola, Seville is bounded by Tarragona and Barracks streets to the west, Wright Street to the north, and Florida Blanca Street to the east.

Today, the fortunate visitor to the Seville District can sample an eclectic offering of the past's treasures. First-time callers should begin their visit at the so-called Historic Pensacola Village. This collection of memorabilia includes the

Museums of Industry and Commerce (850-595-5994), the Julee Cottage Museum of Black History, the Dorr House, Lavalle House, and Quina House. Visitors are welcomed between 10:00 A.M. and 4:00 P.M., Monday through Saturday. There is no better introduction to Pensacola's rich heritage.

The Palafox Historic District sits astride the center portion of downtown Pensacola and includes the city's commercial seaport. In the early 1900s, when the city was experiencing a boom based on the belief that the Panama Canal would make Pensacola an international trade center, this area became the city's principal business center and included a large collection of hotels and foreign trade offices. The boom went away, but it left behind a wide assortment of old buildings, stores, and hotels which are today being restored to their former glory. Chief among these points of interest are the Saenger Theater (118 Palafox Place, 850-444-7686) and the so-called Bear Block (402-410 Palafox Place).

The North Hill Preservation District is found (as its name implies) north of Palafox. According to "A Historical Guide to Pensacola," it long ago hosted British and Spanish forts, and "North Hill residents still unearth the occasional cannonball while digging in their gardens." From 1870 to the 1930s, North Hill developed as a residential area. It contains "over 500 homes and is one of the most intact residential historic districts in Florida. Queen Anne, Neoclassical, Tudor Revival, Craftsman Bungalow, Art Moderne, and Mediterranean Revival are among the architectural styles found in North Hill." Visiting cruisers will probably need a rental car to visit this district, unless you happen to like long hikes.

After you have finished your tour of historic Pensacola, you might be in the mood for something a bit more modern. The nearby Pensacola Air Station is justly known as America's "birthplace of naval aviation." This proud tradition is recalled by a fascinating museum on the base. Again, a taxi ride or rental car will be necessary for most nautical visitors who choose to take advantage of this unique attraction.

When it comes time to select a spot for your evening repast, Pensacola is ready. A vast selection of modern restaurants are available within the confines of the Seville and Palafox historic districts.

For something really different, make reservations at Hopkins Boarding House (900 N Spring Street, 850-438-3979) for your evening meal. Huge, Southern, home-cooked meals are served family-style at long common tables. Tuesday, Friday, and Sunday are fried chicken nights—arrive early.

How does a French restaurant housed in a Victorian cottage grab you? The management of Jamie's French Restaurant chose the former homeplace of a Pensacola schoolteacher to set up shop in. Located in the heart of the Seville Historic District (426 E Zaragosa Street, 850-434-2911), the house dates to 1860. Heavenly!

The Pensacola dining spot with what may very well be the most unusual name is known as "1912 The Restaurant" (200 E Gregory Street, 800-384-3336). In 1984 the Hilton Corporation purchased the old L&N Railway Depot in the Seville Historic District and began extensive renovations. The Hilton created a restaurant in what was once the baggage room. Its interior is magnificently set off by monstrous gilded mirrors. The menu ranges from prime rib to sauteed scallops. This is one of Pensacola's most distinguished restaurants. Reservations are definitely recommended.

McGuire's Irish Pub (600 E Gregory Street, 850-433-6789) has become synonymous with good times and good food in Pensacola. Located in an old firehouse, it offers hearty fare from seafood to Irish stew in either a rollicking pub room or quieter quarters, if you prefer. Diners will enjoy memorable dishes and times here.

Pensacola History   As the history of eastern Florida was inextricably interwoven with the story of St. Augustine, so the progress of western Florida has always been tied to Pensacola. As Gloria Jahoda comments in her famous book *The Other Florida*:

> To see Pensacola is to see a Florida reluctant to part with the Old World. Tall shutters, lacy balustrades, and rampant grapevines are seldom approximations but usually survivals. Spain is in the names of the streets. . . . On hot afternoons couples stroll hand in hand in Plaza Ferdinand VII and there is more than a suggestion of the siesta in their slowness. . . . History in Pensacola today is as inescapable as conquering Andrew and Rachel Jackson found it in 1821. American has been added onto it, but not allowed to submerge it.

Indeed, Ms. Jahoda's glowing words are more than apt. With the sole exception of St. Augustine, there is not a more historic site to be found in all of Florida. It goes far beyond the confines of this work to present more than a quick sketch of Pensacola's fascinating story. Cruisers are urged to acquire their own copies of *The Other Florida* and Dr. Charlton W. Tebeau's *A History of Florida* (among many other works) to learn the rest of the story. Believe me, it is a story worth learning!

Since earliest exploration, the English, French, and Spanish alike have recognized Pensacola as one of the finest natural harbors on the Northern Gulf Coast. This has made the city a prize for competing armies and navies. At one time or another, Pensacola has been under Spanish, French, British, Confederate, and finally United States control. This fragmented past is still recalled in modern-day Pensacola by the festival of the "Five Flags."

The story began in 1559 when Spain sent Don Tristan de Luna to Pensacola Bay to establish a colony. A hurricane smashed his fleet, destroyed his supplies, and decimated the huts his 1,500 colonists had built ashore. After two years of backbreaking toil, the colony was deserted. Western Florida was abandoned by the Spanish for the next 150 years.

The Spanish returned in 1698, narrowly beating the French, who arrived in January of 1699 to find the Spanish comfortably settled in their new fort. Pensacola swapped hands between the two numerous times until the British acquired the area with the Treaty of Paris in 1763, losing it to the Spanish again in 1781.

In 1814 Andrew Jackson routed the combined Spanish, British, and Indian forces in western Florida and took Pensacola by storm. This was but a prelude to Jackson's magnificent victory over the British at the end of the War of 1812 in New Orleans. We shall hear more of this struggle later.

Surprisingly, Spanish Florida held on until 1821, when the land was at last sold to the United States. Andrew Jackson arrived in Pensacola as western Florida's first territorial governor. He stayed only a short time. National politics soon called him north to Washington and eventually the presidency.

Between Florida's acceptance into the American fold and the beginning of the Civil War, the United States established Pensacola as its primary Gulf coast naval base. Local commerce boomed and ships and more ships slid off the ways. Forts Pickens, McRee, and Barrancas were built to defend the harbor. The three stockades ringed Pensacola Inlet. Any foe entering the inlet would find themselves in a deadly crossfire.

As the Civil War began, local Confederate militia took Fort McRee and Barrancas, but Union forces held onto Fort Pickens. The strongest of the three structures, Pickens could rain fire and shot down on the city and all shipping on the bay. Pensacola was soon abandoned by the Confederacy and remained a virtual ghost town throughout the war.

Pensacola suffered through Reconstruction along with the rest of the South. During the early 1900s Pensacola's economy was boosted by a local lumber boom. Railroads were built and the Pensacola Railway Company promoted its parent city as the "Naples of America."

In 1914 modern Pensacola was born with the establishment of the United States Naval Air Station on the lands bordering the bay, just west of the city. Since that time, the base has grown ever larger and more important. It remains an integral part of the local economy.

The reader will appreciate that the sketch presented above gives only a bare-bones account of this marvelous city's storied past. Mariners and landlubber visitors alike are urged to learn all they can of Pensacola's history before their arrival. Your visit will be far the richer for the extra effort.

PENSACOLA AND PENSACOLA BAY NAVIGATION

Pensacola Bay is a large, well-marked body of water which nevertheless calls for careful navigation. While shallow water is not much in evidence, there are several long runs between markers with which captains must contend. Strong or even moderate winds have more than enough room to raise a very uncomfortable, occasionally dangerous chop on the wider sections of the bay. Small-craft skippers should be particularly cautious about the approach of strong thunderstorms and take shelter at once if one of these powerhouses heads their way.

With good weather in the offing, passage through Pensacola Bay is a pleasant experience. The shoreline is generally an eye-pleasing alteration between totally natural stretches, residential development, and the urbanized city waterfront. The various channels can usually be relied upon to see you safely into one of the sheltered bayous or other regional facilities. As usual, plot long runs between markers in advance, watch for leeway, and observe the sounder. Follow these rules and you will hopefully come through with nothing worse than a little salt spray.

Entry from Santa Rosa Sound   From a position abeam (to the south) of flashing daybeacon #144, south of Deer Point, set a careful compass/GPS course to come abeam of flashing daybeacon #145 east of the charted turning basin. It is a long run of some 2.6 nautical miles between #144 and #145, but luckily there are no shoals to contend with during this passage. Be sure to come abeam of #145 well to its northerly side, as some shallow water is found to the south of the aid.

As you approach #145, don't be surprised to find that the waters are becoming more choppy. You are now entering the wide waters of Pensacola Bay and leaving the relative security of Santa Rosa Sound behind.

At flashing daybeacon #145 you must decide whether to follow the buoyed route west to Pensacola Inlet and the westward-flowing ICW, or swing north and visit the Pensacola waterfront. We shall now turn our attention to the Pensacola regional bays, bayous, and waterfront. Navigational coverage of the ICW and Pensacola Inlet will be reviewed later in this chapter.

North to Pensacola   To cruise north to Pensacola, set course from flashing daybeacon #145 for the gap between flashing buoys #21 and #22, marking the main Pensacola Harbor (Bay) channel. Once between #21 and #22, set course to come between flashing buoy #23 and unlighted nun buoy #24. From this point, cruisers can choose to head north to Pensacola, northeast to the long Pensacola/Gulfbreeze Bridge and the open waters of eastern Pensacola Bay, or west to Bayou Grande.

Bayou Grande   Remember that the eastern reaches of Bayou Grande are spanned by a fixed bridge with only 14 feet of vertical clearance. The section of the creek east of the bridge offers very few anchorage or gunk-holing possibilities, so if you can't clear the span, it would be best to drop this attractive body of water from your cruising plans.

Successful navigation of Bayou Grande is considerably more complicated than a glance at chart 11378 would suggest. Read the navigational information presented below carefully, proceed cautiously, and keep a sharp eye on the sounder. With these elementary precautions in mind, boats under 45 feet in length and drawing 4 feet or less should come through safely.

The entrance to Bayou Grande from Pensacola Bay looks quite different on the water than it appears on 11378. When cruising into the creek, it appears as if you must turn a sharp angle to port in order to traverse the bayou's small mouth, squeezed between the two unnamed points. To reach the entrance, you will actually cruise parallel to the port side shoreline.

To enter the creek, set a course to come abeam of flashing daybeacon #1 well to its easterly side. Then turn into the marked channel, passing red markers to their southerly sides (your starboard side) and green markers to their northerly quarter (your port side). After passing between unlighted daybeacons #5 and #6, the channel will swing sharply to the south. *Be sure* to avoid the northerly point while cruising through the entrance. A shoal seems to be building out from this promontory. Favor the southern side of the channel while cruising through the entrance.

Point to pass between unlighted daybeacons #7 and #8, and soon thereafter come abeam of unlighted daybeacon #10 by some 20 yards to its southerly side. At this point, the marked channel cuts south on its way to a military personnel marina. The main body of Bayou Grande lies to the west. Captains cruising upstream on the bayou should abandon the marked cut at #10 and continue cruising west while holding scrupulously to the centerline. Be on maximum alert for the correctly charted 4-foot waters stretching south from Jones Point and the equally disturbing finger of 3-foot shoals impinging on the channel's southerly flank. Proceed slowly and keep a sharp watch on the sounder.

Even by carefully following these instructions, it's quite possible to stray briefly into waters with only 3 to 4½ feet of depth. Take heart, deeper waters are ahead.

Head west for the fixed bridge, favoring the northern shore slightly to avoid the charted tongue of 3-foot shoal water to the south.

Shortly after passing under the fixed, 14-foot bridge, the deep, unnamed creek discussed earlier will come abeam on the northern shore. Minimum 9-foot depths with plenty of swinging room render this stream a very desirable anchorage. Enter on the mid-width and drop the hook anywhere along the centerline, short of the low-level, 9-foot, fixed bridge spanning the creek to the north.

Cruising west on Bayou Grande, you need only hold to the middle as far as the first set of charted power lines. Here the channel is squeezed between two charted shoals. Cruise between the two center poles. On a sunny day you can easily see the two flanking shallows. This narrow passage can be a bit unnerving, but the channel does carry minimum 7-foot depths. Just be *sure* to identify the unmarked channel before proceeding through!

Redoubt Bayou Successful entrance into Redoubt Bayou calls for some care. The charted shoal on the western shore has built much farther out into the entrance than is shown on the present edition of chart 11378. Favor the southeasterly shore when cruising through the entrance to avoid this hazard. However, you must be careful not to approach the eastern banks too closely, or the charted shallows abutting this shoreline will land the hapless navigator in 1 to 2 feet of water.

Once past the tricky entrance, good depths open out almost from shore to shore. For best protection and maximum swinging room, cruise under the charted power lines (vertical clearance 35 feet) and drop the hook in the pool-like area to the south.

West on Bayou Grande West of Redoubt Bayou, excellent depths continue on a broad channel straddling Bayou Grande's mid-width. Soon you will cruise under a second set of power lines (vertical clearance 35 feet), but fortunately there are no shoals to contend with at this set of high-tension sentinels.

Soon after leaving the power poles, the docks of Mac's Marina will come abeam on the northern shore. If you choose to visit, cruise straight into the slips from deeper water. Remember, dockside depths can run as shallow as 4½ feet.

Beyond Mac's Marina intrepid cruisers will encounter a sharp point of land on the northern shore. Continue holding to the centerline and avoid both shorelines. West of the point, the creek opens out into a baylike area. This would be a very protected spot to drop the hook in 5 to 6 feet of water. Just be sure to anchor in the middle, as both shorelines are shoal.

Bayou Chico Bayou Chico, home of many of Pensacola's pleasure-boating facilities, can be readily entered from the main Pensacola Bay shipping channel. Simply follow the big ships' cut to a position between flashing buoy #27 and unlighted nun #28. From #27, set a course for flashing daybeacon #2 at the southeastern foot of the charted Bayou Chico channel. Come abeam of #2 to its southwesterly side.

From a position abeam of flashing daybeacon #2, it's a straight shot down the well-marked channel into Bayou Chico. Slower-moving craft should watch their stern as well as the course ahead to guard against lateral leeway easing them out of the channel. As you would expect, pass all red, even-numbered markers to your starboard side, and green beacons to port.

Immediately upon entering the bayou, you will spot the enclosed harbor and large clubhouse of the Pensacola Yacht Club to starboard. Moving farther upstream, the covered slips and piers of Bahia Mar Marina can be seen to starboard.

Next up, you will observe a closed commercial shipyard to starboard, followed by the docks of Mahogany Landing and Harbour View Marine to the south.

The old 12-foot bascule bridge that used to cross Bayou Chico just past Bahia Mar is now nothing more than a distant, bad memory. The new, fixed, 65-foot span crosses the bayou a bit farther upstream from where the now-removed bascule counterpart once was (a short hop northwest of Harbor View Marine).

Shortly after leaving the new high-rise in your wake, the docks and wharves of Brown's Marine Service will be found to the south. No problems should be encountered when entering this facility.

Opposite Brown's Marine Service, on the northern banks, the large metal dry-stack storage building of Day Break Marina will be quite obvious. Unless you happen to have a permanent berth here, visiting cruisers need only enter for gasoline, some mechanical repairs, or the on-site ship's and tackle store.

Northwest of Brown's docks, Bayou Chico is bisected by two small islands. The deeper, main channel passes to the north, but the southerly cut leads to one additional facility. Two unlighted daybeacons (#1 and #2) lead you into the southerly channel, but even so, depths quickly climb to 5-foot levels or occasionally less. You will soon encounter Bell's Marine Service. Retrace your steps to the southeast when leaving.

Moving back to the main Bayou Chico channel, which runs north and northeast of the two small, charted islands, cruisers will encounter the newly marked, southerly-running channel leading to Island Cove

Marina, immediately northwest of unlighted daybeacon #13.

This cut is now outlined by easy-to-identify floating markers. Boy, talk about a serious improvement over the old so-called markers! Cruisers bound for Island Cove Marina will cut off on the main Bayou Chico channel just northwest of #13, and then follow the new markers through a U-turn back to the south and southeast. The channel will then lead you straight to the dockage basin. Stick strictly to the marked cut. Depths outside of the channel run to 3 feet or less!

Northwest of unlighted daybeacon #13, the main Bayou Chico cut maintains minimum 8-foot depths. Soon the vast crane and extensive docks of Pensacola Shipyard will be sighted on the northeastern banks. Those captains with long-legged vessels would do better to coil their lines at the southeasterly set of docks, which maintain 7-foot minimum depths, with 9- to 10-foot soundings being more typical.

Pensacola Waterfront and Palafox Pier Yacht Harbor   To visit the principal Pensacola waterfront, continue following the main ship channel to flashing buoy #29. Those wishing to enter the inner harbor, home of Palafox Pier Yacht Harbor, should track their way from #29 to flashing buoy #PMT2. Come abeam of #PMT2 to its immediate easterly side. Cruise north to the center of the three coves

dead ahead. Soon you sight a concrete breakwater fronting this protected harbor. A second breakwater flanks the entrance to the west. The entrance between these two protective structures will be found on the southwesterly corner of the basin.

Seville Harbour   Enter this impressive facility by continuing on the main Pensacola, "East" channel to flashing buoy #29. From #29 cruise due north towards the commercial port terminal. Some 100 yards before reaching the wharves, cut 90 degrees to the east and follow the shoreline around as it curves to the north. Soon you will see the well-marked but uncharted channel leading to Seville Harbour. Keep to the mid-width of the cut and you should not experience any difficulty.

Old Navy Cove   If you should choose to enter Old Navy Cove, depart from the main channel at unlighted nun buoy #28. Follow a compass/GPS course into the bay's middle. Protection is only sufficient to anchor in a southerly wind. Do not approach the shoreline too closely, as shoal water extends well out from the banks.

Danger Area   East of Seville Harbour a collection of derelict piers and other concrete junk guards the northwestern corner of the Pensacola Bay Bridge. Pleasure craft of all sizes should keep well clear of these waters.

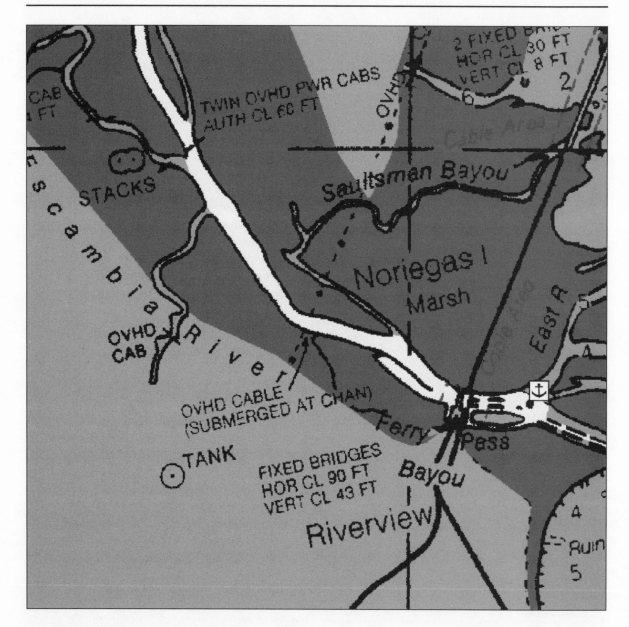

Escambia Bay and River

East of the 3½-mile Pensacola Bay Bridge, the broad waters of Pensacola Bay strike north to form two additional bays, which in turn flow into deep-water rivers. The westernmost of these northerly offshoots is Escambia Bay. While not quite as attractive as its easterly sister, a cruise on this body of water is certainly a visually appealing experience. The westerly shore at the bay's mouth is guarded by high, earthen cliffs which make for a magnificent sight from the water. The eastern banks exhibit some light residential development, but the mix of attractive houses alternating with undeveloped patches will further enhance the visual aspect of your cruise.

Farther to the north, a well-marked, dredged channel leads cruisers through two 50-foot fixed bridges into the foot of the Escambia River. This attractive waterway features cypress-lined, largely undeveloped shores that seem to beckon the passing cruiser to explore and observe some of the abundant wildlife that make their homes along this fortunate strand. However, Escambia River supports a fair amount of barge traffic, courtesy of the charted, twin "stacks" power plant and, farther upstream, the Solutia Plant (charted as "Chemstrand"). With the very real risk of a barge and tow coming along in the dead of night, we no longer recommend anchoring on Escambia River, with the possible exception of one shallow haven on tiny East River (see below).

Be advised that cruising craft must also be able to clear the fixed, 43-foot twin spans that cross the Escambia west of East River in order to take advantage of the most scenic upstream stretch.

Northwest of Hernandez point on Escambia Bay, flashing daybeacon #2 signals the beginning of the marked channel leading north-northwest to the Escambia River. South of #2 captains can expect minimum 9- to 10-foot depths, and at least 8 feet of water can be counted on in the buoyed cut all the way to the Escambia River. Good minimum 8-foot depths

continue on this stream at least to a point just above the power plant.

Powerboats can take maximum advantage of Escambia Bay's cruising opportunities. With these crafts' easy maneuverability, it is a simple matter to keep to the marked channel and avoid the long, charted spoil area to the west. Sailcraft, on the other hand, may find cruising space a little cramped north of flashing daybeacon #2. Also, the 50-foot vertical clearance of the two bay bridges and the 43-foot spans on Escambia River may very well be a problem for wind-powered boats.

Surprisingly, there is not a single marina facility, large or small, to be found anywhere on the banks of Escambia Bay or river. Be sure your tanks are topped off before entering these waters.

There are no protected coves or creeks on the bay itself, but the story is slightly different on Escambia River. As mentioned above, the possibility of passing barge traffic negates anchorage on the river's main path. This is really too bad, as the Escambia would otherwise feature minimum 8-foot depths with plenty of swinging room. Set against the stream's great natural beauty, many would like to spend an evening or two here, but unless you can fit into the shallow and rather small East River anchorage outlined below, you're better to confine your Escambia cruising to day-long explorations.

The only Escambia River anchorage safe from barge traffic is found on the small offshoot charted as the East River, striking north-northeast from the main stream, east of the twin fixed bridges. This tiny stream holds minimum 4½- to 5-foot depths along its centerline for the first 50 yards of its passage. Captains who pilot craft 36 feet and smaller, drawing less than 4 feet, could consider dropping the hook here. Protection is quite good from all but strong northerly blows.

During our last visit to this haven in the fall of 2002, there was a goodly quantity of construction equipment and barges moored near the southerly mouth of East River. This gear was part of a project to erect a second (twin) highway bridge at the charted location of "Ferry Pass." It appeared that this construction was nearing completion, so there is good reason to believe that all this paraphernalia will be long gone by the time of your arrival.

East River boasts undeveloped, tree-covered shores that are perfect for exploring and fishing by dinghy. Entry into these waters does call for some caution. Please read the navigational information on the East River presented later in this chapter before attempting the stream.

To summarize, Escambia Bay and its deep river present a great gunk-holing opportunity, with plenty of all-natural shores and abundant wildlife. Just don't look for a potpourri of protected, barge traffic-less anchorages.

ESCAMBIA BAY AND RIVER NAVIGATION

Escambia Bay and its adjoining river are not navigationally difficult. The lower reaches of the bay present a broad swath of deep water, while the well-marked channel leading to the river's foot is easy to follow and maintains minimum depths of 8 feet. Entry into the Escambia River does call for somewhat more caution, but all navigators need do is hold to the centerline of the main channel for excellent depths. About the only hazard of any real consequence on the bay is the long spoil bank west of the main channel. Avoid this area, watch for excessive leeway, keep an eye on the sounder, and you should find your cruise of the bay and river to be trouble-free.

To enter Escambia Bay, set a course from the Pensacola Bridge's central pass-through for the mid-width of the bay's southerly reaches. This course need not be too exact. There is plenty of latitude. You only need to avoid the clearly charted shoals around Emanuel and Hernandez points to remain in deep water.

Once past the bay's entrance, begin using the Escambia Bay inset of chart 11378 for continued upstream navigation. You will discover that the entire region is well charted. On-site research revealed the designated soundings to be accurate.

Continue north on the bay, pointing to avoid the charted sunken wreck and designated dump area. Soon you will catch sight of flashing daybeacon #2, marking the southerly beginnings of the buoyed cut. As you are cruising toward #2, look west and you will catch sight of the high, earthen shores described earlier. This land mass is charted as Magnolia Bluff.

From #2, follow the various markers to the first of the fixed high-rise bridges. Both spans have a vertical clearance set at 50 feet.

As you pass through the twin bridges, a large industrial complex to port and some additional plants in the distance to the northeast will come into view. For the most part, however, the shores remain undeveloped.

North of the bridges, continue holding to the marked cut until you come between flashing daybeacon #18 and unlighted can buoy #17. From this point the channel swings sharply to the west-northwest and enters the mouth of the Escambia River. Set course to pass unlighted can buoy #19 to its fairly immediate northerly side and continue on the same course into the main river channel's mid-width. Take all subsequent red markers to your starboard side and all green aids to port.

West-northwest of the gap between unlighted nun buoy #22 and unlighted daybeacon #21, the channel soon passes into the interior reaches of Escambia River. There are actually several other uncharted markers along this stretch. Just continue to follow the good, old red-right-returning rule and all should be well.

Eventually, the entrance to East River will come abeam to the north, within sight of the new twin 43-foot highway spans.

East River Anchorage   If you choose to enter, remember minimum depths are only 4½ to 5 feet. Chart 11378 shows a small island bisecting the entrance. We did not find this small land mass during on-site research. Either it has eroded into the waters or has become so enlarged as to appear to be a part of the easterly banks. To maintain best depths, favor the northwestern side of the entrance, but don't get too close to the shoreline. Once past the mouth, immediately cruise back to the mid-width. Drop

the anchor before proceeding more than 50 yards upstream. Pass this point numerous unmarked shoals and questionable depths render passage too hazardous for all but small fishing skiffs.

Upper Escambia River   Northwest of the East River intersection, the Escambia River flows under twin fixed bridges with 43 feet of vertical clearance. To continue upstream past the bridge, simply hold to the middle of the main channel. Be careful to avoid cruising accidentally into the charted Saultsman Bayou entrance, which will appear on the northerly shore. Continue on the Escambia River to the northwest.

Minimum depths are held almost from shore to shore to a point at least 100 yards upstream from the large power plant on the western shore. Soon after passing the plant, you will cross under the charted power lines with 60 feet of vertical clearance. Several new, unlighted, and uncharted nun and can buoys outline the channel at this point. They must be meant for local barge traffic. All pleasure craft need do is continue holding to the centerline!

Farther upstream, the Escambia splinters into two branches, the easternmost being known as the White River. Depths become uncertain. Larger pleasure craft are urged to cease their explorations well short of the White/Escambia rivers intersection.

East Bay and the Blackwater River

The Florida Panhandle is blessed with many beautiful, isolated bodies of water with rich cruising possibilities. Few, however, can boast more positive qualities than East Bay and its adjoining Blackwater River. Visiting cruisers will find just about anything they might ever desire, except for marina facilities. In the past, visiting skippers have seldom visited the waters of East Bay and Blackwater River. To say the least, those who pass by on the ICW without a sidelong glance are missing some of the Gulf coast's finest backwater cruising.

East Bay

East Bay breaks off from the eastern reaches of its larger sister, Pensacola Bay. This body of water features well-wooded, lightly developed shores, along with a general absence of shoals and other navigational problems. The bay is certainly wide enough for a good sail, and local wind boats are often found skimming across the tranquil waters, particularly on weekends. While there are no good anchorages on the bay itself, the Blackwater River can boast any number of fine overnight havens.

Eastern East Bay

The extreme easterly reaches of East Bay lead inland for several miles pass Miller and Axelson points. Unfortunately, numerous unmarked shoals surround this portion of the bay. Captains of larger craft are strictly advised to bypass this portion of the bay and confine their cruising to the main portion of the bay and the Blackwater River.

Bay Point and the Amazing Miss Adelia Rosasco-Soule

In 1904 Bay Point, guarding the westerly shores near the intersection of Blackwater Bay and the Blackwater River, received an immigrant family from Italy that was to leave its mark on Panhandle history. The Rosascos took up residence in a huge, white-columned mansion facing the water. Mr. Rosasco assumed the management of the sawmill at Bay Point, which he had bought in partnership with his brothers in Italy. The native timbers were cut and loaded aboard vessels under the watchful eye of Mr. Rosasco and a trusted employee named "Uncle Manuel." The ships then transported the lumber to Italy, where it was disposed of by one of the brothers. All in all, a thoroughly American enterprise which was so typical of the enthusiastic immigrants who entered the United States during the early 1900s. Of course, unlike many of these new citizens, the Rosascos arrived with money in hand and their economic future set out before them.

Anyway, what really made the arrival of the Rosasco family so notable was their only daughter. Miss Adelia, as she is known today, would, in the ensuing years, become one of the great voices in Florida Panhandle literature. Her poems are legendary. There are perhaps no other collections of verse which do so much to capture the character and heritage of this imaginative land. In her book entitled *Panhandle Memories*, Miss Adelia turns her considerable literary talents towards a highly colorful description of Panhandle life as it was at the turn of the century. *Panhandle Memories* should be required reading for everyone visiting northwestern Florida. Listen to just a few of her vivid descriptions as she details her new home, the famous removal of a backyard stump with the aid of a stick of dynamite, and a ghostly vision by the family's black cook:

> The Big House, as it was known, sat at the head of Front Street, facing the river with a serpentine walk that edged from the back side porch to the lower gate. . . . Where Front Street ended and led with a curve to Back Street, was a rivulet of sorts where Mr. McCarthy's geese laid their eggs and made their nests. These were the geese that, hissing at my inquisitiveness, pecked the seat of my pretty, Swiss-lace panties divers times. (I still do not like geese!)
>
> The house was "guarded" by alligators in the log booms in front, panthers to the rear of the Bicker cottage (resident caretaker) on the left facing the river, and rattlesnakes that nested in the oak tree stump by the kitchen back door.
>
> . . . thunderous explosion . . . splinters of wood rained in every direction and so did 17 baby rattlers hurled out of their nest, plus an irate mother. . . . Mama, riven to the spot, lapsed into her native tongue and kept repeating, "Purissima! Sempre serpenti, serpenti!" With the Virgin Mary . . . Mama was on intimate terms. She called on her with all her titles.
>
> "Don't you come no closer, Sam. You know we give you a good funeral, had a good preachin' too. We buried you right. How come you'se back and actin' like a haint? Go back across the Big Branch and stay gone!"
>
> This parley from the kitchen was directed to the invisible (to all except Aunt Jane [the cook]) ghost loitering around the bread table in the dining room. . . . Being new in this part of the world and never having heard of ghosts or "haints," I was paralyzed with fear and suspicious of the powers of the Big Branch. . . . The Big Branch is

still near what was once Bay Point—larger, more swiftly rushing, reed hidden, wider and hauntingly eerie with past spectres of death and violence, some imagined, some real.

This writer would be happy to go on relating story after story told with such wry humor and penetrating insight by Miss Adelia. However, we must press on to detail the Blackwater River's cruising potential.

The Blackwater River
(Various Lats/Lons—see below)

Blackwater Bay, leading to the Blackwater River, intersects the headwaters of East Bay on its northerly reaches. The river stretches some 6 nautical miles upstream to the historic, backwater villages of Bagdad and Milton. A reliable, well-marked channel with minimum 8-foot depths allows easy passage by most pleasure craft, large or small. However, a fixed bridge with a vertical clearance of 45 feet will prevent many sailboats from exploring the stream's upper reaches, site of the river's best (though not all) anchorages. Power boats and smaller sailcraft will find a cruise of the Blackwater to be an absolute delight.

Moving upstream on the Blackwater River, the first good anchorage is found on the cove northeast of flashing daybeacon #30 (near 30 34.380 North/086 59.200 West). Skippers who pilot craft drawing 4-feet, or preferably a bit less, can track their way to within .15 nautical miles of the easterly banks and hold minimum soundings of 4½ to 5 feet. Closer to shore, depths rise markedly. There is good shelter from eastern, southeasterly, northeastern, and, to a lesser extent, southern and northern breezes, but this haven is wide open to fresh breezes blowing from the west and southwest. The

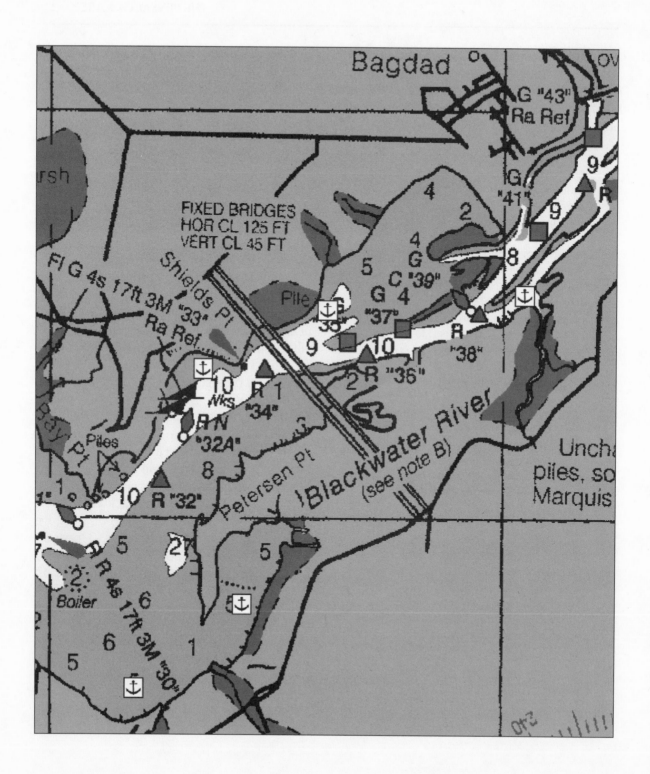

adjoining shoreline supports both moderate residential development and untouched tracks. All in all, the view is quite eye pleasing. This would be an excellent haven for the night, without the necessity of messing with the 45-foot fixed bridge, always supposing the fickle wind chooses to cooperate.

Are there any brave captains out there? Well if, and only if, you are willing to risk finding the bottom, and if you can follow a barely marked channel, there is another extremely well-sheltered haven just northwest of the anchorage described above.

Take a gander at chart 11385 and notice the almost-enclosed cove northwest of Petersen Point. There is a channel into the deeper interior reaches of this cove, *but* it is barely marked, and if you stray outside of the entrance cut, you could easily find yourself in about 6 inches of water!

However, should cruisers be able to negotiate the very tricky entrance cut, they can anchor in 5-foot depths near 30 34.846 North/086 59.590 West. Here you will find enough elbowroom for a 50-footer and protection about as good as it gets. The cove's shoreline is guarded by a few attractive homes and private docks, but believe you me, this is a visually appealing place to spend an evening afloat.

Don't even think about trying to access this anchorage unless your vessel draws *less than* 4 feet. Personally, I wouldn't want to pilot any boat larger than 36 feet into this haven. Even then, read our navigational hints in the next section of this chapter with the greatest of care. Be warned, however, even with all these precautions in hand, it's still quite possible to find the bottom.

West-northwest of unlighted nun buoy #32A (just southeast of Shields Point-I-10 Bridge), minimum 5- to 6-foot depths run to within 75 yards of the westerly banks in the charted cove south of Shields Point. In all but strong easterly blows, boats up to 45 feet can easily drop the hook on these welcoming waters (near 30 34.664 North/087 00.722 West) for the night. The shoreline exhibits the area's typical light, visually pleasing residential development.

Soon after leaving the 43-foot Shields Point-I-10 Bridge in your wake, captains will come across yet another potential anchorage. Notice the charted tongue of deep water west of unlighted daybeacon #35. Boats as large as 45 feet will find good depths of 6½ to 7 feet near 30 35.219 North/087 01.032 West. These soundings hold to within 75 yards of the southwesterly shoreline. The surrounding banks are mostly undeveloped, though a few houses do peep out a bit farther upstream. Don't anchor here if strong winds are wafting from the north, northeast, or northwest, but otherwise, there should be good protection from inclement weather.

North of unlighted daybeacon #37 good depths stretch out almost from shore to shore. The river is narrow enough at this point to afford sufficient protection from all but major storms. The pristine shores make an enchanting backdrop for setting the anchor anywhere you might choose.

One of the best anchorages along the river is found on the charted offshoot abutting the main stream's eastern banks near unlighted daybeacon #38. There is some scattered residential development on the eastern shores, but the opposite banks are in their natural state. Minimum depths of 7 to 8 feet, with enough swinging room for boats up to 45 feet, are found on the waters abeam of the first charted offshoot making off to the east, near 30 36.095 North/087 01.116 West. Protection should be sufficient for even the heaviest of weather.

Craft under 40 feet can follow the above creek as it meanders first northwest, then west, and finally rejoins the main river near unlighted daybeacon #42. Minimum depths remain at 8 feet, with most of the passage being considerably deeper. The stream narrows as it winds its way to the north and west, but even so, boats up to 35 feet should be able to anchor on this stretch of the stream as well.

Farther upstream, passage on the Blackwater River is blocked by a low-level swing bridge at the village of Milton. While a sign on the span promises that the bridge will open with 8 hours' notice, it appears to have been in the closed position for some time.

EAST BAY AND BLACKWATER RIVER NAVIGATION

With the exception of a few shoals guarding the northern quarter of East Bay's entrance, navigation of the bay and the Blackwater River is simple coastal navigation. As always, don't forget the sounder and stay alert.

Entry into East Bay   Use chart 11378 for your initial entry into East Bay. From the deep waters of Pensacola Bay, south of Escambia Bay, follow the wide swath of deep water that flows under the mid-section of the new, fixed, 65-foot bridge south of Hernandez Point. Once through the bridge, set a careful compass/GPS course to come abeam of flashing daybeacon #3 by some 200 yards to its southerly side. Be sure to stay well away from Garcon Point to the north. There are extensive shoals building out from here and jutting out from the banks to the north.

Once abeam of #3, switch to chart 11385 for further upstream navigation. Now the deep waters of East Bay open out to the north and east. While an improved, marked channel leads north from #3, sailors can safely tack their way into the large pool of deep water to the east. Just avoid the shoreline. Shoal water extends out into the bay for some .4 of a nautical mile from almost all the banks.

Don't attempt to enter the extreme easterly reaches of East Bay. As noted earlier, the entrance is surrounded by numerous unmarked shoals waiting to trap the unwary cruiser.

North to the Blackwater River   To continue upstream on the marked channel to the Blackwater River, swing sharply north from #3 and set course to come abeam of unlighted daybeacon #4 to its fairly immediate westerly side. From #4 all the way to flashing daybeacon #30, you need only hold to the marked cut for minimum 8-foot depths. Be sure to avoid the charted spoil banks west of the marked track between unlighted daybeacons #10 and #16, and a similar section west of the gap between unlighted daybeacon #18 and flashing daybeacon #21. Also, be on guard against the charted patch of shallower water east of unlighted daybeacon #22.

Cove Anchorages   To enter the anchorage northeast of flashing daybeacon #30, come abeam of unlighted can buoy #31 to its easterly quarter. Cut northwest toward the next river-channel aid to navigation, unlighted daybeacon #32, as if you were continuing upriver. After proceeding about 150 yards, swing to the east and set course for the easterly shores of the large cove that will open out before you. Be sure to set the hook before approaching to within less than .15 nautical miles of the easterly banks. Depths rise sharply as one moves in closer to the cove's shoreline.

Those brave souls bent on a visit to the protected but navigationally difficult cove northwest of Petersen Point (just northwest of the anchorage outlined above) had better be ready for a bit of a white-knuckle experience. Begin by cruising as if you were going to drop the hook in the haven described above. When you are within some .2 nautical miles of the easterly banks, swing sharply north and use your binoculars to watch for two small markers. One consists of a white PVC pipe, and the other is a small white floater. *Pass both these decrepit markers by some 20 yards to your port side. Do not try to pass between them.*

After leaving the twin markers behind, begin favoring the southwesterly (Petersen Point) side of the channel. If you're lucky, and believe me it will take luck, deep water will eventually open out before your craft in a wide pool. Drop the hook on the centerline of the cove and stand ready to laugh at any rough weather that comes along. Of course, you still have to retrace your steps without finding the bottom, so don't laugh too loudly!

Shields Point Anchorage   To drop the hook in the cove lying along Blackwater River's westerly banks between unlighted nun buoy #32A and flashing daybeacon #33, cut west toward the north-to-south centerline of the large cove that lies west-northwest of #32A. Sound your way carefully toward the westerly banks. Good depths of 5 to 6 feet run to within 75 yards of the shoreline.

On Blackwater River   Northwest of flashing daybeacon #33 and unlighted daybeacon #34, the Blackwater River channel flows through the Shields Point-I-10 Bridge. This fixed span has a vertical clearance of 45 feet, thereby restricting entry into the upper reaches of the Blackwater for tall sailcraft.

Once through the Shields Point span, set course to come between unlighted daybeacons #35 and #36. Another anchorage possibility is accessible short of #35.

Upper Blackwater River Anchorage   Take a gander at chart 11385 and notice the ribbon of deep water west of unlighted daybeacon #35. If you decide to anchor on these fortunate waters, abandon the main Blackwater River Channel about halfway between the Shields Point-I-10 Bridge and #35. Cut to the north-northwest and feel you way along for some 200 yards with the sounder. Good water runs to within 75 yards of the western and southwesterly banks. We suggest dropping anchor abeam of the point you will spot to the southwest.

On Blackwater River   Continue following the well-marked channel as it strikes to the north. Soon you will come abeam of unlighted daybeacon #38 to its westerly side. At this point, the charted offshoot to the north beckons.

Unnamed Loop Anchorage   Just before coming abeam of #38, cruisers can cut to the northeast and enter the charted, deep-water loop on the eastern banks. The entrance is wide and lacks any shallow-water bar. The waters featuring maximum swinging room are found abeam of the first charted offshoot making off from the easterly shoreline.

Craft up to 40 feet can follow the loop all the way north and west until it rejoins the main river channel near unlighted daybeacon #42. Minimum depths are 8 feet, with most of the route being considerably deeper.

Swinging room does decrease on the upper reaches of the loop. Boats larger than 32 feet might not find sufficient swinging room on this section without setting a Bahamian moor.

On the Blackwater   Look west just upstream from unlighted can buoy #39, and you will see a few abandoned structures along the shoreline. This is apparently all that's left of the old logging community of Bagdad.

North of unlighted daybeacon #43 there are no further markers. Good depths, however, open out almost from bank to bank and boats of almost any draft can continue cruising safely upriver to Milton. There are no dockage or marina facilities available to cruising craft in this community.

Eventually your passage will be blocked by a low-level bridge with 8 feet (or less) of vertical clearance. While you may see a sign promising to open the span with eight hours' notice, due to appearances this writer feels that may no longer be an option.

Pensacola Inlet and the ICW Passage to Big Lagoon

Let us now return to the ICW passage across the lower reaches of Pensacola Bay and the much-used inlet leading to the Gulf of Mexico. From the western terminus of Santa Rosa Sound, the ICW passage darts almost due west across the southern foot of Pensacola Bay. Eventually the Waterway leads through the naval turning basin northeast of Fort Pickens, and then across the northern headwaters of Pensacola Inlet. When wind and tide go head to head, this can be one of the roughest sections of the entire Gulf Coast ICW.

West of the inlet intersection, the ICW flows through a short, dredged land cut into the calmer waters of Big Lagoon. Many a captain has breathed a sigh of relief upon sighting the lagoon.

Pensacola Inlet is very well marked and carefully maintained. Most markers are clearly charted, which bodes well for a stable seaward passage. The cut is used on a regular basis by the large naval and commercial vessels frequenting Pensacola Harbor. We lowly, pleasure cruisers can most assuredly make use of the inlet without undue difficulty. As with all seaward passages, the waters can be rough. Try to pick a day of fair breezes for your passage.

This portion of Pensacola Bay is totally without marina facilities. Anchorages are also in very short supply. In southerly breezes, adventurous captains might try easing into the charted deep water southeast of flashing buoy #18, but shelter from inclement weather is quite minimal. Most cruisers will wisely choose to cruise north to Pensacola's ample facilities, west down the ICW to the Big Lagoon marinas, or seaward on the inlet. Except for some very nice scenery, there is little reason to linger on this portion of the Waterway.

Tracking across the ICW channel and Pensacola Inlet is indeed a visually interesting experience. West of flashing buoy #18, you can gaze northward to the extensive piers and support buildings of the Pensacola Naval Air Station. During one of our visits to these waters, a leviathan aircraft carrier dominated the waterfront.

South of flashing buoy #16, passing mariners can readily observe the fascinating structure of Fort Pickens. Fort Barrancas can also be observed on the northern banks north of flashing buoy #15.

The Apaches of Fort Pickens

Soon after Florida was acquired by the young United States in 1819, the American navy began to use Pensacola as a base of operations. There were smugglers to chase and pirates to root out, tasks which were made ever so much more difficult by the long naval supply chain which stretched all the way around Florida's southern tip to St. Augustine. Before long a large naval base was planned in Pensacola's naturally deep and sheltered harbor. To protect the base, federal authorities commissioned the construction of three forts set about Pensacola Inlet. Fort McRae was built on the seaward cut's western shores, and Fort Barrancas guarded the naval yard to the north. Largest of the three was Fort Pickens, set on the shores of Santa Rosa Island east of the inlet.

Begun in 1829 and finished in 1834, the fort was composed of earth and over 21 million bricks. Thought to be impregnable at the beginning of the Civil War, masonry forts such as Pickens were rendered obsolete during the latter years of the War Between the States by highly accurate rifled cannon.

During the Spanish-American War and into the early 1900s, new works were added to Fort Pickens, while the old walls were allowed to deteriorate. This resulted in a confusing hodgepodge of defenses that the modern visitor can only sort out with the help of the official park brochure.

In 1899 a black powder magazine blew up, leveling one corner of the edifice. The fort consequently presents a lopsided appearance to the present-day visitor.

Meanwhile, the site of old Fort McRae, west of the inlet, had completely eroded into the surrounding waters. Nothing is left of this one-time historical site.

Fort Barrancas has been partially restored by the navy. Its remarkably intact walls can be readily observed from the waters just east of Pensacola Lighthouse.

In October of 1886 *The Pensacolian,* a weekly newspaper, ran the following article:

> The powers that be in Washington have at last come to their senses and selected Fort

Pickens as the most suitable place to incarcerate the greatest living American general and his principal officers. Fort Pickens is well suited as an abiding place for one of Geronimo's genius, for there he can be like his great prototype, Napoleon at St. Helena, live again his conquests without being disturbed by the outside world. . . . We welcome the nation's distinguished guests, and promise to keep them so safely under lock and key that they will forget their hair-raising proclivities and become good Indians.

The parallel between Napoleon and the Apache chief Geronimo is not entirely apt. The "general" left the reservation on which his people had been placed by the federal government due to harsh and less than humane conditions. He took to warring in the southeastern United States and northern Mexico, not from dreams of conquest, but as a way of demonstrating his people's desperate plight.

Finally, starving and battle weary, Geronimo and his small band surrendered to General Miles in Arizona. Miles promised protection and forgiveness for all past "crimes." Geronimo had no sooner been transferred to Texas than the government reneged on its bargain and decided to send the great chief to Fort Pickens in Pensacola as a prisoner of war.

On October 12, 1886 the train containing the prisoners pulled into the Pensacola railway station at 2:00 A.M. A large crowd met the train, hoping for a look at the Apaches. They were not disappointed. The prisoners were marched to a waiting steamship, which began the journey across Pensacola Bay to the remote Fort Pickens. Contrary to the claims of some historians, the Indians were given the run of the old fort. Their living conditions were actually rather comfortable for the period and

by some accounts Geronimo and his band soon adapted to the seashore life.

At first there was some understandable concern on the part of Pensacolians about the loose guard kept on Geronimo and his followers. Eventually though, when it was seen that the Indians were well behaved, boatloads of the curious began to visit the fort on weekends. Young ladies making the excursion often brought flowers and food for the imprisoned Native Americans. Geronimo was an obvious favorite with the visitors. He is supposed to have told one visitor that everyone coming to the fort "ought to be liberally assessed [a fee], for he was poor, yes, very poor."

Finally, due to pressure from liberal elements of the national press, the Apaches' families were moved from St. Augustine and allowed to join the men at Fort Pickens. The grateful Indians held a party for the local townspeople. All who traveled over to the fort were permitted to view the tribal dances. The novel celebration caused quite a stir among the townspeople and was discussed for many years afterward.

In May 1888, the Apaches were suddenly transferred from Fort Pickens to the reservation at Fort Sill, Oklahoma. The Pensacola citizenry was incensed by the sudden departure. The Indians had become so popular that volumes of letters were written in protest to the military authorities in Washington. The letters were in vain and Pensacola had to bid a reluctant farewell to some of the most unusual visitors who ever lived along its waters.

Pensacola Lighthouse

Hard by the walls of Fort Barrancas, the valiant Pensacola Lighthouse gazes defiantly out over the waters of the inlet it has marked since 1858. Successor to a weak, much smaller light which was erected in 1824, it's more than slightly amazing that the taller lighthouse has stood until the present day. During the Civil War's early days, the tower was shelled by Northern forces seeking to dislodge Confederate gunners positioned beside Fort Barrancas. Prior to the fall of Pensacola to Union forces, Southern troops stole the light's lens. It was not recovered until after the war.

Lightning seems to like the Pensacola Lighthouse. It has been struck repeatedly by strong bolts. In 1875 the entire lens apparatus was melted during a tremendous thunder and lightning cavalcade.

As if all that weren't enough of an assault, a strong earthquake shook the light soundly in 1885. The keeper mistook the rumbling for a party of visitors ascending the tower's spiral stairway.

Today, the Pensacola Lighthouse still stands proudly, a lasting monument to its builders' prowess with brick and mortar. With an original construction cost of only $25,000, one can only conclude that the taxpayers have gotten their money's worth.

PENSACOLA INLET AND ICW PASSAGE NAVIGATION

Considering the often rough conditions of the ICW's passage across lower Pensacola Bay and the upper reaches of Pensacola Inlet, it's fortunate indeed that the track does not stray anywhere near shoal water. Even the inlet is mostly free of shallows, except for the one charted patch on its westerly quarter.

If winds exceed fifteen knots, it would be prudent to wait for fairer breezes at one of the marinas on Big Lagoon or in Pensacola before tackling the ICW route or the inlet.

ICW to Pensacola Inlet   From a position well north of flashing daybeacon #145, where our discussion of the Pensacola region began, set course to come abeam of flashing buoy #20 well to its northerly side. It is a run of some 1.25 nautical miles between #145 and #20.

As you are now following the Pensacola Bay Inlet channel, subsequent red, even-numbered aids should be passed to your port side and green markers taken to starboard. This color configuration holds until the ICW abandons the inlet channel at unlighted can buoy #1 and flashing buoy #2, as it begins its entrance into Big Lagoon.

Continue through the naval turning basin by setting course to come abeam of and pass flashing buoy #18 to its northerly quarter and flashing buoy #17 to its southerly side. As you are cruising between #20 and #18, watch to the north for the naval wharves and any large vessels that happen to be in port. Soon you will come abeam of flashing buoy #16, south of your course. Once abeam of #16 you should have a good view of Fort Pickens on the western tip of Santa Rosa Island.

Follow the same track past #16, pointing to come abeam of flashing buoy #14 well to its northerly side. At #14 the ICW meets up with the northerly headwaters of Pensacola Inlet.

Pensacola Inlet   From a position abeam of flashing buoy #14, well to its northerly side, follow a lazy turn to the south into the centerline of the Pensacola Inlet channel. West of unlighted can buoy #11, a tongue of shoal water extends well seaward. Stick to the marked cut to avoid this hazard. Otherwise, you need only follow the charted channel for successful passage to the open sea, remembering always that swells on the inlet can be prodigious, even when the surrounding waters are calm.

ICW to Big Lagoon   From flashing buoy #14, set a careful compass course to pass between flashing buoy #2 and unlighted can buoy #1. These aids mark the beginning of the dredged channel leading to Big Lagoon. Marker colors now revert to the normal ICW pattern, with westbound cruisers passing green beacons to their (the cruisers') port side and red markers to starboard.

The channel from Pensacola Inlet to Big Lagoon (north of the charted position of Fort McRae) is subject to shoaling and markers are often shifted to follow the ever-moving sands. Be prepared for different markings than those shown on your chart or presented in this account.

Once between #1 and #2, set course to pass between unlighted nun buoy #4 and unlighted can #3. Bend your course a touch to the south and point to pass between unlighted nun #6 and unlighted can #5. Continue straight ahead to the dredged land cut. As you exit the cut on its western terminus, flashing daybeacon #7 will come abeam south of your course. The waters of Big Lagoon will spread out before you.

This portion of the ICW passage is not too complex during daylight hours, though you must be careful to watch for lateral leeway. At night, however, the narrow passage, coupled with the absence of any lighted aids on the channel leading to the land cut, make successful navigation of the channel a real chore. Navigators lacking local knowledge should definitely plan to arrive during the day. If you can't make the passage before nightfall, retreat to the Pensacola or Big Lagoon facilities and wait for morning.

CHAPTER 5

Big Lagoon to Mobile Bay

West of Pensacola Inlet, the Gulf Coast ICW enters Big Lagoon. Cruising along this section of the Waterway, visiting mariners will begin to notice a radical transformation in the Northern Gulf waters. As you move ever closer to Mobile Bay, the gin-clear depths of the Florida Panhandle begin to cloud. The waters become ever muddier as you cruise to the west. This is only as it should be. Soon after leaving Big Lagoon behind, the Waterway cruises into Alabama and begins its trek to Mobile Bay. The rivers feeding this historically rich bay comprise the second largest drainage basin in the United States, outdone only by the mighty Mississippi. It's not too hard to understand that this vast delta system carries tons and tons of mud, sediment, and other debris in its restless waters. While some may cast a longing backward glance at the Panhandle shores, you can rest assured that the warm, brown waters of Alabama, Mississippi, and eastern Louisiana have more than their own share of cruising opportunities to tempt recreational cruisers.

As the waters begin to change, the landscape between Big Lagoon and Mobile Bay continues to resemble the shoreline to the east which has become so familiar. Numerous creeks and bayous break the lightly developed landscape all along the ICW. Many of these streams have deep channels and can provide secure shelter for almost any pleasure craft. One creek, Ingram's Bayou, has the enviable reputation of offering the loveliest haven on the entire run between Carrabelle and New Orleans.

Mobile Bay itself is a large body of water that is much frequented by commercial barge and tow traffic. For the first time, cruisers will be able to observe the offshore drilling rigs which mine the waters of the Northern Gulf for crude oil and natural gas. Two historic Civil War forts guard the bay's southern mouth, a constant reminder of the region's rich and varied historic heritage. The bay is rather shallow overall, but there is a whole system of well-marked channels which captains and crew can use for cruising to a surprisingly limited number of destinations.

Marinas and boatyards are prolific on the ICW and more than adequate on Mobile Bay. Most of these marinas are first-rate operations that enjoy excellent reputations. One even serves "the best cheeseburgers on earth!"

Shoreside scenery remains a treasure chest for the eyes. Lightly developed patches along the Waterway east of Mobile Bay are interspaced with large, all-natural woodlands and marsh. Mobile Bay presents some of the most dramatic vistas available anywhere. The extensive Mobile commercial port facilities guard the bay's northerly reaches and make for an unforgettable sight from the water.

The city of Mobile, Mobile Bay, and Dauphin Island can lay claim to some of the most colorful figures and dramatic events in the long and dramatic history of the Northern Gulf. This writer suggests that you make every effort to acquire a working knowledge of this heritage before you visit. Your journey will be far the richer for the extra effort.

So now it's time to move along and begin our explorations of Mobile Bay and its approaches. Some of the most exciting cruising to be found anywhere awaits you.

Charts   Only two NOAA charts are required for complete navigation of this region:
11378—follows the ICW from Pensacola Bay to Mobile Bay, and across the bay's southern foot to Dauphin Island—also gives good details on the various side-waters and bayous along the way
11376—principal Mobile Bay chart—will be needed by all navigators cruising on the bay's waters north of the ICW

Bridges
Perdido Key-Gulf Beach Bridge—crosses the ICW at standard mile 172—Fixed—73 feet
Perdido Pass Bridge—crosses the northerly reaches of Perdido Pass south of Terry Cove and west of Bayou St. John—Fixed—54 feet
Foley Beach Express Bridge—crosses the ICW at standard mile 159, southwest of unlighted can buoy #95A—Fixed—73 feet
Portage Creek Bridge—crosses the ICW at standard mile 155—Fixed—73 feet
Fowl River Bridge—crosses Fowl River southwest of unlighted daybeacons #15 and #16—Fixed—24 feet
Dog River Bridge—crosses the mouth of Dog River west of flashing daybeacon #13—Fixed—65 feet
Dauphin Island Causeway—crosses the ICW-Pass Aux Herons channel at standard mile 128—Fixed—83 feet

Big Lagoon to Mobile Bay

Any writer attempting to describe the waters between Carrabelle and Mobile is bound to have a problem. How many times can you use words and phrases like "beautiful, lovely, enchanting, tremendous cruising potential, etc." without becoming repetitive? Eventually one just simply runs out of new adjectives. Well, all these words and more could be used to accurately describe the run from Pensacola to Mobile Bay, so I guess you'll just have to put up with the repetition. By the way, if you happen to think of some new synonyms, please let me hear from you for the next edition.

The Gulf Coast ICW departs the approaches to Pensacola Inlet and enters the broad waters of Big Lagoon via an artificial land cut. While strong breezes can certainly stir up a healthy chop in the lagoon, it's usually a lot smoother than Pensacola Bay.

From Big Lagoon, the Waterway follows a dredged channel for some 15 nautical miles to Portage Creek. This section of the ICW is indented by numerous bays, creeks, and bayous. With only a few exceptions, these prolific side-waters offer excellent gunk-holing and superior anchorage. There is even one inlet which might be considered as a reasonably reliable outlet to the briny blue.

The entrance into Portage Creek heralds a long, mostly man-made canal portion of the ICW that generally leads west for some 8.5 nautical miles to Bon Secour Bay, an auxiliary water of larger Mobile Bay. This is most certainly *not* the most attractive section of the Gulf Coast Waterway. The route is flanked by banks of rock and mud which appear to be eroding in many places. For a portion of this run, the highway serving the resort community of Orange Beach parallels the canal.

Marinas are numerous east of Portage Creek.

A host of facilities are clustered along the ICW, while another group of marinas is found near Perdido Pass Inlet on Cotton Bayou and Terry Cove. Once into the canal-like passage, there are no real facilities available for pleasure craft until reaching Mobile Bay.

Even with its muddier waters, few will dismiss their cruise from Big Lagoon to Portage Creek as merely a voyage to mark time. The shoreline along the way is simply beautiful. Vast natural stretches are split from time to time by light development. Perdido Pass Inlet and the nearby community of Orange Beach feature heavier commercial development, but even this region is not unattractive.

Those who enjoy anchoring off should plan to spend a night under the stars tucked snugly into one of the many side-waters. Even those who usually frequent marinas will find a bonanza of memorable overnight refuges on this stretch of the Gulf Waterway. Take your time and enjoy the sights. With but a few exceptions, cruisers will not find such sheltered, anchorage-rich waters throughout all of the Alabama and Mississippi coastlines to the west.

Big Lagoon (Standard Mile 178.5)

Big Lagoon is a very popular body of water. During the summer months, weekends usually bring out a horde of local cruisers somewhat similar in size to the Spanish Armada. Small power and sailing craft descend on the Perdido Key anchorages by the dozen. Swimming, sunning, and the consumption of a few "cold ones" is the order of the day. Visiting cruisers are always welcome in this friendly fraternity.

Two marinas offer transient dockage on Big Lagoon. There are also any number of good spots to drop the hook in fair weather adjacent to the undeveloped south shoreline. One haven is appropriate for nasty weather.

Big Lagoon has the good fortune to be bounded to the south by Perdido Key. The eastern third of this long island is part of the Gulf Islands National Seashore and is completely protected from development. The landscape consists of low-lying dunes covered by sparse scrub growth and sea grasses. The oceanside beaches are all that could be asked for, and the sound offers good swimming and fishing. In short, what more could you want?

South Cut

Some years ago, a few local captains made use of the channel skirting south of the large spoil island north of charted Fort McRee as an alternate passage from Pensacola Inlet to Big Lagoon. This passage, known locally as the South Cut, has shoaled and become far more complicated. It is no longer advisable for any size vessel to attempt entry into its east-side entrance, cutting in from Pensacola Inlet. On the other hand, vessels drawing *less than* 4 feet could possibly enter the channel along its westerly reaches and drop the lunch hook for a pleasant hour or so. These waters are an official no-wake zone, and your time at anchor is likely to be a pleasant experience, if the weather chooses to cooperate.

Big Lagoon Anchorages (Various Lats/Lons—see below)

The charted tongue of deep water that strikes south to the east of Spanish Point (standard mile 178, near 30 19.336 North/087 19.649 West) can provide sheltered anchorage when winds are not blowing from the north or west.

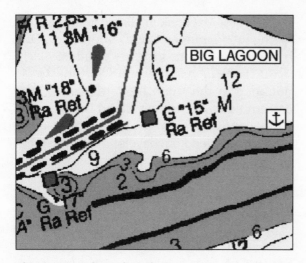

The surrounding shoreline is in its natural state and the oceanside beaches are only a short walk away. Minimum depths are about 6 feet in the anchorage but unmarked shoals are prolific, and it's all to easy to wander into grounding depths. Great care must also be taken to avoid the charted shallows to the south. Please read the Big Lagoon navigational information presented later in this chapter before attempting to make use of this haven. Swinging room should be sufficient for vessels as large as 40 feet.

Another set of popular anchorages is found on the deep waters east of Redfish Point (standard mile 177, near either 30 19.128 North/087 20.210 West or 30 19.068 North/087 20.536 West). Careful captains can ease their way to within 100 yards of shore in 8-foot minimum depths. A patch of shoal water bisects this anchorage. You can choose to enter the deep holes either east or west of these shallows. Both anchorages require you to navigate around unmarked shoals. Swinging room should be sufficient for boats up to 48 feet. The adjacent shores are completely undeveloped and are particularly appropriate

for swimming, sunbathing, and tossing the Frisbee. On weekends you can expect to be joined during the daylight hours by any number of local pleasure craft. Northerly winds over 10 knots or easterly breezes of 15 knots or better would render this haven downright uncomfortable and possibly dangerous. However, in fair weather, boats of practically any size can drop the hook here for a beautiful evening.

The charted patch of deep water east of unlighted daybeacon #15 (standard mile 174, near 30 18.478 North/087 23.195 West) is an even better open-water anchorage. It's a simple matter to cruise to within 100 yards of shore and hold minimum 9-foot depths. Swinging room is sufficient for even the largest pleasure craft. The undeveloped shores are just a short dinghy ride away. The best shelter, of course, is afforded from southerly breezes. Winds from any other quarter exceeding 10 knots call for a different strategy.

Big Lagoon Facilities

Two side-by-side marinas grace Big Lagoon's northerly shores just west of flashing daybeacon #10 (standard mile 177). The easternmost facility is Rod and Reel Marina (30 19.665 North/087 21.381 West).

Cruising visitors calling at Rod and Reel will no longer find the smiling face of former owner, Les Westerman, to greet them. However, the new caretakers have made some noteable improvements in this facility, and we recommend it highly in all but heavy weather.

Rod and Reel features extensive transient dockage at fixed wooden piers with every power and water connection. Depths alongside range from an impressive 12 feet or better at the outer docks to soundings ranging from 5

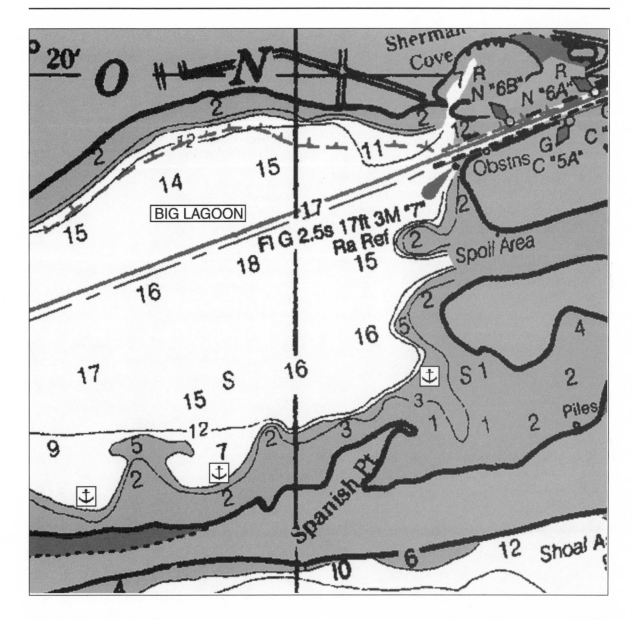

to 7 feet at low water at the inner-harbor berths. Gasoline, diesel fuel, and waste pump-outer service are readily available.

Rod and Reel's dockage basin does lack shelter from strong southerly blows. This is also a problem (ironically) for Southwind Marina, next door. Unless winds exceed 20 knots out of the south, however, this lack of protection should not be too large a problem.

Shoreside, cruisers will discover fair,

nonclimate-controlled showers. Wooden slats in the walls of the shower room let in fresh air. There is also a semi-open-air Laundromat on the premises.

Rod and Reel Marina also features full haul-out repair capability. The yard's travelift is rated at 25 tons. Mechanical servicing can usually be arranged through independent local contractors.

The latest addition at this facility is a small grill and restaurant set in the location of the old ship's/variety store and snack bar. This modest eatery features plentiful open-air dining and some seriously good cheeseburgers. It is open for all three meals of the day, seven days a week.

Veteran cruisers who remember the nearby Rusty's Restaurant will be sad to learn that it is now closed. There is a convenience store within walking distance, but it would be a lengthy journey, even by automobile, to reach a supermarket.

Rod and Reel Marina (850) 492-0100
- Approach depth—12-17 feet
- Dockside depth—5-12 feet
- Accepts transients—yes
- Transient-dockage rate—below average
- Fixed wooden piers—yes
- Dockside power connections—20-, 30-, and 50 amp
- Dockside water connections—yes
- Showers—yes
- Laundromat—yes
- Waste pump-out—yes
- Gasoline—yes
- Diesel fuel—yes
- Mechanical repairs—yes (independent contractors)
- Below-waterline repairs—yes
- Haul-out repairs—yes
- Restaurant—on-site

Rod and Reel Marina, Big Lagoon

Southwind Marina, just to the west (30 19.602 North/087 21.440 West), also gladly accepts transient craft for overnight berths at fixed, wooden piers with 30- and 50-amp power connections and water connections. During the summer season, the docks are attended until 10:00 P.M. Telephone and cable-television hookups are available as well. Very long-legged craft can tie to the outer docks, which have impressive 9-foot dockside depths, while the inner berths feature 5- to 6-foot soundings. A portable pump-out system is at your disposal with advance appointments only. Gasoline and diesel fuel are ready for pumping. The on-site showers are truly bleak, but there is a nice Laundromat. Mechanical repairs can be arranged.

The real attraction at Southwinds is the very popular Ryan's Catch Restaurant (850-492-0335), located just behind the dockage basin. Judging from the impressive numbers of diners we observed during our last visit, this attraction draws many cruisers off the Waterway for the sole purpose of sampling the fare. May you, too, be so lucky!

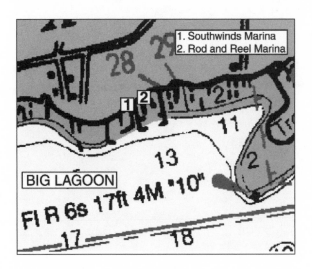

Southwinds Marina (850) 492-0333
   http://www.ryan'scatchrestaurant.com

Approach depth—9-17 feet
Dockside depth—5-9 feet
Accepts transients—yes
Transient-dockage rate—average
Fixed wooden piers—yes
Dockside power connections—30- and 50-amp
Dockside water connections—yes
Showers—yes
Laundromat—yes
Waste pump-out—advance appointment only
Gasoline—yes
Diesel fuel—yes
Restaurant—on site

Oyster Bar Restaurant and Marina (Standard Mile 172) (30 18.696 North/087 25.516 West)

The docks of Oyster Bar Marina (also known as Perdido Key Marina) grace the Waterway's southern shore just west of flashing daybeacon #31 (hard by the Perdido Key-Gulf Beach fixed bridge). Transients are accommodated at fixed, wooden piers with both fresh-water and 30- and 50-amp power hookups. Gasoline and diesel fuel are available, as is one dark but clean and air-conditioned shower.

Depths at Oyster Bar's outer docks run around 8 to 9 feet, while the inner piers hold some 5 to 6 feet of water. This marina has a powercraft flavor, but visiting sailors should still find it comfortable for an overnight stay.

The on-site Oyster Bar Restaurant has changed hands several times during the last several years, and we have not yet had the opportunity to try its latest incarnation. The most we can say is that there were a goodly number of cars in the adjacent parking lot during our last stop here.

Oyster Bar Marina (850) 492-5600

Approach depth—10 feet minimum

Dockside depth—5 to 9 feet
Accepts transients—yes
Transient-dockage rate—average
Fixed wooden piers—yes
Dockside power connections—30- and 50-amp
Dockside water connections—yes
Showers—yes
Gasoline—yes
Diesel fuel—yes
Restaurant—on site

Holiday Harbor Marina (Standard Mile 170) (30 18.628 North/087 26.284 West)

The marked but mostly uncharted entrance channel to Holiday Harbor Marina strikes south from the ICW, immediately west of flashing day-beacon #35. Transients are gratefully accepted for overnight or temporary dockage in a well-sheltered basin featuring berths at fixed, wooden piers. Newer, fixed wooden slips now front the north-to-south-running entrance cut along its easterly flank. For my money, I would request a slip in the sheltered inner harbor every time.

Full power and water connections are found at every berth. The entrance channel boasts minimum 6½-foot depths with some 5 to 6 feet of water at dockside. The dockmaster can easily

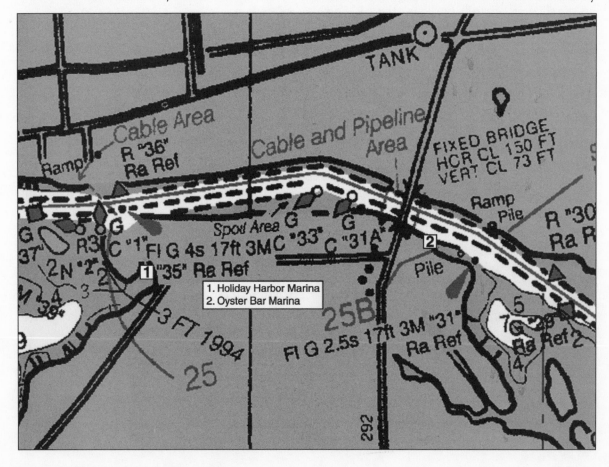

1. Holiday Harbor Marina
2. Oyster Bar Marina

direct deep-draft vessels to an appropriate berth. Gasoline and diesel fuel are readily available, both in the inner basin and at a new fuel dock that fronts directly onto the ICW. There is also one small but air-conditioned shower and a cramped Laundromat.

Full-service mechanical repairs for both gasoline and diesel engines are also offered, as is a ship's store. Smaller power craft can be hauled out via forklift. The marina features a huge dry-stack storage for smaller power craft.

Holiday Harbor now features its own on-site grill, which is currently open for lunch and dinner. The days of operation vary with the season. The Oyster Bar Restaurant, described above, is accessible via a half-mile (or slightly less) walk.

Holiday Harbor Marina (850) 492-0555

Approach depth—6½ feet (minimum)
Dockside depth—5-6 feet
Accepts transients—yes
Transient-dockage rate—average
Fixed wooden piers—yes
Dockside power connections—30- and 50-amp
Dockside water connections—yes
Showers—yes
Laundromat—yes
Gasoline—yes
Diesel fuel—yes
Mechanical repairs—yes
Ship's store—yes
**Restaurant—one on-site and another a long walk
   away**

The Old River (Standard Mile 170)

The upper reaches of the Old River intersect the ICW on its southern shores near unlighted daybeacon #43. This stream flows first south and then west around the popular resort communities on Ono Island and Perdido Key. Ono

is a true island, bordered by Old River to the south and the Intracoastal Waterway to the north. A narrow bridge spanning Old River near its southern foot connects Ono Island to Perdido Key and allows for the passage of automobile traffic onto the island.

During the last two decades, Ono Island and Perdido Key have become some of the most sought-after real estate in eastern Alabama. Dozens of fine homes have been built alongside (unfortunately) more than a few high-rise condo complexes. Today, the popularity of Ono Island-Perdido Key continues, with little in sight to check this trend.

For us cruisers, Old River can serve as a reasonably good anchorage in all but the roughest weather. The east-side entrance channel from the ICW (at unlighted daybeacon #43) is officially unmarked and more than slightly tricky. However, some homemade aids to navigation help cautious navigators to find minimum 8-foot depths into the river's deeper, inner reaches west of Rabbit Island.

By the time Old River winds its way west to the small bridge connecting Ono Island to Perdido Key, unmarked shoals begin to appear with increasing frequency. On a clear, sun-splashed day it's usually possible to bypass these hazards while navigating by eye, but this is certainly not a completely reliable procedure. By all accounts, visiting cruisers should avoid the western portion of Old River at night or in low-light conditions.

Only small, shallow-draft power craft should consider trying to follow Old River under its 24-foot, fixed bridge to Perdido Pass. Even these petite vessels are subject to finding the bottom.

While you could anchor most anywhere

along the course of the Old River channel, short of its westerly shallows, one of the most convenient spots for ICW cruisers is discovered on the charted 7- and 8-foot waters south of Rabbit Island (near 30 17.937 North/087 27.445 West). Here, with only a short cruise from the ICW, you can have good protection from southern, southwestern, northern, and (to a lesser extent) northeastern airs. Strong winds from the east or particularly the west are another matter.

Perdido Bay (Standard Mile 167.5) (Various Lats/Lons—see below)

The broad mouth of Perdido Bay opens into the Waterway's northeastern flank near flashing daybeacon #59. This large body of water runs north and east for 6.7 nautical miles to the Lillian/Highway 98 fixed bridge. At its widest point, Perdido spans some 2.3 nautical miles. Obviously, this is not an inconsequential bay.

Two sheltered anchorages wait to greet cruisers on the wide waters of Perdido Bay. Another overnight haven, Soldier Creek, will be considered separately below.

The main body of Perdido Bay is much too broad and unsheltered for overnight anchorage. Winds over 10 knots can foster a hefty chop. The shoreline is almost entirely in a virgin condition, with a few comely homes breaking the well-wooded shores here and there. As you approach the Lillian Bridge, several attractive houses will be spied on the western banks near Chagrin Point.

Tarklin Bay is actually an offshoot of the Perdido, cutting off from the larger bay's eastern shores north of Bayou Garcon. Visiting skippers can make their way to the southerly approaches of Tarklin Bayou and drop the hook in some 7 feet of water near 30 21.405 North/087 25.341 West. The heavily wooded, undeveloped shores give excellent protection from northern, western, and eastern blows, but there is very little shelter from fresh southerly breezes. Mariners should not attempt to enter Tarklin Bayou under any circumstances. A bar with less than 3 feet of water has built completely across the entrance.

During fair weather, cruisers with time on their hands might consider anchoring off the shallows surrounding Du Pont Point. This promontory is found on Perdido Bay's eastern banks, north of Tarklin Bay. It is surrounded by a beautiful white sand beach set amidst a completely undeveloped shoreline. While you must anchor at least 400 yards to the north or south of the point to avoid shoal water (near 30 22.088 North/087 26.578 West or 30 21.860 North/087 26.635 West), it's a simple matter to dinghy ashore and enjoy the gorgeous surroundings.

Northeast of the Lillian/Highway 98 fixed bridge (vertical clearance 39 feet), Perdido Bay continues to be deep for another 3 nautical miles. The northwestern corner of the bay leads to the mostly deep Perdido River. To enter this stream, you must bypass numerous unmarked shoals. Even with careful navigation, it's all too easy to land in 4 feet (or less) of water. While local captains make the trip on a weekly basis, this trek is not recommended for visiting cruisers. As there are no other protected side-waters on the bay's upper reaches, most cruisers will choose to confine their explorations to the waters south of the fixed bridge.

Soldier Creek
(Various Lats/Lons—see below)

If it were not for one nagging problem, Soldier Creek would provide what would undoubtedly be the finest overnight anchorage between Pensacola and Ingram Bayou. The creek features near perfect protection from even the most violent weather. If I were looking for a hurricane hole along this stretch of the ICW, Soldier Creek would be the clear favorite, assuming I could successfully navigate its tricky entrance.

Soldier Creek is located on the northern shores of Perdido Bay, just a hop, skip, and a jump from the ICW. This fortunate position is very convenient for cruisers traveling the Waterway. It's a run of just over 2 nautical miles from flashing daybeacon #59 to the creek's entrance.

The stream's shoreline alternates between undeveloped patches and light to moderate residential development. No one will ever fault the creek for its scenery.

Now for the bad news. Soldier Creek has a narrow, twisting entrance channel that is more than just slightly difficult to negotiate. While several uncharted, private aids help navigators keep to the deeper water, it's still very possible to wander into 4-foot depths, even when taking the greatest of care. Consequently, this anchorage can only be recommended for vessels drawing 4 feet or preferably less, and no larger than 36 feet. *Be sure* to read the navigational account of Soldier Creek presented later in this chapter before attempting to enter the stream.

Once the evil entrance is to your stern, there are many choices for a snug overnight stay. Minimum depths on the creek's interior are 6 feet, with soundings of 7 to 9 feet being the norm. Perhaps the stream's best anchorage is found on the first cove cutting into the eastern shores, immediately past the entrance. The cove's outer reaches provide ample elbow-room for any-sized pleasure craft in 7 to 9 feet of water (near 30 20.839 North/087 29.546 West). In really terrible weather, boats up to 38 feet can ease into the southeastern corner and drop the hook in one of the more cozy spots you are ever likely to find (near 30 20.771 North/087 29.483 West). While there is one unmarked shoal to avoid in reaching this inner haven, simple caution should see you safely through.

Another anchorage worthy of consideration is located on the mid-width of Soldier Creek, just north of the first sharp point protruding from the stream's easterly banks (near 30 21.313 North/087 29.796 West). Here, good depths of 6 to 8 feet spread out almost from shore to shore. There is plenty of swinging room for most sizes of pleasure craft. The surrounding shoreline exhibits pleasant, moderate, residential development. Protection is quite good from all winds, even if not quite so solid as that found on the cove described above.

Farther upstream, development ceases on both banks of Soldier Creek. Unfortunately, as suggested on chart 11378, depths soon peter out and 4½-foot waters are encountered.

Adventurous captains whose craft fit the size and draft requirements outlined above should give Soldier Creek their most careful consideration before moving on. In my opinion, there is only one other anchorage on this entire stretch that can lay claim to such a healthy share of protection, swinging room, and natural beauty.

Palmetto Creek and Spring Brook

Palmetto Creek cuts the northern shores of Perdido Bay just west of Soldier Creek. Unfortunately, a bar with only 2 to 3 feet of depth has built completely across the entrance to this stream. While the interior depths on Palmetto Creek and its auxiliary water, Spring Brook, are in the 7- to 11-foot range, all but the smallest outboard craft will be forced to bypass this side-water due to its shallow mouth.

Perdido Pass, Bayou St. John, and Cotton Bayou (Standard Mile 167) (Various Lats/Lons—see below)

Southwest of the ICW's flashing daybeacon #57, Bayou St. John leads west and southwest to Perdido Pass Inlet. Cruisers traversing this shoal-flanked route will have access not only to the inlet, but to the marinas and boatyards along both Cotton Bayou and Terry Cove.

While great care must still be taken to avoid the prolific shallows that flank the Bayou St. John channel in all directions, it is quite possible for careful mariners to track their way west and southwest to Perdido Pass with minimum 6-foot depths. Most of the route shows soundings of 7 to 12 feet.

As you might have guessed already, buoys, daybeacons, and other aids to navigation are frequently added, removed, and shifted to follow the ever-changing bottom strata of the Bayou St. John channel. Be sure to read the navigational data presented later in this chapter *before* attempting this passage. You'll be too busy to read it when you're there.

Perdido Pass Inlet offers reasonably safe passage for both power and sailcraft. The seaward cut is spanned by a fixed bridge with 54 feet of vertical clearance. Minimum depths in the marked inlet channel are now 7 feet, with much of the route being deeper. While visiting cruisers should probably check at one of the area marinas concerning the latest channel conditions

Cruising on Bayou St. John

before attempting the inlet, Perdido Pass can currently be rated as an acceptable passage for craft that can clear the 54-foot fixed bridge.

Cotton Bayou cuts into the western edge of the channel leading north from Perdido Pass Inlet. Entrance into the bayou is complicated by a shoal flanking the center of the creek's easterly mouth. A small channel cuts northwest from Perdido Pass Bridge and temporarily hugs the southern banks as it passes into the interior reaches of Cotton Bayou. The initial portion of this cut holds 5 feet of water at low tide, but a navigational mistake can land luckless navigators in 2-foot depths.

Soon after entering Cotton Bayou, the one-time location of Perdido Pass Marina will come abeam to the south. This facility has fallen victim to condo sprawl, and it is now being redeveloped as a completely private facility.

A marked but mostly uncharted channel leads cruisers down the remainder of Cotton Bayou to four additional marina facilities and one waterside restaurant.

The first to come up will be Sanroc Cay Marina (30 16.732 North/087 33.644 West), just south of the split in the channel that leads to Sun Harbor Marina (see below). Transients are accepted at fixed wooden piers. One set of slips fronts the marina and looks out on the Cotton Bayou Channel, while a second, better-sheltered, set of berths are located in a U-shaped harbor. Depths at the outer slips run at least 6½ feet, with even better soundings of 7 to 8 feet (at low water) on the inner dockage basin. Some 5½-foot soundings may be encountered between the main channel and Sanroc Cay. Fresh-water and 30- and 50-amp power hookups are in the offing, as are gasoline, diesel fuel, and a waste pump-out service. A small ship's and variety store is located at the outer end of the main dock.

Shoreside cruisers will find two sets of adequate showers—one climate-controlled, the other not. There is no Laundromat on site or within walking distance.

Come mealtime, there is an almost embarrassment of riches when it comes to your choices, all within easy walking distance. Perhaps the largest dining attraction is known as Louisiana Lagniappe (251-981-2258). They feature Cajun-style seafood. Then, there's Cafe Grazie (251-981-7278), with Italian fare, and Jumbos Grill (251-981-8889), with a more American theme. Still not enough for you, well don't overlook Sunroc's Delicatazza (251-981-8466). They have some fine sandwich makings.

Sanroc Cay Marina (251)981-7263

Approach depth—5½-7 feet
Dockside depth—
    6½-feet minimum (outer slips)
    7-8 feet (inner harbor)
Accepts transients—yes
Transient-dockage rate—average
Fixed wooden piers—yes
Dockside power connections—30- and 50-amp
Dockside fresh-water connections—yes
Waste pump-out—yes
Showers—yes
Gasoline—yes
Diesel fuel—yes
Ship's/variety store—small
Restaurant—many within walking distance

Abeam of the entrance to Sanroc Cay Marina (to the north), the Cotton Bayou Channel splits. As chart 11378 correctly indicates, a narrow ribbon of (slightly) deep water runs back to the east. This side cut can be tricky for first-timers, and even under the best of circumstances, depths run as skinny as 4½ feet at low water.

If they can stand these less-than-impressive soundings, cruisers following this cut can gain access to a waterside dining attraction and a large high-dry marina. Be *sure* to read the Cotton Bayou navigational information in the next section of this chapter *before* attempting first-time entry.

First up will be Tacky Jack's (251-981-4144). This is a new, far more elaborate incarnation of a longstanding restaurant and tavern that has overlooked the northern shores of Cotton Bayou for many a year. Now, where once there was a rather forgettable, dingy structure, there is a large, bright restaurant with its own fixed, wooden dock. Dining

Sanroc Cay Marina, Cotton Bayou

patrons are welcome to tie here while eating, and overnight stays are allowed after paying a $35 fee. There are no dockside connections or other marine services available.

A quick hop farther to the east, the huge, dry-stack storage building associated with Sun Harbor Marina (251-981-6111) will come abeam to the north, near 30 16.878 North/087 33.611 West. Besides the obvious dry storage, cruisers will find gasoline, diesel fuel, a ship's store, and outboard mechanical repairs here. There are also some wet slips, but these are fully occupied by resident vessels.

Continuing west on the main Cotton Bayou channel, low-tide 4½- to 5-foot depths can be expected as you cruise toward two additional marinas. Zeke's Landing Marina (30 16.548 North/087 34.159 West) is a premium-grade

facility guarding Cotton Bayou's southern shores at the western terminus of the marked channel. Transient cruisers are enthusiastically accepted for overnight berths at modern, wooden, fixed piers with every power and water connection. Depths at dockside are a very impressive 6 to 9 feet, though captains piloting deeper-draft vessels will still have to concern themselves with those 4½- to 5-foot low-water soundings on the approach cut. While more power cruisers seem to make use of this marina than their sailing brethren, cruising sailors can also expect a warm welcome. Shoreside, a single shower makes its hard-to-find home in the adjacent dry-stack storage building. The good news is that this unit is air conditioned. There is also a full-service Laundromat on the premises. Gasoline,

Sun Harbor Marina

diesel fuel, waste pump-out service, mechanical repairs (via independent technicians), and dry-stack storage are offered.

Of particular interest to cruisers suffering hunger pains after a long day on the water is the adjacent Zeke's Landing Restaurant and Oyster Bar (251-981-4001). Trust me, you need look no further for superb seafood dining. For more informal dining, take a look at Zeke's Down Under restaurant (251-981-1865). As its name implies, this eatery is located on the first floor of the large building that overlooks the dockage basin, while its larger sister is upstairs.

Just behind Zeke's Landing's dockage basin, visitors will discover a mini shopping center. This complex offers several art, gift, and card shops. Those wanting a few nights off the wa-

ter will find a hotel just across the street from the shopping center.

Zeke's Landing Marina (251) 981-4007

Approach depth—4¹/₂-5 feet
Dockside depth—6-9 feet
Accepts transients—yes
Transient-dockage rate—average
Fixed wooden piers—yes
Dockside power connections—30- and 50-amp
Dockside water connections—yes
Showers—yes
Laundromat—yes
Waste pump-out—yes
Gasoline—yes
Diesel fuel—yes
Mechanical repairs—yes (independent technicians)
Ship's and variety store—yes
Restaurant—two on site

Finally, Romar Harbor, High-Dry Marina is located on Cotton Bayou's northern banks, a bit to the west of Zeke's Landing. This smaller facility specializes in dry storage for power craft up to 28 feet and no services other than gasoline are available for cruising captains. Approach depths run to as little as 4½ feet.

Terry Cove Facilities

It's a straight shot almost due north from Perdido Pass Inlet to the lakelike body of water known as Terry Cove. The entrance cut holds minimum 7-foot depths, with most readings in the 10-foot range. Three pleasure-craft facilities wait to greet cruisers on Terry Cove. Anchoring on the cove is also a viable possibility.

If you follow the channel from Perdido Pass straight into Terry Cove, you will sight the extensive docks and piers associated with Sportsman Marina along the northern banks, just east of your direct course line (near 30 17.507 North/087 33.004 West). The covered slips of yesteryear are now gone, courtesy of some hurricane callers, but believe me, the present-day berths are in first-class condition.

Zeke's Landing Marina, Cotton Bayou

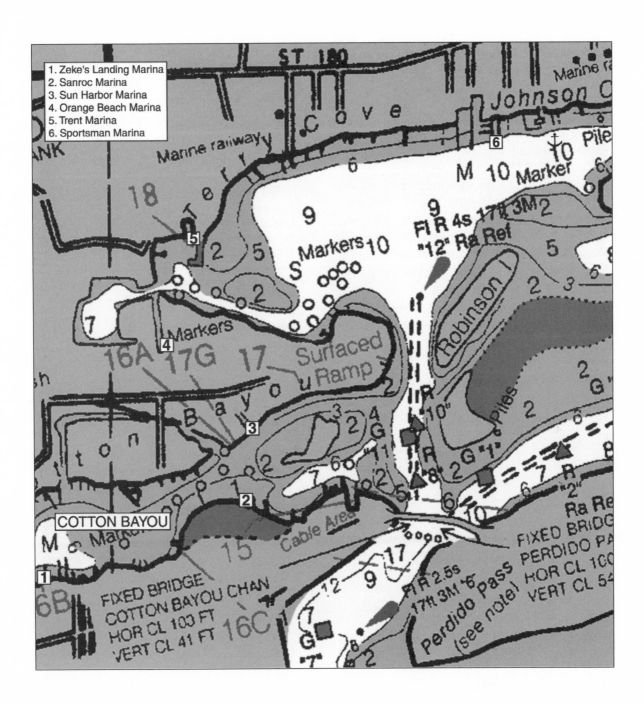

Overnighters are readily accepted at fixed, wooden piers with every power, water, telephone, and cable-television connection. Gasoline and diesel fuel can be purchased from the outer dock, and waste pump-out service is also available. Mechanical repairs are available through the on-site firm of Legendary Marine (251-971-8300).

Good, new, air-conditioned showers are available just behind the dockage basin, as is a climate-controlled Laundromat. There is also a small ship's and variety store at the dockside office. Sportsman has a large metal building dedicated to dry storage for smaller power craft. The on-site restaurant is known as Bayside Grill (251-981-4899). We have not yet eaten here, but Bayside has now survived for several years, a sure sign of a winner in the volatile restaurant game.

Visiting cruisers will agree, I am sure, that Sportsman Marina is a pleasure-craft facility of the first order, offering exceptional services to all mariners. Advance dockage reservations would be a wise precaution at this popular spot.

Sportsman Marina (334) 981-6247
  http://www.sportsmanmarina.com

Approach depth—7-10 feet
Dockside depth—7½-9 feet
Accepts transients—yes
Transient-dockage rate—average
Fixed wooden slips—yes (both covered and open)
Dockside power connections—30- and 50-amp
Dockside water connections—yes
Showers—yes
Laundromat—yes

Sportsman Marina, Terry Cove

Waste pump-out—yes
Gasoline—yes
Diesel fuel—yes
Mechanical repairs—yes (independent
  contractors)
Ship's and variety store—small
Restaurant—on site

Trent Marina (30 17.288 North/087 33.783 West) flanks the northwesterly corner of Terry Cove. This somewhat sleepy facility has 88 covered slips and only 6 open berths, so dockage is primarily for resident power craft. It is a rare event for an overnighter to be accommodated at Trent Marina. The management has informed me that their facility is "not really set up for transients." There are no power or water hookups for visitors, though resident craft enjoy fresh-water and 30- and 50-amp power connections. Both gasoline and diesel fuel can be purchased dockside. Low-key showers can also be found on site. Mechanical repairs can sometimes be arranged through independent contractors.

Trent Marina (251) 981-4850

Approach depth—6 feet
Dockside depth—5-8 feet
Accepts transients—very limited
Transient-dockage rate—below average
Fixed wooden piers—yes (mostly covered)
Dockside power connections—30- and 50-amp
Dockside water connections—yes
Showers—yes
Gasoline—yes
Diesel fuel—yes

Trent Marina, Terry Cove

Orange Beach Marina (30 17.044 North/087 33.849 West), yet another of Terry Cove's full-service, pleasure-craft facilities, is reached via a small (but relatively deep) canal that eases off from the southwestern corner of Terry Cove. A well-marked but uncharted channel carrying 7 to 9 feet of water leads to the canal from flashing daybeacon #12, at the southern entrance of Terry Cove. Orange Beach has always struck this writer as an unquestionably first-class operation with a definite power-boating flair.

Transient craft are accepted for temporary dockage at the marina's fixed wooden piers. Most, though not all, of the berths are in covered slips. Full-service power and water connections are easily accessible dockside. Gasoline and diesel fuel can be purchased, and there is a full-line ship's and variety store just behind the fuel dock. A pump-out station is also found at the docks.

Grimy cruisers will be pleased to learn that Orange Beach maintains two sets of showers. One consists of small-but-adequate, air-conditioned units, while the more northerly set features larger showers that are also climate controlled. There is on-site Laundromat as well.

Orange Beach Marina now boasts two on-site dining attractions. Mangos on the Island (251-981-1416) is open for the evening meal only, while the Calypso Fish Grille and Market (251-981-1415) serves both lunch and dinner. We were most impressed with Calypo's during a recent mid-day meal. We recommend this dining spot to our fellow cruisers.

Now, as if all that weren't enough to put Orange Beach on every cruiser's chart, the marina also features full mechanical and below-waterline, haul-out repair service. The yard's travelift is rated at 60 tons. While visiting, this writer has always observed any number of large power craft hauled out of the water, awaiting a bottom job.

To be succinct, there is probably not a single marina or boatyard between Pensacola and Mobile Bay that can lay claim to a greater variety of services than Orange Beach can. Powercraft skippers, particularly, will want to give this fine facility their attention and, perhaps, their business before continuing their voyage west.

Orange Beach Marina (251) 981-4207

Approach depth—7-9 feet
Dockside depth—7-foot minimum
Accepts transients—yes
Transient-dockage rate—above average
Fixed wooden piers—yes (majority are covered)
Dockside power connections—30- and 50-amp
Dockside water connections—yes
Showers—yes
Laundromat—yes
Waste pump-out—yes
Gasoline—yes
Diesel fuel—yes
Mechanical repairs—yes
Below-waterline repairs—yes
Ship's & variety store—yes
Restaurant—two on site

Some cruisers occasionally anchor on the eastern portion of Terry Cove in the charted bubble of 9- and 10-foot waters (near 30 17.490 North/087 32.821 West). While you are surrounded by rather extensive residential development, this haven does provide good protection from all except strong westerly winds. Minimum depths are in the 7- to 8-foot range and there is enough swinging room for most boats.

Orange Beach Marina, Terry Cove

ICW Marinas

Two good marinas face each other across the Waterway near unlighted daybeacon #65 (standard mile 165), west of Mill Point. Both businesses welcome cruising craft and can make for memorable overnight stops.

The marked entry channel to Bear Point Marina (30 18.573 North/087 31.572 West) flows to the south just east of #65. Believe it or else, this is yet another of the friendly marinas so typical of eastern Alabama waters.

Overnight berths are provided at fixed wooden piers with all power and water connections. The inner harbor is well sheltered and makes a good spot to ride out any weather short of a full gale, while the outer slips are a bit less protected. Entrance depths run from 7 to 10 feet and the docks actually carry 8 to 10 feet of water. Even deep-draft, fixed-keel sailcraft should not have any depth problems. Gasoline, diesel fuel, and a waste pump-out service are on hand. The shoreside showers are small but adequate and air conditioned. There is also a Laundromat.

Mechanical repairs for diesel-powered plants can be performed by the marina's own personnel, while service for gasoline engines can be farmed out to local, independent technicians.

This writer has often been accused of never meeting a restauraunt he didn't like. Well, let that myth end here. The on-site eatery at Bear Point Marina, the Back Porch Restaurant (251-981-2225, open for lunch and dinner) serves out meager portions of mediocre food and charges a pretty penny for it. We suggest exercising your own galley while staying at Bear Point.

In spite of its dining shortcomings, we have consistently liked Bear Point Marina over the years, even as it has changed ownership. We see no reason to change this favorable viewpoint.

Bear Point Marina (251) 981-2327

Approach depth—7-10 feet
Dockside depth—8-10 feet
Accepts transients—yes
Transient-dockage rate—below average
Fixed wooden piers—yes
Dockside power connections—30- and 50-amp
Dockside water connections—yes
Showers—yes
Laundromat—yes
Water pump-out—yes
Gasoline—yes
Diesel fuel—yes
Mechanical repairs—yes
Restaurant—on-site

Bear Point Marina

Yes, I know it's getting tiresome, but yet another good (how about "unique") facility stands ready to greet visiting cruisers just across the Waterway from Bear Point, hard beside the mouth of Roberts Bayou (standard mile 165, 30 19.290 North/087 32.021 West).

You don't see marinas like Pirate's Cove Yacht Club much anymore, and that is a real crime. While no one will ever accurately describe this facility as *sophisticated*, there is a backwater feeling here that is almost tangible. Cruisers who regularly frequent glitzy marinas will probably

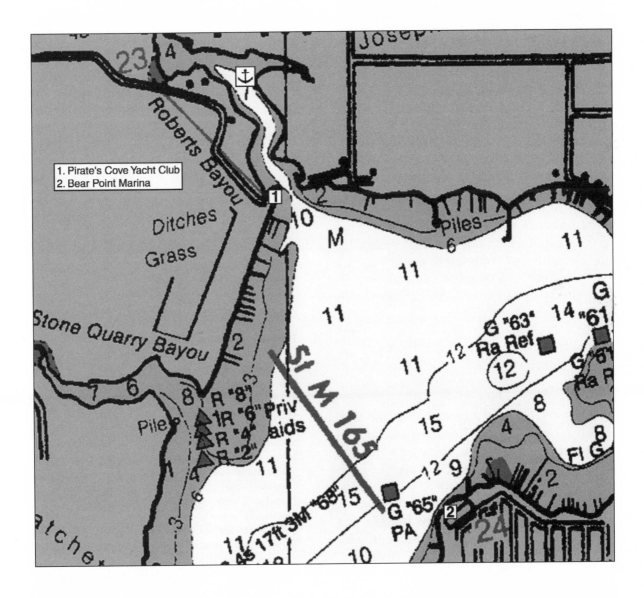

only stop here once, but others (like this writer) will be drawn back time and time again to partake of Pirate Cove's unique atmosphere of earlier, simpler times. Every passing cruiser should give this marina at least one visit. As long as you don't wax too eloquent about the latest New York fashion trends, your welcome should be memorable.

Pirate's Cove is what one might describe as a "good ol' boy"-type marina (in the very *best* sense of that term). There is a tangible feeling of Southern-style bonhomie at Pirate's Cove that, even in this land of friendly marinas, is unique among Alabama dockage facilities.

Pirate's Cove is actually divided into two sections. The first consists of the on-site restaurant surrounded by some small piers and slips along the northern section of Roberts Bayou. Depths at these berths run 5 to 7 feet. The principal dockage basin is found a short jog to the west, opening onto the Waterway. This harbor is almost completely enclosed by a concrete and wooden breakwater and is well protected from all winds. Soundings in this basin range from 6 to 7 feet.

Most cruising craft will want to select overnight berths in the enclosed harbor. If you are just tying up for lunch, the less formal dockage behind the restaurant might be your choice.

In any case, transients are gladly accepted and the marina offers gasoline, diesel fuel, waste pump-out, and full mechanical and haul-out repair services. The yard's travelift can haul up to 18 tons. Dockage (in both basins) is at fixed wooden piers, with 30-amp power connections and water connections. A few basic food supplies can be bought at a small variety-store operation associated with the restaurant.

The big news at Pirate's Cove for this new edition is the construction of a new, first-class bathroom, shower, and Laundromat building. Cruisers who remember the old, unhappy unisex shower (which drained directly onto the ground) will find these new, modern, air-conditioned facilities to be nothing short of amazing.

There is more to Pirate's Cove than just its good dockage, fuel, and service facilities. The marina restaurant claims to serve "the best cheeseburgers on earth." Now, that may be pushing it just a bit, especially since there's this restaurant in New Orleans named, nautically enough, Port of Call, but if you like hamburgers made from lean meat and spiced with a special Cajun sauce, then this extravagant claim may seem more than justified. All passing cruisers are urged to give the burgers a try, even if you only stop for lunch. I think you will agree that they are unforgettable.

Pirate's Cove Yacht Club (251) 987-1224
  http://www.piratescoveriffraff.com
Approach depth—9-10 feet (outer, enclosed
  harbor)
Dockside depth—6-7 feet (outer harbor)
                  5-7 feet (Roberts Bayou docks)
Accepts transients—yes
Transient-dockage rate—above average
Fixed wooden piers—yes
Dockside power connections—30-amp
Dockside water connections—yes
Showers—yes
Laundromat—yes
Waste pump-out—yes
Gasoline—yes
Diesel fuel—yes
Mechanical repairs—yes
Below-waterline repairs—yes
Variety store—small
Restaurant—on site

Rush hour at Pirate's Cove Restaurant

Roberts Bayou (Standard Mile 165) (30 19.520 North/087 32.108 West)

Roberts Bayou is a nicely sheltered stream which can serve as a good foul-weather anchorage for pleasure boats as large as 40 feet. Minimum entrance depths are around 5½ feet. Once on the interior of the stream, soundings improve to 7-, 8-, and 9-foot levels. The westerly shores along the lower portion of the creek show moderate residential development, but most of the banks are still in their natural state.

Probably the best spot to anchor is found upstream of the first sharp point of land on the western banks (near 30 19.520 North/087 32.108 West). Here you can drop the hook in some 7 feet of water with excellent protection from all winds.

Hungry cruisers should note that dinghies issuing forth from boats anchored in Roberts Bayou are happily accepted at the docks of Pirate's Cove Marina Restaurant (see above). Have a cheeseburger and a cold one for me!

Ingram Bayou (Standard Mile 163.5) (30 19.208 North/087 33.449 West)

Ingram Bayou has long had the reputation of being one of the most beautiful anchorages on the entire Gulf Coast ICW. This writer would certainly not argue with that assessment. The creek wanders into the northern shores of the ICW north of unlighted daybeacon #72.

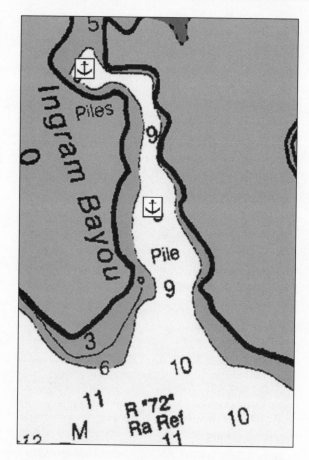

is good for all except strong southerly blows. This anchorage can accommodate even the largest pleasure craft.

By far, the best spot to anchor in Ingram Bayou will be discovered after cruising upstream through the creek's charted 90 degree bend to the west. Soon after cutting to the west, captains can anchor on the stream's mid-width (near 30 19.208 North/087 33.449 West) in some 7 to 8 feet of water. Boats as large as 40 feet will find plenty of elbowroom.

Once the anchor is down, you can settle in for about as secure an evening as could ever be imagined. Even if you normally don't go for anchoring off, you owe it to yourself to look Ingram Bayou over.

Wolf Bay (Standard Mile 161.5) (Various Lats/Lons—see below)

The southern mouth of Wolf Bay, measuring some 1.3 nautical miles in breadth, fronts the ICW's northerly flank between unlighted daybeacon #80 and flashing daybeacon #87. At first glance, captains studying chart 11378 might think that the bay is a bit open for effective shelter. Such a conclusion would overlook some hidden attractions, including one of the most spectacular, but unknown, waterside dining attractions in Alabama.

The shoreline on lower Wolf Bay is completely natural and quite attractive. The upper reaches of the bay are flanked by some light residential development, which only serves to add to the water's appeal.

North of Mulberry Point, Wolf Bay splits into two large branches. The northeasterly arm remains quite spacious for some distance upstream. Cruisers would have to traverse

High, heavily wooded, completely virgin shorelines overlook the creek and reach out, grab you by the neck, and demand that you explore them by dinghy. Protection is excellent, particularly in the upstream portion of the bayou. Minimum entrance depths are 7 feet, though most of the stream carries better than 8 feet of water. There are practically no surrounding shallows to worry with—a true rarity on the Gulf shoreline.

Boats needing maximum swinging room can drop the hook in the broad pool of 9-foot water just north of the creek's entrance, near 30 18.892 North/087 33.265 West. Protection

Anchoring on Ingram Bayou

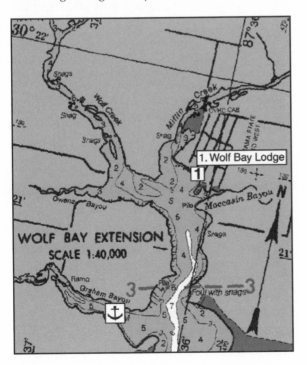

waters with only 4 to 5 feet of depth to find enough shelter for an overnight stop.

The westerly branch has more possibilities and one great, big surprise. Careful cruisers can follow this arm of Wolf Bay north to the intersection with Graham Bayou. This enchanting stream holds 5½- to 6-foot minimum depths on its mid-width for the first 250 yards of its passage. Protection is excellent from all winds and there is enough swinging room for boats as large as 45 feet. This is a great off-the-beaten-path haven that few cruisers have heretofore used. We like to drop the hook near 30 20.463 North/087 36.485 West.

Cruisers can carefully follow the main westerly branch of Wolf Bay north to charted Moccasin Bayou and hold 5 to 7 feet of depth. North of this intersection, Wolf Bay splits again and depths become much too uncertain for cruising-size craft.

However, those captains in the know, and that now includes you, can anchor in the 5- to 7-foot water abeam of Moccasin Bayou and then dinghy ashore to the dock, which cuts the easterly banks just to the north, near 30 21.392 North/087 36.133 West. (Or, if your vessel can stand 4-foot low-water soundings, you can cruise directly to this pier).

This small, nondescript dock serves the famous Wolf Bay Lodge Restaurant. It's really incredible that a dining spot of this quality could be located in such an out-of-the-way location. Wolf Bay's seafood platters are spoken of with reverence all up and down Alabama's coastline. After making several game, but thoroughly unsuccessful, attempts to down an entire order myself during our many visits here, I can only echo the locals' sentiments. By all accounts, you should make *every* effort to visit this outstanding restaurant. If the fried oysters don't convince you to come back time and time again, be sure to let this writer know. He'll be glad to eat your portion for you.

Oh, yes—you may see a sign at the door to Wolf Bay Lodge saying "Members Only." Don't be concerned. The restaurant is glad to serve the public.

Portage Creek
(Standard Mile 159.5—Eastern Entrance)

The canal-like section of the ICW west of flashing daybeacon #94, known as Portage Creek, currently lacks any real dockage facilities for pleasure craft. There is one full-service boatyard to consider.

A short hop east of the charted Highway 59-Gulf Shores fixed bridge, passing cruisers will sight the high, wooden piers of Southport Seafood. Obviously, this facility is geared to-ward commercial vessels and tug traffic.

Just west of the bridge, the basin associated with Garris Propeller Services (251-968-6400) will be sighted on the northern banks. This friendly yard offers complete below-waterline, haul-out repair services. If you have bent shafts, dinged props, or just need a bottom-painting job, the helpful professionals at Garris can fix you up. The yard features a 100-ton travelift and a 300-ton marine railway. Mechanical repairs for both gasoline and diesel engines can be arranged through independent local contractors. No overnight or transient dockage is available.

Gulf Shores History   The resort community of Gulf Shores lies south of the westernmost set of the twin bridges crossing Portage Creek. Today, Gulf Shores is thought of as a modern beach retreat for citizens of nearby Mobile, but in the recent past, the situation was very different.

On Thanksgiving Day in 1946, the Buskens family moved from Mobile to the sparsely settled peninsula of land running between Portage Creek and the Gulf. The sands ran west to Mobile Bay's southern entrance and contained a shallow body of fresh water known simply as "Little Lagoon." In fact, many people simply called the small settlement "Little Lagoon." The name of Gulf Shores was settled upon some time later.

In later years, the Buskenses' daughter, Joy Callaway Buskens, was to become the unofficial historian of Gulf Shores and surrounding Baldwin County. Her enjoyable book *Well, I've Never Met A Native* is a fascinating collection of oral history gleaned from many of Gulf Shore's most venerable citizens. The fortunate reader can discover almost firsthand what life was really like on the Alabama coast before the coming of good roads and modern development.

Perhaps Ms. Buskens' most memorable story is her account of Hurricane Frederic, which slammed into Gulf Shores in 1979. It was a calm Tuesday evening when the residents of Gulf Shores heard that a hurricane was on the way. As they had done on so many previous occasions, they boarded up their homes and packed a few essential belongings before heading inland to wait out the storm. Little did they realize that "this would be one of the worst and most devastating storms" to ever strike the Alabama coast.

Joy describes with eerie detail what followed on that fateful night and its aftermath:

> That night, the water came in a 12 foot tide and pushed the Buskens home 20 feet back [off its foundation]. The wind and water ripped off the front porch which went all the way across the width of the home. Nothing was left of the beautiful china cabinet in the dining area but the very top piece. Grandmama had a beautiful collection of antique dishes and glassware and some of the pieces had floated into the bathroom and settled into the bathtub unbroken. . . . A year later, our daughter Brenda found the Corning ware teapot loaded with barnacles. . . . The giant old trees looked like match sticks that had been twisted and broken. Some of these trees were probably 100 years old.

If you would like to learn more about hurricane Frederic and the life on Gulf Shores during the mid-1900s, Ms. Buskens' book, *Well, I've Never Met A Native,* is highly recommended. It is available at many of the bookstores in Fairhope and Mobile.

Oyster Bay (Standard Mile 152.5)

The ICW runs east and west along the northern reaches of Oyster Bay between flashing daybeacons #97 and #101. While the bay's undeveloped shores are a captivating sight from the Waterway, depths outside of the improved channel quickly rise to as little as 1 foot. Stick strictly to the ICW cut while traversing Oyster Bay. Woolgathering at the wheel will rapidly provide you with the opportunity to hop out and stretch your legs.

Sailboat Bay (Standard Mile 151.5)

Sailboat Bay is a private condo development that occupies the northerly banks of the *U*-shaped creek, east of flashing daybeacon #103. Even though this creek is shown as marsh on chart 11378, on-site research revealed that the *westerly* entrance (only) carries 5 to 6 feet of depth.

Signs at the westerly entrance to the *U*-shaped stream warn that no dockage, anchorage, or other facilities for visitors are available at Sailboat Bay. The anchorage that this writer used to recommend on the easterly portion of the creek is now surrounded by new condos and pretty much off-limits.

BIG LAGOON TO MOBILE BAY NAVIGATION

There is nothing complicated or unusual about navigating the Gulf Coast ICW between Big Lagoon and the Waterway's eastern entrance into Mobile Bay. East of Wolf Bay, the well-defined track works its way to the west by following an improved channel through naturally deep bodies of water. West of flashing daybeacon #94, the ICW enters lengthy Portage Creek Canal. A run of some 8.5 nautical miles leads cruisers through this sheltered but not terribly attractive section of the Waterway into Bon Secour Bay. Bon Secour comprises the southeasterly reaches of Mobile Bay.

While a portion of this run borders on more open water (particularly near Perdido Bay), it is unlikely that chop will ever reach the dangerous stage for cruising-size craft in anything short of a full gale.

Tidal currents do run swiftly. All mariners must be on guard against lateral leeway. As this writer has warned repeatedly throughout this volume, watch your course over the stern as well as ahead to quickly note any leeway slippage.

Navigation of the various side-waters along the Waterway, particularly Perdido Pass Inlet and its surrounding creeks, is an exacting process. While most of these gunk holes can be successfully navigated with a little patience, skippers who go plunging ahead without studying their charts or the information contained in this account are going to buy into some underwater real estate.

Entry into Big Lagoon   As mentioned in chapter 4, the dredged channel leading west

from Pensacola Inlet is a changeable cut which is subject to rapid shoaling. The Waterway's passage is currently marked by a host of floating, (mostly) unlighted nun and can buoys, some of which are charted and some not. All these various aids to navigation really make daylight passage from Pensacola Bay (and Inlet) into the connecting canal a rather simple matter as long as you observe all markers most carefully. Westbound craft should pass all red, even-numbered aids to their (the markers') southerly sides and take green, odd-numbered markers to their (the markers') northerly quarter.

Be advised that there could be a very different configuration of aids present along the easterly approach to the connecting canal by the time you visit. Attempting to run this channel at night is the type of foolish behavior that keeps the widow's walks crowded.

Eventually you will come abeam of flashing daybeacon #7 to its northerly quarter. This aid heralds the ICW's entrance into Big Lagoon.

South Cut   All mariners are strictly advised not to attempt entry into South Cut, found north of charted Fort McRee, between Pensacola Inlet and Big Lagoon. This cut has now shoaled and the channel, such as it is, is more than slightly convoluted.

On the other hand, cautious cruisers in search of a good lunch spot can enter the mid-width of this same cut on its *western* reaches from Big Lagoon. Again, shoals are not marked, but on a clear day, it's easy to spot the surrounding shallows by the water color. During low light conditions, this task is considerably more daunting. Good luck—you may need it!

Spanish Point Anchorage   The first of Big Lagoon's anchorages is accessible immediately upon entering the lagoon's eastern reaches. To enter the haven at Spanish Point, continue on the ICW channel until you are some .3 nautical miles west of flashing daybeacon #7. Then curl around to the south-southeast and set a careful course for the tongue of deep water east of Spanish Point. For once, it's actually easier (in daylight) to enter this gunk hole than a study of chart 11378 would lead you to believe. Be on guard against the shoal coming out from Spanish Point.

As you cruise into the charted tongue of deeper water, shoals begin to encroach on both sides of the cut. The navigable track to the south becomes narrower and narrower. Boats drawing 4 feet or more, or those larger than 35 feet, would do well to drop their anchor in the deeper section to the north. Farther to the south, it's a snap to stray onto the shoal building out from Spanish Point or the shallower waters to the east. Even shallow-draft boats should enter this inner area with maximum caution.

Redfish Point Anchorage   Entry into the anchorage east of Redfish Point is complicated by a shoal that divides the anchorage. You may choose to enter the deeper water either east or west of the shallows. The easterly anchorage is probably the easier of the two to navigate. Set your course for the 7-foot charted depths between the marshy point west of Spanish Point, and the mid-line shoal. Pay particular attention to the correctly charted patch of 2-foot waters lying northwest of Spanish Point. Drop the hook before cruising to within 100 yards of the southerly shoreline.

The west-side anchorage is complicated by the broad shoal abutting Redfish Point. To enter this haven, you must set a careful compass/GPS course from the Waterway channel to pass between the two shallows. This process is made even harder by the absence of any nearby aids to navigation on the ICW to use as a navigational reference. This would be a great spot to try out your GPS interfaced with a laptop computer running the "Cap'n" or Nobeltec's "Navigational Suite" and loaded with up-to-date digitized charts. Otherwise, I can only suggest that you take your time and keep your eyes glued to the sounder. After cruising between the two shoals, be sure to set the anchor at least 100 yards short of the banks.

On Big Lagoon   There is very little shallow water to be concerned with on Big Lagoon. Good depths stretch almost to the northerly banks and to within several hundred yards of the southern shoreline. One exception to this rule is the long shoal building out from Trout Point, north of Redfish Point. To avoid this hazard, set your course to come abeam of and pass flashing daybeacon #10 by at least 100 yards to its southerly side.

West of #10, there are no additional buoys or daybeacons for some 1.9 nautical miles. Don't worry. The route does not stray near any shallow water. Continue following the northerly shoreline, maintaining about the same distance from the banks. Eventually you will spy unlighted can buoy #11. Come abeam of #11 to its northerly quarter.

At #11, the ICW channel takes a sharp jog to the south-southwest. Point to eventually come abeam of and pass flashing daybeacon #13 by at least 75 yards to its westerly side. The charted shoal east of #13 seems to be building outward. After a while, you should pass between flashing daybeacon #16 and unlighted daybeacon #15. Be sure to come abeam of #15 to its northwesterly quarter. At this point the Waterway again turns to the west and continues on its well-marked way.

Deep Water Anchorage   As reviewed earlier in this chapter, the bubble of deep water east of unlighted daybeacon #15 makes up the largest and most easily entered of the three primary Big Lagoon anchorages. All you need to do is set a compass/GPS course from #15 to the middle of the anchorage to the east. As long as you don't cruise more than .5 nautical miles east of #15, or approach the southerly banks closer than 100 yards, you're in fat city.

Next morning when it's time to leave, be sure to retrace your steps to the west to reenter the ICW. The charted 3- to 5-foot waters to the east make an exit from this quarter impractical.

On the ICW   West of flashing daybeacon #18, the waters of the ICW begin to narrow. By the time you reach the 73-foot-high fixed Gulf Beach Bridge, your craft will be cruising through a man-made land cut connecting the Waterway with the broader waters flowing north and east of Perdido Pass Inlet.

All mariners should take careful note of the strong tidal currents that *rip* through this cut between #18 and flashing daybeacon #39. Sailcraft and trawlers should proceed on maximum alert. Fortunately, the highrise span at least means you won't have to wait for a bridge to open.

As you might expect, this swift water flow can lead to shoaling. Be on the lookout for additional markers not shown on your chart. Be sure to yield to any of these aids. They will undoubtedly mark recent encroachments by the ever-shifting sands. Westbound navigators should continue to pass all red markers to their (the cruisers') starboard side and take green markers to port in order to keep to the channel.

West of flashing daybeacon #31, the Waterway passes under the Perdido Key-Gulf Beach Bridge. This fixed high-rise span has a vertical clearance of 73 feet.

Slow down as you approach the Perdido Key Bridge in order to protect the boat docks at Oyster Bar Marina along the southerly banks. Also, be on guard against unusually swift currents as you approach and pass under the span.

Eventually the Waterway passes out into broader waters near the charted village of Inerarity. Soon you will come between flashing daybeacon #44 and unlighted daybeacon #43. The Old River cuts into the southern shores of the ICW just west of these aids.

The Old River   To make good your entry into Old River, abandon the ICW some 25 yards west of unlighted daybeacon #43. Cut south and use your binoculars to pick out several small, somewhat nondescript stakes marking the western side of the southward-flowing entrance channel. These unofficial markers denote the eastern edge of the shallows and are most helpful in avoiding the extensive west-side shoals at the river's entrance. Of course, you must not cut too far to the east either. As chart 11378 clearly and correctly shows, 2-foot shallows wait to trap the careless in this quarter.

To keep to the good water, pass all the short stakes by some 50 yards to your starboard side. Follow the channel carefully as it cuts south of Rabbit Island and begins bordering the southerly banks. As you are cruising through this westerly bend, you may spot some additional stakes outlining the southerly edge of the charted shallows bordering the north side of the channel.

To continue west on the Old River as far as the first charted offshoot making in from the southern banks, favor the southern shoreline heavily. A quick study of chart 11378 correctly shows that this strategy will help keep you to the deep water.

Unless you possess specific local knowledge, cease your explorations before coming abeam of the first south-side (charted) offshoot. Farther to the west, numerous, unmarked shoals impinge on the channel. The *only* way to bypass these shallows successfully is to navigate by eye, and this will only work on sunny days. By all accounts, only small, shallow-draft power craft captained by the adventurers among us should attempt to follow the Old River past the western tip of Ono Island and join up with the waters flowing north from Perdido Pass.

On the ICW   The Waterway channel runs west via an exceptionally well marked cut toward Perdido Bay and Bayou St. John. Some shallow water flanks the channel along this run. Observe all markers carefully and take care not to wander from the improved track.

Eventually you should come abeam of flashing daybeacon #57 to its northeasterly side. At #57 skippers must choose whether to continue northwest on the Waterway to the Perdido Bay intersection and the good facilities on Arnica Bay and Roberts Bayou, or turn south and follow the Bayou St. John channel to Perdido Pass Inlet and its associated marinas on Cotton Bayou and Terry Cove. This latter route will be reviewed first, followed by a continuing account of the ICW passage west.

Bayou St. John   The marked channel leading through Bayou St. John to Perdido Pass Inlet is well marked and quite passable for most pleasure craft. Currently the channel holds minimum 6-foot depths, with most soundings in the 8- to 12-foot range, all the way to the bridge spanning Perdido Pass.

However, this cut is subject to shoaling along its edges. Great care must be exercised to stay within the various markers or a hard grounding could be the less than desirable result. This process is made even more exacting courtesy of the strong tidal currents from Perdido Pass. Keep a sharp watch for leeway at all times!

While a portion of the Bayou St. John channel is fairly wide, other parts are squeezed between growing shallows. Don't be surprised, though, to find other shoals and new aids to navigation by the time you visit. Truly, this is a channel in constant flux.

It should also be noted that practically all the aids to navigation on Bayou St. John and nearby Terry Cove and Cotton Bayou are unlighted. Nighttime entry into this area by strangers is a very risky proposition.

To depart the ICW and enter Bayou St. John, continue on the Waterway past flashing daybeacon #57 for some 100 yards. Then turn almost due south and set course to come between unlighted daybeacon #17 and flashing daybeacon #18. From this point, mariners bound south and then west to Perdido Pass should take all red markers to their (the cruisers') port side and green beacons to starboard. As you are now headed toward the Gulf by way of Perdido Pass, this color scheme makes sense.

Once between #17 and #18, set a new course to come abeam of unlighted daybeacon #15 to its immediate easterly side. As can be seen from a study of chart 11378, this run will lead you close by the shoal water to the east.

Cruisers eastbound on the Bayou St. John channel, making their way from Perdido Pass toward the ICW, should be on guard against some local channel markers lying east of unlighted daybeacon #15. It's all too easy to mistake these errant beacons for the main channel markers. If you are headed toward the ICW, be sure to swing north at #15 and set course to pass between unlighted daybeacon #17 and flashing daybeacon #18.

At #15, westbound captains should cut west-southwest and begin following the numbered markers to the Perdido Pass Bridge. The channel twists a bit in places, so keep a sharp watch for the next marker(s) as you work your way along.

After passing unlighted daybeacon #12, set course to come abeam of unlighted daybeacon #11 to its southerly side. This track will run you hard by the south-side banks, and you will remain close by this body of land until reaching unlighted daybeacons #3 and #4.

Eventually you will pass between unlighted daybeacons #4 and #3. The waters lying to the west-southwest between #3 and the bridge are some of the most troublesome on the entire Bayou St. John channel.

Point to come abeam of unlighted daybeacon #1 to its southerly side. In the past, this aid to navigation has sometimes been replaced by a floater. During our last visit in the fall of 2002, the daybeacon version was present, but things may be different as you go cruising by.

From #1, point directly for the central section of the Perdido Pass Bridge. Don't be tempted to cut the corner and swing north before coming hard by the bridge's northerly face. This maneuver is a sure recipe for disaster. Don't encroach too closely on the south-side banks either.

Once abeam of the fixed bridge's north-side, central passthrough, cruisers will find themselves at a critical intersection. A turn to the south will carry you under the bridge and out to sea, while a careful cruise to the west and then northwest will lend access to Cotton Bayou and its marinas. A sharp turn to the north will eventually lead you to Terry Cove.

Perdido Pass Inlet   The Perdido Pass Inlet channel is well marked and currently carries minimum 7-foot depths. The charted bridge crossing this channel has 54 feet of vertical clearance, a distinct improvement over the old 37-foot span. Some sailcraft can now make use of this well-located inlet.

Many of the markers on the inlet are clearly charted on 11378. As mentioned, this is a good indication of a relatively stable seaward cut.

Cotton Bayou   The mid-width of Cotton Bayou's easterly mouth is spanned by a large shoal with less than 2 feet of depth. This hazard is clearly charted on 11378. Currently, there is only one channel that provides reliable access from the deeper waters lying about the Perdido Pass Bridge to Cotton Bayou.

Once past the tricky entrance, a marked cut continues first north and then west up Cotton Bayou to Zeke's Landing Marina. The aids to navigation on this cut consist of privately maintained, unlighted daybeacons. Some are of the arrow type, with pointers specifying on which side they should be passed.

To gain entrance into Cotton Bayou from Perdido Pass, cruise from a point just north of the central section of the Perdido Pass Bridge towards the western banks. Cut to the northwest some 30 yards before reaching this shoreline and, heavily favoring the port-side (southerly) banks, cruise into the southern reaches of Cotton Bayou's broad mouth. You should spot several private aids to navigation outlining the shallow water to the north.

Take your time on this cut and watch the sounder. With luck, you can hold 6 to 7 feet of water in the entrance channel as far as Sanroc Cay Marina.

As you pass through the easternmost section of the Cotton Bayou channel, the old dockage basin of Perdido Pass Marina will come abeam to the south. Stay away from these waters. We sounded only 4 feet when we got too close to this old harbor.

Those cruisers who choose to continue upstream on Cotton Bayou can follow the privately maintained markers as the channel sweeps briefly to the north. Just before the cut turns back again to the west, cruisers whose craft can stand some 4½-foot depths can break off to the east and visit the pier associated with Tacky Jack's Restaurant and, just next door, the facilities at Sun Harbor Marina. Both these firms guard the creek's northern banks near the charted marsh island to the south. Cruisers visiting either Tacky Jack's or Sun Harbor Marina would do well to retrace their steps through the channel outlined above. The direct passage leading east to the deeper water of the Terry Cove channel has very questionable depths and no markings of any kind.

Continuing on to the west, some 4½- to 5-foot depths will be encountered on the Cotton Bayou channel. Eventually you will spy the docks of Zeke's Landing Marina almost dead ahead.

Incidentally, it would not be a bad idea to proceed at idle, no-wake speed throughout Cotton Bayou and Terry Cove. A number of private docks line the shores and the potential for damage to moored vessels by a strong wake is quite high.

Terry Cove   Successful navigation of the channel into Terry Cove from a position just north of Perdido Pass Bridge has always been a bit complicated, courtesy of the frequent changes in the aids to navigation marking this channel. The current edition of chart 11378, for instance, shows three unlighted daybeacons outlining this cut. During our last visit in the fall of 2002, however, we observed two pairs of nun and can buoys marking the channel. Who knows? By the time you make your way to these waters, the configuration of aids to navigation could be different yet again.

For the moment, all navigators cruising north to Terry Cove need do is to pass between the two sets of markers. As you have almost certainly guessed by now, keep red, even-numbered markers off your starboard side and take green markers to port.

Point to eventually come abeam of flashing daybeacon #12 to its westerly quarter. This aid to navigation had been temporarily replaced by a lighted, floating marker in the fall of 2002, but it will almost certainly be morphed back into its daybeacon form by the time of your visit.

Once abeam of #12, you can continue north through minimum 7-foot depths to Sportsman Marina or cut west and visit Trent Marina or Orange Beach Marina.

An uncharted channel marked by privately maintained, unlighted daybeacons skirts along the cove's southerly banks to the canal allowing access to Orange Beach Marina. If you should choose to visit Trent Marina instead, just depart from the Orange Beach channel as Trent's piers come abeam to the north.

If you decide to anchor on Terry Cove's easterly reaches, continue due north from #12 until you are some 150 yards from the northerly banks. Then turn due east and follow the deep water along the shoreline. You can select any likely spot to drop the hook as long as you don't approach the thin, charted fringe of shoal water flanking the bay's northern and eastern shores.

On the ICW   Northwest of flashing daybeacon #57, the Waterway channel is quite broad. Nevertheless, it borders on very shoal water that protrudes out from Mill Point to the west and southwest and Inerarity Point to the east and northeast. Be sure to come abeam of and pass flashing daybeacon #58 to its westerly side and flashing daybeacon #59 well to its easterly side. At #59, cruising skippers may choose to enter Perdido Bay to the northeast.

Perdido Bay   While Perdido Bay lacks navigational markings of any kind, navigators need only avoid the band of shallow water flanking most of the shoreline to successfully navigate the bay. To enter Perdido Bay, set a compass course from flashing daybeacon #59 to avoid the large shelf of shallows abutting Inerarity Point. Eventually the entrance to Palmetto Creek will come abeam to the north. Bend your course a bit more to the east and cruise directly into the broad expanse of good depths on the main body of Perdido Bay to the east.

Captains who choose to enter Tarklin Bay need only avoid the shoal water along the southerly and easterly banks and a similar patch of shallows stretching out from Tarklin Point to the north. During on-site research we repeatedly discovered a tendency to mistake the shoreline to the east for the anchorage area. You can recognize this patch of shore by several houses on the banks. The actual anchorage to the north is flanked by completely natural shores.

Study chart 11378 for a moment and you will readily note that 2- and 3-foot waters extend west for better than .3 nautical miles from Du Pont Point on Perdido's easterly shoreline. Obviously, you must stay well away from this hazard. If you decide to anchor off and dinghy ashore to the isolated beach on the point, be sure to drop the hook well before reaching the shoal water.

Continued passage north on Perdido Bay to the Lilian fixed bridge is about as easy as it gets. Just keep away from the shoreline and you will not encounter any problems.

The waters northeast of the Lilian span are not recommended for visiting cruisers. While there is a large swath of deep water on the remainder of the bay, numerous unmarked shoals are also present. These shallows are a particularly acute problem for navigators attempting to enter the otherwise deep Perdido River. Lacking specific local knowledge, you had best leave this portion of the bay (and river) to residents.

Soldier Creek   Remember that the entrance channel to otherwise deep Soldier Creek is tricky and currently carries only 4½ to 5 feet of depth. It's only a hop, skip, and a jump into even thinner water.

To enter Soldier Creek, set a compass/GPS course from flashing daybeacon #59 (on the ICW) for the triangle of deep water west of Red Bluff. As you approach the creek, be very mindful of the charted 2-foot waters shelving out from Red Bluff.

At the mouth of the creek you should sight several private markers which will help lead you through the twisting entrance. As you would imagine, pass all red marks to your starboard side and green beacons to port. Proceed at idle speed and ask a crew member to watch the sounder constantly.

The marked channel runs immediately beside the northeasterly banks until reaching the first turn to the north around the sharp easterly entrance point. It's really hard to believe that the best water is this close to shore, but, at least for the moment, it most certainly is.

As the marked cut swings sharply to the north around the point abutting the easterly reaches of the entrance, favor the eastern side of the channel a bit. On-site research revealed that this point is building out a bit, but currently depths along the western side of the entrance are even worse. Pass the east-side point by some 15 to 20 yards to your starboard side. Once past this difficult portion of the channel, good depths open out on the creek's interior reaches.

If the above procedure sounds confusing,

there's a good reason—it is! For those entering Soldier Creek for the first time, it can be a nail-biting experience. However, considering the natural protection and beauty of the stream, many captains who yearn for waters far from the beaten track may choose to make the attempt anyway. Just keep in mind that you may find the bottom in the process.

Once inside Soldier Creek, you would just about have to be drunk or asleep to run aground. Simply hold to the mid-width and good depths are held upstream to the 4-foot soundings clearly charted on 11378.

One exception to this rule is the charted shoal water abutting the southwesterly shoreline of the eastward-running cove just past the entrance. Favor the northeasterly shores a bit to avoid this hazard.

On the ICW   Northwest of flashing daybeacon #59, mariners must contend with the large tongue of shallow water extending northeast and east from Mill Point. Unlighted daybeacons #59A, #61, #61A, and #63 help cruisers around this problem stretch. Come abeam and pass all these aids to their northeastern and northerly sides. Also, be sure to pass flashing daybeacon #60 to its southerly quarter. This aid marks another shoal running south from Ross Point.

West and southwest of #63, a pool of naturally deep water opens out almost from shore to shore. If you observe all markers carefully, there are not any unusual navigational problems moving west to Portage Creek Canal. Three side-waters along this stretch offer excellent overnight anchorage for cruising craft.

Roberts Bayou   Entry into Roberts Bayou is vastly simplified by a series of uncharted markers placed at the creek's entrance, courtesy of Pirate's Cove Marina. These aids help skippers avoid the charted 2-foot shoals flanking the east and west side of the creek's mouth.

As you enter Roberts Bayou, with Pirate's Cove Restaurant immediately abeam to port, favor the starboard shores slightly. A small rim of shallow water seems to have built out from the western banks.

Once past the entrance, good depths of 7 feet or better open out almost from shore to shore. These deep soundings finally fall off as you approach the first offshoot on the easterly banks, near the charted position of Josephine.

Ingram Bayou   Now, my fellow cruisers, pay attention! Overnight anchorage doesn't get a whole lot easier than this. To enter Ingram Bayou, just cruise up the bayou's middle and avoid the two points flanking the entrance. Good depths continue along the centerline until just after the bayou takes a sharp jog to the west and then cuts back north. All but very small, shallow-draft vessels will want to cease their exploration shortly after passing through this last northerly turn.

On the ICW   The Waterway skirts rather close to the southerly shoreline as it passes between flashing daybeacon #74 and unlighted daybeacon #73. Favor #74 a bit when passing to avoid the shallows abutting the banks.

The charted deep-water cove north of #74 could serve as an emergency anchorage. Minimum 8-foot depths run to within 300 yards or so of the northerly banks. Shelter from all but northerly winds would be minimal. You would also be exposed to the wake of all passing vessels. With Ingram Bayou and Wolf Bay so close by, most cruisers will wisely choose one of these more isolated havens.

Sapling Point runs hard by the ICW's northerly flank when passing between flashing daybeacon #78 and unlighted daybeacon #77. Favor #77 to avoid any conflict with the shallows to the north. Also, be sure to pass well south of unlighted daybeacon #80.

At unlighted daybeacon #82, cruisers have access to the last major side-water short of Bon Secour and Mobile Bay.

Wolf Bay   The westerly banks of lower Wolf Bay are flanked by a broad zone of shoal water. Conversely, the easterly banks have a much narrower belt of shallows. Enter Wolf Bay by setting a compass/GPS course from unlighted daybeacon #82 for the easterly half of the bay's waters. As you approach charted Mulberry Point, guarding the western banks, cruise back to the mid-width for best depths.

Some .6 nautical miles north of Mulberry Point, Wolf Bay splits into two large branches. Under no circumstances should you approach the point separating the two forks. As is clearly and correctly forecast on chart 11378, a shoal extends for .3 nautical miles south from the point.

Also, be warned that the separating point appears as much higher ground from the water than you might expect from studying 11378. From a distance, it almost looks like an island bisecting Wolf Bay. Don't be fooled! Again, stay well away from this point.

Most captains will choose to bypass the northeasterly arm of Wolf Bay. As mentioned earlier, these waters become much too thin for cruising-sized boats before the bay narrows enough for effective protection. If you should choose to explore the arm regardless, favor the southeasterly banks when entering. Eventually the fork follows a bend to the north. Depths rise to 5-foot levels through this turn, and deteriorate to 4 feet or less shortly thereafter.

Wolf Bay's westerly fork is a much better choice. Stick to the middle and you can maintain minimum 6- to 7-foot depths as far north as the intersection with Graham Bayou on the western banks.

If you choose to make use of the excellent anchorage on Graham Bayou, simply enter the stream on its centerline. Be mindful of the charted shallows abutting the northerly entrance point. This shoal seems to be building southward. As the charted cove on the southern shore comes abeam, good soundings stretch out almost from shore to shore. We suggest dropping the hook just a touch to the west, where chart 11378 indicates a 6-foot soundings. Farther upstream, depths soon climb to less than 5 feet.

To proceed north on the main body of Wolf Bay's westerly branch, north of Graham Bayou, begin using the "Wolf Bay extension" on chart 11378. Continue on the mid-width until the sharp, charted point on the easterly banks comes abeam. From this point to Moccasin Bayou, best depths are maintained by slightly favoring the westerly side of the stream.

Halt your forward progress as Moccasin Bayou comes abeam to the northeast. Farther north, Wolf Bay soon splits for a second time and depths worsen markedly.

To visit the fabulous Wolf Bay Lodge, drop the anchor once abeam of Moccasin Bayou. Look to the northeast and you will find a beautiful private home surrounded by a luscious green lawn, perched on the charted northerly entrance point to Moccasin Bayou. Don't attempt to approach this promontory, as it is surrounded by very shoal water. Look north of the point occupied by the house and you will spy the pier associated with Wolf Bay Lodge on the northern banks northwest of Moccasin Bayou. Break out the dinghy and head ashore with appetites at the ready. Only boats comfortable with 4-foot soundings should attempt to moor to Wolf Bay Lodge's small dock. Be sure to have a fried oyster for me.

Moccasin Bayou itself is narrow and only carries 4- to 4½-foot depths. It eventually leads to a small commercial boatyard, but there are no services for transients.

On the ICW West of its intersection with Wolf Bay, the Waterway flows through a well-marked, improved channel to the easterly entrance of Portage Creek Canal. Observe all markers carefully. This is not the place to go exploring outside of the ICW.

Captains cruising west from flashing day-beacon #94 will soon encounter the eastern entrance into Portage Creek Canal. As expected, it's only necessary to hold to the canal's centerline for good water.

Do not attempt to enter either of the charted loops that cut into the Waterway's northern banks, or the one on the southerly shore near the canal's easterly entrance. All are shoal and treacherous.

Soon after leaving the errant loops behind, passing cruisers will sight a gravel barge loading wharf on the northern banks. Reduce your speed and pass the docks idling.

Some .35 nautical miles southwest of unlighted can buoy #95A, the new Foley Beach Express Bridge spans the Waterway. Withe a healthy 73-foot vertical clearance, this span is not a cause for concern or delay.

The Gulf Shores twin bridges cross the ICW near Standard Mile 155. These are fixed spans having a prodigious 73 feet of vertical clearance. As you approach this bridge, slow your speed again. This maneuver will avoid the chance of damage to boats docked at the small facilities near the bridge.

At flashing daybeacon #97 the Waterway begins its trek through Oyster Bay. Depths outside of the ICW rise to 1-foot levels. Watch your stern as well as the course ahead to guard against leeway easing you out of the channel.

From #97 set course to pass between flashing daybeacon #100 and unlighted daybeacon #99. Continue straight ahead on the same heading, pointing to come between flashing daybeacon #101 and unlighted daybeacon #102. At this point the Waterway leaves Oyster Bay and follows a canal for about 1 nautical mile before it flows into Bon Secour Bay (standard mile 151), an easterly branch of Mobile Bay. Flashing daybeacon #103 heralds the Waterway's entrance into the bays.

Sailboat Bay   The condo development known as Sailboat Bay is served by a U-shaped creek snaking into the ICW's northerly banks. As this facility is now completely private, and there is no longer any overnight anchorage available, visitors should probably keep clear.

Mobile Bay

It had been a long, long day way back in 1990. Bad weather early that morning had sent me traveling overland from Mobile to Panama City, Destin, and Fort Walton Beach to revisit the marinas along the ICW that had been researched some weeks before by water. I figured if I couldn't spend my time cruising, at least I could check on any recent changes in the facilities to the east.

As anyone who has driven the roads from Panama City to Mobile knows, it can be a long and frustrating route for the motorist, and I was not in the best frame of mind when I recrossed the Highway 98 bridge and causeway that span the northern reaches of Mobile Bay. Suddenly, a panoramic view swept out before me to the south and west. The sun was setting over the bay's western shores, and the sky was painted with every imaginable shade of red and gold. I pulled my tired car off to the side of the road and rushed down to the water's edge with camera in hand.

Looking towards Blakely Island, I could see the World War II battleship, the USS *Alabama*, bathed in its own bright lights and backlit by the sunset. A glance to the south revealed the black shores of the bay starkly set out against a golden sky. Red and white lights winked in the distance on Hollingers Island. As I stared out on the horizon to the south, it was just possible to make out a large ship coming up the main bay channel from the lower bay, with its brave forts, Middle Bay Light, and the mysterious Sand Island Lighthouse.

In about 15 seconds, my fatigue was replaced by intense eagerness to hit the water early the next morning and partake of Mobile Bay's wonders as they should be experienced—from the water. After taking a few photographs, I reluctantly turned my back on the darkening scene and headed home for a late supper of crab and shrimp. To say that I felt recharged falls far short of the mark. I hope that you will have the good fortune to come to this magnificent bay with that same feeling of excitement and anticipation which found its way into my weary soul on that golden evening.

Mobile Bay Geography

Mobile Bay is formed by six rivers that feed into its northern reaches. The huge drainage of these six streams ferries uncounted gallons of water rich in sediment down the bay into the

Gulf of Mexico, resulting, of course, in more than a little shallow water. In fact, depths on the deeper, lower section of the bay average only some 7 to 10 feet. Shoal water is rife on the northerly reaches.

Mariners should also be warned that strong, sustained northerly winds (a frequent occurrence during the winter months) can lower water levels on Mobile Bay below charted soundings and the depths presented in this guide. If a long northern blow has been in progress just prior to your arrival, approach any and all side-waters with extreme caution. Conversely, in the absence of strong winds, lunar tides average 2 feet or less on Mobile Bay.

A large, well-marked ship's channel traverses the entire length of Mobile Bay from south to north. While this cut is heavily used by commercial vessels of all descriptions, it can also serve as a ready artery of travel for pleasure craft. Various side channels cutting off of the main track lead to the bay's several harbors that are appropriate for cruising craft.

Mobile natives can often be heard discussing the "East Shore" or its westerly counterpart. As you might guess, they are discussing a particular shoreline of Mobile Bay, south of the city. Each bank has its own attributes. The Eastern Shore is known for its quiet, attractive communities which seem to slumber contentedly in the summer sun. The western shores are host to the region's finest facilities for pleasure craft, found on Fowl and Dog Rivers.

Surprisingly enough for a body of water of its size, Mobile Bay has a limited number of destinations for cruising craft. Some anchorages can be found on the Fowl and Dog rivers, while marinas are available on the East Shore at Point Clear, and Fly Creek. As already mentioned, the Western Shore plays host to a huge collection of facilities on Dog River, with an equally appealing marina on Fowl River.

The southernmost section of Mobile Bay is constricted by historical Dauphin Island to the west and the Gulf Shores peninsula to the east. The remains of two Civil War forts frown at each other across Mobile Bay Inlet, recalling the tragic days of that ill-starred conflict. Dauphin Island boasts several anchorages and one marina facility for vessels that are not too long legged. There is also a well-placed marina at Navy Cove on the eastern peninsula leading to the resort community of Gulf Shores.

Mobile Bay's East Shore

Many cruisers familiar with Mobile Bay might well term the East Shore as the bay's quiet bank. Indeed, this shore is lined with small, quaint communities interspaced with hauntingly lovely residential sections. Some of these old homeplaces speak eloquently of Southern society before the Civil War. Their peaceful facade reminds us all that this was a gracious, if inequitable, time that will never come again. If you are one of those cruisers who, like this writer, looks forward to piloting his or her craft to quiet villages and peaceful shorelines, then by all means Mobile Bay's East Shore should certainly be your cruising destination.

Facilities along the East Shore are adequate, though widely spaced. A marina and luxurious motel welcome cruising craft at Great Point Clear, while several high-quality marinas are found on Fly Creek to the north. The charming community of Fairhope also offers a long city pier with very minimal dockage for visitors.

Anchorage on the East Shore is quite hard to find. There is but one remote side-water with sufficient depth and shelter to consider as an overnight haven.

Cruising skippers and their crew will delight in the visual aspect of Mobile Bay's eastern banks. Beautiful homes alternate with undeveloped patches in a pattern that seems to have been arranged by some omnipotent landscape architect. At no point will the passing cruiser observe a shoreline which is overcrowded with rampant commercial development.

The Bon Secour River
(30 17.200 North/087 44.210 West)

A charted channel breaks off from the ICW near its easterly entrance into Bon Secour Bay and leads northeast to the inner reaches of the Bon Secour River. This stream serves as the home for one of the last commercial fishing and shrimping fleets on Mobile Bay. These salty craft make for interesting viewing from the water. Based solely on this criterion, this writer suggests Bon Secour River as a good gunk hole for any vessel not limited by the 6-foot minimum channel depths. Be warned that depths outside of the marked cut rise quickly to dangerous levels.

On the other hand, marina facilities are nonexistent on the river and anchorage possibilities are scant as well.

At unlighted junction daybeacon #SF the Bon Secour River channel divides. The southerly offshoot leads to some additional commercial docks, but it is eventually cut off by a low-level fixed bridge. Craft that can stand some 5-foot depths might try anchoring just south of unlighted daybeacon #10, near 30 17.200 North/087 44.210 West. This is not the most attractive of overnight stops, and you may well be bothered during the early morning hours by the coming and going of the local fishing fleet.

Conversely, there is plenty of swinging room for most any size pleasure vessel and the anchorage is well sheltered from all but particularly strong northern and southern winds.

For those willing to make a considerably longer upstream trek on the main Bon Secour River channel, you can pitch out the hook immediately upstream of the last aids to navigation on this cut, unlighted daybeacons #37 and #38. By favoring the westerly shores, minimum 6-foot depths can be maintained. Swinging room should be adequate for vessels as large as 36 feet, and there is superb shelter from foul weather. Be sure to read the navigational information presented below before attempting first-time entry into this haven.

Weeks Bay

Weeks Bay is found some 3.5 nautical miles north of flashing daybeacon #123 (on the ICW's passage across lower Mobile Bay). While at first glance this side-water might be looked upon as a good gunk hole or anchorage, an entrance bar with only 3-foot depths renders Weeks Bay off limits to all but very small, shallow-draft vessels. Unless you pilot a small outboard, I/O, or sailcraft with a retractable keel, you had best leave Weeks Bay out of your cruising plans.

Middle Bay Light

Mariners cruising north to the East Shore via Mobile Bay's ship's channel will come upon Middle Bay Light north of flashing daybeacon #46. While chart 11376 terms this aid as "Mobile Bay," all the locals know it as Middle Bay Light. This interesting structure dates back to 1885, when it was supposed to be one of five "screw pile"-type lighthouses built on

Mobile Bay. The other lights were never constructed, leaving Middle Bay the sole aid to navigation of its type on Mobile Bay.

For those of you who don't know, a screw-pile lighthouse is simply a house which is perched atop pilings "screwed" into the bottom strata. A light is then attached to the roof of the structure.

Those cruisers from the Chesapeake or North Carolina coast will recognize Middle Bay Light as a structure typical of their region. Indeed, Middle Bay is the only screw-pile lighthouse ever built on the Northern Gulf, while the aforementioned coastlines were once dotted with these structures.

Construction crews ran into quite a problem when erecting the lighthouse in 1885. After setting the steel pilings, and placing the "house" atop the structure, the entire assembly began to sink into the muddy bottom. Fortunately, even though it sank some 7 feet, the pilings descended evenly and the decision was made to proceed with the lighting of Middle Bay anyway.

For many years now the strong beacon which once perched atop Middle Bay's light has been extinguished. A red daybeacon-type light now shines from the rooftop. Mariners still use the old beacon as an aid to navigation. It is kept in good repair and cruisers observing it for the first time could be readily excused for thinking it a relatively modern structure. The whitewashed walls of the house look as if they were just painted yesterday.

Point Clear and Grand Hotel Yacht Basin (30 29.182 North/087 56.006 West)

A marked entry channel leads east just to the north of charted Great Point Clear to the Grand Hotel Yacht Basin. This venerable hostelry, owned by the Marriott chain, features a sheltered harbor partially protected by a curving concrete breakwater flanking the entrance channel. Minimum entrance depths run to 5½ feet with typical soundings of 6 to 7 feet. Once within the sheltered dockage basin, soundings improve to between 6 and 7½ feet.

Grand Hotel Yacht Basin accepts transients at its fixed wooden slips featuring fresh-water and 30- and 50-amp power hookups. Gasoline and diesel fuel are available at the adjacent fuel dock, as is a waste pump-out service.

The dockmaster has informed this writer that visiting craft "must make an advance reservation. We stay booked up here." Let this be a word to the wise. Be *sure* to call ahead!

Cruisers looking to spruce up after a salty day on the water must make their way to either of two sets of showers adjacent to the swimming pools (see below) or a third set in the motel. Either way, it's a bit of a trek and not

particularly convenient, especially for an early morning shower. There is no on-site Laundromat, but the hotel does have its own laundry and dry-cleaning service.

The adjacent Marriott Grand Hotel is an unbelievably sumptuous resort complex that features no less than four restaurants, two swimming pools, tennis courts, a golf course, a spa, and a work-out room. All these amenities are readily available to transient visitors.

The grounds are immaculately landscaped and manicured. Many rooms feature magnificent views of the bay, and the sunsets can be spectacular indeed. Service in the hotel is reminiscent of more gracious, far-removed days. If you are in any wise considering a few days living off the water, this magnificent hostelry should definitely be at the top of your list.

Oh, by the way—the Sunday brunch buffet at the Grand Hotel's main dining room is legendary. My best friend, Andy Lightbourne, once described sailing back across Mobile Bay to the Dog River after one of these feasts. As he said, "if you had overflown our sailboat and looked down, you would have seen four people sprawled out flat on the deck, seemingly spent from their efforts."

Grand Hotel Yacht Basin (251) 928-9201

Approach depth— 5½-7 feet (mean low water)
Dockside depth— 6½-7½ feet (most slips)
**   5 feet (a few southern slips)**
Accepts transients—yes (advance reservations
**   recommended)**

Grand Hotel Yacht Basin, Great Point Clear

Transient-dockage rate—slightly above average
Fixed wooden slips—yes
Dockside power connections—30- and 50-amp
Dockside water connections—yes
Showers—yes
Waste pump-out—yes
Gasoline—yes
Diesel fuel—yes
Restaurant—on site

Point Clear History   The modern Marriott Grand Hotel sits almost directly over the site of the Gunnison House Inn, built about 1830. Until the Civil War, Point Clear was a popular summer retreat or watering place for the well-to-do planters in Alabama. During the hot-weather months, whole families would journey down to the water to escape the dreaded heat and swamp fever. During those times it was believed that the disease we know as malaria was caused by noxious vapors rising from the nearby swamps. Of course, today we know that the ignoble mosquito was the planters' real enemy, and the cooling sea breezes simply helped to scatter their foe.

Those planters who chose not to lodge at the Gunnison House often built beautiful summer homes, which they called cottages. These serene structures usually overlooked the bay to catch the cooling breezes from the water. A number of these time-honored homes remain and can be observed from the highway by walking south from the Grand Hotel.

With the advent of the Civil War, the idyllic life at Point Clear came to an abrupt end. Writing in her wonderful book, *Seeing Historic Alabama*, the author, Virginia Van Der Veer Hamilton tells of a young man writing his sweetheart at the beginning of the conflict. The simplicity of his farewell belies the horrible

suffering that the author would find in his new home:

> Dearest, I fear I shall not see you at Point Clear this summer. I am leaving for Vicksburg.

The old hotel was converted to a Confederate hospital. After the war the original building fell into disrepair and was finally destroyed. During the battle of Mobile Bay, one of the Union ships shelled a private home near the present site of the Grand Hotel. The hole made by the cannonball remains and today is covered with a brass plate that reads, "Compliments of Admiral Farragut."

**Fairhope City Marina
(30 31.488 North/087 54.857 West)**

The absolutely charming bayside village of Fairhope maintains a city dockage and fishing pier almost due east of unlighted daybeacon #S, some 2.8 nautical miles north of the Point Clear entrance channel. Navigators studying chart 11376 will easily spy the long, charted pier east of #S.

This facility's uncharted entrance channel runs parallel to the long pier's northerly face. It is outlined by pairs of pilings. While most of this passage carries 6 to 7 feet of water, there is one lump between the second and third set of pilings which raises soundings to some 4½ feet at MLW. Deep-draft vessels take note!

The Fairhope city dockage basin is also located on the north side of the pier. This harbor is protected by a concrete breakwater, which should provide adequate protection in all but gale-force (or stronger) winds. Slip space (5 to 6 feet MLW) is theoretically managed by the adjacent Yardarm restaurant (251-928-0711),

Fairhope City Pier

which sits perched directly on the pier about halfway between the shore and the dock's westerly tip. However, after many visits to this basin over the years, we have yet to see anything in the way of a dockmaster or, for that matter, find anyone to even ask about the dockage facilities. Besides, during our last sojourn on these waters in the fall of 2002, all the available berths were occupied by resident craft. For all these reasons, we strongly suggest that you search for overnight dockage elsewhere.

Fairhope Ashore

Those cruisers who do somehow find a berth at the city pier—or, more likely, those who take advantage of motorized transportation from one of the Fly Creek facilities (see below)—will find a beautifully landscaped park overlooking the waters of Mobile Bay just behind the city pier. Walking up the main street to the east, you will sight some of the community's beautiful Southern-style homes. The serenity of a stroll by these venerable homeplaces is definitely recommended for those cruisers who feel the need to walk anywhere that is not their deck.

Continue up the street and you will soon come to the picturesque business district. Here you will find small shops and stores at which you can readily resupply your larders.

You can pick from gift, book, hardware, and grocery stores and expect a warm, friendly greeting from everyone.

By now, if you have noticed a somewhat rampant enthusiasm on the part of this writer for the fair town of Fairhope, then you are, indeed, perceptive. Even if you can't find dockage at the city facilities, consider driving back into town from Eastern Shore Marine (described below) on nearby Fly Creek. Your cruise will be far the richer for the extra effort.

Fairhope History   In 1894 one of the most inscrutable groups to ever arrive on the eastern banks of Mobile Bay, or the western banks, for that matter, founded the "Fairhope Single Tax Colony." This collection of pioneers were followers of Henry George and his "single tax philosophy." According to E. B. Gaston, writing in *A Brief History of Baldwin County,* "Single Taxers hold as a 'self-evident' truth that all men have equal rights to the use of the earth. . . . They hold that, as a natural result of the coming of people together in communities . . . land values rise, and that these land values . . . are therefore obviously a proper source of public revenue."

To institute this unique philosophy, no land was sold at that time in Fairhope. Rather, the local residents "leased" their land from the city government, paying yearly fees that were reevaluated annually. These moneys were then used to pay for municipal functions such as police, fire, and garbage services and, most important of them all, education.

The Fairhope "Single Taxers" were apparently very interested in promoting new and novel educational techniques. In addition to more public facilities, the "Marietta Johnson School of Organic Education" was founded in the early twentieth century. This school practiced a concept of unstructured education that did not include the pressure of grades. Creativity and free thought were encouraged above all else.

While today much of the nonpublic property in Fairhope is privately owned, the Single Taxers and their unique philosophy are still remembered. Who knows, with all our governmental problems, maybe this approach should be tried afresh.

**Fly Creek Facilities
(Various Lats/Lons—see below)**
The dredged channel leading to Fly Creek strikes east from flashing daybeacon #2, some 1.2 nautical miles north of the Fairhope City Pier, near the charted village of Seacliff. This small but well-protected stream is home to several pleasure-craft-oriented facilities. Minimum entrance depths are 6½ feet, but most soundings are in the 7½- to 8-foot range.

Moving west to east, Fly Creek's first facility will soon come abeam along the northerly banks. Eastern Shore Marine (30 32.544 North/087 54.146 West) is, in this writer's opinion, the premier pleasure-craft facility on Mobile Bay's eastern shore. This marina offers just about everything cruising skippers could ever imagine needing.

Visitors to Eastern Shore Marine can count on finding at least 6 to 8 feet of water at all berths. Transients are readily accepted at modern, fixed wooden piers with all power and water connections. There are adequate, non-climate-controlled showers and a fair Laundromat shoreside. The marina also maintains a small ship's store and a large parts department.

Fly Creek entrance, Mobile Bay

Gasoline, diesel fuel, and waste pump-out service are all readily available.

Full-service boating repairs are also available at Eastern Shore Marine. The helpful and knowledgeable staff offers mechanical service for diesel or gasoline engines, as well as complete haul-out, below-waterline repair capability. The yard's travelift is rated at a 35-ton capacity. Cruisers can make use of these impressive servicing capabilities with confidence. While this writer has yet to meet the completely perfect boatyard, visitors are certainly as likely to find the job done right the first time at Eastern Shore as anywhere else on the Northern Gulf.

Eastern Shore Marine is also associated with Nautica, Ltd., Sailing Charters and School (251-990-5557). This relatively new operation offers four sailcraft (ranging from 25 to 40 feet) for bareboat charter. Give Beverly a call and tell her you found out about Nautica from us.

Finally, as if all that weren't enough, Eastern Shore Marine is within striking distance of the quaint community of Fairhope and its several fine restaurants. Transients are cheerfully extended the use of a courtesy car to drive into Fairhope for sight-seeing, provisioning, or sampling the local gastronomical climate. For those desiring a more extensive landside excursion, Eastern Shore can arrange for car rentals to be delivered dockside.

A new addition to Fly Creek is the nearby Fly Creek Cafe (see below). Now, even cruisers lacking motorized landside transportation can find excellent dining on site.

Clearly this impressive roster of services, coupled with the marina, yard, and charter personnel's helpful attitude, places Eastern Shore Marine in the top-10 pleasure-boating operations along the Northern Gulf coastline. In short, don't dare pass this outstanding facility by.

**Eastern Shore Marine (251) 928-1283
http://www.easternshoremarine.com**

**Approach depth—6½-8+ feet
Dockside depth—6-8 feet
Accepts transients—yes
Transient-dockage rate—below average
Fixed wooden piers—yes
Dockside power connections—30- and 50-amp
Dockside water connections—yes
Showers—yes
Laundromat—yes
Waste pump-out—yes
Gasoline—yes
Diesel fuel—yes
Mechanical repairs—yes
Below-waterline repairs—yes
Ship's store—yes
Restaurant—on site and courtesy transportation
   available to visit restaurants in nearby
   Fairhope**

Eastern Shore Marine, Fly Creek

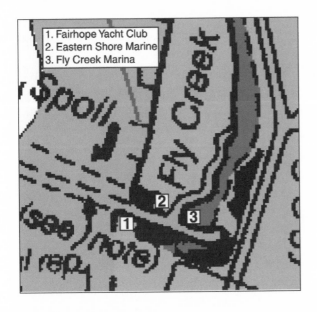

1. Fairhope Yacht Club
2. Eastern Shore Marine
3. Fly Creek Marina

Lying opposite Eastern Shore Marine on the southern banks of Fly Creek, friendly Fairhope Yacht Club (30 32.495 North/087 54.193 West) is glad to accept visitors who are members of other yacht clubs with appropriate reciprocal arrangements. Berths are provided at fixed, wooden piers with fresh-water and 30-amp power hookups. Depths alongside run around 6 feet or better at low water. Shoreside, you will find showers at the clubhouse as well as a full-service dining room and bar open Wednesday through Sunday.

Fairhope Yacht Club (251) 928-3276
  http://www.fairhopeyachtclub.com
Approach depth—6½-8 feet
Dockside depth—6-7 feet (MLW)

Fairhope Yacht Club, Fly Creek

Accepts transients—members of other yacht clubs with reciprocal privileges
Transient-dockage rate—well below average
Fixed wooden piers—yes
Dockside power connections—30-amp
Dockside water connections—yes
Showers—yes
Restaurant—on site

Though it is barely noted on chart 11376, Fly Creek splits as it moves a bit farther to the east. These waters used to play host to a collection of small marinas and pleasure-craft service firms. Now, all the wet slips and service functions have been combined under the auspices of one ultrafriendly firm, Fly Creek Marina (30 32.499 North/087 54.051 West). Trust me on this one, fellow cruisers, you're never going to find a warmer welcome anywhere.

The owners of Fly Creek Marina have been upgrading their physical plant ever since they acquired the property. The wet slips are now in excellent condition, and new, air-conditioned showers and a Laundromat have just been completed as this account is being tapped out on the keyboard. A new, city-installed waste pump-out system is also in the offing.

Transients are readily accommodated at fixed wooden piers featuring 30-amp power connections and fresh-water hookups. Depths pierside run around 6 feet. Maneuvering room is at a bit of a premium on this part of the creek, and I would be hesitant to try and jockey a 50-footer into a slip here, but otherwise, you should be in very good shape.

Eventually, dry-stack storage, a ship's store, and mechanical repairs will be in the offing, but the timing for these new services could not be concretely ascertained at the time of this

writing. As the amiable owner put it to this writer, "Our marina is still very much a work in progress."

For the last two years, Fly Creek Marina has been the informal gathering spot for a fall meeting of "big loopers." For those of you who don't already know about this *hot* topic in the cruising community, big loopers are those who cruise all the way up the Eastern Seaboard, then up the Hudson River, through the Great Lakes, south down the Illinois, upper Mississippi River, Ohio and Tennessee Rivers, then south through the Tennessee Tombigbee Waterway to Mobile. Time will tell whether this informal get-together grows into something larger, but the big loopers could not have picked a better spot.

By the way, if you really want to get something done at Fly Creek Marina, you'd better see Manhole. Of course, your request will probably be met with a *meow*, since Manhole is actually the marina cat. We are told he sometimes does a good job waking visiting cruisers up in the morning by jumping aboard and meowing.

One of the very *best* things to look forward to when visiting Fly Creek Marina is the informal, on-site dining spot known as Fly Creek Cafe (251-990-0902). This *delightful* restaurant offers both open-air and climate-controlled dining. The cafe is open for lunch and remains in operation until about 8:00 P.M. The burgers and seafood sandwiches are simply superb. I can't say enough about what a genuine delight it is to find a dining spot so well placed (diners have a great view of Fly Creek and all its many docked vessels) and offering such wonderful fare. Give it a try—you won't be disappointed.

Fly Creek Marina (251) 928-4868

Approach depth—6½-8 feet
Dockside depth—6 feet
Accepts transients—yes
Transient-dockage rate—well below average
Fixed wooden finger piers—yes
Dockside power connections—30-amp
Dockside water connections—yes
Waste pump-out—yes
Showers—yes
Laundromat—yes
Restaurant—on-site

Blakely and Apalachee Rivers

Two rivers, the Apalachee and the Blakely, flow into the northeasterly corner of Mobile Bay. While the Blakely has a marked entrance channel, both streams are buffered against the bay's waters by a large band of shoals with less than 4 feet of depth. While local outboard fishing skiffs make use of both rivers on a daily basis, cruising-size craft, both power and sail, should discontinue their East Shore explorations long before reaching the shallows fronting these two rivers.

EAST SHORE NAVIGATION

Captains piloting craft entering Mobile Bay via the ICW on Bon Secour Bay (near standard mile 151) may choose to visit the East Shore in one of two fashions. The shorter but more navigationally exacting route leads from flashing daybeacon #135, north of Edith Hammock, through the relatively deep water abutting the eastern shoreline. Aids to navigation on this run are a bit sparse and you must follow several runs of 6 to 8 nautical miles between beacons.

Other captains will choose to continue on the ICW to the Waterway's intersection with Mobile Bay's large ship's channel. You can then cut north and follow a very well-defined track until coming abeam of your destination to the east. While chart 11376 shows spoil banks flanking most of this primary channel, 10-foot depths can be carried over these underwater islands.

Eastbound cruisers on the ICW will almost certainly want to choose the ship channel route. Distance wise, it doesn't make sense to cruise all the way across the foot of Mobile Bay, only to turn back north and work your way back to the northwest.

Be warned! Mobile Bay is relatively shallow and winds over 15 knots can raise a scary chop. Strong blows call for a day spent at the dock and one more bridge game. This is not a body of water to be trifled with in foul weather. Your cruise will be far better served by a bit of patience than foolhardy bravado.

Bon Secour River   Cruisers who choose to explore or attempt overnight anchorage on commercially (fishing) oriented Bon Secour River should stick strictly to the marked channel. Depths outside of this passage are more than suspect.

To enter Bon Secour River, depart the ICW channel just east of unlighted nun buoy #106. The marked and charted river entrance channel sweeps back to the east-northeast and then cuts north. Point to pass between unlighted daybeacons #3 and #4. From this point, vessels cruising upstream should pass all red markers to their (the cruisers') starboard side and take green beacons to port.

After passing between unlighted daybeacons #5 and #6, the marked channel swings sharply north-northeast until it passes between unlighted daybeacons #9 and #10. At this point the cut bends sharply to the east-northeast and hurries on to a split in the channel.

Use your binoculars to watch ahead and pick out unlighted junction daybeacon #SF. If you plan to visit the southward-running channel that eventually leads under an ultra-low-level bridge to Oyster Bay, depart the main river passage just short of #SF and follow the markers south, still passing all red aids to your starboard side and green to port. Do not attempt to cruise more than 75 yards south of unlighted daybeacon #10. Depths soon poop out to 4½ feet or less.

Those continuing upstream on the main Bon Secour River channel should ignore #SF and point to come abeam and pass just south of unlighted daybeacon #11. Continue cruising east-northeast on the channel by following the same course to come abeam of unlighted daybeacon #14 to its northerly side.

From #14, you need only remember your good old red-right-returning rule to follow the cut all the way upstream to its marked limits. North of unlighted daybeacon #24, switch to the Bon Secour River Extension section on chart 11378.

Adventurous souls who track their way to the most upstream set of markers, unlighted daybeacon #37 and #38, in search of overnight anchorage, should ease just far enough northwest of #37 so that they will not swing into the marker. Favor the western banks as you pick out a spot to drop the hook. Shallow water shelves out from the opposite shores.

Only shoal-draft craft should attempt to continue cruising upstream past the anchorage described above. Depths quickly rise to 3 feet or less.

East Shore Passage Route   Westbound cruisers on the ICW who choose the direct passage up Mobile Bay's eastern shore should depart the Waterway at flashing daybeacon #135. While the next westerly (lighted) aid, flashing daybeacon #147, would serve just as well, the additional run of 2 nautical miles between #135 and #147 would be wasted.

Note the "Subm Pile" notation on chart 11378 south of #135. Reports from local captains indicate that this warning is for real. Be sure to stay north of flashing daybeacon #135.

From #135, set a careful compass/GPS course to come abeam of flashing daybeacon #2 off Mullet Point by some .4 nautical miles to its westerly side. Do not approach #2. This aid marks a shoal building to the west from Mullet Point.

The run between #135 and #2 crosses some 7.6 nautical miles of 7- to 10-foot waters. Pay attention to your compass (and/or GPS) and stay on course. This passage does not stray near any shallow water until you begin your approach to flashing daybeacon #2.

Between #135 and #2, it is theoretically possible to break off to the east and visit Weeks Bay. However, as described earlier, this sidewater has a very shallow entrance bar, and it is pretty much off-limits to cruising vessels.

Once abeam of #2, set a new course to come abeam of flashing daybeacon #4, west of Great Point Clear, by at least .6 nautical miles to its westerly side. Boats drawing 5 feet or more should not approach #4 any closer than .9 nautical miles to its westerly quarter. This maneuver will help to avoid the two charted 6-foot patches, which might give especially deep draft vessels a spot of trouble.

Point Clear   If your destination is the Marriott Grand Hotel Yacht Basin at Point Clear, follow a due northerly course from your position abeam of flashing daybeacon #4 for some .4 nautical miles. You can then cut east into the well-marked channel leading to the marina. Keep all red aids to starboard and green markers to port, of course.

North on the Eastern Shore   To continue north on the direct Eastern Shore route, set course from a position abeam of flashing daybeacon #4 to come abeam of flashing daybeacon #C by a good 500 yards to its westerly quarter. Daybeacon #C marks a large tongue of charted shallow water northwest of Battles Wharf. Once abeam of #C, alter course and point to come abeam of privately maintained (but charted) unlighted

daybeacon #S to its northwesterly side.

From #S, you may choose to cruise almost due east to the charted Fairhope pier, or continue north to Fly Creek. Cruisers making for the Fairhope pier should turn almost due east from #S. Watch ahead and you should soon spy the long city dock stretching far out into the bay's waters. Point to come abeam of the pier to its northerly side. Eventually you will catch sight of a series of unadorned pilings outlining a channel paralleling the pier's northerly face and leading to the city dockage basin. Pass between the various pairs of pilings. The shallowest stretch lies between the second and third set of pilings. Eventually, the entrance to the breakwater-enclosed dockage basin will come abeam to starboard.

If Fly Creek is your destination, set course from #S to come abeam of unlighted daybeacon #E to its westerly side. Then, cut sharply to the east-southeast and enter Fly Creek's entrance channel by coming abeam of and passing flashing daybeacon #2 to its immediate northerly side. The creek's mouth will then be dead ahead and fairly obvious.

Most cruising skippers will wisely choose to discontinue their northerly trek at Fly Creek. As you will remember, the Blakeley and Apalachee rivers, feeding into the northeastern corner of Mobile Bay, have shallow entrances which are not appropriate for larger vessels.

Large Ship's Channel to the Eastern Shore
Following the large ship's channel north on Mobile Bay is as simple a navigational challenge as you are ever likely to meet. The cut is

exceptionally well marked with a blaze of lighted aids. While the channel is surrounded by spoil islands, most of these carry at least 10 feet of water.

Entry into the ship's channel from the ICW will be discussed in the last section of this chapter. Turn to this account and study it before attempting to enter the cut for the first time.

Access to all the eastern ports of call can be gained by abandoning the channel at flashing daybeacon #58. An easterly course to Point Clear or a northeasterly run to Fairhope and Fly Creek will lead you over minimum 9-foot depths to your destination. Alternately, southbound mariners on Mobile Bay can depart the marked cut south of flashing daybeacon #66.

Mobile Bay's West Shore

The western banks of Mobile Bay are, as one might say, clearly where the action is. The Fowl River provides one good marina and some anchorage possibilities, while the Dog River, to the north, boasts the largest collection of marinas and boatyards this side of New Orleans. Moving still farther to the north, the bay's ship's channel eventually leads to the city of Mobile and the entrance to the Mobile River. This vital, commercially successful city has a rich history which is still remembered with pride and honor in these modern days of rapid progress. Surprisingly, at the current time there is not a single marina catering to pleasure craft anywhere on the Mobile waterfront. This is a major impediment for cruising captains who want to experience Mobile's many delights. However, a cruise of the commercial waterfront is fascinating nevertheless. Huge containerized cargo ships and oil-drilling rigs line the wharves. Careful captains can even cruise to within sight of the World War II battleship, the USS *Alabama*, permanently moored at Blakely Island.

It should also be mentioned that the Mobile River is the southern terminus of the Tennessee

Tombigbee Waterway (known to most cruisers simply as the "Tenn-Tom"). This route, often described accurately as a classic federal boondoggle, can lead intrepid mariners far north into Tennessee and even Ohio. Increasing numbers of pleasure craft are now beginning to make use of this waterway.

While the various destinations on Mobile Bay's western banks are widely separated, they do provide wonderful cruising with the expectation of good harbors and protection at the end of your explorations. Unless you are in a great hurry, this writer suggests allocating several days in your cruising itinerary to experience the charms and outstanding facilities of the bay's western shoreline.

The Fowl River
(Various Lats/Lons—see below)

Fowl River heads off from Mobile Bay's western shores almost due west of Middle Bay Light (and flashing daybeacon #49). Note the spelling of the word *Fowl,* which denotes the many birds that frequent this stream. The name does *not* imply a "foul" bottom.

The big news on this stream is the first-class condition of Fowl River Marina (see below). Where once there was a very forgettable facility, new owner Bill Brehm has done amazing things in just a few years. The on-site restaurant, Pelican Reef, is nothing to sneeze at either!

The Fowl River can provide anchorage for craft drawing 6 feet or less and able to clear a *24-foot fixed bridge.* Minimum entrance depths are now a good 6 feet, but there is one shoal near the stream's juncture with Mobile Bay that must be scrupulously avoided.

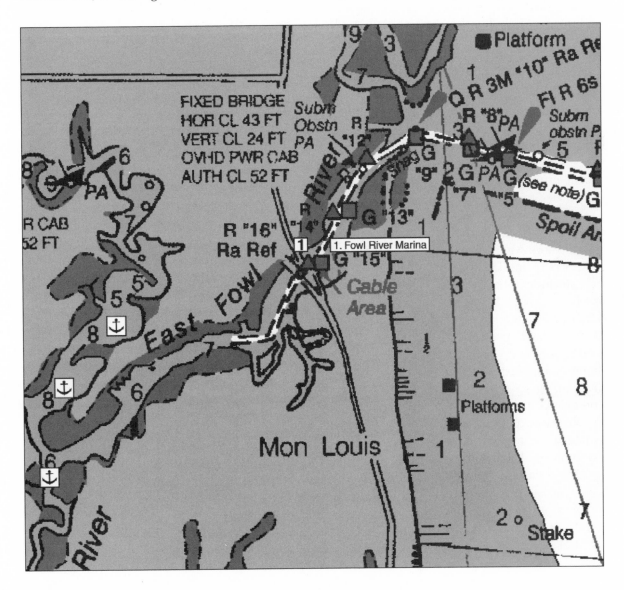

Generally, the Fowl River shoreline is quite attractive. Modest but comely homes overlook much of the banks, alternating with undeveloped patches. The river is quite popular with local small craft during weekends and this can be a bit of a problem for anchored cruisers. For the most part, though, visiting mariners will find a Fowl River cruise to be a visually appealing experience that can only engender fond memories.

Just short of the bridge, newly invigorated Fowl River Marina (30 26.665 North/088 06.819 West) guards the northwesterly banks. It's hard to overstate how many wonderful changes new ownership has brought to this once down-on-its-luck facility. In its present form, cruising craft can make use of Fowl River Marina with every confidence.

Transient vessels as large as 50 feet are eagerly accepted at low-lying, fixed, wooden piers featuring fresh-water and 30- and 50-amp power hookups. Depths alongside at most slips run around 5 feet. There are also some berths, clearly intended for smaller powercraft, in the innermost section of the harbor that have only 4 feet of water alongside. Gasoline, diesel fuel, and waste pump-out service are all readily at hand. Some mechanical repairs for both gasoline- and diesel-powered plants can be arranged through local, independent technicians.

Shoreside, grimy cruisers will find one adequate, air-conditioned shower per sex. There is no on-site Laundromat, however.

One of the real stars at Fowl River is the adjacent Turtle Reef Restaurant (251-973-2670), open for lunch and dinner seven days a week. Put quite simply, everything here is good. Prices are not inexpensive; however, so hold on to your wallet.

It is always a pleasure to bring to light new and/or greatly improved facilities, particularly when they are managed as competently as Fowl River Marina. We suggest that our fellow cruisers put a big, red circle around this marina's location and track their way there during their next visit to Mobile Bay.

Fowl River Marina (251) 973-2670

Approach depth—6 feet (minimum)
Dockside depth—5 feet (most slips)
4 feet (innermost berths)
Accepts transients—yes
Transient-dockage rate—average
Fixed wooden piers—yes
Dockside power connections—30- and 50-amp
Dockside water connections—yes
Showers—yes
Waste pump-out—yes
Gasoline—yes
Diesel fuel—yes
Mechanical repairs—independent technicians
Restaurant—on-site

Fowl River meanders to the southwest for some 1.4 nautical miles past the fixed bridge, and then splits into northern and southern branches. The magnificent Bellingrath estate overlooks the river's split and will be considered in a separate section below. The southern branch of the Fowl River (designated as "East Fowl River" on chart 11376) can provide some limited anchorage for vessels as large as 35 feet on its initial run to the south from the split (near 30 25.676 North/088 08.148 West). Protection is good from all winds and the surrounding shoreline is only lightly developed.

Soon the southerly stream follows a hairpin turn to the east and then back to the south.

Fowl River Marina

Unmarked shoals begin to encroach on the river as it winds through this bend. Cruising vessels are advised to avoid the upper portions of eastern Fowl River.

Happily, northern Fowl River provides even better shelter than its southern sister. There are *at least* two excellent overnight havens worthy of consideration. The first is found on the charted 8-foot, baylike waters just north of the split (near 30 26.053 North/088 08.073 West). Here craft of almost any size can drop the hook with good protection from all winds. The eastern banks exhibit moderate, though not unseemly, residential development while the western banks are in their natural state.

Even better sheltered is the next bay, just to the northeast, boasting correctly charted 8-foot soundings (near 30 26.334 North/088 07.803 West). Minimum depths of 6 feet run in quite close to both shorelines and in a really hard blow, you could ease over to the lee shore for maximum protection. Swinging room (if not the depth) would just about be enough for the famous *Trump Princess*, or whatever she's called by now. These waters are this writer's favorite anchorage on the Fowl River and are well worth every cruiser's consideration.

Farther upstream, depths decline somewhat on the Fowl River, though local craft can find an 8-foot unmarked channel continuing for several miles to the northwest. Many visiting captains will wisely choose to discontinue their exploration at the anchorage described above, but if you are feeling daring, careful skippers can gunk hole upstream for a nautical mile or two and enjoy the many attractive riverside homes overlooking the dark waters.

Bellingrath

The magnificent Bellingrath house and gardens (251-973-2217) overlook the split in the Fowl River from the western banks. This former private residence is now open to the public and has become quite a showplace. The gardens include azaleas, roses, chrysanthemums, camellias and poinsettias. In the spring and summer, they are a riot of color.

The house itself contains huge collections of English silver and Boehm porcelain sculptures. Tours begin at 8:00 A.M. and continue to 5:00 P.M. The gardens are open from dawn to sunset. Admission is charged for both the house and gardens.

While Bellingrath has a dock on the Fowl River with 6- to 8-foot depths, advance arrangements are necessary to obtain a temporary berth. Many cruisers will find this extra effort justified. Call the house ahead of time and make the appropriate reservations. Trust me. A cruising stop at this magnificent attraction is certainly worth a little extra bother.

Hollingers Island

Navigators studying chart 11376 will note two channels leading northwest and west respectively to Hollingers Island. The two cuts flank an exceptionally large spoil island that appears as a substantial body of land from the water. The southerly passage is known as the Theodore ship channel.

Hollingers Island is a large industrial complex with at least one mammoth chemical plant.

Cruising craft should probably bypass both of the Hollingers Island channels. There are no facilities or provisions for pleasure craft and both cuts are used heavily by commercial waterborne traffic. Especially adventurous captains might cruise in for a quick look, but I suggest leaving as quickly as you came.

Dog River
(Various Lats/Lons—see below)

Visiting cruisers entering Dog River for the first time will be nothing short of amazed by the huge collection of marinas and boatyards waiting at the beck and call of cruising craft. If there is a more impressive collection of facilities on a single stream anywhere else along the Northern Gulf Coast, this writer has not found it.

Entrance into the Dog River used to be a bit of a problem. Fortunately, dredging has minimized this difficulty. Cruisers can now expect minimum 6½- to 8-foot entrance depths. However, the cut is subject to shoaling and the situation could be very different in several years or following a major storm. To resolve any doubts, check on current conditions with one of the Dog River marinas before attempting entry.

In spite of 3- and 4-foot soundings on the Dog River's inner reaches, noted on chart 11376, mariners will find minimum 6-foot soundings on the river's centerline for many miles upstream. Typical depths are in the 8-foot plus range. Of course, as is true on all of Mobile Bay, sustained northerly blows can occasionally raise soundings to shallower levels.

Captains approaching the Dog River Bridge from Mobile Bay may catch sight of a harbor bristling with sailcraft masts to the northwest.

Dog River Bridge

This is the Buccaneer Yacht Club. Unfortunately, the entrance channel to this private facility is completely unmarked and strays through very shoal water. Considering these problems, this writer cannot recommend Buccaneer for strangers unless a club member can be found to lead you in.

The Dog River entrance is spanned by a 65-foot, high-rise bridge. This structure is a great improvement over the old 11-foot bascule bridge that was replaced almost a decade ago.

After passing the bridge, the river's first facility will come abeam on the northern banks. Turner Marine Supply (30 33.996 North/088 05.285 West) is the first in the incredible series of full-service marinas and yards on the Dog River. Turner has a fuel dock fronting directly onto the river, but most boats are docked in a well-sheltered basin entered just upstream from the fuel pier. Transients are gladly accepted for temporary berths and the high-quality, fixed wooden piers feature all power and water connections. Acceptable, nonclimate-controlled showers and a semi-open-air Laundromat are found on the marina grounds. Waste pump-out service is also available. Turner Supply specializes in below-waterline service work for sailcraft. Their travelift is rated at a 25-ton capacity. Complete mechanical, marine electrical, fiberglass, and refrigeration repairs are also available. There is a good ship's store on the premises and Turner Marine can

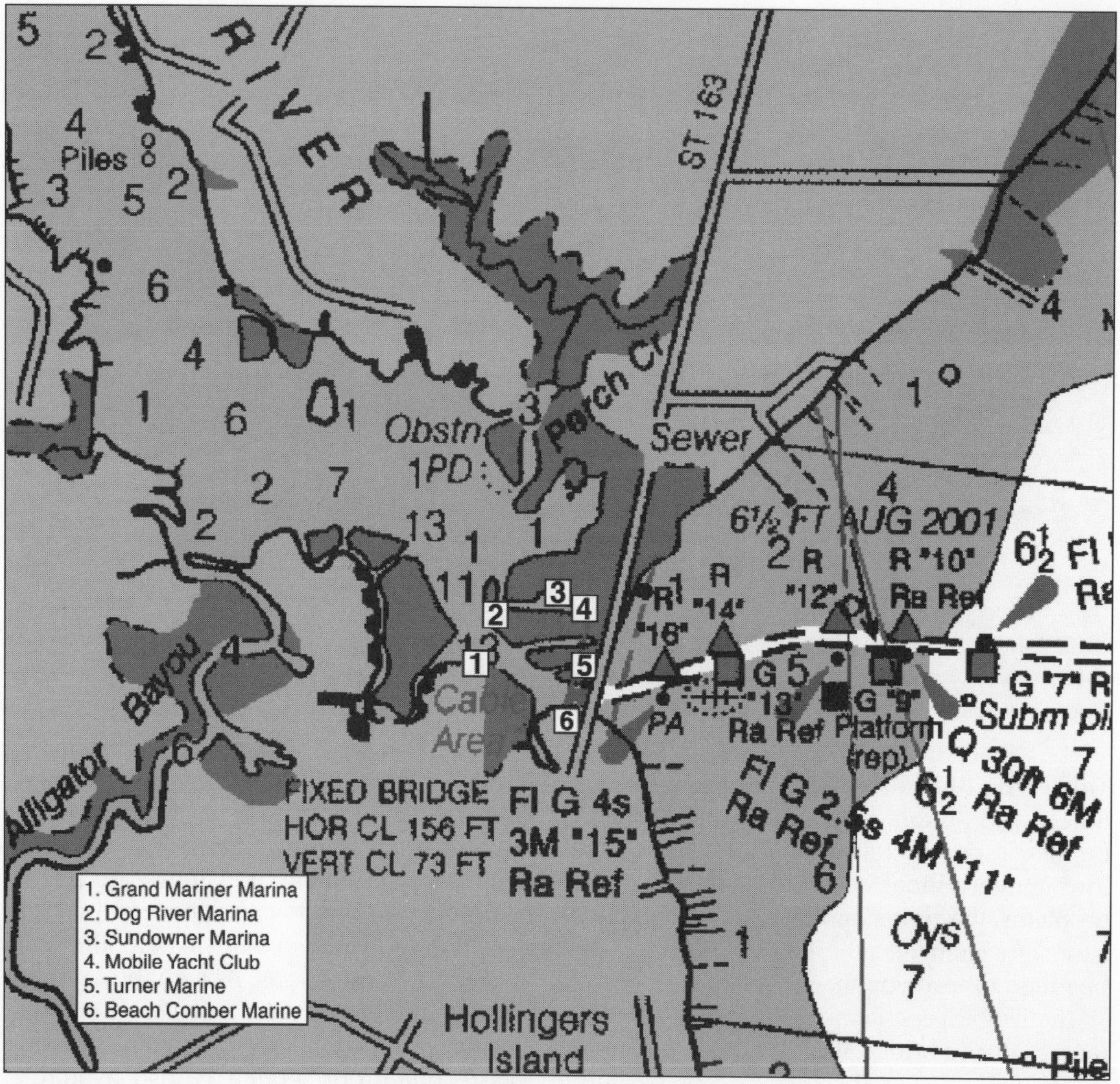

1. Grand Mariner Marina
2. Dog River Marina
3. Sundowner Marina
4. Mobile Yacht Club
5. Turner Marine
6. Beach Comber Marine

arrange for transients to dine at the nearby Mobile Yacht Club. While sailcraft are certainly a bit more in evidence at Turner's dock than powercraft, we spotted any number of "stinkpotters" comfortably ensconced during our visit. During the summer months, advance dockage reservations would be an excellent precaution. The marina and repair yard are closed on Sundays.

Turner Marine Supply (251) 476-1444

Approach depth—7-10 feet
Dockside depth—8-10 feet
Accepts transients—yes
Transient-dockage rate—below average
Fixed wooden piers—yes
Dockside power connections—30- and 50-amp
Dockside water connections—yes
Showers—yes
Laundromat—yes
Waste pump-out—yes
Gasoline—yes
Diesel fuel—yes
Mechanical repairs—yes
Below-waterline repairs—yes
Ship's and variety store—yes
Restaurant—nearby

Almost opposite Turner's, Beach Comber Marine (251-443-8000) makes its uncertain home along the river's southerly banks, near 30 33.875 North/088 05.331 West. During our last visit in late summer 2002, the restaurant fronting onto the river was closed, and we could find no one on duty in the adjacent marina/repair yard. This facility currently seems to be in a rather precarious state, and at least for the moment, we suggest that mariners seek dockage and repairs elsewhere.

Also on the southern banks and a bit farther upstream, fortunate cruisers will discover the extensive docks of Grand Mariner Marina & Restaurant near 30 33.948 North/088 05.565 West. The old tradition of Southern hospitality reaches new heights at Grand Mariner. Visiting cruisers can be totally assured of a warm and professional welcome at this very well-appointed facility.

Grand Mariner Marina and Restaurant, Dog River

Transient cruisers patronizing Grand Mariner are offered overnight or temporary berths at fixed wooden piers with 30- and 50-amp power connections and water connections. Some vessels are accommodated at a long pier fronting the Dog River, while others are moored in a sheltered basin that sports some covered slips. Dockside depths are an astounding 12 to 17 feet at the outer pier, so if you're weekending in your minesweeper, you're in luck. The inner slips display soundings from 6 to 7 feet. Adequate, nonair-conditioned showers and a fair Laundromat are available shoreside, as are gasoline, diesel fuel, and waste pump-out services. There is even a courtesy car for those who need to make a run to the nearest supermarket. The well-stocked ship's and variety store can supply some of your basic provisioning needs.

Grand Mariner features full repair services for both sail and power craft. A 35-ton travelift can handle practically all haul-out needs. The yard has an experienced staff of diesel and gasoline mechanics as well as marine paint, fiberglass, electrical, and carpentry specialists. Wow! How's that for full service?

It should also be noted in passing that the Grand Mariner gets the nod for service work year after year from a majority of the local sailing crowd on Dog River. There are few better recommendations for any nautical establishment.

On-site, S. S. Marina Restaurant (251-443-5700, open evenings only) is, quite simply, one of the best coastal dining choices on the Alabama coastline. Owned by the same friendly family that manages the marina operations, visitors can be assured of a mouth-watering, gut-busting experience. We always manage to plan our cruising itinerary so that we partake of the fare at the S. S. Marina restaurant at least two nights running. We just want to be sure our research is always sufficiently in-depth, you understand.

A new attraction at Grand Mariner is the schooner *Joshua*. This very impressive, traditional, wooden-hulled sailing craft was finished in 2002, having been built from scratch over a nine-year period and fashioned after sailing vessels constructued during the last years of the 1800s. She is 72 feet long and has a beam of 18.5 feet. *Joshua* is available for personalized charters by calling Making Waves Charters at (251) 443-9463 or (251) 209-1168.

Grand Mariner Marina & Restaurant
(251) 443-6300
(251) 443-5300 (repairyard)

Approach depth—7-15 feet
Dockside depth—12-17 feet (outer dock)
                           6-7 feet (inner slips)
Accepts transients—yes
Transient-dockage rate—below average
Fixed wooden piers—yes
Dockside power connections—30- and 50-amp
Dockside water connections—yes
Showers—yes
Laundromat—yes
Waste pump-out—yes
Gasoline—yes
Diesel fuel—yes
Mechanical repairs—yes
Below-waterline repairs—yes
Ship's & variety store—yes
Restaurant—on site

Well, are you getting tired of hearing about "first-rate" facilities? Hold on a bit longer. Almost directly across from Grand Mariner, the extensive piers and dockage basin of Dog River Marina (also known as Middleton Marine) guard the northern banks near

30 34.042 North/088 05.474 West. As seems to be the usual arrangement on this river, the fuel dock flanks the main stream, while a canal leads inland to sheltered dockage that features mostly covered slips.

In spite of its obvious powerboat leanings, Dog River Marina will gladly dock transients arriving by either sail- or motor-driven craft. As the exceptionally friendly dockmaster put it to this writer, "If it floats, we'll dock it." That really about sums it up.

Transient dockage is provided at fixed wooden slips with 30- to as much as 100-amp power connections and fresh-water connections. Soundings on the outer berths run 7 to 8 feet, with typical 6-foot soundings on the inside slips. Gasoline, diesel fuel, and waste pump-out services are readily available, as is one adequate, unisex (nonclimate-controlled) shower and a small Laundromat. The dockmaster's office at the fuel dock doubles as a small variety store, and it now offers an e-mai/Internet connection for the exclusive use of visiting cruisers. How's that for going above and beyond the call of duty?

When it comes time for dinner, visiting cruisers can go across the street to the Wharf House restaurant (251-473-5733) or, better yet, hike across the bridge to the S. S. Mariner restaurant (see above).

Need I say it? *Complete* mechanical (gas and diesel) and haul-out repair services are readily available at Dog River Marina. The yard features two travelifts, rated at 30 and 60

Dog River Marina/Middleton Marine, Dog River

tons respectively. The resources devoted to the repair of large diesel-powered plants is very impressive indeed. In fact, Middleton Marine is the only Detroit Diesel dealer in the region. Of course, you can also count on full marine painting, electrical, and refrigeration services. As you might well imagine, there is also a most impressive parts department on the premises. Again, the service work is geared almost exclusively to larger power craft rather than their sailing brethren.

While visiting Dog River Marina, don't fail to make the acquaintance of Di-Di and Slick. This comical pair of canines are the marina pets, and you will never meet a pair of happier dogs.

Dog River Marina/Middleton Marine
   http://www.dogrivermarina.com
   (251) 471-5449
   (251) 471-4517 (fuel dock and dockmaster)

Approach depth—7-10 feet
Dockside depth—6-8 feet
Accepts transients—yes
Transient-dockage rate—below average
Fixed wooden piers—yes
Dockside power connections—30-, 50-, and 100-amp
Dockside water connections—yes
Showers—yes
Laundromat—yes
Waste pump-out—yes
Gasoline—yes
Diesel fuel—yes
Mechanical repairs—yes (extensive)
Below-waterline repairs—yes (extensive)
Variety store—small
Restaurant—2 nearby

Just upstream from Dog River Marina, a canal leads east to several docks associated with the Mobile Yacht Club (near 30 34.078 North/088 05.280 West). These berths consist of fixed piers with widely varying depths ranging from 5½ to 10 feet. Power (30-amp) and water connections are provided. Visitors who are members of clubs with appropriate reciprocal privileges are accepted for temporary dockage. Guests have the use of all club facilities, including the swimming pool and yacht-club dining room, located in the clubhouse across the street. Evening meals are served Thursday through Sunday. Showers are also available for visitors.

Mobile Yacht Club (251) 471-3131
   http://www.mobileyachtclub.com

Approach depth—7-10 feet
Dockside depth—5½-10 feet
Accepts transients—members of accredited clubs
Transient-dockage fee—well below average
Fixed wooden slips—yes
Dockside power connections—30-amp
Dockside water connections—yes
Showers—yes
Restaurant—on site (open Thursday through Sunday)

Newly minted Sundowners Marina (30 34.092 North/088 05.348 West) guards the northerly banks of the same eastward-running cove serving Mobile Yacht Club. This facility is still in a state of transition into a fully operational condition, but the services already offered are encouraging. New, fixed wooden piers are ready for transients or month-to-month tenants. Depths alongside at mean low water run 5 to 6 feet. Fresh-water and 30-amp power connections are provided at all berths. There are also a few slips that feature 50-amp hookups. A waste pump-out system should be up and running by the time this account finds its way into your hands. Just to be on the safe side, call ahead to check on the availability of this service. Future plans call for the construction of a shoreside support building that will house showers and a Laundromat. The exact completion date of this new structure was still an open question at the time of this writing. Sundowners does not have a fuel dock, but all the restaurants described below and above are within an easy walk of the docks. By the time the next edition of this guide appears, we feel confident that the situation at this facility will have stabilized to a point where we can give far more details. For the moment, however, any new transient dockage on Dog River is something to be thankful for, and we suggest that you give Sundowners Marina a look. Tell dockmaster Cliff we sent you!

Sundowners Marina (251) 471-5999

Approach depth—6-10 feet
Dockside depth—5-6 feet (MLW)
Accepts transients—yes
Transient-dockage rate—below average
Fixed wooden piers—yes
Dockside power connections—30-amp (a few
   50-amp hookups also available)
Dockside water connections—yes
Mechanical repairs—independent technicians
Restaurant—several nearby

Past charted Perch Creek, Dog River soon follows a significant jog to the north. In the crook of this curve, *shallow-draft* vessels can drop the hook in the cove leading to Alligator Bayou, near 30 34.454 North/088 06.269 West. Depths are only some 3½ to 4½ feet and you cannot enter the bayou itself. There are also some unmarked shoals to avoid.

If you can stomach all these negative points, captains can drop the hook with excellent protection from all winds except particularly strong northerly blows. The adjacent shoreline is only lightly developed and makes for a great

evening backdrop. Believe it or else, this is probably the best overnight haven available on lower Dog River.

Continuing to the north, cruisers exploring Dog River will note the extensive docks of the Alba Club on the easterly banks. While there are no services available for transients at this private facility, you might be on the lookout for a 35-foot Pearson sailboat bearing the name *Chaconne.* This sleek vessel belongs to this writer's best friend in the world. If you need advice on cruising Mobile Bay, Andy Lightbourne is the one to ask.

Soon the Dog River opens out to the west. A large cove fronts two offshoots, Rabbit and Halls Mill creeks. While it seems that locals enter these streams and anchor in the cove on occasion, there are many unmarked shoals to avoid. Visiting cruisers lacking specific local knowledge should bypass this area.

North of the cove, the Dog River narrows perceptibly and depths on the mid-width improve to 7 feet or better. Farther to the north, Dog River narrows enough for sheltered anchorage about anywhere on its mid-width. Don't approach any of the shorelines or try to enter various coves along the way. They are invariably shoal.

This upstream portion of Dog River is particularly lovely, with many beautiful homes overlooking the water. Even if you don't have occasion to anchor for the evening, the upper Dog River is a great gunk hole for craft as large as 40 feet. Larger vessels might find maneuvering room a bit skimpy.

Mobile Waterfront and the Mobile River

North of flashing daybeacon #78, the Mobile Bay channel leads into the mouth of the Mobile River. Suddenly cruisers are plunged headfirst into the highly commercial Mobile city waterfront. While there is no dockage for pleasure craft, a trip through the wharves, dry docks, and oil-drilling rig service docks is more than fascinating. At one point you will actually cruise *over* Interstate 10, which passes below you in the Mobile Highway Tunnel. Eventually the commercial waterfront comes to an end near the charted Cochrane Bridge.

North of the bridge, cruising craft enter the southerly reaches of the Tenn-Tom Waterway. This popular route leads, in turn, to the Tennessee River, the Cumberland River, the Ohio River, the upper Mississippi River, and, finally, via the Illinois River to Chicago and the Great Lakes. Anyone who has been around the cruising community for the last several years knows these heartland waters are part of the Big Loop passage. There is no hotter topic among cruisers today than the Big Loop!

Unfortunately, this guide's coverage of the Mobile River ends at the Cochrane span. Cruisers venturing north into the Tenn-Tom and points beyond are enthusiastically referred to Fred Myer's three absolutely first-class guide books: the *Tenn-Tom Nitty Gritty Cruise Guide,* the *Tennessee River Cruise Guide,* and the *Cumberland River Cruise Guide.* Call (800) 803-0809 to order these wonderful books.

Thrillseekers with boats that draw less than 3½ feet can follow the unmarked channel between Little Sand and Pinto islands and join the deep water leading north to the Raft and Tensaw rivers. This track will soon take you abeam of the massive World War II battleship, the USS *Alabama,* permanently moored to the southeastern banks of Blakeley Island.

Farther to the north, the Raft River channel

meets up with the bridges of Interstate 10 and Battleship Parkway (Highway 98). This guide does not cover the waters past the bridge, but let it be noted that few cruising-sized vessels will want to follow this route (past the bridges) anyway.

City of Mobile

Mariners currently have a real problem with a visit to the city of Mobile. The nearest pleasure craft dockage facilities are located on the Dog River, a goodly drive from downtown Mobile. Considering the historical city's many attractions, the additional effort to roust out some landside transportation is more than justified.

Mobile is today a vital, commercially important port with diverse industries. A quick cruise along the waterfront is all that's necessary to evidence the tremendous amount of shipping entering and leaving Mobile daily. Usually you will also spot several oil-drilling rigs in for servicing. These massive towers bear mute testimony to the importance of the offshore oil industry in Alabama. While this part of the Mobile economy has suffered during the last few years, as it has in almost all of the Northern Gulf Coast, the city's diversified economic base has helped it to survive the injury far better than some communities.

Visitors interested in Mobile's fascinating heritage will want to visit Fort Conde (251-208-7304). This impressive visitor's center is actually a re-creation of a Spanish fort. Guests can watch an interesting sound and slide show that will do much to put you in touch with Mobile's colorful past. A quick stroll leads to the historic district and several museums. While this writer found Mobile's historic area to be somewhat in its infancy, new attractions are being added all the time.

When it comes time to dine out in Mobile, the choices are almost mind-boggling. However, for those who (like this writer, as you may have surmised) love partaking of the day's fresh catch, one dining spot stands out. Wintzell's Oyster House (251-432-4605), located at 605 Dauphin Street, may just have the finest fried seafood on the Northern Gulf. The freshest of fish, shrimp, scallops, oysters, and (unforgettable) crab claws are rolled in a very special cornbread mix and lightly fried in oil. The result might make out-of-towners contemplate a change of address.

Wintzell's offers even more than its superb food. The restaurant's walls are covered with the most incredible selection of humorous, occasionally thought-provoking signs that I have ever seen. These many placards add immeasurably to the tangible down-home atmosphere of this unique dining spot. To be succinct, those who have not eaten at Wintzell's have not really seen Mobile.

If you are up for a cholesterol-enriching experience, not to mention some good ol' American food, spare no effort to find your way to the Dew-Drop Inn (1808 Old Shell Road, 251-473-7872). This all-American dining spot was recently featured on NPR as having some of the best cheeseburgers and hot dogs anywhere in the USA. Have one for me!

There are still many private residential sections of Mobile which contain lovely, old, Southern mansions. You will almost certainly need the services of a local to find these districts, but they are well worth your attention.

Those interested in touring Mobile would do well to acquire a copy of Virginia Van Der Veer Hamilton's book, *Seeing Historic Alabama*. It contains the most concise information on Mobile that this writer has discovered. Numbers to know in Mobile:

Checker Taxi—251-476-7711
Yellow Cab—251-476-7711
Avis Rent A Car—251-633-4743
Enterprise Rent-A-Car—251-661-4446
Boat/US (3654 Airport Boulevard)—
    251-414-5447
West Marine (3744 Government Boulevard)—
    251-661-6244

Mobile History   It has been said of Mobile that the city was born in war, battered by war and finally prospered in peace. It certainly goes without saying that Mobile has an incredibly rich historical heritage. Within the confines of this guide, it is only possible to present a bare bones sketch of this fascinating story. Readers are encouraged to research further and learn all they can of Mobile's past. This writer has always believed that all travelers should have an understanding and appreciation of the heritage of the land and waters through which they are traveling to enjoy their voyage to the fullest. Mobile is certainly a shining example of this maxim.

In December of 1701 the intrepid French leader and explorer Pierre LeMoyne, Sieur d'Iberville sailed into Pensacola to be greeted by the Spanish governor with "open arms." In the years preceding this time, Iberville, his younger brother Bienville, and a host of other farsighted French leaders had founded French Louisiana in modern Mississippi. Now Iberville was returning from France after a trip to confer with his king and obtain needed supplies for the colonists.

During Iberville's time in France, the War of Spanish Succession had commenced. England was worried over the French king's successful plan to put his grandson on the throne of Spain. The British felt that the alliance of these longtime enemies would be a serious blow to their own power and prestige. Never one to muck about with a problem, Great Britain promptly declared war on both France and Spain. Suddenly the French on the Northern Gulf found the Spanish in Pensacola as allies rather than potential enemies.

Iberville arrived in the New World with orders to strengthen the French settlement at Biloxi. Casting about for a more defendable position, he selected the western banks of the Mobile River, several miles above the bay.

Iberville's brother Bienville took over the command of the new fortress. It was the beginning of a long and arduous struggle by this amazing leader. In many ways, Bienville was almost solely responsible for the health and well-being of all of French Louisiana until the end of the Seven Years' War. After a few years, Bienville moved the colony downstream and built a new fort, Fort Conde, at the site of the present-day Mobile visitor's center.

In 1717 a strong hurricane closed the channel west of Dauphin Island, severely crimping the shipping trade to Biloxi. Casting about for a new capital, Bienville first selected the French settlement at New Orleans. The colony's council vetoed his decision and Mobile became the capital until 1722, when Bienville finally got his way.

In 1763 England took possession of Mobile as a provision of the Treaty of Paris, which brought the Seven Years' (French and Indian) War to a close. Under English trading practices Mobile began to grow and prosper. However, this enlightened "rule of trade" was not to last for very long, for Spain took the area, including Pensacola, back from the weakened British at the end of the American Revolution.

They were to hold Mobile until April of 1813, when it passed into American hands.

As peace again settled about Mobile, the city began to prosper. Alabama was admitted to the union as a state in 1819. According to Virginia Van Der Veer Hamilton, writing in *Seeing Historic Alabama,* "During the antebellum period, its [Mobile's] port was a busy scene of exchange between steamboats from interior Alabama and oceangoing vessels from around the world, with cotton and lumber its major commodities."

As the Civil War settled its gloom about Mobile, the brave city acted as a vital link in the chain of Confederate supply. Stealthy blockade runners would steal offshore during the night and sail for England and France. The swift ships would soon return, stealthily find their way pass the Union blockade, and unload their vital cargo on the city wharves.

The battle of Mobile Bay in 1864 (described later in this chapter) finally closed this vital artery of the Confederacy. Mobile itself held out for nine more months and was one of the last cities in the South to fall to Northern forces.

Today, the city of Mobile can boast one of the finest commercial ports in America. Heavy industry has also been recruited. Wood pulp, textiles, furniture, and steel are only some of the products now produced in this thriving city.

Still, on a quiet fall evening, those wandering about the walls of reconstructed Fort Conde may still hear the sturdy voice of Bienville urging his colonists and fellow soldiers to greater effort. Though his dream of a French empire in the New World was doomed to failure, the effort is no less glorious for its eventual demise. The modern city of Mobile remains a lasting tribute to the efforts of this extraordinary man.

MOBILE BAY NAVIGATION—WESTERN SHORE

Virtually every cruiser visiting Mobile Bay's western shoreline will want to cruise north via the large ship's channel. Again, if you need help entering the cut from the Gulf Coast ICW, please refer to the "ICW and Mobile Bay Navigation" section at the end of this chapter.

The big ship cut is lighted up like a Christmas tree. You would have to be snoozing at the helm to come to grief here, but stranger things have happened, so stay alert. You wouldn't want to run into a tanker.

Most of the spoil islands flanking the channel have 10-foot depths. There are exceptions and the smart skipper will only depart the channel at the points listed below.

Remember that winds over 10 knots quickly stir up a sharp, steep chop on Mobile Bay. Blows over 20 knots are downright dangerous. Pick a day of fair winds for your passage on Mobile Bay and you can leave the meteorological worries behind.

The Fowl River   For best depths, leave the Mobile Bay large ship's channel just south of flashing daybeacon #49, a short distance north of Middle Bay Lighthouse. Set a careful compass course for flashing daybeacon #2 at the eastern edge of the Fowl River entrance channel. A run of some 3.5 nautical miles separates #49 and #2.

West of flashing daybeacon #2, the channel is well marked to the fixed bridge spanning the stream some 1.7 nautical miles upriver. However, there is one trouble spot that calls for navigational caution. Generally speaking, you should follow the old "red, right, returning" rule and keep all red beacons to your starboard side and all green aids to port.

Immediately after passing between unlighted daybeacon #9 and flashing daybeacon #10, the channel takes a sharp jog to the southwest. There seems to be a tendency to ease over onto the northwestern side of the channel between #9 and the next upstream aid, unlighted daybeacon #12. To avoid this problem, cut sharply southwest after passing between #9 and #10 and point to come abeam of #12 to its immediate southeasterly side.

Be advised that shoals are building out from the northwesterly banks and are beginning to encroach on #12. Be sure to pass this aid to navigation to its southeasterly side.

Eventually Fowl River Marina will come abeam to the northwest, shortly before reaching unlighted daybeacons #15 and #16. The Fowl River Bridge will be obvious as well.

After passing between unlighted daybeacons #15 and #16, navigators will soon encounter the fixed Fowl River Bridge. As my sailing friend Andy put it to me, "Many a sailcraft captain has cursed this span heartily." This bridge has only 24 feet of vertical clearance, plenty for most powercraft but not enough for any but very small sailboats. Perhaps at some time in the future a swinging or bascule bridge will replace the fixed structure. Until that time, the beautiful upper reaches of the Fowl River are pretty much restricted to powercraft.

West of the Fowl River Bridge, stick strictly to the river's centerline until the stream splits at Bellingrath. Don't be tempted to explore any of the side-waters. Depths outside of the mid-width soon rise to 4 feet or less.

At Bellingrath, visiting cruisers must decide whether to enter the north or south branches of the Fowl River. As mentioned earlier, the northerly branch is the better choice. If you insist on exploring south Fowl River (noted as "East Fowl River" on chart 11376), enter the stream's mouth on its mid-width. Good depths continue until the river takes a turn to the east and then another to the south. Past this point numerous unmarked shoals are encountered and depths are much too uncertain for any but local navigators.

North Fowl River, by contrast, is a cruising delight. You need only hold to the mid-width for many wonderful, worry-free miles upstream. This is a cruise which is highly recommended for powercraft under 46 feet.

Hollingers Island and Theodore Ships' Channel

The deep cut known as Theodore ships' channel leads northwest from the big ships' channel between flashing daybeacons #51 and #55. A lighted range marker to the southeast helps large ships keep to the cut. As this channel leads only to a large industrial complex lacking any facilities for pleasure craft, it will not be reviewed further.

Dog River

When entering Dog River, stick to the marked channel. Depths outside of the cut are questionable, particularly on the westernmost portion of the channel. Many more of the aids marking the Dog River channel are now lighted, in contrast to years past. Still nighttime entry by visiting cruisers could be a bit tricky.

The Dog River channel cuts northwest between flashing daybeacons #63 and #65. To enter the passage, continue on the big ships' channel until unlighted daybeacons #1 and #2 are directly abeam to the west. Then, cut between these aids and immediately set a new course to pass between the next pair of markers, flashing daybeacon #3 and unlighted daybeacon #4.

After passing flashing daybeacon #6 to its southwesterly side, the Dog River channel takes a bend to the west. Point to pass between flashing daybeacon #8 and unlighted daybeacon #7. Between #8 and the bridge, the channel is most subject to shoaling. Fortunately, these waters are frequently dredged and, for the moment, the cut has good depths. In the future shoaling could, and most likely will, recur. Don't be surprised to find different or additional markers than those aids shown on the latest edition of chart 11376 by the time you visit.

West of flashing daybeacon #15, mariners will meet up with the 65-foot, fixed, high-rise bridge. Point for the span's central passthrough.

Once through the Dog River Bridge, simply stick to the mid-width as you cruise along this pretty stream. Minimum 6-foot depths can be held on the centerline for several miles upstream. Just don't be tempted into any sidewaters, or depths could rise to 4 feet or less.

To enter the shallow anchorage on the cove leading to Halls Mill and Rabbit creeks, favor the southern shore heavily, but don't approach the point guarding the southerly quarter of the entrance. Be sure to drop the hook before proceeding more than 50 yards into the cove. Even by following this procedure, expect some 4-foot soundings.

On to Mobile   Don't attempt to use the marked and charted cut north of flashing daybeacons #69 and #70, which breaks off to the southwest and heads in the direction of Dog River. This so-called channel shoals to 4 feet or less.

North of flashing daybeacon #74, the Mobile Bay large ships' channel begins to knife its way through surrounding shoals. Stick to the marked cut and watch your stern carefully for any lateral leeway.

West of flashing daybeacon #78, chart 11376 correctly identifies a marked westward-running channel. This cut leads to a U.S. Coast Guard base, but there are no facilities for cruising boats. There is not really even room enough to anchor.

North of #78, switch to the "Mobile Ship Channel—Northern End" section of chart 11376 for further upstream navigation. North of flashing daybeacon #82, you will enter the southerly mouth of the Mobile River and begin your approach to the heavily commercialized Mobile city waterfront. Heavy, oceangoing cargo ships and oil rigs in for repair are usually very much in evidence. While you need not give any concern to depth problems, this portion of the river is usually dotted with flotsam and jetsam. This writer has observed large logs and tree branches floating in the swift current. Keep a sharp eye out for any such obstructions, or a bent prop and shaft could

be the unhappy result.

Be on guard against the swift river current north of flashing daybeacon #78. Low-powered trawlers and sailcraft under auxiliary power should be particularly alert for the water movement. While there is not too much chance of finding shallow water, there is always the dread possibility of being shoved into the docks or some commercial traffic. Keep alert!

After cruising north for some 5 nautical miles, you will encounter the Cochrane Bridge. This guide's coverage of the Mobile River ends at the Cochrane Bridge. To the north the "Tenn-Tom" Waterway beckons. But, as I've said before, that's an entirely different story.

Passage to USS **Alabama**   East of flashing buoy #84, especially *adventurous* captains piloting craft that draw no more than 3½ feet and that are not over 38 feet in length can try and follow the unmarked but well-charted channel between Little Sand and Pinto islands. This cut leads to a large swath of water sweeping north to the Raft and Tensaw rivers and the moorings of the USS *Alabama.*

To enter this questionable cut, continue north from flashing buoy #84 for some 20 yards and then cut sharply to the southeast. Favor the southerly side of the channel but do not approach the southerly banks too closely. As can be seen from a study of chart 11376, this procedure has the best chance of keeping you to the unmarked channel.

Eventually, the northeasterly point of Little Sand Island will come abeam to the south. Continue on course for another .4 nautical miles, and then cut sharply to the north. As you begin your trek north to a point abeam of the USS *Alabama*, be mindful of the large shoal building out from the southern shore of Pinto Island. Don't allow the current to push you to the west onto these shallows.

Notice also the charted partially submerged jetty to the east pictured on the small-scale portion of chart 11376. On-site research revealed a broad channel between the Pinto Island shallows and this obstruction, but in low-light or poor visibility conditions, the jetty can be hard to spot. Don't drift too far to the east or you could be in for a rocky surprise.

Switch back to the small-scale portion of chart 11376 for continued navigation to the north. Cruisers can now follow a broad path of deep water with minimum depths of 10 feet all the way to the Battleship Parkway (U.S. Highway 98) Bridge. Soon you will have the opportunity to observe the massive dignity of the USS *Alabama* just west of your course.

This guide's navigational coverage ends at the Battleship Parkway Bridge. Most skippers of cruising-sized craft should probably end their exploration of these waters once abeam of the battleship.

The Gulf Coast ICW and Mobile Bay

After the mostly protected Florida Panhandle waters to the east, it can be quite a shock for westbound skippers to come upon the lower reaches of Mobile Bay at flashing daybeacon #103. You might be excused for looking back wistfully over your stern. Those are the last sheltered waters you will see directly on the Waterway until reaching Louisiana.

The Gulf Coast ICW enters Mobile Bay on its wide southeasterly lobe, known as Bon Secour Bay. If winds are blowing from the north or west, it can be a very bumpy introduction. Should bad weather be in the offing, retreat to a sheltered haven and wait for better conditions. Mobile Bay is not to be messed with in a hard blow.

Eventually the ICW leads to an intersection with the Mobile Bay ship channel. Mobile Bay Inlet is just to the south. This seaward cut is exceedingly well marked and offers as reliable an access as you will ever find to the Gulf of Mexico.

Two forts, Morgan and Gaines, occupy the points of land flanking Mobile Bay Inlet to the east and west. Both of these proud military structures are quite interesting and have a fascinating historical tale to relate.

West of the Mobile Bay ship channel the Waterway markings resume north of Dauphin Island. This interesting body of land has quite a history of its own.

Facilities on the ICW's trek across lower Mobile Bay are rather scanty, though one and possibly two marinas are worthy of attention from cruising captains. One is located near Fort Morgan on Navy Cove, and the other is found on Dauphin Island. This latter facility can be reached by two different routes. One approach calls for a long cruise through channels that sometimes have only 5 feet of depth, while the other traverses a passage under a fixed bridge with only 25 feet of vertical clearance.

Anchorages are practically nonexistent on this portion of the Waterway east of Dauphin Island. Several overnight havens are accessible along the inner portion of Dauphin Island Bay to vessels that can stand some 5-foot depths. Do not attempt to anchor on Mobile Bay itself. In 1993 an anchored sailcraft was tragically run down by a commercial barge while spending the night near the passage from Mobile Bay to Mississippi Sound.

The southern shoreline of Mobile Bay and the ICW passage across the inlet make for quite a contrast. To the east, the Gulf Shores peninsula is only lightly developed. Numerous all-natural patches are readily visible from the Waterway. Dauphin Island, west of the inlet, features moderate but not unsightly residential development. Cruisers will also have their first chance to view oil-drilling rigs just north of the inlet. Seen for the first time from the water, these huge, ungainly structures are hard to pull your eyes away from.

On a day with fair winds and sunny skies, the ICW passage across lower Mobile Bay can be a fascinating experience. In heavy weather, you may rue the day that your boat set bow on this often choppy body of water. Plan your cruise with an ear to the latest NOAA weather forecast.

Bon Secour Bay (Standard Mile 151)

Mobile Bay widens out on its southerly reaches, particularly on its easterly banks. This broad patch of deep water to the southeast is known as Bon Secour Bay. Besides the river bearing the same name, discussed earlier, there are no side-waters, anchorages, or marinas accessible to cruising-size craft on Bon Secour.

Weeks Bay, to the north, has a very shallow entrance bar with 3 feet (or less) of depth.

Only small, very shallow-draft outboard and I/O craft should attempt entry.

Edith Hammock Anchorage (Standard Mile 144) (30 14.654 North/087 52.662 West)

If winds are blowing from the south, some boats occasionally anchor on the large patch of deep water north of Edith Hammock, south of flashing daybeacon #135. Waters with only 2 feet of depth run out for at least .3 nautical miles from the southern shoreline. Consequently, you must drop the hook well away from the beach. Obviously, this doesn't make for good protection. Considering these disadvantages, the Edith Hammock haven is strictly a light-air anchorage and is not particularly recommended as an overnight stop.

Fort Morgan Marina (Standard Mile 135) (30 13.979 North/087 59.703 West)

This small, friendly facility is located near the charted position of Fort Morgan, just east of the charted ferry docks (well southwest of the ICW's flashing daybeacon #157). Fort Morgan Marina welcomes smaller cruising craft but entrance depths are a continuing concern at this facility. Despite on and off dredging, visiting cruisers can only expect to find about 4 feet at MLW in the entrance cut. Also, the marina management has informed this writer that they can only accommodate craft as large as 34 feet. As they put it to me, "We are mostly a small-craft marina." Be sure to call the marina before your arrival to ascertain the latest channel conditions.

Fort Morgan Marina features a wooden breakwater-enclosed harbor with fixed wooden slips. Depths in the basin are some 4½ to 5 feet. Protection is good in all but the heaviest weather. Power connections of the 30-amp variety and fresh-water hookups are available dockside, as are gasoline and diesel fuel. Mechanical repairs can be arranged, and there is a small ship's, variety, and grocery store on the premises. The marina even has good shoreside shower and laundry facilities.

The Fort Morgan Marina Restaurant (251-540-4665) is located just next door to the marina harbor. Reportedly, this dining spot serves the very freshest of local seafood.

Skippers piloting craft that can dodge the draft requirements may want to give Fort Morgan Marina some consideration. It is the only facility offering fuel and overnight dockage directly adjacent to the Waterway for many miles to the east or west.

Fort Morgan Marina (251) 540-2336

Approach depth—4 feet
Dockside depth—4½-5 feet
Accepts transients—yes
Transient-dockage rate—below average
Fixed wooden piers—yes
Dockside power connections—30-amp
Dockside water connections—yes
Showers—yes
Laundromat—yes
Gasoline—yes
Diesel fuel—yes
Mechanical repairs—yes (independent technicians)
Ship's, variety, and grocery store—yes
Restaurant—on site

Fort Morgan and "Damn the Torpedoes"

During the War of 1812, the young United States government built a small sand and wooden fort on the eastern shores of Mobile Bay Inlet. This structure was known as Fort Bower.

Later strengthened at the insistence of Gen. Andrew Jackson, the fort successfully repulsed a combined British and Indian attack in 1814.

Following their defeat by Jackson at the Battle of New Orleans, the English fleet entered Mobile Bay and overwhelmed the small fortification. The treaty ending the war had already been signed and the fort was soon returned to the Americans. After being abandoned, Fort Bower was destroyed by a violent hurricane in 1820.

The United States Congress was quick to see the need for stronger military fortifications along the Northern Gulf Coast. From 1819 to 1834, the present fort was constructed by slave labor. Designed by a French engineer, Fort Morgan resembles a "five-point star" and is considered "one of the finest examples of brick architecture in America." The fort was named for the revolutionary war general Daniel Morgan.

It was quite hot in August of 1864 as the forces of war began gathering at the southern mouth of Mobile Bay. Fort Morgan had been seized by the Confederates early in the War Between the States, as had its sister fortification, Fort Gaines on Dauphin Island to the west. Between the two forts stretched an almost unbroken chain of underwater mines, which in the vernacular of the day were called "torpedoes." Powerful cannon glared over the bay's entrance from both forts. The Southerners felt as ready as they could be to meet the threat waiting offshore.

Rear Adm. David Farragut had been ordered to take possession of Mobile Bay in January. The bay was a nest of swift blockade runners that served as a vital supply line for the Confederate cause. It was not until August that the intrepid sailor felt he had enough naval power to challenge the bay's defenses.

On August 5, 1864, Farragut stood in to the southern mouth of Mobile Bay with a strong fleet of gunships. Faced with the line of underwater mines, he is supposed to have said, "Damn the torpedoes, full speed ahead." His courageous ploy worked. Even though his own flagship was sunk by a mine, the rest of the armada sailed through the "torpedoes." For some reason they failed to explode, even though the frightened sailors could hear them scraping against their hulls.

As the federal vessels (minus Farragut) sailed into the bay, they were met by the Confederate gunboat *Tennessee*. In what was surely one of the most courageous but futile acts of this tragic war, this lone vessel sailed out to meet the might of the great fleet. The *Tennessee* was soon sunk and that was the end of the Confederate Navy on Mobile Bay.

Meanwhile, both Fort Morgan and Fort Gaines had damaged several ships with cannon fire. The Union ships moved out of range and regrouped. The next day the attack on the forts resumed. Historians claim that more than 3,000 cannon balls were fired at gallant Fort Morgan before the shell-shocked defenders were finally forced to surrender.

Both forts Morgan and Gaines returned to federal control, but Farragut did not have enough firepower to challenge the city of Mobile. It was to remain one of the last bastions of the Confederate cause at the end of the war.

In later years Fort Morgan was again briefly strengthened during the Spanish-American War. It was used as a training base during World War II. The fort was purchased by the state of Alabama in 1927 and, following a brief reactivation during the second World War, was declared a national historic monument. Today, it is open to the public. Cruisers docking at Fort Morgan Marina can visit the site via a quick walk.

While those of us living in these times may question the wisdom of the Confederates' stand, there can never be any doubt as to their loyalty and gallant bravery. Fort Morgan remains a living monument to all the men who fought so vainly but courageously during that dark conflict.

Mobile Bay Inlet (Standard Mile 133.5)

The Mobile ship channel follows a broad and very well marked channel through the southern mouth of Mobile Bay into the Gulf of Mexico. This seaward passage can be confidently rated as an all-weather inlet, keeping in mind that the easily run channel between inland and offshore waters has yet to be invented. Many large, oceangoing ships use the inlet on a regular basis and, as such, the channel is carefully maintained. All markers are clearly charted and are likely to remain so. This is a very stable cut.

Of course, when wind and tide are opposed, or breezes exceed 15 knots, the inlet can get nasty. Craft under 50 feet would do well to plan their passage to coincide with fair weather if at all possible.

Sand Island Lighthouse

Study chart 11376 for a moment and note the "Aband Lt Ho" (abandoned lighthouse) marked "Tower" northwest of flashing buoy #11. This is Sand Island Light, surely one of the strangest aids to navigation in the United States.

The original Sand Island Lighthouse was built in 1838 on (appropriately enough) Sand

Island. The 150-foot lighthouse cost $35,000 to construct and was outfitted with a "first-order" lens. Under ideal conditions it could be spotted for up to 20 miles at sea.

During the Civil War, Confederate forces discovered that the light was being used by artillery spotters for the invading Northern forces. Under the cover of night a stealthy party of Confederates rowed out to the light and successfully dynamited it out of existence.

In the years following the war, mariners called on the federal government to replace this necessary aid to navigation. It was finally rebuilt and again lit in 1872.

As the years passed, the island around the lighthouse began to erode severely into the surrounding bay. By the late 1800s there was very little land left and a strong hurricane in 1906 washed away the keeper's quarters, drowning all the occupants.

Yet, astonishingly, Sand Island Lighthouse continues to stand, perched atop a concrete riprap left over from its construction. Only recently was its light extinguished in the face of the numerous flashing buoys marking the inlet channel. As Bruce Roberts and Ray Jones comment in their fascinating book *Southern Lighthouses*, "Abandoned, isolated, and completely surrounded by the inky waters of Mobile Bay, the black Sand Island tower stands today only as a monument to its own violent and tragic past."

Dauphin Island (Standard Mile 132— Easterly Entrance via Billy Goat Hole Channel) (Various Lats/Lons—see below)

The eastern reaches of Dauphin Island thrust into the southwestern flank of Mobile Bay. The oblong island runs west for many miles, well into Mississippi Sound. One chan-

nel flows from the bay into the island's interior reaches, while three others are accessed from the ICW passage traversing the sound.

It was somewhat difficult for this writer to decide where to place the account of this historic body of land. Considering its importance in the history of Mobile Bay, as well as its marina and anchorage facilities, I have decided to discuss the island in this chapter. However, some of the channels leading from Mississippi Sound will be detailed in the following chapter.

Today Dauphin Island is home to an active resort community. The tranquility of the modern day hides the ravages of war and nature which have savaged this lonely land in times past. The cruising visitor is a beneficiary of this new development. One marina and at least three anchorages await mariners on the island's easterly reaches.

In discussing Dauphin Island from a nautical point of view, we must first mention the differing routes to its marina and anchorages. Billy Goat Hole channel leads from Mobile Bay Inlet and is well marked and charted (though not named on chart 11378—the chart you need to use for navigation around Dauphin Island). This cut follows a rather tortuous path from Mobile Bay, through a canal, and finally around the southern shores of Dauphin Island Bay. While numerous uncharted markers help passing cruisers to stay in the channel, some depths come up to 4½- and 5-foot levels. Several excellent anchorages (discussed below) are found along the course of this passage on Dauphin Island Bay. Eventually, this long route turns to the north and approaches Dauphin Island Marina.

Cruising craft entering Billy Goat Hole from Mobile Bay will see a pilot boat dock on the northwesterly corner of the small baylike area west of flashing daybeacon #17. Apparently many pleasure craft have stopped by this pier to

inquire if overnight dockage was available. A sign posted on the dock reads, "Dockage $250 a day." I guess that answers that question. There is

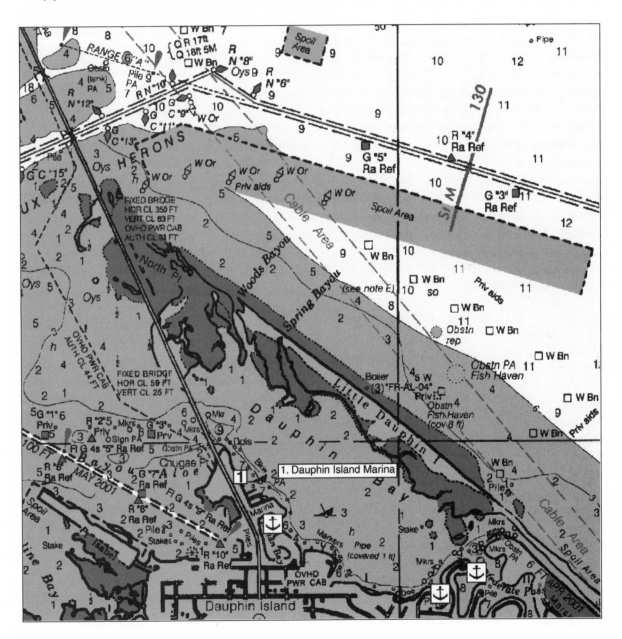

1. Dauphin Island Marina

also a U.S. Coast Guard station located on this small bay.

A second cut strikes southeast and east from the ICW passage through Mississippi Sound and goes under the fixed Dauphin Island Bridge. This fixed span has a vertical clearance (on this portion of the bridge) of only 25 feet. Most sailcraft will be therefore barred from utilizing this useful route. Powerboats can turn south from the bridge and follow a marked channel for a short distance to the marina. This channel has excellent minimum depths of 7 feet, with soundings going all the way to 15 feet.

Several additional Dauphin Island channels will be discussed in the next chapter covering Mississippi Sound. While none of these cuts lead to additional facilities, there are some anchorage possibilities.

Dauphin Island Marina (30 15.838 North/088 06.819 West) has the distinction of being noted by the word *marina* on chart 11378, though the real position is a bit north-northwest of this designation. This facility is found on the eastern side of the southern terminus of the long Dauphin Island Bridge and Causeway.

A new owner has made a tremendous difference in this facility during the last several years. Where in times past we were reluctant to recommend this marina, now cruising captains may choose to berth here with the expectation of enjoying their stay.

The new incarnation of Dauphin Island Marina gladly accepts transients at its refurbished, fixed, wooden piers featuring full power and water connections. Minimum soundings at the docks run 5½ to 6 feet at low water. The dockage basin is a bit open to strong eastern and northeasterly winds, but it is well sheltered from fresh western, southwestern, and (to a lesser extent) northwestern breezes.

Gasoline, diesel fuel, waste pump-out, and dry-stack storage for smaller powercraft are all readily available. There is also a brand-new ship's/variety store on the premises that we found unusually attractive and well merchandised. A convenience store and a hardware store are located within walking distance.

There is also an on-site shower, which we found to be one black mark for this marina. The single unit was unacceptably dirty during our last visit.

Dauphin Island Marina can boast a good, on-site dining attraction. Boats Restaurant and Lounge (251-861-8300) may not be too much to look at from the outside, but the interior holds far more promise. We found the seafood surprisingly good, and the owners seem intent on offering the best of service and fare to their customers. We suggest that you give Boat's (open year round) your most serious gastronomical attention!

Dauphin Island Marina (251) 861-2201
http://www.dauphinislandmarina.com

Approach depth—5-10 feet (Billy Goat Hole)
7-10 feet (Mississippi Sound channel)
Dockside depth—5½-6 feet
Accepts transients—yes
Transient-dockage rate—average
Fixed wooden piers—yes
Dockside power connections—30- and 50-amp
Dockside water connections—yes
Showers-yes
Waste pump-out-yes
Gasoline—yes
Diesel fuel—yes
Ship's/variety store—yes
Restaurant—on-site

At least three anchorages of note are available to cruisers traversing the southern reaches of Dauphin Island Bay. These havens are reached through Billy Goat Hole channel or via the Mississippi Sound cut that travels south past Dauphin Island Marina.

Moving east to west, the first of these havens is charted Confederate Pass (near 30 15.429 North/088 05.551 West). This anchorage is well protected from all winds and features plenty of swinging room for most vessels. Minimum depths are 6 feet, with 7 to 8 feet of water being the norm. For once, the soundings noted on chart 11378 appear to be totally accurate. There is an unmarked shoal at the entrance to Confederate Pass which must be avoided, but captains should be able to bypass this hazard with elementary caution. The cove's shoreline is lined by heavy residential development. Although it has good depths and excellent protection, Confederate Pass cannot be considered an isolated hideaway.

The small charted but unnamed cove just west of Confederate Pass (30 15.331 North/088 05.781 West) can serve as a haven for boats up to 34 feet and drawing less than 4 feet. Minimum entrance depths are 5 feet, though again you must avoid an unmarked shoal. On its interior reaches, the cove sports 6-foot soundings. Strong northerly winds could raise a rough chop, but there is good protection from all other breezes. As with its larger sister to the east, this cove is surrounded by a thick maze of resort homes.

Indian Bay cuts into the southwestern corner of Dauphin Island Bay just south of the marina. Minimum depths are 6 feet and there is enough elbowroom for a 45-footer on the wide, northerly portion of the cove (near 30 15.635 North/088 06.680 West). The more sheltered southerly section (near 30 15.513 North/088 06.647 West) lends enough room for a 38-footer. While this body of water is also surrounded by residential development, it's not quite as heavy as that on the two anchorages to the east.

Dauphin Island History   Dauphin Island began its recorded history on a ghoulish note. The French explorers Iberville and Bienville, exploring the island in 1699, found so many skulls and skeletons that they named the land "Massacre Island." No modern historian has ever been able to find an explanation for this grisly phenomenon.

Later the island was renamed "Dauphine" after the French crown prince. Gradually the "e" was dropped from the name until the land became known as Dauphin Island.

During the heyday of French Louisiana, Bienville built Port Dauphin along the western shores of the island. In those days a deep channel ran along Dauphin's western tip to the Gulf of Mexico, and the port served as a trading center with the Spanish and Indians. However, a strong hurricane in 1717 filled the channel with sand, and though the French maintained a small garrison on Dauphin Island until 1742, it was finished as a trading port.

In 1821 President James Monroe recommended construction of a fort to guard Dauphin's eastern tip. This fortification was finally completed in the 1840s. The Confederates seized the fort, Fort Gaines, at the beginning of the Civil War, but it fell to Admiral Farragut's forces in 1864. A National Historic Monument today, the fort houses a museum of Confederate memorabilia and the anchor and chain recovered from Admiral Farragut's flagship, the only vessel to be sunk by Mobile Bay's "torpedoes" during the Civil War.

330 CRUISING GUIDE TO THE NORTHERN GULF COAST

In 1986 Hurricane Frederick roared into Dauphin Island, destroying many homes and damaging a host of other residences. The bridge leading to the mainland was swept away entirely. By 1990, the span had been completely rebuilt and there was little physical evidence left on the island from the great tempest. Frederick should serve as a reminder to all of us of the awesome destructive power of a killer hurricane. Man, and most certainly his boats, are no match for nature's wrath.

MOBILE BAY—ICW NAVIGATION

The Gulf Coast ICW crosses the wide southern foot of Mobile Bay before ducking under the Dauphin Island Bridge and entering Mississippi Sound. The wind has even more fetch in this portion of the bay, which allows steeper, teeth-rattling chop to develop when winds exceed 15 knots. Clearly, this is not a portion of the Waterway to be taken lightly. All cruising skippers, regardless of the size of their craft, must take the latest weather forecast into account when traversing this portion of the Gulf Coast ICW.

Most of the Waterway channel across Mobile Bay is well marked. There is one glaring exception. North of Navy Cove, the various daybeacons cease and navigators must follow careful compass/GPS courses to intersect the large ship's channel. You must then negotiate yet another markerless run to reach a set of beacons that outline the Pass Aux Herons channel leading to the Dauphin Island Bridge. Fortunately, all these various passages are quite broad and do not stray near shoal water. Nevertheless, mariners running Mobile Bay for the first time should plan their journey well ahead of time and plot all necessary courses at the comfort and safety of their home charting table.

Several shortcuts are possible on this portion of the ICW, both for cruisers headed east or west on the Waterway, or north into the heart of Mobile Bay. These various time-saving maneuvers are outlined below.

Entry into Bon Secour Bay   The ICW wanders into the easterly portion of Bon Secour Bay just west of flashing daybeacon #103. Be ready for an increase in wind and ch-ch-ch-chop.

The initial portion of the Waterway channel running west borders on shallow water to the north and south. Be sure to stay strictly in the marked cut until reaching flashing daybeacon #115, where deeper water opens out on both sides of the cut.

On the ICW   West of the Bon Secour River junction, the Waterway continues west in an almost arrow-straight line. Though charts 11367 and 11378 show a spoil bank south of the channel, on-site research revealed that 7 feet can currently be carried over this underwater mass.

Note the "Subm Pile" notation on chart 11378 south of flashing daybeacon #135. Reports from local cruisers indicate that this warning is to be taken seriously. Be sure to stay north of #135.

North on Mobile Bay Captains heading north on Mobile Bay can save a huge chunk of distance by leaving the ICW at flashing daybeacon #135 and setting course for Middle Bay Light (denoted as "Mobile Bay" on chart 11376). Be advised that you must cover a run of some 11.5 nautical miles between #135 and Middle Bay Light. While this passage does not stray near shallow water, some navigators will not be comfortable with such a long run lacking any navigational reference. Others will be glad of the shortcut and time saved.

If you decide to try this route, set a careful compass/GPS course from #135 for Middle Bay Light. Don't worry about the spoil bank east of the light. On-site research revealed minimum 10-foot depths over the spoils.

ICW to Mobile Ship Channel The marked ICW passage continues almost due west from flashing daybeacon #135 to flashing daybeacon #147. At #147, the Waterway takes a cut to the southwest. Shallow water flanks this run to the south. Pay attention to the markers and watch for south-setting leeway.

While the Waterway continues on to flashing daybeacon #157, many cruisers short-cut this corner by leaving the channel at flashing daybeacon #155 and setting course for the charted cut across the spoil banks at flashing buoys #25 and #26. Some 3.9 nautical miles separate #155 and #26, while a run of 3 nautical miles will be covered between #157 and #26.

In either case, point straight for the two flashing buoys. You can pass either to the north or south of #25 and #26 with good depths. This is not a narrow passage. The charted spoil banks to the north and south carry almost as much water as the charted passthrough.

As you approach the intersection of the ICW and Mobile ship channel, a large drilling rig will be visible. Surprisingly enough, this massive structure actually extracts natural gas instead of liquid petroleum products.

Once abeam of #25 and #26, you can cut north into the large ship's channel to visit ports of call on the east or west banks of Mobile Bay, turn south into Mobile Bay Inlet, or continue on the ICW channel running west.

Mobile Bay Inlet This writer cannot add much to the staggering array of charted aids on Mobile Bay Inlet. Suffice it to say that this is inlet-running at its best. Of course, it's never *too* good, so just keep that in mind.

Just north of flashing buoys #17 and #18, look toward Mobile Point to the east for a good view of Fort Morgan. Similarly, you can gain a distant view of Fort Gaines on the eastern tip of Dauphin Island to the west.

As you approach flashing buoy #11, Sand Island Lighthouse will be readily spied to the west. Be sure to take the opportunity to get a closer look at this miracle of the Gulf Coast if your schedule permits.

Dauphin Island and Billy Goat Hole Channel If you have been using chart 11376 for navigation across Mobile Bay, switch back to 11378 west of the Mobile ship channel intersection. This chart's larger scale gives much better resolution for these waters.

For those who decide to make the approach to Dauphin Island Bay via Billy Goat Hole channel, it's probably best to proceed south on the large ship's channel as if you were running the inlet, until reaching a point about halfway between flashing buoys #23 and #21. You can then cut sharply to the west. Be sure to pass south of the charted, sunken wreck, marked by an unnumbered, 30-foot flashing light. Point to come between flashing daybeacon #1 and unlighted daybeacon #2, the easternmost aids on Billy Goat Hole.

Simply follow the markers west into the entrance north of Fort Gaines. As you come abeam of flashing daybeacon #14, look to the south and you will have a good view of the old fort. You will also spot a launching area flanking the southerly shoreline. Be sure to proceed at idle speed as you pass.

West of unlighted daybeacon #16, Billy Goat Hole channel passes into a small bay. Flashing daybeacon #17 is actually located on the end of the Coast Guard dock. With the pilot boat, Coast Guard, and commercial traffic, anchoring is not a practical possibility.

To continue on to Dauphin Island Bay and the marina and various anchorages to the west, follow the charted channel as it strikes to the northwest. Cruisers coming into this cut will see an uncharted marsh island bisecting the stream. Be sure to pass this small mass to its northeasterly side. The southwestern side is quite shoal.

Eventually the canal intersects the southeastern corner of Dauphin Island Bay. Charts 11376 and 11378 show a channel to

the northeast labeled "Pass Drury." Actually this cut has been entirely closed for many years. Wake up NOAA!

From the head of the canal leading to Dauphin Island Bay, the channel cuts sharply to the west and follows the bay's southerly shoreline closely. The cut is outlined by numerous, obscurely charted markers. Usually, if depths start to rise, hug the shoreline closely. In most cases the deeper water abuts the banks.

Confederate Pass   As correctly noted on chart 11378, a 3-foot shoal is found on the mid-width of the entrance to Confederate Pass. To avoid this shallow patch, favor the port side (eastern side) of the entrance heavily. Once on the cove's interior reaches, good depths open out almost from shore to shore. In heavy weather you can pick whichever arm is the most sheltered and settle in for a snug evening. A small shelf of shallow water does flank the shoreline, so for added safety, drop the hook on the mid-width.

On the Dauphin Island Bay Channel
West of Confederate Pass, navigators will encounter the shallowest section of the channel leading to Indian Bay and Dauphin Island Marina. Even by staying strictly to the marked cut, you can expect some 4½- to 5-foot soundings.

Unnamed Cove Anchorage   To enter the small anchorage on the unnamed cove west of Confederate Pass, favor the starboard (western) side of the stream's mouth. Several tree stakes were present when we visited, outlining shallow water on the port banks. Drop the hook on the mid-width of the cove.

On to Indian Bay and Dauphin Island Marina   As you cruise the channel leading first west and then north to Indian Bay, be sure to hug the shoreline. Depths worsen very quickly as you move out into the bay's waters. Indian Bay itself is easily entered on its mid-width. Good depths stretch almost from shore to shore on the stream's interior reaches. Select any likely spot and settle down for a comfortable evening.

North of Indian Bay, the marked channel quickly leads to Dauphin Island Marina. Several semisunken barges flank the channel to the east, giving some protection against easterly breezes.

On to Mississippi Sound   North of Dauphin Island Marina, the marked channel continues north for .25 nautical miles and then cuts sharply west and passes under the Dauphin Island Bridge. Keep all red markers to your port side and all green beacons to starboard. Take your time, watch the sounder, and you should come through fine.

This particular section of the Dauphin Island span carries 25 feet of vertical clearance. Most sailcraft who have made it this far will be forced to retrace their steps and pick the ICW back up on Mobile Bay.

West of the bridge, several charted and some uncharted markers lead you to flashing daybeacon #5 on the charted cut leading northwest to the ICW and Mississippi Sound channel. Additional information about this cut is presented in the next chapter.

ICW to Mississippi   Back on Mobile Bay, where our discussion of Dauphin Island and Billy Goat Hole Channel began, skippers cruising west on the ICW should set course from flashing buoys #25 and #26 for flashing daybeacon #2 to the west-northwest. It is a run of 2.45 nautical miles between #25 and #2.

The ICW channel is easily followed between flashing daybeacon #2 and unlighted nun buoy #8. At #8 the Waterway meets up with the charted Pass Aux Herons channel and follows a sharp jog to the southwest. The ICW quickly hurries on toward the high-rise section of the Dauphin Island fixed bridge. Be on guard to keep to the marked channel. Shoal water flanks the Waterway to the north and south both east and west of the bridge. This area is subject to shoaling. Don't be surprised to find different or additional markers present by the time you cruise through these waters.

This portion of the Dauphin Island Bridge carries an amazing 83 feet of vertical clearance, enough for just about any vessel short of an aircraft carrier. West of the span the Waterway passes under a power line with 93 feet of vertical clearance and enters Mississippi Sound on its way to Pascagoula, Biloxi, and Gulfport.

CHAPTER 6

Mississippi Sound to Lake Borgne

Most veteran cruisers traveling the Atlantic Coast ICW soon discover a pattern to the Waterway. Though there are exceptions, an open stretch on the ICW is usually followed by a sheltered canal or small river. This allows cruising skippers and their crew a welcome respite from strong winds and the resulting chop. For example, in North Carolina the dreaded Albemarle Sound is followed by the long Alligator/Pungo River Canal. In Eastern Florida, the 100-mile Indian River leads to the sheltered waters stretching from Palm Beach to Fort Lauderdale and Biscayne Bay.

Using this logic, first-time cruising visitors to the Northern Gulf might expect the ICW to enter protected waters after crossing the often bumpy southern foot of Mobile Bay. In reality, nothing could be farther from the truth.

Instead of a protected canal, the Gulf Coast ICW flows under the Dauphin Island Causeway Bridge via the Pass Aux Herons channel into the easterly reaches of Mississippi Sound. This daunting body of water is the longest, most open stretch of any so-called intracoastal waterway that this writer has ever encountered. The Waterway's run through Mississippi Sound stretches east to west for almost 80 nautical miles. The sound's width of 9 to 10 nautical miles contributes plenty of wind fetch to help keep the waters choppy. Runs between aids to navigation are often several miles or better, and shallow water is present in abundance. Winds over 15 knots from any quarter can raise seas guaranteed to make things more interesting than you may like to have them. Stronger blows are most assuredly dangerous

for any size and style of pleasure craft. While in fair weather this stretch of the ICW can be enjoyable, it is not a passage to be undertaken lightly or without proper planning.

On the other hand, sailors may find a run through the ICW portion of Mississippi Sound to be a most enjoyable sail when winds of 10 to 15 knots are blowing (as they frequently do) from the north or south. With these sorts of breezes in the offing, it's possible to beam reach down a goodly portion of the channel without the least need to consult with the iron jenny.

The ICW finally leaves Mississippi Sound and enters Lake Borgne near Heron Bay. This open but much less lengthy body of water leads, in turn, to the Rigolets and several approaches to New Orleans and Lake Pontchartrain. This portion of the Waterway will be dealt with in the next chapter.

Mississippi Sound is bounded by the mainland shoreline of Mississippi to the north and a series of small, uninhabited barrier islands to the south. Although these small bodies of land do shelter the sound from some of the worst swells moving north from the Gulf, they do not provide nearly enough shelter to keep the waters calm. None of the islands provide secure overnight anchorage in stormy conditions and there is a complete lack of marina facilities. Most are surrounded by extensive shoals.

Conversely, during times of fair weather, it is quite possible for cautious mariners to drop the hook along certain portions of the barrier island's northern banks. You can then dinghy ashore to explore the unspoiled beaches and, in some cases, surprisingly well-wooded shorelines. As my good friend Tim Murray, former publisher of the now-defunct *Mid-Gulf Sailing* magazine, put it to this writer some years ago, "Watching the sun rise over the beaches of Horn Island can make you a believer in Mississippi Sound." I would only add that if there is even a hint of unhappy weather in the offing, this sort of idyllic experience could have a very different ending.

In between the barrier islands are a series of inlets known in these waters as "passes." While there are any number to choose from, only three provide reliable access to the Gulf of Mexico. The well-marked cuts at Pascagoula, Biloxi, and Gulfport can be used with relative confidence. The other inlets are suspect at best.

Mississippi Sound does boast a collection of ports along its northerly shores. Pascagoula, Biloxi, Gulfport, Long Beach, Pass Christian, and Bay St. Louis offer good harbors and facilities for pleasure craft. While you often must travel several miles from the Waterway to reach these various ports of call, the visiting cruiser can be reasonably assured of finding dockage and some repair facilities.

Some of the smaller harbors along northern Mississippi Sound are man-made. These havens usually consist of large, concrete breakwaters enclosing a roomy dockage basin. Gulfport, Long Beach, and Pass Christian fall into this category.

With but four exceptions, Mississippi Sound lacks any navigable sidewaters, and with the open nature and shallow surrounding waters of the southern barrier islands, there is a decided lack of well-protected anchorages. Thankfully, there are exceptions. Pascagoula River, Biloxi Back Bay, and Bay St. Louis do indeed provide good anchorage for captains willing to take a trek of several miles from the ICW.

Shoreside scenery along Mississippi Sound runs the full gamut from natural, sandy barrier islands to heavy urban-casino development in Biloxi and Gulfport. In between are lightly developed sections of the mainland, which make for a pretty view. Of course, most cruisers will see very little of this shoreline, as the ICW channel is located several miles from shore in the heart of the sound.

Within the last decade, the state of Mississippi has legalized shoreside gambling. Mariners who have not visited (for instance) Biloxi or Gulfport for some time will be astounded to discover that the once quiet waterfronts are now overlooked by a bewildering maze of huge casinos, hotels, and other support complexes. As I stated in the introduction to this guide, if you are the sort who enjoys gambling and glitzy night life, then you'll like the changes—otherwise you are likely to hate them. The crowds, snarled automobile traffic, and honking horns are enough to turn anyone off to this region!

If you can stomach the auto congestion, there is still value in perusing Highway 90, which spans the northern Mississippi Sound coastline. This major artery leads pass an ethereal collection of old Southern mansions that seem almost dreamlike in their beauty and grandeur. If you can ignore the casinos, this can be one of the most pleasurable drives on the Northern Gulf Coast. Indeed, the Mississippi coastline has a rich history that stretches far back into French Louisiana. In the course of this chapter, we will explore a portion of this storied past. Wherever possible, cruisers will be directed to ports of call that allow a visit to the many landside historical attractions, not least of which are the old homeplaces. Let us begin our cruise.

Charts   Many navigators cruising the waters of Mississippi Sound will need only the first three NOAA charts listed below. Cruisers planning to make use of the various inlets might want to consider the larger-coverage charts.

11378—details the ICW's entrance into Mississippi Sound from Mobile Bay—also covers the Dauphin Island channels

11374—ICW chart that follows the Waterway from Mississippi Sound's eastern entrance to Dog Keys Pass

11372—follows the Waterway through Mississippi Sound to Bay St. Louis—gives good details on all sidewaters along the northern coastline, including Pascagoula River, Back Bay of Biloxi, and Bay St. Louis

11367—covers the ICW's passage into Lake Borgne

11375—detailed chart of Horn Island Pass and the Pascagoula channel

11373—larger coverage chart of Mississippi Sound—useful for running the sound's inlet passes

11371—another large-coverage chart that outlines the westerly reaches of Mississippi Sound and its intersection with Lake Borgne

Bridges

Dauphin Island Causeway—crosses the ICW-Pass Aux Herons channel at standard mile 128—Fixed—83 feet

Pascagoula River Railway Bridge—crosses Pascagoula River north of flashing buoy #4—2 feet (closed)—usually open unless a train is due

Pascagoula River-Highway 90 Bridge—crosses Pascagoula River north of the railway span detailed above—Bascule—31 feet (closed)—does not open at all between 6:15 A.M. and 7:15 A.M., 7:25 A.M. and 8:00 A.M., and 3:30 P.M. and 4:45 P.M.; at all other times the span will open on demand—new bridge now under construction immediately adjacent to existing span

Escatawpa River-State Road 613 Bridge—crosses the Escatawpa River east of unlighted daybeacon #2–Fixed—77 feet

Escatawpa River-State Road 63 Bridge—crosses the Escatawpa River east of flashing daybeacon #9—Fixed—73 feet

Escatawpa River Railway Bridge—crosses the Escatawpa River east of flashing daybeacon #9—5 feet (closed)—usually open unless a train is due

Biloxi-Ocean Springs Highway 90 Bridge—crosses the entrance to Back Bay of Biloxi northwest of unlighted daybeacon #31—Bascule—40 feet (closed)—opens on demand

Biloxi Railway Bridge—crosses the entrance to Back Bay of Biloxi northwest of Highway 90 Bridge detailed immediately above—14 feet (closed)—usually open unless a train is due

Old Fort Bayou Bridge—crosses Old Fort Bayou east of unlighted daybeacon #30—Bascule—20 feet (closed)—does not usually open

Back Bay-Highway 110 (D'Iberville) Bridge—crosses the Back Bay of Biloxi west of unlighted daybeacon #10—Bascule—60 feet (closed)—opens on demand

Back Bay-Pops Ferry Road Bridge—crosses the Back Bay of Biloxi southwest of unlighted daybeacon #24—Bascule—25 feet (closed)—opens on demand

Bernard Bayou Bridge—crosses Bernard Bayou west of Kremer Marine—Bascule—12 feet (closed)—does not open at all between 6 A.M. and 8 A.M. and 4 P.M. and 6 P.M.; at all other times the span will open on demand

Bayou Portage Bridge—crosses Bayou Portage

east of unlighted daybeacon #9—Bascule—11 feet (closed)—opens on demand **Bay St. Louis Railway Bridge**—crosses the entrance to Bay St. Louis well north of flashing daybeacon #2—13 feet (closed)—usually open unless a train is due

Bay St. Louis-Highway 90 Bridge—crosses the entrance to Bay St. Louis a short distance north of the railway span detailed immediately above—Bascule—17 feet (closed)—opens on demand

Pass Aux Herons Bridge to Dog Keys Pass

A run of 28 nautical miles spans the gap between the ICW's easterly entrance into Mississippi Sound at the Pass Aux Herons (Dauphin Island Causeway) Bridge (standard mile 128.5) and the inlet between Horn and Ship islands known as Dog Keys Pass. This is one of the loneliest sections of the entire passage to Lake Borgne. While the seafaring city of Pascagoula is located on the mainland shore near the midpoint of this run, there is only one marina available to cruising craft here or anywhere else on the sound short of Biloxi and Ocean Springs. A few acceptable anchorages are to be found on Dauphin Island near the sound's easternmost corner, and several excellent havens are available on the Pascagoula River. During times of fair breezes *(only)*, a stopover at the popular anchorage northeast of Sand Island (hard by Horn Island Pass) or the "horseshoe" anchorage just north of Horn Island are enticing possibilities. However, with the exceptions outlined above, cruisers are on their own to Ship Island, Dog Keys Pass, and Biloxi. Check your fuel gauge and your craft's operating condition before leaving the Mobile Bay and Dauphin Island facilities.

Pass Aux Herons Channel History   The year 1827 saw the first regularly scheduled steamboat service from New Orleans to Mobile.

Two seemingly insoluble problems became immediately apparent. The shoals and sandbars stretching from Dauphin Island to the Alabama mainland barred passage by all but shallow-draft vessels. Steam-powered craft were forced to leave the shelter of Mississippi Sound at Ship Island Pass and cruise through open waters to Mobile Bay's inlet.

Mobile Bay itself was found to be too shallow for the stern-wheelers. Passengers and goods had to be unloaded at Dauphin Island and ferried 30 miles inland to Mobile.

A visionary named Capt. John Grant was destined to solve these difficulties. As a young man, Grant invented what came to be called the "Baltimore Harbor Dredge." Shortly thereafter the inventor was commissioned by the federal government to dredge Mobile Bay. Beginning in 1827, Grant worked for two years to dig a broad channel from Mobile Bay's southerly entrance to within five miles of Mobile. In 1839 Captain Grant successfully dredged a channel north of Dauphin Island between Mississippi Sound and Mobile Bay. Now powered ships could travel from Lake Pontchartrain and New Orleans to Mobile without having to brave the often choppy waters of the Gulf of Mexico. For his efforts, Grant was honored with the unofficial title,

"Father of Gulf Coast Transportation." Following the successful completion of his prodigious projects, the waterway pioneer settled happily in Pascagoula and lived there amid the esteem of his fellow citizens until the end of his days.

Bayou Aloe (Standard Mile 126)

A fairly well-marked channel with 6- to 7-foot minimum depths breaks off to the southeast between unlighted nun buoys #20 and #22 (on the ICW) and leads to wide Bayou Aloe. At flashing daybeacon #5 (on the Bayou Aloe channel), captains may choose to break off to the east and follow a channel under the Dauphin Island Bridge to Dauphin Island Marina. This passage was detailed in the last chapter.

Bayou Aloe itself is surrounded by heavy residential and commercial fishing-type development. While there are some docks along the cove's shoreline, all the piers are commercial in nature and there are no berths for cruising craft.

At the end of the huge Dauphin Island sailboat race held every April, the participants usually anchor in Bayou Aloe. As you will recall, the 25-foot clearance of the bridge spanning the channel that runs east to Dauphin Island Marina precludes sailcraft from making use of this route.

In light breezes, passing cruisers might consider throwing out the hook in Bayou Aloe for an evening. If winds are blowing from the north or northwest, it could be a very uncomfortable night. By all accounts the stream's protection is not sufficient for heavy weather.

Lafitte Bay and Heron Bayou (Standard Mile 126) (30 15.313 North/088 08.370 West)

Captains who pilot craft no more than 45 feet in length and drawing less than 4 feet might consider dropping the hook on protected Lafitte Bay, near 30 15.313 North/088 08.370 West. This haven is reached by departing the Bayou Aloe channel at flashing daybeacon #2. You can then follow an indifferently marked cut almost due south as if you were going to enter Heron Bayou. Eventually the entrance to Lafitte Bay will come abeam hard by the westerly side of the channel.

Protection is quite good from all winds on Lafitte Bay. There should also be enough elbowroom for most pleasure craft. However, the entrance channel outlined above is marked

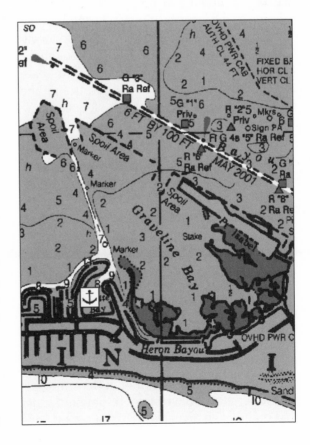

only by a few stakes that are privately maintained and not particularly reliable. With this restriction in mind, boats larger than 40 feet might run into problems. Minimum depths in the entrance channel and Lafitte Bay are 6 feet, while most soundings reveal much deeper water.

Heron Bayou, to the south, has shallow depths of 4 feet or less. Only small, shallow-draft outboard or I/O vessels should attempt to cruise this small stream.

Bayou La Batre (Standard Mile 115)

Deep Bayou La Batre slices into the mainland shores of Mississippi Sound well north-northwest of the ICW's flashing daybeacon #49. This stream is home to the largest shrimping fleet this writer has ever witnessed, and several years ago, it was featured in the movie *Forrest Gump* (though the actual on-the-water scenes were shot in Beaufort, South Carolina). As my good friend and research assistant, Andy, put it so eloquently:

> During the weekdays on Bayou La Batre, the main activity is *shrimping*. Of course, on Saturdays the local inhabitants can generally be found *shrimping*. Sunday, however, brings on the task of *shrimping*. During the evening hours, Bayou La Batre sees quite a bit of *shrimping*. . . .

Tongue in cheek it may be, but any cruiser who has the opportunity to gunk hole on this fascinating stream will be amazed by the huge collection of shrimping craft. They cover the whole range of sizes, shapes, and conditions. Some boats are bright and freshly painted, seemingly straining at their lines to be away. Others have stained, patched hulls that speak of an owner who has fallen on hard

times. In fact, Bayou La Batre claims to be the "largest producer of fishing and work boats in the world."

On the last weekend in July the usually stolid banks of Bayou La Batre come alive with the "Blessing of the Fleet" festival. The whole fleet is blessed for the season by a visiting bishop, and a seafood festival and all sorts of other fun activities follow. There is a parade down the bayou of all the creek's fishing craft decked out in gaily colored bunting and streamers. Visitors by the hundreds line the shores to cheer on the boats and their crews. As Virginia Van Der Veer Hamilton comments in *Seeing Historic Alabama*, "The fleet blessing takes on the aura of a summer Mardi Gras." If you happen to be in the region when this notable event is scheduled, it is well worth your time.

While it is a super gunk hole, dockage for pleasure craft is completely lacking on Bayou La Batre. Similarly, there is not enough room to anchor. The particularly diplomatic captain might try to negotiate some diesel fuel, or even an overnight berth at one of the many commercial docks, but don't count on it. Most cruisers will enter Bayou La Batre strictly for the sight-seeing and depart thereafter.

Bayou Coden (Standard Mile 115)

A marked channel cuts off to the east at flashing daybeacon #BC on the Bayou La Batre channel and leads to Bayou Coden. Formerly this creek was a smaller version of Bayou La Batre, with more than a few commercial fishing craft in evidence. On-site research reveals that a bar with less than 4 feet of low-tide depth has now built completely across the entrance (between flashing daybeacon #10 and unlighted daybeacon #11). While any number of commercial craft still dock on Bayou Coden, these vessels obviously enter and leave at high water. They may also know of a particular portion of the entrance which is deeper and not apparent to strangers. Unless future dredging removes the entrance bar, cruising-size craft would be well advised to bypass Bayou Coden entirely.

Petit Bois Pass (Standard Mile 114)

South-southeast of flashing daybeacon #5, broad Petit Bois Pass (or inlet) spans the 4-nautical-mile gap between the western tip of Dauphin Island and the easterly reaches of Petit Bois Island. Much of the pass is plagued with shoals that often exhibit less than 3 feet of low-tide depth. While a few locals occasionally venture onto the Gulf's waters through Petit Bois, visiting cruisers are urged to continue on to well-marked Horn Island Pass, just a few additional miles to the west.

Petit Bois Island (Standard Mile 107) (Various Lats/Lons—see below)

Petit Bois Island is the easternmost in the strip of lonely, uninhabited barrier islands which buffer Mississippi Sound from the Gulf of Mexico. Petit Bois was actually the westerly portion of Dauphin Island until a violent hurricane in 1717 cut an inlet completely through the land. The remaining sand spit to the west was renamed Petit Bois and, as far as this writer has been able to learn, the island has never been permanently inhabited.

Today Petit Bois Island is a national wildlife refuge and part of the Gulf Islands National Seashore. The land is protected from commercial development. While it is certainly possible

to anchor in the lee of the island's northerly banks, this procedure is not without risk. True, the body of Petit Bois does shelter the northern havens from the prevailing summertime southerly winds. On the other hand, if one of the Gulf's infamous thunderstorms comes up suddenly during a spring, summer, or fall afternoon, you could be caught many miles away from real shelter.

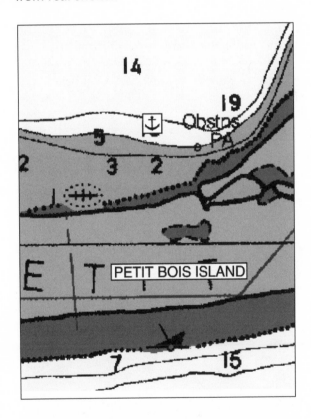

If good weather seems to be in the offing and you have assessed and accepted the risks, there are two spots that might merit attention as anchorages (however temporary). The easternmost is found on the charted 10-foot waters north and a bit west of the "Obstns PA" notation on chart 11374 (near 30 12.267 North/088 26.716 West). A large shelf of 1- and 2-foot waters extends .2 nautical miles offshore, necessitating a long dinghy ride to the island. Protection from all but southerly winds is practically nonexistent.

Somewhat better protected and undoubtedly more convenient is the cove south of flashing daybeacon #2, east of the Pascagoula/Horn Island Pass channel (near 30 12.626 North/088 29.414 West). Here the careful skipper can cruise to within .1 of a nautical mile of the northerly banks and hold minimum 7-foot depths. Again, this anchorage is not sheltered enough for anything like heavy weather.

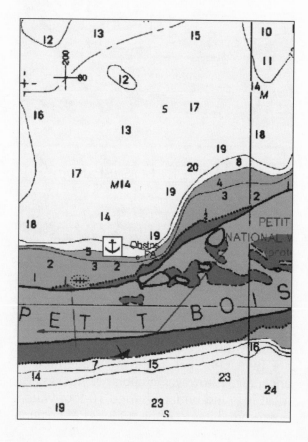

Cruisers who are able to drop the hook and dinghy ashore to Petit Bois will find a fascinating, undeveloped landscape with often lonely beaches and some surprising maritime forests. Walk across to the Gulf side of the island and you should come upon numerous sand dunes piled up by the prevailing southerly breezes. Just remember to keep an eye on the sky conditions. If a thundercloud is sighted, it's time for a quick trip back to the boat and a hurried cruise to better shelter.

Sand Island Anchorage (Standard Mile 104)

Unnamed on chart 11374, Sand Island lies almost due west of flashing buoy #19 (one of the markers on the Pascagoula/Horn Island Pass channel). Though you would never guess it from a study of chart 11374, this small body of land hosts what is possibly one of the most popular anchorage on the Mississippi Sound barrier islands. *(Note that we will not be giving lat/lon positions for the anchorage described below. This is due to the fact that the best place to drop the hook tends to wander a bit from month to month.)*

Sand Island itself is a completely undeveloped, artificial body of land that has been formed by continual dredging of adjacent Horn Island Pass. Over the years, more and more sand has been pumped out of the pass and dumped into the waters just to the west. All this activity has now produced a good-sized island, which, if they didn't know better, most visiting cruisers would mistake for a natural body of land.

As recently as several years ago, an uncharted hook on the island's northeasterly tip formed a small but well-sheltered harbor that was often crowded with local powercraft on weekends. Unfortunately, this harbor has now been completely filled in by shoaling. Obviously, this one-time haven is no longer of any use to pleasure craft.

It is still quite possible to anchor during fair weather only in 6- to 8-foot depths off the northerly shores of Sand Island, a short hop northwest of the island's northerly tip. During our several visits to these waters, we have always observed a large collection of cruising craft anchored along this stretch during weekends.

While minimum 6-foot depths can be held from the well-marked Horn Island Pass channel to the anchorage off Sand Island's northerly shore, navigation can be a bit tricky for first-timers. Be sure to read the navigational account of Sand Island in the next section of this chapter before making the attempt for the first time.

Horn Island Pass (Standard Mile 104)

The ICW intersects the Pascagoula/Horn Island Pass channel some .6 nautical miles west of flashing daybeacon #1. This extremely deep, exceptionally well marked channel leads north to Pascagoula and Bayou Casotte and south to Horn Island Pass. This cut is, without a doubt, one of the three most reliable inlets on Mississippi Sound. If you are planning to put to sea short of Biloxi, Horn Island Pass should most certainly be your choice.

Round Island

The small land mass known as Round Island is found some 3.1 nautical miles west of flashing daybeacon #39 on the main Pascagoula channel. A large body of shoals completely surrounds the island, cutting it off from all but very shallow-draft vessels. While it is isolated, undeveloped, and even sports an old, abandoned light, most cruisers will probably

decide that the hazards and the long dinghy trip necessary to get ashore are not worth the trouble. With this contention in mind, navigational coverage will not be provided in this guide for Round Island.

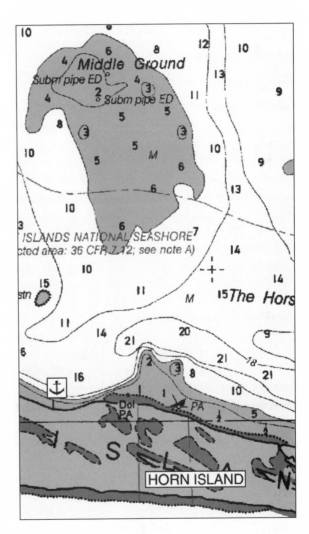

Round Island History In 1849 Round Island became home for an unlikely "army" of mercenaries termed "Filibusters." These soldiers of fortune had been drawn to Mississippi Sound by promises of land and fortunes for any who would enlist in the cause of Cuban independence.

Even though the war for Cuban independence enjoyed wide support throughout Florida and the Northern Gulf Coast, President Zachary Taylor issued a proclamation of strict neutrality for the United States. A federal naval squadron under Commander Victor Randolph blockaded Round Island and threatened to shell the would-be soldiers. These actions incensed the people and state governments of Mississippi and Louisiana. The local press screamed that states' rights were being trampled upon by the government in Washington.

Both sides eventually backed down. Randolph, faced with legal action by the state of Mississippi, lifted his blockade, while the Filibusters, knowing that they would surely be sunk if they tried to reach Cuba, disbanded. This seemingly isolated event attracted nationwide attention and served to signal the widening chasm between Northern and Southern interests.

Bayou Casotte (Standard Mile 104)

A wide, deep, and well-outlined channel breaks off from the main Pascagoula entrance channel at flashing buoy #36 and leads almost due north to Bayou Casotte. This small stream is home to a huge industrial complex, including a most malodorous paper mill. Considering the stench and the heavy commercial traffic on the Bayou Casotte channel, most mariners would be well advised to either continue west on the ICW or visit Pascagoula to the northwest.

Pascagoula (Standard Mile 104)

The coastal city of Pascagoula has its roots in the far-distant past of French Louisiana. Today, it is one of the two most successful commercial ports on the Mississippi coast. Huge oceangoing commercial and naval ships are usually crowded along the harbor's wharves. During an earlier on-site research visit, we were fascinated by a small, helicopter aircraft carrier docked near the southern mouth of the Pascagoula River. Farther upstream, we observed a huge grain elevator and barge-loading facility rubbing shoulders with numerous offshore oil rigs in for servicing and repair. There is also a U.S. Coast Guard base on the western banks near the river's southern mouth.

Obviously, Pascagoula must have a first-rate harbor to support this sort of commercial waterborne traffic. In fact, the city boasts one of the most extensive tracts of inland waters on the Northern Gulf Coast. An exceptionally deep, unbelievably well marked channel leads north from Horn Island Pass, across the ICW, and into the southern mouth of Pascagoula River. Just in case you have any worries of running aground, be advised that full-size battleships can visit Pascagoula without difficulty. Anybody have more draft than that?

Farther to the north, the Pascagoula River becomes the Escatawpa River. Several deep sidewaters provide some overnight anchorage possibilities for vessels willing to undertake a long cruise from the ICW. There is another anchorage on charted Lake Yazoo, near the channel's southerly entrance into Pascagoula River, that skippers whose craft draw 4 feet or less can use.

The principal Pascagoula waterfront is completely without facilities for pleasure craft. Cruisers in search of a good marina must make the somewhat tricky trek to West Pascagoula River (discussed later in this chapter).

Despite its relative lack of amenities, visiting

Huge harborside grain elevator—Pascagoula

Hauled-out naval vessels at Pascagoula shipyard

cruisers are urged to explore lower Pascagoula River if their schedule permits. The impressive wharves, mammoth dry docks, and colossal ships make for a very special sight from the water which should be the subject for many cruising yarns to come.

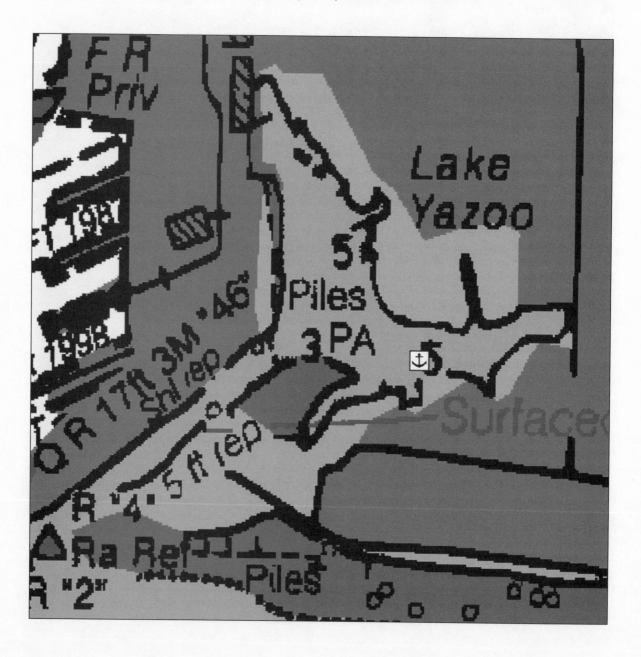

Lower Pascagoula River Anchorages (Various Lats/Lons—see below)

Anchorage on the Pascagoula River along the industrial waterfront is, of course, not a good idea, except on the waters of protected Lake Yazoo. The river's upper reaches support several overnight havens, which are reviewed below. Those captains wishing to drop the hook in closer proximity to the industrial district can consider two potential spots.

The charted channel striking northeast to Lake Yazoo is found east of flashing daybeacon #52. With careful navigation, visiting cruisers can now carry at least 4½ feet (typically 5 feet) of water east into a snug overnight stop on the interior reaches of southerly Lake Yazoo near 30 20.838 North/088 33.401 West. One mistake on the (mostly) unmarked approach passage can, however, land you in about 6 inches of water. Considering these limitations, this anchorage is pretty much restricted to vessels drawing 4 feet or less.

Assuming your craft fits the above outlined draft requirements, once on the waters of Lake Yazoo you will discover excellent protection from all winds. The lake is dotted here and there with permanent moorings, but there is just enough elbowroom for a 36-footer on the southerly arm of the lake. Try dropping the hook abeam of the short, charted, rectangular cove along the southerly banks (near the lat/lon specified above).

Lake Yazoo is surrounded by a hodge-podge of moderate, mostly residential development. There is a launching ramp flanking the southerly shores of the canal leading from the main Pascagoula/Horn Island Pass channel to Lake Yazoo, and a city-owned dockage complex

guards the lake's easterly reaches. No services are available at either facility for visitors.

Back on the main body of the Pascagoula River, the charted cove south of unlighted daybeacon #4 holds minimum depths of 6 feet and sports enough elbowroom for a 36-footer with good protection from inclement weather. This cove is surrounded by fairly heavy development and supports a goodly amount of local boating traffic, particularly during the weekends. There is a launching ramp just to

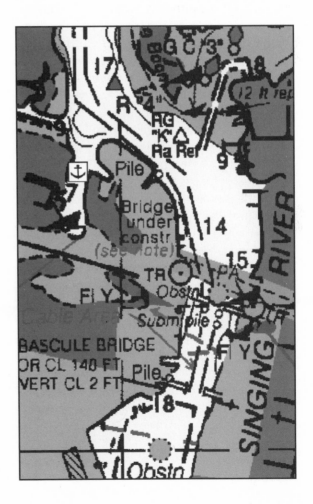

the south, which adds to the confusion. Those who can put up with the traffic might consider anchoring near 30 22.597 North/088 34.108 West, but for my money, I would either drop the hook in Lake Yazoo (if my vessel had a sufficiently shallow draft) or continue upriver to a more isolated haven.

Pascagoula History   In his early explorations of the Mississippi Coast, Jean Baptiste LeMoyne, Sieur de Bienville visited a deep river emptying into Mississippi Sound east of Biloxi. He discovered a tribe of Indians living along the stream's shores and calling themselves the Pascagoulas. The name stuck and today is used to refer to the river and its surrounding communities.

As the early settlement of French Louisiana went forward, the colonists from France were augmented by Canadians traveling south down the mighty Mississippi River. Two of these northerly colonists arriving about 1700 settled along the Pascagoula River and built plantations. By the time Pascagoula passed into British hands following the Seven Years' War, the region was producing a cash crop of cotton.

As was true all along the entire Mississippi coastline after the Louisiana purchase, local agitators stirred up plots to make the region part of the United States. On December 4, 1810, a group of militia wrested control of the city from the weak Spanish authorities and raised the American flag above Pascagoula for the first time.

During the South's antebellum period, Pascagoula become one of the Mississippi coast's "Six Sisters." These coastal communities were summer retreats or watering places for the well-to-do. The wealthy planter would pack up his entire household and escape to the cooling coastal breezes to avoid the dreaded "swamp vapors" that we today know as malaria.

As related in his wonderful book *The Mississippi Gulf Coast* author Charles L. Sullivan quotes a letter of Gov. W. C. D. Claiborne describing Pascagoula in 1813:

> The village of Pascagoula is three miles in length and contains about twenty families, each family having a little farm. They are not . . . wealthy . . . but are independent and accommodating. The situation of this place is elegant, a most beautiful bay in view affording always a sea breeze and abounding in fish and oysters. We are plentifully supplied with butter, fish, fowls of various kinds, vegetables, melons, peaches, grapes, figs, and in fact, everything the heart could wish.

During the Civil War, Pascagoula was one of the few Southern communities to be raided by a squadron of exclusively black troops. Stationed at nearby Ship Island (under Union control) and commanded by Col. Nathaniel Daniels, 200 recently freed slaves marched on Pascagoula on April 9, 1863. Confederate pickets delayed them while Southern reinforcements were hastily summoned. A large Rebel force finally arrived and Daniels' troops were forced to withdraw.

As the Civil War drew to its close, bitter feelings of resentment led to excesses by both sides. In 1864 Brigadier Gen. John W. Davidson launched a drive from Baton Rouge to cut the lines of communication with still Confederate Mobile. Marching along the Mississippi coast, the Union troops got completely out of hand. As described in Sullivan's *The Mississippi Gulf Coast*, the invaders "fired houses, barns, bridges and corn cribs, shot cattle and sheep, and gave way to rape and pillage. In at least one case a man died in a futile effort to protect his sister from them. Reaching West Pascagoula on December 13, they ran amok, smashing into burial vaults, robbing the bodies and strewing the remains about." Is it any wonder that hard feelings persisted between North and South for many decades following the end of this conflict?

In October of 1870 the long-awaited railroad running from Mobile to New Orleans was at last completed. Pascagoula's future was assured. The railway ran directly through town. With the railroad and its naturally deep harbor, the village became a central point for shipping and naval maneuvers.

Since that time Pascagoula has seemingly never looked back. While a few of us might yearn for the simpler village of days gone by, there is no denying that the wharves of modern Pascagoula provide many jobs and the grease to keep coastal Mississippi's wheels of commerce turning. It is indeed gratifying to learn that this venerable coastal town has so completely recovered from the horrible times of the Civil War.

Singing River Yacht Club

This writer's good friends at Singing River Yacht Club maintain a small clubhouse and a set of fixed, wooden piers on the northeasterly reaches of the charted Bayou Chico channel, well east-northeast of flashing daybeacon #42. I fondly remember speaking to this organization's membership following a fabulous banquet of barbecued ribs. I'll be *glad* to come back anytime!

Currently, the entrance and dockside depths carry only 4 to 4½ feet at low water. If you can stand these soundings, visitor's berths are provided for members of other yacht clubs with appropriate reciprocal privileges. Fresh water

and mostly 20-amp power connections are available dockside. The club dining room is open for lunch Monday through Saturday and in the evening on Wednesday and Friday.

Singing River Yacht Club (228) 769-1876

Approach depth—4-4½ feet (low water)
Dockside depth—4-4½ feet (low water)
Accepts transients—members of other yacht club with reciprocal privileges
Fixed wooden piers—yes
Dockside power connections—20-amp (a few 30 amp)
Dockside water connections—yes
Restaurant—on site (see hours of operation above)

West Pascagoula River (Marina—30 23.472 North/088 36.798 West)

West Pascagoula River is a large stream in its own right. It boasts the only marina catering to cruising craft in the Pascagoula region. Located, as you would expect, west of Pascagoula River, this stream is accessible by two channels convenient to the main Pascagoula commercial waterfront. Access can be gained by following the narrow but charted channel west-southwest of unlighted daybeacon #4 (on the Pascagoula River), or from Bayou Chemise, which intersects the upper reaches of the Pascagoula River near unlighted daybeacon #10. The former passage maintains minimum 6-foot depths, but does require navigational caution when crossing charted Marsh Lake. The latter route boasts at least 7 feet of water, with many soundings exceeding 15 feet. The southern intersection of West Pascagoula River and Mississippi Sound is quite shoal and should not be attempted by even the most shallow-draft pleasure vessel.

Mary Walker Bayou makes its way into the

western banks almost opposite the entrance channel from Marsh Lake. While there is one unmarked shoal to avoid at the entrance, visiting mariners can hold 7-foot minimum depths with elementary caution. Mary Walker Bayou plays host to one pleasure-craft-oriented marina as well as a fishing camp. Cruising craft looking for overnight marina dockage on Pascagoula waters must, by necessity, set their course for this stream.

Moving upstream on Mary Walker Bayou, cruisers will first spy Tucei Fish Camp on the western banks. This small-scale facility offers gasoline, but 4-foot dockside depths may be a bit skimpy for many larger cruising craft.

Soon Mary Walker Bayou follows a sharp bend to the west. After rounding the turn, the extensive docks of Mary Walker Marina will be spotted on the southern shore near 30 23.472 North/088 36.798 West. This obviously well-managed facility welcomes transient cruisers at well-sheltered, fixed wooden piers. Most dockage is on the bayou, while some additional slips are found on a small, southward-running canal. A few piers are shielded by unusual half-moon aluminum covers. Dockside power and water connections are readily available, as are gasoline and diesel fuel. Mary Walker features mechanical and haul-out repair services. The yard has an electric lift that can haul most boats as large as 32 feet. Judging from the number of hauled craft that we have always observed here during our many visits, this facility handles much of the local small-craft repair trade. There is no surer recommendation for any yard. A small ship's and variety store is located on the marina grounds. The Tiki restaurant (228-497-1591) is within a short walk of the docks.

While this writer was not privileged to partake of this dining spot's fare, it was highly recommended to me by the local crowd.

Veteran cruisers reading the above account will agree, I am sure, that Mary Walker Marina is a very well-appointed facility. It is fortunate, indeed, that such a full-service marina is available in a region otherwise lacking in pleasure-craft facilities.

Mary Walker Marina (228) 497-3141

Approach depth—7-10 feet
Dockside depth—6-8 feet
Accepts transients—yes
Transient-dockage rate—well below average
Fixed wooden piers—yes
Dockside power connections—30- and 50-amp
Dockside water connections—yes
Gasoline—yes
Diesel fuel—yes
Mechanical repairs—yes
Below-waterline repairs—yes (32 feet and under)
Ship's and variety store—small
Restaurant—nearby

North of its intersection with Mary Walker Bayou, West Pascagoula River continues to be quite deep all the way to the Interstate Highway 10 bridge. Some soundings reach an astonishing 50 feet. However, as the river soon leaves chart 11374, it would probably be best for all but very small craft to avoid this portion of the river.

While it can serve as an excellent gunk-holing opportunity, anchorage on upper West Pascagoula River is not particularly recommended. The surrounding marsh shores to the east give only minimal protection. Add this to the fairly rapid current and you can formulate a good notion of why it would be better to choose another haven.

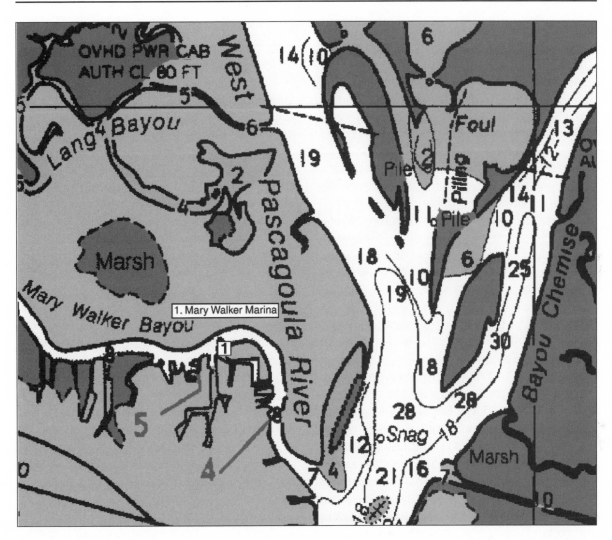

1. Mary Walker Marina

Wide and deep Bayou Chemise leaves West Pascagoula River and flows first northeast and then east to rejoin the Pascagoula River near unlighted daybeacon #10. Basic navigation allows mariners to make use of this fortunate connecting stream and hold minimum 7-foot depths. Be sure to read the navigation sketch of Bayou Chemise presented later in this chapter before trying to run the stream.

Upper Pascagoula and Escatawpa River (Various Lats/Lons—see below)

North of its juncture with Bayou Chemise, upper Pascagoula River follows a marked track to the north and east. The heavily industrial waterfront is soon left behind and the river begins to run between delightful shorelines with only light development. At flashing daybeacon #14, the Pascagoula follows a long bend to the east and splits near unlighted daybeacon #1. The northerly fork is shoal and should not be entered, but the stream that continues on to the east is known as the Escatawpa River and provides many miles of gunk-holing and some possible anchorages.

Before we go on to detail the anchorages and gunk holes on the Escatawpa, it should be noted that both a large paper mill and a menhaden processing plant overlook the river to the east. If winds are blowing from this quarter, the smell of progress can be downright suffocating. Cruising craft that choose to anchor on the Escatawpa River should take the paper mill and fish house into account. Check on the forecast wind direction before dropping the hook.

After crossing under the 77-foot fixed bridge, east of unlighted daybeacon #2, a deep cut that we shall call the Moss Point Channel makes off to the south at flashing daybeacon #3. While there is an unmarked shoal to avoid, most navigators can hold minimum depths of 10 feet to O'Leary Lake.

The lower reaches of this side channel, short of the lake, border on the quaint community of Moss Point. Watch the western shores and you will see twin launching ramps with an adjacent dock. Boats as large as 36 feet can tie to this primitive pier in 10-foot depths. No power or water connections, nor any other marine services, are available. There do not seem to be any local regulations concerning overnight dockage at this pier, but I would not suggest staying more than a few days at the most.

The Moss Point Channel veers sharply east at the launch area and quickly leads to O'Leary Lake. If winds are not blowing from the paper mill or fish-processing plant, this lake makes an acceptable overnight anchor-age for almost any pleasure vessel. Try dropping the hook near 30 24.850 North/088 31.963 West. Depths of 7 to 8 feet guard the centerline, and 5 to 6 feet of water is held quite close to shore. Protection is particularly good from southerly winds, though strong (over 30 knots) northerly breezes blowing across the marsh-grass shores could raise a rough chop. The lake's mainland banks are composed of high ground with light residential development and one commercial plant. The northerly shores are natural salt marsh. The southeastern tip of O'Leary Lake is blocked by a very low-level fixed railroad bridge. Cruising vessels should drop the hook well before reaching this span.

Cruisers can follow the northern branch of the Moss Point Channel past O'Leary Lake and hold 10-foot-plus depths to McInnis Lake. This body of water can also be accessed directly from the Escatawpa River by following the deep cut south of flashing daybeacon #9. Minimum depths on the southern portion of the lake are 9 feet, and there is enough swinging room for boats as large as 45 feet. However, portions of the bottom strata in McInnis Lake are littered with debris, and you just might lose an anchor. Should you feel compelled to drop the hook here anyway, one spot to consider is found near 30 24.880 North/088 31.360 West. The marsh-grass shores render enough protection for light to moderate breezes, but are insufficient for really foul weather.

Back on the main Escatawpa River channel, the passage soon passes under a high-rise (73 foot) fixed bridge east of flashing daybeacon #9, and then encounters a low-level railway span. This span is usually open unless a train is due.

Soon, passing cruisers may spy one or two oceangoing trawlers and related craft docked

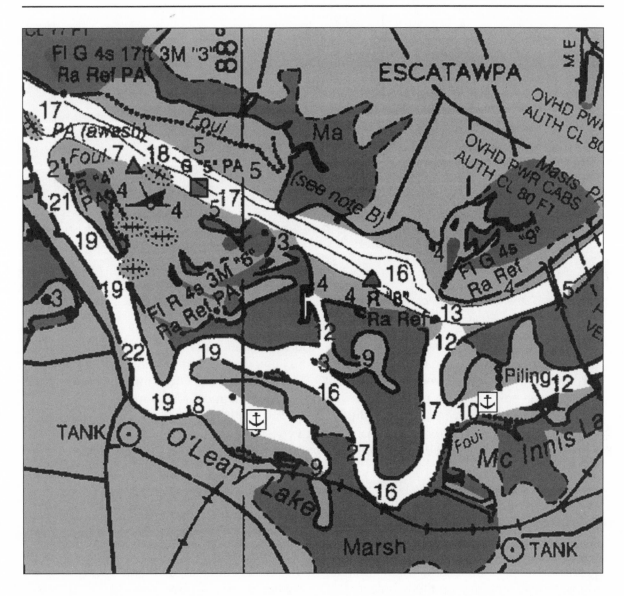

along the Escatawpa's northern shores, east of the railway bridge. These rather grim-looking vessels are associated with an adjacent menhaden plant. Believe you me, when these oily fish are actually being processed, the stench is almost unbelievable, and it's never too good, even when the plant isn't in operation. We always try to leave this place in our wake at the earliest possible moment.

After leaving the menhaden plant behind, the Escatawpa River splits into two branches. The northerly arm features soundings of 10 feet

Railroad bridge on Escatawpa River, Pascagoula

or better. Some depths approach 20-foot levels.

A pipeline-underwater cable crosses this northerly branch of the river about halfway between the split and the point where the stream splinters into several small offshoots. This hazard is noted by signs on the shore. Be sure to drop your hook well away from this dangerous obstruction.

One of the best anchor-down spots on the Escatawpa's northerly branch is found just short of the splinter area, near 30 25.577 North/088 30.157 West. Here the shoreline opens out a bit for better swinging room and depths are not quite so cavernous. Protection is good from all winds, though best from northerly breezes.

The entire shoreline of the northern fork is wonderfully undeveloped. Cruisers who make it this far can enjoy the feeling of accomplishment that comes from knowing you have dropped the hook where few cruising craft have ever been before. Unfortunately, the pulp mill

and menhaden plant may well detract from the full enjoyment of this off-the-beaten-path feeling. Remember to check the wind before making a commitment for the night.

The southern fork of the Escatawpa River is very similar to its northerly sister except that some 5-foot soundings are in evidence, and this stream eventually leads hard by the pulp and paper mill. Skippers anchoring on this body of water should consider dropping the hook as soon as the charted higher ground comes abeam to the south, near 30 25.285 North/088 30.009 West. Although depths here are in the 15- to 20-foot range, there is only enough swinging room for boats up to 36 feet. Protection is quite good, even for heavy weather.

Frankly, unless you have some reason to prefer the southern branch, the northern fork will probably better serve as an overnight haven. However, if you can stand the somewhat thinner water, there is nothing wrong

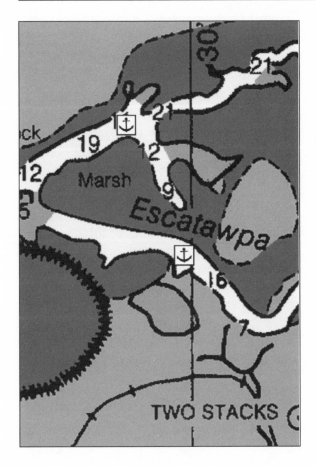

with the stream to the south, so, if you are of a mind to do so, gunk hole away.

Horn Island (Standard Mile 98)
(30 14.137 North/088 39.405 West)

Horn Island is the second (moving east to west) in the series of uninhabited barrier islands flanking the southerly limits of Mississippi Sound. It has the enviable reputation of being the most attractive of the lot. Horn Island is quite long, spanning a length of almost 11 nautical miles, while averaging only half a nautical mile in width. It too is a

national wildlife preserve and part of the Gulf Island National Seashore. There is no development nor any marine facilities on the island. However, during fair weather, anchoring off the northerly shores and then dinghying ashore can make for a truly memorable trip, particularly if the beaches and maritime forests are bathed in the warm light of a fall or spring afternoon.

Cruisers who decide to visit Horn Island should consider anchoring in the deep cove along the northern banks, west of "The Horseshoe," near 30 14.137 North/088 39.405 West. These waters can be reached by departing the ICW at flashing daybeacon #3.

Minimum 12-foot depths run to within 200 yards of shore south of Middle Ground Shoal. The main body of Horn Island allows shelter from southerly winds while the point to the east gives some protection when (no more than) moderate winds are blowing from this quarter. Be sure to read the navigation information presented in the next section of this chapter before attempting to access this haven.

Remember that this anchorage, like all the others on Mississippi Sound's barrier islands, lacks sufficient shelter for thunderstorms or high winds.

Dog Keys Pass (Standard Mile 87.5)

While not nearly as well marked as Horn Island Pass or Gulfport Inlet, Dog Keys Pass nevertheless supports fairly heavy local waterborne traffic. A few aids are charted, while a host of other buoys are shifted much too often to appear on 11374 or 11372.

While with appropriate caution Dog Keys Pass can be used by strangers, it would seem wise to choose nearby Horn Island Pass instead. The latter cut's mass of markings is to be much preferred over Dog Key's sparse aids to navigation.

PASS AUX HERONS BRIDGE TO DOG KEYS PASS NAVIGATION

Navigation of the ICW through Mississippi Sound will never be dull. Besides the potential for nasty wind and wave already mentioned elsewhere in this chapter, the Waterway channel itself calls for more than its share of caution. To the east, the ICW briefly follows the dredged Pass Aux Herons channel through numerous shoals north of Dauphin Island. Then, as the deeper waters of Mississippi Sound open out to the west, aids to navigation become fewer and fewer. Runs between the various daybeacons and buoys sometimes exceed several nautical miles. Visiting and resident cruisers alike should plan their cruise carefully and chart all necessary compass/GPS courses well ahead of time. It just won't do to try to plot a course on a heaving cockpit or flybridge floor while frantically wondering where the next marker might be. Of course, this is also a section of the Waterway where a well-functioning GPS interfaced with a laptop computer can be a real advantage.

Fortunately, the Waterway borders very few shoals on most of its passage between the western tip of Dauphin Island and Dog Keys Pass. The infrequent exceptions to this rule are noted within the body of this text.

Pascagoula and Bayou La Batre, the two major ports of call on this section of the ICW, have well-marked entrance channels of their own that cruising captains can use with confidence. The Pascagoula cut is lined with one of the largest collections of flashing buoys and daybeacons that this writer has ever observed.

Pass Aux Herons Channel   The ICW leaves Mobile Bay and enters Mississippi Sound by crossing under the fixed high-rise Dauphin Island Causeway/Pass Aux Herons Bridge (83 feet of vertical clearance). The Waterway then follows a dredged cut for some 4.5 nautical miles to the deeper sound waters. The eastern portion of this channel, particularly the section adjacent to the bridge, cuts through very shallow water and is itself subject to shoaling. Be prepared to discover new and different markers from those discussed in this guide or pictured on chart 11378. Pass all red beacons to their southerly sides and all green aids to their northerly quarter. A charted set of lighted range markers southwest of unlighted nun buoy #28 helps captains keep to the cut. Nighttime passage of the Pass Aux Herons channel by outsiders is definitely not recommended. West of unlighted nun buoy #20, passing cruisers have access to two possible sidewaters on the northern shores of Dauphin Island.

Bayou Aloe   Mariners bound for the Bayou Aloe channel should depart the Waterway almost midway between unlighted nun buoys #20 and #22 as they come abeam of the charted, unnumbered flashing daybeacon just south of the ICW channel. Pass the unnumbered flashing daybeacon to its immediate southwesterly side and set course to come abeam of unlighted daybeacon #1 to its immediate southwesterly quarter. While this portion of the channel is quite narrow, it borders on waters with at least 5 feet of depth. Craft that do not draw more than 4 feet need not be too meticulous in their navigation. Skippers of fixed-keel sailcraft that need more than 5 feet of water to stay off the bottom must exercise far greater caution.

From unlighted daybeacon #1, continue on course, pointing to come abeam of flashing daybeacon #2 to its immediate northeasterly side. From #2, the Bayou Aloe channel continues on its well-marked and merry way to the southeast. After passing between the last set of aids, flashing daybeacon #9 and unlighted daybeacon #10, the inner reaches of Bayou Aloe will be dead ahead. Pick any likely spot to drop the anchor, but don't approach the shoreline too closely.

Lafitte Bay   The entrance channel leading south to Lafitte Bay and Heron Bayou departs the Bayou Aloe channel at flashing daybeacon #2. Set a careful compass/GPS course from #2 for the narrow channel leading towards Heron Bayou. Keep a sharp watch for several privately maintained stakes outlining the eastern side of the cut. If these indifferently placed aids are still present when you visit, pass them just to their westerly sides.

Soon the wide and deep entrance to Lafitte Bay will come abeam to the west. Enter the mouth on its mid-width and settle in for a night without fear of wind or wave.

Do not attempt to continue south into Heron Bayou past the Lafitte Bay entrance. Depths of 4 feet or less are quickly encountered.

As can be readily appreciated by a perfunctory study of the above procedure and associated charts, the Lafitte Bay channel is not for everyone. It is narrow and borders on waters with less than 2 feet of depth. The cut is only recommended for boats under 38 feet in length, and drawing 4 feet or preferably less. Even then, only adventurous captains should make the attempt.

On the ICW   At unlighted nun buoy #28, the ICW cuts to the west and leaves the path outlined by the lighted range markers behind. As you approach unlighted nun buoy #32, it's time to put our old friend chart 11378 away and break out 11374. If you are like this writer, it will seem as if you have been using 11378 forever.

The ICW continues to follow its improved, well-marked channel until coming abeam of flashing daybeacon #49 to its northerly side. Westbound mariners might take a moment to wave to the markers behind them. They are the last set of such closely packed beacons you will see short of Lake Borgne.

From flashing daybeacon #49, set a careful compass course to come abeam and pass flashing daybeacon #5 to its southerly side. A gap of 4.1 nautical miles separates #49 and #5. Stay on course and be on guard against side-setting currents.

Let's stop right here to explore a cartographical abnormality on this portion of the Northern Gulf ICW. Between flashing daybeacon #49 and the Waterway's intersection with the Horn Island Pass- Pascagoula channel, there are three aids to navigation marking the passage: flashing daybeacons #5, #3, and #1. Note that these are all green markers. Following the normal east-to-west Northern Gulf Coast ICW pattern, most any navigator would expect to pass these aids to navigation to their northerly side. Wrong! For whatever reason, the magenta line on chart 11374 specifies that all three of these lighted daybeacons should be passed to their *southerly* quarters. I know this doesn't make too much sense, but notice the charted obstructions north of #3 and #5. Consequently, it only makes sense to pass south of these beacons, but why #5, #3, and #1 are not designated as #6, #4, and #2, I can't begin to tell you.

Anyway, once abeam of #5, you should continue cruising west on the same course, pointing to come abeam of flashing daybeacon #3 by some 100 yards to its southerly side. From this aid, brave cruisers have access to one of the anchorages on Petit Bois Island to the south.

Petit Bois Island Remember that neither of the two anchorages adjacent to the northern shores of Petit Bois Island is recommended in anything short of fair weather. If you choose to make use of the cove west of the "Obstns PA" symbol on chart 11374, set a careful compass/GPS course from flashing daybeacon #3 for the charted obstructions. A run of some 2.5 nautical miles will bring the cove into sight. Alter course a bit to the west to avoid the underwater obstructions and, *at idle speed*, feel your way carefully south with the sounder. *As soon as* depths start to rise, reverse course for some 50 yards and drop the hook. You can then dinghy ashore without having to worry about whether your boat will swing into the shallows.

The deep cove south of flashing daybeacon #2 can also be reached directly from flashing daybeacon #3. Again, a carefully plotted compass course from #3 to the cove's interior reaches is called for. Navigators traversing this route will have a run of some 4 nautical miles from #4 to the cove.

Most captains will wisely choose to enter the westerly Petit Bois anchorage from the Pascagoula/Horn Island Pass channel. Cruisers following this route can depart the inlet channel at flashing buoy #14 and set course to pass between the shallows abutting the shoreline to the south and the tongue of charted 5- and 6-foot water to the north. Along the way you will pass a series of pilings which serve as a dredge berth. Avoid this hazard by passing to its northeasterly side.

Once on the western cove's inner reaches, be sure to drop the hook at least .1 nautical miles from shore. Closer in, depths rise quickly and dramatically.

Sand Island Anchorage Cruisers bound for the haven off the northerly shores of Sand Island can safely depart the Horn Island Pass channel (see below for more details on this cut) at flashing buoy #19. Set course for the waters lying northwest of the island's charted, sharp northeasterly tip.

Now that the Sand Island interior harbor has been closed by shoaling, all vessels should anchor on the deeper waters off the island's northerly shores, northwest of the charted, sharp northeasterly tip. Here you will find good water and some protection from southerly winds.

Once again, we must caution all cruisers that this haven has virtually no shelter from foul weather. If an afternoon thunderstorm should come along, as it often does, things could get far more exciting than you might wish. As with all the Mississippi barrier island anchorages, we suggest that you look elsewhere for a more sheltered haven to spend nights comfortably swinging on the hook. One good possibility would be the anchorage on Lake Yazoo off the Pascagoula River!.

ICW to Pascagoula/Horn Island Pass Channel A run of 3.75 nautical miles west-northwest from flashing daybeacon #3 will bring westbound ICW cruisers abeam of flashing daybeacon #1 to its southerly side. It's then only a quick hop west of .6 nautical miles to intersect the Pascagoula/Horn Island Pass channel. Both east- and west-bound Waterway cruisers will come abeam of this major channel between flashing buoys #29 and #30 (north of the ICW's east-to-west passage) and flashing buoys #27 and #BB (south of the ICW channel).

In a late-breaking development, we have just learned that all the markers on the Pascagoula-Horn Island Pass Channel have been renumbered between the sea buoy and the mouth of the Pascagoula River. This new scheme *is* reflected in the aid-to-navigation numbers contained in this guide, but it is *not* shown on the latest editions of charts 11375 and 11374, available at the time of this writing. Please proceed cautiously!

A turn to the north will lead navigators to the Pascagoula River's southern entrance. At flashing buoy #36, the Pascagoula channel veers off to the northwest while an alternate northward-running cut goes into Bayou Casotte. Due to the heavy industrial traffic on this latter channel, Bayou Casotte is not recommended for pleasure craft.

On the Pascagoula River Flashing daybeacon #52 introduces cruising captains to the broad, lower reaches of the Pascagoula River. Depths are 20 feet or more almost from bank to bank in the industrial section. Look west at the river's entrance and you can observe the huge ships often docked along the wharves of Ingalls Shipyard. If you're lucky, one or more large naval vessels might be in port.

Lake Yazoo Anchorage The small canal leading to Lake Yazoo cuts to the northeast abeam of flashing daybeacon #52. Two un-lighted daybeacons, #2 and #4, guide you into the canal's westerly entrance. As usual, pass #2 and #4 to your starboard side. Expect some low-water soundings of only 4½ to 5 feet between #46 and the canal's south-westerly entrance.

Once past the canal's mouth, hold to the mid-width as you cruise toward the lake. Soon you will pass a large, public launching-ramp facility to your starboard side. No-wake regulations are in effect well southwest and northeast of this area.

Immediately after coming abeam of the public launching ramps, begin favoring the port side (northwesterly banks). This prohibition is just a taste of things to come!

The trickiest portion of the passage will come up just as the approach canal enters the westerly reaches of Lake Yazoo. It looks as if all you need do is continue straight ahead. Wrong! This course of action will carry you into some 2 feet of water.

Instead, turn a bit to the northeast as you cruise out into the lake. Use your binoculars to pick out one small, low-lying green buoy that will be, hopefully, spied to the east-northeast. Set course to bring this tiny marker abeam hard by your port side. Then, at last, you can safely turn southeast and eventually east into the main body of the lake's southerly arm. We suggest anchoring on this water body's midline soon after coming abeam of the charted, rectangularly shaped cove along the southerly banks.

Don't attempt to explore the northern half of Lake Yazoo. Depths run as thin as 1 foot. Anyone got a vessel with that little draft?

On the Pascagoula River   Farther upstream, watch the western banks for a large grain elevator and barge-loading dock. This structure is more than slightly impressive from the water.

As you cruise north on the Pascagoula, your way will first be barred by a low-level railway bridge with only 2 feet of closed vertical clearance. This span is generally open, unless one of the frequent trains serving the port is due.

Soon after leaving the railroad behind, the river is spanned by a highway bascule bridge that presently has 31 feet of closed vertical clearance. Sailcraft that cannot clear this height must contend with restrictive opening times. Currently, the bridge will not open at all between 6:15 A.M. and 7:15 A.M., 7:25 A.M. and 8:00 A.M., and 3:30 P.M. and 4:45 P.M. At all other times of the day, the span supposedly opens on demand. Maybe so, but my experience leads this writer to believe that the bridge tender can be a bit slow on the draw when pleasure craft signal for passage.

Be advised that a new bridge is now under construction just upstream of the present span. For some time to come, cruisers will need to take extra care to avoid the work barges and other construction equipment as they cruise through this section of Pascagoula River. Eventually, after completion of the new span and removal of the old bascule bridge, things will take a definite turn for the better.

Cruising farther upriver, the stream takes a jog to the northwest. Favor the southwestern banks slightly to avoid the charted shallows along the easterly and northeasterly shoreline. Point to come abeam of unlighted daybeacon #4 to its southwesterly quarter.

At #4, captains may choose to enter the second of the Pascagoula's anchorages to the south or follow the Marsh Lake channel to West Pascagoula River and the facilities on Mary Walker Bayou.

Second Pascagoula Anchorage   Enter the cove south of unlighted daybeacon #4 on its mid-width. Consider dropping the hook before proceeding more than 100 yards to the south. The northerly section of the anchorage has a bit more privacy than the southern corner.

Marsh Lake Channel to West Pascagoula River   Cruisers entering Pascagoula late in the day, or those wanting to rest from their travels for a bit, will want to make their way to the marina off West Pascagoula River (on Mary Walker Bayou). While it is quite possible to reach West Pascagoula via Bayou Chemise, the shortest route for mariners cruising north from the ICW is by way of the channel crossing Marsh Lake.

This cut holds minimum 6-foot depths and is easy to run, with the exception of the passage across Marsh Lake. Here the channel is unmarked and borders on very shallow water to the north and south. Keep your stern lined up with the canal opening behind you, and your bow pointed for the opening in front of you. By using the two entrances almost as range markers, you can avoid trouble. Stick to the centerline on the remainder of the passage and no difficulty other than possibly some floating debris should be encountered.

The western terminus of Marsh Lake channel flows into West Pascagoula River almost opposite Mary Walker Bayou. The close proximity of these two sidewaters is quite convenient for visiting cruisers.

West Pascagoula River   The southern mouth of West Pascagoula River is littered with shoals and marsh islands. It is completely surrounded by a wide bar with only 2 feet of depth. Absolutely no craft, not even shallow-draft outboard boats, should attempt to enter West Pascagoula River directly from Mississippi Sound. Instead use either the Marsh Lake cut described above or Bayou Chemise, reviewed below.

South of the Marsh Lake channel intersection, West Pascagoula River is traversed by the same two bridges that cross its easterly sister on the industrial waterfront. The majority of cruisers will not need to trouble with these spans. South of the bridges, the shoals and bar surrounding the river's entrance (mentioned just above) are soon encountered. All mariners will want to confine their cruising to the waters north of the twin bridges.

Mary Walker Bayou   Enter the mouth of Mary Walker Bayou by favoring the port side banks. As accurately portrayed on chart 11374, a tongue of 4-foot water flanks the northern tip of the entrance.

Once on Mary Walker Bayou, simply follow the mid-width upstream to the marina. Don't attempt to cruise west of the charted split in the creek. Depths past this point become much too uncertain for larger cruising craft.

Bayou Chemise   The southerly entrance of Bayou Chemise is bisected by an oblong marsh island. Best depths are maintained on the stream running east of the marsh island. Simply hold to the center and follow the creek as it cuts to the east.

Shortly after its turn to the east, Bayou Chemise opens out to the north. Don't attempt to enter this portion of the bayou. Even though chart 11374 predicts an unmarked channel running north, on-site research failed to discover this cut. Instead, favor the southern banks slightly as you continue east toward the intersection with the Pascagoula River.

Don't be tempted to enter the small offshoot that wanders off from the northeastern banks soon after you leave the shallow northerly waters behind. This small stream has depths of 4 feet or less.

As you approach the Pascagoula River, begin favoring the northwesterly shoreline. This maneuver will help you avoid the correctly charted shoal bordering the southeasterly point of the intersection between Bayou Chemise and the Pascagoula River. Eventually, if all goes well, you will intersect the main Pascagoula River channel southwest of unlighted daybeacon #10.

Upper West Pascagoula River   The main branch of West Pascagoula River runs north-northwest from Bayou Chemise. Even though surprising depths of 15 to as much as 50 feet continue for some distance upriver, the stream soon leaves the confines of chart 11374. Without the benefit of charted waters, boats over 28 feet should probably leave the upper portion of the West Pascagoula to our outboard brethren.

Upper Pascagoula and Escatawpa River The principal Pascagoula River channel runs generally north and then west to the Bayou Chemise intersection. It remains well marked and reasonably easy to follow. Be warned that unlighted daybeacon #8 can be difficult to spot. It's anchored hard by the easterly banks. Craft traveling downstream will have to look carefully to find this beacon.

East of unlighted daybeacon #17 the river splits. Don't attempt to cruise into the northerly fork. Depths of 3 feet or less are immediately encountered.

The main stream continues to the east and takes on the name of Escatawpa River. Markings resume, but are now renumbered, beginning with unlighted daybeacon #1. This is as it should be; you are entering a new river and the numbering of aids to navigation starts anew as well.

Don't try to enter the charted channel leading south to Beardslee Lake, east of unlighted daybeacon #2. During on-site research, we discovered that the bottom of the lake's entrance channel is littered with concrete debris. Our bent prop bears mute witness to the very real danger for those who attempt this errant side trip.

East-northeast of unlighted daybeacon #2 the Escatawpa River flows under a fixed high-rise bridge. This span has a vertical clearance of 77 feet. Just east of this bridge, skippers can turn to the south and follow a deep channel to Moss Point, O'Leary Lake, and McInnis Lake.

Moss Point Channel   The charted shoal flanking the east side of the entrance to Moss Point channel appears to have built out farther to the west than is shown on the latest edition of chart 11374. Be sure to favor the westerly banks when entering the Moss Point cut.

Once past the shoal, simply hold to the centerline for excellent depths all the way to the Moss Point dock. If you choose to explore or drop the hook in O'Leary Lake, continue following the channel until the entrance to the lake opens out to the east. Enter through the centerline and drop the hook anywhere near the lake's middle.

You can continue on to McInnis Lake by

following the stream's mid-width as it meanders to the east, then southeast, then north. Don't be tempted to try the small, charted stream running north to the Escatawpa River west of unlighted daybeacon #8, or the adjacent spiral-shaped creek. Both streams are too narrow for larger craft and depths are more than suspect.

The Moss Point channel eventually follows a hairpin turn to the north. Soon the entrance to McInnis Lake will come abeam to the east.

Cruise into this lake on the mid-width of its entrance. Favor the southerly shores a bit to avoid the charted pilings and other debris on the northern banks. To the east, you should spy the charted, semi-sunken wreck. Our research revealed this old derelict to be an abandoned dredge. Be sure to cease your forward progress and drop the hook well before reaching the wreck. Remember, the bottom may well prove to be foul with debris in McInnis Lake, so set a trip line on your anchor.

The Moss Point Channel continues on to the north and rejoins the Escatawpa River south of flashing daybeacon #9. Hold to the center as you cruise back into the larger stream. The points to the east and west are somewhat shoal.

On the Escatawpa River
East and southeast of flashing daybeacon #3, the Escatawpa River channel is encroached upon by shallows to the north and south. Observe all aids to navigation carefully and stick strictly to the marked cut. Fortunately, the prolific daybeacons make this a fairly routine process.

Flashing daybeacon #9 marks the northern edge of the Escatawpa at the point where the Moss Point channel cuts into the river from the south. This aid can be hard to spot. It is actually located on a small sandspit.

East of #9, the Escatawpa River begins a long, slow turn to the northeast. Good depths again open out almost from bank to bank. The visiting (or the resident) cruiser will soon pass under a high-rise highway bridge with 73 feet of vertical clearance. This span is soon followed by a railway bridge with only 5 feet of closed vertical clearance. If the latter should be closed when you arrive, it could mean a long wait.

After leaving the railroad bridge, you will observe the menhaden-processing plant and possibly several old, steel trawlers (described earlier) lining the northern banks. Be sure to proceed at idle speed through these waters. A strong wake could bring on more than just a few shouted curses.

Soon the Escatawpa splits into two branches. An obscurely charted marsh island actually sits out from the point separating the two arms of the river. Don't approach this small body of marsh. Enter either branch of the river by cruising the centerline between the mainland and the marsh island.

The northerly branch is by far the better of the two for anchorage. There is a pipeline crossing on this stream, amply noted by signs on both shores. Be sure to drop your anchor well away from this underwater hazard.

Enter the northern branch on its mid-width and proceed on the centerline. Eventually the river breaks up into numerous shallow passages. The waters just short of the splinter point make for an excellent overnight stop. Discontinue your explorations here. The multiple streams to the east are too small for cruising boats.

The southerly branch of the Escatawpa should also be entered on its mid-width. Follow the middle of the river until you begin your approach to the pulp mill, quickly recognized by the charted stacks to the southeast. Of course, the smell will let you know their proximity long before you see the stacks.

Discontinue your upstream explorations as the industrial stacks come abeam to the south. Depths finally begin to fall off east of this point.

Back on the Gulf Coast ICW From its intersection with the Pascagoula/Horn Island Pass channel, the Gulf Coast ICW strikes west for 5 nautical miles passing flashing buoy #1 to its northerly side and then coming abeam of flashing daybeacon #2's southerly side. This run does not stray near any shallows, but its length does call for careful attention to one's compass or GPS.

Note that the strange color reversal of the three ICW markers east of the Pascagoula-Horn Island Pass channel ceases as you approach flashing buoy #1. Westbound mariners should once again generally pass north of green, odd-numbered aids to navigation and south of even-numbered, red markers. Go figure!

Flashing daybeacon #3 marks the southern side of the Waterway a short distance to the west of #2. Come abeam of #3 to its northerly side.

At flashing daybeacon #3 the ICW route takes a sharp swing to the northwest and heads for flashing daybeacon #5 and unlighted can buoy #5A. Pass both #5 and #5A well to their northeasterly and northern sides, and then follow the Waterway as it turns to the west. Eastbound navigators will want to bring #5 and #5A abeam to their (the markers') northerly quarters.

From #3, visiting cruisers can choose to journey to an anchorage on the northern shores of Horn Island.

Horn Island Anchorage To enter the anchorage southwest of the Horseshoe, on the northern banks of Horn Island, set a compass course from flashing daybeacon #3 to pass between the charted 6-foot water of "Middle Ground" to the north and the 1- and 2-foot depths jutting north from the island's point to the south. There is a broad swath of deep water between these two hazards, but you must be cautious to avoid the shallow waters abutting the point to the south. It would be far better to err in your course a bit to the north than to the south.

Once past the southerly shallows, feel your way carefully in towards the southerly banks with your sounder. Be sure to drop the hook before cruising to within less than 200 yards of shore.

On to Dog Keys Pass From flashing daybeacon #5 it is an arrow-straight run to the west of some 2.5 nautical miles before coming abeam of flashing daybeacon #6 to its southerly side. Again, skippers need not be concerned about adjacent shallows. Simply stay on course and no undue difficulties should be encountered.

West of #6, another 4.6 nautical miles will bring you abeam of the Biloxi entrance channel to the north and Dog Keys Pass to the south. Along the way you will pass south of flashing daybeacon #8.

Dog Keys Pass   If you choose to run this inlet, set a course from flashing daybeacon #8 to bring charted, unlighted can buoy #3 abeam to its easterly side. Be mindful of the large body of shoals west of #3.

Continue cruising south to the Gulf by following both the charted and uncharted markers you will encounter. As you would expect, pass all green markers to their easterly sides and all red beacons to their westerly quarters.

Biloxi (Standard Mile 87.5)

The seaport city of Biloxi (bill-LUCK-see) shares the honor of being the oldest European-founded settlement on the Northern Gulf Coast with Pensacola, Florida. Founded in the first struggling days of French Louisiana, the memories of those times are still very much alive in this timeless city.

Today the Biloxi waterfront presents an all-too-modern face to visiting cruisers, with mammoth gambling casinos rubbing shoulders with the few traditional commercial fishing craft that have not been squeezed out quite yet. Excellent marina facilities are readily found in Biloxi. Additionally, waterborne visitors will find a world of things to see and do upon coming ashore.

One recent happening in Biloxi centers around several of the region's mammoth casinos. Some of these establishments have recently added marinas to their list of offerings. *However*, during repeated visits to Biloxi in the spring and fall of 2002, we could not help but notice a curious phenomenon. While the two Biloxi city marinas (see below) were bulging at the seams with pleasure craft, hardly a single vessel was to be seen in *any* of the casino marinas. We can only conclude that local captains know something, and coupled with the lack of any dockmasters (at least any we could find) at the casino marinas, we are only going to mention these questionable facilities in passing.

Without putting too fine a point on it, Biloxi and its surrounding waters can lay claim to a goodly quantity of cruising destinations and facilities. In earlier, simpler times, this writer used to term Biloxi as "the Mississippi coastline's yachting capital," as a consequence of all these many and varied cruising opportunities. However, these days—with the ever-increasing throngs of gamblers, snarled, angry automobile traffic, and honking horns never ending—cruisers more inclined to a quite anchorage may want to just keep on trucking west to Louisiana. Others may find much to experience in the city's rich entertainment and dining attractions. We suggest newcomers try Biloxi once and see if the new incarnation of this historic city fits their tastes. Thereafter, you'll know whether to set your course to Biloxi or head elsewhere.

Numbers to know in Biloxi:

City Cab—228-436-4655
Yellow Cab—228-436-3788
Enterprise Rent-A-Car—228-868-6004
Avis Rent A Car—228-864-7182
National Car Rental—228-863-5548
West Marine (2406 Pass Road)—
   228-388-9090

Biloxi Geography

In order to comprehend the many ins and outs of Biloxi from a cruising point of view, you must first come to understand the region's unique geography. If you could look at a satellite photo of Biloxi and its surrounding waters, it would appear as if nature had erected two barriers between the city and hostile weather moving north from the Gulf of Mexico. To the south, historic Ship Island guards Mississippi Sound's southern flank. Immediately south of the Biloxi waterfront, refreshingly undeveloped Deer Island provides a welcome lee from the prevailing southerly breezes. Even with these barriers, though, violent hurricanes have brought about a fair share of havoc and damage over the years.

Biloxi itself appears as a peninsula, fronted by Mississippi Sound to the south and the Back Bay of Biloxi to the north. It would take only an additional glance by any true pleasure-craft skipper to appreciate the numerous cruising opportunities afforded by the prolific auxiliary streams feeding into Back Bay.

The Gulf Coast ICW intersects the main Biloxi channel well southeast of the city waterfront at standard mile 87.5. This cut runs northwest through an improved channel until reaching a very strategic intersection at flashing daybeacon #26. A cut to the northeast will carry cruisers to the Ocean Springs small-craft harbor, while a turn to the southwest (then west) leads to the principal Biloxi waterfront, protected by Deer Island to the south. Two city marinas welcome transient craft along this waterfront.

A cruise to the northwest from the juncture of the Ocean Springs and Biloxi channel will lead captains and their crew through a third cut into the Back Bay of Biloxi. This body of water has hitherto been largely overlooked by cruising skippers. What a mistake! The many gunk holes on adjacent Old Fort Bayou, Biloxi River, and Bernard Bayou are enough to addle the mind of any true waterborne explorer. There is even a full-service boatyard on Bernard Bayou, just where you might least expect to find a facility of this type.

Biloxi and Ship Island History   The old town of Biloxi lies at the heart of what was once French Louisiana. In fact, it is second only to St. Augustine as the oldest permanently occupied European settlement in the United States.

On February 10, 1699, a French expeditionary force dropped anchor in the lee of Ship Island. In command was Pierre LeMoyne, Sieur d'Iberville. His younger brother Jean Baptiste LeMoyne, Sieur de Bienville, was with the expedition as a midshipman. These two dominant personalities were to be the shepherds of French Louisiana for the next forty years.

Within a few days of his arrival, Iberville had wined and dined the local Indians and concluded an alliance that would hold throughout the sixty-four-year history of French Louisiana. Within months a fort was erected on the mainland north of Ship Island. Some of Iberville's documents refer to this fortification as Fort Maurepas, but it was generally known as Biloxi, after the local Indian tribe.

During the War of Spanish Succession, Iberville was forced to move his military headquarters to Mobile, returning in 1719, when the capital of French Louisiana was moved from Mobile to Biloxi. This change of venue was in response to the devastating hurricane of 1717, which virtually closed the channel west of Dauphin Island. Eventually, Bienville would convince the colony's council to move the capital to New Orleans, which he had founded some years earlier.

From 1719 to 1722 an avalanche of colonists, most of them women in search of husbands, poured into Biloxi. These immigrants were known as "*Femmes de Casquette* because they carried . . . chests containing marriage outfits. . . ." These wretched refugees were quartered on Ship Island while Bienville desperately tried to find husbands and lodging on the mainland. As Charles Sullivan comments in *The Mississippi Gulf Coast*, "Hundreds died as Bienville stood by helplessly."

Prior to the Civil War, the character of Biloxi changed markedly. A trading center under the British and Spanish, the town became one of the Mississippi coast's "Six Sisters," or summering locales. Wealthy cotton planters built fine vacation residences. Whole families would travel to Biloxi to spend the hot weather months amid the cooling ocean breezes. By 1838 the town was the largest of the "Sisters."

In 1848 a grand ball was held at the new Biloxi Hotel to mark the beginning of the "season." A reporter from the *New Orleans Daily Delta* wrote, "We have seen some of the Biloxi girls dance, they wear no curls nor corsets, and throw their entire souls into their substantial heels." It sounds like a good old time in Biloxi to this writer.

Nature heralded the arrival of the Civil War on the Mississippi coast with a furious hurricane. On September 14, 1860, a storm of incredible strength plowed head on into southern Mississippi. As recounted in *The Mississippi Gulf Coast*, a ship's captain arriving from New Orleans the next day described the destruction:

> The scene before us beggars description—not only are the wharves gone but the houses unroofed, and some blown down and entirely destroyed. . . . The whole beach, as far as the eye can reach, is one mass of wrack and ruin. A more desolate prospect I never beheld.

During the War Between the States, Biloxi Confederates resorted to guile in the face of a lack of supplies and munitions. In December of 1861, 18,000 Union soldiers landed on nearby Ship Island. They took possession of Fort Massachusetts, which had been abandoned by the Confederates, but were dissuaded from attacking Biloxi by a strong battery of cannon protecting the waterfront. Union scouts in small vessels had reported that this well-placed fortification would play havoc with the Northern gunboats. Finally, on New Year's Day, 1862, the federal navy stood in to Biloxi. No shots were heard from the

Confederate battery. Upon closer inspection the mollified Union forces realized that the so-called cannon were actually none other than black-painted logs. Biloxi quickly surrendered and was occupied on and off by Northern forces until the war's end. Ship Island remained a staging ground for federal offensives against New Orleans and the Alabama coast.

Following the war's conclusion, Biloxi looked more and more to the sea's harvest as a mainstay of the local economy. The invention of the ice machine and the introduction of European canning methods to New Orleans in 1867 provided the impetus that was to transform Biloxi into the United States' largest exporter of seafood.

The impact of the industry on the city was enormous. By 1885 a New Orleans newspaper reported that citizens of Biloxi were "losing their southern shabbiness . . . [and] taking on the . . . thrifty appearance of Eastern seashore cities." The seafood industry's demand for labor soon exceeded the local supply of workers, and the city received an influx of immigrants from Yugoslavia, Poland, and other European countries. These diverse immigrants enriched the city's cultural life.

In 1888, the rival Biloxi seafood companies began holding annual races between their fastest schooners. The competition was described as "fierce," with every crew clamping on maximum canvas and doing all in their power to cross the finish line ahead of their rivals. It does not require too much imagination to see these trials as the beginnings of Biloxi's yacht-racing tradition.

Having survived its twentieth-century hurricanes, Biloxi remains a city on the move. Visitors can still tie their lines to the city's facilities and gain a quick sense that here is a community with a great boating tradition. Pause a few moments in your cruise along the town waterfront and reflect on all those who have gone before you—the French, English, Confederates, and the young United States Navy. Their stories are more than fascinating.

The reader will appreciate that it has only been possible to present the briefest sketch of Biloxi's past in the above account. Those who would like to learn more about this venerable city are referred to Charles L. Sullivan's marvelous book *The Mississippi Gulf Coast*. The author presents the history of coastal Mississippi in a most readable and enjoyable manner which this writer can only envy.

Davis Bayou

A well-marked channel leads almost due east from unlighted daybeacon #24 on the principal Biloxi entrance channel to broad and shallow Davis Bayou. While most of the creek has depths of only 1 and 2 feet, the marked cut maintains minimum 5-foot soundings, with typical readings of 6 to 7 feet.

The Davis Bayou channel leads to a U.S. Park Service ferry dock. Tour boats leaving this channel carry visitors offshore to Ship Island and its historic fort. This battered piece of land will be reviewed in the next section of this chapter.

There are no services for cruising vessels on the Davis Bayou channel, but the cut does make for good gunk-holing. There are assorted attractive homes lining the northerly banks short of the Park Service dock. Mariners piloting boats 34 feet and smaller, with time on their hands, might consider exploring the bayou, while other cruisers will hurry on by to Biloxi and Ocean Springs.

Ocean Springs

The small community of Ocean Springs sits astride the Biloxi entrance channel northeast of flashing daybeacon #26. A marked channel leads to a canal that serves as the community waterfront. Minimum entrance depths are around 7 feet (assuming you can keep to the sparsely marked channel), while dockside soundings range from from 6 to 7 feet.

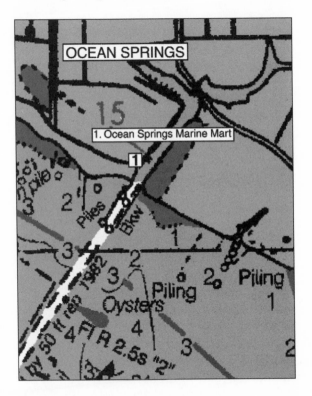

Cruisers entering the Ocean Springs canal will first catch sight of Ocean Springs Marine Mart on the northwestern banks near 30 24.208 North/088 49.418 West. This small, privately owned facility offers limited transient dockage, gasoline, diesel fuel, ice, snacks, bait, and cold drinks at a dockside variety store. Two slips are usually kept open for overnight visitors. Dockage is found at smaller, fixed wooden piers featuring 30- and 50-amp power connections and fresh-water hookups. No other services (such as showers) are available, and there are no restaurants or grocery stores within walking distance. All in all, Marine Mart is a bit on the primitive side, but we were given a warm welcome during our last visit, so if you don't mind docking well away from the beaten track, and the lack of shoreside amenities doesn't bother you, then give this facility a look.

Ocean Springs Marine Mart (228) 875-0072

Approach depth—7 feet
Dockside depth—6-7 feet
Accepts transients—yes (2 slips for visitors)
Transient-dockage rate—average
Fixed wooden piers—yes
Dockside power connections—30- and 50-amp
Dockside water connections—yes
Gasoline—yes
Diesel fuel—yes
Variety store—yes

A bit farther upstream the creek borders on a series of commercial fishing docks along the northwesterly banks. Here, you can often see several shrimping trawlers either unloading or simply resting from their labors.

Still farther along, the stream opens out to the northwest. This offshoot serves as the Ocean Springs city small-craft docks. While we were told a few years ago that visitors could sometimes find slip space here, that appears to no longer be the case. This time around, we have been unable to located anything in the way of a city dockmaster, despite repeated attempts. We conclude that all available slip

Ocean Springs Marine Mart

space in this city facility is now occupied by resident craft.

Biloxi Waterfront and Marina Facilities (Various Lats/Lons—see below)

The channel leading to Biloxi's waterfront cuts west-southwest at flashing daybeacon #26. North of unlighted daybeacon #26, Point Cadet Marina will come abeam near 30 23.349 North/088 51.573 West. This facility is owned by the Biloxi Port Commission and now sits in the heart of one of the largest gambling complexes on the Biloxi waterfront. Over 30 transient slips wait to greet visiting cruisers. Even so, advance reservations are accepted and encouraged by this writer. With this marina's popularity, wise skippers will most cer-

tainly want to make advance arrangements rather than risk disappointment upon arrival.

During our last stopover at Point Cadet in the fall of 2002, we found everything to be in reasonably good condition. However, we have received reports from numerous fellow cruisers that they found the marina to be in "not the best of repair" and that "the quality of the place has really deteriorated." So persistent have these comments become, we feel obligated to pass them along in this guidebook.

Point Cadet's entire dockage basin is surrounded by a thick, concrete breakwater. This barrier provides excellent protection from all winds and promises a secure night tucked snugly in your slip without unwelcome chop. Incidentally, concrete breakwater-enclosed

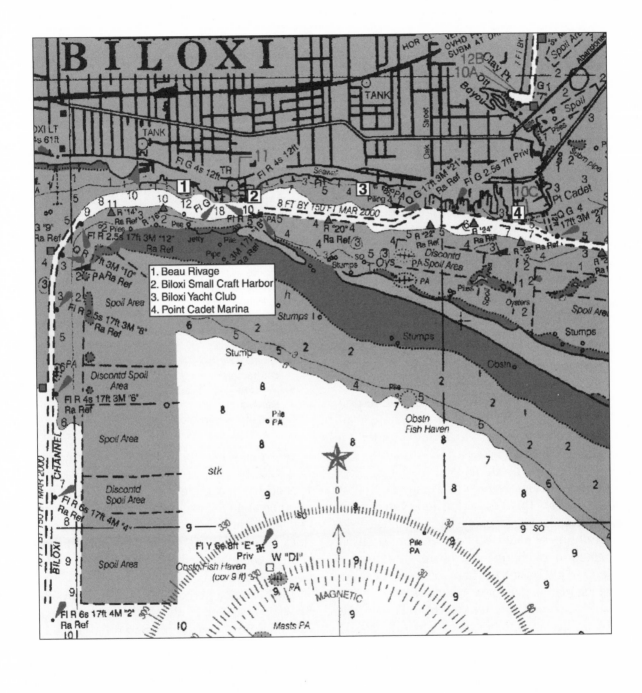

harbors are quickly becoming the standard on the Mississippi and Louisiana coastlines. To be sure, there are exceptions, but the relative lack of protected sidewaters often necessitates this sort of construction.

Overnight berths are provided at fixed, concrete-decked piers with all power and water connections. Depths in the enclosed harbor range from a minimum of 6½ to as much as 10 feet. That should be enough depth for most any pleasure craft short of the former *Trump Princess*.

Waste pump-out service is offered, and very good, air-conditioned shoreside showers and a climate-controlled Laundromat are readily at hand. Light mechanical repairs can be arranged through independent local contractors. Gorenflo's Tackle & Marina Store (228-432-7387) now occupies the second floor of the towerlike structure (readily visible from the harbor). This is a very cruiser-friendly store whose management seems to be quite responsive. Gasoline and diesel fuel are now available at an adjacent fuel dock under the auspices of Gorenflo's.

For more in-depth nautical shopping, check out Pitalo's Hardware (116 Cedar Street, 228-432-0381). This firm is located within a 2½-block walk of the dockage basin. Pitalo's carries a full line of nautical charts and an extensive selection of marine hardware. The store is located just behind the Catholic church. Ask any of the marina staff for walking directions.

It's also only a quick step from Point Cadet harbor to any number of the restaurants associated with the adjacent gambling casinos. Several offer spectacular buffets at very reasonable prices. Again, ask any of the friendly dockmasters for directions.

You will also discover a convenience store within 6 blocks of Point Cadet's docks, but you will probably need to hail a taxi for more serious grocery shopping. The nearest supermarket is several miles away.

Point Cadet Marina (228) 436-9312

Approach depth—10-12 feet
Dockside depth—6½-10 feet
Accepts transients—yes
Transient-dockage rate—average
Fixed concrete piers—yes
Dockside power connections—30- and 50-amp (plus a few 100-amp)
Dockside water connections—yes
Showers—yes
Laundromat—yes
Waste pump-out—yes
Gasoline—yes
Diesel fuel—yes
Mechanical repairs—light (independent local contractors)
Ship's store—on site and nearby (Pitalo's Hardware)
Restaurant—several nearby

Between Point Cadet and flashing daybeacon #21, the Biloxi waterfront is now overlooked by one huge gambling casino after another. With the exception of a few commercial shrimpers who are hanging on at the odd dock here and there, this portion of the Biloxi shoreline is scarcely recognizable from what it was a decade ago.

The Biloxi Yacht Club (30 23.479 North/088 52.419 West), yet another in the rather incredible chain of ultrafriendly and reliable yacht clubs along the Northern Gulf coastline, maintains a small complex along the northerly banks, a short hop west of flashing daybeacon #21. The amiable club manager has informed

Point Cadet Marina, Biloxi

Shrimper on the Biloxi waterfront

this writer that his club is glad to accept visitors from other yacht clubs who have appropriate reciprocal privileges in place. As space is somewhat tight, it would be a good idea to call ahead. Berths are cheerfully provided at fixed, wooden slips with 5½- to 6-foot minimum depths. Low-water soundings on the approach to the harbor run 6 to 8 feet. The docks are partially sheltered by wooden planks affixed vertically (side by side) along the southernmost pier. Nevertheless, this is not the spot to get caught in a really hard blow.

All slips feature 30-amp power connections and fresh-water hookups. Showers are available across the street in the well-appointed clubhouse. Lunch is served Tuesday through Friday from 11:30 to 1:30 P.M. Evening meals are available Wednesday and Friday nights only from 7:00 to 9:00.

Biloxi Yacht Club (228) 435-5455

Approach depth—6-8 feet (MLW)
Dockside depth—5½-6 feet (MLW)
Accepts transients—members of other yacht
   clubs with reciprocal privileges
Fixed wooden piers—yes
Dockside power connections—30-amp
Dockside water connections—yes
Showers—yes
Restaurant—on site (dining room)

A second, public pleasure-craft facility is available on the Biloxi waterfront north-north-west of flashing daybeacon #18, a short hop west of the Biloxi Yacht Club (near 30 23.468 North/088 53.000 West). The Biloxi Small Craft Harbor is found in a concrete-breakwater-enclosed basin on the northern banks. The two charted lights between #18 and unlighted

Biloxi Lighthouse

daybeacon #16 mark either side of the breakwater's entrance. This marina is also owned and managed by the Biloxi Port Commission.

None of the problems discussed above at Point Cadet Marina seem to be present at this facility. Thus, at least for the moment, we are now picking the Biloxi Small Craft Harbor as our marina of choice in Biloxi.

Transient dockage is readily available at a host of improved docks. Some are composed of fixed wooden piers, while other berths consist of wooden pilings set out from a concrete seawall. All feature full power and water connections. The surrounding breakwater gives good protection in all but the very heaviest weather. Depths in the harbor run from 6½ to as much as 10 feet. First-class, air-conditioned shoreside showers are available and visitors can ride the city trolley to and from Point Cadet to use the Laundromat there. Gasoline and diesel fuel can be purchased at Biloxi Bait and Fuel shop (228-436-6592), which is found to starboard just inside the dockage basin's entrance. Waste pump-out is available at this fuel dock as well as a small ship's and variety store. Minor mechanical repairs can sometimes be arranged through local independents.

The adjacent McElroy's Harbor House Restaurant (228-435-5001) is absolutely fabulous. This dining attraction has been a fixture in Biloxi for many years now, and it seems to just go on as it always has, oblivious of the monumental changes taking place around it.

McElroy's serves the *best* stuffed flounder that this writer has ever had the pleasure of enjoying. The entire dish seems to be marinated in some sort of buttery concoction. The result is a rich taste you are not likely ever to forget.

Beach Manor Inn (228-436-4361) is located just across the street from the small-craft dockage basin. This older, but still very nice, hostelry is ultraconvenient for those wanting to spend a night or two with dry land under their feet.

Visiting cruisers can reach the Big Star Supermarket via a two-block walk, while a convenience store is found within one block of the docks.

Biloxi Small Craft Harbor (228) 436-4062

Approach depth—10 feet plus
Dockside depth—6½-10 feet
Accepts transients—yes

Transient-dockage rate—average
Fixed concrete piers—yes
**Dockside power connections—15-, 30-, and 50-
    amp**
Dockside water connections—yes
Showers—yes
Waste pump-out—yes
Gasoline—yes
Diesel fuel—yes
**Mechanical repairs—limited (independent
    technicians)**
Ship's and variety store—yes
Restaurant—on site

Side by side with the Biloxi Small Craft Harbor, an adjacent breakwater encloses a commercial dockage basin reserved for local fishing vessels. While there are no facilities for pleasure craft, the many shrimpers and trawlers do make for a picturesque sight from the water.

Northeast of unlighted daybeacon #16, the behemoth Beau Rivage Casino overlooks the Biloxi Channel. An associated marina sits just east of the huge casino near 30 23.495 North/088 53.357 West. This is one of the dockage basins (mentioned above) where we have seldom seen any pleasure craft docked. Again, we suggest that you make use of the Biloxi Small Craft Harbor (see above), just to the east.

Downtown Biloxi

The Biloxi Visitor's Center (228-374-3105) is very convenient to the small-craft dockage basin, as is a goodly portion of the historic district. Visitors can shop and dine at a wide variety of establishments in what is often called the "Old Market" district. Many fine, old, Southern homes still grace downtown Biloxi. A walking tour of the district is highly recommended. Inquire at the marina office for directions to the Visitor's Center. Here you can acquire a map which will facilitate your visit to the district.

In March many of Biloxi's private homes are open during the "Gulf Coast Pilgrimage." If you happen to be in the area during this time, be sure to take advantage of this most noteworthy event.

Biloxi Lighthouse

The Biloxi waterfront channel begins to curl back around to the south at the western tip of the Deer Island shoals. Eventually the cut leads to the deeper waters of Mississippi Sound to the south. At flashing daybeacon #12, located in the middle of the southerly turn, passing mariners will have an excellent view of the historic Biloxi Lighthouse.

Originally lit in 1824, the light today stands in the midst of the Highway 90 median. It may be the most "seen" lighthouse in the United States.

The Biloxi Lighthouse is built of brick and is surrounded by a cast-iron shell. The unusual construction has kept the lighthouse standing through a host of violent hurricanes.

Following the Civil War, the Biloxi Lighthouse was painted black for a time. Some years later a tale arose that this color was to commemorate the death of Abraham Lincoln. As Bruce Roberts and Ray Jones comment in *Southern Lighthouses,* "It is an unlikely story, especially when one considers that from the tower you can see Beauvoir, the home of Jefferson Davis who, as president of the Confederacy, was Lincoln's most implacable enemy."

From 1867 to 1920 the Biloxi Lighthouse had one of the only female keepers ever stationed at a light in the Southern states. Maria Youghans finally retired in 1920 only after her daughter agreed to take over her duties.

Ocean Springs Yacht Club

From unlighted daybeacon #31, the charted channel leading to the Back Bay of Biloxi runs on to the northwest and soon approaches a 40-foot (closed vertical clearance) bascule bridge. Just short of this span, the good folks at Ocean Springs Yacht Club (228-875-1917) have built a small but nice clubhouse guarding the northeasterly banks. At the present time, this facility only has a single, fixed wooden pier at which low-water depths run only 3 to 3½ feet. There is usually a family dinner on Wednesday evenings and a "cook your own steak" barbecue Friday nights. You will seldom find a warmer cruising crowd than at Ocean Springs.

Ott Bayou Facilities

Captains cruising between the three Plummer Point bridges spanning the channel leading to Back Bay will notice an alternate cut leading southwest, just short of the northernmost span (the railway bridge). This passage holds 10-foot depths and leads to Ott Bayou, south of Clay Point. While this small stream is mostly commercial in nature, two boatyards offer some repair services for pleasure craft. Both yards are located on the bayou's northern banks, west of unlighted daybeacon #7.

First up is Bay Marine Boatworks (228-432-2992). Full below-waterline, haul-out repairs (60-ton travelift) are offered. Just next door, cruisers will find Rebel Boat Works (228-435-2762). This large, informal yard offers haul-out, fiberglass, and marine carpentry repairs. The firm's travelift is rated at 35 tons.

While entering Ott Bayou, yet another huge casino will be obvious along the southerly shoreline. This outfit is called the Palace, and it has an adjacent marina. There was not a single boat docked here during out last visit.

Old Fort Bayou 30 25.141 North/088 49.838 West

Old Fort Bayou flows from the eastern banks of Biloxi Back Bay north of unlighted nun buoy #2, itself just north of the Plummer Point railway bridge. This stream is lined by heavy residential development on its southern banks. The northern shores are undeveloped marsh. Many of the homes along the creek have private docks, which host a whole fleet of resident pleasure craft. While boats drawing less than 4½ feet can cautiously explore the bayou, there is only one real opportunity for overnight anchorage, and this spot is not terribly sheltered, plus the surrounding waters support a whole passel of small-craft traffic.

The marked Old Fort channel leads from #2 first to the north and then sharply east into the

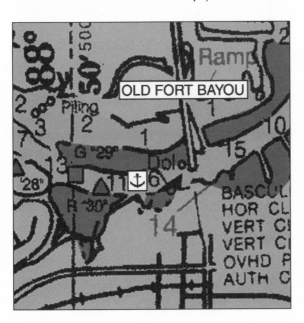

creek. Minimum depths in the marked channel are only 5 feet or so. Outside of the channel, depths rise almost immediately to grounding levels. It's all too easy to miss a marker or cut a corner unintentionally and find yourself in 2 feet of water.

East of unlighted daybeacon #30, the bayou begins its approach to a new 20-foot bascule bridge (seldom, if ever, opened anymore) spanning the creek. High ground fronts the southern banks. The waters immediately west and east of the bridge make for a fair overnight stop. Of course, sailcraft or powerboats that can't clear the 20-foot span must settle for the western haven. Protection is good from southern winds and adequate for northerly and easterly breezes. Strong blows from the west call for another strategy. Try anchoring near 30 25.141 North/088 49.838 West.

Cruisers should also be advised that there is a very active public launching ramp on the northern banks of Old Fort Bayou, immediately east of the 20-foot bridge. During weekends especially, all the comings and goings can make these waters anything but a quiet, secluded anchorage.

While it is not the ideal overnight stop, Old Fort Bayou can boast of being the anchorage closest to Biloxi. While there are better havens to the west on Back Bay, they are a long cruise away. If you prefer to anchor off and don't want to cruise far from the Biloxi waterfront, Old Fort could be a consideration. Just make sure to exercise plenty of caution when entering or leaving the creek!

Back Bay of Biloxi
(Various Lats/Lons—see below)

The main body of Back Bay stretches west from Old Fort Bayou for some 7 nautical miles to the intersection with Big Lake and the Biloxi

River. While much of the bay is shallow, a deep, well-buoyed channel allows for relatively easy passage by most sizes of pleasure craft. This cut is used regularly by commercial tugs entering and leaving the Industrial Seaway beyond Big Lake. As you might expect, the channel receives the best of care.

Back Bay is spanned by two bridges. The easterly Highway 110 (D'Iberville) twin spans clear the water by 60 feet, while the Pops Ferry Road bascule bridge has 25 feet of closed vertical clearance. Fortunately, the latter span opens on demand.

While there is an almost total lack of anchorages and marina facilities open to the general public east of Big Lake and Bernard Bayou, a cruise through Back Bay can make for a very pleasant day on the water. The shoreline alternates between patches of light development and completely natural stretches. West of D'Iberville, the bay borders on Keesler Army Base along the southern shoreline. Several interesting buildings and a marina serving service personnel only are visible from the water, including a large, hospital-like structure south of unlighted daybeacon #19.

Pops Ferry Fish Camp (30 24.868 North/088 58.590 West, 228-388-9980), sporting a small collection of fixed wooden piers, is located on the bay's southern shore just east of the Pops Ferry Road 25-foot bascule bridge. There is a bar and bait shop on the premises. Gasoline can be purchased dockside. Depths run from 5 to 6 feet and there should be enough room for one 30-footer to squeeze in. No overnight accommodations are available.

This writer has always been rather taken with the cruising conditions on the Back Bay of Biloxi. Seen in the golden sunlight of a late spring afternoon, it is one of the loveliest bodies of water on the Mississippi coast. With its collection of good anchorages, many captains will want to include this most attractive body of water in their cruising itineraries.

Biloxi River Anchorage
(30 25.756 North/088 58.959 West)

Biloxi River opens into the northeastern corner of Big Lake, just west of the Pops Ferry Road bascule bridge. This stream has minimum depths of 15 feet, but the marina that used to grace its shores and the isolated anchorage a bit farther upstream are no more. Where once there were undeveloped banks, extensive and rather palatial residential development now graces the eastern shoreline. The old location of Wicks Marina and Fish Camp has been more or less swallowed up in this explosion of development.

There is still good anchorage on these waters, however. One great spot is found just as the river begins to angle to the northwest, near 30 25.756 North/088 58.959 West. Here cruisers can pitch out the hook in 11 to 12 feet of water abeam of an absolutely sumptuous homeplace guarding the northeasterly banks. This anchorage certainly allows cruisers to take a gander at how the upper crust lives.

Farther upstream, Biloxi River sounding notations on chart 11372 cease. As always under these conditions, we strongly suggest you leave these waters to local captains who understand what the channel is doing this week.

Big Lake

Big Lake is a very shallow body of water where depths of 1 to 2 feet are the norm. Happily, the buoyed Industrial Seaway channel cuts a well-defined path from east to west

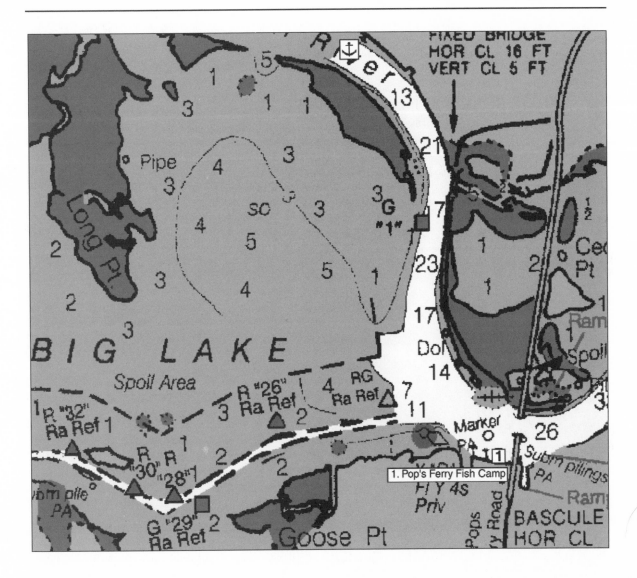

across the lake. No boat, large or small, should attempt to explore the waters of Big Lake outside of the Seaway channel.

Bernard Bayou
(Various Lats/Lons—see below)

The creek known as Bernard Bayou cuts a C-shaped track west and then north from Big Lake's southwesterly corner to an intersection with the Industrial Seaway near flashing daybeacon #5. This surprising stream is chock-full of overnight anchorages and one full-service boatyard. Is that enough reason to cruise this far from the beaten path? It is for me!

Beautiful homeplace and yacht on Biloxi River

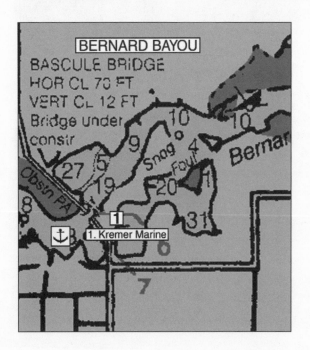

Depths on Bernard Bayou range from a few brief 6-foot soundings near its easterly entrance to an astonishing 30 feet or better. Over the course of the stream's path, there are many baylike patches of water which afford wonderfully protected anchorage. Except for the waters immediately adjacent to the Cowan Road, 28-foot fixed bridge, there simply isn't a bad place to anchor on Bernard Bayou. All you need to do is pick a spot to your liking with enough swinging room for your particular craft and settle back for an unforgettable evening tucked snugly into one of the safest havens on the Mississippi coastline.

Be sure to take the deep depths of the bayou into account when deciding whether to drop the hook. Remember, if you anchor in depths of 20 feet, you should pay out at least 120 feet of anchor rode for a minimally acceptable 6-to-1 anchor scope. If swinging room seems to be a bit of a problem, consider making use of a Bahamian mooring.

One of our favorite Bernard Bayou overnight stops will be discovered on the waters southwest of the 28-foot bridge. Of course, unless you intend to take the long way around via the Industrial Seaway, you must be able to clear this span. Anyway, try anchoring near 30 24.261 North/089 01.750 West, in about 18 feet of water. The surrounding shores exhibit some light development, but there is superb shelter from foul weather.

The shoreline of Bernard Bayou runs the full spectrum from totally natural stretches to banks overlooked by heavy, but appealing, residential development. The creek does support a large volume of small craft boating traffic, particularly on weekends. Cruising vessels anchored on the bayou could be awakened early in the morning by passing speedboats.

The large Kremer Marine (228-896-1629) complex juts out from the southern shores of Bernard Bayou just short of the 12-foot bascule bridge at facility designation #7 on chart 11372 (near 30 24.294 North/089 01.602 West). The dockage basin is located in the charted, square cove to the south of the main stream.

Minimum approach depths run around 6½ feet, but the unmarked channel can be tricky for first-timers. Soundings at the inner harbor's wet slips improve to 9+-foot levels.

Unfortunately, transients are not accepted for overnight or temporary dockage at Kremer Marine. The friendly management has informed this writer that few visiting cruisers have heretofore made the 10-nautical-mile trek from the Gulf to their docks, so all slip space is reserved for resident craft.

Kremer offers full haul-out and (gasoline) mechanical repair services. A large crane (50-ton capacity) and marine railway (100-ton capacity) can haul boats up to 100 feet long. The accommodating management can put skippers in need of diesel engine repairs in touch with nearby mechanics. The shoreside repairs and servicing facilities are top-notch. The two large work barns fronting Bernard Bayou are particularly impressive.

Industrial Seaway

The Biloxi Industrial Seaway canal cuts into the southwestern corner of Big Lake near unlighted daybeacon #36. This deep, artificial stream runs west to several huge barge-loading facilities. While there are no facilities for pleasure craft or spots to anchor on the seaway, some captains may decide to cruise the canal anyway just for the sights.

It should also be noted that Bernard Bayou makes its way into the Industrial Seaway east of flashing daybeacon #5. If you cruise up the industrial canal, you may choose to return to Back Bay by way of this lovely stream.

SHIP ISLAND TO LAKE BORGNE NAVIGATION

There are two terms that aptly describe the waters surrounding the city of Biloxi: "shallow," and "well-marked channels." As this description implies, shoal depths are the standard in and around Biloxi. A vast network of channels crisscrosses the regional waters and allows for ready passage by most sizes of pleasure craft. Visiting mariners *must* remember to exercise great caution in keeping to the marked cuts or a close encounter of the ground kind could be the unpleasant and immediate result. There is a fair amount of current on these waters, so be alert for lateral leeway. Be sure to watch the markers over your stern as well as the course ahead to catch any slippage.

Otherwise, generally speaking, navigational cruising conditions on the waters of Biloxi are nearly ideal. Keep alert, maintain your usual watch on the sounder, and you should not have undue difficulty unless really heavy weather makes an appearance.

Entrance from the ICW   Westbound cruisers on the Gulf Coast ICW can connect with Biloxi's eastern entrance channel west of flashing daybeacon #8. A cut to the north will lead you between Biloxi's southernmost aids to navigation, flashing daybeacon #2 and unlighted daybeacon #1. This cut runs first north and then northwest for almost 7 nautical miles on its way to the intersection of the three principal Biloxi channels at flashing daybeacon #26. Do not approach #26 closely. This aid apparently marks a sunken wreck.

As you approach flashing daybeacon #26, slow down and sort out the various aids to navigation. The sea of markers can be a real source of confusion. Have chart 11372 ready at hand to quickly resolve any questions. Be sure to positively identify the channel that you want to follow before leaving #26.

The southerly section of the eastern entrance channel is well outlined by numerous daybeacons and buoys. Caution must be exercised to keep to the marked passage, particularly between flashing daybeacons #18 and #26. This portion of the channel borders on shoal water. Depths outside of the cut quickly rise to 4-foot levels. Be on guard against leeway.

Eastbound ICW mariners can save a good chunk of distance by making use of the marked entrance channel west of Deer Island. This cut has minimum 6-foot depths and is generally easy to follow. Again, keep to the channel. Depths outside of the buoyed route are suspect.

To reach the *western* entrance channel from the ICW, set a course from flashing daybeacon #S to come between flashing daybeacon #2 and unlighted daybeacon #1. These latter two aids denote the southern genesis of the western entrance cut.

Continue following the plentiful daybeacons on the western channel until coming between flashing daybeacon #10 and unlighted daybeacon #9. At this point, the passage begins a slow turn to the east and passes around the western tip of the shoals running out from Deer Island. By the time you come abeam of unlighted daybeacon #14 to its northerly quarter, your turn to the east will be complete. The Biloxi waterfront channel will be spread out before you to the east. The city will lie to your north, while Deer Island will flank you to the south. Our discussion will now return to the eastern entrance channel and its auxiliary passages.

Davis Bayou The heavily marked Davis Bayou channel can be entered by cruising east from unlighted daybeacon #24. Captains piloting pleasure craft of any normal size should have no trouble following the cut as far as the Park Service ferry docks.

Discontinue your exploration of Davis Bayou once abeam of the Park Service piers. Farther upstream, depths go to 4 feet or less.

Ocean Springs The channel leading to Ocean Springs strikes northeast from flashing daybeacon #26. To enter the cut, proceed northwest on the Biloxi entrance channel for some 25 yards past #26. Then turn sharply to the northeast and set course to come abeam of flashing daybeacon #2 fairly close to its northwesterly side. Once abeam of #2, continue straight ahead into the harbor entrance.

During our last visit to Ocean Springs, we sighted a pair of unlighted and unnumbered daybeacons marking the entrance into the Ocean Springs Small Craft Harbor. As you have almost certainly guessed, keep the red marker off your starboard side and take its green counterpart to port.

Once the harbor entrance is in your wake, favor the northwesterly (port-side) shores. Soon the wet slips associated with Ocean Springs Marine Mart will be sighted, also to port. Check here for any available transient dockage.

Biloxi Waterfront Channel The channel leading west-southwest from flashing daybeacon #26 to the principal Biloxi waterfront is the most heavily used of the three cuts. This passage is clearly outlined by numerous daybeacons. Use these aids to stay in the improved passage. Again, depths outside of the channel rise dramatically.

From #26, turn to the west-southwest and point to pass unlighted daybeacon #35 to its southerly side. Continue on course by passing all subsequent red aids to their northerly quarters and all green beacons to their southerly sides.

At flashing daybeacon #30, the channel turns more to the west. Point Cadet Marina will come abeam to the north at unlighted daybeacon #26. As you approach flashing daybeacon #27, a semisunken trawler will be sighted south of the channel. The waterfront cut continues to be well marked and easily followed as you cruise farther to the west.

Back Bay Channel A relatively wide channel strikes northwest from flashing daybeacon #26 toward the waters of Biloxi Back Bay. As you are still "returning" from the Gulf of Mexico, the old "red, right, returning" rule is still in force and remains so all the way to and through the Industrial Seaway.

After leaving unlighted daybeacon #31 behind, the Back Bay channel begins its approach to the Plummer Point triple bridges. It is a run of .5 nautical miles between #31 and the first of the spans. While the channel is not terribly narrow along this stretch, you should guard against wandering too far from the marked cut. Outside of the channel, 4-foot waters are waiting to greet your keel.

The first of the Plummer Point spans is the Highway 90 Bridge with 40 feet of closed vertical clearance. Sailcraft that need more height will be glad to know that this span opens on demand.

Next up is an abandoned highway bridge. The center section of this span has been removed to allow passage by boats and ships, but the remainder of the old structure has been left in place for the local fishing crowd.

Finally, the northernmost bridge consists of a railway span with 14 feet of closed vertical clearance. This overpass is usually open unless a train is due, in which case it tends to be closed.

Ott Bayou Channel   The marked channel leading to Ott Bayou strikes southwest between the abandoned Plummer Point highway bridge and the railroad span. To enter the cut, come abeam of and pass unlighted daybeacon #1 to its immediate northerly side. Continue on the same course, pointing to come abeam of unlighted daybeacon #3, also to its northerly quarter.

At #3 the Ott Bayou cut takes a sharp swing to the south. Continue cruising southwest past #3 for some 25 yards and then swing south and point to pass unlighted daybeacon #5 to its westerly side. Moving farther to the south, you should catch sight of unlighted daybeacon #7 ahead. The wide entrance to Ott Bayou will open out to the west just before reaching #7.

On the Back Bay Channel   Once through the Plummer Point railroad bridge, point to come abeam of unlighted nun buoy #2 to its southerly side. Don't attempt the small charted but unmarked channel leading west, south of unlighted daybeacon #3. On-site research revealed only 4 feet (or less) of water here.

Old Fort Bayou   The marked channel leading first north and then east into Old Fort Bayou leaves the main Back Bay route at unlighted nun buoy #2. Remember that this cut has minimum depths of only 5 feet and it is no strain at all to ease out of the channel into 2 feet of water. If you decide to enter the creek anyway, take your time, don't cut any corners, and watch the sounder like a hawk.

To enter Old Fort Bayou, pass #2 to its fairly immediate easterly side and point to come abeam of Old Fort's southernmost aid, unlighted daybeacon #4, to its immediate westerly side.

North of #4 the channel is reasonably easy to follow until it passes between unlighted daybeacons #7 and #8. These two aids are anchored in the waters hard by Fort Point. Past #7 and #8 the channel begins to bend to the east.

Enter Old Fort Bayou by passing unlighted daybeacon #14 to its immediate northerly side and pointing upstream to come abeam of unlighted daybeacon #16 to its northeasterly side.

With appropriate caution, you can follow the marked channel up Old Fort Bayou past #16 to the bascule bridge. This span has a closed vertical clearance of 20 feet.

East of the bascule span all markings cease. However, good depths continue for some distance upstream. Cruising craft should discontinue their explorations before reaching the charted hairpin turn.

On Back Bay Channel   At unlighted nun buoy #2, the channel traversing Back Bay takes a sharp turn to the west. From #2 to flashing daybeacon #7, the channel follows a dredged track. Depths outside of the cut are 3 to 4 feet or less. Stay within the markers and watch for leeway.

At flashing daybeacon #7 the Back Bay channel cuts to the northwest, skirts the westerly marshes of Big Island, and hurries on toward the D'Iberville/I-110 bascule bridge. Before reaching this span, a whole series of charted dolphins lines the cut's southwesterly flank. Be very sure to pass *north* of these piles!

East of the D'Iberville span, a portion of an old low-level bridge has been left in place, but there is a wide passage between the structure's remaining arms. A power line with 85 feet of vertical clearance spans the channel just west of the old bridge. The tall, skeletal, steel supporting towers are a striking sight from the water.

The D'Iberville Bridge has a *closed* vertical clearance of 60 feet. It is surprising that a bridge of this height is not a fixed structure. Apparently the swinging span was introduced to accommodate the heavy commercial traffic entering and leaving the Industrial Seaway to the west.

West of the Highway 110 (D'Iberville) Bridge, the Back Bay channel leading to Big Lake and the Biloxi River becomes much broader and markers are less numerous. Some visiting cruisers may want to run short compass/GPS courses between the various aids to navigation to minimize any chance of finding the charted shallows to the north or south. Even if this procedure does not recommend itself to you, be sure to pick out and identify the various markers as you go along. Have chart 11372 nearby to resolve any conflicts.

A short hop west-southwest of unlighted daybeacon #16, passing cruisers may spot what appears to be a marina on the southerly banks. This is actually a recreational area for military personnel stationed at Keesler Army Base. No facilities or dockage are available to private pleasure boats.

At unlighted daybeacon #23 the broad Back Bay channel takes a slow turn to the southwest and then bends west as it flows under the Pops Ferry Road Bridge. This span has a closed vertical clearance of 25 feet and opens on demand.

West of the Pops Ferry Bridge, the channel splits just east of the charted, unlighted junction daybeacon. By turning northeast of this aid to navigation, cruisers can find their way to Biloxi River.

Biloxi River   Favor the easterly shoreline when entering the Biloxi River, but don't approach the banks too closely. Stay to the east of the river's one aid to navigation, unlighted daybeacon #1, and you should not have any difficulty. As chart 11372 clearly indicates, there is shoal water west of #1.

Good depths continue on the Biloxi River at least until high ground begins to front the eastern banks. This is *the* prime anchorage on the Biloxi River. Depth soundings are not noted on chart 11372 upstream of this point. For this reason, the upper reaches of the Biloxi River are not recommended for cruising-sized craft.

Big Lake   Water depths average between 1 and 2 feet on Big Lake; following the marked channel is encouraged. Enter the Big Lake channel by passing just to the south of the red and green unlighted junction daybeacon. The remainder of the Big

Lake passage is amply marked by unlighted daybeacons. Wise navigators will study chart 11372 before running the cut.

West-northwest of unlighted daybeacon #36, captains can choose to continue following the marked cut to the Industrial Seaway or cut west into Bernard Bayou.

Bernard Bayou   Bernard Bayou is a truly delightful stream with few shallows to worry with. Cruisers staying anywhere near the centerline should find more than ample water under their keel.

Leave the Big Lake channel after passing unlighted daybeacon #36. One small stretch of 6-foot soundings is found abeam of the first marshy offshoot on the southerly banks. This is the shallowest portion of the creek (excepting a few shoal sidewaters).

The charted cove south of the semisunken wreck is quite shallow and should not be entered by any vessel larger than a kayak. Even outboards may well find the bottom.

After passing the second charted, partially submerged wreck, the entrance to Kremer Marine will be spotted on the southern banks. At the present time, this facility's entrance channel is unmarked. Heavily favor the starboard-side banks as you cruise southwest and then south into the dockage basin.

Bernard Bayou runs southwest from Kremer Marine under a new fixed bridge with 28 feet of vertical clearance. Vessels that need more clearance must enter Bernard Bayou by way of its northerly intersection with the Industrial Seaway (see below), east of flashing daybeacon #5.

West of the just-described bridge, the stream's course is bisected by a small island. Be sure to pass to the north of this land mass.

Farther to the west, the bayou bends to the north and follows a winding path to the Industrial Seaway. This portion of the stream contains a number of baylike bodies of water that make excellent overnight anchorages. For best depths, drop anchor near the middle.

West of flashing daybeacon #3 on the Industrial Seaway, the waters of Bernard Bayou and this commercial waterway meet. Depths are questionable across this opening, and cruising craft would be wise to continue following Bernard Bayou until it joins the Seaway near flashing daybeacon #5.

Industrial Seaway   This passage is comprised of a long, man-made canal with deep, carefully controlled depths. Pleasure craft should encounter few navigational problems on the passage.

At flashing daybeacon #5, the channel crosses a larger, lake-like body of water. Pass #5 to its northerly side for best depths.

Eventually the channel cuts a bit to the southwest. Point to come abeam of flashing daybeacon #9 to its northerly side.

West of #9, you will pass several additional barge-loading wharves and a commercial fuel dock. West of flashing daybeacon #13, the Industrial Seaway finally plays out. Some 5-foot depths are encountered on the extreme westerly portion of the canal.

Ship Island to Lake Borgne

The western reaches of Mississippi Sound continue the wide-open Waterway cruising so prevalent to the east. A scant two additional barrier islands buffer the sound from the open waters of the Gulf of Mexico. Again, seas can be more than a little choppy. Fortunately, there are several reliable ports of call along the way in which one can take shelter.

From the foot of the easterly Biloxi entrance channel, the Waterway follows a straight stretch to the prolifically marked Gulfport entrance cut. This channel leads north to Gulfport Harbor and south to Ship Island Pass. This pass is quite reliable and heavily used by pleasure craft, commercial fishing vessels, and even oceangoing ships. It is one of the most reliable seaward passages on Mississippi Sound.

The thriving city of Gulfport maintains a concrete breakwater-enclosed triple-basin harbor. The eastern basin offers full services for cruising craft, including new shower facilities and snug overnight dockage.

A short jump farther to the west, visiting cruisers may choose to enter the Long Beach small-craft harbor. This small facility also offers transient dockage.

Situated just east of St. Louis Bay, Pass Christian offers very protected overnight berths in a community that is steeped in the history of American yachting. Many cruisers will want to include a stop at this port of call for this reason alone.

St. Louis Bay (also known as Bay St. Louis) presents the largest selection of off-the-beaten-path cruising opportunities on western Mississippi Sound. Featuring a single, decrepit marina facility, but many overnight anchorages and a friendly yacht club, this body of water has been largely bypassed by visiting cruisers up to this time. This writer hopes that, after reading the account of Bay St. Louis presented in its own subsection at the end of the chapter, you will help to reverse that trend.

The Gulf Coast ICW finally traverses the so-called Grand Island Channel and leaves Mississippi Sound at St. Joe Pass. To the west is an equally wide open water, Lake Borgne. The waters south of the westernmost section of Mississippi Sound are a maze of islands and shoals which are best avoided by visiting cruisers. The channels are a nightmarish maze and are largely unmarked.

Broadwater Resort Marina (Standard Mile 81) (30 23.344 North/088 57.815 West)

Some 7.7 nautical miles northwest of flashing daybeacon #S on the ICW, a long, marked channel leads north to Broadwater Resort Marina. In times past, this writer used to recommend Broadwater without reservation. Now, however, a large, semi-floating gambling casino (President Casino) has been located in the concrete-breakwater-enclosed harbor, and the emphasis seems to have shifted from pleasure craft to gaming.

Broadwater does retain the advantage of being within walking distance of the Beauvoir Mansion, last homeplace of Jefferson Davis, president of the ill-starred Southern Confederacy. In addition to Beauvoir, Broadwater Beach allows visitors one of the few opportunities to view some of the other magnificent, privately owned historic homes on Mississippi's "Miracle Parkway," Highway 90.

This facility is actually located only a short automobile ride from the Biloxi historic district. By renting a car or taking a taxi, visitors can tour this attraction as well.

Broadwater Beach Resort Marina features a well-marked entrance channel with 10- to 12-foot depths. Similarly impressive readings are found dockside.

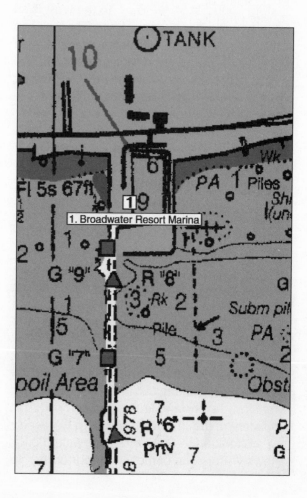

Broadwater's dockage basin is enclosed by a high, well-built concrete breakwater. Heavy weather should never be a problem in any blow short of a hurricane.

Overnight berths are provided at modern, fixed concrete piers with 30- and 50-amp power hookups and fresh-water connections. The vast majority of these slips are covered, with only a few open berths for sailcraft. There are three sets of shoreside showers, but only the units located in the dockmaster's building are climate controlled. There is also an on-site Laundromat. Full fueling and waste pump-out services are available. Mechanical repairs can sometimes be arranged through local, independent contractors.

Cruisers in need of supplies will find a convenience store within easy walking distance. The nearest supermarket is some 1½ miles from the dockage basin, but courtesy transportation to and from this facility is cheerfully provided by the marina staff.

Broadwater Beach Resort Marina is found just across Highway 90 from the marina complex. Captains and crews desiring a respite from their voyages can abandon their vessels for a night or two and recharge their cruising batteries ashore. The hotel features four swimming pools, adjoining tennis courts, plus workout and game rooms. Courtesy transportation is provided to a nearby world-class golf course.

Hungry cruisers can check out any of the three restaurants in the adjacent President Casino. Several other dining choices can be accessed by way of a long walk along Highway 90.

Broadwater Beach Resort Marina (228) 385-4097

Approach depth—10-12 feet

Dockside depth—10-12 feet
Accepts transients—yes
Transient-dockage rate—above average
Fixed concrete piers—yes
Dockside power connections—30- and 50-amp
Dockside water connections—yes
Showers—yes
Laundromat—yes
Waste pump-out—yes
Gasoline—yes
Diesel fuel—yes
Mechanical repairs—yes (independent
   contractors)
Restaurant—3 on site

Beauvoir

In 1877, ten years after his release from federal prison, Jefferson Davis, first and last president of the Confederate States of America, retired to a beautiful mansion overlooking Mississippi Sound. The estate was named Beauvoir, which means "beautiful view." While visiting with the home's former owner, Davis became so enraptured with the "view" that he bought the house and grounds.

Jefferson Davis lived at Beauvoir until his death in 1889. During that time he wrote his authoritative *The Rise and Fall of the Confederate Government* and *History of the Confederate States of America.* By most accounts the former president was happy at Beauvoir, even though the failure of the Confederacy was most certainly to haunt him until the end of his days.

Broadwater Beach Resort Marina and President Casino

Little Dog Keys Pass (Standard Mile 84)

The inlet known as Little Dog Keys Pass lies west of Dog Keys Pass, just off the shoals radiating out from the easterly tip of Ship Island. Do not attempt to use this inlet. It is pocked with shoals and is *completely* unmarked. Instead, use Dog Keys Pass to the east or, preferably, the Gulfport/Ship Island Pass inlet to the west.

Ship Island and Fort Massachusetts (Standard Mile 73) (Various Lats/Lons—see below)

Ship Island sits almost due south of Biloxi and has figured prominently in the history of the community. Today the island is part of the Gulf Islands National Seashore and is protected from development. Regular ferry service is provided between May and October from Davis Bayou, near Biloxi, to Fort Massachusetts near the island's western tip.

In response to English attacks during the War of 1812, then U.S. Secretary of War Jefferson Davis ordered the construction of Fort Twiggs on Ship Island in 1856 to defend the vital inlet passage to Biloxi. This structure was never completed and the island was abandoned by the Confederates and occupied by Union forces early in 1861. The fort was renamed "Massachusetts" and was used as a prison and staging ground for Union attacks, most notably on New Orleans, until the end of the war.

In 1969 Hurricane Camille roared into nearby Pass Christian. The great storm's backlash cut Ship Island in half, leaving a mile-wide swath of waters between the two land masses. The island to the west was renamed Western Ship Island, while the other is (you guessed it) Eastern Ship Island.

Navigators can easily locate Fort Massa-chusetts on Western Ship Island by the designation "Old Fort" just west of the old Ship Island Light Tower, clearly charted on 11372.

The park service has built a long pier that juts out from the island into the sound's deeper waters. Private craft are allowed to dock at the pier, but it's none too easy. Most of the available space is set aside for the various tour boats that bring landlubbers to the fort. Signs on the dock warn that portions are reserved for these vessels. Depths on the outer one-fifth of the pier run from 8 to as much as 15 feet. However, just a trifle closer to shore, soundings shelve upward rapidly to 3 feet. If you can't find space near the northerly end of the pier, it would be far better to anchor in the correctly charted 20+-foot waters north of the dock (near 30 12.916 North/088 58.394 West) and dinghy ashore or into the pier.

For a slightly more secure anchorage, try the waters north of the shallows lying west of Fort Massachusetts, near 30 12.840 North/088 58.871 West. Shoals strike north at least as far as chart 11372 would indicate. Be sure to drop your hook well short of this thin water. This spot affords some shelter from light to lower-moderate southerly winds, but it is wide open to all other airs. There is not really enough shelter for an overnight stay unless there is nary a mention of foul weather or thunderstorms in the forecast.

Snacks, some light food, souvenirs, and, most importantly, ice can be purchased at the concession booth inside Fort Massachusetts. Who would have ever thought you could replenish the icebox this far from the mainland?

Ship Island Pass Inlet (Standard Mile 73)

The heavily marked channel leading north

to Gulfport flows south into the Gulf of Mexico via Ship Island Pass. This cut lies just off the westerly tip of Ship Island and is intersected by the east-to-west-flowing ICW passage between flashing daybeacons #42 and #44. Both #42 and #44 are aids to navigation on the Gulfport/Ship Island channel, not the Intracoastal Waterway. Minimum 25-foot depths are maintained amid the Gulfport-Ship Island channel's host of lighted buoys and daybeacons. In a situation very similar to the Pascagoula channel, many large ships make use of Ship Island Pass on a regular basis. The cut is carefully maintained. Visiting cruisers can enter or put to sea from Ship Island Pass with as much confidence as can ever be mustered when running an inlet.

Cat Island

Cat Island is the last of the major Mississippi Sound land buffers. While its shores are a most attractive mix of white sand beaches and sparse maritime forest, the land mass is surrounded by extensive shoals to the north, south, and west. Unfortunately, given these navigational difficulties, this writer suggests that a visit to one of the other Mississippi Sound barrier islands would be more appropriate.

Gulfport (Standard Mile 73) (30 21.709 North/089 05.233 West)

The city of Gulfport shares honors with Pascagoula as coastal Mississippi's most successful commercial port. For pleasure cruisers, there is an excellent small-craft harbor offering full services, including ultraprotected dockage, good dining, and even a trained-dolphin show.

Numbers to know in Gulfport:

Sun Cab—228-832-3891
Yellow Cab—228-863-1511
Budget Car Rental—228-864-5181
Enterprise Rent-A-Car—228-868-6004
Hertz—228-863-2761

The ICW meets up with the Gulfport channel well west of the Waterway's flashing daybeacon #2, about halfway between the Ship Island Pass channel's flashing daybeacons #42 and #44.

It is a run of 5.9 nautical miles northwest from the ICW-Gulfport Channel intersection to the small-craft harbor. While this is a somewhat lengthy journey, it is typical of the voyages necessary to reach shelter from the Waterway's passage through Mississippi Sound.

Study chart 11372 for a moment and you will see that Gulfport actually has three harbors. The larger, middle basin is geared to jumbo-size, commercial shipping and a large gambling ship. While there are no facilities for pleasure boats, an idle-speed cruise through this harbor often yields fascinating sight-seeing.

The western dockage basin is home to Gulfport's commercial fishing fleet. As you would expect, no facilities are available for cruising boats, though the particularly genial types among us might be able to purchase some diesel fuel or ice. As these services are available in the easterly basin, few pleasure craft will need to make the effort.

The Gulfport Small Craft Harbor occupies the eastern dockage basin. This haven fairly brims with services and shoreside extras for visiting cruisers. We have always received the red-carpet treatment when docking at the city facilities in the Gulfport basin, and conversations with

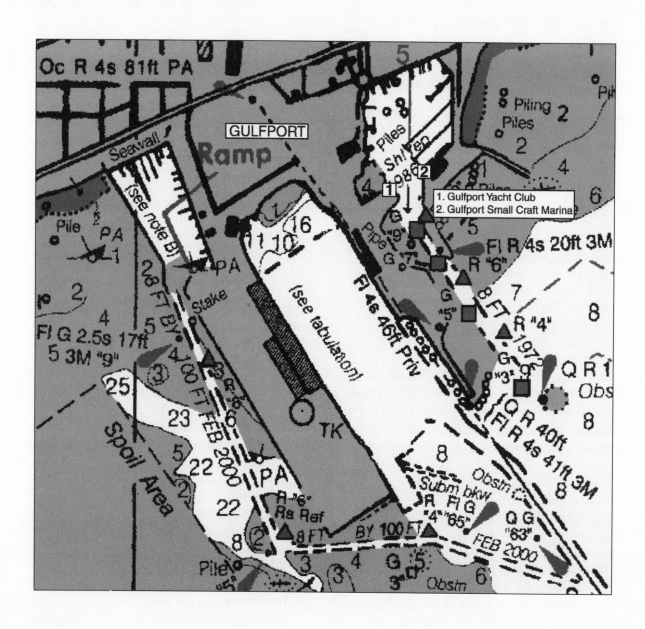

fellow cruisers lead this writer to believe that this happy state of affairs is the norm.

While cruising into the small-craft harbor, you will sight a new, multistory building to starboard. This structures now houses the city dockmaster's headquarters; all-new, fully climate-controlled showers; and a Laundromat. (By the way, how about this for cruiser-friendly services? The Laundromat—with a small paperback exchange library—is run on an honor system. You pay the dockmaster after completion of your washing and drying, so you do not need a fistful of quarters.) Full waste pump-out services are also available at this location.

Soon after passing the new dockmaster's building, the extensive city-maintained piers of the small-craft harbor will be spotted to the east. Transients are gladly accepted for overnight or temporary berths at the fixed wooden piers with all power and water connections.

While no fuel is available immediately adjacent to the docks, the city of Gulfport leases space to a private firm on the northerly side of the harbor. Gasoline and diesel fuel, as well as a small variety, bait, and tackle store are available here. We sounded minimum 6-foot depths while tracking our way to the fuel dock, but a fellow sailor whose craft draws 5½ feet has informed this writer that he touched bottom lightly when making his way in for fuel.

Once ashore, visiting mariners can easily walk to a nearby convenience store. For serious galley restocking, see the harbormaster to arrange courtesy transportation to the nearest supermarket. This service is cheerfully provided, but only by way of advance arrangements.

The adjacent Whitecap restaurant (228-863-4652) serves excellent fried seafood and mouth-watering hush puppies. Diners have a fine view of the Gulfport entrance channel and Mississippi Sound.

For those with a more sophisticated palate, we heartily recommend the nearby Chimney's Restaurant (1640 East Beach Boulevard, 228-868-7020). This fabulous dining spot is located along the northerly margin of Highway 90, just a few blocks from the dockage basin. While it's a bit of walk (or a short cab ride) to get there, Chimney's is worth more than a little inconvenience.

For starters, this dining attraction is housed in a historic Gulfport homeplace that has been beautifully adapted as a restaurant. Patrons cannot help but feel that they are partaking of the finest of fare in the almost tangible atmosphere of the Old South.

And the food—well, words just fail me. We have always found *every* entrée, appetizer, and dessert here to be both imaginatively prepared and, in a word, superb.

Do your palate a tremendous service and put the Chimney's on your dining itinerary. It will never be accurately described as inexpensive, but at least here, you get what you pay for. Oh yes, this might be a good spot to dig out your last clean shirt—you know, the one buried under the forward V-berth. Calling for reservations wouldn't be a bad notion either, particularly on weekends.

Gulfport Small Craft Harbor (228) 868-5713

Approach depth—7½-8 feet minimum
Dockside depth—7-8 feet
Accepts transients—yes
Transient-dockage rate—a real bargain!
Fixed wooden piers—yes

Dockside power connections—30- and 50-amp
Dockside water connections—yes
Showers—yes (one)
Laundromat—transportation provided
Waste pump-out—yes (north side of harbor)
Gasoline—yes (north side of harbor)
Diesel fuel—yes (north side of harbor)
Variety store—yes (north side of harbor)
Restaurant—on site

The Gulfport Yacht Club's piers, slips, and clubhouse are found immediately across the basin from the small-craft city docks on the harbor's western shoreline, near 30 21.651 North/089 05.360 West. This friendly club is glad to accept members of accredited yacht clubs for overnight or temporary dockage. Power and water connections are available at the club's fixed, wooden slips. Shoreside showers are available and the club's dining room is open for lunch seven days a week from 11:30 to 1:30 and for dinner Wednesday and Friday evenings 6:00 to 9:00. There is also a swimming pool for a cool dip after a long day on

New harbormaster and shower building, Gulfport Small Craft Harbor

Gulfport Small Craft Harbor

the water. Advance reservations are recommended.

Gulfport Yacht Club (228) 863-2263

Approach depth—7-8½ feet
Dockside depth—7-8 feet
Accepts transients—members of accredited
**   yacht clubs**
Fixed wooden slips—yes
Dockside power connections—mostly 30 amp
Dockside water connections—yes
Showers—yes
Restaurant—on site

A few docks associated with the Marine Life Exposition will be spotted along the harbor's western shores, north of the Gulfport Yacht Club. This firm presents performances by trained bottle-nosed dolphins throughout the day. The Marine Life building can be identified by three half-moon arches sporting gaily waving flags. Although private craft are not permitted to dock at the piers, the show hall can be reached by walking from the city transient slips.

A United States Coast Guard station overlooks Gulfport harbor's westerly banks just north of Marine Life. Shortly beyond the station, the easterly Gulfport basin

Gulfport Yacht Club

finally comes to an end. The city-leased fuel dock described earlier can be found on this rearward portion of the harbor.

Gulfport History The highly successful modern community that we know as Gulfport began as the dream of but one man. William Harris Hardy began planning a railroad from Jackson, Mississippi to the coast within a year following the Civil War. His idea was to provide a route for goods to enter and leave the state via waterborne shipping. In 1887 Hardy purchased 5,000 acres along the northerly shores of Mississippi Sound. Gulfport was born.

By 1892 the new railway had been partially graded and track had been laid to Hattiesburg. A financial panic temporarily halted construction and spelled financial ruin for Hardy.

In 1895 a former Union officer, Joseph T. Jones, bought the remains of Hardy's railroad "on a whim." Following the war, Jones had become a millionaire by investing in the oil industry. Under his leadership the railway was at last completed in 1895.

The main impediment to progress now was the shallow depth of Mississippi Sound. The state government refused to dredge the harbor, so Jones financed the project himself. Beginning in May of 1899 and stretching into 1902, a "24 feet deep . . . 300 foot wide" channel was dredged from Gulfport to the Gulf of Mexico.

The port was officially opened in January of that year. When London insurance agents, citing the supposed instability of the channel, refused to cover ships entering the new port, Jones personally underwrote the safety of any vessel calling at Gulfport.

The rest, as they say, is history. Gulfport soon proved to be the phenomenal success foreseen by Hardy and Jones. By 1907 Gulfport had become the world's leading exporter of pine board.

As Charles Sullivan comments in *The Mississippi Gulf Coast,* "By the time of his death in 1916 . . . Joseph T. Jones . . . had bequeathed to the Mississippi Gulf Coast a charming legacy. At a personal cost of $16 million, he had created out of lumber and locomotives a thriving all-American city of 8,000 souls on a formerly deserted strand in a land he had once fought to destroy."

Long Beach (Standard Mile 65) (30 20.678 North/089 08.547 West)

The city of Long Beach maintains yet another in the series of concrete-breakwater-enclosed harbors lining Mississippi Sound's northerly banks. This facility is found some 2.8 nautical miles west of Gulfport, but a whole series of shoals separates the two basins. Cruisers traveling east or west on the ICW will want to enter the harbor via a four-mile voyage from flashing buoy #1, north of Cat Island.

The well-marked and charted entrance channel and the city dockage basin was dredged in the summer of 2002, and for the moment, both hold at least 8 to 9 feet of water. This happy situation may change in the future, if past history is any guide.

Even though you may spot a restaurant and the Long Beach Yacht Club fronting the north-

ern shores, avoid the back of the harbor like the plague. These waters have always been shallow, and the recent dredging project did not extend to this part of the harbor.

Transient craft are accepted for temporary dockage at Long Beach harbor. This writer gained the impression that this practice was considerably less frequent here than in Gulfport, but there is no doubt that transient berths are available. Dockage is at older, fixed wooden piers with fresh-water and 30-amp power connections. A few slips sport 50-amp power hookups. The city of Long Beach maintains a small snack bar on the docks, along with two nonclimate-controlled rest rooms, but there are no showers or laundromat. Gasoline, diesel fuel, and waste pump-out services are available.

Two restaurants make their homes on the shores of the Long Beach Small Craft Harbor. Steve's Marina Restaurant (228-864-8988) occupies the old Chimney's location along the basin's northwesterly corner. It is open for lunch and dinner (evening) seven days a week. Long Beach Lookout restaurant (228-575-0737) sits just north of the dockage basin and is open for lunch and dinner Monday through Saturday, while it serves lunch only on Sundays. Both of these attractions feature optional outside dining. We have not yet sampled the fare at either spot but hope to in the future.

Long Beach Small Craft Harbor (228) 863-4795

Approach depth—9 feet
Dockside depth—9 feet
Accepts transients—yes
Transient-dockage rate—below average
Fixed wooden piers—yes
Dockside power connections—30-amp (some 50-amp)
Dockside water connections—yes
Waste pump-out—yes
Gasoline—yes
Diesel fuel—yes
Snack bar—yes
Restaurant—two on site

Immediately across Highway 90 from the Long Beach Small Craft Harbor, visiting cruisers will discover a strip-type shopping center containing a Kmart and a Sav-A-Center supermarket. There is also a host of fast-food restaurants along this portion of the highway.

For more information on Long Beach, pay a visit to the Long Beach Chamber of Commerce (228-863-6666). The office is located just north of the local dockage basin, on the south side of Highway 90.

Pass Christian (Standard Mile 63) (30 18.700 North/089 14.954 West)

How do you tell a visitor with a Southern accent from a Mississippi native? Answer—if you pronounce Pass Christian like it's spelled, you must be from what one local calls the "northern South." This writer was informed respectfully but firmly that the town's name is pronounced "Pass Christi-Ann." Now you can sound like a native, too.

The twin marked channels leading to Pass Christian harbor can be reached from flashing buoy #1 on the ICW. The cut maintains minimum depths of 6 feet, but care must be exercised to avoid several surrounding, unmarked shoals. First-timers should be sure to read the entrance-cut navigational information presented in the next section of this chapter before attempting to enter the harbor.

Pass Christian holds a unique spot in the annals of American pleasure boating. On July 11, 1849, R. H. Montgomery, manager of the famed Pass Christian Hotel, announced that a sailboat race was to be held the following Saturday. The victor's prize was a silver pitcher worth $75. That weekend a dozen "sleek craft" took part in the novel event and the tradition of sailboat racing was born on the Gulf Coast. In fact, this was one of the first races of its kind in the United States.

Following the race, sailing enthusiasts gathered at the Pass Christian Hotel and formed the

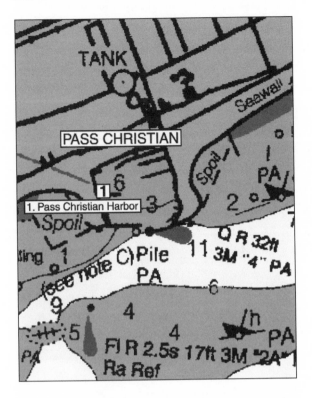

1. Pass Christian Harbor

"Southern Regatta Club." In later years the organization changed its name to the Pass Christian Yacht Club. The club continues in operation to this very day and claims to hold the distinction of being the second oldest yacht club in America—the New York Yacht Club being only six years older. There are those at the Southern Yacht Club in New Orleans who might welcome the chance to engage in lively debate or even livelier fisticuffs on this point, but this writer will leave it to them to sort out.

Today the clubhouse of Pass Christian Yacht Club (228-452-2571) still overlooks the eastern side of the harbor. While the club itself has very little in the way of dockage, visitors from other accredited yacht clubs berthing at the Pass Christian city piers are welcome to make use of the showers, dining room, and bar. No fuel or other marine services are available at the clubhouse.

Pass Christian harbor maintains the now-familiar concrete breakwater to shelter docked craft from the surrounding chop on Mississippi Sound. The city-maintained small-craft docks are found on the basin's western banks.

Transients are accepted for overnight or temporary dockage in Pass Christian harbor. Berths are provided at fixed wooden piers with 30-amp power (a few slips feature 50-amp power hookups) connections and water connections. Depths alongside run around 6 feet. While there are some adjacent rest rooms, no showers or repairs are available.

Gasoline, plus bait, ice, fishing tackle and a few very basic grocery items can be purchased at the leased, dockside store guarding the harbor's westerly banks. Diesel fuel is a bit harder to come by. It can be purchased at the seafood docks fronting the basin's easterly shores, but this practice is clearly more the exception than the rule for pleasure craft.

Highway 90 runs on its merry east-to-west way immediately behind the Pass Christian harbor. Those not wishing to brave the three- to four-block walk into town (see below) will find a Domino's Pizza (228-452-3278) just across the highway from the dockage basin. Just next door, you might also choose to check out the Harbor View Cafe (228-452-3911).

Pass Christian Small Craft Harbor (228) 452-3315

Approach depth—6-8 feet
Dockside depth—6 feet
Accepts transients—yes
Transient-dockage rate—below average

Pass Christian Yacht Club

Fixed wooden piers—yes
Dockside power connections—30-amp (some 50 amp)
Dockside water connections—yes
Gasoline—yes
Diesel fuel—limited
Variety store—mostly bait and tackle
Restaurant—several nearby

Pass Christian Ashore

Cruisers who step ashore at Pass Christian harbor and simply gaze across Highway 90 could be excused for thinking there isn't too much to Pass Christian. Such a conclusion would be more than slightly premature, however. The community sports a small but charming downtown section that affords a surprising array of attractions for both waterborne and landlubber visitors.

Those in search of galley supplies will want to check out the Morning Market (101 E Market Street, 228-452-7593). This natural-food store is well stocked and conveniently located only three blocks from the small-craft harbor.

Ready to leave wind and wave behind for a night or two? Well, we heartily recommend a visit to either the Inn at the Pass (125 E Scenic Drive, 228-452-0333) or the Harbour Oaks Inn (126 W Scenic Drive, 228-452-9399). Both inns are located in historic homeplaces, and both feature a wonderfully tranquil atmosphere. Harbour Oaks boasts a fine view of the harbor, and it is only a very quick step from the docks.

Pass Christian Small Craft Harbor

Any visitor interested in coastal Mississippi history will want to make his or her way to the Pass Christian Historical Society headquarters (228-452-0063, on East Scenic Drive). This facility is open Monday through Friday from 10:00 A.M. to 12 noon, and on Wednesdays from 1:00 P.M. to 3:00 P.M.

The Pass Christian Chamber of Commerce office (228-452-2252) is located just behind (at the southwestern corner of) the dockage basin. If you arrive during business hours, be sure to check here for additional information about visiting the town's historical attractions.

Pass Christian History   During the antebel-lum period, Pass Christian became perhaps the most lavish of Mississippi's fashionable summer retreats known as the "Six Sisters." As Charles L. Sullivan comments in *The Mississippi Gulf Coast,* "Antebellum Pass Christian was not a town that possessed a hotel but rather a hotel that possessed a town. The opening of the Pass Christian Hotel circa 1836 put the village on the map. . . ."

In 1838 a reporter for the *New Orleans Commercial Bulletin* described the Pass Christian Hotel as "one of the best situated and best appointed houses in Mississippi." It was not long before well-to-do tourists began to arrive in Pass Christian by the hundreds. In 1845 one of the hotel's guests labeled the inn as the

"Saratoga of the South." The future seemed bright and assured.

By 1850 a "mile of summer homes" had been built flanking the Pass Christian Hotel. The hostelry held center stage in the village, which by then boasted a post office, grocery store, arcade, and doctor's office.

Many women "summered" at Pass Christian while their husbands stayed behind to mind the store or watch the plantation. The men would come down for a weekend or occasionally a longer stay. In those stiff, Victorian times the activities of the fairer sex were, to say the least, restricted. As described by one frequent visitor:

> We walked the pier to the bath-houses in muslin dresses. Bathing suits were hideous, unsightly garments, high neck, long sleeves, long skirts intended for water only.

The appearance of "Yellow Jack," or yellow fever, in 1853 at Pass Christian marred the summer season. This dreaded disease was to appear sporadically all up and down the coast until the twentieth century, when the real cause of the affliction was finally discovered. With the appearance of modern antibiotics and the partial eradication of the mosquito population, Yellow Jack is now but a dark memory.

During the Civil War, Pass Christian was attacked and shelled by Union forces in 1862. Fortunately the conflict had not attained the bitterness of its later days and invading troops were ordered to scrupulously respect private property.

Following the war, the old Pass Christian Hotel was converted into a boys' school. With the South's devastated economy as a somber backdrop, the old watering hole's days seemed to be at an end.

Such a conclusion would have been premature, however. With the coming of good railway transportation to the Mississippi Gulf Coast, a new era of tourism was born. This time visitors consisted mostly of wealthy Northerners fleeing Old Man Winter. In 1883 the Mexican Gulf Hotel opened in Pass Christian. This hostelry was appointed specifically with the "snowbird" crowd in mind.

Since those days, Pass Christian has remained a favorite resort for both Northern visitors and Southern natives alike. As one of my good friends in New Orleans put it to this writer, "There's old money in Pass Christian." While this assertion is almost self-evident, visitors, particularly of the cruising variety, can be assured of a warm welcome. The long tradition of welcoming guests to Pass Christian has lost nothing in the twentieth century.

SHIP ISLAND TO LAKE BORGNE NAVIGATION

The Gulf Coast ICW continues its wide-open run through Mississippi Sound from its intersection with the Biloxi entrance channel to Lake Borgne. Daybeacons and other aids to navigation become a bit more common on this portion of the run through the sound as the channel frequently borders on shoals and shallow patches. Prudent navigators will still pre-plot compass/GPS courses for long runs between aids to navigation or routes to the various harbors along the way. By following these elementary precautions, this portion of the Mississippi will hold no new surprises for you.

On the ICW   The nominal ICW channel actually passes .7 nautical miles south of flashing daybeacon #2 and unlighted daybeacon #1, the southernmost aids on the Biloxi easterly entrance channel. With good visibility, mariners can hopefully still use these markers as a navigational reference. Have your binoculars ready to help pick up the daybeacons.

From its intersection with the Biloxi channel, the Waterway runs west for 5.7 nautical miles to flashing daybeacon #S. Thankfully, this run does not border on any problem areas. While you can actually pass #S on either side, the aid's color indicates that a passage to the south is to be preferred.

Broadwater Resort Marina   Westbound cruisers choosing to visit Broadwater Resort Marina will probably want to abandon the Waterway's track at flashing daybeacon #S and strike northwest to the southernmost aid on the Broadwater entrance channel, unlighted daybeacon #1. Mariners proceeding east of the ICW can save several miles of open-water cruising by leaving the ICW where the 89 degrees, 58 minutes line of longitude crosses the Waterway, 2.9 nautical miles east of the Gulfport channel intersection. You can then follow this line of position almost directly to #1.

The Broadwater Beach Marina entrance channel is straight, well marked, and easy to follow. The cut's northern terminus is flanked by a small, privately maintained lighthouse

that towers 67 feet over the harbor's entrance. This aid leaves no doubt that you have found the Broadwater channel.

On the Waterway   West of flashing daybeacon #S, the Waterway passes south of flashing daybeacon #2. Another westerly run of 3.7 nautical miles will bring you abeam of the many markers of the Gulfport/Ship Island channel.

Those following the ICW route either east- or westbound will intersect the Gulfport/Ship Island Pass cut between two pairs of markers. The set to the northwest is flashing daybeacons #43 and #44, while the southeasterly duo is composed of flashing daybeacons #41 and #42. From this point, a turn to the northwest allows ready access to Gulfport Harbor, while a veer to the southeast leads to Ship Island Pass inlet.

Ship Island   Skippers wanting to visit old Fort Massachusetts on Ship Island should cruise south and southeast on the Ship Island Pass Channel to a position between flashing buoys #25 and #26. You can then cut to the east of #26 and follow the northerly banks of Ship Island, being sure to remain at least .3 of a nautical mile offshore. Have your binoculars in hand and watch the shoreline for the Park Service's long pier. When this structure is directly abeam to the south, you can turn in to the pier and carefully feel your way in with the sounder. Don't cut either the eastern or western corner. As clearly indicated on chart 11372, there is shoal water to the east and west.

Captains who choose to anchor west of the Park Service dock must take great care to avoid the correctly charted shallows striking north from the Ship Island shoreline. Be sure to set the hook far enough to the north so that your vessel will not swing into the shoal if the tide or wind should change.

Ship Island Pass   The prolific markings on Ship Island Pass make for delightful navigation of this seaward cut. The only problem area seems to be just off the westerly tip of Ship Island. A shoal is building outward from this point and periodic dredging and remarking is necessary to keep up with the shifting sands.

Gulfport   The passage through the Gulfport channel from the ICW intersection to Gulfport's triple harbors is, navigationally, a walk in the park. Not only is the channel outlined with a bevy of daybeacons and buoys, it doesn't border on any shallow water for 85 percent of its track. If you run aground here, let me suggest a quick trip to the eye doctor and a long session with Chapman's.

With the prolific markers, successful navigation of the cut is delightfully simple anyway. Just remember "red-right-returning" and you will quickly divine that cruisers headed from the ICW (or Ship Island Pass) for Gulfport should pass all red markers to their (the cruisers') starboard side and take green aids to port.

Mariners eastbound on the ICW may safely save a good chunk of distance by departing the Waterway at flashing daybeacon #2 and setting a course directly for flashing daybeacon #61. This route will take you over the charted spoil banks, but minimum 6-foot depths are still maintained on these waters. Should your boat draw more than 6 feet, please ignore this route unless you want to give the local Sea Tow some business.

Flashing daybeacon #63, marking the passage's westerly flank, is the northernmost aid to navigation on the Gulfport approach channel. A run to the north-northwest would lead you into the central commercial shipping basin, while a set of additional markers leads northwest to the commercial fishing docks.

Almost all cruisers will want to cut a bit to the north from flashing daybeacon #63 and pick up the north-northwesterly running channel leading into the Gulfport small-craft harbor. A whole series of correctly charted, unlighted and flashing daybeacons will lead you into the harbor, beginning with unlighted daybeacon #3 and flashing daybeacon #2. Just continue passing red aids to your starboard side and green markers to port. After passing between the northernmost set of markers, unlighted daybeacons #9 and #10, continue straight ahead into the harbor. You will first come abeam and pass the new dockmaster's building to the east. Shortly thereafter, the city docks will be spied to starboard, while the clubhouse and wet slips of the Gulfport Yacht Club will be spotted to port. The leased fuel dock and ship's store guards the harbor's northerly banks.

On the ICW   The ICW runs almost due west for 6.6 nautical miles from its intersection with the Gulfport channel to a position just north of flashing buoy #1. Cat Island lies to the south between the Gulfport cut and #1. As this marshy island is surrounded by extensive shoals, navigational information will not be presented in this guide.

Long Beach Small Craft Harbor   Cruisers choosing to berth in the Long Beach small-craft harbor can cut north from flashing buoy #1 and follow a compass/GPS course to the charted and well-marked approach cut leading to the passageway in the basin's concrete breakwater. A gap of 4.6 nautical miles separates #1 and the harbor's entrance.

The ample markings on the entrance channel leading to the Long Beach harbor make the approach a dream. Simply pass between the outermost (southernmost) markers, flashing daybeacons #1 and #2, and continue tracking your way to the northwest, passing all other red daybeacons to your starboard side and green to port. Soon the harbor's entrance will be spotted dead ahead.

Remember to avoid the rear of Long Beach harbor. Shoal water of 1 to 2 feet is waiting there to trap the unwary navigator.

Pass Christian   Entry into Pass Christian harbor from the ICW is complicated by the presence of several large shoals north of the Waterway. Two of these have rather interesting names. Where else have you ever heard shallows referred to as Square Handkerchief Shoal and Tail of the Square Handkerchief?

While their names may be amusing, the 3- to 5-foot depths are no laughing matter. To avoid these problem areas, depart the Waterway at flashing daybeacon #3. You

can then set a compass/GPS course to the northwest and gain Pass Christian while still keeping clear of all the various shoals. Along the way, you will pass unlighted nun buoy #2P and flashing daybeacon #4P well to the southwest of your course line.

There are actually two channels serving Pass Christian. These cuts pass east and west of the large, tail-shaped shoal just south of the harbor's entrance. While both can be used by captains exercising reasonable caution, the eastern cut is wider and simpler.

To make use of this eastern approach channel, set your course to come abeam of flashing daybeacon #2 by some .2 nautical miles to its southeasterly side. Once this aid comes abeam, alter course immediately to the northwest and point to come abeam and pass #2 to its fairly immediate southerly side. This set of maneuvers will help to avoid the charted sunken wreck south of #2.

Once abeam of flashing daybeacon #2, you can continue on to the west, pointing to come abeam of flashing daybeacon #4, which marks the breakwater's entrance to its southerly side. The harbor's mouth will then be obvious. Take note that flashing daybeacon #4 is actually mounted on the Pass Christian concrete breakwater.

Pass Christian's western entrance channel calls for a careful cruise around the southern tip of the shoal running south for 1.8 nautical miles from the harbor. Point to eventually come abeam of flashing daybeacon #1 by some 50 yards (no closer) to its easterly side. Set a new course to come abeam of flashing daybeacon #2A to its westerly side. You must then curl around

#2A to the east and follow the deeper water to flashing daybeacon #4 and the harbor entrance. As suggested above, this procedure is more complicated and risky than those maneuvers required in the eastern channel.

On the ICW   At flashing buoy #1 the ICW takes a sharp cut to the southwest. Markers become more numerous, though there are still some hefty runs between markers along the way. Be prepared to find new and different aids to navigation along this stretch from those pictured on your chart or discussed in this account by the time you visit.

Between flashing daybeacon #3 and flashing daybeacon #8, two large shoals flank the Waterway to the southeast, while a smaller patch of shallows is found to the northwest. Fortunately, none of these shoals bears directly on the ICW channel. You need only stay in the general vicinity of the Waterway for good depths.

At flashing daybeacon #14, the Waterway begins to follow the improved Marianne channel. Merrill Coquille shoal lies northwest of unlighted nun buoy #18 and a sunken wreck is found east of unlighted can buoy #19. Both these hazards are easily avoided by sticking to the Waterway channel.

Flashing daybeacon #1 marks a sharp westward swerve in the Waterway. You are now in the dredged Grand Island channel. Markers are quite numerous, though there is very little shallow water to worry about except for the charted spoil bank to the south. Simply stay in the well-marked cut to avoid this threat.

St. Louis Bay can be reached by a long cruise north from flashing daybeacon #1. This somewhat shallow, but nevertheless cruising-rich, body of water will be considered in the next section of this chapter.

Flashing daybeacon #15 marks the western terminus of the Grand Island channel. The Waterway now bends a bit to the west-southwest and flows between Lighthouse Point and Grassy Island into Lake Borgne. This broad channel is known as St. Joe Pass.

There are no markers directly on the ICW for some 2.7 nautical miles west of #15. Set a careful compass/GPS course from #15 to come abeam of unlighted daybeacon #2, southeast of Lighthouse Point, by some some .2 miles to its southerly side. Another run of 1.1 nautical miles will bring you abeam of flashing daybeacon #3, north of Grassy Island. Stay well north of #3. We suggest coming abeam of and passing #3 by some .4 nautical miles to its northerly quarter. Continued navigation of the ICW channel west to Louisiana will be presented in the next chapter.

Bay St. Louis (Standard Mile 54)

Perhaps it should first be noted that chart 11372 names this body of water as St. Louis Bay. Cruising visitors will quickly discover that all the locals call it Bay St. Louis. Even the chart gives this moniker to the village along the bay's western banks. In this guide the two names will be used interchangeably. Hopefully, this explanation will remove any potential confusion.

Bay St. Louis probably represents the largest body of undiscovered cruising opportunities on the Mississippi coastline. Even with the presence of a low-key marina on the bay, cruising these waters brings forth a sense of privacy and adventure that many mariners will savor like a fine wine. While the bay itself is shallow and careful compass/GPS courses must often be followed between the widely separated aids to navigation, the various sidewaters running off the sound present a host of opportunities for dropping the hook far from the madding crowd.

Captains who pilot craft drawing more than 5 feet may not be able to comfortably experience many of Bay St. Louis's cruising charms. Some of the channels hold only 6 feet of water at low tide, while a few others are in the 5-foot range. Sailcraft with fixed keels should assess their draft requirements with a critical eye before deciding whether to venture upon these delightful waters.

One somewhat seedy marina is located on Bayou Portage, to the east of flashing daybeacon #3. This facility does offer some questionable transient dockage.

While Bay St. Louis may not be the most easily navigated body of water you will ever visit, I urge my fellow cruisers to give it a try. I think you will find that the end justifies the meanders.

Pelican Cove Marina
(30 18.710 North/089 17.436 West)

Between the two Bay St. Louis bridges, tiny Pelican Cove Marina guards the easterly banks, along the banks of the small, charted stream, south of the noted "Ramp." This is a high-dry storage operation that is clearly geared toward smaller powercraft. Gas and diesel fuel can be purchased dockside, but be advised that approach and alongside depths run as little as 3 feet. Obviously, this small facility is off-limits to many cruising-sized craft.

Bay-Waveland Yacht Club
(30 19.499 North/089 19.587 West)

The charted and enclosed dockage basin belonging to the friendly folks at Bay-Waveland Yacht Club (228-467-4592) lies along the lower bay's westerly banks, a short hop north of the northernmost of the two bridges that cross this water body's mouth. This yacht club does not have deep water. Entrance depths run as thin as 4 feet at MLW, with minimum 5-foot soundings dockside.

As far as this writer has been able to determine, no wet-slip dockage is available to visitors without prior arrangements. We found the docks unattended on three widely separated visits to this facility. We did spot a waste pump-out during our last visit.

Bayou Portage
(Various Lats/Lons—see below)

The channel leading to Bayou Portage cuts off to the northeast some .83 nautical miles north of the northernmost Bay St. Louis bridge. At unlighted junction daybeacon #A, this cut further subdivides itself from the Wolf River channel. The Bayou Portage entrance cut maintains minimum depths of 6 feet, with soundings of 8 to 9 feet being typical along much of its length. Depths on the interior reaches of the creek are similar to these readings. The creek is spanned by a bascule bridge with 11 feet of closed vertical clearance which opens on demand.

The shoreline of Bayou Portage carries

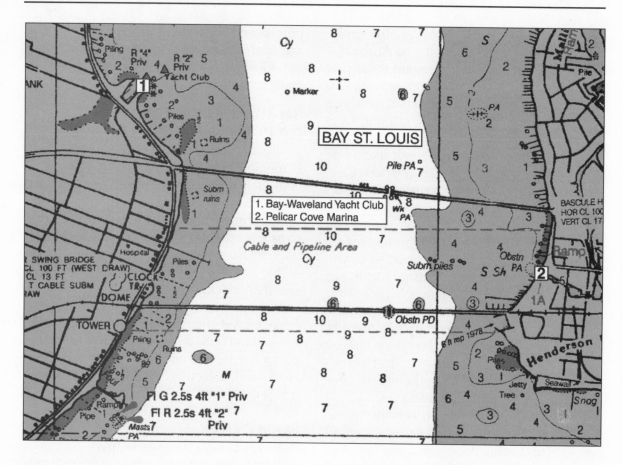

moderate development. Some sections are purely residential, while others are commercial in nature. Still other portions of the creek are flanked by natural marsh.

Bayou Portage offers one very low-key marina facility and several well-protected anchorages.

Pepper's Discovery Bay Marina Resort (30 20.801 North/089 15.418 West) guards the charted dockage basin north of flashing day-beacon #13. While care must be taken to keep to the unmarked entrance channel, 6-foot minimum depths are held in this cut. If you

wander from the desired track, however, depths of 5 feet or less are soon encountered. Dockside soundings are in the 6- to 8-foot range.

Discovery Bay Marina is associated with an adjacent housing development that has quite obviously fallen on very hard times during the last several years. The on-site restaurant has long been shut down and both this building and an adjacent structure are in very poor condition. In fact, we are sorry to report that the atmosphere of decay and of "something has gone very wrong here" is all pervasive. Honestly, folks, this may be one instance when it

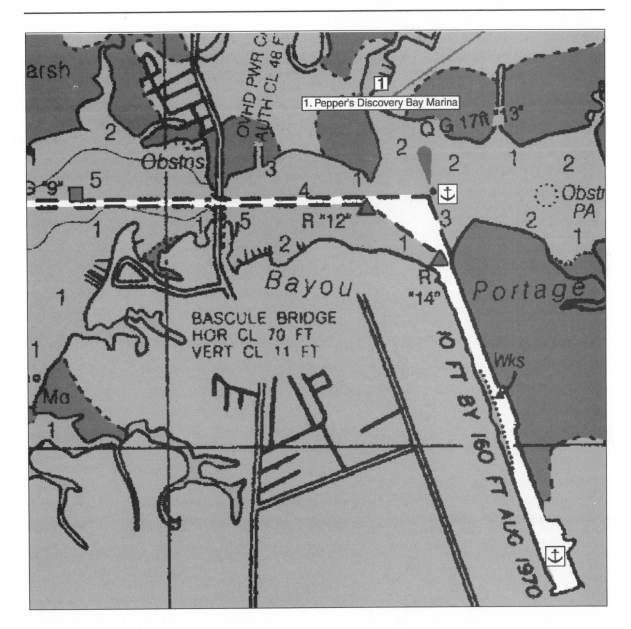

1. Pepper's Discovery Bay Marina

would be better to anchor off rather than tie your lines to Discovery Bay's piers, but the choice is yours.

The marina does offer overnight dockage at fixed wooden piers with 30-amp power connections and water connections. An adjacent swimming pool is open during the summer months to cruisers. There is also an on-site bar that serves "burgers," but one could not describe the atmosphere in this dining spot as savory. All in all, this is one of the most forgettable marina facilities on the Northern Gulf coastline. If you should decide to see for yourself, please let me know if you have a different experience.

Pepper's Discovery Bay Marina Resort
  (228) 452-9441

Approach depth—6 feet
Dockside depth—6-8 feet
Accepts transients—yes
Fixed wooden piers—yes
Dockside power connections—30-amp
Dockside water connections—yes
Bar & snack-sandwich bar—yes

The good news when it comes to any discussion of Bayou Portage are the two (at least) good anchorages that captains can consider. In light-to-moderate winds, it is quite possible to drop the hook south and a bit east of flashing daybeacon #13, near 30 20.551 North/089 15.258 West. Here you can anchor in 20+ feet of water amidst plentiful swinging room. There is shoal water to avoid north of #13, and the protection afforded on these waters is not sufficient for heavy weather. Otherwise, however, this is a fine anchorage with only a smattering of development visible on the adjoining shores.

The second anchorage that one might try

Pepper's Discovery Bay Marina Resort, Bayou Portage

resides on the man-made fork of Bayou Portage that strikes south from unlighted day-beacon #14. This stream once served as a barge-loading area, but all—save one—of these industrial centers now appear to be out of business.

The southern terminus of this canal holds 9 to 11 feet of water and could serve as a well-protected overnight haven for boats as large as 45 feet. Try anchoring near 30 19.746 North/089 14.975 West. The surrounding shoreline is dotted with old, trashy industrial development, but you should not be bothered by any commercial traffic this far down the canal, even if the odd barge should happen along farther downstream (to the north). A roadway flanks the canal's southern tip, but automobile traffic appears to be light. Protection is sufficient for the foulest weather unless very strong winds blow from the north-north-west, directly down the length of the canal.

Wolf River
(Various Lats/Lons—see below)

Are you one of those mariners who, like this writer, treasures secret thoughts about dropping the hook where few pleasure craft have been before you? If this description fits your cruising tastes, then by all means give Wolf River your most serious consideration.

First, the bad news: the Wolf River entrance channel will never be accurately described as simple to run. In fact, it is only sparsely marked and carries low-tide soundings of only 5 to 5½ feet in several places. There are also several unmarked, tricky sections that call for extra caution. Given these restrictions, Wolf River is really only appropriate for boats that draw 4½ feet or (preferably) less and are no longer than 36 feet. Even then, this stream will recommend itself only to adventurous captains.

Now, the good news: of all the coastal Mississippi streams revisited for this new edition, Wolf River is one of the most unchanged of the lot. The river's mostly natural banks are a genuine delight! Two seemingly ancient and beautiful homes overlook the river just as the charted high ground comes abeam to the south. It is quite possible to drop the hook abeam of these home-places in 6 to 10 feet of water near 30 21.480 North/089 16.605 West. Swinging room should be enough for vessels as large as 36 feet, and protection is good from all but the heaviest weather.

Intrepid explorers can continue following Wolf River upstream to the new, 28-foot fixed bridge. Captains piloting craft as large as 40 feet can anchor short of the bridge, along the river's centerline, in some 6 to 10 feet of water near 30 21.443 North/089 16.450 West.

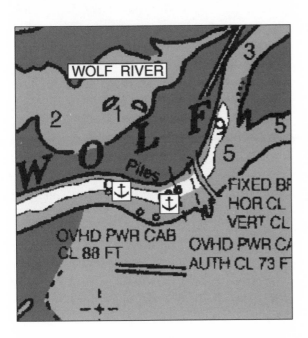

Homeplace on Wolf River

Closer to either shore, soundings rise to 5-foot levels. This spot is also well sheltered and while it lacks the two attractive houses visible from the anchorage to the west, it is still a great spot to spend an evening tranquilly rocking back and forth.

The Jourdan River
(Various Lats/Lons—see below)

The Jourdan River is a deep, mostly uncharted stream cutting into the western shores of Bay St. Louis near Cedar Point. This fascinating river provides many miles of prime cruising grounds and tons of good anchorages.

To be succinct, you would have to look far and wide to find a more charming body of water than the Jourdan River.

Normally, I don't recommend uncharted bodies of water to my fellow cruisers. However, extensive on-site research has led me to believe that the *mid-width* of the Jourdan River can be trusted to hold at least 5 feet of water as far as the high-rise highway bridge. The various sidewaters along the way are not recommended, however. The lack of any cartographical aid on such questionable waters is reason enough to leave them for the locals.

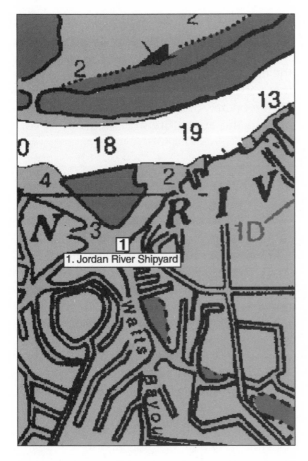

1. Jordan River Shipyard

West of unlighted daybeacon #9, two unlighted daybeacons, #1 and #2, mark a southward-flowing passage leading to an enclosed harbor. This body of water plays host to mammothlike Casino Magic. This gambling establishment once had dreams of operating an adjacent marina, but during our last visit in the fall of 2002, we found the piers immediately adjacent to the marina to be completely unused and cut off from the rest of the complex. A few boats were docked along the basin's easterly banks, but they appeared to be longtime residents, probably left over from the days of now long-defunct Bay Cove Marina. Given all these unfortunate statistics, we suggest that our fellow cruisers avoid Casino Magic entirely.

After cruising west-southwest for another .9 nautical miles, moving upstream on Jourdan River, a wide sidewater will open out along the southerly banks. This stream allows access to Jourdan River Marina and Shipyard, found near 30 19.878 North/089 22.471 West. Be advised that approach depths run as thin as 5 feet.

Study chart 11372 for a moment, and you will notice that it is theoretically possible to alternately approach the shipyard via the charted southeasterly running stream south of Catfish Bayou. Don't attempt this second approach. Soundings run to a mere 3 feet.

Jourdan River Marina and Shipyard (228-467-4771) is a service facility that offers haul-outs by way of a 50-ton travelift. The yard seemed very active during our last visit in early 2003.

Catfish Bayou makes into the northern banks of the Jourdan River just a quick hop farther to the west. This stream is far too small and shallow for cruising-sized vessels, but judging from the numbers of anglers we always see on these waters, the bayou is a very popular fishing spot. Why not break on the dinghy, wet a line, and try your luck?

Moving upstream from a position abeam of Catfish Bayou, Jourdan River winds through some beautiful countryside. Some areas are completely undeveloped, with salt marsh very much in evidence. Other portions of the banks border on higher ground and are overlooked by light to moderate residential development.

Soon the river becomes sheltered enough for light- to moderate-air anchorage almost anywhere on its mid-width. For better protection, continue following the river for several more miles until it turns to the north and eventually approaches the twin I-10 highway bridges.

We now suggest halting your explorations short of these spans. Construction of new bridges along this stretch is ongoing—even at the time of this writing—and we found the river clogged with construction equipment.

Those who do choose to anchor just short of the highway span will be treading upon waters that very, very few cruisers have known. This off-the-beaten-path feeling can add immeasurably to the adventure and pleasure of your cruise.

BAY ST. LOUIS NAVIGATION

Successful navigation of the relatively shallow Bay St. Louis waters is not a task to be taken lightly. Shoal water is the rule rather than the exception and some sections of the channel are marked by widely separated aids to navigation. Be sure to plot the various compass/GPS courses *before* embarking upon a cruise of the bay. Strangers would do well to cruise the various channels at reduced speed until learning the lay of the waters. Read the information presented below, study chart 11372 carefully, and with any luck at all you should come through with nothing worse than a few gray hairs.

Due to its overall shallow nature, St. Louis Bay can foster a sharp, steep, nasty chop when winds exceed 12 knots. While these wave conditions do not usually reach dangerous proportions unless storm conditions are present, they can certainly beat the bejeebers out of you, your boat, and your crew.

Only a few of the markers on Bay St. Louis are lighted. This writer strongly counsels against passage of the various channels after dark without specific local knowledge.

Entrance from the ICW   From flashing daybeacon #1 marking the eastern genesis of the Grand Island channel, set course to come abeam of flashing daybeacon #2 off the western tip of Square Handkerchief Shoal by some .2 nautical miles to its westerly side. It is a long run of 5.5 nautical miles from #1 to #2. This track does not stray near any shallow water as long as you stay to the west of #2. East of this aid the shoal waters of Square Handkerchief could be a problem. Keep an accurate log of your progress north from #1 and use your binoculars to pick out flashing daybeacon #2 when you are within 1 nautical mile of this marker. You can then be sure to avoid Square Handkerchief Shoal by staying well to the west.

Once abeam of flashing daybeacon #2 to its western side, set course for the charted pass-through of the first bridge spanning the bay's entrance. Note that the pass-through is well east of center. As you approach the bridge, be mindful of the charted shallows stretching west from Henderson Point. Be sure to guard against leeway easing you too far to the east.

The entrance to St. Louis Bay is crossed by two bridges. The first is a railroad bridge with 13 feet of closed vertical clearance.

This structure is usually open. The second span is a highway bascule bridge with 17 feet of closed vertical clearance. At the current time, this span opens on demand to vessels that need additional clearance.

North of the highway bridge, mariners have always heretofore set course for flashing daybeacon #1, which marked the southerly apex of the Bayou Portage, Wolf River, and Jourdan River channels. Now, for reasons that this writer can not fathom, #1 has been removed. Go figure.

Navigators lucky enough to have a functioning GPS aboard can set course for the old location of #1, at 30 19.894 North/089 18.263 West. Mariners without one of these electronic marvels will just have to practice their best DR navigation.

Between the bridge and the apex of the three Bay St. Louis channels, watch the western shore and you may catch sight of the docks of the Bay-Waveland Yacht Club. If you should decide to visit this club's somewhat shallow dockage basin, set course for its entrance channel's outermost marker, flashing daybeacon #2. Be advised that the current edition of chart 11372 depicts this aid to navigation as an unlighted daybeacon #2.

As you would expect, pass #2 to its southerly side and continue cruising generally west into the harbor by passing south of unlighted daybeacon #4.

This latter marker (#4), denotes the easterly tip of a stone breakwater that protects a portion of the entrance cut's northerly flank. Obviously, it would behoove all captains to keep their craft south of #4. Once

this marker is in your wake, the entrance to the yacht club harbor will open out dead ahead.

Moving back onto the waters of Bay St. Louis, once you arrive at the old location of #1, it is time to decide whether to cut northeast into the Bayou Portage/Wolf River channel or break off to the northwest and enter Jourdan River.

Bayou Portage   As seems to be the case with all the Bay St. Louis channels, you must keep in the marked cut when entering Bayou Portage, or water levels will quickly rise to 4- and 5-foot levels. Watch over your stern as well as the course ahead to make note of any lateral slippage.

Set course to come abeam of unlighted junction daybeacon #A to its immediate southeasterly side. From #A, continue on course, pointing to come abeam of and pass unlighted daybeacon #2 to its fairly immediate northwesterly side. Swing your course a touch to the east and point as if you were going to come abeam of flashing daybeacon #3 to its easterly side.

The Bayou Portage channel actually takes a sharp turn to the east before reaching flashing daybeacon #3. Some 25 yards short of #3, turn sharply to the east and point to come abeam of and pass unlighted daybeacon #4 to its fairly immediate northerly side. From #4 it is a straight shot east to the bascule bridge spanning the bayou. One unlighted can (incorrectly charted on 11372 as unlighted daybeacon #5) and two green daybeacons help you along the way. Pass each of these markers to their southerly sides.

East of unlighted daybeacon #9, the Portage channel soon approaches a bascule bridge with only 11 feet of closed vertical clearance. This span opens on demand for pleasure craft.

Once through the bascule bridge, set course to come abeam of unlighted daybeacon #12 to its immediate northerly side. If you decide to visit Pepper's Discovery Bay Marina Resort to the north, depart from the marked channel once abeam of #12. *Do not continue east to flashing daybeacon #13 and then attempt to turn into the marina.* From #12, point for the mid-width of the entrance to the charted dockage basin. This course will lead you hard by the western banks.

Cruisers who decide to anchor on the waters south and a bit east of #13 should cruise south on the main channel from #13 for some 50 yards and then feel their way to the east for no more than 25 yards. Be *sure* to stay south of #13. Shoal water strikes out from the northerly banks and has encroached on #13 from this quarter.

Skippers entering the artificial canal to the south should continue on the main branch of Bayou Portage until they are some 20 yards short of flashing daybeacon #13. Then, swing sharply to the south and point to enter on the canal's centerline by passing unlighted daybeacon #14 to its immediate easterly quarter. For best depths, stick to the middle as you cruise south.

Wolf River   The entrance channel to the Wolf River strikes north from unlighted junction daybeacon #A on the Bayou Portage cut. This is a narrow passage that could use some additional markers. Use maximum caution to keep to the marked cut and keep a close eye on the sounder. Detail a hand to watch over the stern for leeway. Proceed at idle speed and be ready to make quick course corrections.

Pass #A by some 10 yards to its easterly side and set course to come abeam of flashing daybeacon #3 by about the same distance to its easterly quarter. At #3, the channel shifts to the northeast. Point to come abeam of flashing daybeacon #5 by about 10 yards to its southeasterly side. As you approach #5, look north and you should catch sight of a large industrial complex overlooking the bay's shoreline.

Immediately after coming abeam of #5, alter course sharply to the east-northeast and point for the entrance into the Wolf River. As the first small marsh island comes abeam to the south, begin favoring the northern side of the channel slightly. Cruise back to the mid-width of the river's entrance as you begin your approach to the charted cut-through leading north to Little Bay. From this point to the bascule bridge, hold scrupulously to the centerline for best depths.

If you decide to anchor abeam of the two old houses on the southern banks, or near the bridge, drop your anchor on the mid-width and use the minimum anchor rode for a proper scope. Even with this procedure, it's possible to swing into 5-foot depths. Vessels drawing more than 3½ feet might want to consider a Bahamian mooring to minimize swinging.

The Jourdan River   The entrance to the Jourdan River is also quite narrow and requires caution. By contrast, the river's interior section carries good depths along a broad path straddling its centerline. Until reaching the deeper water west of unlighted daybeacon #9, keep a close watch on the sounder and, as always, watch out for leeway.

To enter the river, point to come abeam of and pass unlighted daybeacon #3 to its fairly immediate northeasterly side. It's a run of 1.3 nautical miles between #1 and #3. Make every effort to stay on course. Some of the waters outside of the channel, particularly those to the north, are mighty thin.

Continue past #3, pointing to come abeam of flashing daybeacon #5 to its easterly side. Cruise past #5 on the same heading for a very short distance and then cut sharply west-southwest and point to pass unlighted daybeacon #7 by some 10 yards to its northerly side. During our last visit to the Jourdan River in the fall of 2002, we noted some 5-foot depths in the middle of the channel near #7.

Continue on the same course until coming abeam of unlighted daybeacon #9 to its northerly quarter. Now the channel widens, and navigators can breathe a sigh of relief.

The only additional markers west of unlighted daybeacon #9 on the Jourdan River are two unlighted daybeacons outlining the entrance channel into the Casino Magic dockage basin. Unlighted daybeacon #1, on the marina channel, is charted and #2 is not.

The charted shoal north of unlighted daybeacon #1 seems to be building south into the river's mouth. To avoid this hazard, you must guard against slipping too far north. Once abeam of #9, point to pass unlighted daybeacons #1 and #2 by some 25 yards (no more) to their northerly sides. This maneuver should help in avoiding the northern shallows.

West of unlighted daybeacon #1 good depths spread out on the Jourdan River in a broad path. You need only hold to the mid-width of the stream for good depths as far as the fixed twin highway bridges several miles upstream. As reported earlier, the replacement of these bridges is currently underway, and we suggest that you cease your explorations short of the twin spans.

Otherwise, you can anchor just about anywhere you choose along the Jourdan River's centerline. Just be sure to set the hook so as not to swing into the narrow band of shallows that abut the river's various shorelines.

Cruisers bound for the Jourdan River Marina and Shipyard should cut into the mid-width of the broad, charted passage that eventually runs southwest of Watts Bayou. The repair yard will be sighted along the easterly banks, just before reaching the southerly flowing waters of Watts Bayou.

Do *not* try to access Jourdan River Marina and Shipyard by way of the alternate channel running southeast, south of Catfish Bayou. This stream is quite shoal.

CHAPTER 7

New Orleans and Lake Pontchartrain

If ever there was a single region that exemplifies the diverse cruising conditions on the entire Northern Gulf Coast, it would have to be the waters in and about the timeless city of New Orleans. With the exception of the Florida Panhandle's clear depths, you will find just about every imaginable cruising condition. Ranging from the wide-open, often rough surface of Lake Pontchartrain to the almost secret recesses of Lake Maurepas and the Tickfaw River, the waters surrounding the nation's "party city" have something for everyone. Visiting cruisers will most certainly want to allow a week, or preferably longer, to sample the cruising delights of this marvelous port of call.

New Orleans' waterside geography can be more than slightly confusing for first-time cruising visitors. To the east, the Gulf Coast ICW runs through the open reaches of Lake Borgne. Really far more a sound than a lake, this body of water is bounded by the Louisiana mainland to the north and west, and by the confusing Chaudalier Islands to the south.

North of Lake Borgne a bevy of wilderness rivers offer super off-the-beaten-path cruising. Chief among these streams is the Pearl River, but the Old Pearl River, the Middle River, and the West Pearl River all offer many miles of exceptionally cruisable waters.

At Catfish Point and flashing buoy #21, mariners come to a basic parting of the ways. The primary ICW channel continues west (and southwest) straight toward the New Orleans Industrial Canal, while a cut to the northwest carries captains and crew through the broad and deep waters of the Rigolets into Lake Pontchartrain. Surprisingly, the ICW route is by far the least interesting of the two passages. This almost arrow-straight stretch of the Waterway offers only a single marina catering to transient cruising craft. Anchorages are all but nonexistent. Once it joins the Industrial Canal, the Waterway becomes extremely commercial in nature. Pleasure craft are likely to feel a bit lost in this "land of the giants." Finally, the canal passes through a huge lock, also very commercial in nature, and out into the restless, muddy waters of the Mississippi River. The ICW follows the great river only briefly, and while a portion of this passage flanks downtown New Orleans and the French Quarter, there is no dockage available on the waterfront for pleasure craft. Soon the ICW leaves the Mississippi River by one of two alternate routes. For the first time in this guide's history, a new chapter following this section will detail the lower Mississippi River and the ICW moving west to Grand Isle and the Barataria Waterway.

It should also be noted that the Industrial Canal flows north from its intersection with the ICW and connects with the southern reaches of Lake Pontchartrain, thereby allowing cruisers on the lake to have a ready entrance into the Waterway route leading west. If this is all a bit confusing, just look at the excellent overview of the region afforded by chart 11369 and the watery pattern should all become clear (or, at least, clearer).

Mariners who are not in a hurry to leave New Orleans will wisely choose to cruise northwest on the Rigolets and visit Lake Pontchartrain. New Orleans' primary marina facilities are located on the southern shores of this vast lake, while a collection of delightful marinas and charming small towns overlooks the northern banks.

To the west, Lake Maurepas offers isolated cruising grounds, including the little-discovered Tickfaw River.

New Orleans itself is, of course, one of the nation's most popular tourist attractions. This city may well be America's #1 site for conventions. That says a lot, considering the many alternatives. Whether you stroll the French Quarter, stand as a fascinated bystander for a Mardi Gras parade, or partake of the unique Creole and/or Cajun cuisine at one of hundreds of fine restaurants in New Orleans, any visitor will soon come to understand that there is nothing else quite like this in the world!

Every time I contemplate a cruise on the waters surrounding New Orleans and a visit to the "Big Easy" itself, I feel a bit like the diner who has gone through a buffet line and emerged with a plate overflowing with good food. It all looks great, but I know it will take a manly effort to polish it all off. Such is the happy state in which cruising visitors will find themselves in this blessed region. I honestly think you could take three or four months and still not exhaust all the nooks and crannies available for exploration. Take heart, though—even a sampling of these waterborne delights can make for a cruise which will never be forgotten. Let's forge ahead and review these many possibilities.

Charts   Most cruisers exploring the waters about New Orleans need only purchase the first two charts listed below. Only those captains following the Mississippi River to the Gulf of Mexico (see the next chapter) will need 11361.
11367—ICW chart that follows the Waterway through New Orleans. Also gives good details on the Rigolets, the New Orleans Industrial Canal, and the ICW passage through the Mississippi River

11369—detailed chart of Lake Pontchartrain and Lake Maurepas. This map will be needed by any who cruise on either body of water
11364—covers the Mississippi River from New Orleans to Fort Jackson, and the Mississippi Gulf Outlet channel into the Gulf of Mexico
11361—outlines the Mississippi River from Fort Jackson to this great stream's complicated channels leading to the Gulf of Mexico

Bridges
Pearl River Railway Bridge—crosses the Pearl River .9 nautical miles north of flashing daybeacon #8—14 feet (closed)—usually open unless a train is due
Pearl River-Highway 90 Bridge—crosses Pearl River .8 nautical mile north of unlighted daybeacon #38—Swing bridge—10 feet (closed)—opens on demand
Rigolets Railroad Bridge—crosses the Rigolets between Rabbit Island and Pearl River Island—11 feet (closed)—usually open unless a train is due
Rigolets-Highway 90 Bridge—crosses the Rigolets west of flashing daybeacon #4— Swing bridge—14 feet (closed)—opens on demand
Lake Pontchartrain, Point Aux Herbes-Interstate 10 Bridge—crosses the easterly reaches of Lake Pontchartrain west of unlighted daybeacon #15—Fixed—65 feet

Lake Pontchartrain-Highway 11 Bridge—crosses the easterly reaches of Lake Pontchartrain west of the Point Aux Herbes-I-10 Bridge—Bascule—13 feet (closed)—opens on demand

Bayou Bonfouca Bridge—crosses Bayou Bonfouca abeam of the Slidell waterfront—Swing bridge—6 feet (closed)—opens on demand

Lake Pontchartrain Railroad Bridge—crosses the easterly reaches of Lake Pontchartrain immediately west of the Highway 11 Bridge—4 feet (closed)—opens on demand unless a train is due

Lake Pontchartrain Causeway—contains 5 pass-throughs along its 24-mile breadth, listed below moving north to south

    1. Fixed Span (northernmost)—22 feet

    2. Bascule Span—42 feet (closed)—opens with 3 hours' notice via VHF channel 16 except between 6:00 A.M. and 9:00 A.M. and 3:00 P.M. and 6:00 P.M. During these times of peak traffic this span does not usually open at all

    3. Fixed Span—22 feet

    4. Fixed Span—50 feet

    5. Fixed Span (southernmost of the five pass-throughs)—22 feet

Tchefuncte River-Highway 22 Bridge—crosses the Tchefuncte River at Madisonville—Swing bridge—1 foot (closed)—opens on the hour and half-hour seven days a week, year round, between 5:00 A.M. and 8:00 P.M.—does not usually open at night

Pass Manchac Railway Bridge—crosses Pass Manchac just east of Lake Maurepas—Fixed—56 feet

Pass Manchac-Highway 55 Bridge—crosses Pass Manchac just east of Lake Maurepas—Fixed—50 feet

Tickfaw Bridge—crosses the Tickfaw River just east of the split into the Blood River—Swing bridge—½ feet (closed)—opens on demand

New Orleans Inner Harbor Navigation Canal (Industrial Canal)—contains 5 bridges, listed below moving south from Lake Pontchartrain to the turning basin

    1. Highway 47-Hayne Boulevard Highway Bridge—Bascule—46 feet (closed)— does not open during peak traffic hours (7:00 A.M. to 8:30 A.M. and 5:00 P.M. to 6:30 P.M.)—otherwise opens on demand

    2. Seabrook Railway Bridge—1 foot (closed)—opens on demand unless a train is due

    3. Highway 90 Bridge—Lift bridge—50 feet (closed)—120 feet (open)—does not open during peak traffic hours (7:00 A.M. to 8:30 A.M. and 5:00 P.M. to 6:30 P.M.)—otherwise opens on demand

    4. Interstate 10 Bridge—Fixed—115 feet

    5. Gentilly Road Railway Bridge—1 foot (closed)—opens on demand unless a train is due

Chef Menteur Railway Bridge—crosses Chef Menteur north of its intersection with the ICW—10 feet (closed)—usually open unless a train is due

Chef Menteur-Highway 90 Bridge—crosses Chef Menteur north of the railway bridge—Swing bridge—11 feet (closed)—opens on demand

Interstate Highway 510 Bridge—crosses the ICW at standard mile 13—Fixed—138 feet

ICW-Inner Harbor Navigation Canal (Industrial Canal)—contains 3 spans between the turning basin and the Mississippi River

    1. Florida Avenue Railway and Highway Bridge—0 feet (closed)—does not open at all between 6:45 A.M. and 8:30 A.M. and from 4:45 P.M. to 6:45 P.M.—at all other times, supposedly opens on demand unless a train is due—note that a new bridge is currently under construction at this location

2. North Claiborne Avenue Bridge—Lift bridge—40 feet (closed)—155 feet (open)—does not open at all between 6:45 A.M. and 8:30 A.M. and from 4:45 P.M. to 6:45 P.M.—at all other times, supposedly opens on demand

3. St. Claude Avenue Bridge—Bascule—0 feet (closed)—opens in conjunction with the Industrial Canal lock doors—does not open at all between 6:45 A.M. and 8:30 A.M. and from 4:45 P.M. to 6:45 P.M.

Wilderness Rivers

North (and a bit east) of flashing buoy #11 and unlighted nun buoy #12 on the ICW (standard mile 40), intrepid cruisers can follow a reliable channel into the southerly mouth of Pearl River. This gateway, along with its two other counterparts on the Rigolets, ushers cruisers into a vast grass savanna crisscrossed by an incredible collection of undeveloped rivers, creeks, and small passages. While the myriad streams can be a bit confusing, they offer many, many miles of solitary exploration. Opportunities to drop the hook abound, but be warned that the deep soundings require a lot of anchor rode and the surrounding marsh grass shores do not give the best protection in heavy weather. Most of these wilderness waters are only appropriate for vessels as large as 45 feet. Bigger boats may not find enough maneuvering room.

If your craft can fit these requirements and you enjoy cruising where there is very little evidence of man's handiwork, the wilderness streams between the Pearl River and the Rigolets may just be for you. On the other hand, if you prefer to spend your evenings idling at the pier of a well-founded marina, it would be advisable to continue following the Waterway west to the Rigolets. There is not a single marina on any of the wilderness rivers or creeks.

The Pearl River

A well-defined channel with minimum depths of 8 feet runs north from flashing daybeacon #1 (itself northeast of flashing buoy #11 and unlighted nun #12) to the southern mouth of the Pearl River. The largest, deepest, and best marked of the undeveloped streams east of the Rigolets, the Pearl River offers many miles of good cruising. Minimum depths on the stream's mid-width are 9 feet, with some soundings deepening to 30 feet or better. Conversely, there are very few anchorages along the river's track, but this dearth of havens is offset by the potential havens found on the various sidewaters running into the Pearl.

The Pearl River serves as the modern-day coastal boundary between Mississippi and Louisiana. In Colonial times both banks were part of French Louisiana.

The southerly reaches of Pearl River are bounded by huge expanses of marsh grass which seemingly stretch on to the horizon. North of the charted Highway 90 Bridge, the banks rise to higher, well-wooded shores. Development is quite light over the entire course of the Pearl River. A few houses occasionally overlook the stream, especially near the Highway 90 Bridge. For the most part,

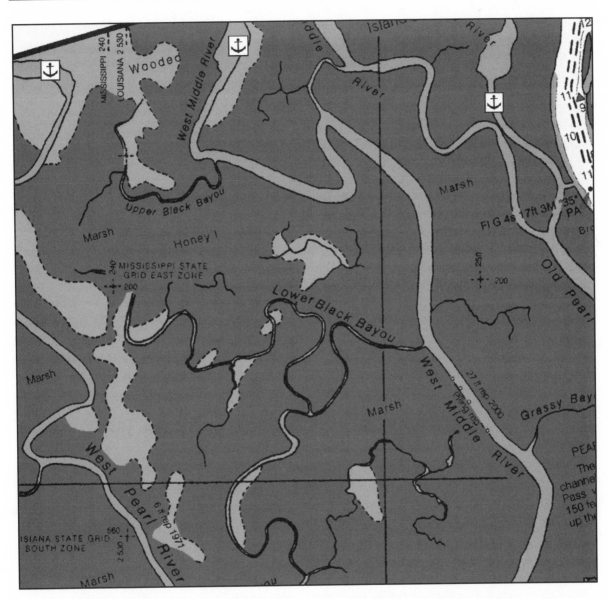

though, visiting mariners can gaze contentedly at a very attractive shoreline in its natural state.

It is a run of better than 7 nautical miles from the Pearl River's southern mouth to the Highway 90 Bridge. Another 8 nautical miles separate this span from the upstream cruising limits for pleasure craft at unlighted daybeacon #73.

Anchorage on the river north of the Highway 90 span is a definite possibility in the absence of any commercial traffic. The higher banks would render good protection from winds short of hurricane force.

Currents do flow swiftly in the Pearl River. If you drop the hook anywhere over the river's course, be sure the anchor is well set and not dragging before settling in for the evening.

Many visitors to the Pearl River will be as surprised as this writer to learn that a NASA manufacturing facility guards the stream's extreme northerly reaches. The presence of this plant accounts for the prolific markings along the river's path. A sign just north of unlighted daybeacon #73 warns against further upstream passage by pleasure craft. During our visit to this river, we were astonished to spy a large tugboat hauling a huge liquid oxygen storage tank down the river. Should you anchor on the Pearl's upper reaches and one of these tugs happens along, it could call for a sudden move. If this unhappy event should occur during the night, the resulting confusion could be considerable.

South of the entrance to Mulatto Bayou, navigators studying chart 11367 will note a small island of higher ground known as "English Lookout." While I have been unable to find any specific references to this area in my historic research, with a name like that it's a good bet that it was once used as a small fort.

North of flashing daybeacon #62, three loops of Pearl River have been bypassed by modern canal dredging. The first of these is found northwest of unlighted daybeacon #63. This small offshoot holds surprising depths of 12 to 20 feet, but there is not really enough swinging room for vessels larger than 28 feet. In a pinch, you might get by with a Bahamian mooring or a stern anchor, but it would still be tight.

The second bypassed loop cuts east, just south of unlighted daybeacon #66. *Do not* attempt to explore this stream. Our on-site research revealed some sort of strange, semisunken underwater obstructions in the otherwise sufficient depths. Also, the northern entrance has a bar with only 4- to 4½-foot depths.

The third and final loop between unlighted daybeacons #70 and #72 is much too small for cruising-sized craft. Just north of this sidewater, skippers are warned to turn back by a sign at unlighted daybeacon #73.

Grand Plains Bayou

The small creek known as Grand Plains Bayou splits off from the eastern shores of the Pearl River just south of the railroad swing bridge. Depths vary from 6 to 8 feet moving east to the stream's charted split. There is only enough swinging room for boats up to 28 feet to anchor. Most cruising skippers will bypass this small creek without another thought.

Mulatto Bayou
(30 12.524 North/089 34.990 West)

Mulatto Bayou opens onto the northern shores of the Pearl River due north of English Lookout Island. Minimum entrance depths are 8 feet (from the Pearl River) and soundings range from 8 to 16 feet over the course of the stream.

The bayou runs generally north for some 2.7 nautical miles to an intersection with the Port Bienville Industrial Park canal. Craft as large as 33 feet can probably drop the hook on Mulatto Bayou short of Port Bienville, but swinging room is skimpy. Again, you might need a stern anchor or a Bahamian moor to avoid swinging into the shoreline. The creek's shores are composed entirely of marsh grass to the south, while the easterly banks rise to higher levels north of the Cross Bayou intersection. With winds from the east, this would be the best spot to anchor (possibly near 30 12.524 North/089 34.990 West).

The Port Bienville Industrial Park canal is overlooked by a huge plant of some sort east of unlighted daybeacon #WR. There is also evidence of barge loading on these waters. With such commercial traffic in mind, this writer does not suggest anchoring on the stream.

The Port Bienville canal runs back to the southwest and rejoins the Pearl River near flashing daybeacon #PB. While some navigational caution must be exercised in this passage, minimum 8-foot depths are held in the canal channel leading to the river's deep waters.

Cross Bayou

Cross Bayou is a small stream that runs from Mulatto Bayou to the southwestern reaches of the Port Bienville canal. While exhibiting fair depths, this creek is too narrow for boats larger than 25 feet.

Little Lake Channel

South of flashing daybeacon #21, a marked channel leads southwest from the Pearl River and across shallow Little Lake to the Rigolets. This passage holds minimum 10-foot depths and is relatively easy to follow during the daylight hours. Nighttime passage is another matter.

Besides providing reliable access directly from the Pearl River to the Rigolets, the channel across Little Lake also allows an approach to West Middle River and West Pearl River via a channel running northwest from flashing daybeacon #11. Entrance depths are only 5½ to 6 feet, and navigational caution is required.

Nevertheless, many cruising craft drawing 5 feet or less will find this cut to be quite useful.

The Old Pearl River

The stream known as the Old Pearl River flows northwest from its bigger sister, the Pearl River, at flashing daybeacon #25. Minimum 8-foot depths are carried at the intersection of the two streams. There are a few unmarked and uncharted shallows to avoid, but elementary precautions should see you through. Soundings on the river's main track range from 15 to 28 feet.

The Old Pearl River is bounded entirely by saltwater marsh. As you might expect, the shoreline does not afford enough shelter for heavy weather. However, with forecast winds less than 20 knots, it is quite possible to drop the hook anywhere on the river upstream of its first long jog to the west. The initial southerly portion of the stream's track is a bit too open for any but light air anchorage. Swinging room should be sufficient for boats up to 40 feet in length.

The Old Pearl River runs northwest for slightly less than 2 nautical miles before it breaks into two alternate streams, East Middle River and the Middle River.

East Middle River
(30 13.847 North/089 37.394 West)

East Middle River is an astonishingly deep stream with some soundings actually reaching 60 feet! Anyone worried about running aground in that?

The river is surrounded by the usual undeveloped salt marsh, which gives only minimal protection from strong winds, but captains can still cruise to one good anchorage. About 1 nautical mile north of the Old Pearl River, East

Middle River runs through a stretch of broad water just south of the small charted offshoot running north from the eastern banks (near 30 13.847 North/089 37.394 West). There is plenty of swinging room but depths of 35 to 60 feet will call for an awful lot of anchor rode to achieve a minimum 6-to-1 scope.

North of the anchorage discussed above, East Middle River soon runs under the Highway 90 swing bridge. This guide's coverage of the river ends at that point.

It is also possible to reach East Middle River directly from the Pearl River. The charted passage at flashing daybeacon #35 (on the Pearl River) holds 15-foot depths for most of its short length, but there is a bar near #35 with only 6 to 7 feet of water. Boats drawing less than 5 feet can readily make use of this handy cut-through.

The Middle River

Middle River is very similar in character to the Old Pearl and East Middle rivers. The same salt grass shores with minimum 10-foot depths characterize the stream.

After cruising north for .5 nautical miles from the Old Pearl River intersection, the Middle River passes through a loop to the west and actually touches East Middle River. On-site research revealed that 5-foot depths can be carried across the bar separating the two streams. However, this passage is not reliable and not particularly recommended by this writer.

South of the charted location of Desert Island, an offshoot cuts southwest to West Middle River. (Yes, that's right—there's East Middle River, Middle River, and West Middle River. Don't look at me; I didn't name them.) This cut carries depths of 10 to 12 feet and can be used with confidence.

North Pass, East Mouth, and West Mouth (30 10.878 North/089 38.202 West)

Shifting our attention to the west, let's review the passage striking northwest from the Little Lake channel and leading eventually to the Rigolets. This stream is known as North Pass on its easterly reaches, East Mouth on its center section, and West Mouth on its approach to the Rigolets. Besides having good depths and anchorage possibilities of its own, the creek allows easy access to the southern mouths of West Middle and West Pearl rivers. If this sounds confusing, and I know it does, just glance at chart 11367 to clear up any doubt.

The entrance to North Pass from Little Lake channel carries only 5½ to 6 feet of low-tide depth. Vessels drawing 5 feet or (preferably) less should be able to cruise through without mishap, but be alert for recent changes in the channel.

The interior portion of the triple-named creek carries depths of from 8 to as much as 30 feet. The entrance into the Rigolets displays 8-foot minimum depths.

By now you must be growing just a bit tired of my references to undeveloped saltwater marsh on the wilderness streams. Well, guess what. This stream is surrounded by (you guessed it) undeveloped salt marsh. Protection is, again, not sufficient for comfortable overnight anchorage when winds exceed 20 to 25 knots.

The North Pass section of the stream is a bit narrow for boats over 35 feet to drop the hook, as is West Mouth. Fortunately, East Mouth is quite wide and affords enough elbow room for boats as large as 45 feet. Depths vary widely from 12 to as much as 40 feet. Unless you have a large quantity of anchor rode aboard,

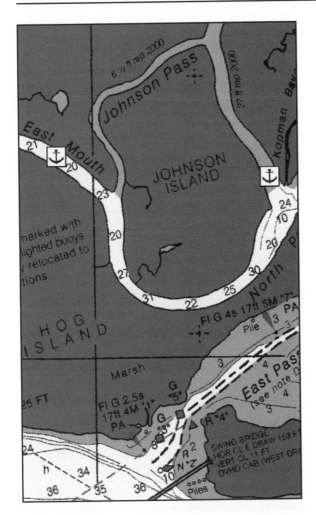

the stream's course moving north to the Highway 90 Bridge.

Boats up to 34 feet can anchor in the southern mouth of West Middle River in some 18 feet of water near 30 10.772 North/089 37.089 West. Protection is fair from all winds but insufficient for a strong blow.

Captains willing to cruise 5 nautical miles upstream to a point just short of the Highway 90 Bridge will discover a first-rate anchorage on the charted lakelike bay near 30 13.904 North/089 38.758 West. Higher ground looks out over the eastern shores and vastly improves protection for winds blowing from this quarter. Swinging room is sufficient for most pleasure craft, but the 30-foot depths again call for a lot of anchor rode.

Johnson Pass

Narrow Johnson Pass, found north of charted Johnson Island, bridges the gap between West Middle River and East Mouth. This stream carries 8 feet of water, but is probably too narrow for boats larger than 34 feet. Small craft can use the pass as a convenient shortcut into the upper reaches of West Middle River.

West Pearl River
(30 13.804 North/089 39.748 West)

The last of the wilderness rivers, moving to the west, is West Pearl River. The stream holds minimum depths of 10 feet on its mid-width upstream to the anchorage discussed below. Unlike its sister streams, the West Pearl is a bit too narrow over most of its length for anchorage by cruising-sized craft.

The one exception to this rule is found some 4 nautical miles upstream, near 30

pick out one of the shallower sections. One good spot is found near 30 10.878 North/089 38.202 West.

West Middle River
(Various Lats/Lons—see below)

As you would expect, West Middle River is typical of its nearby sister streams in every respect. Minimum entrance depths are 12 feet, with soundings ranging from 18 to 47 feet on

13.804 North/089 39.748 West. Here, West Pearl River is flanked by higher ground to the east and west. While on-site research did *not* reveal the wider, baylike section shown on chart 11367, captains who are willing to make the upstream trek and who pilot boats no more than 42 feet in length can drop the hook in a well-sheltered haven adjacent to the higher shores. Protection should be sufficient for minor storms, but not full gale winds.

Sawmill Bayou

Narrow Sawmill Bayou cuts into the northeastern banks of West Pearl River just north of the larger stream's southerly mouth. While Sawmill actually has good depths, it is too small for all but outboard and I/O skiffs. A lone cabin overlooks the point separating the two streams. One can only look and wonder at a domicile out in the middle of all this vast saltwater wilderness.

WILDERNESS RIVERS NAVIGATION

An experienced mariner could almost be trusted to successfully navigate all of the wilderness rivers with the one admonition, "Stick to the mid-width." Indeed, this old saw is so universally true throughout the whole region that I won't bore the reader by repeating it for every individual stream. Only those portions of the various channels that require a bit more maneuvering will be noted below. Frankly, these are waters where few navigators will have any problems with running aground. The streams are uniformly deep and shoals are very few. However, it never hurts to stay alert and keep a watch on the sounder.

The Pearl River   Depart from the ICW some .3 nautical miles east of flashing buoy #11 and unlighted nun #12. Set course to come abeam of and pass flashing daybeacon #1 by some 10 yards to its easterly side. Unlighted daybeacons #3, #5, and #7 lead you through a dredged channel across the river's entrance bar. Flashing daybeacons #7A and #8 mark the Pearl

River's southerly mouth. Stick to the centerline of the gap between #7A and #8.

The Pearl River crosses under a swinging railway bridge .9 nautical miles north of flashing daybeacon #8. This span has a closed vertical clearance of 14 feet. It is usually open during daylight hours unless a train is due. From 9:00 P.M. to 5:00 A.M. the span is closed and special arrangements are necessary for an opening.

North of #8, there are no further markers for a goodly distance upstream. They resume at the intersection of Little Lake Pass. Don't confuse the markers on Little Lake Channel with the Pearl River aids to navigation. Pass flashing daybeacon #21, which marks the northwesterly point separating the Pearl River and the Little Lake channel, to its easterly side.

Northwest of unlighted daybeacon #31, a charted 3-foot shoal seems to be building out from the river's northeastern banks. Favor the southwestern side of the river a bit when passing.

The Highway 90 swing bridge crosses the

Pearl River .8 of a nautical mile north of unlighted daybeacon #38. It has a closed vertical clearance of only 10 feet, but opens on demand except from 9:00 P.M. to 5:00 A.M. The span usually remains closed during these hours.

North of unlighted daybeacon #63, three loops of the Pearl River have been bypassed by the stream's modern course. None of these offshoots is particularly recommended for cruising-size vessels. When cruising downstream on the Pearl River, it can be all too easy to mistake these loops for the river's primary channel. Be sure to keep chart 11367 around to quickly resolve any questions which might arise.

Mulatto Bayou Navigation of Mulatto Bayou remains quite straightforward until reaching the Port Bienville Industrial Park canal. At this point cruisers should either retrace their steps south back down the bayou, or cut southwest and follow the marked canal channel back to the Pearl River. Don't attempt to enter either of the two creeks north of unlighted daybeacon #3. Depths on both streams are quite suspect.

If you follow the industrial canal to the Pearl River, be sure to use the passage south of the small marsh island, west of unlighted daybeacon #2. Follow the mid-width of the channel, pointing to come abeam of flashing daybeacon #PB to its immediate southerly side.

Little Lake Channel The easterly portion of the channel leading southwest from the Pearl River across Little Lake to the Rigolets is wide and easily followed. Southwest of flashing daybeacon #14, the cut narrows a bit and markers are slightly farther apart. Watch for leeway and stick strictly to the marked cut. Depths outside of the dredged channel rise very quickly to grounding levels.

Southwest of #14, you must be on guard against confusing the markers leading northwest to North Pass with the Little Lake channel aids to navigation. Be sure to pass just southeast of flashing daybeacon #11 and continue on course, pointing to pass between unlighted daybeacon #9 and flashing daybeacon #10. Unless you are planning to enter North Pass, ignore the unlighted daybeacons to the northwest.

Immediately after passing between unlighted daybeacons #4 and #5, the channel takes a jog to the south. Care must be taken to avoid straying too far east into the charted 2-foot shoal. Set course to come abeam of unlighted daybeacon #3 to its fairly immediate easterly side. You can then proceed southwest out into the Rigolets through the broad and deep passage between flashing daybeacon #1 and unlighted nun buoy #2.

The Old Pearl River Entrance into the southerly mouth of the Old Pearl River from the Pearl River calls for caution. One of the few shoals on these waters is found adjacent to the river's entrance.

For best depths, depart the Pearl River channel some .1 nautical miles after passing unlighted daybeacon #24 and point to come abeam of flashing daybeacon #25 by some 25 yards to its southwesterly side. Immediately after leaving #25 behind, begin favoring the easterly banks while cruising upstream for the next 100 to 150 yards. You can then cruise back into the center and good depths open out almost from shore to shore.

East Middle River and the Middle River
The point of marsh on the Old Pearl River, separating the southern mouths of East Middle and Middle rivers, has built south for quite a distance. Avoid this point and enter either stream on its mid-width. Hold to the centerline on both rivers, as well as on the passages from East Middle River to the Pearl River and the Middle River to West Middle River, for best depths.

North Pass, East Mouth, and West Mouth
The channel running from Little Lake into North Pass has shoaled somewhat. Minimum low-tide depths are only 5½ to 6 feet. If this is a bit thin for your craft, consider entering West Mouth from the Rigolets. This passage carries 8 feet of water or better.

To enter North Pass from Little Lake, depart the Little Lake channel some 50

yards east-northeast of flashing daybeacon #11. Turn to the west-northwest and set a course to pass unlighted daybeacon #2 to your immediate starboard side. Continue dead ahead, pointing to pass unlighted daybeacon #3 by some 10 to 15 yards to its northerly quarter. Continue on the same course from some .15 nautical miles, and then bend your track a touch to the west. Point to come abeam of unlighted daybeacon #5 by about 15 yards to its northerly side.

As you cruise into the easterly mouth of North Pass, favor the southerly banks. On-site research revealed that shoal water is present just to the north. As the southerly mouth of West Middle River comes abeam to the north, good depths again open out from shore to shore.

West Middle and West Pearl Rivers   No unusual navigational problems are encountered on either of these streams as far north as their respective Highway 90 bridges. Simply stay to the mid-width and you should have a delightful cruise.

The Rigolets, Lake Pontchartrain, and Lake Maurepas

We shall now turn our attention to the cruising grounds north of New Orleans. This vast region provides most of the city's cruisable waters and marina facilities. Mariners interested in visiting New Orleans or simply in sampling the Northern Gulf's most spacious cruising grounds should give every consideration to the waters north of the "Big Easy."

The Rigolets is a broad inlet that leads directly

from the ICW (standard mile 35) to the extreme easterly reaches of Lake Pontchartrain. Along the way, there is one marina that offers some overnight dockage for smaller cruising craft.

The Rigolets (French speak for "Little Canal") flows into huge Lake Pontchartrain by way of a well-marked channel. Take a moment to glance at chart 11369. You will see that Lake Pontchartrain resembles a colossal turtle. The head is outlined by the lobe leading from the Rigolets, while the vast round body encompasses the lake's north and south shores.

The north shore provides superb cruising via several small rivers. During the last few years marina facilities on these various streams have been growing at a breakneck pace. Fortunately, the quaint Louisiana towns along the shores of these backwaters have not yet succumbed (and hopefully never will) to rampant commercial development.

While cruising on these waters it is still quite possible, even likely, to hear a local discussing the fishing conditions in an inimitable Cajun accent. Visitors can frequently savor an unforgettable Creole-style meal in a charming restaurant that seems like more of a secret than a tourist attraction. To say that this writer is enthusiastic about cruising the northern banks of Lake Pontchartrain just doesn't cover it. This region deserves recognition by all cruisers. Read the account below carefully. Hopefully, you will agree that the north shore deserves a place in every mariner's itinerary.

Pontchartrain's south shore is home to New Orleans' marina facilities. One vast harbor is found a short distance east of the mammoth Lake Pontchartrain Causeway, while a well-protected basin is located just east of the charted Lakefront Airport. Visiting cruisers can be assured of finding every imaginable service at these facilities, including plentiful overnight dockage.

West of the Lakefront Airport, the New Orleans Inner Harbor Navigation Canal joins Lake Pontchartrain. After passing a bevy of low-level bridges, cruising craft can rejoin the ICW and journey through the industrial lock to the Mississippi River.

Pontchartrain's shoreline runs the full gamut from undeveloped stretches to intense urban and residential development around New Orleans and Slidell. Oil and natural-gas drilling rigs are back in operation on the lake and, while environmentalists may question the utility of these operations, they make for undoubtedly interesting viewing from the water.

Lake Pontchartrain is crisscrossed by several underwater pipelines and overhead power cables. All of these various obstructions are well charted and outlined with aids to navigation and, in the case of the power lines, lighted towers. Obviously, you should never anchor anywhere near a pipeline and sailcraft should take very careful note of the overhead clearances of the various power lines.

The rear of the Lake Pontchartrain turtle is the western shore. While there are very few cruising opportunities on this portion of the lake, notice that the turtle has a tail. This stream is known as Pass Manchac and it leads, in turn, to Lake Maurepas. This body of water is smaller than Pontchartrain, but still impressive in its size. The lake itself is almost completely lacking in marina facilities or anchorages. However, one of its three feeder rivers, the Tickfaw, is a genuine cruising pleasure with one marina and a waterside restaurant. In addition to these modern conveniences, the Tickfaw River has a charm of its own that is rooted in the stream's largely isolated, undiscovered character. While cruisers of all descriptions have been learning the delights of this beautiful river during the last several years, it can still be classified as a practically private experience.

When it comes to Lake Pontchartrain and Lake Maurepas, the two operative terms to describe these bodies of water are "big" and "rough." Lake Pontchartrain is better than 20 nautical miles in width on its north-to-south axis and almost 28 nautical miles across from east to west. Depths average only 10 to 15 feet, with some spots being considerably shallower. It doesn't require the brains of Einstein to understand that Pontchartrain's waters can produce a considerable chop when winds exceed 10 knots. In fact, stories about dangerous winds and waves on Lake Pontchartrain have been making the rounds over the last several years in the national boating press. Most of these on-the-water disasters have come about due to the afternoon thunderstorms that are so very much a part of the local meteorological climate in the spring, summer, and fall. Visiting and resident cruisers alike should check the forecast before leaving the dock and listen to updates regularly while on the water. If you see a dark cloud on the horizon heading your way, *don't muck about*! Head for the nearest harbor or anchorage immediately!

Cruising sailors should be aware that Lake Pontchartrain is crossed by four bridges. The shorter three spans cross the head of the turtle near the Rigolets and are not too great a problem. The 21-nautical-mile Lake Pontchartrain Causeway straddles the lake's mid-width. With only one opening span, sailboats that cannot clear a 50-foot fixed pass-through must contend with a restrictive opening schedule and often cruise a goodly distance out of their way to travel east or west of this barrier.

So, in a nutshell, there you have it. The Rigolets, Lake Pontchartrain and Lake Maurepas— prime cruising grounds, but nevertheless waters that must be approached with the greatest respect and caution. Whether you choose to visit the backwater towns of the north shore, the vastly unique city of New Orleans on the south shore, or the almost secret recesses of Lake Maurepas and the Tickfaw River, the waters around New Orleans never fail in their cruising reward. Just remember to keep a sharp watch at all times for bad weather and have the chart and this guide ready to help plot a quick course to the nearest harbor!

The Rigolets

The Rigolets is a large, wide-open stream that leads north and west from the Gulf Coast ICW to the easterly reaches of Lake Pontchartrain. While most captains hurry through this passage, intent on reaching the great lake, the Rigolets has a few cruising possibilities of its own.

The main body of the Rigolets is much too wide open for effective anchorage. The presence of strong currents in the cut can cause dragging anchors. No matter what you may read elsewhere, this writer strongly recommends that all skippers look elsewhere for overnight anchorage.

One marina offers overnight dockage and other services for cruising craft on Geoghegan Canal, just off the Rigolets. If bad weather is on the way, it makes more than a little sense to wait out the wind and rain at this facility, rather than venture out onto the often choppy water of Pontchartrain.

West Mouth and East Pass (Little Lake Channel)

Both of these routes provide access to the wilderness river region to the east. Each was covered in the preceding section of this chapter. Please consult this account for descriptive and navigational information.

The Blind Rigolets and Counterfeit Pass

The creek known as the Blind Rigolets opens

Rigolets Railway Bridge

into the southwestern banks of the Rigolets northwest of charted Rabbit Island. Small Counterfeit Pass cuts off just northwest of the larger stream's mouth. In spite of the seemingly broad channel shown entering the Blind Rigolets on chart 11367, any number of on-site research visits over the years have revealed an entrance bar with only 4 feet (or less) of depth. Cruising-sized vessels are warned against attempting to enter either of these risky streams.

Lagoon Anchorage

This writer used to recommend the water-tank-shaped lagoon north-northeast of flashing daybeacon #3, on the Rigolets' northerly banks, as an overnight anchorage. However, the entrance, which was never too deep, has now shoaled to only 3½-foot depths at MLW. We now suggest that all mariners bypass this errant body of water, even though you may see some local shrimp craft moored on the small bay's interior reaches.

Sawmill Pass and Lake St. Catherine (30 09.166 North/089 43.747 West)

The wide passage known as Sawmill Pass strikes south to shallow Lake St. Catherine, well southwest of flashing daybeacon #4. While the channel running through Sawmill Pass carries minimum depths of 7 feet, soundings on Lake Catherine quickly rise to 3- and 4-foot levels. Sawmill Pass is much too open for any but light-air anchorage.

If winds are calm and are forecast to remain

so, you might consider anchoring near 30 09.166 North/089 43.747 West, astride the Sawmill Pass's interior reaches. However, we strongly suggest that all mariners piloting cruising-sized craft avoid Lake St. Catherine entirely.

Fort Pike Canal

Historic Fort Pike gazes out over the southwestern shores of the Rigolets just short of the Highway 90 swing bridge. The seemingly ancient masonry walls of this fortification were actually built between 1819 and 1828. Following the War of 1812, the federal government built a whole series of forts along the Gulf Coast to guard against an enemy invasion such as had occurred during that conflict. This fort was designed to safeguard the back-door approach to New Orleans via the Rigolets. Today, Fort Pike is a state park and is open to the public.

The charted canal southeast of Fort Pike carries entrance and interior depths of 5 to 5½ feet. The stream leads to a series of private docks. There is not enough swinging room for boats larger than 25 feet to anchor comfortably. If you choose to visit Fort Pike itself, it would probably be best to anchor off on the Rigolets' deeper depths and dinghy ashore.

Rigolets Bait and Seafood—Geoghegan Canal (30 10.540 North/089 43.578 West—marina)

Deep Geoghegan Canal splits off from the Rigolets' northeastern banks directly across from Fort Pike, southeast of the Highway 90

Fort Pike, the Rigolets

swing bridge. This fortunate stream carries minimum depths of 7½ feet, with most soundings considerably deeper. Two possible anchorages and one small marina are available on Geoghegan Canal.

Rigolets Bait and Seafood, now under new ownership, overlooks the western banks a short distance upstream of the canal's southerly mouth. This facility has changed hands several times over the last three or four years, but the new management team seems to be the most cruiser friendly of the bunch.

Nevertheless, clearly the emphasis here is on sportfishing. During our last visit, the waiting line to launch small craft at the marina ramp was impressive indeed. Rigolets Bait and

Seafood must possess one of the most popular launching ramps in the state of Louisiana.

Larger cruising craft are accepted for overnight dockage, if space is available. The numbers of wet slips are limited. Dockage is provided at fixed wooden piers with both fresh-water hookups and some 30-amp power connections. Low-water dockside soundings run in the 5- to 6-foot region. Most of the marina's slips are far more appropriate for vessels 40 feet and smaller. Gasoline and diesel fuel are readily available for dockside purchase, and there is also an extensive tackle and variety store on the premises, just behind the fuel dock. Unfortunately, the on-site restaurant has been closed for some time, and its future, if any, is very uncertain. No grocery stores or other shopping facilities are within easy reach of this marina.

All in all, we found Rigolets Bait and Seafood to be a small but friendly marina that transients who pilot smaller cruising craft and who don't need a great deal of shoreside support might well consider. In light of the relatively few slips set aside for visitors, it might be a good idea to call ahead of time and check on availability before committing to a plan for an overnight stay.

1. Rigolet's Bait and Seafood

Rigolets Bait and Seafood (985) 641-8088

Approach depth—7½-12 feet
Dockside depth—5-6 feet
Accepts transients—yes
Transient-dockage rate—below average
Fixed wooden piers—yes
Dockside power connections—30-amp
Dockside water connections—yes
Gasoline—yes
Diesel fuel—yes
Variety and tackle store—yes

Rigolets Bait and Seafood

The broad northwesterly flank of Double Bayou Lagoon intersects Geoghegan Canal some .6 nautical miles northeast of the marina. Depths of 18 to 40 feet are found on the mid-width of this lagoon, near 30 10.977 North/089 43.055 West. The surrounding shores are composed exclusively of the usual salt marsh. This would be an acceptable spot to drop the hook when winds are not forecast to exceed 15 knots. Stronger blows would call for another strategy. There should be enough swinging room for vessels as large as 40 feet on the lagoon.

Eventually, Geoghegan Canal dead-ends into a small, charted stream that runs northwest for a short distance. Just before reaching the primary canal's northeasterly terminus, captains piloting craft up to 32 feet might consider dropping the hook in some 8 feet of water. While boats as large as 34 feet may find enough swinging room, it would probably be wise to use a Bahamian-style mooring. The surrounding shores are marsh, but high ground does front the canal a short distance to the northeast. Considering the canal's narrow width, protection should be sufficient for nasty weather, even if not enough for a full gale.

RIGOLETS NAVIGATION

Successful navigation of the Rigolets to Lake Pontchartrain is quite straightforward. Markings are adequate and good depths stretch almost from bank to bank. In general, you need only be concerned about the relatively strong current and sometimes rough conditions caused by winds over 15 knots. Otherwise, sit back and enjoy the scenery.

Entrance from the ICW   From flashing buoy #21, set a careful compass course to the central pass-through of the "Rigolets L&N Railroad Bridge" spanning the stream between Rabbit and Pearl River islands. Be mindful of the small shoal extending east and northeast from Catfish Point to the west. Be sure to use the east-side pass-through, as the western one is crossed by an overhead power cable. I always think it's a good idea to avoid shocking overhead obstructions!

This railway swing bridge has a closed vertical clearance of 11 feet. The span is supposed to open on demand. However, we once watched a passing cruiser blow his horn repeatedly and listened to numerous unanswered calls on the VHF before the tender deigned to open the bridge for a mere pleasure craft. I suggest long and loud horn action if you encounter a similar state of affairs.

On the Rigolets   Immediately after you pass through the Rigolets L&N Railroad Bridge, the passage to Little Lake will open out to the east-northeast. As you will

remember, this route was covered in the last section of this chapter.

A range marker is visible to the northwest immediately after you leave the railroad span behind. With the broad channel, pleasure boats can pretty much ignore this aid to navigation.

Simply hold to the mid-width as you work your way upstream toward flashing daybeacon #2. This aid is almost on the shore and can be somewhat difficult to spot. Come abeam of #2 well to its southerly side.

Southeast of #2 the entrance to West Mouth (also detailed in the last section of this chapter) opens out on the northern shores, as does the mouth of the Blind Rigolets to the south. Remember, do not attempt entry into this latter stream. Entrance depths are 4 feet or less.

West of flashing daybeacon #2, the Rigolets takes a small jog farther to the northwest and hurries on for some 2.1 nautical miles to a sharp westerly turn, marked by flashing daybeacon #3. This aid is found hard by the southern banks and is particularly hard to spot for westbound navigators. Use your binoculars to pick out the daybeacon among the flanking marsh grasses.

Lagoon Anchorage   *Please remember that we no longer recommend anchoring on the waters of the water-tank-shaped lagoon found on the northern banks of the Rigolets opposite flashing daybeacon #3. During our last visit, we observed a local shrimper* moored on the interior reaches of this lagoon. How he got over the 3½-foot depths at the entrance is a mystery to this writer.

On the Rigolets West of flashing daybeacon #3, the already broad Rigolets widens into a very impressive stream indeed. Good depths continue on the vast majority of the stream, though one stretch of shallows is located along the southern banks. Anyone within shouting distance of the mid-width will avoid this hazard by a very wide margin.

You should point to eventually come abeam of flashing daybeacon #4, on the northern banks, well to its southerly side. At #4, the Rigolets cuts to the northwest and begins to narrow as it hurries toward the Rigolets-Highway 90 swing bridge. To the south, deep Sawmill Pass channel runs to shallow Lake St. Catherine. A bit farther to the northwest, the entrance to the Geoghegan Canal will come abeam to the northeast, just short of the highway span.

Geoghegan Canal Enter the canal on its centerline and continue holding to the middle as you work your way upstream. If you decide to enter Double Bayou Lagoon, do so on the center of its southwest to northeast axis. Drop the hook anywhere near the middle of the lagoon for good depths.

Boats continuing northeast on the canal to the anchorage just short of the stream's terminus should continue holding to the mid-width. Be sure to set the hook at least 50 yards short of the point where the canal

cuts sharply to the northwest. Don't attempt to enter this upper extreme of the creek unless your craft is no more than 28 feet long.

Fort Pike If you should decide to visit historical Fort Pike, drop the hook just southeast of the charted semisunken wreck. Fort Pike Canal is a bit shallow and narrow for boats over 28 feet. Once the hook is down, you can dinghy ashore to view this old monument from Louisiana's past. Please don't trespass on private property.

On to Lake Pontchartrain From flashing daybeacon #4, set course to eventually pass through the charted swinging section of the Rigolets-Highway 90 Bridge. This span has a closed vertical clearance of 14 feet, but fortunately, it opens on demand. Again, the operator has been known to be a bit slow on the trigger. Try calling the bridge tender on VHF channel 13 or, if that doesn't work, blowing your horn.

After passing the highway bridge, set a careful compass course to eventually come abeam of flashing daybeacon #5, off the point of land guarded by Fort Pike, by at least 200 yards to its northern side. As you come abeam of #5, you might be shocked to see your sounder indicating depths of 90 to 100 feet. Grounding should not be a problem in this section (ha, ha). Be mindful of the charted shallows well to the north. At #5, you may be able to catch sight of the old, wooden Rigolets Lighthouse to the south.

To the west, the broad reaches of Lake Pontchartrain will be readily visible. Believe it or else, this is the "narrower" turtle's-head portion of the lake. This knowledge can bring quite a shock when you first see the wide swath of open waters before you. To the west, one of the few shoals on Lake Pontchartrain complicates entry into the main body of water. Fortunately, there is a dredged, well-marked passage which leads off to the northwest. This cut will be covered in the next navigational section of this chapter.

Lake Pontchartrain—Northern Shore

One bright, summer morning in the early 1990s, my ace research assistant Andy Lightbourne and I were working our way up the Tchefuncte River toward the village of Madisonville. We were admiring the heavily wooded, lightly developed shores when we spotted a large, full-service marina. The friendly dockmaster unhurriedly detailed all the marina's services in a slow, Cajun accent that rolled off her tongue like pickled honey. She pointed out at least three restaurants with dockage of their own within sight of the marina, and we visited one of them for a very memorable lunch. Then it was upriver past beautifully natural shores teeming with anchorage possibilities. Just when we least expected it, a marina with a well-sheltered basin popped up. As we continued our explorations, Andy summarized our collective mood by saying, "This is the kind of stream on which one could go cruising and forget to ever come home."

That simple statement really says it all about cruising the northern shore of Lake Pontchartrain. The shoreline is dotted with wide, deep rivers, creeks, and bayous which lead north to a host of anchorages and a growing number of marinas. Some of these streams have beautifully undeveloped shores, while others are overlooked by small, intensely Southern towns which still look very much as they did fifty years ago. The natives are universally friendly, particularly to those arriving by water. Dining out can be the experience of a lifetime, as this writer once discovered in nearby Mandeville. Hey, what more do you want?

Oak Harbor
(30 12.929 North/089 47.616 West)

One of the largest and best-appointed facilities on Pontchartrain's northern shore is found just inside the well-marked, charted channel immediately west of the Interstate Highway 10 Bridge. This span is the first bridge you will encounter west of the Rigolets. Oak Harbor Marina features 10-foot minimum entrance depths. Dockside soundings are even better, with 16 to 19 feet at the outer piers and 10 to 11 feet of water on the inner slips.

Cruising into the harbor's improved channel leading northeast, you will first spot a large concrete seawall to starboard. Soon the entrance to the well-protected dockage basin will be spied, also to starboard.

Visiting transient craft are gratefully accepted for overnight or temporary dockage in the protected basin on the northeastern side of the entrance canal. Berths feature both

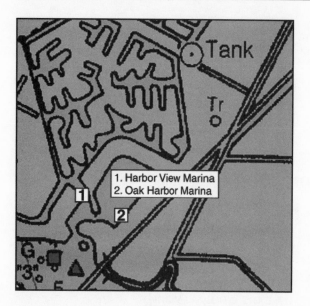

1. Harbor View Marina
2. Oak Harbor Marina

Oak Harbor Marina (985) 641-1044

Approach depth—10 feet
Dockside depth—10-19 feet
Accepts transients—yes
Transient-dockage rate—below average
Concrete floating docks—yes
Fixed wooden docks—yes
Dockside power connections—30- and 50-amp
Dockside water connections—yes
Showers—yes
Laundromat—yes
Mechanical repairs—limited
Restaurant—2 nearby

superior-quality floating concrete docks and fixed wooden piers. Oak Harbor is one of the very, very few marinas on the Northern Gulf Coast that offers this first-rate construction. As you might expect, all power and water connections are available, as are shoreside, climate-controlled showers and laundry facilities. Mechanical services can sometimes be arranged through an independent mechanic, but the assistant dockmaster has informed this writer that such a practice is rare. The nearby Marine Cafe restaurant (985-641-0464) is very convenient and seems to serve good seafood. This writer's good friends at the Tammany Yacht Club use this facility as their meeting spot for dinner get-togethers.

While it most certainly lacks the small-town charm found in Mandeville and Madisonville, Oak Harbor Marina can lay claim to some of the most impressive facilities on the north shore. If you are looking for a full-service marina with every amenity, your search is over.

Another small marina, plus fuel pier, is found just short of the entrance to Oak Harbor. Cruisers can cut to the northwest before entering Oak Harbor and discover Harbor View Marina overlooking the canal's southerly banks near 30 13.016 North/089 47.819 West. This minimal facility is often closed during the winter months. Harbor View offers some minimal overnight transient dockage at its fixed wooden face docks. Space can be at a bit of a premium. Depths alongside are 6 feet or better. Fresh-water connections and 20-amp power hookups are available as well. If the on-site lounge is in operation during your visit, it can make for a noisy evening.

Gasoline and diesel fuel, as well as a shoreside variety/convenience store, are available. A very healthy walk will lead you to Vera's Restaurant (337 Lakeview Drive, 985-643-9291).

Harbor View Marina (985) 649-3320

Approach depth—8-10 feet
Dockside depth—6+ feet
Accepts transients—limited
Fixed wooden face docks—yes
Dockside power connections—20-amp
Dockside water connections—yes

Oak Harbor Marina

Gasoline—yes
Diesel fuel—yes
Variety store—yes
Restaurant—long walk

Skippers following the canal that curves off to port past Harbor View Marina can find their way to two additional low-key facilities. Be advised that all these waters are an official no-wake zone. Proceeding at idle speed, it can take just short of forever to reach your goal. Most cruising-size boats will probably want to take advantage of the Oak Harbor facility rather than go traipsing off on a long trek. Tall sailcraft should also be warned that they must pass under a power line with 50 feet of vertical clearance to continue upstream on the canal.

As the canal takes a sharp turn to the north, the docks of North Shore Marine (985-863-3834) will come up to port. This firm specializes in the sales of smaller powercraft. It does have a fuel dock with both gasoline and diesel fuel fronting the canal. Dockside depths are about 5 feet.

Continuing upstream, you will soon encounter a fuel dock associated with a convenience store, also to port. Gasoline and diesel fuel can be purchased while you float in some 5 to 6 feet of water.

To the north and east, a whole series of mostly deep canals serve a highly developed but reasonably attractive by-the-water residential community. While you are certainly free to cruise the canals at idle speed for a closer look, no additional facilities are to be found.

Liberty Bayou and Bayou Bonfouca (Various Lats/Lons—see below)

The marked entrance channel leading north to the twin streams known as Liberty Bayou and Bayou Bonfouca lies to the northwest of Big Point. Minimum depths are a very respectable 8

feet, with many soundings being deeper. The two streams offer some marina facilities and good anchorage.

Some .5 nautical miles north of its intersection with Pontchartrain, the wide stream leading from the lake splits into two branches. Liberty Bayou runs on to the north and northeast while Bayou Bonfouca cuts to the south and then northeast on its way to the city of Slidell. The lower reaches of this latter stream are surrounded by undeveloped saltwater

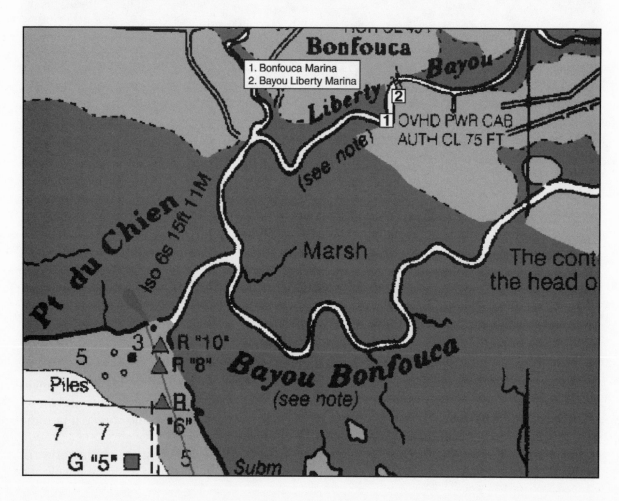

marsh. Excellent 8-foot depths continue on the mid-width, with good water often stretching almost from shore to shore. Boats up to 38 feet will find plenty of swinging room to drop the hook with fair protection afforded by the low, surrounding shores. Captains should be aware that they might have to move aside at a very disagreeable hour for a tug and towed barge coming down or going up the bayou to Slidell. Granted, your luck would have to be pretty down for such an instance to actually occur, but there is always the possibility.

After traveling upstream on Bayou Bon-fouca for a mile or two, you will begin to notice development picking up on both shores. At first this modern construction con-sists only of attractive homes, but as you get closer to Slidell, passing cruisers will note a whole collection of large barges moored to huge wharves. Sometimes you can watch loading in progress as you pass.

After a cruise of several additional miles, the creek takes a sharp turn to the east and flows toward a low-level swing bridge. You are now nearing the principal Slidell waterfront. As you begin making your way toward the span, watch the northern shore and you should catch sight of Slidell Marine (30 16.295 North/089 47.692 West). This petite but friendly facility boasts one transient slip with 6- to 7-foot soundings. Month-to-month wet-slip rentals are featured as well. Slidell Marine's fixed wooden pier dockage is designed for boats 40 feet and smaller. Fresh-water connections and 20- and 50-amp power hookups are readily available dockside, as is gasoline (but no diesel fuel). Shoreside visi-tors will be delighted with the full-line ship's store (with a few basic variety-store-type food

items) and extraclean bathrooms. Mechanical servicing is available for gasoline engines, I/Os, and outboards. A hefty one-mile walk will lead you to several restaurants and a con-venience store. You might also choose to call Parish Cab at 985-641-9479. Ask the friendly marina management for recommendations.

Slidell Marine (985) 649-4412
   http://www.slidellmarine.com

Approach depth—8-12 feet
Dockside depth—6-7 feet
Accepts transients—one slip kept open for visitors
Transient-dockage rate—below average
Fixed wooden piers—yes
Dockside power connections—20- and 50-amp
Dockside water connections—yes
Gasoline—yes
Mechanical repairs—gasoline, I/Os, and outboards
Ship's and variety store—yes
Restaurant—very long walk

A bit farther upstream, Maritime Systems (985-726-6022, formerly Pontchartrain Boat Works) will come abeam on the south shore after you pass under the swing bridge, near 30 16.306 North/089 47.564 West. This full-service repair yard offers mechanical (gasoline- and diesel-powered plants) and below-waterline repairs. The two on-site travelifts are rated at 35 tons and 100 tons, respectively.

Returning now to Liberty Bayou, this stream wanders generally northeast for 1.5 nautical miles or so to a low-level swing bridge. This stream is surrounded by somewhat higher, lit-tle-developed banks. While this shoreline would render fair protection for overnight anchorage, the creek is a bit narrower than its sister to the east. Thirty-six feet may be the size limit for boats dropping the hook and having sufficient swinging room. You may be able to offset this limitation by using a Bahamian mooring or setting a stern anchor. For maximum room, consider dropping anchor in a bend of the creek where the water spreads out a bit.

Some .1 nautical miles short (south) of the charted "Pontoon Bridge" crossing Liberty Bayou, Bonfouca Marina will come abeam along the easterly banks, near 30 15.891 North/089 50.730 West (hard by the charted location of Bonfouca). This facility is very friendly to live-aboards, and visitors will find quite a community of those who spend their days and nights on the water moored at the facility's fixed wooden piers. Very few slips are usually open for transients. Call ahead of time to check on overnight-berth availability.

Bonfouca Marina features 30-amp power connections and fresh-water hookups. Dockside

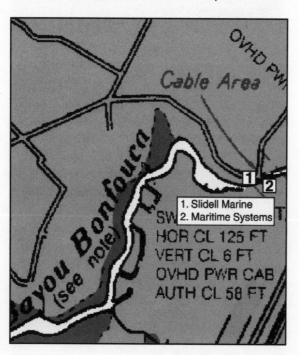

soundings run 6 feet or better. All berths afford excellent shelter. In fact, this is one of the best places to ride out heavy weather on Pontchartrain's northern shore. Shoreside, visitors will discover two sets of nonair-conditioned but heated showers. There are no restaurants or grocery stores within walking distance, so be sure to bring all your own supplies.

While its transient services are minimal, we are happy that live-aboards have a welcoming port of call on the northern banks of Lake Pontchartrain at Bonfouca Marina. This service is becoming rarer and rarer in these days of burgeoning condos.

Bonfouca Marina (985) 781-0709

Approach depth—8 feet
Dockside depth—6 feet (minimum)
Accepts transients—limited
Transient-dockage rate—below average
Fixed wooden piers—yes
Dockside power connections—30-amp
Dockside water connections—yes
Showers—yes

A touch farther upstream, the small dockage basin of Bayou Liberty Marina (985-641-1529, 30 16.017 North/089 50.667 West) guards the easterly shoreline, just short of the charted pontoon bridge. All slips in this dockage basin are set aside for month-to-month dockers.

Also located here is Cassadaban Marine Services (985-643-6505). This firm offers mechanical repairs for both gasoline- and diesel-powered plants.

Lacombe Bayou
(Various Lats/Lons—see below)

The happy stream known as Lacombe Bayou, located west of charted "Pt. Platte," offers superb anchorage for cruising craft traveling along Lake Pontchartrain's northerly banks. Minimum depths over the entrance bar are 6 feet, while 9 to 11 feet of water can be carried on most of the interior sections. There is one unmarked shoal at the creek's mouth to avoid, but the most elementary caution should see you safely by this hazard.

Soon after leaving Pontchartrain behind, Lacombe Bayou takes a sharp turn to the west. Boats up to 38 feet can anchor anywhere on the mid-width along this portion of the stream. One good spot is found near 30 15.867 North/089 57.209 West. Maximum elbowroom is found just before the creek takes a second sharp turn, this time back to the north. The surrounding banks are the usual low marsh grass and are an inadequate buffer for heavy weather.

Continuing upstream, passing cruisers will spot a small collection of private homes and fishing houses as the creek turns sharply east, where chart 11369 indicates that the paralleling road is right alongside the creek's westerly banks. A small offshoot cuts to the north and serves a host of residential docks, while the principal channel strikes east. Follow the stream to a point just above this small village. You can then drop the hook on a wide pool of water in 10- to 12-foot depths on the mid-width of the bayou, near 30 16.921 North/089 57.006 West. The surrounding shores are delightfully undeveloped and a bit higher. While still not sufficient for a gale, this would be a good spot to ride out smaller tempests.

Mandeville and Bayou Castine
(Various Lats/Lons—see below)

Fortunate indeed is the mariner who finds his or her way to the marked entrance of

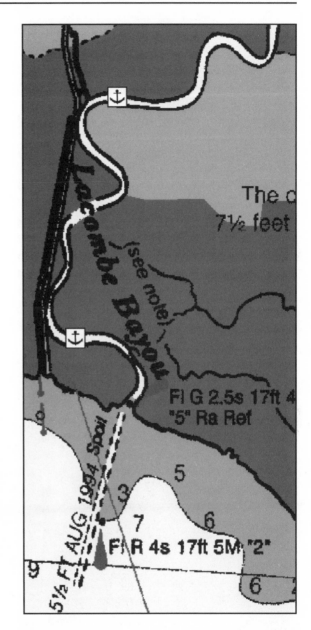

Bayou Castine, west of Green Point. This stream provides deep and ready access to the superfriendly community of Mandeville. Good marina facilities and fabulous dining

are only some of the many qualities that will endear this town to all cruising visitors. In fact, it's not going too far to say that Mandeville, along with its cousin to the west, Madisonville, are *the* ports of call on northern Lake Pontchartrain. Even if you are one of those cruisers who usually anchors out for the night, try docking for an evening in Mandeville. You won't regret the experiment.

The town of Mandeville itself is a quiet, restful community which still retains many of its fine, older homeplaces. A leisurely stroll along its streets (Lakeshore Drive in particular) is highly recommended for those who have seen one too many waves on their voyage. This writer found the friendly locals more than willing to take their time for questions or advice. The atmosphere was truly down home. I will always hold my times spent in Mandeville as some of my best cruising memories on the Northern Gulf.

The well-marked Mandeville entrance channel was dredged in August 2002 and now carries minimum soundings of 9 to 10 feet. In the future, shoaling may reduce these depths, but at least for a year or two, all should be well.

Soundings deepen to between 8 and 11 feet once on the stream's interior reaches. Even though some upstream portions of Bayou Castine are rather narrow, these excellent depths continue far upstream to the many, many docks lining the creek's banks. An armada of large cruising boats, particularly sailcraft, uses the bayou on a daily basis. Given these conditions, skippers need not be too concerned about navigational problems while visiting this delightful port of call.

Mandeville town docks, Bayou Castine

Flashing daybeacons #2 and #3 mark the Mandeville harbor entrance through a breakwater that gives some protection to the lower reaches of Bayou Castine. Soon after you leave the lighted aids behind, Mandeville's city docks will come up on the port-side banks near 30 20.973 North/090 03.563 West. Visiting cruisers are welcome to tie to these fixed-wooden face docks for an overnight stay. No power or water connections seem to be currently available at these berths. Dockage for the first 24 hours is without charge. Thereafter, you may be asked for a nominal daily dockage fee, but reports from locals indicate that this charge is seldom actually collected. It is a four- or five-block walk to many of the town's fine restaurants (see below). Just behind the docks, there is a public telephone, which can facilitate a call home to see who's minding the store.

The good folks at Pontchartrain Yacht Club maintain a friendly clubhouse overlooking the northwesterly banks of lower Bayou Castine, just across the street from the city docks. While this organization lacks any wet-slip facilities, members of other Gulf Yachting Association clubs are welcome at the clubhouse. This writer has twice been lucky enough to address more than 200 fellow cruisers here. Those evenings are a fond memory indeed.

If you are lucky enough to have the necessary affiliations and find your way to this yacht club's bar, you will undoubtedly find a warm welcome and the opportunity to share more than a few cruising yarns.

Moving upstream on Bayou Castine, the stream splits. The port branch serves some local docks, while the starboard fork leads to a repair yard and a superfriendly marina complex.

First up is Northshore Marine (985-626-7847, formerly the Yacht Works Boat Yard http://www.northshoremarine.net), located in the body of an almost 90 degree turn to starboard on Bayou Castine (near 30 20.990 North/090 03.441 West). This repair firm (closed on Mondays) offers full mechanical, electrical, painting, and below-waterline haul-out service work. It also specializes in rigging large sailcraft. The yard boasts a 15-ton travelift, a 25-ton travelift, and a 5-ton crane. Needless to say, if you need repair work of any description, your search has ended. The boatyard also maintains a ship's and parts store on the premises.

Farther upstream the 200 wet slips of Prieto Marina will be spotted along the bayou's western and northwestern banks. The dockmaster's office overlooks a central basin near 30 20.999 North/090 03.223 West.

Prieto Marina's dockage for both transient and month-to-month customers is at wonderfully sheltered fixed, wooden piers. It would take a very strong storm, indeed, to threaten boats docked on Bayou Castine. Typical soundings at dockside are a very respectable 8 feet. Fresh-water connections and 30-amp power hookups are available at all slips. There are three sets of shoreside showers at hand to wash away the day's salt and grime, but none are climate controlled. Mandeville's many fine restaurants are within a walk of several blocks or a half-mile.

Prieto Marina (985) 626-9670
  http://wwwprietomarina.com

Approach depth—9-11 feet
Dockside depth—8 feet
Accepts transients—yes
Transient-dockage rate—below average
Fixed wooden slips—yes
Dockside power connections—30-amp

Dockside water connections—yes
Showers—yes
Restaurant—several nearby

Incidentally, Bayou Castine's eastern and southeastern shores are part of Fontainebleau State Park and, as such, are beautifully undeveloped. Sometimes it's quite possible to catch sight of an alligator as you work your way quietly upstream. If the wildlife isn't enough to hold your interest, just take a gander at the rows upon rows of large, beautifully outfitted sailcraft, with a few power boats thrown in from time.

Mandeville Restaurants and Shoreside Businesses

The Mandeville Branch Library (985-626-4293) resides at 845 Gerard Street. This library is of particular interest to sailors, as it contains, among its many offerings, an impressive collection of old, long-out-of-print nautical books that have been donated by the Prieto family, one of the oldest families in Mandeville. Any sailor worth his or her salt will want to give these books a good perusal.

If you are fortunate enough to arrive in Mandeville at meal time, then the lucky stars are

Prieto Marina, Mandeville

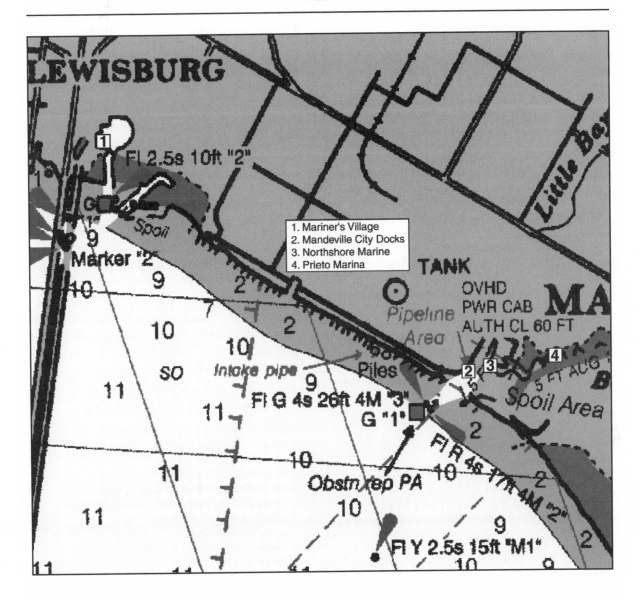

indeed shining upon you. A host of fine dining attractions overlooks Lake Pontchartrain on nearby Lakeshore Drive. It's a bit of a walk from either the free city piers or Prieto Marina, but the effort is more than justified. Besides, a stroll down Mandeville's wonderfully quiet lanes will allow for a close view of the town's many fine homes. Simply ask any local for directions.

If all this sounds just a bit too far for a comfortable walk, help is available. Give either Good Old Days Taxi (985-674-0161) or Parish Cab (985-892-2010) a call.

It's really a shame that we don't have the space to review each of Mandeville's notable dining spots in the course of this discussion. Practically any could make for a very happy evening ashore.

Let us, however, mention three dining attractions that should be on every cruiser's gastronomical itinerary. If fresh seafood is your bailiwick, spare no effort to find your way to Rip's On the Lake (1917 Lakeshore Drive, 985-727-2829). This restaurant is under new management, and the fresh regime seems intent on improving an already good dining choice.

Up for a little historic dining? Then check out Bechac's Restaurant (2025 Lakeshore Drive, 985-626-8502). This firm has been in operation overlooking the shores of Lake Pontchartrain since 1885.

And, finally, if some really elegant dining is your forte, dig out your last clean outfit and find your way to Nouvolari's (246 Gerard Street, 985-626-5619). This is one of the most sophisticated restaurants in Louisiana. As our dear friend, Mary Boshart of Bay Sails, put it, "Nouvolari's is the ultimate!"

Lewisburg Harbor
(30 21.977 North/090 05.433 West)

Yet another in the long list of northern Pontchartrain's marina facilities is found just west of Mandeville in charted Lewisburg Harbor. A marked, charted channel leads north just to the east of the northern terminus of the Lake Pontchartrain Causeway to Mariner's Village Marina. Unfortunately, this cut and the dockage basin to which it leads are now suffering through shoaling problems. Entrance and dockside depths have risen to 4- and 5-foot levels at low water. Plans call for future dredg-

ing to alleviate this situation, but the actual beginning date for this project could not be determined at the time of this writing.

Mariner's Village accepts transients for overnight dockage at fixed, wooden slips with all power and water connections. The basin is quite sheltered and should be snug and secure in any winds up to hurricane force.

Gasoline, diesel fuel, waste pump-out service, and dockside ice are on hand, and mechanical services can be contracted through local, independent technicians.

The on-site restaurant at Mariner's Village is now closed, but you could always take the two-block walk to Trey Yuen Chinese Restaurant (600 Causeway Boulevard, 985-626-4476). This dining attraction has been consistently rated one of the top Chinese restaurants in the United States.

Mariner's Village Marina (985) 626-1517
  http://www.marinersvillagemarina.net

Approach depth—4-5 feet (low water)
Dockside depth—4-5 feet (low water)
Accepts transients—yes
Transient-dockage rate—below average
Fixed wooden piers—yes
Dockside power connections—30- and 50-amp
Dockside water connections—yes
Waste pump-out—yes
Gasoline—yes
Diesel fuel—yes
Mechanical repairs—independent technicians
Restaurant—nearby

Lake Pontchartrain Causeway

The Lake Pontchartrain Causeway crosses the great lake from a point just west of Lewisburg on the northern shore to New Orleans on the south bank. Spanning a length of better

Mariner's Village Marina, Lewisburg Harbor

than 24 miles, this structure has the distinction of being the longest bridge in the world. Seen from the lake, its twin concrete ribbons seem to stretch on to the north and south forever and ever, amen. Long before you actually spot the bridge itself, the raised spans rise above the horizon like some mammoth sentinel of old. It is an awe-inspiring sight from the water.

Unfortunately, the causeway is a special cause of concern for sailcraft. Four out of the five pass-throughs are fixed, three of which have only 22 feet of vertical clearance. The one 50-foot fixed span is located convenient to the south shore, but a very long cruise would be required of those following the northern banks.

Only the central span, somewhat offset to the north, opens. This bridge now opens more or less (see below) on demand with advance notice (except during peak traffic times). Keep this in mind if your craft cannot clear the closed vertical clearance of 42 feet.

The Tchefuncte River and Madisonville (Various Lats/Lons—see below)

The magnificent Tchefuncte River cuts into the northern shores of Lake Pontchartrain 3.9 nautical miles west of Pontchartrain Causeway. The well-marked entrance leads to one of the most cruisable streams anywhere in this region. Graced by the absolutely charming community of Madisonville and blessed by numerous marinas and prolific anchorages, the Tchefuncte deserves the attention of *every* serious cruiser.

The Tchefuncte River is easily navigable for 6 nautical miles upstream to the Interstate 10 twin bridges. North of the Madisonville waterfront, passing mariners will observe long stretches of all-natural shores interspersed with attractive residential development. Along the way there are countless spots to drop the anchor, whether just for lunch or even for a few days' rest. Those who don't find the Tchefuncte attractive may as well go home and announce the sale of their boat.

The local cruising crowd from New Orleans has been discovering the charms of the Tchefuncte River in ever-increasing numbers during the last several years. The river can still be described as uncrowded, particularly on weekdays. As traffic inevitably increases, this situation could change. For now, mariners can rejoice in the many cruising opportunities that can still be described as being a bit off the beaten path.

The Tchefuncte River's entrance from Lake Pontchartrain is a bit complicated, but well marked. Caution is required to maintain the minimum 9-foot depths found in the channel. The whitewashed Tchefuncte River Lighthouse

Madisonville waterfront, Tchefuncte River

overlooks the outer portion of the cut and serves as the rear aid of a range marker. The light is quickly identified by its one black vertical stripe. Surprisingly, this modern-looking structure has adorned the shores of Pontchartrain since 1839.

Once past the entrance, the shores of the lower Tchefuncte River are mostly undeveloped. Watch the eastern banks and you will spot what will appear to be long sections of a concrete bridge to nowhere paralleling the river's track. Just how this structure came to be here is a mystery to this writer.

Some .6 nautical miles north of the Tchefuncte's mouth, the river takes a small jog to the northeast. At this point the stream narrows a bit and provides enough protection for overnight anchorage in light to moderate winds. Depths are in the river's usual range of 9 to 25 feet. Be sure to anchor a bit to one side of the mid-width to allow for the passage of any commercial traffic.

As high ground begins to overlook the westerly banks, the Tchefuncte River begins its approach to the Madisonville waterfront. Large power cruisers should slow to idle speed. Soon the entrance to the notable Marina Del Ray will come abeam on the eastern banks near 30 24.051 North/090 09.199 West.

Two unlighted and uncharted daymarkers lead you off the Tchefuncte into Marina del Ray's dockage basin. This friendly facility is the most modern marina on the river. The staff and management are eager to attract visiting cruisers.

An old barge fronting the river combines with a wooden breakwater to give the harbor excellent protection. The fuel dock and ship's store are located just in front of (north of) the protective barge, directly on the river. Believe it or else: there is actually a swimming pool (available to transient customers of the marina) located atop the barge. To say the least, this is an unusual, albeit a welcome, arrangement.

Entrance depths into Marina del Ray are an impressive 10 to 15 feet, with 8 to 11 feet of water at dockside. Even the longest-legged sailcraft should not have any problems with this much water. Surprisingly, soundings at the fuel dock on the river are only 7 to 8 feet, though that is still plenty for 99 percent of all cruising craft.

Transients are gratefully accepted for overnight or temporary dockage at floating wooden-decked piers with 30- and 50-amp power hookups and water connections. These floating docks are a considerable advantage during strong southerly blows and heavy rains, when water levels rise considerably. Five slips are usually available for overnight visitors, but this writer has been informed that additional transient vessels can sometimes be accommodated at other berths that have been temporarily vacated by resident craft. Good, climate-controlled shoreside showers and a Laundromat (no a/c) are nicely done. Gasoline, diesel fuel, waste pump-out service, and a small variety store (just behind the fuel dock) are available on the pier fronting the Tchefuncte. Pumps at the fuel pier are open 24 hours a day for those with credit cards. Some mechanical repairs can be arranged through an on-site, independent contractor.

A walk across the bridge will bring you to the River Food Mart, a small grocery store (see below). Ask any local or the marina staff for directions.

Marina Del Ray now features its own on-site dining choice, known as the Marina

Restaurant and Bar (985-792-1555). We have not eaten here, but this small restaurant has been highly recommended by fellow cruisers. There are so many other outstanding dining spots in Madisonville within an easy walk across the bridge (see below) that you will be faced with an embarrassment of dining riches.

Marina del Ray (985) 845-4474

Approach depth—10-15 feet
Dockside depth—8-11 feet (dockage basin)
                7-8 feet (fuel dock)

Accepts transients—yes
Transient-dockage rate—average
Floating wooden piers—yes
Dockside power connections—30- and 50-amp
Dockside water connections—yes
Showers—yes
Laundromat—yes
Waste pump-out—yes
Gasoline—yes
Diesel fuel—yes
Mechanical repairs—yes (on-site independent)
Variety store—yes
Restaurant—one on-site and several others nearby

Marina del Ray, Madisonville

Before leaving our discussion of Marina Del Ray, we would be very remiss not to point out that this marina is the new and greatly expanded home of our dear friends at Bay Sails (985-626-8820). Operated by two of the most wonderfully salty people you will ever meet (Bob and Mary Boshart), Bay Sails offers visitors first-class nautical clothing (with custom monogramming) and also brokers super sail- and powercraft. All visiting mariners will want to be sure to make the acquaintance of the good people at Bay Sails!

Another point of interest also on the grounds of Marina Del Ray is the Barge Inn (985-845-8048, 888-832-2743). As its name implies, this unique hostelry makes its home aboard a mammoth, floating barge permanently moored along the banks of the Tchefuncte River. To say that the guest rooms are elegant simply falls short of the mark. If you have seen one too many waves lately, and yearn to spend a night or two somewhere other than your own vessel, give Tim a call at the Barge Inn and tell him we sent you!

Across the Tchefuncte River from Marina Del Ray, visiting craft are welcome to tie to the long city face dock without charge. This facility will be spotted near 30 24.175 North/090 09.307 West. Apparently there is no time limit for these pier-side stays, so just go nuts. Be sure to use plenty of fenders, as the city docks consists of wooden pilings set against a concrete seawall. Visiting craft can moor either north or south of the Highway 22 Bridge. No power or water connections or other marine services are currently available at the city piers, but there is an "artesian well" in front of the adjacent town hall. A looong garden hose might allow you to top off your fresh water tanks.

Madisonville

If ever you set out to pick the prime example of a small Louisiana lake or river town, Madisonville would certainly have to rank near the top of the heap. Within the last three years, extensive residential development has sprung up along the Madisonville waterfront, but all these fine new homes can only be accurately described as being quite attractive when seen from the water. However, many of the community's older, historic homeplaces have also been restored. A stroll through this quiet, sleepy community is an experience not to be missed.

Madisonville is blessed with a ton of fine places to satisfy an appetite whetted by a long day of cruising. Cajun, Creole, and good old Southern-style American dishes are offered by any number of restaurants, some directly overlooking the river. First up, at least in this writer's gastronomical opinion, is Morton's Seafood (702 Water Street, south of the Highway 22 Bridge, 985-845-4970). Saying that this dining spot is popular with the local crowd is like saying the Beatles were popular musicians. One weekday in February a few years ago, we thought there could not possibly be any wait for lunch. Boy, were we surprised when we saw the line of people waiting for admittance. Fortunately, it turned out that the food was worth standing for a week in the rain. The Cajun and Creole dishes were outstanding and, for those with less adventurous palates, the fried seafood is as good as it can be.

A short cruise north of the Highway 22 Bridge (or an equally short walk north on Water Street) will bring you to the Friends on the Tchefuncte Restaurant (407 Tammany Street, 985-845-7303), also on the western

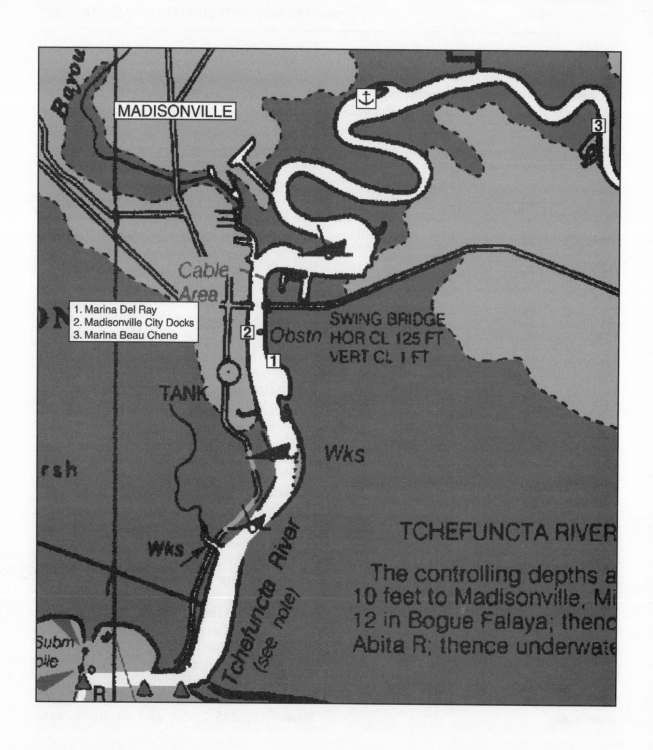

banks. This just may be the most attractive dining spot in Madisonville. Large plate-glass windows overlook the river, and outdoor dining is available. The restaurant has its own dock with 9- to 12-foot depths. There should be enough room for at least one 40-footer. While this writer was not privileged to sample Friends' cuisine, its high quality is a very safe bet.

Cruising chefs in need of supplies are not completely forgotten in Madisonville, though you should not expect to find a full-line supermarket. Instead, track your way to the River Food Mart (101 Highway 22 W, 985-845-4328). This firm is a bit of a cross between a convenience store and a neighborhood supermarket.

Cruisers up for a bit of historic sight-seeing will want to check out the Madisonville Museum (201 Cedar Street, 985-845-2100), open weekends only. Housed in the former courthouse above the old jail, it is listed in the National Register of Historic Places. Exhibits include Civil War, Native American, and wildlife themes, with seasonal attractions thrown in as well. The museum is open from noon to 4:00 weekdays.

For a community of its size, Madisonville hosts quite a series of special events. Chief among these festivals, at least to those of us with salt water in our veins, is the Madisonville Wooden Boat Show, usually held the third weekend in September. Wooden vessels from all over the East and Gulf coasts are on display this fun weekend, and coveted prizes are awarded to the "best" vessels in many different categories. Water Street becomes a local "fairground" and even this writer has been known to participate by holding free seminars on cruising the Northern Gulf

coastline. If you are anywhere near the Tchefuncte or Madisonville while this event is in progress, do yourself a huge favor and be sure to attend. For more information call (985) 845-9200.

That's not all, folks. If you happen to be cruising the waters of northwestern Lake Pontchartrain on Mother's Day, don't miss the "Rhapsody on the River." This event comprises a boat parade on the Tchefuncte River with a "symphony orchestra" aboard the various vessels. A good time is usually had by all.

With all these fortunate attributes, Madisonville deserves a red circle on any cruiser's chart. A simple stroll along the quiet streets is guaranteed to cure fevered brows that have seen one too many waves. Couple this peaceful atmosphere with the fine restaurants, historic attractions, and great special events, and it's not too hard to understand why this writer is drawn back to Madisonville time and time again. I think you will be too!

Upper Tchefuncte River
(Various Lats/Lons—see below)

After leaving the Friends on the Tchefuncte Restaurant dock behind, the main branch of the Tchefuncte River cuts sharply east, while a small offshoot strikes to the north. Most captains piloting cruising-size craft will want to avoid the smaller stream. It serves only local vessels and does not lead to any active facilities.

Farther upstream, the Tchefuncte River follows a hairpin turn back around to the west. Development becomes much sparser on both banks. From this point to the Interstate 10 twin bridges, the river is especially attractive. Long stretches of completely undeveloped cypress shores are interspersed with beautiful homes.

Some are absolutely magnificent. There is even a golf course and a state park visible from the river. Few will find a cruise of the upper Tchefuncte to be less than visually memorable.

Surprising depths of 40 feet or better are held through the broad reaches of the first hairpin turn. During our on-site research, we observed several large commercial barges and tugs moored to the banks along this stretch. Considering the depth and the commercial traffic, it would be better to drop the hook a bit farther upstream.

Soon the river enters yet another sharp turn. The charted offshoot striking west leads to a barge-loading facility and is best avoided by cruising craft. North of this small intersection, the Tchefuncte River narrows enough for anchorage almost anywhere along its track. Maximum swinging room is found downstream from the charted island on the northerly banks. Depths continue to range from 10 to as much as 25 feet. Be sure to leave plenty of swinging room to avoid a rude meeting with the shoreline should the wind or current change during the night. Also, don't forget to anchor at least a short distance off the centerline to allow for passing river traffic. Fortunately, there seems to be little in the way of large commercial traffic on this upper portion of the river, but it would still be best to anchor slightly off the mid-width for maximum safety. Be sure to show an anchor light at night.

In heavy weather you can drop the hook behind the small charted island along the river's northern banks, near 30 25.209 North/090 08.694 West. Minimum depths run in the 6- to 7-foot range, and there should be enough elbowroom for vessels up to 40 feet. The surrounding shores are beautifully undeveloped and make for a very peaceful evening spent far from civilization. There are some shallow-water concerns associated with this anchorage. Be sure to read the navigational account presented later in this chapter before attempting entry.

A well-placed marina facility graces the starboard banks (moving upstream) of the upper Tchefuncte some 1.4 nautical miles above the just-discussed anchorage, near 30 25.026 North/090 07.538 West. Marina Beau Chene accepts transients on a space-available basis only. No slips are reserved specifically for visitors. Call ahead of time to check for available space.

Cruisers who find an open berth at Marina Beau Chene will tie their lines in a very well-protected harbor featuring slips composed of wooden pilings set out from a concrete seawall. All slips have full power, water, cable-television, and telephone connections. The basin is surrounded by attractive, widely spaced homes and condos. Entrance and dockside depths are 7 to 10 feet. Shoreside showers and a coin Laundromat are available. Beau Chene is in the process of acquiring a waste pump-out facility at this time, but the date for the onset of this new feature could not be accurately determined at the time of this writing. No fuel can be purchased and there is not a restaurant within easy walking distance. (The dockmaster told this writer that Marina Beau Chene is a "quiet marina" where the residents don't want a noisy restaurant crowd nearby). Live-aboards are gladly accommodated without additional charge. After talking with several resident cruisers, this writer can accurately report that the marina and its management are very popular with its patrons. There are few better claims to fame for any pleasure-craft facility.

Marina Beau Chene (985) 845-3454

Approach depth—7-10 feet
Dockside depth—7-10 feet
Accepts transients—limited
Transient-dockage rate—average
Fixed wooden slips—yes
Dockside power connections—30- and 50-amp
Dockside water connections—yes
Showers—yes
Laundromat—yes

The Tchefuncte continues to wind its way first east and then north for some miles to the I-10 twin bridges. Mariners cruising this portion of the river will observe many beautiful homes overlooking the banks, interspersed with patches of shoreline that remain completely undeveloped. Superb shelter and enough swinging room for vessels as large as 36 feet are available almost anywhere along the way. A charted overhead power line with 85 feet of vertical clearance spans the river's upper reaches. Extremely tall sailcraft and low-flying planes take note.

At one point, a private country club with its own docks overlooks the easterly banks. Signs on the piers clearly warn against dockage by any but club members and their guests.

This guide's coverage of the Tchefuncte River finally ends at the twin I-10 high-rise bridges. While the river probably remains deep for some distance upstream, it is now well off the chart and too risky for cruising-size craft.

The Tangipahoa River

The marked entrance channel leading from Pontchartrain to the Tangipahoa River breaks off to the northwest some 5.3 nautical miles southwest of the Tchefuncte River cut. The Tangipahoa has quite a collection of navigational problems that will cause most captains to bypass its track. While 6-foot minimum depths can theoretically be held in the channel, some of the river's markers are placed improperly to warn against the surrounding shoals. Without special precautions, it's a cinch to land smack (and I do mean smack) in 1-foot waters, even within the marked cut. If you should choose to make the attempt anyway, please *be sure* to read the navigational account on the Tangipahoa presented later in this chapter *before* making the attempt. And, if you still run aground, don't say I didn't warn you!

Even if they manage to traverse the tricky entrance successfully, cruisers entering the Tangipahoa will find a relatively narrow stream lacking any facilities or even enough swinging room for ready anchorage. The few sidewaters flowing into the river within a mile of its mouth are universally shallow and unusable by cruising-sized craft. The river is overlooked by a large collection of small, fishing camp-type houses. Many have their own docks where small powercraft are often moored, so be sure to pass by at idle speed. During on-site research, our progress was monitored by a large bull, seemingly grazing at random in someone's backyard.

Frankly, the Tangipahoa River is rather uninteresting. This fact, coupled with its assorted shoals and shallows, should probably prompt most wise cruising captains to forgo this small stream. However, for those who just gotta see it all, navigational information is presented in the next section.

LAKE PONTCHARTRAIN—NORTH SHORE NAVIGATION

Navigation on Lake Pontchartrain calls for the cautious cruising recommended at the beginning of this chapter. Remember that thunderstorms can arise quickly and foster extremely rough conditions. Know your position and the route to the nearest port or sheltered anchorage at all times, and be ready to make a run for it if bad weather threatens. The lazy mariner on Lake Pontchartrain can be in for a heap of trouble just when problems are least expected.

Cruising the northern shores of Lake Pontchartrain requires first traversing the "head" of the turtle-shaped lake. A marked channel leads you through three bridges into the main body of water. All traffic entering the lake must follow this cut, even if the south shore is your destination.

With the exception of the Tangipahoa River, almost all the various sidewaters on northern Pontchartrain have marked entrances with respectable depths. Surrounding shoals are frequent, however, so proceed with caution.

Entrance from the Rigolets   The vast majority of cruising vessels will enter the easternmost "turtle's head" region of Lake Pontchartrain via the Rigolets. It is also possible to safely traverse Chef Menteur Pass to the south, providing access to Pontchartrain from the main ICW route. This passage is fraught with difficulty and unmarked shoals. It will be discussed in the "ICW to New Orleans" section at the end of this chapter.

The turtle's head is rife with shoal water and depths of 3 to 5 feet are all too common. While it is theoretically possible to follow several unmarked routes from the Rigolets, prudent navigators will stick strictly to the marked channel detailed below.

The buoyed entrance channel leading to the main body of Lake Pontchartrain hugs the northern banks and leads through three bridges. This cut is subject to shoaling, but repeated maintenance dredging can usually be relied upon to maintain sufficient depths for pleasure craft. *Be ready to discover additional uncharted markers placed along the cut that warn of recent encroachments by surrounding shoals.*

On-site soundings revealed that minimum depths of 7 to 8 feet could be expected on the Pontchartrain entrance channel (from the Rigolets). The situation could be different by the time you visit. Proceed with caution and keep a careful watch on the sounder.

As you leave the western mouth of The Rigolets, watch to the north for flashing daybeacon #6. This aid marks the sharp northwestward swing in the marked channel. Point to pass unlighted daybeacons #3, #5, and #7 within 20 yards of their northeasterly sides. Continue on course, pointing to come abeam of unlighted daybeacon #9 to its immediate northeasterly quarter. At the time of this writing, an uncharted aid, unlighted daybeacon #7A, has been placed between #7 and #9. This beacon may or may not be present by the time you visit. If you should spot #7A, be sure to pass it also to its fairly immediate northeasterly side. This is the most difficult portion of the entrance channel. Use the charted range to help keep to the good water. Maintain a close eye over your stern to quickly note any leeway and, as always, keep checking the sounder.

At #9 the channel takes a sharp jog to the west and heads toward the I-10 high-rise fixed bridge. While a series of unlighted daybeacons helps you to keep to the marked cut, depths outside of the channel are not quite as suspect in this portion of the passage.

West of unlighted daybeacon #15, all markers cease. Head straight for the central pass-through of the I-10 fixed bridge. A vertical clearance of 65 feet should be enough for almost any pleasure craft. Immediately west of the I-10 span, captains may choose to cut northeast and visit the first of the north shore's many facilities.

Oak Harbor   To visit impressive Oak Harbor Marina and/or Harbor View Marina, simply cruise between the pair of charted aids to navigation leading into the northern banks. As you would expect, keep all red markers to starboard and all green beacons to port.

After passing between unlighted daybeacons #3 and #4, continue holding to the mid-width as you follow the broad entrance channel. Watch to your starboard side and you should spot a large, concrete sea wall just as the stream takes a jog to the north. Soon the channel turns back to the northeast. The Oak Harbor dockage basin will be spotted to the east, while Harbor View Marina can be found on the southern shore of the first west-running canal to your port side.

If you should choose to explore part of the intricate network of canals surrounding the Oak Harbor area, simply hold to the mid-width for best depths and proceed at idle speed.

On Lake Pontchartrain   After passing under the I-10 span, set course for the common central pass-through of the twin bridges about one nautical mile to the west. The first span is the Highway 11 Bridge with 13 feet of closed vertical clearance, and the second is a railway span with only 4 feet of closed vertical clearance. Both bridges open on demand unless a train is due.

West of the railway span, the routes to the north and south shores of Pontchartrain diverge. This account will go on to consider the various north shore ports of call. The south shore will be reviewed later in this chapter.

From the twin bridges, north-shore-bound mariners should consider setting course for flashing daybeacon #2 at the southern head of the Liberty Bayou/Bayou Bonfouca entrance channel. Even if you don't plan to visit the twin creeks, this aid makes a good navigational reference.

Bayou Bonfouca/Liberty Bayou   The entrance channel to the side-by-side streams known as Bayou Bonfouca and Liberty Bayou is, for once, actually easier to run than would appear to be the case from a study of chart 11369. In actuality, the channel is rather broad and the numerous aids help even sloppy navigators to stay in the cut. Nevertheless, the channel is subject to shoaling and skippers should be on the lookout for new markers. Be sure to pass all red beacons, charted or not, to your starboard side and all green markers to your port.

Unlighted daybeacon #10 leads cruisers into the shared mouth of the two streams. Hold to the mid-width and you should not encounter any depth problems.

Some .4 nautical miles upstream, the creeks divide. Liberty Bayou strikes to the north and northeast. This stream continues holding excellent depths on its mid-width to the charted bridge some 1.3 nautical miles upstream. Don't be tempted to try the charted fork leading north. It is shoal and should not be entered by any save very small, shallow-draft vessels.

Eventually, Bonfouca Marina will be spotted along the easterly banks, just as the stream swings sharply north, followed soon thereafter by Bayou Liberty Marina. It is then only a quick hop, skip, and jump farther upstream to the charted pontoon bridge. Most cruisers should confine their explorations to the bayou south and west of the bridge. North of the span, the stream soon narrows considerably.

Bayou Bonfouca cuts sharply to the south at the fork with Liberty Bayou. Eventually the stream meanders back to the northeast and heads for Slidell. Good depths are held on the centerline all the way to Slidell Marine, the charted 6-foot swing bridge and Maritime Systems.

North of this point, the stream is choked for a time by commercial barges and loading facilities. It peters out soon thereafter.

As you approach Slidell on Bayou Bonfouca, commercial barges, tugs, and loading wharves will become ever more in evidence. Be sure to pass these industrial facilities at reduced speed to minimize the possibility of damage from your wake.

The docks of Slidell Marine will be spotted on the port shore near the charted 6-foot swing bridge. This will be followed by the Maritime Systems dockage basin to starboard after passing the bridge (which opens on demand).

On Lake Pontchartrain   From flashing daybeacon #2 at the foot of the Liberty Bayou/Bayou Bonfouca channel, navigators might want to consider setting course to come abeam of yet another flashing daybeacon #2, this one denoting the southerly reaches of the Lacombe Bayou entrance channel, by some 2 nautical miles to its southerly side. This strategy will help to avoid the charted pipelines and gas wells. At this point, a turn to the north will carry cruisers to Lacombe Bayou.

Lacombe Bayou   The entrance channel into Lacombe Bayou is scantily marked. Leeway can ease you out of the improved cut into 3- and 4-foot water. Be sure to watch over your stern for any lateral slippage.

Turn north from the deeper lake waters and point to come abeam of flashing daybeacon #2 by some 10 yards to its westerly side. Continue on course, pointing to pass unlighted daybeacon #4 by some 20 yards to its westerly side.

As you approach the mouth of Lacombe

Bayou, be sure to pick out flashing daybeacon #5. Swing a bit to the northeast and pass #5 to its fairly immediate easterly side.

Be sure to hold to the centerline as you continue your upstream explorations on Lacombe Bayou. The shoreline along this portion of this creek is very shoal. If you drop the hook, do so on the mid-width and use only enough anchor rode for the minimally acceptable scope.

On Lake Pontchartrain   It's a long cruise of almost 10 nautical miles from a position south of Lacombe to Mandeville Harbor and Bayou Castine. Skippers can follow the northern shore safely by staying at least 1 nautical mile offshore. A closer approach invites disaster from encroaching on the broad shelf of shallows extending well out from the shoreline.

Two shoals of particular concern on this run are the broad banks of shallows abutting Goose and Green points. Be sure to steer well away from these promontories.

Just before reaching Mandeville, a marked pipeline runs to the southwest across Lake Pontchartrain. Flashing daybeacon #M1, the northeasternmost of the pipeline aids, is useful for marking a point well suited for entering Mandeville Harbor.

Mandeville and Bayou Castine   The entrance into Mandeville Harbor has recently been dredged, and it is well marked, to boot. Just be sure to pass all red markers to your starboard side and take green beacons to port.

Flashing daybeacons #2 and #3 actually sit on the southwestern tips of the twin concrete breakwaters that partially enclose the harbor's entrance. Once past #2 and #3 and inside the breakwater, you will quickly spot the city docks lining the northwestern banks.

To continue upstream on Bayou Castine to Northshore Marine and Prieto Marina, follow the right-hand (northeasterly) branch of Bayou Castine. The short left-hand fork leads only to private docks with no room for anchorage.

As usual, hold to the mid-width for best depths. Watch the port shore for the office of Northshore Marine. Farther upstream, the extensive docks and dockmaster's office of Prieto Marina line the western and northwestern banks.

Lewisburg Harbor   The entrance to Lewisburg Harbor and Mariner's Village Marina is found on Pontchartrain's northern shore, just short of the long causeway spanning the lake. Please remember that this channel and its adjacent harbor have shoaled to depths of 4 and 5 feet at the time of this writing. Hopefully, dredging will relieve this situation in the near future, but at least for the moment, captains piloting boats that draw more than 3 feet should approach this basin with extreme caution.

Two sets of daybeacons lead you through a narrow opening in a wooden breakwater. Once into the harbor, you will spot the marina complex on the western banks.

On Lake Pontchartrain   West of Mandeville the entire 24-mile breadth of Lake Pontchartrain is spanned by a huge causeway. While undoubtedly a boon for motorists visiting the lake's northern shore and commuters coming into the city, the long bridge presents special problems for cruisers.

The Lake Pontchartrain Causeway contains only 5 pass-throughs along its lengthy stretch. Three of these openings are fixed and have only 22 feet of vertical clearance. A fourth span is found 6 nautical miles from the south shore and has 50 feet of vertical clearance. Only the marked central span can open. This pass-through has a closed vertical clearance of 42 feet. This bascule span now supposedly opens mostly on demand, except during peak traffic hours (see below). The bridge operators (on duty 24 hours a day) request that all boats who know that they will need the bridge to open, call on VHF channel 16 or 17 well before they actually reach the span (at least 3 hours ahead of their arrival). At this time, the operators can make captains aware of any potential traffic or mechanical problems. During peak traffic times, from 6:00 A.M. to 9:00 A.M. and 3:00 P.M. to 6:00 P.M., this bridge does not normally open.

Obviously, power cruisers have the best of the causeway. Those traveling along Pontchartrain's northern shore can make use of the first (moving north to south) 22-foot-clearance span, some 3.2 nautical miles south of Lewisburg. Most sailcraft will be required to journey another 3.5 nautical miles farther to the south to reach the bascule span.

Once the impressive but pesky causeway is left behind, most cruisers will set their courses for the entrance to the Tchefuncte River, serving the charming community of Madisonville.

Tchefuncte River and Madisonville   The Tchefuncte River is mostly free of shoals and obstructions all the way north to the I-10 bridges. Generally speaking, mariners need only hold to the mid-width for excellent depths. The cut leading from Pontchartrain to the Tchefuncte River is another ball of wax.

This channel is anything but straightforward. You must follow several twists in the cut or a grounding in 3-foot waters could be the rapid and less than desirable result. A goodly number of markers and a range help you keep to the deep water. Read the account presented below carefully, proceed at a cautious speed, taking careful note of all markers, and keep those eyeballs glued to the sounder. With these simple precautions, good navigators should be able to cruise into the river's deep interior reaches without mishap.

To enter the Tchefuncte River, come abeam of flashing daybeacon #2 by some 25 yards to its westerly side. Look towards the northern shore. In all but heavy weather you should be able to readily spot the range markers denoting the outer portions of the entrance channel. The rear marker is none other than the Tchefuncte River Lighthouse, readily identifiable by its snowy white exterior bisected by one black vertical stripe.

Follow the range as you come abeam of and pass unlighted daybeacons #4 and #6 to their fairly immediate westerly sides. Do not stray too far away from #4 and #6. There is shallow water to the west.

After passing #6, continue on course for some 15 to 20 yards and then cut sharply to the east, pointing to come abeam of and pass unlighted daybeacons #8 and #10 to their fairly immediate northerly sides. North and a bit east of #10 the wide and deep mouth of the river opens out before you.

Navigation of the Tchefuncte remains quite simple upriver to Madisonville. While the river is deep almost to its banks, smart navigators will hold to the centerline to avoid any possible underwater obstructions.

As you approach the Madisonville swing bridge, Marina del Ray dockage basin will be spotted to starboard, while the southern section of the city docks will be found to port.

The Tchefuncte River-Highway 22 swing bridge has a closed vertical clearance of only 1 foot! As it also has a restricted opening schedule, visiting cruisers will want to make advance plans to avoid delays. The bridge opens only on the hour and half-hour, seven days a week, all year, between 5:00 A.M. and 8:00 P.M. During the evening and nighttime hours, the span does deign to open on demand.

North of the Madisonville bridge, some additional city piers line the western banks, followed by the dock fronting Friends on the Tchefuncte Restaurant. Just past Friends, a small branch of the river strikes to the north. Most cruising-size craft will want to avoid this questionable offshoot and follow the main river channel as it swings sharply to the east.

North of this point, the Tchefuncte River follows a whole series of hairpin turns. At the first bend, surprising depths of 40 feet or more will be noted on the sounder. If you are searching for a spot to drop the hook, it would be better to continue upstream for a bit until depths rise to normal 10- to 15-foot readings.

To enter the anchorage behind the charted island flanking the river's northern shore, use the westerly entrance as the stream arcs to the east. Local captains have informed this writer that underwater stumps line the easterly passage. While our on-site research failed to turn up any of these silent hazards, I have never thought it a good policy to ignore native advice. Consequently, be sure to make your approach and exit from the west, not the east.

Depart from the main river track well before reaching the island. Cruise carefully towards the northern shores. Once you are within 25 or 30 yards of the banks, point your course to the east and pass between the mainland banks and the island. Avoid the island's westerly tip. Shoals seem to extend out for a goodly distance from this point.

Successful passage farther upstream on the delightful Tchefuncte to the I-10 twin bridges can be summed up by the usual saw of holding to the mid-width. Avoid the various points along the way and no undue difficulty excepting possibly some flotsam should be encountered.

On Lake Pontchartrain From Madisonville, most mariners cruising Pontchartrain's northern shores will either choose to retrace their steps, enter Lake Maurepas through Pass Manchac (8.6 nautical miles from Madisonville) or voyage across the breadth of the lake to New Orleans on the southern shore. The Maurepas passage will be covered in the next section of this chapter, followed by a complete discussion of the south shore. A very few skippers may decide to explore the Tangipahoa River to the west, but such risky cruising is not encouraged by this writer.

Under no circumstance should any boat, be it large, small, or indifferent, attempt to follow the marked and charted channel between the Tchefuncte and Tangipahoa rivers that cuts northwest to Port Louis. This work of the devil leads unsuspecting cruisers into a mud bank *directly between the markers* with less than a foot of depth. This writer once had to work for an hour up to his knees in evil-smelling muck to extract his craft from this unseen menace. Unless this so-called channel is dredged, these markers represent a hazard and should be removed forthwith.

Take a moment to glance at chart 11369 and you will note a charted power line running between the head of the Port Louis "channel" and the Tangipahoa River entrance cut. Sailcraft should take note that the overhead clearance is only 40 feet. Seen from the water, this power line is an impressive sight, and readily outlines a path to the Tangipahoa.

The Tangipahoa River   Remember that the Tangipahoa River is not really recommended for cruising size vessels. The tricky entrance combines with a total lack of facilities or anchorages to render this stream basically uninteresting for most cruisers.

For those who won't take *my* word for it, enter the Tangipahoa by coming abeam of flashing daybeacon #2 to its fairly immediate southwestern side. Then turn to the northwest and point to come abeam of and pass unlighted daybeacons #4 and #6 to their fairly immediate southwesterly sides.

The real trouble spot on the Tangipahoa entrance channel is encountered between #6 and the next upstream aid, flashing daybeacon #8. A large shoal has built into the channel from the northeast and has completely surrounded #8. Depths of 2 feet or less are now found well to the southwest of this aid. To enter the river, stay way away from #8 and favor the southwestern side of the entrance.

Once past the annoying entrance, good depths open out on the narrow stream's main track. Do not attempt to enter any of the sidewaters that you might spot along the way. They are, without exception, cheats and blinds waiting to trap the unwary navigator.

Lake Maurepas

For many years Lake Maurepas and its adjoining Tickfaw River were the undiscovered cruising grounds of New Orleans. During those happy times, only a few fishing skiffs were usually to be found on the lake's broad waters. Now that situation is beginning to change. Smaller powercraft, in particular, are seen more and more often, particularly on the Tickfaw River. However, for the next few years at least, mariners can still rejoice in these waters as a secluded cruising opportunity. While weekend boating traffic is undoubtedly on the upswing, it is still possible to anchor and feel that you have left civilization far behind.

Lake Maurepas sits due west of its larger sister, Lake Pontchartrain, and is joined to this latter body of water by a deep stream known as Pass Manchac. Lake Maurepas is over 10 nautical miles in length on its north-to-south axis and some 8 nautical miles from east to west. As such, the lake is an impressive body of water in its own right. The wide dimensions, coupled with average depths of only 7 to 12 feet, can give rise to a very sharp chop when winds exceed 10 knots. Smaller powercraft in particular should take a long look at the expected winds before venturing out onto the main body of the lake.

Lake Maurepas is an almost perfect oval and, except for its three feeder rivers and Pass Manchac, it lacks any protected coves or sidewaters. Thus, while the lake can provide good grounds for day sailing, there are no opportunities for sheltered anchorage. The main reaches of Lake Maurepas are completely without facilities for cruising craft, though, fortunately, this situation is not reflected on its sidewaters.

Lake Maurepas is surrounded by a remarkably wild-looking shoreline that has only light development. Most of the banks are overlooked by the usual tall cypress marsh and swamp which is so indicative of Louisiana. This natural character can lend a special flavor to your cruise.

Three rivers flow into Lake Maurepas. The Blind River is found on the lake's southwestern corner, while the Amite River strikes into the middle of the western banks. Both these streams are a bit narrow. For this reason they are not covered in this guide.

The third feeder stream, Tickfaw River, presents a very different situation. Featuring a broad and mostly deep channel, this most attractive river leads to a low-key marina. The entire stream is sheltered enough for overnight anchorage almost anywhere along its length. Happy indeed is the cruiser who finds his or her way to this somewhat remote body of water.

All in all, Lake Maurepas and Tickfaw River can be evaluated as an appealing, somewhat remote cruising opportunity that requires a long cruise to reach its confines. During our various on-site research trips on these waters, it has become quite obvious that far more powercraft are willing to make the effort than sailors. In fact, we have never spied a single wind-powered vessel on the entire length of the Tickfaw River. Nevertheless, sailcraft skippers should take note—if you can clear the Pass Manchac fixed 50-foot highway bridge, Lake Maurepas can offer good day sailing, with overnight anchorages just to the north on the Tickfaw River. Why not be a pioneer and check it out?

Pass Manchac

Pass Manchac is a surprisingly broad and deep body of water which cuts into the western shores of Lake Pontchartrain south of the Tangipahoa River. The stream flows west and enters Lake Maurepas south of Jones Island. The pass provides ready access between the two lakes.

While the inner reaches of Pass Manchac exhibit depths running up to 50 feet, both ends of the channel are somewhat shoal. Two channels (one currently unmarked) lead into the pass from Pontchartrain, and both have some 5-foot depths. Two additional cuts lead around a shoal fronting Pass Manchac's western mouth into Lake Maurepas. The northern cut is reasonably well marked and has minimum 8-foot depths.

Anyone studying chart 11369 might conclude that Pass Manchac is a sheltered body of water that provides a welcome respite from the often choppy conditions of its two adjoining lakes. However, cruisers should be aware that in strong easterly or westerly breezes, winds blow directly up or down the stream, giving rise to a very substantial chop. During our initial on-site research in the early 1990s, we just about had our teeth jarred out of our heads in an easterly wind of some 15 knots.

Except for some light development near the bridges on its western reaches, most of Pass Manchac's shoreline remains undeveloped marsh. The swamps seem deep and almost forbidding, but fascinating nevertheless.

Just short of its western terminus, Pass Manchac is spanned by twin fixed bridges. Just west of the twin spans, an uncharted creek strikes north to a collection of small homes and fishing camps. Minimum entrance depths are 6 feet, with most soundings being considerably deeper. While there are no facilities for cruising craft, nor really enough room to anchor, the offshoot does at least provide a way to get off the main track should you be desperate for shelter.

North Pass

North Pass is a small stream that breaks off from the northern shores of Pass Manchac near unlighted daybeacon #2 and meanders to the north and west until finally emptying into Lake Maurepas north of Pass Manchac. While deep over most of its length, the entrance into Lake Maurepas is shoal, with depths of only 2 to 3 feet in one spot. This stream is best left to the many small fishing craft that ply its reaches on a regular basis.

Tickfaw River

If you have ever dreamed of cruising on a beautiful river with abundant anchorages and at least some minimal facilities, and don't mind a bit of a trip to get there, then the Tickfaw is most definitely for you. Seldom in all my wanderings on the Northern Gulf Coast have I come across a body of water which I found to be more attractive. The shores are very lightly developed, with just a few homes here and there to provide a pleasing contrast with the heavily wooded, marshy banks.

The Tickfaw's entrance from Lake Maurepas is found near the center of the lake's northern shoreline. Minimum depths of 6 to 8 feet can be maintained by staying strictly to the marked cut. Outside of the channel, soundings deteriorate to 4- and 5-foot levels.

The southern portion of Tickfaw River is rather wide and is only sheltered enough for anchorage when winds do not exceed 10 to 12 knots. If light airs are forecast, these waters are quite attractive and could make for a memorable overnight stay.

Soon the Tickfaw follows a sharp bend to the west-southwest, near which you will find an intersection with the Natalbany River. This small stream intersects its larger sister on the northern banks. Surprising depths of 20 feet or more exist at the intersection of the two streams. Due to the large amount of anchor rode necessitated by these depths, only boats up to 28 feet will find enough swinging room for anchorage. While depths remain deep moving north on the Natalbany, the river soon becomes a bit narrow for cruising boats.

West of the Natalbany intersection, the Tickfaw River narrows somewhat and becomes sheltered enough for anchorage in all but heavy weather. Simply pick a spot to your liking and drop the hook.

The Tickfaw continues a wandering course to the northwest until finally reaching the Warsaw Landing swing bridge some 6 nautical miles upstream. Just before reaching the bridge, facilities are available on both the northern and southern banks.

The first is Tickfaw Marina. This facility is found in its own protected cove on the southern banks. The entrance cuts south immediately before reaching Tin Lizzie's Restaurant (discussed below). Entrance depths range from 6 to 12 feet and dockside soundings are some 6 to 7 feet. Tickfaw Marina accepts transients for overnight or temporary dockage if any slips are available. Most of the marina's slips are usually occupied by resident craft. Give the marina a call well ahead of time and you may be able to arrange an advance reservation. Dockage is at fixed wooden piers with 15- and 30-amp power hookups and water connections. Gasoline and diesel fuel are sold here, and there is a ship's and variety store on site.

Tickfaw Marina (225) 695-3340

Approach depth—6-12 feet
Dockside depth—6-7 feet
Accepts transients—very limited
Transient-dockage rate—below average
Fixed wooden piers—yes
Dockside power connections—15- and 30-amp
Dockside water connections—yes
Gasoline—yes
Diesel fuel—yes
Ship's and variety store—yes
Restaurant—next door

Tin Lizzie's Restaurant overlooks the Tickfaw River's southern banks just short of the swing bridge. Built to resemble a huge old barn with a rusty tin roof, the restaurant is actually a favorite dining spot of locals and visitors alike. It is open from April 1 through the first weekend in September only.

For us cruisers, the restaurant management has thoughtfully provided a whole mass of dockage. Some of the piers front directly onto the river, while others are found on the west side of the cove leading to Tickfaw Marina. Dockside depths are 6 to 7 feet. Patrons of the restaurant are welcome to tie up while dining, though no overnight accommodations or other marine services are available.

Riverside Tavern & Oyster Bar is found just opposite Tin Lizzie's on the northern banks of the Tickfaw. This eating and drinking establishment features one long face dock with impressive depths of 12 to 14 feet. Unfortunately, the docks are so low that boats over 30 feet will find it necessary to put out quite a bit of fendering to avoid damage to the hull.

West of the Warsaw Landing swing bridge, the Tickfaw River soon splits. The southern fork retains the name of Tickfaw and winds its way through several very sharp turns to the west. For the first 300 yards or so, the stream is plenty wide enough for anchorage by any pleasure craft up to 38 feet. Depths are 15 feet or better. Protection is excellent from all winds, courtesy of the higher ground to the north and south. The surrounding shoreline is mostly undeveloped and can certainly contribute to the aesthetics of your stay. Farther upstream, the Tickfaw narrows considerably. Cruising-size vessels should probably confine their explorations to the waters short of the river's first hairpin turn to the south.

The northerly fork in the Tickfaw is known as the Blood River. Good depths of 10 feet or better continue upstream at least to the charted location of Warsaw Landing. This stream is well sheltered but somewhat narrower than the waters to the south. Anchorage by boats larger than 28 feet would be cramped indeed.

LAKE MAUREPAS NAVIGATION

Successful navigation of Lake Maurepas, Pass Manchac, and Tickfaw River is very much akin to cruising on Lake Pontchartrain. If you've learned to put up with the sometimes wicked chop, relatively shallow lake depths, and shoal entrances to sidewaters, you are ready to visit Lake Maurepas.

Pass Manchac   Two somewhat obscurely marked channels lead north and south from the deeper waters of Lake Pontchartrain to the eastern mouth of Pass Manchac. A direct approach from the east is impossible due to a large shoal with 3-foot depths directly east of the pass's entrance. Take just a moment to glance at chart 11369 and you can easily pick out these bothersome shallows.

The approach from the south is deeper and far better marked, but both passages are subject to some 5-foot depths. Neither is recommended for boats that draw more than 4½ feet. For my money, I would pick the south channel every time, and no further information will be given here for the north-side cut, which now definitely requires up-to-date local knowledge.

The southern Pass Manchac entrance channel is fairly well marked and reasonably easy to run during daylight. Point to come abeam of flashing daybeacon #1 to its fairly immediate easterly side. You should then turn north and track your way past unlighted daybeacons #3 and #5, passing both markers within about 20 yards of their easterly sides.

After passing #5, slant your course just a shade farther to the north-northeast. This procedure will help to avoid the correctly charted tongue of shallower water which is building into the approach channel's western flank.

Eventually you should point to come abeam of flashing daybeacon #7 by some 200 yards to its easterly quarter. Now, the entrance to the mouth of Pass Manchac will come abeam to the west. At this point you should turn west and enter the pass by favoring the northern banks slightly.

Chart 11369 correctly forecasts two large patches of shoal water flanking the northern and southern sides of Pass Manchac's eastern mouth. The channel itself is actually quite deep. If depths rise above 18 feet as the northern and southern entrance points come abeam, it's a safe bet that you are beginning to encroach on the shallows to the north or south. Make corrections at once before soundings rise to even shallower depths.

Once the tricky entrance is left behind, you need only hold to the pass's centerline for depths of better than 20 feet all the way to the twin bridges. One aid, unlighted daybeacon

#2, marks the intersection of North Pass, Stinking Bayou, and Pass Manchac. Pass this aid to its southerly side. As discussed earlier, these small sidewaters are not recommended for larger craft.

The first bridge crossing Pass Manchac is a railway span with a closed vertical clearance of 56 feet. There is also an overhead power line with 64 feet of clearance. Immediately adjacent to the railroad is a fixed highway bridge with 50 feet of vertical clearance. One small swath of charted shallows abuts the northeastern corner of the railway bridge. This hazard is easily avoided by sticking to the mid-width.

Cruisers passing through the Pass Manchac bridges will find the wide-open waters of Lake Maurepas spread out before them. You cannot continue directly to the west into the lake, however. A crescent-moon-shaped shoal is found just to the west of Pass Manchac's westerly mouth. Reliable channels pass to the north and south of these shallows. Only the northerly cut is marked. While locals make use of the southern channel all the time without problems, strangers are advised to traverse the northern cut. The markings remove any doubt about the right course to follow.

To follow the northern channel, set a course immediately after passing through the fixed highway span to come abeam of unlighted daybeacon #2 by some 75 yards to its southwesterly side. Continue on the same course until coming abeam of unlighted daybeacon #4 by about the same distance to its southwestern quarter. Bend your course slightly to the south and point to come abeam of flashing daybeacon #6 by a short distance to its southerly side. You are now in deep water and #6 is the last marker you will see short of the various channels leading to the lake's sidewaters.

Tickfaw River The Tickfaw River can be reached by setting a course from flashing daybeacon #6 to a point well south of flashing daybeacon #1, the southernmost aid on the river's entrance channel. Turn north and point to pass #1 by at least 20 yards to its easterly side. Be sure to stay away from the daybeacons on the entrance channel, as they seem to be surrounded by shallow water.

Be alert when traveling this cut. It is surrounded by shoal water to the east and west. You may spot some old stumps to the east, which warn not only of shoal water, but also of foul bottom conditions on that side of the channel.

Continue cruising north by passing unlighted daybeacon #3 by some 20 to 25 yards (no more) to its easterly quarter. Soon the southern mouth of Tickfaw River will be obvious to the north. Enter the river on its centerline.

Once on the Tickfaw River's interior reaches, you need only keep anywhere near the centerline for good depths all the way to the Warsaw Landing swing bridge. Don't be tempted to explore too far upstream on the Natalbany River if your craft is larger than 28 feet. This stream soon narrows too much for comfortable maneuvering.

The Warsaw Landing bridge is now a fixed structure with 50 feet of vertical clearance. Just short of the span, passing cruisers will spot Tickfaw Marina and Tin Lizzie's Restaurant to the south and Riverside Tavern and Oyster Bar to the north.

West of the swing bridge, Blood River joins the Tickfaw. The Tickfaw River continues west. Cruising pass the first hairpin turn to the south on this stream is not recommended for any but small craft.

Excellent depths are held on the Blood River to Warsaw Landing by holding to the old practice of following the mid-width. Avoid the various points along the way.

Lake Pontchartrain—Southern Shore

The south shore of Lake Pontchartrain is inextricably interwoven with that sometimes-fascinating-sometimes-confusing-but-never-dull city known as New Orleans. Indeed, all of the city's marina facilities are located along Pontchartrain's southern reaches. Hard as it is to believe, there is not a single marina to be found along the ICW's track between Lake Borgne and the New Orleans Turning Basin. Mariners wanting to spend some time getting to know the Big Easy are almost required to moor their craft along southern Lake Pontchartrain.

With the exception of the New Orleans marinas and the Inner Harbor Navigation Canal, Lake Pontchartrain's southern shores are without anchorages or side trips. If you pass the city facilities by, your next stop is Pass Manchac and Lake Maurepas, some 18 nautical miles to the west. So, unless you are headed for the north shore or Lake Maurepas, your most likely south-shore destination will be one of the two New Orleans marina complexes.

The city of New Orleans now features not one but two extensive dockage basins. The newer, eastern facility is under unified management and features a well-sheltered, man-made harbor that, unfortunately, also houses a large gambling ship. The westerly basin is chock full of marinas, yards, and marine service organizations of every description, not to mention one of the most prestigious yacht clubs in America. If you can't meet your marine needs at the New Orleans facilities, give up.

Let us first turn our attention to a shamefully brief review of New Orleans' fascinating attractions and rich history. We shall then review the northern portion of the Inner Harbor canal, followed by a complete review of the regional facilities.

New Orleans

As a young boy around the turn of the century, Lyle Saxon visited New Orleans for the first time with his grandfather during the festival of Mardi Gras. After leaving their paddle-wheeled steamer behind, the duo walked along the cobblestone streets and breakfasted at a nearby coffeehouse. The young boy was "intoxicated" by the new sights and sounds. A beggar woman happening by asked for a nickel. Lyle's grandfather produced the requested coin and the woman gaily burst out, "May all the saints bless you for it. I hope you enjoy yourself. Have a good time while you can. . . . That's what *I* always say!"

In his later life Mr. Saxon was to become one of the driving forces in New Orleans' quest for a thriving tourist industry. His classic book *Fabulous New Orleans* has become the standard by which all other works purporting to describe the "Crescent City" are judged. In thinking over that first early morning visit to the city so long ago, Mr. Saxon muses:

> And this is my first impression of the fabulous city, when I went there with my grandfather. . . . I have never forgotten the gay old beggar woman, for her voice might have been the voice of the city itself. It has always seemed that New Orleans cries out: "Have a good time while you can. . . . That's what *I* always say!"

Since its earliest days as part of the young United States, it would seem that New Orleans has always had a keen interest in good times and good food. Even in these modern, more predictable times, this writer is happy to report that the party attitude is still very much intact. Visitors to the "Big Easy," whether they arrive by land or water, cannot help but be caught up in the lively and colorful spectacle which is the true heart of New Orleans.

The city of New Orleans has more than its share of nicknames. Some call it the "Crescent City." This moniker refers to the town's location on a crescent-shaped bend in the mighty Mississippi River. New Orleans has also been called the nation's "Party City." It doesn't require too much imagination to decide from whence comes this title. Now, as for the nickname "The Big Easy," that one is a little harder to figure. Perhaps it refers to native New Orleanians' easygoing attitude and general penchant for laughter, mirth, and a good time enjoyed by all, as this is what seems to be implied by yet another of its nicknames, "The City That Care Forgot."

New Orleans' greatest and most diverse resource lies in its colorful and varied peoples. There is perhaps no other city in the nation (with the possible—I say *possible*—exception of New York) which can lay claim to so many different nationalities and cultures living in harmony. Indeed, the varied population of the city is its most crucial source of variety and originality.

In any discussion of New Orleans and its people, one must first mention the Creoles. This unique strain of people has resulted from the intermarriage over the years between the original well-to-do French and Spanish colonists of old Louisiana, often with a dash or two of Negro and/or Indian blood thrown in for good measure. Over the years the Creoles have been one of New Orleans' most colorful elements and staunch defenders of the city they love. The "French Quarter" or "Vieux Carré" was the heart of the Creole population until recent times. Even today, the district bears the Creoles' indelible stamp. By all accounts, Creole-style dining is *the* most popular cuisine in this city of varied foods.

Visitors not familiar with New Orleans often confuse the Creoles with another of Louisiana's unique peoples, the Cajuns. Their background is actually very different. In 1755 the French settlers in Nova Scotia (known as Acadians) were ordered off their land by the British government. The peninsula had been ceded to the English following one of the many conflicts between France and Britain. Many of the Acadians returned to France, where they yearned for the New World. Beginning in 1764 and stretching into the period of Spanish rule (1785), many of the homeless settlers immigrated to southwest Louisiana. Since that time, the word "Acadian" has been "vernacularized" to "Cajun."

Since their first appearance in Louisiana, the Cajuns have preserved their own particular speech and culture. Cajun cooking is another very popular cuisine in New Orleans. Such Cajun cooks as Justin Wilson have developed a nationwide following through their cookbooks.

Mixed in with the Creoles and Cajuns are other Americans from an incredible variety of racial, religious, and cultural backgrounds. Working, living, and marrying together has produced the melting pot of peoples that is New Orleans. There is really nothing just like it anywhere else in the world!

New Orleans' visitors have the opportunity to see and experience a mind-boggling array of attractions. Readers are advised to obtain copies of *A Marmac Guide to New Orleans* and *The Pelican Guide to New Orleans* well before their visit. Call 1-800-843-1724 to order your copies. Study the books religiously. It is only with adequate preparation that you can hope to have anything like a full appreciation of the many sights, sounds, and foods of this fabulous community by the Mississippi.

The city of New Orleans is built upon a plot of land which is actually below sea level. A series of well-maintained levees and dikes protects the city from flooding when water levels on the Mississippi River or Lake Pontchartrain are higher than normal. This phenomenon has resulted in an unusual New Orleans characteristic. Until recently, it was not possible to dig a grave below ground. Before you could turn around, the hole would be full of water. For this reason, New Orleans cemeteries consist of often elaborate mausoleums built above ground. They are some of the most unusual burial places in the world. Visitors to New Orleans should take the opportunity to view these unique sites.

New Orleans' citizens are justifiably proud of their Superdome, one of the largest completely enclosed, environmentally controlled stadiums in the world. The National Football League's New Orleans Saints make their home in the Superdome. The city has never failed to support the Saints with anything less than wild enthusiasm.

Speaking of wild enthusiasm, let's not forget the fiesta that made New Orleans a household word—Mardi Gras! Almost every year since 1857, the day before Ash Wednesday is filled with costumed merrymakers riding floats through the city and tossing out tons of plastic beads, colorful "coins," frisbees, plastic cups, and you name it to the cheering crowds. The spectacle just cannot be described. It has to be experienced to be believed, and even then you probably won't believe it.

Cruising visitors wanting to attend Mardi Gras should make their plans far in advance of the actual event. Dockage reservations can be very hard to come by. Call for your space several months, even a year, in advance rather than risk disappointment. Remember, with the lack of anchorages around New Orleans, a marina berth is your only viable alternative for taking part in the festival.

Another of the city's top-notch festivals is the New Orleans Jazz and Heritage Festival, commonly known as the "Jazz Fest." Every year both world-famous and relatively obscure musicians and their followers make pilgrimages to the New Orleans Fair Grounds to partake of two weekends of great food, great music, and various arts and crafts shows. If you are *crazy* about music (not just jazz), simply *like* music, or *hate* music and need to be set straight, make a bee-line for the Big Easy the last weekend in April or the first weekend in May. The same precautions about slip reservations that apply to Mardi Gras apply here, too.

Dining at a few of the hundreds and hundreds of fine restaurants in New Orleans is, for many, the city's chief attraction. Those in the know about such things will tell you that this city has more fine restaurants than any other community in the nation. While those from Charleston, South Carolina might take exception to this claim, there is actually a very good reason for this tradition of fine dining. New Orleans has a secret resource. There is a whole cadre of mostly African-American Creole cooks who make the rounds year after year working in one city restaurant or another. Their art is carefully passed on to assistants or sometimes family members. It is just about impossible to imagine any finer foods than those produced by this incredibly talented group. Add to that a good measure of hot and spicy Cajun cuisine and good old Southern-style cooking, and you can readily appreciate why New Orleans can truly lay waste to your waistline.

There have been books and books written about the "best" restaurants in New Orleans. This writer could not even begin to sort out the best from the good. It should be noted that I have yet to eat a meal in this city that I consider less than good. Again, I suggest that you study both the Marmac and Pelican guides for suggestions. Strictly as a starting point, allow me to suggest Mandina's (3800 Canal Street, 504-482-9179) and NOLA (534 St. Louis Street, 504-522-6652) and, for Cajun-style cuisine, Patout's (501 Bourbon Street, 504-524-4054) and K-Paul's (416 Chartres, 504-524-7394). Another good choice is Feelings Cafe, found just outside of the Quarter at 2600 Chartres (504-945-2222), and the Red Maple Restaurant and Lounge (1036 Lafayette Street, 504-367-0935), across the river in Gretna. Call for reservations. Trust me, you'll be glad you took this tip!

Note that with the exception of a few restaurants near West End and South Shore Harbor (see below), visiting cruisers will need to acquire a rental car or take a taxi to access most of the city's dining attractions. Again, the extra effort and expense is more than justified!

New Orleans is the birthplace of American jazz music. A unique blend of classical and popular music with a liberal dose of experimentation, the unmistakable sound of New Orleans jazz can still be heard every night of the year wafting its way through the streets of the city. Walk along just about any lane in the French Quarter and your ears will lead you to many a club where you can sample this quintessentially New Orleans musical fare.

When talking about New Orleans' attractions, everyone will eventually find his or her way to a discussion of the French Quarter. This is the heart of old New Orleans and there is no better place to put you in touch with the city's unique culture. Nothing else in America is quite like a stroll through the narrow lanes and cobblestoned ways of the "Quarter." Wander down raucous Bourbon Street, or maybe stroll through the French Market. See lovely Jackson Square, with its artists and performers. The old Creole homes, with their cool, stucco walls and elaborate wrought-iron balconies dripping with flowers, will take you back to another time. Unfortunately, at times it seems as if the whole nation is trying to undergo this experience and the Quarter can become rather crowded, to say the least. Nonetheless, the joys of discovering New Orleans' French Quarter are *not* to be missed.

Numbers to know in New Orleans include

Metry Cab—504-835-4242
Yellow Cab—504-525-3311
United Cab—504-524-9606
Avis Rent A Car—504-523-4317
Budget Car Rental—504-467-2277
Enterprise Rent-A-Car—504-522-7900
West Marine (827 Harrison Avenue)—
    504-482-5090

Cajun Legend

Ever wonder why Canadian lobsters are so large and Louisiana crawfish are so small? The Cajuns have a ready explanation for this. According to legend, the lobsters so missed their Cajuns after they were forced to depart Nova Scotia that they migrated south down the Mississippi River to be with them again. Their Herculean efforts so depleted the lobsters that their size was much reduced and remains so to this day.

Fanciful as it may be, this humorous tale serves to show visitors how the once-lowly crawfish is part and parcel of Louisiana Cajun cuisine. Cruisers docking in New Orleans, or anywhere in Louisiana, should take the opportunity to try several of the Cajun or Creole dishes containing this Southern delicacy.

New Orleans History In 1685 Henri de Tonti, a French Canadian, descended the Mississippi with a party of soldiers to make contact with the explorer La Salle at the river's mouth. Actually, La Salle had completely missed the southern mouth of the great river and eventually returned to Canada. Unable to find La Salle, Tonti established an alliance with the local Native Americans and proclaimed the lands about the lower Mississippi "Louisiana," in honor of his king. The French party returned north up the river, but not before Tonti left a letter for La Salle with one of his trusted Indian chiefs.

It was not until 1699 that the French returned to Louisiana. Landing in modern-day Mississippi, Pierre Le Moyne, Sieur d'Iberville thought the waters too shallow and the land a bit low for development. Iberville explored the Mississippi but found no suitable site for his colony. Leaving his brother Bienville to continue explorations, Iberville returned to the small French settlement at Biloxi and then to France.

Bienville continued his explorations of the Mississippi and was rewarded for his efforts when friendly Native Americans presented him with Tonti's letter for La Salle, left with them fourteen years previously. This humble document established French claims to the lower Mississippi beyond question.

In September of 1699, Bienville portaged across the future site of New Orleans with two canoes and a few men. The next day he came upon an English warship in a bend of the Mississippi River. This force had been dispatched from Virginia to oppose French settlement of the region. Resorting to guile, Bienville informed the captain that a fleet of French men-of-war waited just around the next bend, and if he did not depart at once, his ship would be blown out of the water. The ruse worked and this portion of the great river has ever after been called "English Turn."

After the strong hurricane of 1717 Bienville, by then the undisputed leader of French Louisiana, selected his old portage between Lake Pontchartrain and the Mississippi River as the site of the colony's new capital. Even though Mobile actually served as the center of government until 1722, construction of New Orleans began in 1718.

Bienville personally directed this early phase of development. First, he had his men chop out a small clearing amidst the cane and willow trees growing about the banks of the Mississippi. This site became the "Place d'Armes," which we today know as Jackson Square.

All did not proceed according to Bienville's careful plans. One year after its inception, the new settlement of New Orleans consisted only of three houses and a hundred huts. In order to increase the population, prisoners and prostitutes from French jails were deported to New Orleans. Negro slaves began to arrive in quantity during 1720. By 1721 the city had a population of some 1,700 persons, almost half of whom were black slaves.

In 1721 a strong hurricane struck New Orleans a great blow. By this time the Vieux Carré (the modern French Quarter) occupied a 4,000-foot section on the Mississippi waterfront. Almost two-thirds of the houses in the city were flattened. The loss of life was great and it was to be many years before the city would recover entirely.

Following the end of the Seven Years' War in 1762, New Orleans and all of French Louisiana west of the Mississippi was ceded to Spain. From 1788 to 1794 New Orleans suffered two great fires which almost completely destroyed the old Vieux Carré. The district was rebuilt, and thus almost all of the buildings in what we today call the French Quarter were actually built under Spanish rule.

Napoleon forced his vassal state of Spain to cede New Orleans and most of Louisiana back to France in 1802. Shortly thereafter, Napoleon sold the entire region, along with New Orleans, to the United States for much-needed cash. Spain retained control temporarily of what it called "West Florida," which included the modern-day coastlines of Alabama and most of Mississippi. The Louisiana Purchase remains one of the crowning achievements of Thomas Jefferson's presidency.

At first there were bad feelings between the local mix of Spanish, French, black, and Indian populations, which by then had assumed the name of Creoles, and the backwoods Americans or "Kaintucks," as they were often called in disdain. Soon, however, events were to force these two groups to work in close harmony to save their city.

In 1812 war was declared between the United States and England. Fearful of the new nation to the north, Spanish authorities along the Northern Gulf Coast allowed British naval forces unrestricted access to their port facilities and incited the Creek Indians to violence. In August 1812, a Creek war party attacked and massacred 500 settlers at Fort Mims on the Alabama River above Mobile.

The governor of the Mississippi territory called out the local militia. This band of soldiers was to become the core of one of the most courageous fighting forces in America's military history. All it needed was an extraordinary commander.

Far to the north in Nashville, Tennessee, Gen. Andrew Jackson lay in bed recovering from two bullet wounds. When news of the Fort Mims disaster reached his ears, he sprang into the saddle and led a group of Tennessee militia south. On March 27, 1814, with the help of the Cherokee Indian tribe, Jackson routed the Creeks at the battle of Horseshoe Bend. The general was soon appointed by the Department of War to the command of the Northern Gulf Coast defenses.

Meanwhile, England had at last exiled its old enemy Napoleon, thereby crushing the threat on its eastern flank. This allowed the British military command to send a huge army to attack the American Gulf. Even while its ministers talked peace with American representatives, the army sailed with orders to "attack even if a peace pact were signed."

Informed by spies of the English intentions, Jackson first worked feverishly to reinforce Mobile's defenses. After an English attack on Mobile was firmly repulsed in September of 1814, the English turned their attention to New Orleans.

Jackson dashed overland to New Orleans in a near superhuman journey and reached the city on December 1. Here he met with the local Creole leaders, principal among them the sometimes pirate Jean Lafitte. All differences were hastily laid aside in the face of a common foe.

On December 12 the British armada arrived. The force consisted of 20,000 veteran soldiers and ships mounting over 1,000 guns. Jackson's forces numbered some 4,500 troops and a few small gunships. The outcome seemed preordained.

After a gallant delaying action by ragtag American forces fighting from barges on nearby Bay St. Louis, the main British army marched against the American lines on the Plain of Chalmette, south of New Orleans, on January 17, 1815. Jackson's forces laid down a murderous fire in the foggy weather. The British forces were hindered by the swampy ground and their slow progress allowed the Americans to cut them down like wheat before the scythe. At the end of the battle, it was learned that 2,036 British soldiers had died, while only 71 Americans lost their lives.

New Orleans was ecstatic in this great victory and the optimistic attitude carried the city into an unprecedented era of progress during the 1830s. In 1836 two of the largest hotels in the nation, the St. Charles and the St. Louis, opened their doors for business in New Orleans. The Mobile to New Orleans railway was completed during this period and the port on the Mississippi River boomed. Goods of all descriptions were shipped upriver from the Gulf or downstream from the territories to the north and then loaded upon rail cars for transshipment inland. If not for the Civil War, New Orleans could well have grown into the largest city in the South.

New Orleans fell to Union forces early in the Civil War. Using Ship Island off Mississippi Sound as a staging ground, naval forces under the command of Admiral Farragut and ground troops under Gen. Ben Butler attacked the city. Fortunately, there was relatively little damage to the city. Compared to later campaigns by Northern forces, the occupying troops had at least a nominal respect for private property and New Orleans emerged from the war in much better shape than many of its Southern sister cities.

Nevertheless, the Reconstruction period spelled hard times for New Orleans. It was not really until the coming of riverboat traffic in the early 1900s that the city's economy revived. In the late 1880s the mouth of the Mississippi River was finally stabilized by a system of stone jetties. Now ships of all drafts could call at the port and have their goods shipped upriver by stern-wheeled, steam-driven riverboats.

Since those glorious days of the riverboats, New Orleans has almost never looked back. From 1884 to 1885 the Cotton Centennial Exposition was held in the city. This was the world's fair of its day and did much to put New Orleans on the economic map of the twentieth century. In 1984 this tradition was continued with the Louisiana World Exposition, almost one hundred years to the day after the Cotton Exposition.

The reader will understand that the above sketch, lengthy as it is, only begins to scratch the proverbial surface of New Orleans' fascinating story. I again urge you to acquire copies of *Fabulous New Orleans*, *A Marmac Guide to New Orleans*, and *The Pelican Guide to New Orleans* and learn more about the city's fascinating past before you visit. For knowledgeable visitors, the Crescent City never fails in its reward.

New Orleans' South Shore Harbor (30 02.360 North/090 00.937 West)

Moving east to west, the first and newest New Orleans marina facility is large South

South Shore Harbor, New Orleans

Shore Harbor, found just east of the charted location of Lakefront Airport. Its location is clearly noted on chart 11369. This well-sheltered, artificial harbor is owned and managed by the Orleans Levee Board, an agency of the state government.

This writer has, in times past, been critical of the decision to locate a huge, garish gambling ship on the southeasterly corner of South Shore Harbor. However, there have been some recent improvements. The marina's dockmaster has assured this writer that the "noise pollution" problems (once generated by the casino and its crowds) are now minimized and that the marina parking and casino parking are now separated by a chain-link fence. However, I still consider the presence of the gambling ship a black mark on this otherwise excellent pleasure-craft facility. Cruisers who are into gambling may well disagree with me on this point, but most other mariners will want to take the casino's presence into their plans.

Transients are gladly accepted for overnight or temporary dockage at South Shore Harbor's fixed, concrete-decked slips. Fresh-water, 30- and 50-amp electrical, and telephone connections are available at all berths. Soundings alongside run in the 9- to 10-foot range. Some slips are of the covered variety, but most are open and appropriate for both power and sailcraft.

Waste pump-out service is available, and mechanical repairs can sometimes be arranged through independent contractors. There are two sets of showers at South Shore Harbor. The smaller, nonclimate-controlled set overlooks the southeasterly banks of the dockage basin. We found these units to be barely adequate. The larger, air-conditioned showers are located in a free-standing building just

behind and beside the large gambling ship. Here, cruisers will find three small, individual shower rooms and a petite Laundromat. Unfortunately, visitors must make a goodly trek across the parking lot and then pass under the covered walkway leading to the gambling ship to reach these showers and the Laundromat. There is more bad news. These facilities share the same building with a small cafeteria that serves the casino employees. We found a distinct smell of old French fries in the showers and Laundromat.

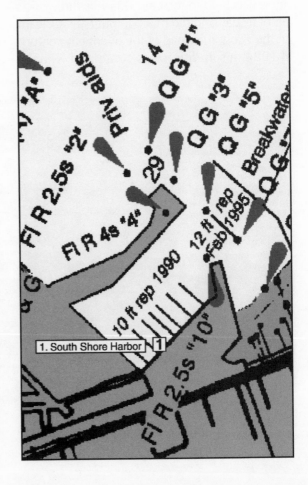

1. South Shore Harbor

The South Shore Harbor dockmaster's office is located in a separate building, just outside of the southwestern corner of the parking lot. The headquarters for the good folks at South Shore Yacht Club (504-241-8863) is also located in this structure.

The only restaurant within easy foot access is the buffet served aboard the on-site gambling ship. Otherwise, you will want to call a taxi to visit any of the city's many fine-dining spots.

South Shore Harbor (504) 245-3152
   www.marinasinneworleans.com/ssharbor.htm

Approach depth—12 feet
Dockside depth—9-10 feet
Accepts transients—yes
Transient-dockage rate—below average
Fixed concrete slips (on wooden pilings)—yes
Dockside power connections—30- and 50-amp
Dockside water connections—yes
Showers—yes
Laundromat—yes
Waste pump-out—yes
Mechanical repairs—independent technicians
   only
Restaurant—on site (or taxi ride necessary)

Inner Harbor Navigation Canal

Study either chart 11367 or 11369 for a moment and you will quickly spot the New Orleans Inner Harbor Navigation Canal connecting the Mississippi River and Lake Pontchartrain. Near the mid-point of its north-to-south passage, the ICW intersects the canal from the east (standard mile 8). The lower portion of the canal will be reviewed in the next section of this chapter, but for now let us look at the northerly branch leading south from Lake Pontchartrain.

First, let it be duly noted that most New Orleans natives shorten the impressive title of this body of water to its simpler name, the Industrial Canal. We shall follow this same practice in our discussions.

Captains and crews voyaging on the ICW and wishing to visit New Orleans can use the northern leg of the Industrial Canal to reach southern Lake Pontchartrain and its associated marina facilities. Hard as it may be to believe, there is not a single marina located directly on the ICW in the New Orleans area. The stretch of the Mississippi River bordering on downtown New Orleans and its famous French Quarter is also *completely* without facilities for pleasure craft.

Conversely, mariners who are ready to slip their southern Pontchartrain moorings and leave New Orleans can follow the Industrial Canal south to the lock which gives access to the Mississippi River and the ICW's continued passage to the west. It's ironic that such an important artery of pleasure-craft traffic has been all but taken over by commercial waterborne interests.

You might think it a simple matter to cruise from Pontchartrain's southern shores to the Industrial Canal's junction with the ICW after a quick glance at chart 11367. Let me assure you that nothing is farther from the truth. The canal is overlooked by closely packed industrial facilities of every description. Commercial wharves are everywhere, often in use by barges being loaded and unloaded. Tugboats and tows are a very frequent companion on a cruise through the stream. These vessels' limited maneuverability calls for a wide berth and extreme caution.

As if all that were not enough, the northerly

leg of the Industrial Canal is a steeple chase of bridges. Some of these are extremely low level railroad spans which do not even allow for a small motor vessel to pass without opening. Just to make matters a little more interesting, some of the other spans now sport a restrictive opening schedule as well. In short, you had best leave plenty of time in your cruising plans to traverse any and all portions of the Industrial Canal. Proceed at idle speed and be ready to avoid any commercial traffic quickly.

With all its commerce, the canal is kept deep to its banks. This is one watery passage in New Orleans where your last worry is running aground. Spend your time instead worrying about being run *over*.

It does not require too much imagination to conclude that a cruise along this crowded waterway is anything but a relaxing ecological experience. The industrial facilities are not exactly clean and the smog and pollution can seem thick enough to cut with a knife. Yet, this writer cannot deny having felt a certain fascination with this passage. For a time or two at least, the sight of these giant plants from the water can be awe-inspiring. Just remember to keep a lookout for commercial traffic as you rubberneck.

West End Harbor
(Various Lats/Lons—see below)

West End Harbor, about 4.1 nautical miles west of the Industrial Canal's northern entrance, is home to most of New Orleans' yachting facilities. The list is quite long indeed. It includes one of the nation's most prestigious yacht clubs, two major dockage facilities, and a host of service organizations, not to mention numerous fine restaurants. As you might expect, the harbor is teeming with boats of all descriptions. It's a long way from an isolated anchorage on the Tickfaw River, but there is also every marine service you might ever require ready at hand.

West End Harbor actually consists of two well-sheltered basins split apart by a long tongue of land running from west to east. This gives the harbor something of *W* shape, with the two principal basins located on the outside arms of the *W* to the north and south. A small but deep canal runs along the eastern banks of the harbor and connects the two dockage harbors.

The land separating the two basins is actually a park with luscious green grass and tall shade trees. Small ponds and feeder canals add greatly to the general peace and serenity of this delightful respite from on-the-water problems. A stroll through this charming park is highly recommended after a rough day fighting the chop on Pontchartrain.

Entrance depths from Lake Pontchartrain into West End Harbor run in the 9- to 12-foot range and dockside soundings measure some 8 to 9 feet of water. Running aground need not be a concern unless your craft draws more than 7 feet of water.

Mariners entering West End Harbor will be greeted by the sight of New Canal Light dead ahead. This light is part and parcel of the origins of West End. It seems that in the early 1830s the city fathers of New Orleans authorized the construction of an ambitious canal that would connect Lake Pontchartrain with the Mississippi River. This project failed for lack of funding, but the initial portion of the work became an active harbor which would one day be the city's principal dockage basin.

New Canal Light, West End Harbor

In 1834 a brick lighthouse was erected at the entrance of West End Harbor for $25,000. In those days that was quite a sum of money. The government obviously didn't get much of a deal, for the light was only in use for 20 years before it became unusable. Shortly thereafter a cottage-style lighthouse was constructed at a cost of only $6,000 and served the harbor through the Civil War. This structure was replaced by a similar-house-style light in 1890 that remains in place to this day.

The "house" part of the light used to house the Lake Pontchartrain Coast Guard base, but that facility has now been moved elsewhere. The old light remains, however, and it is just as great a sight from the water as ever. As you enter the harbor, pause for a moment to reflect upon all the history that has flowed pass this venerable structure.

A turn to the west will lead visiting cruisers into West End's northerly dockage basin. You will immediately sight the Southern Yacht Club's impressive clubhouse to port. Founded in 1848, the Southern Yacht Club (504-288-4221) claims to be the second-oldest organization of its type in the country. It has been instrumental in the social and sporting life of New Orleans for almost 150 years.

The Southern Yacht Club welcomes members of other accredited clubs with reciprocal agreements to their clubhouse facilities. Visitors can make use of the club's many amenities, including the cool swimming pool and first-class dining room (closed on Mondays). The Southern Yacht Club no longer has any wet slips of its own, but the club is readily accessible from either the adjacent New Orleans Municipal Yacht Harbor or the Orleans (Levee Board) Marina.

Most remaining dockage in the north basin is taken up by the concrete piers of the New Orleans Municipal Yacht Harbor (30 01.525 North/090 07.128 West). This facility keeps better than 20 slips open for transients. However, most are usually spoken for well in advance, so make your reservations early. The marina's fixed, concrete-decked berths feature full power and water connections. No fuel or repairs are offered, but free waste pump-out service is in the offing.

New Orleans Municipal Yacht Harbor boasts new, climate-controlled showers on the first floor of the large building overlooking the harbor's southerly banks. The city dockmaster's office and the headquarters of the New Orleans Yacht Club (504-283-2581) are located on the second floor of this structure. We found these showers and the adjacent Laundromat to be more than adequate.

The many restaurants described below are all within walking distance of this facility, though the dining spots overlooking the harbor's western shores are the most convenient. The nearby shopping center and its first-class grocery store, detailed below, are also within hiking distance,

though it's a much longer walk from the New Orleans Municipal Harbor than from the Orleans Marina (see later in this chapter).

**New Orleans Municipal Yacht Harbor
    (504) 288-1431**

Approach depth—9-12 feet
Dockside depth—8-9 feet
Accepts transients—yes
Transient-dockage rate—well below average
Fixed concrete piers—yes
Dockside power connections—30- and 50-amp
Dockside water connections—yes
Showers—yes
Laundromat—yes
Waste pump-out—yes

New Orleans Municipal Yacht Harbor, West End Harbor

Returning now to the entrance of West End Harbor, and cruising south on the canal connecting the two basins, the entrance to the southern dockage basin will open out to the west. We shall review this harbor shortly, but let's continue for just a moment down the connecting canal.

Soon you will come abeam of and pass both the Hong Kong Restaurant, without dockage, and AmberJack's Down Under Restaurant (7306 Lakeshore Drive, 504-282-6660), which does have one face pier with 7- to 8-foot depths. One 38-footer should be able to squeeze in.

The canal finally ends amidst a host of private docks associated with a condo development. Condos seem to be springing up all around both dockage basins of West End Harbor. While great for the residents, they certainly add to the general congestion.

Now, turning our attention to the south harbor, the southern banks are occupied by the Orleans Levee Board-owned Orleans Marina (30 01.357 North/090 06.972 West), while the northern shore teems with yachting facilities of every description.

In actuality, the Levee Board owns all of West End Harbor. Except for its own extensive docks in the south basin, the remainder of the harbor is leased out to the various private and municipal concerns. Orleans Marina keeps 10 to 12 slips open for transients. Advance reservations are a wise practice. The piers are composed of fixed, concrete-decked structures set atop wooden pilings. The central docks (but not the finger piers serving the boat slips) are covered (which is ever so nice in inclement weather) without inconveniencing those of us who captain wind-powered vessels. Some berths have 30-amp power hookups, while

others feature 50-amp connections. All have fresh-water hookups, and waste pump-out service is available. The on-site, climate-controlled showers and Laundromat are housed on the first floor of the two-story building, overlooking the southeastern corner of the dockage basin. No fuel or other marine services are present. All of the restaurants described below are within easy walking distance, and the nearby shopping center with its wonderful grocery market is only a short hike away.

Orleans Marina (504) 288-2351
    **http://www.marinasinneworleans.com/orlean
    smarina.htm**

Approach depth—9-12 feet
Dockside depth—8-9 feet
Accepts transients—yes
Transient-dockage rate—below average
Fixed concrete slips (atop wooden pilings)—yes
Dockside power connections—30- and 50-amp
Dockside water connections—yes
Showers—yes
Laundromat—yes
Waste pump-out—yes
Restaurant—several nearby

Beginning on the eastern end of the south harbor's northern shore, Schubert's Marine's extensive shoreside facilities and docks overlook the harbor near 30 01.461 North/090 06.838 West. This firm has changed ownership recently, but it is still operating under the same name. Only time will tell what effect the new owners might have on this operation.

Schubert's offers the only private, commercial dockage for transients in West End Harbor. Berths are provided at fixed, wooden-face docks with fresh-water hookups and 30- to

Orleans Marina, West End Harbor

50-amp power connections. Additionally, the marina features complete mechanical, generator, and below-waterline, haul-out repairs (60-ton crane). The management has informed this writer that they engage mostly in diesel-engine repairs but do service some smaller gasoline-powered plants. Schubert's is a designated Detroit Diesel, Perkins, and Northern Lights dealer. We have always seen far more power-craft than sailing vessels undergoing work in Schubert's repair yard, but my talks with the management indicate that sailboats can be served as well. Full fueling facilities are available at a fuel dock on the western shore of the connecting canal. A variety store (undergoing renovation at the time of this writing) with a small selection of snacks and basic food items is found just behind the fuel pier. Obviously, Schubert's is one of the most comprehensive full-service facilities in West End Harbor. Mariners can make use of their services with confidence.

Schubert's Marine (504) 282-8136

Approach depth—9-12 feet
Dockside depth—10-14 feet
Accepts transients—yes
Transient-dockage rate—below average
Fixed wooden slips—yes
Dockside power connections—30- and 50-amp
Dockside water connections—yes

Schubert's Marine, West End Harbor

Gasoline—yes
Diesel fuel—yes
Mechanical repairs—yes
Below-waterline repairs—yes
Variety store—yes
Restaurant—several nearby

Moving farther west, M. G. Mayer Yacht Services (504-282-1700) offers full mechanical gas- and diesel-engine repairs, as well as haul-outs by way of a 35-ton travelift.

The northwestern corner of West End's southern dockage basin is overlooked by what may be the friendliest and most knowledgeable repair yard in all of New Orleans. Sintes Boat Works (30 01.403 North/090 07.139 West, 504-288-7281) offers every imaginable haul-out, engine, generator, air-conditioning, painting, fiberglass, and marine carpentry service. If you can't get it fixed here, better find out how new boat prices have been doing lately. The yard has extensive work buildings and shoreside facilities to accommodate these varied repairs solidly. Haul-outs are accomplished by a crane with an 18-ton capacity. The impressive physical plant is ably manned by an unusually competent body of workers. This writer found the management of Sintes to be quite willing to go that extra mile to satisfy the cruiser's every need with quality work. Not to put too fine a point on it, Sintes is unreservedly recommended by this writer for both sail- and powercraft in need of service.

Finally, Sea Chest Marine (504-288-1250) occupies the northwestern corner of Sintes Boat Works. This firm is under the same family ownership as the boatyard but has different managers. Sea Chest is undoubtedly one of the best-stocked and most efficiently organized independent marine stores this writer has ever had the privilege to review. Whether you need that certain part, new galley china, or just the latest chart or cruising guide, you can be sure of finding what you need at Sea Chest. In the unlikely event that the store does not have what you need in stock, it can be quickly ordered. I have always found the staff and management to be friendly, knowledgeable, and highly efficient. If you need anything nautical, the Sea Chest is your ticket.

West End Harbor Ashore

West End Harbor is surrounded by a gaggle of fine restaurants. These sumptuous dining choices can be divided into three camps: those which guard the eastern, southern, and western banks of the harbor.

Let's begin with those restaurants on the eastern shore. Here you will find Joe's Crab Shack (8000 Lakeshore Drive, 504-283-1010). This restaurant occupies the one time location of Bart's.

The southern shore of West End Harbor plays host to the largest collection of dining spots in the area. Famished cruisers in search of fine fare should check out Russell's Marina Grill (8555 Pontchartrain Boulevard, 504-282-9980) and the West End Cafe (8536 Pontchartrain Boulevard, 504-288-0711). This latter dining spot is also open for breakfast Saturdays and Sundays only. For those with a taste for fine beef, don't miss the Red Steer Grill (124 Lake Marina, 504-283-4582).

While all of these dining choices have merit, this writer particularly recommends Russell's Marina Grill. Open for all three meals of the day, you simply can't go wrong by setting your gastronomical sights on this port of call. For lunch or dinner, please take my advice and sample the Shrimp and Crab Cakes Patricia. Topped with a light and creamy crawfish sauce, this dish alone will bring you back time and time again.

Cruisers strolling West End Harbor's western shores will find Keith Noonan's Saloon (7354 W Roadway Street, 504-282-1466) and, last but certainly not least, Bruning's Seafood Restaurant (West End Park, 504-288-4521). Bruning's has been delighting patrons with their fine seafood and landlubber dishes since an incredible 1854. As Darlene, manager of the nearby Sea Chest Marine Store, put it to this writer, "this is 'the' place to dine on West End Harbor."

So, you prefer to cook up your evening meal n the pleasant confines of your vessel's galley. Well, West End Harbor is still a good place for you to set your sails. Walk east on Lake Marina Drive, then turn south on Lakeshore Boulevard and east again on Robert E. Lee Boulevard. Depending on where you have chosen to coil your lines, a walk of only three to four blocks will bring you to a nice strip shopping center guarding the northern side of Robert E. Lee Boulevard. Here you will find a Walgreen's Drug Store and a useful enterprise known as Dry Cleaning by Louis (504-288-8236). Of even greater promise, however, is the Robert Fresh Market (504-282-3428). This is a very upscale, gourmet supermarket with a wonderful deli, super bakery, and simply dreamy wine selection. Oh yes, the prime beef and poultry are nothing to sneeze at either. Please listen to me on this one—you could scarcely do better than restock your larders at this fine market. Your on-board chef will be ever so glad that we sent you to Robert's.

Visiting cruisers should also note that inexpensive bus service is available from this strip center. You can quickly and cheaply ride downtown to the French Quarter or Canal Street. Ask any of the local dockmasters for advice concerning the bus schedules.

LAKE PONTCHARTRAIN—SOUTH SHORE NAVIGATION

Navigation of Lake Pontchartrain's southern shore is complicated by the relative lack of aids to navigation. This can and usually does result in long runs between points of reference. These are excellent waters in which to try out your new GPS interfaced with a laptop computer system. In any case, be sure to plot the various compass/GPS courses needed to reach your destination before taking to the water. As always, watch for aids to navigation and keep well clear of any commercial traffic.

Entry from the Rigolets   Skippers bound for Pontchartrain's southern shoreline from the Rigolets will follow the same channel through the three bridges spanning the eastern "turtle's head" portion of the lake as their brethren cruising to the northern shore. This route was outlined in a preceding section of this chapter. Once through the westernmost railway span, it's time for a long, markerless run.

On to the South Shore   From the westerly face of the railway bridge's pass-through, we suggest setting course for unlighted buoy #Y, just off the northern tip of the charted Lakefront Airport. You will pass through a little better than 12.6 miles of open water along the run. Stay on course and use your GPS and/or GPS/laptop computer combination if you have them.

As you approach Lakefront Airport, you will spy the long runways leading out well into the water. You can cut east of the airport and enter South Shore Harbor, or continue west to West End Harbor. The Industrial Canal (Inner Harbor Navigation Canal) cuts south immediately west of the airport.

South Shore Harbor is clearly shown on the current edition of chart 11369. Successful entry is simplified by a series of flashing daybeacons that outlines both sides of the approach channel. Eventually the entrance cut will bring you between a stone jetty to your port side and a concrete-wall breakwater to starboard. To make good your entry into the inner harbor, you must follow an almost 180-degree turn through the breakwater. During daylight, this approach is fairly straightforward, even for strangers.

On to the Industrial Canal   Be sure to pass well north of the outermost runway of Lakefront Airport to continue on to the west past South Shore Harbor. If you want to pick up the ICW or continue on to the Mississippi River, cut south into the northern mouth of the Industrial Canal.

Industrial Canal   Switch to chart 11367 for navigation on the Industrial Canal. Its larger scale details these waters far better than the other broad-coverage charts.

The New Orleans Industrial Canal is well named. The shores are packed full of commercial facilities, including quite a number of barge-loading wharves. Cruise through at idle speed and give any commercial traffic the widest possible buffer zone. These vessels usually have limited maneuverability and it's up to you to keep clear. Fortunately, the canal is deep almost to its banks and there is usually plenty of room to clear other traffic.

No fewer than 5 bridges span the Industrial Canal between Lake Pontchartrain and the ICW's intersection with the canal. One is a high-rise fixed span, while two others have 46 and 55 feet of closed vertical clearance. The remaining two railway bridges are so low that they must open even for the passage of small outboard craft. Two highway bridges among this collection of spans have restricted opening schedules. The low-level railway bridges are supposed to open on demand, but be warned that pleasure craft carry a very low priority. We have always found the bridge operators to be more than slightly slow on the trigger. Most can be raised on VHF channel 16 or 13 eventually. We found it often took repeated calls to get any response.

To leave Pontchartrain, cruise through the first, high-rise bascule span (the Highway 47-Leon C. Simon Highway Bridge). This bridge has a closed vertical clearance of 46 feet. It does not open at all from 7:00 A.M. to 8:30 A.M. and again from 5:00 P.M. to 6:30 P.M. Otherwise it opens on demand.

The highway bridge is closely followed by one of the two ultralow-level railway spans. This one is known as the Seabrook Railway Bridge. Try calling on your VHF and blowing the horn. Don't be surprised if you don't get a response. If a train is due, the bridge may be closed for a good fifteen minutes or more without radio explanation.

Once the low-level railway span is in your wake, you will cruise through a mercifully bridgeless portion of the canal spanning some 1.4 nautical miles. You will next meet up with the Highway 90 lift bridge. This span has a closed vertical clearance of 50 feet and an open clearance of 120 feet. It also does not open between the hours of 7:00 A.M. and 8:30 A.M. and between 5:00 P.M. and 6:30 P.M. At other times, the bridge deigns to open on demand for us peon pleasure craft.

Another .2 nautical mile will bring you to the fixed, high-rise Interstate 10 bridge. This span's 115-foot vertical clearance should be sufficient for any cruising craft.

Unfortunately, the high-rise is immediately followed by the second of the low-level railway bridges (Gentilly Road Railway). The same rules of delay apply here.

Once this last bridge is left behind, you can watch the sights for the next .7 nautical mile while cruising south to the charted 34-foot-deep turning basin. At this point, the ICW passage from Lake Borgne comes in from the east, while the locked passage to the Mississippi River cuts sharply south. Continued navigation of the Industrial Canal and the ICW will be presented in the next section of this chapter.

On to West End Harbor West of the

Industrial Canal, the southern shores of Lake Pontchartrain are protected by a concrete seawall. Just behind the banks a park overlooks much of the lake's shoreline. This is a great place to stroll during the early morning or afternoon hours, though a nighttime visit is most assuredly in the realm of the foolhardy.

By staying at least .3 nautical mile north of the banks, you can follow the shoreline west to West End Harbor. Along the way, you will note several of the seemingly random white, yellow, and orange buoys charted on 11369. I suggest ignoring these aids. They are of no use to the pleasure-craft navigators.

The entrance to West End is found on the harbor's northeastern corner. It is easily identified by the white New Canal Lighthouse described earlier. This "cottage-style" lighthouse can be spied from a goodly distance on the water. Use your binoculars to verify recognition.

At night, the south shore seawall is well illuminated by street lights. While making sure to maintain an adequate buffer of at least .3 nautical mile from the banks, you can follow the shore to West End Harbor. Use your binoculars to aid your nighttime vision.

The New Canal Light just behind West End's entrance is also quite useful for spotting the harbor at night. This old sentinel can be a welcome harbinger of safe harbor.

West End Harbor   West End Harbor is noted on chart 11369 with the words "New Canal C. G.," abbreviation for New Canal Coast Guard Station, which is just east of the twin basins.

It doesn't get much simpler than this, people. Simply cruise through the protective breakwater's entrance on its mid-width, keeping flashing daybeacon #2 to starboard. Once you are inside, good depths stretch from shore to shore.

Lake Pontchartrain Causeway   Mariners cruising west on Pontchartrain's waters pass West End Harbor will have to contend with the 24-mile Lake Pontchartrain Causeway. Moving south to north, the first pass-through is found some 3.5 nautical miles from the southern shore. Although it is unmarked, most powerboats should probably choose to make use of this convenient passage. With its vertical clearance of 22 feet, it is perfect for these sorts of craft but unusable by all but the smallest sailboats. It is the closest passage to West End Harbor.

Set a compass/GPS course from West End or some other ready point of navigational reference for the first pass-through. On clear days, you should spot it riding high out of the water long before you arrive.

Sailcraft or any vessel needing more than 22 feet but no more than 50 feet of vertical clearance should set their course for the second (south to north) of the causeway's pass-throughs. This passage is well defined by a whole series of charted and lighted daybeacons. It has a vertical clearance of 50 feet, which should be sufficient for all but larger sailcraft.

Set a course from either West End or some other charted navigational reference to come between flashing daybeacons #1 and #2, the easternmost aids leading to this second Pontchartrain Causeway pass-through. Once you are between #1 and #2, the raised span is directly to the west.

Note the charted sunken wreck southwest of flashing daybeacon #6, west of the causeway. If you draw 6 feet or better, be sure to bypass this underwater hazard by passing far closer to flashing daybeacon #5 than #6.

Vessels requiring more than 50 feet of vertical clearance must cruise far to the north and make use of the causeway's swinging bascule span. This passage is also well outlined by flashing daybeacons. It is a run of 13.1 nautical miles from West End Harbor to this opening span. This could be a voyage encompassing several hours for a sailcraft. Obviously, you must make use of this pass-through if none of the others have sufficient clearance.

This bascule bridge now supposedly opens mostly on demand (with 3 hours' advance notice), except during peak traffic hours (see below). The bridge operators (on duty 24 hours a day) request that all captains who know that they will need the bridge to open, call on VHF channel 16 or 17 well before they actually reach the span (at least 3 hours ahead of their arrival). At that time, the operators can make captains aware of any potential traffic or mechanical problems. During peak traffic times, from 6:00 A.M. to 9:00 A.M. and 3:00 P.M. to 6:00 P.M., this bridge does not normally open.

It should also be noted that a second fixed 22-foot elevated span is available between the 50-foot pass-through and the bascule section. Powerboats on the middle section of Lake Pontchartrain can make use of this passage.

West on Lake Pontchartrain   West of the Lake Pontchartrain Causeway, a broad shelf of shallow water juts out from the southern banks. Stay well away from these shallows.

There are no additional ports of call or anchorage possibilities on the south shore west of the causeway. In fact, those captains cruising west will not find any passages off often choppy Lake Pontchartrain until reaching Pass Manchac, far to the northwest.

Cruisers traveling this long and sometimes arduous route can make use of the charted flashing daybeacons outlining a long pipeline crossing the lake diagonally from the northeast to southwest. Any of these aids can make a good mid-course correction point for navigators journeying to Madisonville or Pass Manchac and Lake Maurepas.

Sailcraft skippers should also take very careful note of the charted 40-foot power line stretching south from Pass Manchac to Pontchartrain's southern shore. A second power line parallels the southern banks for 4.9 nautical miles from the lake's southwestern corner to two charted but unnumbered (privately maintained) flashing daybeacons. Skippers should also note that the southern power line is founded in shoal water for the most part and should be avoided by all vessels.

ICW to the Mississippi River and New Orleans

From Rabbit Island and the Blind Rigolets, the ICW follows an almost arrow-straight track generally west to the turning basin on the New Orleans Industrial Canal. Beginning as a wild, undeveloped stream surrounded by fearless marsh grass and low shores, this canal-like passage becomes ever more commercial as you approach New Orleans. Cruisers who see the city skyline before them and have not taken the time to read an account of what to expect often wonder if they have somehow strayed into a commercial waterway where pleasure craft are not welcome.

From the turning basin on the Inner Harbor Navigation (Industrial) Canal, cruising craft pass south through a tall lock where commercial traffic is again dominant. Often, pleasure-craft skippers feel somewhat akin to a flea on an elephant. Plan for delays when cruising through the lock. Long waits are often necessary in order to accommodate the considerable commercial traffic.

After you leave the lock (hopefully without being squashed), a short passage leads you to the restless Mississippi River. Strong currents here can be a problem for sailcraft and trawlers.

The ICW boasts two alternate routes on the mighty river. Skippers can turn downstream away from New Orleans and follow the so-called Algiers route or, preferably, turn west and parallel New Orleans' French Quarter while making the short hop to the Harvey lock and canal.

Occasionally the Industrial Canal lock and the adjacent St. Claude Avenue Bridge are closed for repairs. In this unlikely instance, mariners traveling west on the ICW must follow one of the several routes by way of Lake Borgne and/or the artificial Mississippi Gulf Outlet waterway south to Breton Sound, thence west into Bayou Baptiste Collette, and finally to the Mississippi River, all described in the next chapter. Cruisers must then retrace their steps north on Old Man River to New Orleans. This passage encompasses a trek of better than 200 nautical miles to actually traverse only a short distance on the ICW. Call the Industrial Canal lock (504-945-2157) well in advance of your arrival and check on current conditions.

It would be really going too far to say that pleasure craft are not welcome on the New Orleans section of the ICW, but it almost goes without saying that commercial vessels of all descriptions dominate the Waterway. Clearly, pleasure boats are in the minority and they certainly do not have priority. Proceed carefully, watch your wake, and give any commercial vessels you meet a very wide berth. As "Note C" on chart 11367 says, "Small craft operators are warned to beware of severe water turbulence caused by large vessels traversing narrow waterways."

The Waterway passage from its intersection with the Rigolets and Rabbit Island (standard mile 34.5) to New Orleans and on to points west is almost completely without anchorages and features only a single marina, which is friendly to cruising craft. One good overnight haven can be found near the eastern genesis of this track.

Frankly, few will count this portion of the Gulf Coast ICW as an attractive cruise. Most captains are glad to get through the Industrial Canal's lock without getting crushed, ogle at the sights of New Orleans' French Quarter from the mighty Mississippi, and then cut west on the Waterway to less developed waters. It cannot be denied, though, that there is a certain fascination to these quickly flowing waters. Seen from the cockpit or flybridge of a cruising craft, the industrial parks and huge commercial wharves are a sight that few will forget. The short Mississippi River section of the ICW, in particular, brings with it sights which most of us will look back on for the rest of our lives. So take your time, be careful, and get ready for some really different cruising.

Rabbit Island Loop (Standard Mile 34) (Various Lats/Lons—see below)

West of flashing daybeacon #26, a deep loop cuts north into the shores of Rabbit Island from the ICW. This stream can be used as a light- to moderate-air anchorage for boats up to 40 feet in length. You can drop the hook near the eastern entrance in some 12 to 15 feet of water near 30 08.928 North/089 38.165 West. The surrounding undeveloped marsh grass shores give only minimal protection. Better sheltered is the patch of charted 16-foot

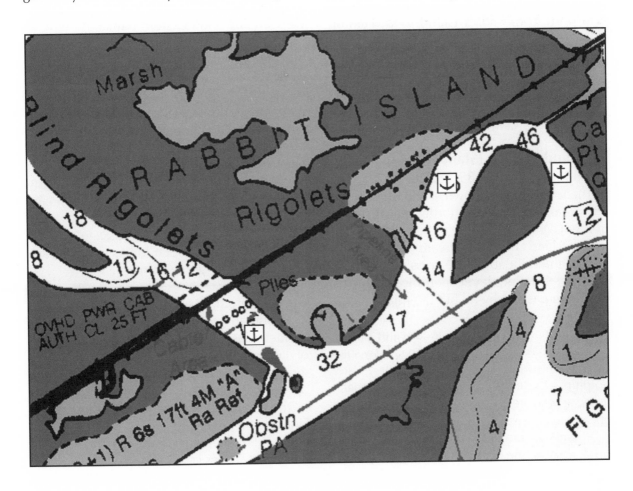

water just up from the loop's westerly mouth, near 30 08.891 North/089 38.451 West. This anchorage fronts high ground to the west and affords fairly good protection when the wind blows from that quarter. Strong easterly breezes would still raise an uncomfortable chop.

The rear of Rabbit Island loop is quite deep, with depths of 35 feet or better. The stream narrows a bit here and this factor, coupled with the deep water, means there is not really enough swinging room for cruising-size vessels.

Visiting navigators should also note that a railroad runs hard by the rearward (northwestern) portion of Rabbit Island loop. Passing trains may disturb you during the night with their whistles and bright lights.

For many years now, a huge, abandoned oil-drilling rig has sat along the eastern shores of the loop near its western entrance. This old derelict gets shabbier every year, but it is easily avoided.

The Blind Rigolets (Standard Mile 33) (30 08.566 North/089 38.962 West)

The wide stream known as the Blind Rigolets breaks off from the northwestern shores of the ICW immediately to the southwest of Rabbit Island Loop. This stream can be identified by the railroad bridge crossing its upper reaches. This low-level span blocks further upstream passage by all but the smallest outboard powercraft.

Additionally, a series of underwater pilings guards the passage southeast of the railway span between the bridge and the charted above-water dolphins. These hazards present a real menace for boats who are not aware of their presence and attempt to cruise as far as the railway bridge.

Vessels as large as 45 feet can drop the hook short of the charted above-water pilings

in about 20 feet of water. Higher ground to the southwest gives some protection when winds are blowing from this direction, but the other surrounding, low-level marsh grass shores render only minimum shelter from other breezes. The anchorage is also open to the wake of vessels passing by on the ICW. Clearly, this is not a heavy weather overnight haven. Captains should choose this spot only after carefully consulting the overnight weather forecast.

Unknown Pass (Standard Mile 29.5)

Unknown Pass intersects both the northwestern and southeastern banks of the ICW just southwest of standard mile 30. Do not attempt to enter either branch of this wayward stream. Depths have shoaled to 4 feet or less.

Alternate Channel (Standard Mile 26.5)

At flashing daybeacon #1, east of Chef Menteur Pass, an alternate man-made loop has been dredged south of the ICW. While this passage is deep and easily run, it is obviously meant for commercial traffic and would not be appropriate as an overnight anchorage. As there is no advantage to this passage over the ICW (in fact, it's a touch longer), most cruisers will want to ignore it entirely.

Chef Menteur Pass (Standard Mile 22.5)

The broad and deep passage known as Chef Menteur Pass crosses the ICW just southwest of flashing daybeacon #4. The southern half of the stream leads to the Gulf and is too wide open for anchorage.

The northern branch of the pass is found a bit farther to the southwest and is a bit more worthwhile. This stream can be identified by the railroad bridge that crosses its southerly reaches. The span

Chef Menteur Railway Bridge

is clearly visible from the Waterway. One possible anchorage and a single rather low-key facility are found on the cut. It is also possible for captains piloting shallow-draft vessels to cruise into the southern reaches of Lake Pontchartrain by making use of this cut.

Chef Menteur runs generally north and northwest to a meeting with Lake Pontchartrain. The stream is unusually deep, with soundings of better than 30 feet being the norm. There are even a few holes with 80 feet of depth. These impressive readings stretch almost from shore to shore.

The intersection between Chef Menteur Pass and Lake Pontchartrain is shoal. While the passage into the great lake is mischarted on 11367 and 11369, careful navigators can

still enter Pontchartrain with 5-foot minimum depths. Be sure to read the navigational detail of the pass presented later in this chapter before making the attempt.

In times past, there was a low-key marina located along Chef Menteur's southwestern banks, southeast of the highway swing bridge, behind historic Fort Macomb. A late check in the fall of 2002 showed this facility to be closed and out of business.

The southern portion of Chef Menteur Pass, north of the ICW, is surrounded by undeveloped marsh on its western banks, while the higher eastern banks are overlooked by a plethora of private residences.

Old Fort Macomb, built in 1828, guards the pass's southwestern banks southeast of the highway swing bridge. The old walls are in poor repair. At some point in the future perhaps the state of Louisiana will restore the fortification and open it to the public. This writer's research has revealed that a shot was never fired in anger from the fort's walls.

As Chef Menteur winds its way to the north and northwest, Bayou Sauvage cuts into the western banks just before the pass's first sharp turn to the east, northwest of the highway swing bridge. This sidewater carries minimum 8-foot depths for the first mile or two of its passage to the west and leads to a whole series of private homes and docks. Boats drawing no more than 5 feet can purchase gasoline at a small facility near the stream's eastern mouth. You might also consider dropping the hook along the mid-width of the bayou. However, this stream does support some local traffic, and swinging room is not sufficient for vessels larger than 32 feet. If you should anchor here, be *sure* to show an anchor light!

This writer specifically no longer recommends the overnight haven that I used to spotlight on the charted, squared-off cove lying along Bayou Sauvage's northern banks, near this stream's easterly mouth. Depths on this errant cove have now shoaled to grounding levels.

North and northeast of the Bayou Sauvage intersection, the eastern banks of Chef Menteur are lined with a rather motley collection of private homes. Undoubtedly this shoreline will undergo extensive renovation and development in the years to come as the New Orleans suburbs continue to grow.

Michoud Canal (Standard Mile 15)

By the time you approach Michoud Canal, cutting into the northern banks, west of flash-

ing daybeacon #2, the ICW is well on its way to becoming a commercial waterway. Michoud Canal is nothing more than a huge, man-made cove surrounded by industrial structures. While it is theoretically possibly for pleasure craft to anchor on the canal's southerly reaches, all cruisers will find this a taxing place to spend an evening. The noise from the surrounding industrial facilities is considerable. Plus, there is always the possibility of having to move aside at some ungodly hour for a commercial tow.

So, we strongly suggest that you look elsewhere to spend the night. If you should choose to ignore this advice, be *sure* to show an anchor light!

Mississippi Gulf Outlet (Standard Mile 14)

One nautical mile west of Michoud Canal, the ICW meets up with the Mississippi River Gulf Outlet. This useful channel will be covered in chapter 8.

Bayou Bienvenue and Gulf Outlet Marina (25 59.460 North/089 56.551 West) (Standard Mile 14)

Just southeast of the Gulf Outlet-ICW intersection, Bayou Bienvenue makes into the former channel's southwesterly banks. This stream is home to Gulf Outlet Marina, the only marina facility offering transient dockage just off the ICW between Bay St. Louis and the Barataria Waterway, well west of New Orleans.

Bayou Bienvenue is entered via a floodgate fronting the Gulf Outlet. Currents can be strong here. Low-powered trawlers should proceed with caution. Depths near the floodgate run around 6 to 7 feet, with 6 to 10 feet of water in the channel.

Local powercraft of considerable size use the

Bayou Bienvenue channel ever day without mishap. However, we have received e-mails from several cruisers over the last two years who have failed to identify the correct track to the marina. We strongly recommend that you call Gulf Outlet Marina at either (504) 277-8229 or (504) 277-9980 and let owner Joe Medina, or a member of his fine staff, direct you through the best possible approach.

Sailcraft skippers take note! Bayou Bienvenue is crossed by a power line with 55 feet of clearance. If your mast is anywhere near or more than this height, avoid these waters entirely.

The friendly folks at Gulf Outlet Marina are glad to accept transients at their fixed wooden piers. Fresh-water hookups and 30-amp power connections are available. The harbor is well sheltered and makes a good foul-weather hidey-hole. Dockside soundings are in the 6- to 14-foot range. Shoreside, showers, a Laundromat, gasoline, and diesel fuel are available, and there is a small variety store beside a popular, local launching ramp. Mechanical repairs can sometimes be arranged. An adjacent Econo-Lodge offers first-class shoreside accommodations. There is an on-site, twenty-four-hour combination café, casino, and lounge, or you can take a taxi into New Orleans to sample its gastronomical delights. Gulf Outlet Marina is actually as close to downtown New Orleans and the French Quarter as the marinas on southern Lake Pontchartrain.

So, there you have it. Gulf Outlet Marina is the only game in town along the ICW route to New Orleans. Just be sure to call for the latest approach information!

Gulf Outlet Marina 504-277-8229 (office) 504-277-9980 (boat launch and dock)

Approach depth—6-10 feet (call marina for best route)
Dockside depth—6-14 feet
Accepts transients—yes
Transient-dockage rate—below average
Fixed wooden piers—yes
Dockside power connections—30-amp
Dockside water connection—yes
Showers—yes
Laundromat—yes
Gasoline—yes
Diesel fuel—yes
Variety store—yes

New Orleans Industrial Canal

By the time cruisers find their way to the charted 34-foot turning basin (Standard Mile 8), the ICW will have completed its transformation to an industrial passage. Everywhere you look, there are huge commercial vessels, barges, and tugs.

From the turning basin, the Industrial Canal and the ICW bend sharply south, pass through several restricted bridges (including one ultra-low-level span), and continue on to the infamous Industrial Canal lock. The northern leg of the Industrial Canal was covered in the preceding section of this chapter.

The northern door of the Industrial Canal lock will be spotted dead ahead after passing under the 40-foot (down) lift bridge. The entrance is surrounded by large groups of pilings known as dolphins. While these tie-offs are designed mostly for commercial vessels, pleasure craft are welcome to tie up as well while waiting for entry into the lock.

Industrial Canal Lock (Standard Mile 6)

To say that the New Orleans Industrial

Quadruple barges and tug on ICW approaching New Orleans turning basin

Canal lock has an infamous reputation with cruising skippers and their crews is to be guilty of gross understatement. Stories of pleasure craft being bumped and jostled by commercial vessels are all too common. In times past, the lockmasters were not always kind to pleasure craft, sometimes leaving them dangling in the strong currents and bumpy conditions by a single

Dry docks on New Orleans turning basin

line. Fortunately, this situation has improved somewhat and cruising captains can breathe a bit easier.

During a recent conversation with one of the Industrial Canal lockmasters in January 2003, this writer learned that, unlike the Algiers and Harvey Canal locks, pleasure craft and commercial vessels are often locked through together here. This practice is in marked contrast to the latter two locks, where, normally, cruising craft and commercial tonnage are locked through in separate cycles.

The Industrial Canal Lock is one of the largest and most potentially confusing locks that you will ever enter. Be sure to read the "Locking Through" account in the following navigational section before getting anywhere near this imposing structure.

Immediately south of the lock, the passage goes under the low-level St. Claude Bridge. This span is synchronized with the lock doors and skippers need not worry with any additional signals.

A quick run down the southernmost section of the Industrial Canal leads cruisers to one of the most famous rivers in all the world. The restless, muddy waters of the Mississippi River wait to greet you.

Florida Avenue Bridge, approaching Industrial Canal Lock

Barge and tug cruising under the St. Claude Bridge into the Industrial Canal Lock

Mississippi River and the ICW

The storied Mississippi River is one of the mightiest streams in the world. Its history is interwoven with the fabric of our nation's past like the red, white, and blue cloth of the American flag. It would take its own mammoth cruising guide to even begin to address its boating possibilities. Our purpose in this chapter will simply be to review the small section of the Mississippi shared by the ICW. We'll take a far more extensive look at the lower reaches of the Mississippi River in chapter 8.

At the Harvey lock (see below), just off the Mississippi River, cruising craft will pass through mile "0" on the Gulf Coast ICW. As you may have noticed, the standard mile markings have been dropping as we have worked our way west on the Waterway. Perversely, the standard mileage begins to increase again as you move westward on the ICW. Obviously some Washington bureaucrat must have thought up this scheme.

As you cruise from the southern mouth of the Industrial Canal into the Mississippi River, it's time to make a basic choice. Two entirely different routes are available to connect with the ICW. You might choose to turn downstream (east-southeast) and follow the current for some 4 nautical miles to the Algiers Alternate Route. This waterway opens into the southern banks of the Mississippi. Mariners must pass through yet another lock and thereafter follow an artificial canal for some 7.6 nautical miles until meeting up with the principal Harvey Canal portion of the ICW.

This passage is sometimes necessitated for sailcraft and single-engine trawlers by the swiftly moving currents on the Mississippi River. If you discover that your power plant cannot make headway against the water flow, it's nice to know that you can at least run with the water east and south to the alternate passage.

Most captains will want to turn west-northwest from the Industrial Canal and head upriver to the Harvey Canal lock. This portion of the Mississippi borders on the French Quarter in downtown New Orleans. Jackson Square, the St. Louis Cathedral, and the many paddle-wheeler excursion boats docked along the shores make for fascinating, unforgettable sights. As mentioned previously, there are, strangely enough, no marina or dockage facilities of any description on either bank of the Mississippi between the Algiers Alternate Route and the Harvey Canal. Maybe someday some enterprising individual or corporation will correct this dearth of facilities.

After a cruise of slightly less than 5 nautical miles, the ICW cuts south on the Harvey Canal. You guessed it. Cruising craft must pass through yet another lock to leave the Mississippi. As already noted above, cruising vessels and commercial craft are usually segregated at this lock.

ICW TO MISSISSIPPI RIVER AND NEW ORLEANS NAVIGATION

The considerable commercial traffic which all but dominates the Gulf Coast ICW between Rabbit Island and New Orleans means that a constant vigil must be kept from the flybridge or cockpit to avoid trouble. Keep alert at all times and give any barges that you meet the widest possible berth. With these simple rules, you should come through the passage with nothing more than a passel of cruising stories to share with your fellow mariners.

Entry from Lake Borgne   From a position abeam of flashing buoy #21 to its northerly side, set course for the mid-width of the passage directly to the west. Along the way you will pass between unlighted can buoy #23 (to its northerly quarter) and unlighted nun buoy #24. Point to pass between flashing daybeacon #26 to its southerly side and flashing daybeacon #25 well to its northerly quarter. Don't approach #25 too closely. It is surrounded by shoal water. In fact, shallows flank the entire southerly side of the entrance into the protected passage of the ICW. Favor the northern side of the entrance for best depths.

These waters *are* plagued with some current, so check your course over the stern, as well as your track ahead, to quickly note any lateral slippage.

Rabbit Island Loop   Rabbit Island Loop can be entered from either its eastern or western mouth. While good depths stretch practically from bank to bank, smart navigators will hold to the mid-width. The rear of the loop is fairly narrow and quite deep. This characteristic will persuade most skippers to drop the hook in the somewhat shallower water near either of the two entrances.

The Blind Rigolets   Enter the Blind Rigolets on the mid-width. Be sure to discontinue your forward progress before reaching the charted line of dolphins. Between these structures and the low-level railway bridge, submerged pilings are waiting to trap luckless mariners. Even small powercraft should not attempt this passage.

On the ICW   It's a straight shot southwest on the ICW for several nautical miles to flashing daybeacon #1. At this point an alternate industrial loop channel swings to the southwest and intersects the southern leg of Chef Menteur Pass. As this sidewater does not lead to any facilities or anchorages, it is best ignored by cruisers.

Chef Menteur Pass   The northern passage on Chef Menteur Pass can be recognized by the swinging railway bridge which is easily spotted from the Waterway. Enter the stream on its broad mid-width.

Soon you will approach the railway span. It has a closed vertical clearance of only 10 feet, but it is usually open unless a train is due.

From the railway, it is a short hop northwest to the highway swing bridge. Just before reaching this structure, old Fort Macomb will be visible on the southwestern banks. As the marina that used to sit behind the old fort is now closed, we suggest that all visiting vessels avoid the obscure channel just southeast of the fort.

The Chef Menteur-Highway 90 swing bridge has a closed vertical clearance of 11 feet, but it does open on demand. Watch for restrictive hours of operation in the future.

Bayou Sauvage cuts west off Chef Menteur just northwest of the highway bridge. Captains can enter this cut on its centerline and possibly drop the hook along the bayou's mid-width. As this passage does support a fair amount of local boat traffic, this is not a particularly good overnight stop. If you should anchor here, be sure to show an anchor light.

Do not attempt to enter or anchor on the waters of the charted square cove to the north. Depths have now risen to grounding levels on this sidewater.

A small marina just to the south of the shallow square cove offers gasoline. Boats drawing more than 4½ feet might find the water a bit thin at this facility.

Visiting cruisers are advised to discontinue their explorations of Bayou Sauvage at least before reaching the charted sharp northerly swing in the stream. Past this point, the stream is uncharted and depths are too unsure for larger pleasure craft.

North of Bayou Sauvage, Chef Menteur Pass cuts sharply east and then begins a slow turn back to the north and northwest on its way to Lake Pontchartrain. As mentioned earlier, it is possible to enter Pontchartrain from Chef Menteur, but the passage is incorrectly shown on chart 11367. The charted deep water northwest of flashing daybeacon #6 shoaled years and years ago. The NOAA charting folks have still not caught on to this fact. Those who stick their bows into these waters (*don't do this!*) will discover soundings of 4 feet or less.

Instead, cut sharply east-northeast just before reaching #6 and pass south-southeast of the daybeacon and between the small is-land to the northwest and the marshy mainland to the southeast. Proceed at idle speed and keep a steady watch on the sounder. This route is not for the faint of heart and should only be attempted by especially adventurous captains.

On the ICW   The ICW continues on its merry, straightforward way west from Chef Menteur Pass to Michoud Canal. The northern banks become diked along this run and commercial plants are sighted for the first time.

Michoud Canal   There are no worries about running aground in deep, artificial Michoud Canal. Depths of better than 25 feet stretch from bank to bank. Remember, though, there is a considerable amount of commercial traffic and shoreside activity on this sidewater. If you do decide to drop the hook here, show an anchor light (several would be preferable) and be prepared to move aside at any hour for commercial traffic. An all-night anchor watch would be a very wise precaution.

Mississippi Gulf Outlet   The artificial canal known as the Mississippi Gulf Outlet will be covered in the next chapter as part of our discussion of how to reach the waters of the lower Mississippi River.

Bayou Bienvenue and the Gulf Outlet Marina   The entrance to Bayou Bienvenue will be spotted on the southwestern shores of the Gulf Outlet some .9 nautical miles from this route's intersection with the ICW.

As noted earlier, this creek is home to Gulf Outlet Marina, the only cruiser-friendly facility on this portion of the Waterway. As the passage to the marina can be confusing for first-timers, we strongly suggest that you call Gulf Outlet Marina at either (504) 277-8229 (office) or (504) 277-9980 (boat launch and dock) for advice on the best route to the marina. These good folks will quickly set you straight on the best deep-water route to their docks.

On the ICW   West of the Gulf Outlet intersection, the Waterway becomes increasingly commercial in nature. West of flashing day-beacon #129, the ICW passes under the fixed, high-rise Interstate Highway 510 Bridge with 138 feet of vertical clearance. If that's not enough, head back out to sea, Captain Ahab. Another 4 nautical miles or so will lead you to the charted turning basin on the Industrial Canal. By the time you reach this point, you may feel as if you have wandered into the land of the giants.

Industrial (Inner Harbor Navigation) Canal
To reach the Mississippi River and continue west on the Gulf Coast ICW, cut south from the turning basin and follow the Industrial Canal to the lock. Proceed at reduced speed and watch your wake. You will soon come upon the low-level Florida Avenue combined highway/railroad bascule bridge. This span does does not open at all between 6:45 A.M. and 8:30 A.M. and from 4:45 P.M. to 6:45 P.M. At all other times it supposedly opens on demand, unless a train is due.

All cruisers should be aware that construction is currently underway on a higher, replacement bridge for the Florida Avenue span. Be on guard against the presence of barges and other construction equipment as you approach and pass through this span. Proceed at idle speed and expect the unexpected!

Next up is the North Claiborne Avenue vertical lift bridge with 40 feet of closed vertical clearance. This span also does not open between 6:45 A.M. and 8:30 A.M. and from 4:45 P.M. to 6:45 P.M. At all other times it supposedly opens on demand, but again, you can expect the operator to be a bit slow on the trigger. When open, this span has a 155-foot clearance from the water line.

Finally, after leaving the lift bridge in your wake, you will spot the dolphins fronting the northern doors of the Industrial Canal lock. Slow to idle speed! *Stay well back* from the lock unless you should be lucky enough to arrive when the doors at your end are open. Either mark time in the water or moor to one of the pilings until you are specifically signaled to enter. Stay clear of any commercial tows waiting to enter. Use the time to put out every fender you have on both sides of your vessel.

You can call the lock on VHF channels 12 and 14 to check on the next scheduled opening. Curiously enough, the usual calling channels, 16 and 13, are not monitored continuously. As you might have guessed, the Industrial Canal lock does not operate during the peak automobile traffic hours between 6:45 A.M. and 8:30 A.M. and from 4:45 P.M. to 6:45 P.M.

When the doors finally open, stay out of the way. On many occasions, a huge flotilla of commercial craft will have to exit the lock before you can even begin to consider entering. The lockmaster may call you on the VHF or (more likely in the case of pleasure boats) use a loudspeaker perched atop the lock gate to guide the various vessels into the lock. Follow the lock attendant's instructions exactly! When you're the smallest craft on the water, it's not the time for wanting to do it your way.

After finding your way to the designated space along the lock wall, hand up fore and aft lines to the lock attendants. This lock does *not* have any movable cleats on the lock walls, so you must depend on these lines to keep you in place.

Occasionally, you will be instructed to raft up against a commercial vessel. Again, your fenders are the only insurance to protect your boat from the often rusty and oily hulls of these ships and barges.

After the lock doors close, be ready for turbulence as water is pumped into or out of the lock. You will be raised or lowered a considerable distance before the process is completed. Conditions are often at their worst when the doors at the opposite end finally open. All crew members should be ready to fend off during the whole locking process. Remember, though, that feet and hands are no match for the bulk of large vessels. Exercise extreme caution to avoid crushed limbs. Better to get a gash on the gelcoat than a trip to the hospital.

When the doors on the opposite end finally do open, wait for instructions before proceeding on your way. Often the lock attendants have to play an intricate jigsaw game to sort out the various ships and tows.

By the time you are instructed to leave, the St. Claude Avenue Bridge should be up. It's now a straight shot down the remainder of the canal to the Mississippi River.

The Mississippi River and the ICW   Pleasure-craft captains and crews traveling on the mighty Mississippi need to be prepared for swiftly moving waters, lots of flotsam and jetsam, plus a raft of commercial traffic. Low-powered boats such as sailcraft and single-engine trawlers must be particularly alert to stay well clear of commercial vessels. With the strong currents, your boat will not always go where it is pointed. Don't become so engrossed in the sights that you end up becoming a New Orleans accident statistic.

During times of maximum current, some low-powered vessels may have to turn east-southeast from the southern mouth of the Industrial Canal Lock canal and reconnect with the ICW on the Algiers Alternate Route. In the absence of these conditions, this writer suggests that you turn west-northwest and follow the river to the Harvey Canal lock.

As you pass through the sharp southerly turn near the charted location of Algiers on the eastern banks, look to the north and northwest, and you will have a good view of the French Quarter and Jackson Square. You may also sight any number of gleaming white paddle-wheeler riverboats, which take tourists on sight-seeing expeditions from New Orleans. Again, give these vessels plenty of room. They have even less maneuverability than you.

A bit farther upriver, you will cross the

route of the Canal Street ferry. If the ferry should be en route across the river, stay clear. Soon you will pass under two high-rise fixed bridges, which have better than 75 feet of vertical clearance.

Finally, you will sight the entrance to the Harvey lock on the southern banks. There are no aids to navigation to mark the lock, so keep up with your progress on chart 11367.

Both this lock and its counterpart on the Algiers Alternate Route are very similar in character to the Industrial Canal structure. The same cautions should be exercised. The routes west from both these locks, as well as the waters of the mighty Mississippi downstream of the Industrial Canal Lock, will be detailed in the next chapter.

CHAPTER 8

South and West from New Orleans

For the first time, in this 2003 edition of *Cruising Guide to the Northern Gulf Coast,* we are going to cover the waters of the lower Mississippi River and a small portion of the ICW as it pushes on to the west. As part of this latter passage, we will also review the alternate Barataria Waterway as it moves south to Grand Isle, Louisiana.

Those cruisers not familiar with Louisiana waters might think this chapter will break down into two neat, logical sections. Sadly, this simplistic view does not take into account the many vagaries of these restless waters. On the one hand, while it is certainly possible to cruise through the New Orleans Industrial Lock and then turn downstream on "Old Man River" and follow the great stream all the way to its multiple mouths, there are four other alternate routes by which captains can cut a huge chunk of distance from this passage. All of these various cruising schemes have their own advantages and disadvantages, but each requires a cruise across a greater or lesser portion of totally open waters. All four passages will be considered comprehensively below.

Similarly, cruisers cutting west from the Mississippi River on the ICW must choose between the two alternate channels mentioned briefly in the last chapter. Within the body of this discussion, we will take an in-depth look at the differing characters of both the Algiers and Harvey Canal ICW routes.

Finally, the Barataria Waterway (not an official part of the Louisiana ICW) must be separately considered as it wends its way south to Grand Isle. Trust me when I tell you that, with very few exceptions, this is *not* the place to go exploring outside the marked channel.

The waters covered in this chapter are *very* different from the other cruising grounds to the east, considered earlier in this volume. Suddenly, cruisers are plunged into a region with only a few marina facilities and a minimum number of anchorages. Conversely, the shorelines become ever wilder and less developed. At times, you may look around and realize that this is what "off the beaten path" cruising is really all about. Of course, if you are one of those skippers who expects to stop every night at a first-rate marina, you might want to keep trucking to the west on the ICW at full speed. Most of the rest of us will count an exploration of the lower Mississippi or the Barataria Waterway as a real gem in the way of cruising experiences. Study the information below, access your needs and preferences, and make your decision accordingly.

Charts 11367—important ICW chart that covers both the Harvey Canal and alternate Algiers Waterway routes—also follows the Waterway to an intersection with both the Mississippi River Gulf Outlet and, much farther to the west, the Barataria Waterway—it even provides detail of the Barataria Waterway's northernmost section

11371—excellent chart for the passages across Lake Borgne to the Mississippi River Gulf Outlet—gives the best details of the wide-open waters of Lake Borgne, even though this same area is covered on several other charts

11364—important chart for two regions—provides coverage of the Mississippi River Gulf

Outlet to the open waters of Chandeleur Sound and details the lower Mississippi River to Venice—a necessity for all navigators plying the waters between New Orleans and Venice

11363—follows the outer and middle sections of the Baptiste Collette Bayou channel from the Mississippi River Gulf Outlet cut

11361—details the Mississippi through its many mouths into the Gulf of Mexico

11365—provides detailed coverage of the Barataria Waterway from Lafitte to Grand Isle—also includes a good account of Barataria Pass

11366—necessary to run the outermost section of Barataria Pass to the Gulf of Mexico

Bridges

Crescent City Connection—Highway 90 Bridge—crosses the Mississippi River between the Industrial Canal Lock and the entrance to the Harvey Canal Lock—fixed—150 feet of vertical clearance

Combination Harvey Canal Railway Bridge and State Road 18 Highway Bridge—crosses the Harvey Canal ICW route immediately south of the Harvey lock—bascule—7 feet—closed vertical clearance—opens on demand unless a train is due

West Bank Expressway Twin Bridges—crosses the Harvey Canal ICW route near Standard Mile 1—fixed—95 feet of vertical clearance

Lapalco Boulevard Bridge—spans the Harvey Canal ICW route near Standard Mile 3—bascule—45 feet closed vertical clearance—does not open at all between the hours of 6:30 A.M. and 8:30 A.M. and from 3:45 P.M. to 5:45 P.M.—at all other times, opens on demand

State Route 407 Bridge—crosses the Algiers Alternate ICW Route near Standard Mile 1—fixed—100 feet of vertical clearance

Mississippi-Pacific Railway Bridge—spans the Algiers Alternate ICW Route near Standard Mile 4—vertical lift bridge—2 feet closed vertical clearance—125 feet open vertical clearance—usually open unless a train is due

Belle Chasse Highway Bridge—spans the Algiers Alternate ICW Route near Standard Mile 4—vertical lift bridge—40 feet closed vertical clearance—100 feet open vertical clearance—does not open at all between the hours of 6:00 A.M. and 8:30 A.M. and from 3:30 P.M. to 5:30 P.M.—at all other times, opens on demand

Crown Point Bridge—crosses the ICW near Standard Mile 12—fixed—73 feet of vertical clearance

Lafitte Bridge—spans the Barataria Waterway about 1 nautical mile south of this channel's intersection with the ICW—bascule—7 feet of closed vertical clearance—opens on demand

Lower Mississippi River

Every American who has taken even the most rudimentary United States history course has heard of the great Mississippi River and how it twists and snakes its way through the story of this great nation. Thus, it is oftentimes true that waterborne visitors look upon a cruise on this mighty river as an almost mystical experience.

This writer cannot really argue with that rose-colored view of this potent stream. Both my first-rate, first mate and I always look forward to an exploratory cruise of the Mississippi. From the cockpit, we have sat entranced as the high-diked shores slip past, while in other spots, mammoth oil refineries tower over the banks. We could not help but feel that we were following in the giant footsteps of those water-borne pioneers who have gone before us. That was, and is, a special experience, indeed!

However, there is another very different and very real aspect of Mississippi River cruising. As you may already know, this river has the largest drainage basin of any stream within the confines of the North American continent. South of St. Louis, Missouri, there are no locks or dams on the Mississippi to impede the swift flow of these sometimes raging waters. It is not by accident that ninety-eight percent of all cruisers who are plying the waters of American's heartland, as part of a Big Loop passage, choose the Ohio River—Tennessee River—Tennessee Tombigbee route to reach the Gulf of Mexico at Mobile, Alabama, rather than run the uncontrolled section of the Mississippi River south of St. Louis.

So, what does this mean to skippers and crew intent on exploring the Mississippi south of New Orleans? Well, it means lots of current and lots of flotsam and jetsam, not to mention a wealth of large, oceangoing freighters, tankers, barges, and tows. This does not exactly make for carefree cruising.

Fortunately, there are alternatives. While some mariners will choose to pass through the Industrial Lock and then cruise downstream to Venice (site of the only pleasure-craft-oriented marinas on the lower Mississippi River), an intriguing body of water known as Baptiste Collette Bayou provides a cut-through into the lower river. There are at least four alternate routes by which one can access Baptiste Collette, but all require a substantial cruise through the open waters of either Breton Sound and/or Lake Borgne. Three of these passages make use of the man-made, Mississippi River Gulf Outlet channel.

Then, of course, the truly adventurous among us might choose to enter by way of the Mississippi River's multiple entrance channels leading from the Gulf of Mexico. There's nothing easy about this route, and we do not particularly recommend it for first-time visitors. Nevertheless, we shall take a quick look at this passage below.

So, there you have it, the lower Mississippi River, with all its glories and warts. There are some incredibly scenic and historic waters for us to consider in these climes, so let's get started!

Approach to Lower Mississippi River via Industrial Canal Lock

We have already verbally traversed the first half of this most-sheltered route to the lower Mississippi River in the last chapter. After cruising through the New Orleans Industrial Canal Lock, all captains need do is simply turn downriver and begin the 82+-nautical-mile sojourn to Venice, site of the only pleasure-craft-oriented marinas on the Mississippi south of New Orleans. From this port of call, it's another 10 nautical miles or so before reaching the northerly genesis of the several river mouths that eventually, and hopefully, lead mariners traversing these complicated waters to the Gulf of Mexico.

With foul weather in the offing, this is probably the passage you should choose, winding and lengthy as it is. It would take some strong winds to raise a really menacing froth on these waters. As we shall learn below, all of the other possible routes require cruisers to venture out into open waters to a greater or lesser degree.

Conversely, this run down the full length of the lower Mississippi River will bring you fully face to face with the strong currents, potentially dangerous underwater debris, and the prolific, commercial river traffic alluded to above. These conditions can be a bit daunting to captains used to the sheltered confines of the Northern Gulf Coast ICW, and all mariners must proceed with their attention fully engaged.

It should also be noted that the lower Mississippi is anything but a straight shot from New Orleans to Venice. The river winds this way and that, at times turning back to the north. Skippers would do well to keep a good DR track of their progress as they wend their vessels hither and yon through the many bends and turns.

Two marinas welcome cruising craft at the small river village of Venice. One of these is a new facility that also features shoreside lodging and on-site dining.

Anchorages are completely nonexistent on the lower Mississippi. Don't even think about dropping the hook along the length of the river in anything but the direst emergency! The frequent commercial traffic could easily run down your vessel in the dark—or even during daylight. Remember, these large vessels have very limited maneuverability.

After passing through the Industrial Canal Lock and turning downstream, passing cruisers will sight a whole range of industrial and commercial facilities associated with New Orleans. Near flashing buoy #R (29 55.539

Chalmette Ferry, Mississippi River

North/089 57.900 West), a huge oil refinery will be spied along the northern banks. A car ferry also crosses the river just west of #R.

A bit farther downstream, the industrial development drops away, and the scenery becomes much more repetitive. Virtually all the riverbanks are diked from New Orleans to Venice, and while these impressive man-made structures are essential to keep the Mississippi from flooding the surrounding lands on a regular basis, they do block your view pretty effectively from a cockpit or even a flybridge.

Perhaps we could sum up our discussion of this approach to the lower Mississippi by saying it's clearly the longest but also the most sheltered approach. Check out our account of the alternatives below, consult the latest NOAA weather forecast, and decide which is right for you and your vessel.

Gulfport to Venice via Baptiste Collette Bayou

Let's now take a look at the other end of the proverbial stick. Are you one of those cruisers who thrives on passages across open waters? Perhaps you pilot a larger sailcraft and yearn to leave the restricted confines of the Waterway. If this description fits, then perhaps you might want to consider the shortest but least sheltered route to Venice.

Fuel-cracking plant, Mississippi River

Did I say "least sheltered"? How about no shelter? Captains who choose this route will first run the incredibly well-marked Gulfport channel seaward, through Ship Island Pass. Then, at flashing buoy #7, just where the Gulfport cut takes a sharp swing to the east, you will depart the marked channel and begin a 36.4-nautical-mile, markerless run through the wide-open waters of the Chandeleur Sound, until finally striking (hopefully—not explicitly) flashing daybeacon #38 (29 34.232 North/089 13.985 West) on the Mississippi River Gulf Outlet channel. It's then a run of another 9.8 nautical miles through the waters of Breton Sound—on the initial but completely unprotected outer portion of the Baptiste Collette Bayou channel—before this cut swings to the south and enters a more sheltered passage. Count all that up, and you'll see it's a lengthy trek of better than 46 nautical miles between the Gulfport channel's #7 and more sheltered waters. If the wind is whistling, this can be a long, dusty crossing. However, on fair days, this could just be the way to go, particularly for sailors.

The good news is that once you are on the interior reaches of Baptiste Collette Bayou, it's a reasonably sheltered run of about 8.9 nautical miles to the waters of the Mississippi River. And, talk about convenient, the two marinas at Venice lie just a hop, skip, and a jump southeast of Baptiste Collette Bayou's entrance into the great river, on the opposite bank.

As if life was not exciting enough on an open-water passage such as this, the waters of Chandeleur Sound have an average depth of 7 to 13 feet. Now, obviously, that's enough for most pleasure craft. However, given the long wind fetch across this broad expanse of water, coupled with these relatively shallow soundings, the stage is set for a short (read that as "close together"), steep wave pattern that, if the fickle wind gets its dander up, can jar the fillings out of your teeth.

It doesn't take a rocket scientist to guess that marina facilities are naught along this route short of Venice, and anchorages are simply not in the offing. As for scenery, how do a lot of waves and whitecaps grab you?

So, now we have seen the antithesis of the first route described above to the lower Mississippi River. This passage is the shortest, but the most open to wind and wave. The three passages described below fall somewhere between the two.

Route to Venice by Way of Lake Borgne and the Mississippi River Gulf Outlet

Now, let's turn our attention to what might be described as the midline set of two passages to Venice and the lower Mississippi River. Both of these routes involve cruising the wide-open waters of Lake Borgne to a greater or lesser degree, but they are still more sheltered than the direct jump from Gulfport. Both passages also ply a goodly portion of the man-made Mississippi River Gulf Outlet channel, met briefly in the last chapter.

Lake Borgne, really more of a sound than a lake, lies south of the ICW's trek between Mississippi Sound and the Rigolets. Two partially man-made passes allow access from the "lake" to the interior reaches of the Mississippi River Gulf Outlet channel. The Gulf Outlet channel leads, in turn, to the wide, thoroughly unprotected waters of Breton Sound. The well-marked, outer portion of the Mississippi River Gulf Outlet channel continues southeast through this sound. A turn to the south at flashing daybeacon #37 (29 34.083 North/089 14.073 West) will point cruisers through the outer, unsheltered 9.8 nautical miles of the Baptiste Collette Bayou approach channel. Finally, at flashing daybeacon #1, mariners will slip into the sheltered interior reaches of this bayou and begin the 8.9-nautical-mile run to the waters of the Mississippi River. And, once again, talk about convenient, the two marinas at Venice lie just a hop, skip, and a jump southeast of Baptiste Collette Bayou's entrance into the great river, along the opposite bank.

The easternmost of the two approaches to the Mississippi River Gulf Outlet channel from Lake Borgne (which we shall hereafter refer to as Lake Borgne Route #1) departs the Waterway at unlighted can buoy #7 (30 09.159 North/089 31.068 West), just southeast of the ICW's intersection with the Pearl River approach channel. It's then a trek of 18.7 nautical miles through the shelterless waters of Lake Borgne to flashing daybeacon #2 (approximately 29 52.307 North/089 40.373 West), the outermost marker of the Bayou Yscloskey cut. This useful channel carries minimum 6-foot depths all the way to the deep waters of the Mississippi River Gulf Outlet passage.

There are a few navigational concerns when cruising the Bayou Yscloskey cut. Please check out our navigational account of these waters in the next section below before attempting first-time entry.

Captains and crew working their way south on the Bayou Yscloskey passage from Lake Borgne have some scenic attractions to enjoy.

Shell Point ruins, Bayou Yscloskey cut-through from Lake Borgne

Along the easterly banks, a whole series of old docks and pilings will be sighted. This venerable woodwork is actually the remnants of the delta community of Shell Beach. When the Mississippi River Gulf Outlet was built, this small town was moved south of the new channel—lock, stock, and barrel. The village now guards the easterly shores of Bayou Yscloskey, south of the Mississippi River Gulf Outlet channel. There is one tiny marina located here, which we will consider briefly below.

But wait, there's more. Look west as you enter the northerly mouth of the Bayou Yscloskey cut, and you will gaze in wonder at an old fort that almost seems to breathe musty old age. This dilapidated structure is Fort Beau-regard, and its location is noted on chart 11364 with the notation "Old Fort Beauregard." Check out our historical account of this fort just below for the whole story.

From the southerly mouth of the Bayou Yscloskey cut, skippers bound for the lower Mississippi should turn east and southeast on the Mississippi River Gulf Outlet for a 29-nautical-mile run to flashing daybeacon #37 in the Breton Sound portion of the Gulf Outlet channel. From this marker, the passage to Venice via Baptiste Collette Bayou is described at the beginning of this subsection.

The good news is that all but the southeasternmost 12.8 nautical miles of the trek down the Mississippi River Gulf Outlet is well sheltered.

Old Fort Beauregard, Bayou Yscloskey cut-through from Lake Borgne

Bayou Yscloskey commercial fishing craft

Southeast of flashing daybeacons #68 and #67 (themselves southeast of charted Lake Athanasio), the Gulf Outlet channel darts out in the wide-open waters of Breton Sound. Things can get a little exciting on this portion of the cut if the wind exceeds fifteen knots.

Skippers opting for the westernmost of the two routes across Lake Borgne (hereafter referred to as Lake Borgne Route #2) should first take a long look at their craft's draft. The initial portion of this route carries a mere 5 feet of water at low tide. For this reason, we strongly suggest that only those piloting vessels that draw 4 feet or (preferably) less opt for this passage.

Those who choose Lake Borgne Route #2 should continue following the Waterway gen-erally west to its intersection with the seaward branch of Chef Menteur Pass. This portion of the ICW was covered in the last chapter. You must then skip south-southeast down Chef Menteur Pass to flashing daybeacon #2 (30 02.215 North/089 45.814 West). From this marker, navigators will set a southwesterly course across Lake Borgne for some 5.8 nautical miles to flashing daybeacon #1 (29 57.256 North/089 49.355 West), the north-easternmost marker on the Martello Castle cut. This latter passage carries minimum 6-foot soundings and provides reliable access to the Mississippi River Gulf Outlet channel from Lake Borgne.

Notice that Lake Borgne Route #2 crosses open water for only 5.8 nautical miles, instead of the 18.7-nautical-mile jaunt required by Lake Borgne Route #1. On the other hand, Lake Borgne Route #1 is considerably shorter overall, as you are cutting a big corner with this approach that must be trekked when following Route #2.

Again, it is a trade-off—more shelter for more distance or vice versa. Access the weather conditions, your vessels cruising characteristics, not to mention your own preferences, and make your decision accordingly.

Old Fort Beauregard History The venerable structure that cruisers see today lining the westerly flank of the Bayou Yscloskey cut-through from Lake Borgne was never actually finished, nor did it ever fire a shot in anger.

Prior to the War Between the States, one spur line of the Mexican Gulf Railway ended at this location, and it was decided that the site would be a good spot for a military fortification. The idea was to not only defend the railroad, but also guard against invasion of New Orleans by this backdoor route.

Money was appropriated by the United States Congress in 1855, and construction began the following year. The interior walls were completed and the ground arches rose to their full height. However, by September 1858, construction had ceased due to lack of funds. The breakout of hostilities at the beginning of the Civil War spelled the end of any further improvements.

During the first few months of this dark struggle, the never-completed fort was used as a watchtower. This practice was soon abandoned, and no military activity took place in and around the fort for the remainder of the

conflict. A fort keeper was stationed here for some years after the war, but in 1916, the structure came under private ownership.

For much of its life, this military structure was actually known as Proctor's Tower. It came to be called Fort Beauregard during the twentieth century, after Maj. P. G. T. Beauregard, the supervising engineer over the forts in this region of Louisiana and a Confederate general.

So, take a good, long look as your cruise past and reflect on all the moneys spent to build this fort that was never completed and never defended anything!

Mississippi River Gulf Outlet to Venice

Those wise cruisers who have been following these confusing discussions of the various routes to Venice and Baptiste Collette Bayou with their charts will have already guessed the track of the final, fourth passage. Quite simply, you may opt to continue cruising generally west on the comfortable confines of the Northern Gulf Coast ICW to its intersection with the Mississippi River Gulf Outlet. Mariners choosing this passage must then cruise the entire 45-nautical-mile length of the Mississippi River Gulf Outlet to flashing daybeacon #37 (29 34.083 North/089 14.073 West). You can then turn to the south and run the Baptiste Collette channel as described above.

The advantages of this fourth route are obvious. There are no open-water runs across either Lake Borgne or the Chandeleur Sound with which to worry. The only unprotected waters here are the 12.8 nautical miles of the outer, Breton Sound portion of the Mississippi River Gulf Outlet channel, and the 12 nautical miles of the Baptiste Collette Bayou's approach channel.

Conversely, this passage is second in distance only to the Industrial Canal Lock route to the lower Mississippi, described earlier. Even so, this is the approach we usually pick with a powercraft. Yes, it's longer, but it's ever sooo nice to simply sneer at the wind blowing over your shoulder, at least until you reach Lake Athanasio. Then, the wind may well have its say anyway.

Under sail, however, we usually pick Lake Borgne Route #1 (the deeper of the two Lake Borgne routes). This approach provides enough open water for a rousing afternoon of running before the wind without requiring the lengthy, outside run needed to traverse the direct route from Gulfport to Baptiste Collette Bayou. That's our opinion, anyway. You are certainly encouraged to reach your own conclusion. In fact, if you have a different on-the-water experience, we would very much like to hear from you. Please e-mail your impressions to opcom@cruisingguide.com.

Mississippi River Gulf Outlet Marinas (Various Lats/Lons—see below)

First of all, it must be said that the pleasure-craft facilities that lie near the Mississippi River Gulf Outlet channel are not what this writer would really call marinas. They are, rather, what most cruising captains would refer to as fish camps. Clearly, their facilities are geared toward the impressive fleet of small, mostly outboard-powered runabouts that ply these waters for the wonderful fishing enjoyed here. There is nothing in the way of real transient dockage at any of these tiny marinas, though gasoline and diesel fuel can sometimes be purchased by cruising craft 40 feet and (preferably) smaller. Larger vessels simply will not find enough space at the various fuel docks to tie up comfortably, even just to take on petroleum distillates.

The four marina/fish camps guard the shores of Bayou Yscloskey. This loop-shaped stream intersects the Mississippi River Gulf Outlet just east of flashing daybeacons #101 and #102 (immediately south of the cut-through to Lake Borgne) and, again, a short hop northwest of flashing daybeacons #93 and #94 (southwest of charted Bayou la Loutre).

The westernmost fish camp, Shell Beach Marina (29 51.250 North/089 40.749 West, 504-252-6891), lies along the easterly shores of Bayou Yscloskey, just south of this stream's northerly cut into Lake Borgne. Shell Beach is the largest of these small marinas. It features gasoline, diesel fuel, and a medium-sized variety/bait-and-tackle store. Approach and dockside depths run 5½ to 7 feet.

Hopedale Marina (29 49.505 North/089 40.021 West, 504-676-1244) is a medium-sized fish camp lying along the northerly shores of Bayou Yscloskey near the charted, unnamed stream that runs south to Lake Ameda. Again, gasoline and diesel fuel can be found here, as well as a small ship's/variety store. Typical approach and dockside soundings run 5 to 6 feet.

Pip's Place (29 48.853 North/089 38.633 West, 504-676-3747) is even smaller, and dockage is extremely limited here. We did spot gasoline and diesel pumps, but cruising-sized craft will find it very difficult, if not impossible, to jockey their way to this petite fuel dock.

Finally, Breton Sound Marina (29 49.093 North/089 36.697 West, 504-676-1252) overlooks the northwesterly shores of Bayou Yscloskey as it loops back to rejoin the

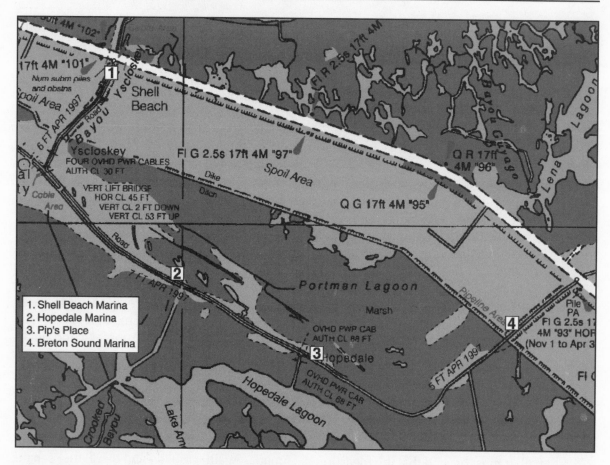

Mississippi River Gulf Outlet near Bayou la Loutre. Depths are more impressive here, in the 10- to 13-foot range (though approach soundings can still run as thin as 5 feet), but only gasoline is available.

By now you have probably gained the correct impression that there is really little of interest to the cruising community to be found among these four Bayou Yscloskey fish camps. Unless you are in dire need of fuel, we suggest you keep on trucking to the facilities at Venice (see below). Of course, there are always those among us who just have to see it all, so for these hardy souls, a quick navigational account of Bayou Yscloskey will be included in the next section of this chapter.

Venice Marinas and Tiger Pass
(Various Lats/Lons—see below)

In a complete about-face, the two marinas at Venice on the lower reaches of the Mississippi River offer good transient dockage, full fueling services, and sheltered harbors. Both of these marinas are to be found on the northernmost reaches of Tiger Pass. This large stream combines with a sister, Grand Pass, and intersects the "Old Man River" just northwest of flashing buoy #10A, at the charted location of Venice.

Well, you may be asking at this point, why is Venice the home of the only two pleasure-craft-oriented marinas on the lower Mississippi River? I was asking myself this same question until my publisher, Dr. Milburn Calhoun, drove me to Venice from his home in English Turn. I quickly learned that Venice is "as far as one can drive an automobile downstream on the Mississippi." Indeed, when we returned later by water, it became instantly obvious that the great river's extensive system

of dikes ends at Venice. Downstream of this point, the Mississippi is no longer bounded by the works of mankind, and it often shifts and changes directions. Indeed, one who studies a general chart of this section of coastline will quickly discern that over the expanse of years, the Mississippi has flowed through many mouths to find the open sea.

The northernmost of the area facilities, Cypress Cove Lodge, occupies the charted harbor cutting into the westerly shores of Tiger Pass, south of the charted "Tower" (near 29 15.010 North/089 21.632 West). Cypress

Venice Marina, Tiger Pass

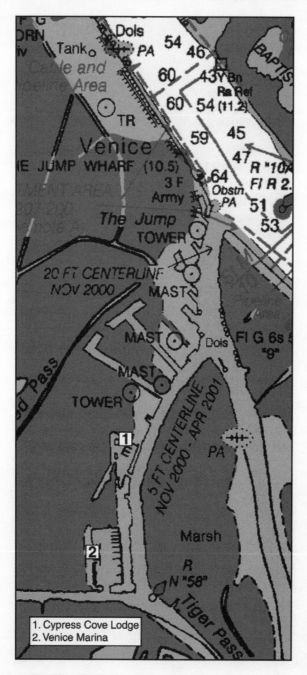

1. Cypress Cove Lodge
2. Venice Marina

Cove is clearly the new, flashy kid on this

block. Everything about this marina speaks of being brand new and fresh. That's probably because this marina only opened a few short years ago, along with an adjacent restaurant and shoreside motel.

Transients and regulars will find well-sheltered dockage at Cypress Cove at (mostly), fixed concrete piers with 50-amp power hookups and fresh-water connections. There are also a few slips with 100-amp electrical service and a few other berths at floating, wooden-decked docks. Minimum approach depths run 7 to 8 feet, with at least 6-foot soundings dockside. Waste pump-out services, gasoline, and diesel fuel are all readily available. While there is a shoreside Laundromat that cruisers may use, strangely enough for a marina of this obvious quality level, there are no showers available to transients. Of course, you could always rent a room at the adjacent motel, but many cruisers will, obviously, wish to remain aboard.

Just behind the dockage basin, an unusually nice ship's and variety store overlooks the piers. Perched atop the store, Cypress Cove Grill offers lunch and the evening meal. We did not have a chance to sample the fare here, but the grill seems very popular with the local crowd, a sure and almost always certain recommendation. No other restaurants or grocery stores are close by.

As mentioned above, Cypress Cove also features an on-site motel. We visited here briefly and found a clean, quiet establishment that is more than adequate, even if a bit run-of-the-mill. If you want to take a break from the live-aboard routine, this motel is obviously superconvenient.

It is obvious that Cypress Cove is a first-class

well-managed facility that visiting cruisers can make use of with confidence. All we have to do is convince the management to install showers, and we'll have it made!

Cypress Cove Lodge (985) 534-7777

Approach depth—7-8 feet
Dockside depth—6 feet
Accepts transients—yes
Transient-dockage rate—below average
Fixed concrete piers—yes (mostly)
Wooden floating docks—yes (a few)
Dockside power connections—50-amp
  (also a few 100-amp connections)
Dockside fresh-water connections—yes

Laundromat—yes
Waste pump-out—yes
Gasoline—yes
Diesel fuel—yes
Mechanical repairs—can call some inde
  pendent technicians
Ship's/variety store—yes
Restaurant—on-site

Next up is Venice Marina (29 14.413 North/089 21.870 West). This ultrafriendly establishment makes its home on the charted, well-sheltered basin just south of Cypress Cove Lodge (also on the western banks of Tiger Pass). New ownership has taken over this facility within the last year, and this bunch

Cypress Cove Marina, Venice

seems intent on offering the best it has to the cruising community. The dockage here is not as new as that found at Cypress Cove, but it is certainly adequate. Transients will find berths at fixed wooden piers with 10- to 12-foot dockside depths. Minimum approach soundings are in the 7- to 8-foot region. Power hookups of the 30- to 50-amp variety are to be found at all slips, as are fresh-water connections. There is an on-site Laundromat, and, while there is no dedicated shower room, the owners can often arrange for transients to use one of the bathrooms contained in several on-site guest cabins. Gasoline and diesel fuel are available as well, and there is a small ship's and variety store perched on the second story

of a small building along the harbor's westerly shoreline. No restaurant or grocery store is within walking distance, so come with a fully supplied galley.

Plans are in the works to add waste pump-out to the offerings at Venice Marina, but a date for the availability of this service could not be definitely determined at the time of this writing! If you are in need of waste pump-out, be sure to call ahead prior to your arrival and ask whether this service is yet up and running.

Of course, if you really want something done at Venice Marina, you'll probably have to speak with Beau. He may answer you with a woof, as Beau is the marina's yellow Labrador retriever. He really makes a splash

Beau the Lab, Venice marina

when jumping off the dock going after a thrown stick or plastic bottle. Just watch out for all the cascading water. This writer did not heed this wise advice and spent the rest of the afternoon with wet socks.

As you may have already gathered, Venice Marina is a warm, friendly place, where visiting cruisers can expect a knowledgeable welcome. Tell Michael we sent you!

Venice Marina (985) 534-9357

Approach depth—7-8 feet
Dockside depth—10-12 feet
Accepts transients—yes
Transient-dockage rate—below average
Fixed wooden piers—yes
Dockside power connections—30- and 50-
  amp
Dockside fresh-water connections—yes
Showers—limited
Laundromat—yes
Gasoline—yes
Diesel fuel—yes
Ship's/variety store—yes%er

Tiger Pass

Study chart 11361 for a few moments and notice that south of the above-described marinas a marked passage continues generally south on Tiger Pass. It would seem that here lies another useful outlet to the briny blue. However, local captains have repeatedly warned this writer of underwater debris and shoaling on the southerly reaches of Tiger Pass. One local skipper informed this writer that he will not even traverse the pass in his outboard-powered fishing craft for fear of bent props. I've always thought it a very good thing to pay attention to local captains. So, with this advice in mind, the remainder of Tiger Pass will not be further detailed in this guide.

Mississippi River to the Gulf of Mexico

South of flashing buoy #1, those few cruisers who choose to continue following the Mississippi River to the Gulf of Mexico will come to the charted "Head of Passes." South of this point, the great river fractures into alternate mouths. This can, to say the very least, be a confusing region that calls for very careful navigation.

In the most general sense, cruisers should know that the Pass A Loutre—Southeast Pass—is shoal and dangerous. South Pass has depths adequate for pleasure craft, but the deep-draft, commercial, river traffic uses Southwest Pass.

Otherwise, we will not pretend to know all the ins, outs, and vagaries of these complicated waters. Good luck if you decide to come this way—you may need it!

LOWER MISSISSIPPI RIVER NAVIGATION

It's a bit difficult to make many general remarks about navigation on the various routes that access the lowest regions of the Mississippi River. Some require a greater or lesser passage across open stretches of water, while others demand knowledge of "river navigation," which is very different from coastal navigation. We will take a look at the differing navigational concerns in the several passages below.

For now, however, this writer would like to pass along an abbreviated version of my good friend and fellow author Fred Myers' river-navigation advice. As many of you know, Fred writes the incomparable *Tennessee River Cruise Guide, Cumberland River Cruise Guide,* and the *Tenn-Tom Nitty Gritty Cruise Guide*. No one knows more about river navigation than Fred! So, Fred tells me that, besides flotsam and jetsam, one of the greatest concerns that one might face while traversing the lower Mississippi River comes when encountering large tows, freighters, and other unwieldy commercial vessels. Tows in particular are a real concern because they may require all, or almost all, of the navigation channel when rounding a bend or making a sharp turn in the river. Again, according to Fred, the only real insurance in these sorts of circumstances is communication. Call every tow you sight on VHF Channel 16 (and then switch to a working channel) as soon as possible, identify your vessel by position, and ask the tow captain on which side you should plan to pass his vessel (or combination of vessels and barges). He or she will reply that you should pass on the "one" or on the "two."

This seemingly enigmatic answer refers to the old rules of the road, which specify that when two vessels are traveling in the opposite direction, and are about to pass each other, "one" whistle directs captains to pass port side to port side, while "two" whistles means that the two meeting vessels should pass starboard side to starboard side. So, if the tow captains tell you to pass him on the "one" keep him to your port side. Conversely, if he says pass him on the "two," keep him to your starboard side. Remember, these directions apply when you are meeting other vessels traveling in the *opposite* direction. Thanks, Fred!

Gulfport to Venice via Baptiste Collette Bayou

There is nothing elegant or complicated about navigating this easternmost route to Baptiste Collette Bayou. On the other hand, let's recall that this passage requires cruisers to take a looonnnng look at some really open water.

Mariners choosing this passage must first traverse 11.2 nautical miles of the Gulfport-Ship Island Pass channel from this cut's intersection with the ICW to flashing buoy #7, southeast of Ship Island Pass. This entire run is wide open, except for a very short stretch where it is fronted by Ship Island to the east.

At #7, the Gulfport channel takes a sharp turn to the east. However, captains bound for Baptiste Collette Bayou and the lower Mississippi should leave the marked passage at this point and strike south-southwest on a careful compass/GPS course for flashing daybeacon #38 on the outer, unprotected portion of the Mississippi River Gulf Outlet channel.

From #7 to #38, cruisers will cross approximately 36.4 nautical miles of the Chandeleur Sound's unprotected waters. Just to add a bit more spice to your passage, depths along this passage can run as thin as 7 feet. While that's plenty of depth for most pleasure craft, the sound's prodigious wind fetch, coupled with these rather meager soundings, can result in short (close together), steep chop, which can—quite literally—rattle your bones.

This would be a marvelous passage on which to try out your new GPS or, better yet, a chart plotter or a GPS interfaced with a laptop computer. If you are short of having these electronic marvels aboard, be sure to keep a good DR track. It's all too easy to wander off from your intended course with such a long run between aids to navigation in the offing.

As your craft begins its approach to flashing daybeacon #38 and the Mississippi River Gulf Outlet channel, some oil- and gas-drilling platforms will be spotted northwest and southeast of your course line. Stay well away from all these structures.

By the way, these commercial platforms are just one reason why you will never catch me undertaking this passage during the nighttime hours or in weather conditions resulting in lowered visibility. We strongly suggest that you adopt a similar approach and confine your exploration of this route to fair-weather, daylight crossings.

Pass #38 to its fairly immediate northwesterly side and then continue cruising across the breadth of the Mississippi Gulf Outlet channel to the marker opposite #38, flashing daybeacon #37.

Just south of #37, the first two markers of the Baptiste Collette Bayou approach channel will be spotted. Cruise between flashing daybeacon #2 and unlighted can buoy #1. Once the gap between these two markers is in your wake, a continuing series of aids to navigation outlines a track running (more or less) to the southwest for some 9.8 nautical miles to flashing buoy #21.

At #21, the channel turns south into a dredged, well-marked cut. South of flashing daybeacon #1, the passage at last begins to come under the lee of low, marshy shores to the east and west. The open-water portion of this route is now behind you.

Eventually, after passing between flashing daybeacons #17 and #18, the markers cease for a bit, but the bayou's passage is pretty obvious at this point. Soon, the stream takes a bend to the south-southwest and hurries on its way to the Mississippi River.

Just short of Baptiste Collette Bayou's intersection with shallow Kimbel Pass, unlighted daybeacon #19 marks the channel's easterly flank. This aid to navigation is a welcome sight after the long markerless run from #17 and #18.

Unlighted daybeacons #22 and #21 mark a southwesterly turn in the track of Baptiste Collette Bayou. Now, it's only a relatively short trek of 1.4 nautical miles to the restless waters of the Mississippi River.

Cruise out into the mid-width of the Old Man River and turn southeast (downstream). Use your binoculars and soon you will spy flashing buoy #10A. Some .25 of a nautical mile before reaching #10A, cut off to the south and point to enter the mid-width of the wide, combined mouths of Tiger Pass and Grand Pass.

Another .7-nautical-mile cruise to the south will bring skippers and crew face to face with a fork in the watery road. Grand Pass continues on to the south, while Tiger

Pass cuts to the south-southwest. All but small, shallow-draft vessels should enter Tiger Pass on its mid-width.

Eventually, the entrance to the Cypress Cove Lodge dockage basin will come abeam to the west, south of the charted "Tower," followed soon thereafter by the harbor serving Venice Marina, also guarding the westerly shoreline.

To access Venice Marina, cut to the west at unlighted nun buoy #58 and cruise along the centerline of the stream that will open out before you. Very soon after leaving this creek's easterly mouth behind, the entrance to the Venice Marina basin will open out to the north.

As mentioned earlier, based on conversations with several local captains, we do not recommend continued exploration of Tiger Pass south of Venice Marina. Those who choose to ignore this advice will proceed at their own peril.

Lake Borgne Route #1 Okay, here we have less open water than what will be encountered on the direct passage from Gulfport to of Baptiste Collette Bayou described just above, but still more than any of the other routes detailed below. Study wind and wave and make your decision accordingly.

To make use of Lake Borgne Route #1, continue cruising generally west on the ICW to unlighted can buoy #7. This aid to navigation lies south and just a bit east of the Waterway's intersection with the marked track to Pearl River. This section of the Gulf Coast ICW was covered in the last chapter.

At #7, set a careful compass/GPS course to the south-southwest, pointing to eventually meet up with flashing daybeacon #2, the northernmost marker on the Bayou Yscloskey cut-through from Lake Borgne. This run treks through better than 18.7 miles of the wide-open reaches of Lake Borgne. You may be tired of me saying it, but, yes, sport fans, this would be yet another good time to try out your GPS, GPS chart plotter, or (best yet) GPS interfaced with a laptop computer.

Study chart 11367 and notice the charted, underwater pipeline that parallels the entire passage from unlighted can buoy #7 to flashing daybeacon #2 to the west and northwest. Don't even think about dropping anchor on this portion of Lake Borgne.

Also, notice the spoil area to the southwest of unlighted can buoy #7. Be sure to stay east and southeast of this hazard on the initial portion of the run from #7 to #2.

Flashing daybeacon #2, along with unlighted daybeacons #3 and #4, outline the Bayou Yscloskey cut-through from Lake Borgne to the Mississippi Gulf Outlet channel. Observe all these markers very carefully. By all accounts, do *not* slip to the west. The waters between the marked track and Fort Beauregard are fowl with both above-water and below-water stumps.

Once south of unlighted daybeacon #4, look west for a good view of Old Fort Beauregard, but don't even think about a closer approach. The stumps mentioned above are waiting to greet your keel and underwater hardware.

Eventually, the passage comes under the

cover of shores to the east and west and narrows. Craft over 45 feet in length may feel a bit cramped on this stream. Soon, the bayou runs through a sharp turn to the east and then quickly cuts back again to its original southerly track. A cruise of another .25 of a nautical mile or so will bring mariners face to face with the wide, deep, well-marked and easily identified Mississippi Gulf Outlet channel.

If you should be making for the tiny fish camps on the interior reaches of Bayou Yscloskey, Shell Beach Marina guards this stream's easterly shores, a short hop south of the outlet. The remainder of the marinas require a far longer trek off the main channel. Be advised that all the interior loop portion of Bayou Yscloskey, south of the Gulf Outlet, is an official no-wake zone. Our conversations with local captains led to the sure and certain conviction that these regulations are enforced.

An alternate entrance to the easterly reaches of Bayou Yscloskey makes into the southwesterly banks of the Gulf Outlet, opposite charted Bayou la Loutre, just northwest of flashing daybeacon #93. Breton Sound Marina lies along the bayou's northwesterly banks a short distance southwest of this intersection.

Cruisers bypassing the tiny facilities on Bayou Yscloskey (and that will be most of us) need only follow the wide, deep reaches of the Mississippi Gulf Outlet as its cuts its way to the east and southeast. Southeast of the gap between flashing daybeacons #67 and #68, the Gulf Outlet channel passes out into the open, unprotected waters of Breton Sound. Cruisers must look forward to a run of some 13 nautical miles through this unsheltered portion of the channel until meeting up with flashing daybeacon #37 (opposite flashing daybeacon #38).

Just south of #37, the first two markers of the Baptiste Collette Bayou approach channel will be spotted. Cruise between flashing daybeacon #2 and unlighted can buoy #1. Once the gap between these two aids to navigation is in your wake, a continuing series of markers leads, more or less, south-southwest for some 9.8 nautical miles to flashing buoy #21.

At #21, the channel turns south into a dredged, well-marked cut. South of flashing daybeacon #1, the passage finally begins to come under the lee of low, marshy shores to the east and west. The open-water portion of this route is behind you.

Eventually, after passing between flashing daybeacons #17 and #18, the markers cease for a bit, but the bayou's passage is pretty obvious at this point. Soon, the stream takes a bend to the south-southwest and hurries on its way to the Mississippi.

Just short of Baptiste Collette Bayou's intersection with shallow Kimbel Pass, unlighted daybeacon #19 marks the channel's easterly flank. This aid to navigation is a welcome sight after the long markerless run from #17 and #18.

Unlighted daybeacons #22 and #21 mark a southwesterly turn in the track of Baptiste Collette Bayou. Now, it's only a relatively short trek of 1.4 nautical miles to the restless waters of the Mississippi River.

Cruise out into the mid-width of the Old

Man River and turn southeast (downstream). Use your binoculars and soon you will spy flashing buoy #10A. Some .25 of a nautical mile before reaching #10A, cut off to the south and point to enter the mid-width of the wide, combined mouth of Tiger Pass and Grand Pass.

Another .7-nautical-mile cruise to the south will bring skippers and crew face to face with a fork in the watery road. Grand Pass continues on to the south, while Tiger Pass cuts to the south-southwest. All but small, shallow-draft vessels should enter Tiger Pass on its mid-width.

Eventually, the entrance to the Cypress Cove Lodge dockage basin will come abeam to the west, south of the charted "Tower," followed soon thereafter by the Venice Marina harbor, also guarding the westerly shoreline.

To access Venice Marina, cut to the west at unlighted nun buoy #58, and cruise along the centerline of the stream that will open out before you. Very soon after leaving this creek's easterly mouth behind, the entrance to the Venice Marina basin will open out to the north.

As mentioned earlier, based on conversations with several local captains, we do not recommend continued exploration of Tiger Pass south of Venice Marina. Those who choose to ignore this advice will proceed at their own peril.

Lake Borgne Route #2 For all of those out there who like to take the middle course, this is probably it—if and only if your boat draws 4 feet or (preferably) less. There's less open water here (though still some), but this route is certainly shorter than its two sisters outlined below. Just please don't forget the wide swath of 5-foot, low-water soundings southwest of Chef Menteur, mentioned earlier!

Cruisers bent on plying our so-called Lake Borgne Route #2 should continue gaily cruising west on the ICW until the seaward branch of Chef Menteur comes abeam to the south, just northeast of flashing daybeacon #5.

Cut to the south-southeast, and run this outer portion of the Chef Menteur channel. Keep to the centerline. Eventually, you should point to come abeam of flashing daybeacon #2, the only aid to navigation on this stretch of Chef Menteur, to its westerly side. Switch to chart 11371 as you approach #2. This cartographical aid will serve you well for the remainder of your passage across Lake Borgne.

Now it's time to cut southwest across 5.8 nautical miles of open Lake Borgne, eventually pointing for flashing daybeacon #1, the northeasternmost marker on the Martello Castle cut-through to the Mississippi Gulf Outlet channel. For the first 1.8 nautical miles of this passage between #2 and #1, your craft will be cruising through waters that carry only 5 feet (perhaps slightly less here and there) at mean low water. ***If tides are running unusually low, select another route to the lower Mississippi River!***

With a bit of luck and good navigation, flashing daybeacon #1 will appear over your bow without misfortune. The remainder of the route to the Gulf Outlet is well marked. Just observe all the various markers carefully, and stick to the mid-width of the last, unmarked stretch, which cuts through to the outlet channel.

Cruise out into the mid-width of the Mississippi Gulf Outlet and turn to the southeast along this channel's wide track. After cruising along for some 7.9 nautical miles, the Bayou Yscloskey cut-through to Lake Borgne, which we have already met in our discussion of Lake Borgne Route #1, will come abeam to the north.

From this point onward, the navigation of Lake Borgne routes #1 and #2 is identical. Please refer to our account of route #1 (above) for full details.

Mississippi River Gulf Outlet to Venice

There's not much navigational detail that need be added to this route. Simply continue following the well-worn track of the Gulf Coast ICW west, past the Michoud Canal and flashing daybeacon #2, to the northwesterly genesis of the Mississippi River Gulf Outlet.

Do not cut the easterly corner at the juncture of the two routes. Take a lazy turn around to the southeast, and pass flashing daybeacon #127 to its northeasterly side.

Southeast of flashing daybeacon #125, Bayou Bienvenue makes into the Gulf Outlet's southwesterly banks. As discussed in the last chapter, the marina that once was located on the upstream section of this creek is now closed, and shoaling is rampant. We strongly suggest that you keep on trucking.

A run of some 5.8 nautical miles down the Mississippi Gulf Outlet will bring passing cruisers abeam of the Martello Castle cut-through to Lake Borgne. Another 10.3 nautical miles will bring up the Bayou Yscloskey passage to Lake Borgne along the northerly banks, while the interior reaches of the bayou lie to the south.

If you should be making for the tiny fish camps on the interior reaches of Bayou Yscloskey, Shell Beach Marina guards this stream's easterly shores, a short hop south of the outlet. The remainder of the marinas requires a far longer trek off the main channel. Be advised that all the interior loop portion of Bayou Yscloskey, south of the Gulf Outlet, is an official no-wake zone. Our conversations with local captains led to the sure and certain conviction that these regulations are enforced.

An alternate entrance to the easterly reaches of Bayou Yscloskey makes into the southwesterly banks of the Gulf Outlet, opposite charted Bayou la Loutre, just northwest of flashing daybeacon #93. Breton Sound Marina lies along the bayou's northwesterly banks a short distance southwest of this intersection.

Cruisers bypassing the tiny facilities on Bayou Yscloskey (and that will be most of us) need only follow the wide, deep reaches of the Mississippi Gulf Outlet as its cuts its way to the east and southeast. Southeast of the gap between flashing daybeacons #67 and #68, the Gulf Outlet channel passes out into the open, unprotected waters of Breton Sound. Cruisers must look forward to a run of some 13 nautical miles through this unsheltered portion of the channel until meeting up with flashing daybeacon #37 (opposite flashing daybeacon #38).

Just south of #37, the first two markers of the Baptiste Collette Bayou approach channel will be spotted. Cruise between flashing daybeacon #2 and unlighted can buoy #1. Once the gap between these two markers is in your wake, a continuing series of markers leads, more or less, south-southwest for some 9.8 nautical miles to flashing buoy #21.

At #21, the channel turns south into a dredged, well-marked cut. South of flashing daybeacon #1, the passage finally begins to come under the lee of low, marshy shores to the east and west. The open-water portion of this route is now behind you.

Eventually, after passing between flashing daybeacons #17 and #18, the markers cease for a bit, but the bayou's passage is pretty obvious at this point. Soon, the stream takes a bend to the south-southwest and hurries on its way to the Mississippi.

Just short of Baptiste Collette Bayou's intersection with shallow Kimbel Pass, unlighted daybeacon #19 marks the channel's easterly flank. This aid to navigation is a welcome sight after the long markerless run from #17 and #18.

Unlighted daybeacons #22 and #21 mark a southwesterly turn in the track of Baptiste Collette Bayou. Now, it's only a relatively short trek of 1.4 nautical miles to the restless waters of the Mississippi River.

Cruise out into the mid-width of the Old Man River and turn southeast (downstream). Use your binoculars, and soon you will spy flashing buoy #10A. Some .25 of a nautical mile before reaching #10A, cut off to the south, and point to enter the mid-width of the wide, combined mouths of Tiger Pass and Grand Pass.

Another .7-nautical-mile cruise to the south will bring skippers and crew face to face with a fork in the watery road. Grand Pass continues on to the south, while Tiger Pass cuts to the south-southwest. All but small, shallow-draft vessels should enter Tiger Pass on its mid-width.

Eventually, the entrance to the Cypress Cove Lodge dockage basin will come abeam to the west, south of the charted "Tower," followed soon thereafter by the Venice Marina harbor, also guarding the westerly shoreline.

To access Venice Marina, cut to the west at unlighted nun buoy #58, and cruise along the centerline of the stream that will open out before you. Very soon after leaving this creek's easterly mouth behind, the entrance to the Venice Marina basin will open out to the north.

As mentioned earlier, based on conversations with several local captains, we do not recommend continued exploration of Tiger Pass south of Venice Marina. Those who choose to ignore this advice will proceed at their own peril.

Approach to Lower Mississippi River via Industrial Canal Lock Please refer to our account in chapter 7 for navigational detail involved with following the Gulf Coast ICW to and through the huge New Orleans Industrial Canal (also known as the Inner Harbor Navigation Canal) Lock. Once through this tall lock, and after passing under the St. Claude Avenue Bridge, the short canal soon meets up with the restless waters of the Mississippi River, south of flashing daybeacons #1 and #2.

Cruisers bound for the lower reaches of this mighty river, whether to run its passes or visit the marinas at Venice, should turn east-southeast (downstream) from the lock canal and begin to make their way along this busy, busy waterway.

South of the charted location of "Chalmette," a car ferry crosses the river on a regular basis. Watch out for it as you cruise along. A huge oil refinery looms over the northern shores at this point as well. It makes for an impressive sight from the water.

Soon, flashing daybeacon #A, lying along the southerly banks, will mark the juncture of the Mississippi and the Algiers Alternate ICW Route. This passage will be covered in the next section of this chapter.

It would serve no purpose for this writer to try and verbally describe the entire route to Baptiste Collette Bayou and Venice via the Mississippi River from the Industrial Canal Lock. On the plus side, the river remains deep almost from diked bank to diked bank. Causes for concern are found by way of the, at times, very heavy, commercial waterborne traffic running along this vital avenue of commerce. Please refer to our suggestions at the beginning of this navigational section for important tips on how to communicate with tows and other commercial vessels you will encounter along the way.

Don't be shocked if your compass seems to be pointing to the northwest during the initial portion of the long, 82+-nautical-mile run from the Industrial Canal Lock to Venice. This stretch of the river twists and turns one way and another. Now you know why one of New Orleans' nicknames is the "Crescent City." That's right, it sits on a portion of the Mississippi River that forms a rough crescent.

We suggest making use of NOAA chart 11364 for the entire passage from the New Orleans lock to Venice. While portions of these waters are covered by other charts as well, we have found the concise cartographical information on 11364 convenient and well detailed. Chart 11361 is good for those brave souls who plan to continue south and run one of the Mississippi's many passes into the Gulf of Mexico.

Finally, 1.9 nautical miles south-southeast of flashing daybeacon #14 (labeled as "Michella" on charts 11364 and 11361), the southwesterly mouth of Baptiste Collette Bayou will be spotted along the northeasterly banks. If you have been reading steadily through this chapter up to this point, you know that this passage figures prominently in all the other routes to the waters of the lower Mississippi River.

Break out the old, reliable binoculars, and use them to help pick up flashing buoy #10A.

This aid to navigation will be found along the river's main track, just a little better than 1 nautical mile south of the Baptiste Collette Bayou intersection. Some .25 of a nautical mile before reaching #10A, cut off to the southeast, and point to enter the mid-width of the wide, combined mouths of Tiger Pass and Grand Pass.

Another .7-nautical-mile cruise to the south will bring skippers and crew face to face with a fork in the watery road. Grand Pass continues on to the south, while Tiger Pass cuts to the south-southwest. All but small, shallow-draft vessels should enter Tiger Pass on its mid-width.

Eventually, the entrance to the Cypress Cove Lodge dockage basin will come abeam to the west, south of the charted "Tower," followed soon thereafter by the Venice Marina harbor, also guarding the westerly shoreline.

To access Venice Marina, cut to the west at unlighted nun buoy #58, and cruise along the centerline of the stream that will open out before you. Very soon after leaving this creek's easterly mouth behind, the entrance to the Venice Marina basin will open out to the north.

As mentioned earlier, based on conversations with several local captains, we do not recommend continued exploration of Tiger Pass south of Venice Marina. Those who choose to ignore this advice will proceed at their own peril.

ICW Routes to the Barataria Waterway

Those of you who were following along in chapter 7 should have noticed that the ICW route west from New Orleans divides once through the Industrial Canal Lock. This is the only instance of such a division in the official Northern Gulf ICW from Carrabelle to New Orleans, though veteran cruisers of the Atlantic ICW may recall the differing Dismal Swamp Canal and North Carolina-Virginia Cut ICW routes from Virginia to North Carolina or the alternate Umbrella Cut route around Georgia's St. Andrews Sound.

Whether you choose the primary Harvey Canal passage or the Algiers Alternate ICW Route, both described in detail below, cruisers plying these waters will have a chance to look at a bit of the waterfront associated with that fascinating, ever-restless city known as New Orleans. Of course, the quick hop upstream on the Mississippi River from the Industrial Canal Lock to the Harvey Canal Lock flows past the primary "Big Easy" waterfront. This is a cruise we always enjoy. The many touring, paddle-wheel riverboats sit gaily amidst the colorful shores. Portions of the French Quarter, Jackson Square, and the St. Louis Cathedral are readily visible from the water.

So, check out our accounts of both routes below, access the river current in regards to your craft's power plant, and make a decision accordingly. Whichever way you go, be ready for an unforgettable passage.

ICW-Harvey Canal Route

Most captains will correctly choose to turn upstream (west) from the southerly exodus of the Industrial Canal Lock and set their course for the northerly entrance of the 415-foot Harvey Canal Lock. This is a run of about 5 nautical miles, as the river twists this way and that. As referenced above, the scenery can be, to say the least, memorable.

Eventually, cruisers will meet up with the northerly entrance of the Harvey Canal Lock near 29 54.717 North/090 05.091 West. Good news here—while commercial traffic is still very much in evidence, pleasure craft and commercial vessels are often locked through in separate operations. That may make for a few delays, but it's ever so nice not to have to worry with being squashed. This practice of separate locking operations is in marked contrast to the mixed lockage in the Industrial Canal. Let's be thankful for small favors at the Harvey lock.

Once the Harvey lock is in your wake, cruisers will enter the narrow, well-sheltered but heavily industrialized Harvey Canal #1. Note that ICW Standard Mileage, which has been counting down all along our verbal sojourn from Carrabelle to New Orleans, begins counting up from Mile 0 at this lock.

No one will ever accurately describe a cruise along the Harvey Canal as an idyllic experience. Both shores are overlooked by a heavy concentration of industrial facilities. Moored barges are everywhere, and at times, it can be a tight squeeze to avoid commercial traffic.

There are *no* marinas or anchorages anywhere along the Harvey Canal Route. Be sure your vessel has sufficient fuel and sufficient time to make its way to the facilities on the Barataria Waterway before committing to this passage.

And, just to add a dash more excitement for those who go cruising on wind-powered vessels, the Lapalco Bridge, near the Harvey Canal's southerly limits, has a closed vertical clearance of 45 feet and sports a restrictive opening schedule during peak automobile traffic hours. Check out our navigational account below for specifics.

Eventually, Harvey Canal #1 cuts to the southwest and enters a section charted as "Hero Cutoff." After skirting a barge-chocked stream making in from the charted "Pumping Station" and rounding a small island, this passage joins up with the Algiers Alternate ICW Route. By the time your vessel reaches the juncture with the Algiers passage, you will have cruised about 5 statute miles from the Harvey lock. Thereafter, the ICW continues on its recombined way to an intersection with the Barataria Waterway near Standard Mile 15.

Before taking a quick look at this connecting link between the intersection of the two differing routes and the Barataria, let's turn our attention to the Algiers Alternate ICW Route.

Algiers Alternate ICW Route

Note that in our otherwise rosy description of the initial run of the Harvey Canal Route, by way of the New Orleans waterfront, that the word "upstream" made a prominent appearance. Let us recall that there are no locks or dams on the mighty Mississippi River south of St. Louis to impede the river's sometimes-monumental current. So, if the river happens to be moving swiftly, and/or your craft is a low-powered vessel, it might come to pass that it would be very difficult to make progress "upstream" from the Industrial Canal Lock to the Harvey lock.

Fortunately, this is a situation that the powers that be at the Army Corps of Engineers planned for in the 1930s, when this portion of the ICW was constructed. Consequently, a plan was adopted to also dredge a downstream passage, which came to be known as the Algiers Alternate ICW Route.

Now, while the Algiers route is a real boon to low-powered craft, we think it should only be chosen if you cannot make ready progress upstream to the Harvey lock. There are two principal reasons for this stricture. First and foremost, those who choose this track will miss the many and colorful sights along the principal New Orleans waterfront. Secondly, the Algiers passage is about 2.5 statute miles longer than its Harvey Canal counterpart.

Like the Harvey Canal passage, the Algiers Alternate ICW Route consists of one lock fronting the Mississippi River followed by a man-made canal that eventually intersects its sister track some 8.5 statute miles to the (generally) southwest. There is less heavy industrial development along the Algiers track, but it is still not what we would refer to as an attractive section of the Waterway.

Again, there are absolutely no marinas, anchorages, or even any place to stop along the Algiers Alternate ICW Route. Be sure you and your vessel are ready for this passage, and leave plenty of time to make your intended overnight stop farther to the west before nightfall. I don't even want to contemplate an enforced overnight stop along either the Harvey Canal or Algiers routes.

And, yes (sigghhh), there is also a restrictive bridge along the way for sailors to worry with. Both the Mississippi-Pacific Railway Bridge and the Belle Chase Highway Bridge cross the Algiers route near Standard Mile 4. While the railway span is usually open, the highway bridge is restricted during peak automobile traffic periods.

Eventually, the Algiers Alternate ICW Route skirts southeast of the same small island we met at the end of our discussion of the Harvey Canal and rejoins its sister shortly thereafter.

ICW to Barataria Waterway

The once-again-whole ICW cuts south-southwest and eventually west for some 9 statute miles from the intersection of the two competing routes, skirts past the small community of Crown Point, and finally intersects the Barataria Waterway near Standard Mile 15. Surprisingly, again, there are no marinas or prospective anchorages short of the intersection with the Barataria. The shoreline along this stretch is far more attractive here than on the alternate routes to the east, but the best is yet to come!

ICW ROUTES TO THE BARATARIA WATERWAY NAVIGATION

There are really only two navigational challenges to running either the Harvey Canal or Algiers Alternate ICW Route to their eventual intersection with each other. First, captains must traverse a portion of the busy, current-strewn Mississippi River, and then they must pass through a lock, which can often make for some on-the-water excitement. Neither of these obstacles is extreme by any measure, and most mariners will come through with nothing but good memories of the colorful sights along the New Orleans waterfront.

Harvey Canal Route Those choosing this most popular leg of the ICW will turn to the west-northwest once the waters of the Industrial Canal Lock are in their wake and their craft passes out into the wide waters of the Mississippi River. Immediately, it's time to be on guard against the passage of large commercial tows, freighters, and other vessels.

Stay well clear of any commercial traffic, and remember our hints about communicating with these vessels, presented earlier in this chapter (as part of the "Lower Mississippi River Navigation" section).

After cruising upstream for some 1.4 nautical miles, the Mississippi runs through a sharp bend to the south. The Canal Street-Algiers car ferry crosses the river on a southwest-to-northeast axis just south of this bend. Its location is noted on chart 11367. Be sure to keep well clear of this ferry.

A bit farther to the south, the combined ICW-upriver Mississippi trek crosses under the twin Highway 90-Crescent City Connection bridges. Both spans tower 150 feet over the water. Anyone got a mast that tall?

Eventually the Mississippi slowly bends to the southwest. Begin watching the southerly banks for the entrance to the Harvey Canal Lock. An aid to navigation to mark this important intersection would be ever soooo nice. Are you listening Army Corps of Engineers?

As mentioned earlier in this chapter, pleasure craft and commercial traffic are often locked through separately here and in the Algiers Alternate ICW Route Lock that we will review below. Of course, this is not always the case, and it's entirely up to the lockmaster's discretion as to whether pleasure craft are mixed with commercial vessels or not. However, clearly, things are not as hectic here as is the situation sometimes encountered in the Industrial Canal Lock.

During a recent conversation with the Harvey Canal lockmaster, we were informed that the lock doors fronting the Mississippi (the northern doors) will not be opened if a large ship is due to pass on the river. This stricture has been put in place to prevent large bow waves created by passing ships from actually entering the lock. Well, gee, that sounds OK, but what are we peon pleasure-craft skippers supposed to do while awaiting a lock opening on the Mississippi side and watching large freighter traveling near a bit faster than it should be? The final answer to that question is that we must do the best we can by turning into the wave and riding over it. While we have not yet had this interesting experience, other cruisers we have spoken with have, and it was apparently not any fun.

Once the Harvey Canal Lock is in your wake, you will be cruising through (guess what?) the Harvey Canal #1. Be ready for some serious industrial development along both shores. You will also find large portions of the banks lined by moored barges, sometimes rafted up several deep. Be advised that many of these on-the-water hulks are *not* lighted at night. This could make for some calamitous nighttime collisions. For this reason, more than any other, we strongly suggest that pleasure craft confine their traversal of this canal to the daylight hours only!

Larger powercraft skippers should take a word to the wise and proceed at minimal-wake speed through much of the Harvey Canal. While your wake may not bother the many barges moored here, the same may not always be said of smaller tugboats and working barges. Remember, you are legally responsible for any damage caused by your vessel's wake.

Two bascule bridges cross the Harvey Canal just south of the lock. These spans, thankfully, open on demand.

Some .6 of a nautical mile past the locks, the Harvey Canal passes under the West Bank Expressway Twin Bridges and over the West Bank Expressway tunnel. This interesting complex of structures allows automobile traffic to choose whether to drive under or over the canal. Vertical clearance on the bridges is set at 95 feet.

After another 1.7 nautical miles of the Harvey Canal are behind your stern, cruisers will encounter the Lapalco Boulevard bascule bridge. This span does not open from 6:30 A.M. to 8:30 A.M. and between the hours of 3:45 P.M. to 5:45 P.M. Closed vertical clearance is set at 45 feet, so most powercraft will not have to worry with this restrictive schedule, but on the other hand, sailcraft skippers should be sure to take these hours of nonoperation into account.

Eventually the Harvey Canal Route swings to the southwest and enters the so-called Hero Cutoff. Watch for the charted, sunken barge near Standard Mile 5. This derelict is marked by flashing daybeacon #A. Obviously, it would behoove all mariners to stay well clear of this underwater hazard.

Finally, the route skirts west of the charted, triangular-shaped island and rejoins the Algiers Alternate ICW Route shortly thereafter. Don't even think about trying to drop the hook on the charted stream north of the small island. We found these waters choked with old barges.

Algiers Alternate ICW Route Those mariners choosing the less-visually-appealing but less-current-plagued Algiers Alternate ICW Route should swing downriver (east-southeast) after exiting the Industrial Canal Lock. It's a run of some 3.9 nautical miles to the northeasterly mouth of the canal leading to the Algiers Lock. This intersection is marked by the charted 30-foot light (designated as #A), which actually sits on the shoreline.

Before reaching #A, passing cruisers should watch out for the charted Chalmette car ferry, which crosses the river just west of the Algiers Lock approach canal. Need I say it? Stay well away from this cumbersome craft.

Like its Harvey Canal counterpart, pleasure craft and commercial vessels are often locked through in separate cycles in the Algiers Lock. This is not always the case, however. The lockmaster will direct your vessel according to his wishes.

After locking through, mariners will soon pass under the fixed, 100-foot State Route 407 Bridge. This writer has driven across this span many times traveling to and from his publisher's magnificent homeplace at English Turn.

Another 2.4 nautical miles or so will bring captain and crew face to face with the Mississippi-Pacific Railway Bridge and the Belle Chasse Highway Bridge. The former span has a closed vertical clearance of 2 feet, while the highway bridge sits 40 feet off the water when closed. The railway bridge is usually open unless a train is due, but the Belle Chasse span features a restrictive opening schedule.

This bridge does not open from 6:00 A.M. to 8:30 A.M. and between the hours of 3:30 P.M. to 5:30 P.M.

Continue holding to the centerline, avoiding all the derelicts along the way, some of which are charted and some of which are not. Finally, the route swings southeast of the charted island and intersects the Harvey Canal passage soon thereafter. Don't even think about trying to drop the hook on the charted stream north of the small island. We found these waters choked with old barges.

ICW to Barataria Waterway After rejoining, the ICW works its way down Bayou Barataria (not to be confused with the Barataria Waterway). The first several miles of this run are markerless (simply hold to the mid-width), but finally, unlighted day-beacon #1 marks a southwesterly turn in the channel.

The small community of Crown Point lines the Waterway from Standard Mile 10.5 to Standard Mile 11. This settlement makes for interesting viewing from the water, but no services or dockage is available for pleasure craft.

Soon the ICW exchanges greetings with the Crown Point fixed bridge. This fortunate span has a healthy vertical clearance of 73 feet.

After flowing through a slow but definite bend to the south, the ICW skirts northwest of a charted marsh island and intersects the main entrance of the Barataria Waterway.

Barataria Waterway to Grand Isle

If you have ever treasured the notion of exploring the Louisiana backwaters without having to stick your keel into the all-too-prevalent shallow soundings so typical of this region, boy, have we got good news for you. The Barataria Waterway allows visiting cruisers to experience a little bit of everything there is to see in this unique country of wide lands, marshes, and waters.

The Barataria was constructed by the Army Corps of Engineers during World War II to facilitate the easy delivery of the region's rich petroleum and natural-gas products. Today, cruisers will discover a waterway covering some 40 nautical miles from Lafitte to Grand Isle. The first 30 nautical miles are well sheltered, while the last stretch of slightly better than 10 nautical miles skips between marsh islands on the edge of huge Barataria Bay.

Moving south from the ICW-Barataria Waterway intersection, cruising craft will wend their way by shores that are part of the old river village of Lafitte. Here, palatial homes rub shoulders with rough and ready fish camps. These contrasting styles are like nothing else we have met anywhere along our lengthy trek from Carrabelle to New Orleans. A slow cruise along this northwesternmost section of the Barataria Waterway is sure to produce visual memories that can be savored for years and years to come.

And, Lafitte has something else to boast of, namely, a goodly selection of pleasure-craft-oriented marinas. While some of these establishments are little more than fuel stops, at

Commercial fishing vessel, Barataria Waterway

least two marinas offer secure overnight dockage. One of these firms even has full repair capabilities.

There is also one anchorage available in this region. Check out our account of Bayou Rigolettes below.

South of flashing daybeacon #10, the Barataria leaves most of the development behind. Now, the grass savannahs seem to stretch on almost to the horizon. Here and there, oil- and gas-drilling platforms and equipment are spied to either side of the channel. These structures serve to remind visitors just what an integral part the oil and gas industry plays in the economy of Louisiana.

West of unlighted nun buoy #48, the waters of Bayou St. Dennis play host to the only viable anchorage on the Barataria Waterway south of Lafitte. This is a fair-weather-only haven, and you will never catch this writer trying to ride out foul conditions on these waters.

Finally, after running across a portion of wide Barataria Bay, the waterway comes to an end at flashing daybeacons #1 and #2. These markers denote an intersection with a channel running behind Grand Isle and the Barataria Pass. This latter cut provides reliable access to the Gulf of Mexico and a chance to engage in some historical gazing.

Grand Isle features two marinas of its own, both of which feature some transient dockage. This island is the center of the Louisiana offshore sportfishing industry, and it is, as this writer's publisher put it so succinctly, "the

New Orleans working man's weekend playground." We found Grand Isle to indeed be a grand place, even if a bit on the seasonal side.

So, let's push on to verbally explore this small slice of backwater Louisiana—some might say a "small slice of heaven." There's much to see and do. So let's get started!

Lafitte Marinas and Restaurants (Various Lats/Lons—see below)

The old river community of Lafitte straddles the northerly section of the Barataria Waterway and stretches for many miles to the south. Amidst this often-tasteful development, passing cruisers will find a goodly selection of marinas. Some are obviously ready to serve the needs of overnight visitors, while others offer far less in the way of cruising-craft services.

Moving north to south, the first of these facilities, Cochiara Shipyard and Marina (29 41.510 North/090 05.847 West), will come up along the waterway's easterly banks, just north of the charted cut-through to the "Pen." This latter body of water is huge but quite shallow. Chart 11367 notes the location of Cochiara's by way of facility designation #44.

The marina's fuel dock fronts directly onto the easterly banks of the Barataria Waterway. A very few, smaller craft might be able to tie up here, but we doubt whether any cruising-sized craft have done this anytime lately. Depths run as thin as 4½ feet, and the slips and fuel dock are not in the best of condition. We did not see hide nor hair of any dockside power or water connections.

Small craft that can clear a 10-foot bridge will find some additional slips fronting onto the adjacent motel. These docks we also found to be in very poor shape, and the shoreside

hostelry can only be described as "scuzzy." Depths alongside at these berths are a very thin 2½ feet.

Gasoline can be purchased, but the diesel pump was broken during our last visit. Some very low-key mechanical repairs are reportedly available for outboards. Shoreside, a large ship's, variety, and tackle store overlooks

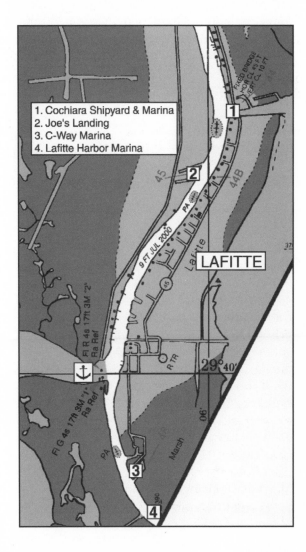

1. Cochiara Shipyard & Marina
2. Joe's Landing
3. C-Way Marina
4. Lafitte Harbor Marina

LAFITTE

the fuel dock on the opposite side of the road. No showers or Laundromat are to be found here. There is a good restaurant located just across the bridge, but many cruisers will probably have trouble finding a place to leave their craft long enough to check out the bill of fare.

Are you beginning to get the idea? Sad to say, but Cochiara's is clearly a facility that's rather down on its luck. Until significant improvements are made here, we suggest that you keep trucking down the Barataria to some of the better-equipped marinas detailed below.

Cochiara Shipyard and Marina
  (504) 689-3701

Approach depth—8+ feet
Dockside depth—4½ feet (outer slips and fuel pier)
  2½ feet (inner berths adjacent to motel)
Accepts transients—extremely limited
Gasoline—yes
Ship's and variety store—yes
Restaurant—close by

Next up is Joe's Landing (504-689-4304, 29 41.113 North/090 06.078 West). This small but friendly facility gazes out from the westerly banks of the Barataria Waterway, just south of Cochiara's, where chart 11367 notes facility designation #45. Joe's is composed of a fixed, wooden fuel pier, backed by a two-story building, the first floor of which houses a variety and tackle store. Gasoline and diesel fuel are available here, though dockside soundings of as little as 3½ to 4 feet will limit this facility's usefulness to cruising craft. The various slips along the fuel dock also looked a bit too small to accommodate vessels over 36 feet. Nevertheless, visiting cruisers can expect a warm welcome

at Joe's, and we are told that their fuel prices are some of the lowest in the region.

Just across from Joe's Landing, passing cruisers will sight a few small piers associated with the legendary Boutte's Restaurant (504-689-3889). This dining spot is spoken of with something akin to awe, even by the locals. Is there any better recommendation? Unfortunately, the docks did not appear to be appropriate for cruising-sized craft. Happily, we can report that complimentary transportation is sometimes available to and from the local marinas. Give Boutte's a call and check to see if a ride is available on the evening of your arrival. There is an almost universal opinion that this effort well be more than worthwhile.

C-Way Marina (29 39.432 North/090 06.507 West) is another of the friendly Lafitte marinas, but this one has a legitimate claim to overnight transient dockage. C-Way occupies the charted, well-sheltered harbor making into the Barataria Waterway's easterly banks, south of the cut-through to Bayou Rigolettes (see below). This position can also be identified by facility designation #48 on chart 11367.

We received a very warm welcome during our last visit to C-Way. To be succinct, these are good people, and they seemed ready to do all in their power to help us along the way. Visiting cruisers can make use of this facility with confidence, always supposing you find one of the 3 slips usually kept open for transients to be available. Call ahead of time to check on availability.

After traversing a short entrance canal, C-Way's dockage basin will open out to port. Berths consist of fixed, wooden piers, some of which are covered, but others are not. Cruising craft 42 feet and smaller will probably be most comfortable amidst these piers. Depths at most berths run from 6 to 10 feet, but a few slips have soundings of a mere 3 feet. Deep-draft vessels should be sure to ask for a deeper water slip. Fresh-water connections and 20-amp power hookups are available, as is gasoline, diesel fuel, and a combination ship's and variety store. No shoreside showers or Laundromat are in the offing, however. Some mechanical repairs for both diesel- and gasoline-powered plants can be arranged through local, independent technicians.

When it comes time for the evening meal, if you are up for a 1½-mile walk, then by all means check out Voleos Restaurant (504-689-2482). We have not yet had the good fortune to dine here, but the C-Way Marina personnel swear

by the food, a sure sign of good things!

Of course, as noted above, you might (and probably should) call Boutte's Restaurant (504-689-3889) and see if transportation can be arranged. Don't overlook this yummy possibility!

All in all, while it would take the rosiest colored glasses to look upon C-Way as a full-service facility, the friendly attitude and well-sheltered dockage will be enough to lure many cruisers off the Barataria.

C-Way Marina (504) 689-3148
   http://www.c-waymarna.com

Approach depth—8+ feet
Dockside depth—3-10 feet (most slips 6-10 feet)
Accepts transients—3 slips set aside for visitors

C-Way Marina, Barataria Waterway

Transient-dockage rate—below average
Fixed wooden piers—yes
Dockside power connections—20-amp
Dockside water connections—yes
Gasoline—yes
Diesel fuel—yes
Mechanical repairs—independent contractors
Ship's/variety store—yes
Restaurant—very long walk

Lafitte Harbor Marina (also known as C&M Bayou Fuel, 29 39.220 North/090 06.388 West) is the village's largest pleasure-craft facility and offers more services than any other marina in the region. The fuel dock and one long, fixed wooden face dock front onto the northeasterly shores of the Barataria Waterway, a short hop southeast of C-Way Marina. There is also a well-sheltered but uncharted dockage basin behind the tongue of land occupied by the marina's extensive ship's store and adjacent motel. Dockage here is of the fixed wooden variety. Depths on the outer piers, directly on the waterway, run at least 6 feet, while some 4 to 4½ feet of water can be expected in the protected basin at low tide.

Transients are readily accepted at Lafitte Harbor Marina. If your vessel draws less than 4 feet, we would suggest requesting a berth in the interior basin. Otherwise, a space along the outer dock is fine, though obviously not as well sheltered. Most everyone seems to have gotten the word, however, and wake from passing vessels does not seem to be a real problem at the outer berths.

Dockside, visiting cruisers will find fresh-water connections and 30- to 50-amp power hookups. Gasoline and diesel fuel are ready for pumping, but at this time, no waste pump-out

is available. Lafitte Harbor hopes to add this service in the future.

Shoreside, as mentioned above, cruisers will discover an unusually well-stocked ship's store with just about everything nautical that might ever be needed. The marina showers and Laundromat are located in a building at the southeasterly end of the motel, overlooking the entrance to the inner dockage basin. It can be a bit of a trek from the outer berths to reach this facility. We found the showers to be in fair to good condition, with some minimal climate control. The same can be said for the Laundromat.

Mechanical repairs are available through local, independent contractors for both gasoline and diesel engines. Boats up to 7½ tons can be hauled with an electric winch, while craft up to 15 tons (and up to 43 feet in length) can be removed from the water by way of a crane. These are the *best* repair capabilities for pleasure craft to be found anywhere in Lafitte.

Once again, let's note that famished cruisers can call Boutte's Restaurant (504-689-3889) and request complimentary transportation. If this service is not available, then be advised that the long walk to Voleos Restaurant (504-689-2482), met in our discussion of C-Way Marina, is a bit longer from Lafitte Harbor. Ask the friendly marina staff if they could help with landside transportation. Failing this, the walk is certainly justified in fair weather, and it will allow visitors to get an up close and personal view of the Lafitte community shore.

Lafitte Harbor Marina (504) 689-2013
http://www.bayoufuel.com/lafitteharbor/

Approach depth—8+ feet

Dockside depth—6 feet (outer piers and
   fuel dock)
   4-4½ feet (inner harbor)
Accepts transients—yes
Transient-dockage rate—below average
Fixed wooden piers—yes
Dockside power connections—30- to 50-
   amp
Dockside water connections—yes
Showers—yes
Laundromat—yes
Gasoline—yes
Diesel fuel—yes

Mechanical repairs—gasoline and diesel
   engines (independent contractors)
Crane haul-out capacity—up to 15 tons
   and 43 feet in length
Ship's store—extensive
Restaurant—very long walk%er

Lafitte Anchorage
(29 39.994 North/090 06.875 West)

There is one fair, overnight anchorage possibility along the Lafitte portion of the
Barataria Waterway. Study chart 11367 for a

Lafitte Harbor Marina fuel dock, Barataria Waterway

moment, and notice that the wide mouth of huge Bayou Rigolettes cuts the western banks north of C-Way Marina. This entrance is outlined by flashing daybeacons #1 and #2.

Skippers piloting cruising craft that draw 4½ feet or (preferably) less can cut between #1 and #2 and drop anchor some .14 nautical miles to the west, amidst 5-foot depths. Care must be taken to avoid encroaching on the surrounding shorelines. Shoal water stretches out for a considerable distance from both the northern and southern banks.

Another concern in regards to anchoring on these waters comes in the form of nighttime commercial fishing traffic. We have been told by local captains that the passage of such vessels is not an infrequent occurrence during the night. For this reason, we strongly suggest that mariners drop the hook just a bit south of the centerline, being sure to set the hook so as not to swing too close to the southern shoals and banks. This can be a tricky procedure for vessels larger than 36 feet. If your craft is larger than this, you might want to look for an overnight stop elsewhere. By all accounts, be *sure* to show a bright anchor light!

Shelter is good from northern, southern, southwestern, and, to a lesser extent, eastern winds. This is not the place to be caught with strong breezes blowing from the west.

To summarize, this is a fair anchorage for shallower-draft cruising craft, with fair weather and gentle breezes in the offing. If your vessel cannot meet these requirements, we suggest one of the Lafitte marinas as a lying-over spot for the night.

Lafitte Cemeteries and Pirogues

The old river village of Lafitte is, to say the very least, a colorful place, and it has a very colorful past as well. Take for example, its cemeteries and burial practices. The community's first cemetery is said to have been founded by sometimes-pirate Jean Lafitte, for whom the town is named. The site was none other than a "shell mound" where the buccaneer was supposed to have hidden much of his ill-gotten booty. Boy, talk about good cover for a hiding spot!

Until very recent times, many funerals in Lafitte were a waterborne event. The funeral procession advanced down Bayou Barataria in a solemn line of local boats. The casket was placed on the first boat in the procession, along with the pallbearers, family, and a local priest. Other craft, peopled by friends and relatives, followed after.

To this day, the residents of Lafitte maintain a unique custom of honoring their dead on Halloween (also known as "All Saints' Day Eve"). Relatives place lighted candles on the graves of their departed family members and ancestors. A local priest blesses the graves, and prayers are offered by the entire party. We have been told that the many, many candles burning during a Halloween evening could make one think a forest fire was in the offing.

A *pirogue* is a traditional Louisiana craft if ever there was one. You can think of a pirogue as a blunt-ended punt. While this design did not originate in Lafitte, one could argue that it certainly achieved fame in this community.

During the early 1900s, perhaps the most prominent citizen of Lafitte was one, Etienne Billiot. He was a giant of a man, weighing in at 248 pounds of solid muscle. It's said that he often wrestled alligators and was quite a fisherman and huntsman, to boot.

Etienne, as he was universally known in Lafitte, was also famous for his fine pirogues. He would build them from hand-hewn cypress logs. The finished craft was usually some 13 feet in length, with a beam of 20 to 22 inches. How's that for a narrow, sleek vessel?

It is said that Etienne would sometimes dive into the murky waters of Bayou Barataria to retrieve sunken cypress logs, from which he would later build his sturdy boats. Today, most pirogues are constructed from plywood. This writer deeply suspects that the modern versions of these craft will not last nearly as long as Etienne's finely wrought products.

In 1934, Etienne and several other local residents organized the first pirogue race. There were only four contestants, and the race was won by, who else, Etienne Billiot. He was awarded $18 and a silver trophy.

Today, these races continue on the waters of the Barataria from time to time. Ask at any of the local marinas to find out if a race happens to be in the offing during your visit.

Etienne continued his boat-building efforts until just a few years prior to his death in 1971 at the age of 94. It is said that every citizen of Lafitte attended his funeral. Truly, he was a dyed-in-the-wool son of the Louisiana backwaters.

Bayou St. Dennis Anchorage (29 29.398 North/090 02.294 West)

South of Lafitte Harbor Marina, the Barataria Waterway leaves the development associated with the community of Lafitte behind and begins a lengthy passage though a marshy section of the Louisiana coastline. A little better than 11 nautical miles farther along, the Barataria intersects the wide reaches of Bayou St. Dennis at unlighted nun buoy #48. A wide but completely unmarked channel stretches on to the west, moving into the bayou's interior reaches. Unfortunately, extensive shoals shelve out from all the adjacent shorelines. So, even though the channel is broad, it's entirely possible that one could find these shallows, even when care is being taken.

If, and only if, you can negotiate the unmarked Bayou St. Dennis channel, it is quite possible to anchor most anywhere along the channel's centerline, at least during fair weather and light breezes. This is clearly not the spot to ride out heavy weather. Shelter from the surrounding marsh is minimal, and strong winds from the east blow right up the entire length of the bayou's lower reaches.

On the other hand, there is plenty of swinging room in the broad channel, and depths (in the channel) run 12 feet or better. If you have a GPS chart plotter or a GPS interfaced with a laptop computer aboard, it's relatively easy to cruise upstream on the mid-width of the broad channel and find a good spot to anchor. Cruisers who lack these electronic wonders are taking a far greater chance of finding the bottom.

We like to anchor in the crook of the bayou's first turn to the northwest, near 29 29.398 North/090 02.294 West. Here you will discover ample swinging room for vessels up to 48 feet and 15+-foot soundings.

There is nothing navigationally easy about this anchorage, and as already mentioned, the shelter from foul weather is certainly less than great. Given the right conditions, and with electronic navigation aboard, you might consider this nightly anchor-down spot. Otherwise, you might want to think long and hard before attempting entry.

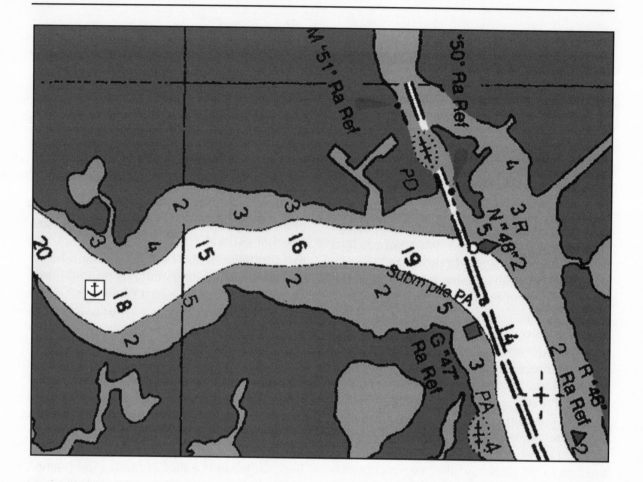

Grand Isle

After running through a rather open section across Barataria Sound, the waterway of the same name comes to an end at flashing day-beacons #1 and #2. From this point, mariners have two choices (at least) to continue their exploration. A straight shot to the southeast will lead to deep and reliable Barataria Pass (see below), while a turn to the southwest at flashing buoy #1 will lead cruisers into the northeasterly genesis of the charted channel running behind (north and northwest of)

Grand Isle. This passage allows access to the island's two marina facilities and affords cruising visitors a shoreside glimpse of this fascinating barrier island.

Grand Isle was first inhabited by European immigrants as early as 1710. Today, it plays host to 1,500 year-round residents, but at times during the summer months, that population swells by another 12,000. As these statistics suggest, Grand Isle (www.grand-isle. com) is the weekend playground for many of those who live and work in the greater New Orleans region. It is the capital of the Louisiana offshore charter-fishing fleet, and its shores house many private homes, two bed-and-breakfast inns, plus a small but interesting selection of restaurants. Unfortunately, both of Grand Isle's marina facilities are located on the island's extreme northeasterly corner. It's a long, long walk of 4 to 5 miles from either to reach the main business district.

Did I say that Grand Isle was the center of Louisiana charter fishing? That description could not be more apt. Www.grand-isle.com/events.htm yields a listing of better than a dozen fishing tournaments throughout the course of the year. That's some serious angling in this writer's book.

If you do decide to make the trek into the central section of Grand Isle, some of the dining spots to consider are Cigar's Cajun Cuisine (985-787-2188), the Lighthouse (985-787-3331) and the Starfish Restaurant (985-787-2711). Those wishing to spend some time with solid ground under their feet might want to call either Gulf Breeze (985-787-4703) or the Landry House (985-787-2207). Both are bed-and-breakfast-type inns.

While it's not particularly convenient for visiting cruisers who lack shoreside motorized transportation, Grand Isle is nevertheless a fascinating place that begs to be explored. Stretch those legs a bit and give it a good look-see.

Grand Isle Marinas (Various Lats/Lons—see below)

While there are a few other small marinas on Grand Isle, only two serve the needs of cruising-sized craft, and one of these seems to be in some sort of transition. Moving northeast to southwest, the first marina to consider is Pirate's Cove. This facility's entrance channel runs south from unlighted can buoy #3A. First-timers might become confused while running this cut, particularly when leaving the marina. Be sure to check out our navigational account of these waters below before attempting first-time entry.

Pirate's Cove Marina (29 15.853 North/089 57.441 West) is, at least at the current time, an enigma. During our last visit in early February 2003, we found a well-sheltered dockage basin sitting behind the dockmaster's building, a fuel dock, and a shoreside support building that probably contains showers and possibly a Laundromat. Furthermore, there was landscaping work underway around the harbor. Everything appeared neat as a pin, the docks were in great shape, and any number of boats were riding comfortably at their berths. There was just one problem. The dockmaster's building was locked tight as a drum, and telephone calls as late as April 1, 2003, were met with a message that said a certain individual's (presumably the marina owner or dockmaster) voice-mail box was full. Has the marina closed? Is it being remodeled? Or just what's going on here? We can't answer that question at this time, much as we have tried to do so. We can only advise our fellow cruisers to call well ahead of their arrival and check on slip availability, if any, at Pirate's Cove.

Those who are lucky enough to secure wet-slip space here will first cruise past the fuel dock, backed by the dockmaster's building. We spotted both gasoline and diesel pumps at the fuel pier. Look across the canal at this point for a good view of the Grand Isle U.S. Coast Guard station. Soon the marina's large dockage basin will open out before you. Here,

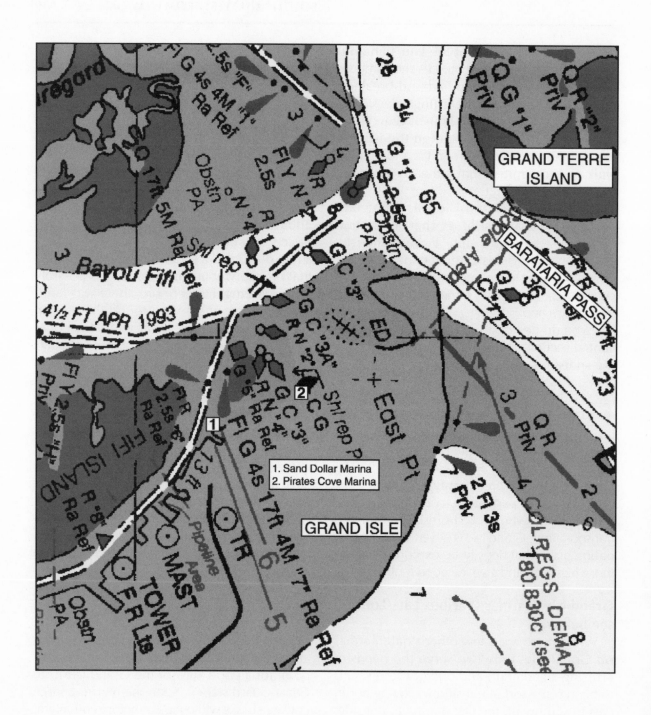

you will find fixed, wooden piers, some of which are covered. Full power and water connections seem to be in place at each berth.

We apologize once again for being so indefinite in our reporting of the services or lack thereof available at Pirate's Cove Marina. Be assured we have pulled out all the stops in trying to answer these questions, but all to no avail.

The other Grand Isle facility fit for cruising-sized vessels is the Sand Dollar (29 15.760 North/089 57.733 West). Its breakwater-protected basin guards the Grand Isle channel's southeasterly flank, southwest of flashing daybeacon #6. Transients are accepted at fixed wooden piers in the marina's harbor. Cruisers will discover 30- and 50-amp power hookups and dockside fresh-water connections. Depths alongside run around 5½ feet at low tide. Gasoline and diesel fuel are available. A large combination dockmaster's office, small ship's store, and motel overlooks the basin's southwesterly banks. Some very poor showers and an equally unappealing Laundromat are housed within this structure as well. The single light bulb in the shower was not working when we inspected this facility, and the room was definitely less than spic and span.

As mentioned above, it is a prodigious walk of 4 to 5 miles to the nearest restaurant or grocery store. If you're not up for such a hike, make sure to arrive with a fully stocked galley.

Sand Dollar Marina (985) 787-2500

Approach depth—7+ feet
Dockside depth—5½ feet MLW
Accepts transients—yes
Transient-dockage rate—below average
Fixed wooden piers—yes
Dockside power connections—30- and 50-amp

Dockside water connections—yes
Showers—minimal
Laundromat—minimal
Gasoline—yes
Diesel fuel—yes
Ship's store—small
Restaurant—very long walk

Barataria Pass

From flashing buoy #1 a wide channel strikes seaward between Grand Isle and Grand Terre Island. This cut is quite deep and boasts a very impressive collection of aids to navigation. Daylight passage out to the briny blue should not be a problem unless the wind is really kicking up her heels.

On the other hand, study chart 11365 for a moment and notice that most of the aids to navigation along this track are unlighted. This does not bode well for nighttime passage.

Otherwise Barataria Pass is an unusually reliable means to enter and exit from the Gulf of Mexico. No wonder the Grand Isle charter-fishing fleet is the envy of the Louisiana coastline.

Fort Livingston

Cruisers running Barataria Pass will undoubtedly catch sight of the impressive masonry walls of Fort Livingston to the northeast as they run the gap between Grand Isle and Grand Terre Island. The old walls you see today are actually made of tabby, a traditional building material composed of shell and limestone. Only the outer face of the tabby walls were later covered with a brick veneer. The secrets necessary for the manufacture of tabby have been lost in these modern times. No other walls of this ilk will ever rear their heads either here, or in the South Carolina low country, where tabby was also used extensively.

Sand Dollar Marina, Grand Isle

As early as 1813, the need for a fort to defend Barataria Pass and Barataria Bay was recognized. Plans for the fort were drawn up by 1817, but construction did not begin until 1842. Most of the fort was complete by 1849.

The eventual design of Fort Livingston changed much during the building process. When complete, the fort had two walls lined with cannon. The southeasterly face defended against an assault from the waters of the open Gulf, while the southwestern walls gazed sternly over Barataria Pass.

Originally named Fort Barataria, the fort underwent a name change to honor Edward Livingston, a New York native who came to Louisiana in 1804 and served as U.S. senator. He also held the post of secretary of state under Pres. Andrew Jackson.

Surprisingly enough, Fort Livingston was never armed or manned until the Civil War. In 1861 four companies of local troops took up station here, but the fort was evacuated in 1862 when the Union schooner *Kittletinny* was sighted. The Confederate "defenders" burned their tents, ammunition, and provisions, but the fort's many cannon were left behind.

Fort Livingston was abandoned for good in 1882 at the recommendation of Gen. W. T. Sherman. The property was ceded back to the state of Louisiana in 1923.

Fort Livingston, Barataria Pass

BARATARIA WATERWAY NAVIGATION

For the first 30 nautical miles or so, the Barataria Waterway consists of a canal-like passage. It's easy to follow this track successfully. Cruisers who keep even a nodding acquaintance with the waterway's centerline should be in good shape.

For the first 8 nautical miles of its southerly trek, the Barataria's banks are lined by the old community of Lafitte. While we have not seen any speed-limit signs along this stretch, there are, in addition to the several marinas described above, any number of private homes with their own docks, which sport a variety of pleasure craft. Always keeping in mind that captains are legally responsible for any damage caused by their vessel's wake, we suggest that larger power craft proceed at slow speed wherever boats are docked along the banks of the waterway.

The Barataria is spanned by the Lafitte swing bridge a short hop southeast of the waterway's northwesterly genesis. This span has a closed vertical clearance of 7 feet, but thankfully, it opens on demand.

Lafitte Anchorage Near the southerly limits of the Lafitte community, the wide mouth of Bayou Rigolettes cuts into the western banks of the Barataria Waterway. Chart 11367 shows two flashing daybeacons, #1 and #2, marking the bayou's entrance. During our on-site research, #1 (shown on chart 11367 as marking the southerly flank of the entrance) was absent.

We discovered that best depths could be maintained by slightly favoring the southerly banks when entering. Drop the hook before proceeding more than .14 nautical miles to the west. Anchor just slightly south of the centerline to help avoid any nighttime commercial fishing traffic that might happen along. Be sure to show an anchor light!

Remember that both shorelines are quite shoal. Don't let out so much anchor rode that you swing into these shallows.

Farther upstream, depths become much too unreliable for cruising craft, particularly after the bayou takes a sharp swing to the south.

On the Barataria Shortly after all development ceases along the banks of the Barataria Waterway, flashing daybeacon #10 will be spotted. After such a long time without sighting any aids to navigation, #10 can be a welcome sight.

Pass flashing daybeacon #10 to its westerly side. As a general rule, cruising craft proceeding south down the Barataria to Grand Isle should pass red, even-numbered aids to navigation to their (the cruisers') port side and take green markers to starboard.

South of flashing daybeacons #2A and #1A, the Barataria transits the long, markerless Bayou Cutler stretch. Stick to the mid-width, and the worse you should encounter might be some floating debris.

Eventually, flashing daybeacon #51 will be passed just west of your course line. Daybeacon #51 marks the northerly genesis of a dredged cut-through from Bayou Cutler to an intersection with Bayou St. Dennis. Be sure to come abeam and pass flashing daybeacon #50 and unlighted nun buoy #48 to their fairly immediate westerly sides. Just south of #48, the westward-running section of Bayou St. Dennis beckons with anchorage possibilities.

Bayou St. Dennis Anchorage Note that chart 11365 shows a deep-water section of Bayou St. Dennis exiting the easterly flank of the Barataria Waterway south of unlighted daybeacon #46. Looks pretty good on the chart, doesn't it? In three words, "don't try it." My publisher, Dr. Milburn Calhoun, and I watched as a local craft came to grief on these waters by way of a muddy grounding. A local captain has also warned this writer that these waters are not nearly so deep as they are shown to be on chart 11365. Indeed, note the "Shl rep 1982" notation. You might think that if these shallows have been around since 1982, NOAA would have gotten the word by now. Sigghhhh!

Happily the westerly branch of Bayou St. Dennis, opposite unlighted nun buoy #48, holds more promise. However, even this broad channel is wholly unmarked, and the lengthy shelf of charted 2- and 3-foot shallows stretching out from both shores is for real! So, we can only recommend this potential overnight haven to adventurous skippers and those with full electronic navigational capabilities aboard.

Mariners who decide to brave the unmarked cut should cruise south of #48 on the Waterway for some 25 yards and then turn west. Favor the northerly banks *slightly,* and follow the bayou as it runs on to the west. Start working your way back to the centerline when the sharp, charted point on the southerly banks is sighted ahead.

Continue on the mid-width until cruising into the crook of the bayou's first turn to the northwest. We suggest anchoring on these waters. Farther upstream, the lack of markings continues, and shelter is not further enhanced.

Good luck, you may need it!

On the Barataria South of the Bayou St. Dennis intersection, mariners need to pay stricter attention to markers. Depths outside of the channel are *quite* shallow, and just to spice up our on-the-water day a bit more, leftover underwater oil and drilling equipment can be encountered from time to time. During a recent cruise, my publisher and I were shocked when the very knowledgeable local captain with whom we were voyaging lost a prop blade by way of a tiny deviation from the marked track.

South of flashing daybeacons #31 and #32, the channel passes out into the open waters of Barataria Bay. From this point to the intersection with the Grand Isle channels, the waterway ducks behind and between a few marsh islands, but this remains a far more open and less protected stretch than the waters farther to the north.

Continue paying attention to business, and note all markers with the greatest care. Just look at the soundings noted on chart 11365 outside of the channel, and the reasoning behind this stricture will become immediately apparent.

Southeast of flashing daybeacons #1 and #2, the Barataria Waterway approaches its terminus at the intersection of the Grand Isle channels. Be sure to come abeam and pass the correctly charted, unnumbered flashing yellow daybeacon to its northeasterly side. Continue cruising on the same course for a good 50 yards or so out into the wide swath of deep waters ahead.

Grand Isle Channels and Marinas After cruising through the southeasterly terminus of the Barataria Waterway and coming abeam of the gap between unlighted nun buoy #2 and flashing buoy #1 to the southwest, cruisers have come to a basic parting of the way. Those bent on meeting up with the Gulf of Mexico need only continue cruising southeast on wide, well-marked Barataria Pass.

On the other hand, skippers bent on a visit to one of Grand Isle's marinas should swing to the southwest and run the initial portion of the Grand Isle channel. To enter this cut, cruise between flashing buoy #1 and unlighted nun buoy #2. Yes, I know that chart 11365 would lead one to believe that such a course would border on shoal water, but my guess is that the markers are far more current than the chart.

Continue on to the southwest by passing unlighted can buoy #3 to its fairly immediate northwesterly side. Next up are unlighted can buoy #3A and unlighted nun buoy #4. Point for the gap between these markers.

South of #3A, the marked channel to Pirate's Cove Marina can be run. Keep all red markers to your starboard side, and take green markers to port. Eventually, you will pass into the interior reaches of a small canal. The Grand Isle U.S. Coast Guard station will be visible to port, while the fuel dock and dockmaster's building will come abeam to starboard. The dockage basin will open out just a bit farther upstream.

We have noted that visiting cruisers leaving Pirate's Cove have a tendency to mistake unlighted daybeacon #5 as a marker on the marina channel. This is an easy mistake to make from the water, but actually, #5 has nothing to do with the marina cut. It marks the continuing southwesterly run of the Grand Isle channel. Those errant navigators who try to cruise directly from the inner markers on the marina channel to #5 will run aground *every* time!

Just west-southwest of the #3A and #4, the channel divides. One cut stretches onto the west by way of Bayou Fifi. This passage is not further detailed in this account.

The main Grand Isle channel moves off to the southwest. Point to come abeam and pass unlighted daybeacon #5 by some 25 yards to its northwesterly side, followed soon thereafter by flashing daybeacon #6, which should be passed to its fairly immediate southeasterly quarter.

The entrance to the breakwater-enclosed harbor serving Sand Dollar Marina will come up along the southeasterly side of the channel, southwest of flashing daybeacon #6. During daylight, the entrance to the dockage basin is obvious.

Barataria Pass The easily run passage from inland to offshore waters has yet to be invented. However, Barataria Pass comes about as close as cruisers are ever likely to find. The channel is wide, deep, and extremely well marked.

Of course that does not mean that things are always easy on these waters. When wind and tide oppose one another, it can still make for an exciting ride.

As mentioned earlier, the vast majority of the prolific aids to navigation on Barataria Pass are unlighted. Smart navigators will plan for a daylight run through these waters.

Be sure to use chart 11365 as you navigate Barataria Pass. While you will also need chart 11366 for the outermost reaches of this cut, this latter chart does not give sufficient detail for the passage's interior section.

I hope you have enjoyed our passage from Carrabelle to Grand Isle as much as I have. Truly, we have seen some wonderful and varied cruising grounds along the way. Good luck and good cruising!

Bibliography

Buskens, Joy Callaway. *Well, I've Never Met a Native.* Columbus, Ga.: Quill Publications, 1986.

Comings, L. J. Newcomb, and Albers, Martha M. *A Brief History of Baldwin County.* Fairhope, Ala.: Baldwin County Historical Society, 1969.

Dartez, Cecilia Casrill, ed. *A Marmac Guide to New Orleans.* Gretna, La.: Pelican Publishing Company, 1991.

Griffin, Thomas K. *The Pelican Guide to New Orleans.* Gretna, La.: Pelican Publishing Company, 1991.

Hamilton, Virginia van der Veer. *Seeing Historic Alabama.* Tuscaloosa, Ala.: University of Alabama Press, 1982.

Jahoda Gloria. *The Other Florida.* Port Salerno, Fla.: Florida Classics Library, 1984.

Marth, Del and Martha. *The Florida Almanac.* Gretna, La.: Pelican Publishing Company, 1998.

Mettee, Vivian Foster. *. . . And the Roots Run Deep.* Destin, Fla., 1983.

O'Brien, Dawn, and Matkov, Becky Roper. *Florida's Historic Restaurants.* Winston-Salem, N.C.: John F. Blair Publishing Company, 1987.

Roberts, Bruce, and Jones, Ray. *Southern Lighthouses.* Chester, Ct.: Globe Pequot Press, 1989.

Rosasco-Soule, Adelia. *Panhandle Memories.* Pensacola, Fla.: West Florida Literary Federation, 1987.

Saxon, Lyle. *Fabulous New Orleans.* Gretna, La.: Pelican Publishing Company, 1995.

Scheib, Flora K. *History of the Southern Yacht Club.* Gretna, La.: Pelican Publishing Company, 1986.

Skinner, Woodward B. *Geronimo at Fort Pickens.* Pensacola, Fla.: Skinner Publications, 1981.

Sullivan, Charles L. *The Mississippi Gulf Coast.* Chatsworth, Calif.: Windsor Publications, Inc., 1985.

Tebeau, Charlton W. *A History of Florida.* Miami, Fla.: University of Miami Press, 1971.

Wright, Sarah Bird. *Islands of the South and Southeastern United States.* Atlanta, Ga.: Peachtree Publishers, Ltd., 1989.

Index